HMH Georgia Science

This Interactive Student Edition belongs to

_____

Teacher/Room

_____

Houghton Mifflin Harcourt

Consulting Authors

Michael A. DiSpezio

Global Educator
North Falmouth, Massachusetts

Michael DiSpezio has authored many HMH instructional programs for science and mathematics. He has also authored numerous trade books and multimedia programs on various topics and hosted dozens of studio and location broadcasts for various organizations in the U.S. and worldwide. Most recently, he has been working with educators to provide strategies for implementing science and engineering practices, including engineering design challenges. To all his projects, he brings his extensive background in science, his expertise in classroom teaching at the elementary, middle, and high school levels, and his deep experience in producing interactive and engaging instructional materials.

Marjorie Frank

Science Writer and Content-Area Reading Specialist
Brooklyn, New York

An educator and linguist by training, a writer and poet by nature, Marjorie Frank has authored and designed a generation of instructional materials in all subject areas, including past HMH Science programs. Her other credits include authoring science issues of an award-winning children's magazine, writing game-based digital assessments, developing blended learning materials for young children, and serving as instructional designer and co-author of pioneering school-to-work software. In addition, she has served on the adjunct faculty of Hunter, Manhattan, and Brooklyn Colleges, teaching courses in science methods, literacy, and writing.

Acknowledgments for Cover

Front cover: *lava ©Bruce Omori/epa/Corbis*

Copyright © 2019 by Houghton Mifflin Harcourt Publishing Company

All rights reserved. No part of this work may be reproduced or transmitted in any form or by any means, electronic or mechanical, including photocopying or recording, or by any information storage or retrieval system, without the prior written permission of the copyright owner unless such copying is expressly permitted by federal copyright law. Requests for permission to make copies of any part of the work should be submitted through our Permissions website at https://customercare.hmhco.com/contactus/Permissions.html or mailed to Houghton Mifflin Harcourt Publishing Company, Attn: Intellectual Property Licensing, 9400 Southpark Center Loop, Orlando, Florida 32819-8647.

Printed in the U.S.A.

ISBN 978-1-328-86821-3

6 7 8 9 10   0928   27 26 25 24 23 22 21 20 19

4500747183   B C D E F G

© Houghton Mifflin Harcourt Publishing Company • Image Credits:

Michael R. Heithaus

Dean, College of Arts, Sciences & Education
Professor, Department of Biological Sciences
Florida International University
Miami, Florida

Mike Heithaus joined the FIU Biology Department in 2003, has served as Director of the Marine Sciences Program, and as Executive Director of the School of Environment, Arts, and Society, which brings together the natural and social sciences and humanities to develop solutions to today's environmental challenges. He now serves as Dean of the College of Arts, Sciences & Education. His research focuses on predator-prey interactions and the ecological importance of large marine species. He has helped to guide the development of Life Science content in this science program, with a focus on strategies for teaching challenging content as well as the science and engineering practices of analyzing data and using computational thinking.

Georgia Reviewers

C. Alex Alvarez, EdD
Director of STEM and Curriculum
Valdosta City Schools
Valdosta, Georgia

Suzanne Salter Brooks
Teacher
Lee Middle School
Sharpsburg, Georgia

Cindy Brown
Teacher
Coffee Middle School
Douglas, Georgia

Monica Dyess, EdD
Pine Grove Middle School
Valdosta, Georgia

Felecia Eckman
Teacher
Carl Scoggins Middle School
Dallas, Georgia

Theresa D. Flanagan
Physical Science Instructor
Arnall Middle School
Newnan, Georgia

Toppy R. Gurley, EdS
Science Dept. Chair
P.B. Ritch Middle School
Dallas, Georgia

Angel James
Middle Grades Educator
Midway Middle School
Midway, Georgia

Keith A. Peterman
Life Science Teacher
Lewis Frasier Middle School
Hinesville, Georgia

Monique Prince, EdD
East Paulding Middle School
Dallas, Georgia

Melanie Smith, MEd
Physical Science Instructor
Arnall Middle School
Newnan, Georgia

Cynthia L. Tupper
Science Teacher
Lewis Frasier Middle School
Hinesville, Georgia

Content Reviewers

Paul D. Asimow, PhD
*Professor of Geology
and Geochemistry*
Division of Geological and Planetary Sciences
California Institute of Technology
Pasadena, CA

Laura K. Baumgartner, PhD
Postdoctoral Researcher
Molecular, Cellular, and Developmental
Biology
University of Colorado
Boulder, CO

Eileen Cashman, PhD
Professor
Department of Environmental Resources
Engineering
Humboldt State University
Arcata, CA

Hilary Clement Olson, PhD
Research Scientist Associate V
Institute for Geophysics, Jackson School of
Geosciences
The University of Texas at Austin
Austin, TX

Joe W. Crim, PhD
Professor Emeritus
Department of Cellular Biology
The University of Georgia
Athens, GA

Elizabeth A. De Stasio, PhD
*Raymond H. Herzog Professor
of Science*
Professor of Biology
Department of Biology
Lawrence University
Appleton, WI

Dan Franck, PhD
Botany Education Consultant
Chatham, NY

Julia R. Greer, PhD
*Assistant Professor of Materials Science and
Mechanics*
Division of Engineering and Applied Science
California Institute of Technology
Pasadena, CA

John E. Hoover, PhD
Professor
Department of Biology
Millersville University
Millersville, PA

William H. Ingham, PhD
Professor (Emeritus)
Department of Physics and Astronomy
James Madison University
Harrisonburg, VA

Charles W. Johnson, PhD
*Chairman, Division of Natural Sciences,
Mathematics, and Physical Education*
Associate Professor of Physics
South Georgia College
Douglas, GA

Tatiana A. Krivosheev, PhD
Associate Professor of Physics
Department of Natural Sciences
Clayton State University
Morrow, GA

Joseph A. McClure, PhD
Associate Professor Emeritus
Department of Physics
Georgetown University
Washington, DC

Mark Moldwin, PhD
Professor of Space Sciences
Atmospheric, Oceanic, and Space Sciences
University of Michigan
Ann Arbor, MI

Russell Patrick, PhD
Professor of Physics
Department of Biology, Chemistry, and Physics
Southern Polytechnic State University
Marietta, GA

Patricia M. Pauley, PhD
Meteorologist, Data Assimilation Group
Naval Research Laboratory
Monterey, CA

Stephen F. Pavkovic, PhD
Professor Emeritus
Department of Chemistry
Loyola University of Chicago
Chicago, IL

L. Jeanne Perry, PhD
Director (Retired)
Protein Expression Technology Center
Institute for Genomics and Proteomics
University of California,
Los Angeles
Los Angeles, CA

Kenneth H. Rubin, PhD
Professor
Department of Geology and Geophysics
University of Hawaii
Honolulu, HI

Brandon E. Schwab, PhD
Associate Professor
Department of Geology
Humboldt State University
Arcata, CA

Marllin L. Simon, PhD
Associate Professor
Department of Physics
Auburn University
Auburn, AL

Larry Stookey, PE
Upper Iowa University
Wausau, WI

Kim Withers, PhD
Associate Research Scientist
Center for Coastal Studies
Texas A&M University-Corpus Christi
Corpus Christi, TX

Matthew A. Wood, PhD
Professor
Department of Physics & Space Sciences
Florida Institute of Technology
Melbourne, FL

Adam D. Woods, PhD
Associate Professor
Department of Geological Sciences
California State University, Fullerton
Fullerton, CA

Natalie Zayas, MS, EdD
Lecturer
Division of Science and Environmental Policy
California State University, Monterey Bay
Seaside, CA

Contents

Contents (continued)

Contents (continued)

Matter

Big Idea

Matter is described by its properties and may undergo changes.

S8P1., S8P1.a, S8P1.b, S8P1.c, S8P1.d, S8P1.f

What do you think?

A large iceberg floats in water, but an anchor sinks. What is different about these two objects that causes them to behave differently in water? As you explore the unit, gather evidence to help you state and support claims that answer this question.

Unit 1
Matter

CITIZEN SCIENCE

Deep Freeze

When outdoor temperatures reach 0 °C (32 °F), liquid water can freeze to form a solid. Snow, ice, sleet, and hail are examples of the solid form of water. Understanding the properties of water in its different states helps people to stay safe during icy weather.

① Think About It

How is liquid water different from solid ice?

_____

_____

_____

_____

This truck is applying salt to an icy road. Do you know what effect this will have on the ice?

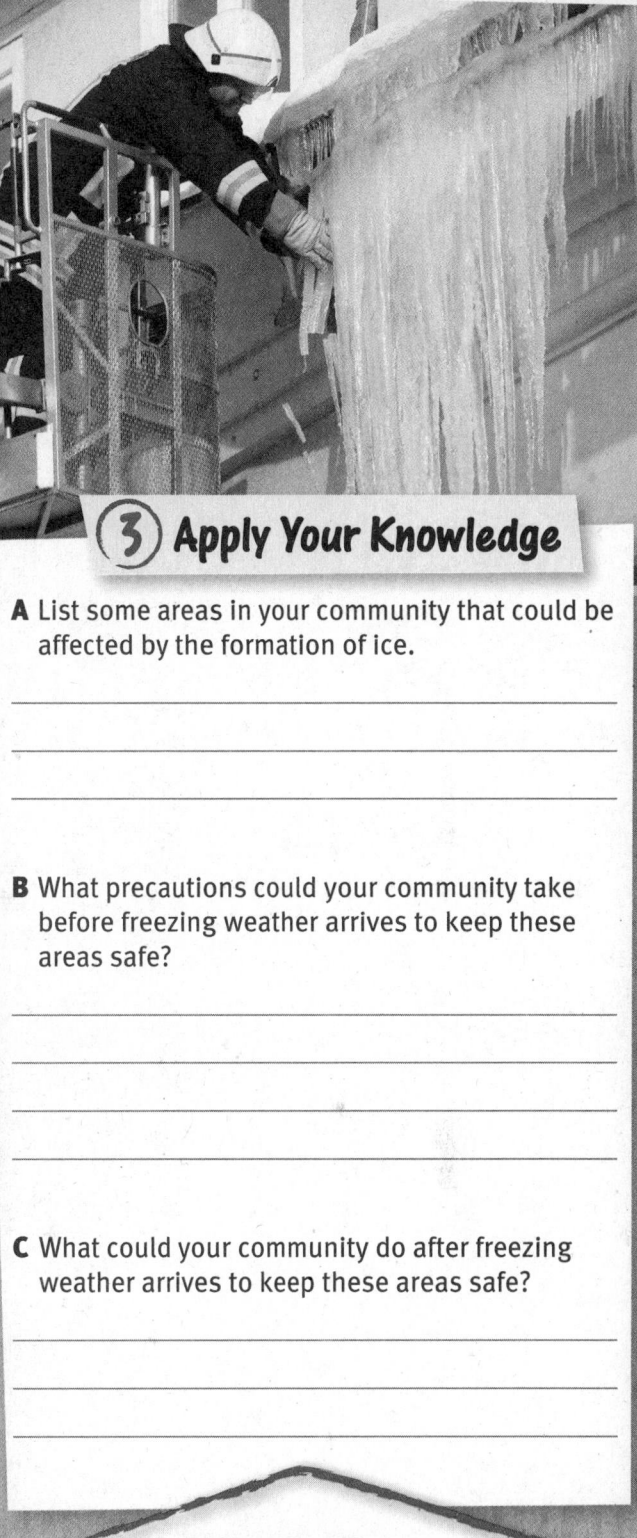

② Ask A Question

What precautions should be taken during freezing weather?

Would you believe that the ice on these fruit trees is actually protecting them? The trees are being sprayed with water, which turns to ice in freezing weather. The formation of ice helps to keep the plants warmer. With a partner, research some of the ways in which people protect other areas and living things during icy weather.

Think about the impact that ice could have on
- ✔ plants
- ✔ people
- ✔ bodies of water
- ✔ pets and other animals

③ Apply Your Knowledge

A List some areas in your community that could be affected by the formation of ice.

_____
_____
_____

B What precautions could your community take before freezing weather arrives to keep these areas safe?

_____
_____
_____
_____

C What could your community do after freezing weather arrives to keep these areas safe?

_____
_____
_____

Take It Home

How do you prepare a home for icy weather? Draw a map of a home and the surrounding area. Identify areas on your map that could become hazardous in freezing conditions. Then, create a plan for protecting these areas. See *ScienceSaurus*® for more information about weather.

Introduction to Matter

ESSENTIAL QUESTION

What properties define matter?

By the end of this lesson, you should be able to relate mass, weight, volume, and density to one another.

Hot air takes balloons aloft because hot air is less dense than the cooler air around it.

 S8P1.c Chemical and physical properties of matter

✋ **Lesson Labs**

Quick Labs
• Mass and Weight
• Finding Volume by Displacement
• How Much Mass?
Exploration Lab
• Comparing Buoyancy

 Engage Your Brain

1 Describe Fill in the blank with the word or phrase that you think correctly completes the following sentences.

A(n) _____ can hold a greater volume of water than a mug.

A hamster weighs less than a(n) _____ .

A bowling ball is harder to lift than a basketball because _____ .

2 Explain List some similarities and differences between the golf ball on the left and the table-tennis ball on the right in the photo below.

_____
_____
_____
_____
_____
_____

🖊 Active Reading

3 Apply Many scientific words, such as *matter*, also have everyday meanings. Use context clues to write your own definition for each meaning of the word *matter*.

Example sentence
What is this gooey <u>matter</u> on the table?

Matter:

_____
_____
_____

Example sentence
Please vote! Your opinions <u>matter</u>.

Matter:

_____
_____
_____

Vocabulary Terms

• matter   • volume
• mass   • density
• weight

4 Identify This list contains the vocabulary terms you'll learn in this lesson. As you read, circle the definition of each term.

What's the MATTER?

What is matter?

Suppose your class takes a field trip to a museum. During the course of the day you see mammoth bones, sparkling crystals, hot-air balloons, and an astronaut's space suit. All of these things are matter.

As you will see, **matter** is anything that has mass and takes up space. Your body is matter. The air that you breathe and the water that you drink are also matter. Matter makes up the materials around you.

However, not everything is matter. Light and sound, for example, are not matter. Light does not take up space or have mass in the same way that a table does. Although air is matter, a sound traveling through air is not.

Active Reading **5 Explain** How can you tell if something is matter?

_____

_____

_____

Visualize It!

6 Identify Name three examples of matter found in this photo.

_____

_____

_____

What is mass?

You cannot always tell how much matter is in an object simply by observing the object's size. But you *can* measure the object's mass. **Mass** describes the amount of matter in an object.

Compare the two balloons at the right. The digital scales show that the balloon filled with compressed air has a greater mass than the other balloon. This is because the compressed air adds mass to the balloon. Air may seem to be made of nothing, but it has mass. The readings on the scale are in grams (g). A gram is the unit of mass you will use most often in science class.

Objects that are the same size can be made up of different amounts of matter. For example, a large sponge is about the same size as a brick. But the brick contains more matter. Therefore, the brick has a greater mass than the sponge.

The readings on these digital scales show that all matter, even air, has mass.

0.010 g

0.005 g

How does mass differ from weight?

The words *weight* and *mass* are often used as though they mean the same thing, but they do not. **Weight** is a measure of the gravitational force (grav•ih•TAY•shuhn•uhl FAWRS) on an object. Gravitational force keeps objects on Earth from floating into space. The gravitational force between an object and Earth depends partly on the object's mass. The greater that the mass of an object is, the greater the gravitational force on the object will be and the greater the object's weight will be.

An object's weight can change depending on the object's location. For example, you would weigh less on the moon than you do on Earth because the moon has less mass—and therefore exerts less gravitational force—than Earth does. However, you would have the same mass in both places. An object's mass does not change unless the amount of matter in an object changes.

The weight of this dachshund on the moon is about one-sixth of its weight on Earth.

Active Reading **7 Explain** Why do astronauts weigh less on the moon than they do on Earth?

_____

_____

The balance below works by moving the masses on the right along the beams until they "balance" the pan on the left. Moving the masses changes the amount of force the levers exert on the pan. The more massive the object on the pan, the more force will be needed on the levers to balance the two sides.

8 Infer Would this balance give the same value for mass if used on the moon? Explain your reasoning.

_____

_____

_____

_____

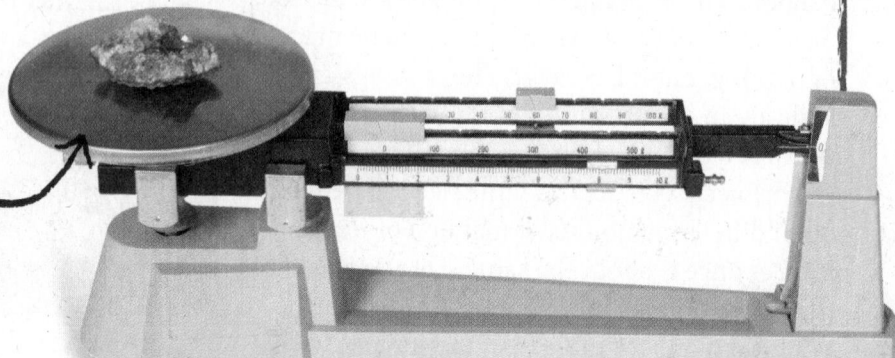

A triple-beam balance can be used to measure the mass of small objects such as this geode fragment.

The spring scale gives weight in pounds (lb).

How are mass and weight measured?

Mass is often measured by using a triple-beam balance such as the one shown above. The balance compares an object's mass to known standards of mass called *countermasses*. The countermasses slide across each of three beams. When the countermasses balance the mass of the object in the balance pan, the pointer will rest at 0. Then, the mass can be read from the position of the countermasses on the beams.

Weight is measured with devices such as the spring scale shown at the left. The spring measures the force between the mass in the pan and Earth. The more massive the object placed in the pan, the more forceful is the attraction between it and Earth, and the more the spring will stretch. Greater stretch means greater weight.

Because weight is a measure of gravitational force, it is given in units of force. You probably are most familiar with weight given in pounds (lb), like the units shown on the scale. The standard scientific unit for weight, however, is the newton (N). A 100-g mass weighs approximately 1 N on Earth. One newton is about one-fourth of a pound.

Measuring Space

How is the amount of space occupied by matter measured?

All matter takes up space. The amount of space that an object takes up, or occupies, is known as the object's **volume.**

Objects with the similar volumes do not always have the same mass. In the photos, the bowling ball and the balloon have about the same volume, but the bowling ball contains a lot more mass than the balloon. You know this because the bowling ball weighs much more than the balloon. The different masses take up about the same amount of space, so both objects have about the same volume.

Active Reading 9 **Define** What does volume measure?

_____

_____

The bowling ball has a lot more mass than the balloon.

The balloon is similar in volume but has much less mass than the bowling ball.

© Houghton Mifflin Harcourt Publishing Company • Image Credits: (bkgd) ©Golden Pixels LLC/Alamy; (b) ©Inspirestock Inc./Alamy

Think Outside the Book Inquiry

10 **Infer** Big things can look very small when seen from far away. Describe how you know big things far away aren't really small.

How can volume be determined?

There are different ways to find the volume of an object. For objects that have well-defined shapes, you can take a few measurements and calculate the volume using a formula. For objects that are irregularly shaped, such as a rock, you can use water displacement to measure volume. For liquids, you can use a graduated cylinder.

Using a Formula

Some objects have well-defined shapes. For these objects, the easiest way to find their volume is to measure the dimensions of the object and use a formula. Different shapes use different volume formulas. For example, to find the volume of a rectangular box, you would use a different formula than if you were to find the volume of a spherical ball.

> To find the volume of a rectangular box, use the following formula:
>
> $$Volume = (length)(width)(height)$$
> $$V = lwh$$

The volume of a solid is measured in units of length cubed. For example, if you measure the length, width, and height of a box in centimeters (cm), the volume of the box has units of centimeters multiplied by centimeters multiplied by centimeters, or cubic centimeters (cm^3). In order to calculate volume, make sure that all the measurements are in the same units.

 **Do the Math** **Sample Problem**

Find the volume of the lunch box.

Identify

A. What do you know?

length = 25 cm, width = 18 cm, height = 10 cm

B. What do you want to find? Volume

Plan

C. Draw and label a sketch:

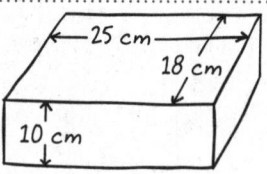

D. Write the formula: $V = lwh$

E. Substitute into the formula: $V = (25 \text{ cm})(18 \text{ cm})(10 \text{ cm})$

Solve

F. Multiply: $(25 \text{ cm})(18 \text{ cm})(10 \text{ cm}) = 4{,}500 \text{ cm}^3$

G. Check that your units agree: The given units are centimeters, and the measure found is volume. Therefore, the units should be cm^3. The units agree.

Answer: $4{,}500 \text{ cm}^3$

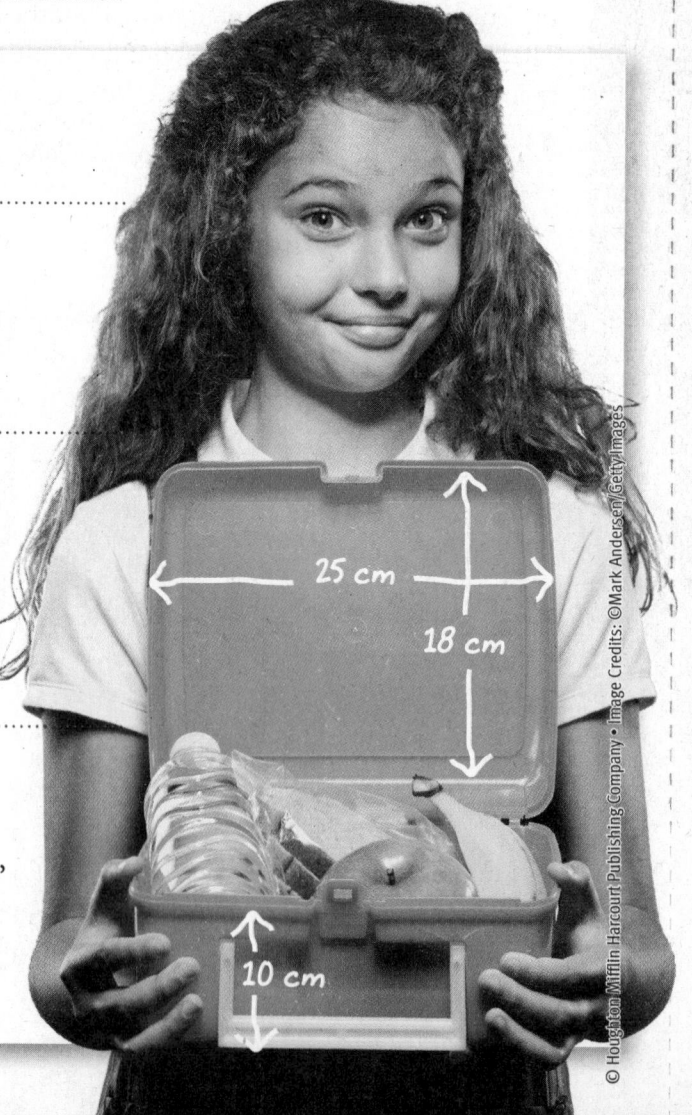

The volume of your locker will tell you how much stuff will fit inside.

30 cm

200 cm

←40 cm→

Do the Math — You Try It

11 Calculate Find the volume of a locker that is 30 cm long, 40 cm wide, and 200 cm high.

Identify

A. What do you know?

B. What do you want to find?

Plan

C. Draw and label a sketch:

D. Write the formula:

E. Substitute the given values into the formula:

Solve

F. Multiply:

G. Check that your units agree:

Answer:

Using Water Displacement

In the lab, you can use a beaker or graduated cylinder to measure the volume of liquids. Graduated cylinders are used to measure liquid volume when accuracy is important. The volume of liquids is often expressed in liters (L) or milliliters (mL). Milliliters and cubic centimeters are equivalent; in other words, $1 \text{ mL} = 1 \text{ cm}^3$. The volume of any amount of liquid, from one raindrop to an entire ocean, can be expressed in these units.

Two objects cannot occupy the same space at the same time. For example, as a builder stacks bricks to build a wall, she adds each brick on top of the other. No brick can occupy the same place that another brick occupies. Similarly, when an object is placed in water, the object pushes some of the water out of the way. This process, called *displacement*, can be used to measure the volume of an irregularly shaped solid object.

In the photos at the right, you can see that the level of the water in the graduated cylinder has risen after the chess piece is placed inside. The volume of water displaced is found by subtracting the original volume in the graduated cylinder from the new volume. This is equal to the volume of the chess piece.

When deciding the units of the volume found using water displacement, it is helpful to remember that 1 mL of water is equal to 1 cm^3. Therefore, you can report the volume of the object in cubic centimeters.

Do the Math

You Try It

12 Calculate The two images below show a graduated cylinder filled with water before and after a chess piece is placed inside. Use the images to calculate the volume of the chess piece.

Volume without chess piece = _____

Volume with chess piece = _____

Volume of chess piece = _____

Don't forget to check the units of volume of the chess piece!

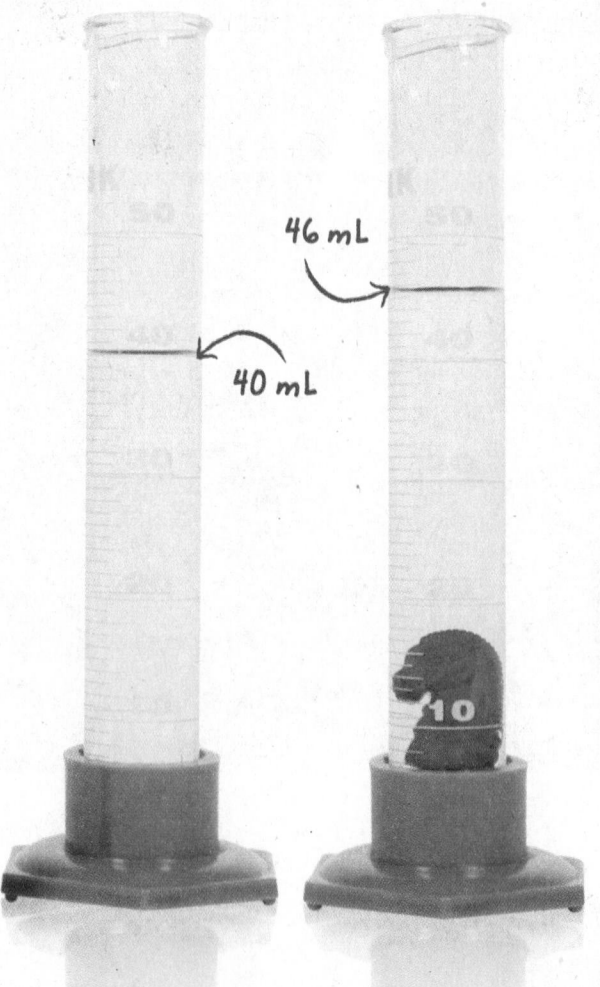

46 mL

40 mL

Packing It In!

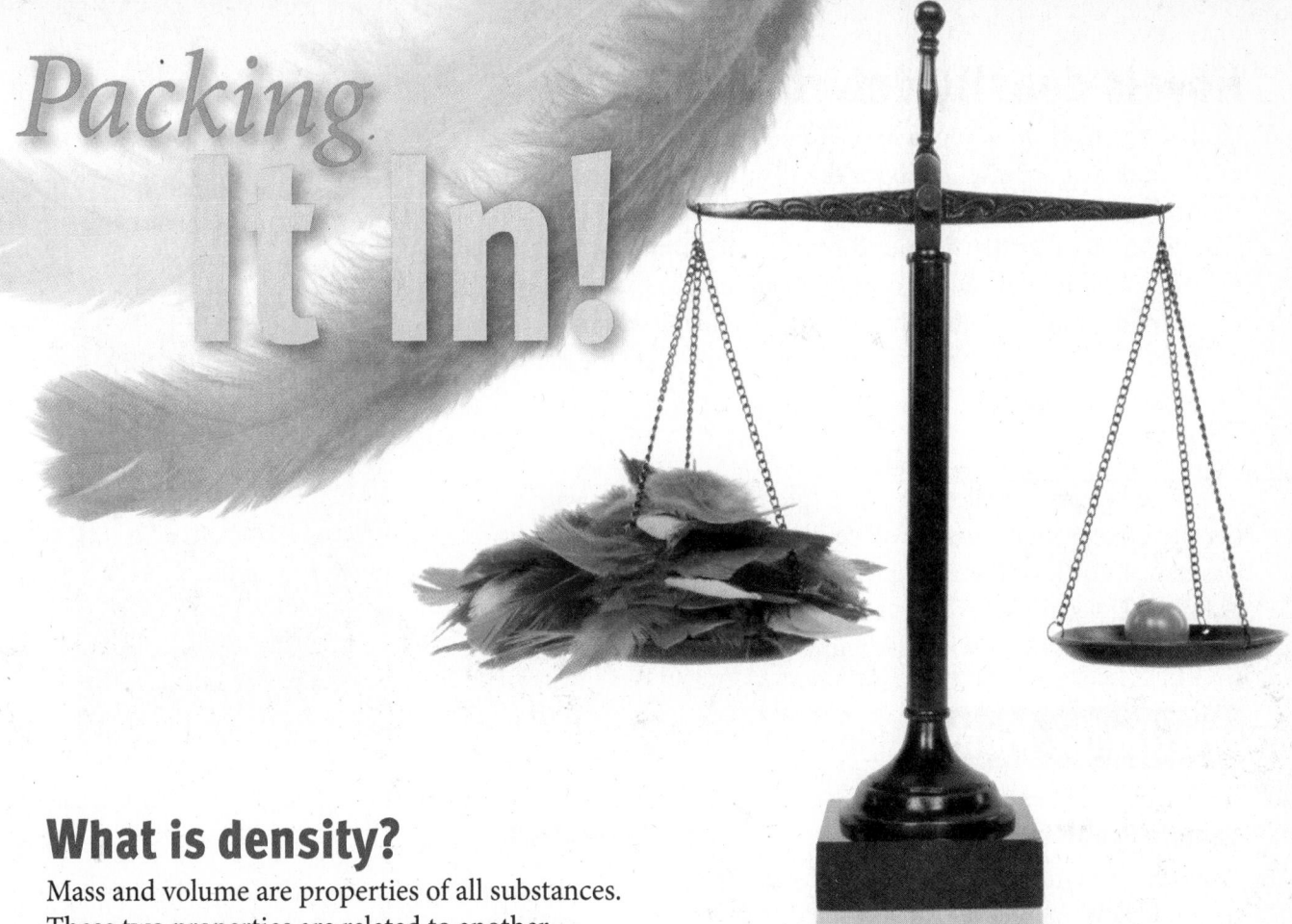

What is density?

Mass and volume are properties of all substances. These two properties are related to another property called density (DEN•sih•tee). **Density** is a measure of the amount of mass in a given volume. Objects containing the same amount of mass can take up different amounts of space. For example, the pile of feathers above takes up more space than the tomato. But they have the same mass. This is because the tomato is more dense. The tomato has more mass in a smaller space.

The density of a given substance remains the same no matter how much of the substance you have. For example, if you divide a piece of clay in half, both halves will have the same density as the original piece.

The tomato and the pile of feathers have similar masses, but the tomato has less volume. This means that the tomato is more dense.

Active Reading

13 Explain What is density?

_____

_____

_____

14 Predict Circle the item in each pair that is more dense.

Golf ball	Empty milk carton	Foam ball
Table-tennis ball	Milk carton full of milk	Baseball

How is density determined?

Units for density consist of a mass unit divided by a volume unit. Units that are often used for density are grams per cubic centimeter (g/cm³) for solids, and grams per milliliter (g/mL) for liquids. In other words, density is the mass in grams divided by the volume in cubic centimeters or milliliters.

To find an object's density (D), find its mass (m) and its volume (V). Then, use the given formula to calculate the density of the object.

$$D = \frac{m}{V}$$

The density of water is 1 g/mL (g/cm³). Any object with a density greater than 1 g/mL will sink in water and with a density less than 1 g/mL will float. Density, therefore, can be a useful thing to know. The sample problem below shows how to calculate the density of a volcanic rock called pumice.

Pumice and obsidian are two igneous volcanic rocks with very different densities.

Do the Math

Sample Problem

Pumice is an igneous volcanic rock, formed by the rapid cooling of lava. What is the density of a 49.8 g piece of pumice that has a volume of 83 cm³?

Identify

A. What do you know?

mass = 49.8 g, volume = 83 cm³

B. What do you want to find? Density

Plan

C. Write the formula: $D = \frac{m}{V}$

D. Substitute the given values into the formula:

$D = \frac{49.8\text{ g}}{83\text{ cm}^3}$

Solve

E. Divide: $\frac{49.8\text{ g}}{83\text{ cm}^3} = 0.6$ g/cm³

F. Check that your units agree: The given units are grams and cubic centimeters, and the measure found is density. Therefore, the units should be g/cm³. The units agree.

Answer: 0.6 g/cm³

You Try It

15 Calculate Obsidian is another type of igneous rock. What is the density of a piece of obsidian that has a mass of 239.2 g and a volume of 92 cm³?

Identify

A. What do you know?

B. What do you want to find?

Plan

C. Write the formula:

D. Substitute the given values into the formula:

Solve

E. Divide:

F. Check that your units agree:

Answer:

 **Do the Math**

Sample Problem

A basalt rock displaces 16 mL of water. The density of the rock is 3.0 g/cm³. What is the mass of the rock?

Identify

A. What do you know?

volume = 16 mL, density = 3.0 g/cm³

B. What do you want to find? Mass

Plan

C. Rearrange the formula $D = \frac{m}{V}$ to solve for mass. You can do this by multiplying each side by *V*.

$$D = \frac{m}{V}$$
$$m = D \cdot V$$

D. Substitute the given values into the formula. Recall that 1 mL = 1 cm³, so 16 mL = 16 cm³.

$$m = \frac{3.0 \text{ g}}{\text{cm}^3} \cdot 16 \text{ cm}^3$$

Solve

E. Multiply: $\frac{3.0 \text{ g}}{\text{cm}^3} \cdot 16 \text{ cm}^3 = 48 \text{ g}$

F. Check that your units agree: The given units are g/cm³ and mL, and the measure found is mass. Therefore, the units should be g. The units agree.

Answer: 48 g

You Try It

16 Calculate A rhyolite rock has a volume of 9.5 mL. The density of the rock is 2.6 g/cm³. What is the mass of the rock?

Identify

A. What do you know?

B. What do you want to find?

Plan

C. Write the formula:

D. Substitute the given values into the formula:

Solve

E. Multiply:

F. Check that your units agree:

Answer:

Kilauea is the youngest volcano on the Big Island of Hawaii. "Kilauea" means "spewing" or "much spreading," apparently in reference to the lava flows that it erupts.

Visual Summary

To complete this summary, check the box that indicates true or false. Then, use the key below to check your answers. You can use this page to review the main concepts of the lesson.

Relating Mass, Weight, Volume, and Density

Mass is the amount of matter in an object. Weight is a measure of the gravitational force on an object.

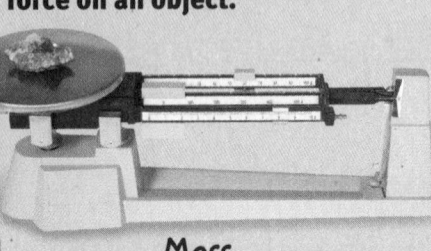

Mass

Weight

	T	F	
17	☐	☐	An object's weight is the amount of space it occupies.
18	☐	☐	The mass of an object is equal to its weight.

Volume is the amount of space that matter in an object occupies.
To find the volume of a rectangular box, use the formula:

$$V = lwh$$

	T	F	
19	☐	☐	The volume of a solid can be expressed in units of cm^3.

Density describes the mass of a substance in a given volume.
To find the density of a substance, use the formula:

$$D = \frac{m}{V}$$

	T	F	
20	☐	☐	An object that floats in water is less dense than water.

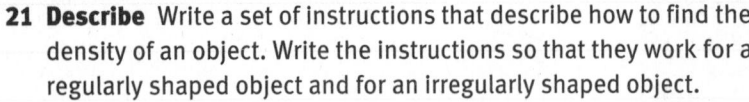

Answers: 17 F; 18 F; 19 T; 20 T

21 Describe Write a set of instructions that describe how to find the density of an object. Write the instructions so that they work for a regularly shaped object and for an irregularly shaped object.

Lesson Review

Vocabulary

Fill in the blank with the term that best completes the following sentence.

1 _____ is the amount of space that matter in an object occupies.

2 _____ is anything that has mass and takes up space.

3 _____ is the amount of matter in an object.

4 _____ is a measure of the amount of matter in a given amount of space.

5 _____ is a measure of the gravitational force on an object.

Key Concepts

6 Classify Is air matter? Describe evidence that supports your claim.

_____

_____

_____

7 Describe Is it possible for an object's weight to change while its mass remains constant? Explain your reasoning.

_____

_____

_____

8 Compare Explain why a golf ball is heavier than a table-tennis ball, even though the balls are the same size.

_____

_____

_____

9 Calculate A block of wood has a mass of 120 g and a volume of 200 cm³. What is the density of the wood?

Critical Thinking

Use this table to answer the following questions.

Substance	Density (g/cm³)
Zinc (solid)	7.13
Silver (solid)	10.50
Lead (solid)	11.35

10 Claims · Evidence · Reasoning Suppose that 273 g of one of the substances listed above displaces 26 mL of water. What is the substance? Explain your reasoning.

_____

_____

_____

11 Evaluate How many mL of water would be displaced by 408 g of lead?

_____

_____

12 Predict How can you determine that a coin is not pure silver if you know the mass and volume of the coin?

_____

_____

_____

_____

_____

13 Calculate A truck whose bed is 2.5 m long, 1.5 m wide, and 1.0 m high is delivering sand for a sand-sculpture competition. About how many trips must the truck make to deliver 7 m³ of sand?

My Notes

Think Science

Evaluating Scientific Evidence

Many people and companies claim to use scientific evidence to support their ideas, arguments, or products. Some of this evidence may be strong and well-supported by scientific investigation. But some evidence may be biased, or may not be supported by valid scientific investigation. How can you recognize the difference?

Tutorial

The advertisement below highlights some things that you should consider as you try to evaluate scientific evidence.

Grow your best Indian blanket wildflowers using new Fertilizer Formulation!

Fertilizer Formulation

We tested 20 patches of Indian blanket wildflowers in the Valdosta, Georgia, area. Plants that received the recommended amount of fertilizer grew an average of 30% taller. This fertilizer is made of all-natural ingredients and provides the best mixture of nutrients for any garden.

Everyone should use this fertilizer!

Weakness This sample is biased. The advertisement says that everyone should use the fertilizer, but the sample plants were all from the Valdosta, Georgia, area. An unbiased test would include samples from other parts of the country.

Weakness "All-natural ingredients" is a vague statement that advertisers use because people tend to believe that "natural" is better. However, in many cases that statement doesn't really mean anything. The minerals found in all fertilizers are "natural".

Weakness This generalization is not supported by the evidence. The fertilizer was only tested on Indian blanket wildflowers. It is impossible to say, based on that evidence, whether the fertilizer would be good for gardens with other types of plants.

You Try It!

Read the following advertisement, and answer the questions below to evaluate whether the evidence supports the claims being made.

GroBig
Soil Additive

GroBig will work on all types of wildflowers!

Buy GroBig today, and watch your flowers grow!
$19.95 per liter

"I've found the secret to the best wildflower garden—using GroBig Soil Additive. Now, you can have your best garden, too."
— A. Gardener

Botanists at a private nursery near Tampa, Florida, selected two tall samples of a common wildflower, the narrow-leaved sunflower. One plant received the recommended amount of GroBig Soil Additive. The other did not. After 2 weeks, the plant given GroBig Soil Additive had grown 4 cm. The other plant had grown just 2 cm. What a difference!

1 Identifying Conclusions Identify the claim that the advertisers are making.

_____

_____

_____

2 Evaluating Evidence Identify two weaknesses in the evidence presented in this advertisement.

_____

_____

_____

_____

3 Applying Concepts List three questions you would need to answer in order to support the claims being made about GroBig.

_____

_____

_____

_____

_____

_____

Take It Home

Find an article or advertisement in a newspaper or magazine that contains a scientific claim and supporting information. Identify the evidence that is being used to support the claims in the article or advertisement. Write a paragraph that summarizes the article or advertisement and its scientific evidence.

Lesson 2

Properties of Matter

ESSENTIAL QUESTION

What are physical and chemical properties of matter?

By the end of this lesson, you should be able to classify and compare substances based on their physical and chemical properties.

To harvest cranberries, the dry beds are flooded with water. Next, water reels loosen the berries from the vines. Since cranberries are less dense than water, they float. Harvesters take advantage of this property to gather and easily float them toward collection sites.

S8P1.c Chemical and physical properties of matter

✋ Lesson Labs

Quick Labs
- Comparing Two Elements
- Observe Physical Properties

Exploration Lab
- Identifying an Unknown Substance

🐟 Engage Your Brain

1 Predict Check T or F to show whether you think each statement is true or false.

T F

☐ ☐ Liquid water freezes at the same temperature at which ice melts: 0 °C.

☐ ☐ A bowling ball weighs less than a Styrofoam ball of the same size.

☐ ☐ An object with a density greater than the density of water will float in water.

☐ ☐ Solubility is the ability of one substance to dissolve in another.

2 Describe If you were asked to describe an orange to someone who had never seen an orange, what would you tell the person?

_____

_____

_____

_____

_____

Active Reading

3 Synthesize Many English words have their roots in other languages. The root of the word *solubility* is the Latin word *solvere*, which means "to loosen." Make an educated guess about the meaning of the word *solubility*.

_____

_____

_____

_____

Vocabulary Terms

- physical property
- chemical property

4 Apply As you learn the definition of each vocabulary term in this lesson, create your own definition or sketch to help you remember the meaning of the term.

Physical Education

What are physical properties of matter?

What words would you use to describe a table? A chair? A piece of cloth? You would probably say something about the shape, color, and size of each object. Next, you might consider whether the object is hard or soft, smooth or rough. Normally, when describing an object, you identify what it is about that object that you can observe without changing the identity of the substances of which it is made.

They Are Used to Describe a Substance

A characteristic of a substance that can be observed and measured without changing the identity of the substance is called a **physical property**. Gold is one metal prized for its physical properties. Gold can be bent and shaped easily and has a lasting shine. Both properties make it an excellent metal for making coins and jewelry.

All of your senses can be used to detect physical properties. Color, shape, size, and texture are a few of the physical properties you encounter. Think of how you would describe an object to a friend. Most likely, your description would be a list of the object's physical properties.

Active Reading **5 Describe** Does observing a physical property of a substance change the identity of the substance? Explain.

_____
_____
_____
_____

Gold is a highly sought-after metal for making jewelry. Gold is dense, soft, and shiny, and it is resistant to tarnishing. Gold is often mixed with other metals to make it stronger.

In this factory, gold is being purified by the process of smelting. This process uses pressure, high heat, and chemicals to remove impurities from the gold.

They Can Be Observed without Changing the Identity of a Substance

Mass and volume are two physical properties. Thus, changing the mass or volume of a substance does not change the identity of the substance. For example, a lump of clay might have a mass of 200 g and a volume of 100 cm³. If you were to break the clay in half, you would have two 100-g pieces of clay, each with a volume of 50 cm³. You can bend and shape the clay, too. Even if you were to mold a realistic model of a car out of the clay, it still would be a piece of clay. Although you have changed some of the properties of the clay, such as its shape and color, you have not changed the fact that the substance you are observing is clay.

One easily observed physical property is state of matter—the physical form in which a substance exists. Solids, liquids, and gases are three common states of matter. Regardless of what state a substance is in, it is always that substance. For example, water is always water whether it is a solid, liquid, or gas.

Visualize It!

6 Observe Describe the physical properties of objects you see in this photo.

_____

_____

_____

_____

_____

Think Outside the Book

7 Apply Describe a common object by naming its properties. Trade your mystery-object description with a classmate's and try to guess what object he or she has described.

Common Physical Properties

On these two pages, you can read about some common physical properties. The physical properties of a substance often describe how the substance can be useful.

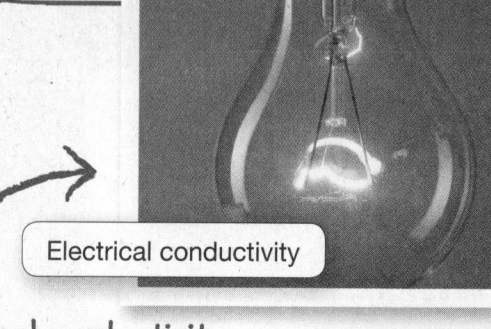

Electrical conductivity

Electrical conductivity is a measure of how well an electric current can move through a substance.

Density

Density is a measure of the amount of mass in a given amount of volume.

8 Explain The photo above shows oil and vinegar in a pitcher. The top layer is the oil. Describe the density of the vinegar compared to the density of the oil. Explain the evidence that supports your claim.

_____

_____

_____

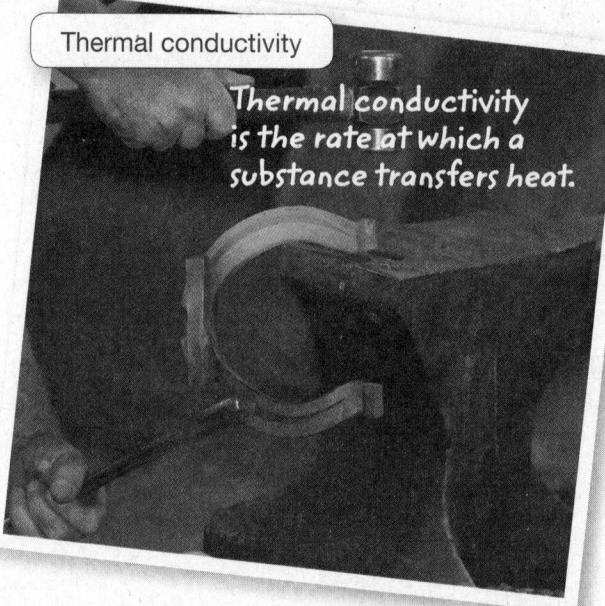

Thermal conductivity

Thermal conductivity is the rate at which a substance transfers heat.

Solubility

Solubility is the ability of a substance to dissolve in another substance. This powdered drink mix is dissolving in water. When fully dissolved, the particles of the drink mix will be spread throughout the water.

9 Predict If you let all of the liquid evaporate out of the pitcher, would you be able to see the solid particles of the drink mix? Explain.

_____

_____

_____

Malleability

Malleability (MAL·ee·uh·bil·i·tee) is the ability of a substance to be rolled or pounded into various shapes. Aluminum has the property of malleability.

10 Identify Name something made of aluminum and explain why malleability is a useful property.

_____

_____

_____

Some metals exert a magnetic attraction. Magnetic attraction can act at a distance.

Magnetic attraction

Luster

Many metals often have a shine, or luster, that make them prized by decorators.

Melting point

The melting point of a substance is the temperature at which it changes from a solid to a liquid.

Boiling water beneath the surface of Earth powers this geyser.

Boiling point

Inquiry

11 Infer Compare what happens when a geyser erupts to what happens when a tea kettle whistles.

_____

_____

_____

_____

Identity Theft

What are chemical properties of matter?

Active Reading **12 Identify** As you read, underline the definition of a chemical property.

Physical properties are not the only properties that describe matter. A **chemical property** describes a substance's ability to change into a new substance with different properties. Common chemical properties include combustibility and reactivity with substances such as oxygen, water, and acids.

They Describe How a Substance Changes

Can you think of a chemical property for the metal iron? When left outdoors in wet weather, iron rusts. The ability to rust is a chemical property of iron. The metal silver does not rust, but eventually a darker substance, called tarnish, forms on its surface. You may have noticed a layer of tarnish on some silver spoons or jewelry. Rusting and tarnishing are chemical properties because the identity of the metal changes. After rusting or tarnishing, a portion of the metal is no longer the metal but a different substance.

The ability to ripen is a chemical property.

13 Predict Why do automobiles rust more easily in wet climates than drier climates?

_____

_____

_____

_____

Iron can form rust, turning a once shiny car into a crumbling relic.

They Can Be Observed by Attempting to Change the Identity of a Substance

One way to identify a chemical property is to observe the changes that a substance undergoes. Wood for a campfire has the chemical property of flammability—the ability to burn. When wood burns, new substances are formed: water, carbon dioxide, and ash. These new substances have different properties than the wood had. Reactivity is another chemical property that can be identified by observing changes. Reactivity is the ability of a substance to interact with another substance and form one or more new substances.

You can also observe a chemical property of a substance by attempting to change the substance, even if no change occurs. For example, you can observe that gold is nonflammable by attempting to burn it. A chemical property of gold is that it is nonflammable.

Reactivity is a chemical property. Vinegar and baking soda react to make water, a salt, and carbon dioxide gas.

Flammability, or the ability of a substance to burn, is a chemical property. For example, the wood building in the photo is flammable, and the suits that help keep the firefighters safe are flame resistant.

Property [Boundaries]

What is the difference between physical and chemical properties?

How do you tell a physical property from a chemical property? A physical property of a substance can change without changing the identity of the substance. The form of the substance may change, but its identity remains unchanged. For example, the size and shape of a sheet of paper changes when the sheet is torn into smaller pieces. Changing these properties alters the form of the paper but does not alter the paper's identity. The smaller pieces consist of the same substance that was present in the original sheet. Therefore, size and shape are physical properties.

A chemical property of a substance changes when the substance undergoes a change in identity. A new substance is formed when chemical properties are changed. For example, consider that burning a sheet of paper demonstrates its combustibility. Burning changes the paper into new substances. One substance produced is carbon dioxide, a gas that is released into the air. A second substance produced is ash. Neither substance has the same identity as the original sheet of paper. Therefore, combustibility is a chemical property.

Active Reading 14 **Describe** In your own words, describe the difference between a physical property and a chemical property.

_____

_____

Think Outside the Book Inquiry

15 **Design** Plan experiments that will distinguish between chemical properties and physical properties using the following two processes: 1) burning a candle, and 2) melting a candle. Describe how your experiments will allow you to distinguish chemical properties from physical properties of wax. Then carry out your experiments to test your predictions.

Visualize It!

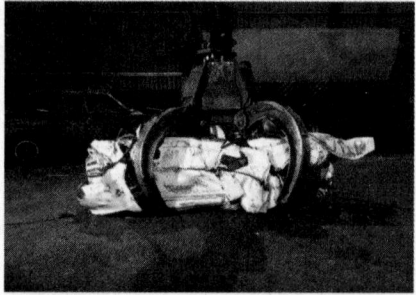

Crushing demonstrates a physical property of metal.

16 **Apply** What observations can be used as evidence that crushing demonstrates a physical property and not a chemical property of metal?

_____

_____

Rusting demonstrates a chemical property of metal.

17 **Apply** What observations can be used as evidence that rusting demonstrates a chemical property and not a physical property of metal?

_____

_____

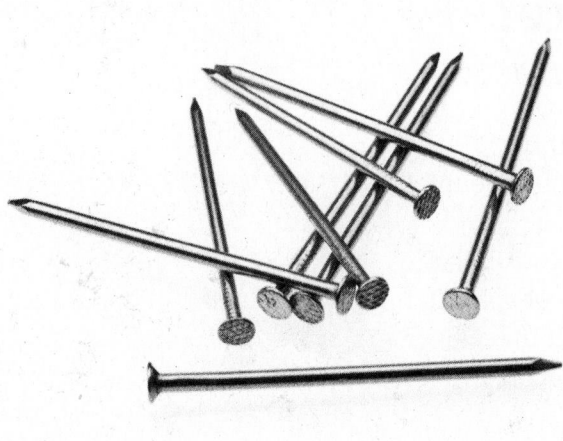

Visualize It!

18 Apply Identify a physical property and a chemical property of the substance shown in each image. Briefly describe evidence to support each of your identifications.

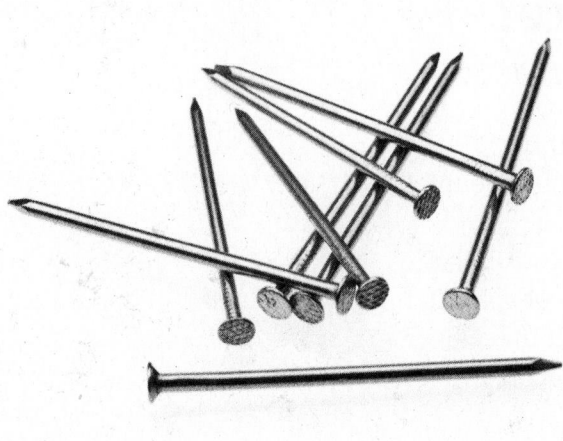

physical property:

_____

_____

chemical property:

_____

_____

physical property:

_____

_____

chemical property:

_____

_____

physical property:

_____

_____

chemical property:

_____

_____

physical property:

_____

_____

chemical property:

_____

_____

How can physical and chemical properties identify a substance?

Properties unique to a substance are its *characteristic properties*. Characteristic properties can be physical properties, such as density, or chemical properties, such as combustibility. Characteristic properties stay the same regardless of the amount of a sample. They can help identify a substance.

Iron pyrite is one of several minerals having a color similar to that of gold. Miners can find iron pyrite near deposits of gold, and sometimes mistake it for gold. Color however, is about the only property iron pyrite shares with gold. The two substances have quite different characteristic properties.

For example, gold flattens when hit with a hammer, but iron pyrite shatters. When rubbed on a ceramic plate, gold leaves a yellow streak, but iron pyrite leaves a greenish black one. Gold keeps its shine even if beneath the sea for years, but iron pyrite turns green if exposed to water.

An easy way for miners to tell iron pyrite and gold apart is by using the property of density. Miners collect gold by sifting through dirt in pans. Because of its high density, gold stays in the pan while dirt and most other substances wash over the side as the miner swirls the contents in the pan. Because gold has a density almost four times that of iron pyrite, distinguishing gold from iron pyrite should be an easy task for the experienced miner.

> To find the density of a substance, use the following formula, where D is density, m is mass, and V is volume:
>
> $$D = \frac{m}{V}$$

19 Infer Check the box to show which would tell you for sure if you had a sample of real gold.

	Yes	No
Color of your sample.	☐	☐
What happens when you strike your sample with a hammer.	☐	☐
The location where your sample was found.	☐	☐

In pan mining, as the contents in the pan are swirled, less dense substances are washed away.

© Houghton Mifflin Harcourt Publishing Company • Image Credits: ©Neil Overy//Getty Images

 **Do the Math**

Sample Problem

A sample of gold has a mass of 579 g. The volume of the sample is 30 cm³. What is the density of the gold sample?

Identify

A. What do you know?

mass = 579 g, volume = 30 cm³

B. What do you want to find? Density

Plan

C. Write the formula: $D = \dfrac{m}{V}$

D. Substitute the given values into the formula:

$$D = \dfrac{579 \text{ g}}{30 \text{ cm}^3}$$

Solve

E. Divide: $\dfrac{579 \text{ g}}{30 \text{ cm}^3} = 19.3 \text{ g/cm}^3$

F. Check that your units agree:

The given units are grams and cubic centimeters, and the measure found is density. Therefore, the units should be g/cm³. The units agree.

Answer: 19.3 g/cm³

Gold

Iron pyrite

You Try It

20 Calculate A student finds an object with a mass of 64.54 g and a volume of 14 cm³. Find the density of the object. Could the object be gold?

Identify

A. What do you know?

B. What do you want to find?

Plan

C. Write the formula:

D. Substitute the given values into the formula:

Solve

E. Divide:

F. Check that your units agree:

Answer:

	Yes	No
Could the object be gold?	☐	☐

Decisions, Decisions...

How are materials chosen?

Materials are chosen because of their characteristics. The characteristics of a material include the material's physical and chemical properties. These properties influence the way a material functions.

By Chemical Properties

Chemical properties describe a material's ability to take part in a chemical reaction. Some materials are chosen because they are nonreactive and do not take part in chemical reactions easily. Stainless steel and some plastics are highly nonreactive. Other materials are chosen because they do react chemically. For example, ammonia is used in cleaners because it reacts with grease. After the ammonia is applied, the grease dissolves more easily in water and can be washed away.

By Physical Properties

Physical properties are the characteristics of a material that can be observed or measured without changing the material's composition. Some physical properties of materials include:

- Density
- Boiling point and melting point
- Transparency, or the ability to let light pass though
- Conductivity, or the ability to carry electric current
- Hardness

Visualize It!

21 Apply How do the physical and chemical properties of the glass cleaner, glass, and paper towels enable these items to be used for their intended purposes?

_____

_____

_____

_____

22 Infer How do you think the chemical properties of stainless steel compare to those of iron? Why are kitchen sinks made of stainless steel rather than iron?

_____

_____

_____

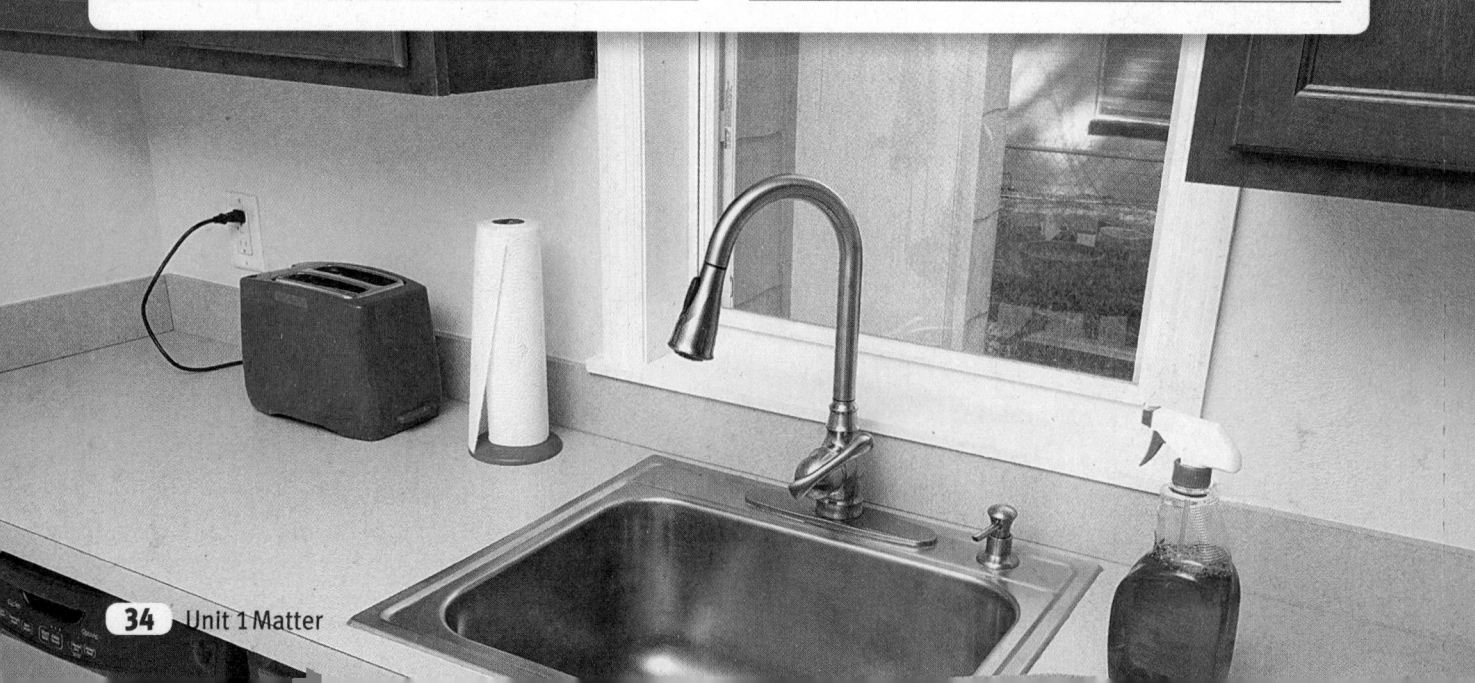

Materials used for products that function in the human body must meet certain requirements. For example, any material that comes into contact with our bodies must be non-toxic. This is important so the material won't cause harm to living tissue.

Dental braces are used to straighten teeth. Braces contain many different materials that are used because of their physical and chemical properties.

The information lists requirements of materials used in the most common type of braces, the parts of braces, and materials that are typically used in these kinds of braces.

Requirements of Materials for Braces
Non-toxic
Rigid
Malleable
Nonreactive
Adhesive
Elastic
Low density

Parts of Braces	Materials Typically Used
Bracket	Stainless steel
Wire	Stainless steel or alloy of nickel, copper, and titanium
Ties for brackets	Rubber bands
Bracket bonding cement	Glue

23 Analyze Use the information provided to explain why each of the materials listed is appropriate to use for the different parts of braces.

_____

_____

_____

_____

24 Infer Some braces are made out of ceramic or a plastic material that is transparent. Why do you think those materials may have been chosen instead of metal?

_____

_____

_____

Visual Summary

To complete this summary, circle the correct word. Then use the key below to check your answers. You can use this page to review the main concepts of the lesson.

Physical and Chemical Properties

A physical property is a property that can be observed or measured without changing the identity of the substance.

25 Solubility / Combustibility is a physical property.

26 The melting point of a substance is the temperature at which the substance changes from a solid to a gas / liquid.

A chemical property is a property that describes a substance's ability to form new substances.

27 Reactivity with water / Magnetism is a chemical property.

28 Combustibility is the ability of a substance to transfer heat / burn.

The properties that are most useful in identifying a substance are its characteristic properties. Characteristic properties can be physical properties or chemical properties.

29 The characteristic properties of a substance do / do not depend on the size of the sample.

Answers: 25 Solubility; 26 liquid; 27 Reactivity with water; 28 burn; 29 do not

30 Claims · Evidence · Reasoning You have two solid substances that look the same. What measurements would you take and which tests would you perform to determine whether they actually are the same? Explain how the evidence you suggest gathering would support a claim made about the substances.

Lesson Review

Vocabulary

Fill in the blanks with the term that best completes the following sentences.

1 Combustibility is an example of a _____ property.

2 Electrical conductivity is an example of a _____ property.

Key Concepts

3 Identify What are three physical properties of aluminum foil?

_____

_____

_____

_____

4 Describe What effect does observing a substance's physical properties have on the substance?

_____

_____

_____

_____

5 Explain Describe how a physical property, such as mass or texture, can change without causing a change in the substance.

_____

_____

_____

_____

6 Justify Must new substances be formed when you observe a chemical property? Explain the reasoning for your claim.

_____

_____

_____

_____

Critical Thinking

Use this table to answer the following question.

Element	Melting Point (°C)	Boiling Point (°C)
Bromine	−7.2	59
Chlorine	−100	−35
Iodine	110	180

7 Infer You are given samples of the substances shown in the table. The samples are labeled A, B, and C. At room temperature, sample A is a solid, sample B is a liquid, and sample C is a gas. What are the identities of samples A, B, and C? (Hint: Room temperature is about 20 °C.)

_____

_____

_____

8 Conclude The density of gold is 19.3 g/cm³. The density of iron pyrite is 5.0 g/cm³. If a nugget of iron pyrite and a nugget of gold each have a mass of 50 g, what can you conclude about the volume of each nugget?

_____

_____

_____

9 Predict Suppose you need to build a raft to cross a fast-moving river. Describe the physical and chemical properties of the raft that would be important to ensure your safety.

_____

_____

_____

_____

_____

My Notes

Houghton Mifflin Harcourt Publishing Company

Lesson 3

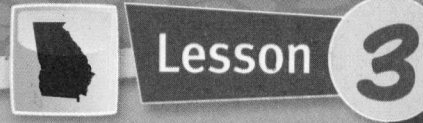

Physical and Chemical Changes

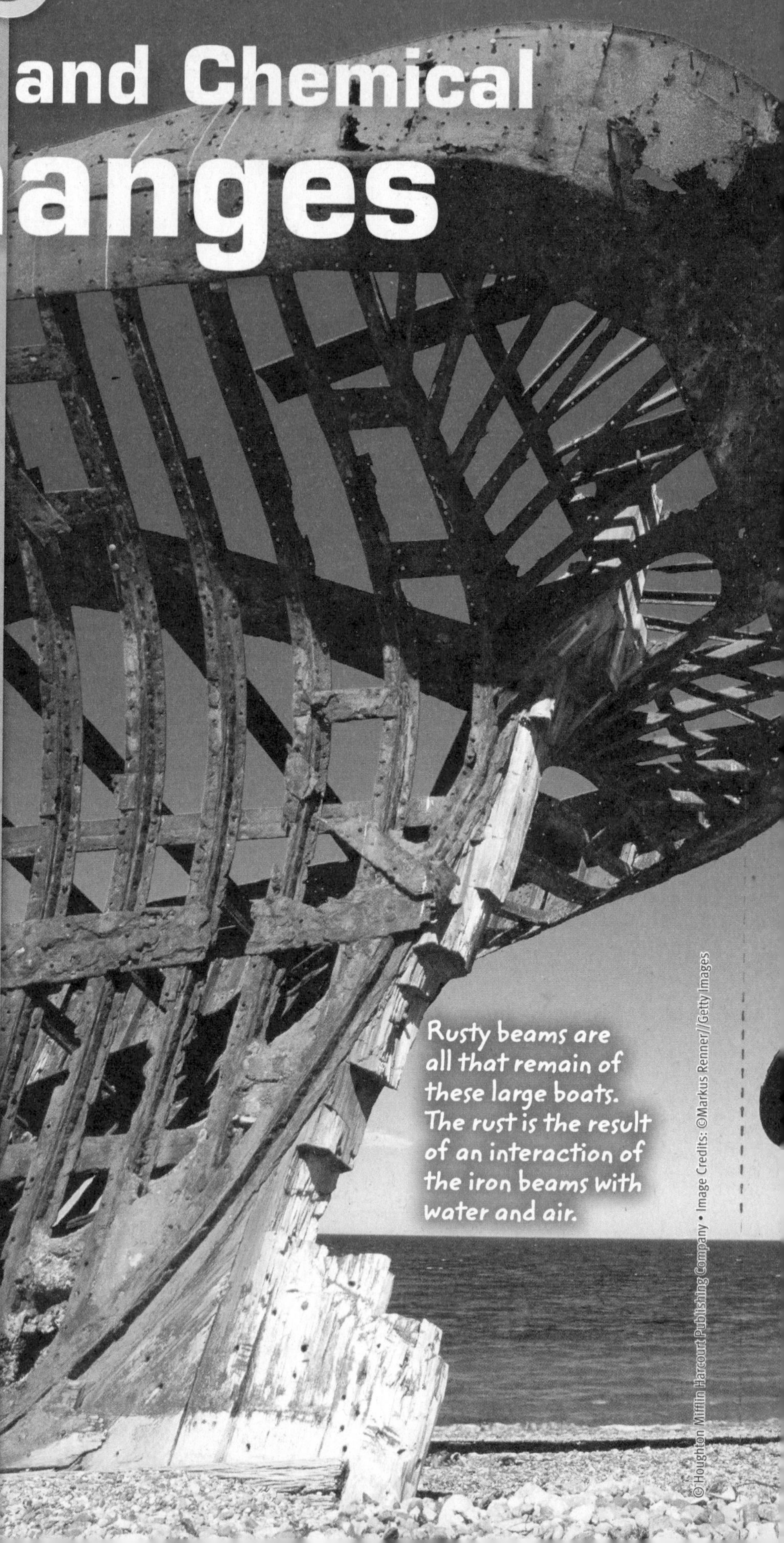

Rusty beams are all that remain of these large boats. The rust is the result of an interaction of the iron beams with water and air.

ESSENTIAL QUESTION

What are physical and chemical changes of matter?

By the end of this lesson, you should be able to distinguish between physical and chemical changes of matter.

S8P1.d Chemical and physical changes in substances

S8P1.f Conservation of matter in chemical reactions

Lesson Labs

Quick Labs
- Physical or Chemical Change?
- Properties of Combined Substances

Engage Your Brain

1 Predict Check T or F to show whether you think each statement is true or false.

T	F	
☐	☐	When an ice cube melts, it is still water.
☐	☐	Matter is lost when a candle is burned.
☐	☐	When your body digests food, the food is changed into new substances.

2 Describe Write a word or phrase beginning with each letter of the word CHANGE that describes changes you have observed in everyday objects.

C ____________________

H ____________________

A ____________________

N ____________________

G ____________________

E ____________________

Active Reading

3 Apply Use context clues to write your own definitions for the words *interact* and *indicate.*

Example sentence
As the two substances interact, gas bubbles are given off.

interact:

____

____

____

Example sentence
A color change may indicate that a chemical change has taken place.

indicate:

____

____

____

Vocabulary Terms

- **physical change**
- **chemical change**
- **law of conservation of mass**

4 Apply As you learn the definition of each vocabulary term in this lesson, create your own definition or sketch to help you remember the meaning of the term.

Change of Appearance

What are physical changes of matter?

A physical property of matter is any property that can be observed or measured without changing the chemical identity of the substance. A **physical change** is a change that affects one or more physical properties of a substance. Physical changes occur when a substance changes from one form to another. However, the chemical identity of the substance remains the same.

Changes in Observable Properties

The appearance, shape, or size of a substance may be altered during a physical change. For example, the process of turning wool into a sweater requires that the wool undergo physical changes. Wool is sheared from the sheep. The wool is then cleaned, and the wool fibers are separated from one another. Shearing and separating the fibers are physical changes that change the shape, volume, and texture of the wool.

Active Reading

5 Explain What happens to a substance during a physical change?

_____

_____

_____

Physical Changes Turn Wool into a Sweater

A Wool is sheared from the sheep. The raw wool is then cleaned and placed into a machine that separates the wool fibers from one another.

B The wool fibers are spun into yarn. Again, the shape and volume of the wool change. The fibers are twisted so that they are packed more closely together and are intertwined with one another.

C The yarn is dyed. The dye changes the color of the wool, but it does not change the wool into another substance. This type of color change is a physical change.

Changes That Do Not Alter the Chemical Identity of the Substance

During the process of turning wool into a sweater, many physical changes occur in the wool. However, the wool does not change into some other substance as a result of these changes. Therefore, physical changes do not change the chemical identity of a substance.

Another example of a physical change happens when you fill an ice cube tray with water and place it inside a freezer. If the water gets cold enough, it will freeze to form ice cubes. Freezing water does not change its chemical makeup. In fact, you could melt the ice cube and have liquid water again! Changes of state, and all physical changes, do not change the chemical makeup of the substance.

6 Identify The list below gives several examples of physical changes. Write your own examples of physical changes on the blank lines.

Examples of Physical Changes
Stretching a rubber band
Dissolving sugar in water
Cutting your hair
Melting butter
Bending a paper clip
Crushing an aluminum can

_____

_____

_____

D Knitting the yarn into a sweater also does not change the wool into another substance. A wool sweater is still wool, even though it no longer resembles the wool on the sheep.

Visualize It!

7 Analyze How does the yarn in the sweater differ from the wool on the sheep?

_____

_____

Change from

What are chemical changes of matter?

Think about what happens to the burning logs in a campfire. They start out dry, rough, and dense. After flames surround them, the logs emerge as black and powdery ashes. The campfire releases a lot of heat and smoke in the process. Something has obviously happened, something more than simply a change of appearance. The wood has stopped being wood. It has undergone a chemical change.

Changes in Substance Identity

A **chemical change** occurs when one or more substances change into entirely new substances with different properties. For example, in the campfire, the dry, dense wood became the powdery ashes—new substances with different properties. When a cake is baked, the liquid cake batter becomes the solid, spongy treat. Whenever a new substance is formed, a chemical change has occurred.

Be aware that chemical *changes* are not exactly the same as chemical *properties*. Burning is a chemical change; combustibility is a chemical property. The chemical properties of a substance describe which chemical changes can or cannot happen to that substance. Chemical changes are the *processes* by which substances actually change into new substances. You can learn about a substance's chemical properties by watching the chemical changes that substance undergoes.

Visualize It!

8 Identify Use the boxes provided to identify the wood, ashes, and flames involved in the chemical change. Then write a caption describing the chemical changes you see in the photo.

_____

_____

_____

_____

the inside

A _____

B _____

C _____

Changes to the Chemical Makeup of a Substance

In a chemical change, a substance's identity changes because its chemical makeup changes. This happens as the particles and chemical bonds that make up the substance get rearranged. For example, when iron rusts, molecules of oxygen from the air combine with iron atoms to form a new compound. Rust is not iron or oxygen. It is a new substance made up of oxygen and iron joined together.

Because chemical changes involve changes in the arrangements of particles, they are often influenced by temperature. At higher temperatures, the particles in a substance have more average kinetic energy. They move around a lot more freely and so rearrange more easily. Therefore, at higher temperatures, chemical reactions often happen more quickly. Think of baking a cake. The higher the temperature of the oven, the less time the cake will need to bake because the faster the chemical reactions occur.

Active Reading **9 Explain** How do higher temperatures influence a chemical change?

_____

_____

_____

Think Outside the Book Inquiry

10 Infer Think of ways you control temperature to influence chemical changes during a typical day. (Hint: Cooking, Art class)

Look for the signs

How can you tell a chemical change has happened?

Physical changes and chemical changes are different. Chemical changes result in new substances, while physical changes do not. However, it may not be obvious that any new substances have formed during a chemical change. Here are some signs that a chemical change may have occurred. If you observe two or more of these signs during a change, you likely are observing a chemical change.

Active Reading **11 Compare** How are physical and chemical changes different?

_____

_____

_____

_____

Production of an Odor

Some chemical changes produce odors. The chemical change that occurs when an egg is rotting, for example, produces the smell of sulfur. Milk that has soured also has an unpleasant smell—because bacteria have formed new substances in the milk. And if you've gone outdoors after a thunderstorm, you've probably noticed a distinct smell. This odor is an indication that lightning has caused a chemical change in the air.

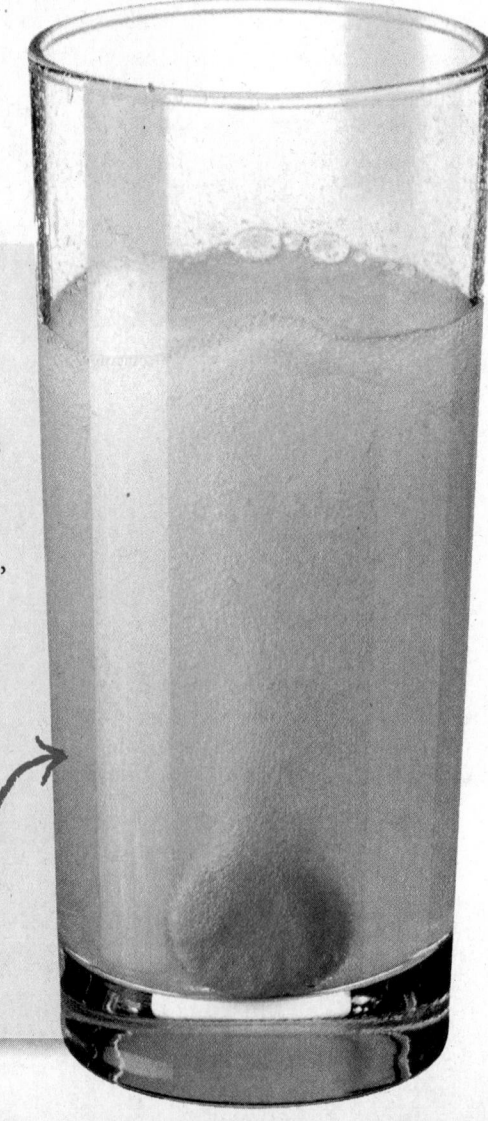

Production of a Gas

Chemical changes often cause fizzing or foaming. For example, a chemical change is involved when an antacid tablet is dropped into a glass of water. As the tablet makes contact with the water and begins to react with it, bubbles of gas appear. One of the new substances that is formed is carbon dioxide gas, which forms the bubbles that you see.

It is important to note that some physical changes, such as boiling, can also produce gas bubbles. Therefore, the only way to know for sure whether a chemical change has taken place is to identify new substances.

Bubbles form when an antacid tablet reacts with water. The bubbles contain a new, gaseous substance, which signals that a chemical change has happened.

© Houghton Mifflin Harcourt Publishing Company • Image Credits: ©PhotoSpin, Inc/Alamy

Formation of a Precipitate

Chemical changes may result in products in different physical states. Liquids sometimes combine to form a solid called a *precipitate*. For example, colorless potassium iodide and lead nitrate combine to form the bright yellow precipitate lead iodide, as shown below.

Bright yellow lead iodide precipitates from the clear solution.

Change in Color

A change in color is often an indication of a chemical change. For example, when gray iron rusts, the product that forms is brown.

Change in Energy

Chemical changes can cause energy to change from one form into another. For example, in a burning candle, the chemical energy stored in the candle converts to heat and light energy.

A change in temperature is often a sign of a chemical change. The change need not always be as dramatic as the one in the photo, however.

The reaction of powdered aluminum with a metal oxide releases so much heat that it is often used to weld metals together. Here it is being used to test the heat-resistant properties of steel.

12 Apply Classify each change listed below as either physical or chemical. Then describe the evidence that supports your claim.

Change	Type of change	Evidence to support your claim
Boiling water		
Baking a cake		
Burning wood		
Painting a door		

Conservation is the Law

What is the law of conservation of mass?

If you freeze 5 mL of water and then let the ice melt, you have 5 mL of water again. You can freeze and melt the water as much as you like. The mass of water will not change.

This does not always seem true for chemical changes. The ashes remaining after a fire contain much less mass than the logs that produced them. Mass seems to vanish. In other chemical changes, such as those that cause the growth of plants, mass seems to appear out of nowhere. This puzzled scientists for years. Where did the mass go? Where did it come from?

In the 1770s, the French chemist Antoine Lavoisier (an•TWAHN luh•VWAH•zee•ay) studied chemical changes in which substances seemed to lose or gain mass. He used experimentation to show that the mass was most often lost to or gained from gases in the air. This was the first demonstration of the *law of conservation of mass*. The **law of conservation of mass** states that in ordinary chemical and physical changes, mass is not created or destroyed but is only transformed into different substances. Matter is conserved as well because the same particles making up a substance are present in the same numbers before and after any chemical or physical change.

The examples on the next page will help you understand how the law works in both physical and chemical changes. In the top example, the second robot may have a different shape than the first, but it clearly has the same parts. In the second example, vinegar and baking soda undergo a chemical change. Mix the baking soda with the vinegar in the flask, and mass seems to vanish. Yet the balloon shows that what really happens is the production of a gas—carbon dioxide gas.

Active Reading **13 Identify** What is the law of conservation of mass?

_____

_____

The water may freeze or the ice may melt, but the amount of matter in this glass will stay the same.

© Houghton Mifflin Harcourt Publishing Company • Image Credits: ©D. Hurst/Alamy

Conservation of Mass in Physical Changes

When the long gray piece is moved from its arms to its waist, the toy robot gets a new look. It's still a toy robot—its parts are just rearranged. This demonstrates that matter has not been created or destroyed. Because matter is conserved, mass is conserved. All physical changes follow the law of conservation of mass.

Before

After

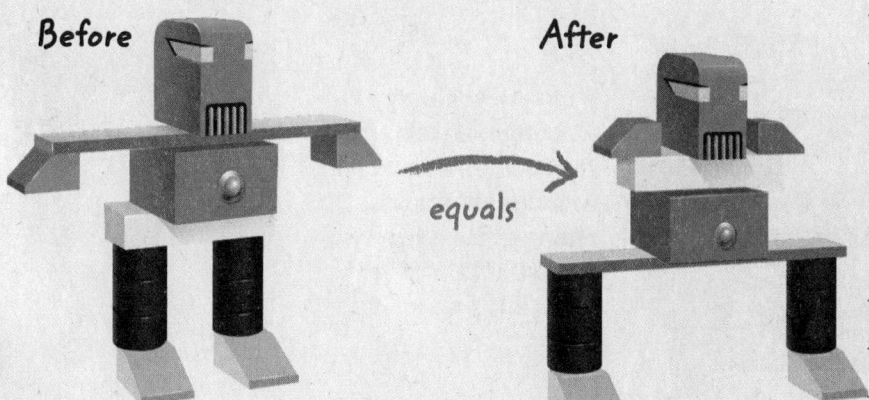

equals

 Visualize It!

14 **Describe** How is the physical change in the robot reversible?

_____

_____

15 **Justify** What numerical data can you use as evidence that matter is conserved in this example? How do the data you suggest support the law of conservation of mass?

_____

_____

_____

Conservation of Mass in Chemical Changes

When vinegar and baking soda are combined, they undergo a chemical change. One of the products is carbon dioxide, a gas, that fills the balloon attached to the reaction flask. Matter is conserved because none of the particles making up vinegar and baking soda are destroyed. Instead, they are rearranged to form new substances. Mass is conserved because there is no change in the total quantity of matter present before and after the reaction.

Before

After

equals

vinegar

baking soda

When vinegar and baking soda combine, carbon dioxide gas is produced.

👁 Visualize It!

16 **Infer** What would you observe about the mass in the flask if you did not put the balloon on top? Explain your reasoning.

_____

_____

Visual Summary

To complete this summary, circle the correct word or phrase. Then use the key below to check your answers. You can use this page to review the main concepts of the lesson.

How Matter Changes

A physical change is a change of matter from one form to another without a change in the identity of the substance.

17 Burning / Dying wool is an example of a physical change.

A chemical change is a change of matter that occurs when one or more substances change into entirely new substances with different properties.

18 The formation of a precipitate signals a physical / chemical change.

Chemical changes often cause the production of an odor, fizzing or foaming, the formation of a precipitate, or changes in color or temperature.

19 This physical / chemical change results in the formation of new substances.

The law of conservation of mass states that mass cannot be created or destroyed in ordinary chemical and physical changes.

20 The mass of the toy on the right is the same as / different from the mass of the toy on the left.

Answers: 17 Dying; 18 chemical; 19 chemical; 20 the same as

21 Explain Do changes that cannot be easily reversed, such as burning, observe the law of conservation of mass? Explain.

Lesson Review

Vocabulary

In your own words, define the following terms.

1 physical change

_____

_____

_____

2 chemical change

_____

_____

_____

3 law of conservation of mass

_____

_____

_____

Key Concepts

4 Identify Give an example of a physical change and an example of a chemical change.

_____

_____

_____

_____

5 Compare How is a chemical change different from a physical change?

_____

_____

_____

_____

6 Apply Suppose a log's mass is 5 kg. After burning, the mass of the ash is 1 kg. Explain what may have happened to the other 4 kg.

_____

_____

_____

_____

Critical Thinking

Use this photo to answer the following question.

7 Analyze As the bright sun shines upon the water, the water slowly disappears. The same sunlight gives energy to the surrounding plants to convert water and carbon dioxide into sugar and oxygen gas. Which change is physical and which is chemical?

_____

_____

_____

8 Compare Relate the statement "You can't get something for nothing" to the law of the conservation of mass.

_____

_____

_____

9 Claims · Evidence · Reasoning A student claims that any change in matter can be classified as either a physical change or a chemical change. Do you agree or disagree? What evidence would you use to support your claim? Explain your reasoning.

_____

_____

_____

_____

My Notes

Engineering Design Process

Skills
Identify a need
Conduct research
✓ Brainstorm solutions
✓ Select a solution
✓ Design a prototype
✓ Build a prototype
✓ Test and evaluate
Redesign to improve
✓ Communicate results

Objectives
• List and rank insulation materials according to effectiveness.
• Design a technological solution to keep an ice cube frozen.
• Test a prototype insulated ice cooler and communicate whether it achieved the desired results.

Building an Insulated Cooler

What do freezers, ovens, and polar bears have in common? They are all insulated! *Insulation* is a type of material that slows the transfer of energy such as heat. Refrigerators and freezers use insulation to keep the food inside cold. Insulation around ovens keeps energy inside the oven. And some animals have hair, fur, and fat layers that provide them with insulation, too.

1 Apply Which items in this picture provide insulation?

_____

_____

_____

_____

_____

2 List Name other everyday objects not shown here where insulation is used to keep objects warm or cool.

_____

_____

_____

_____

_____

_____

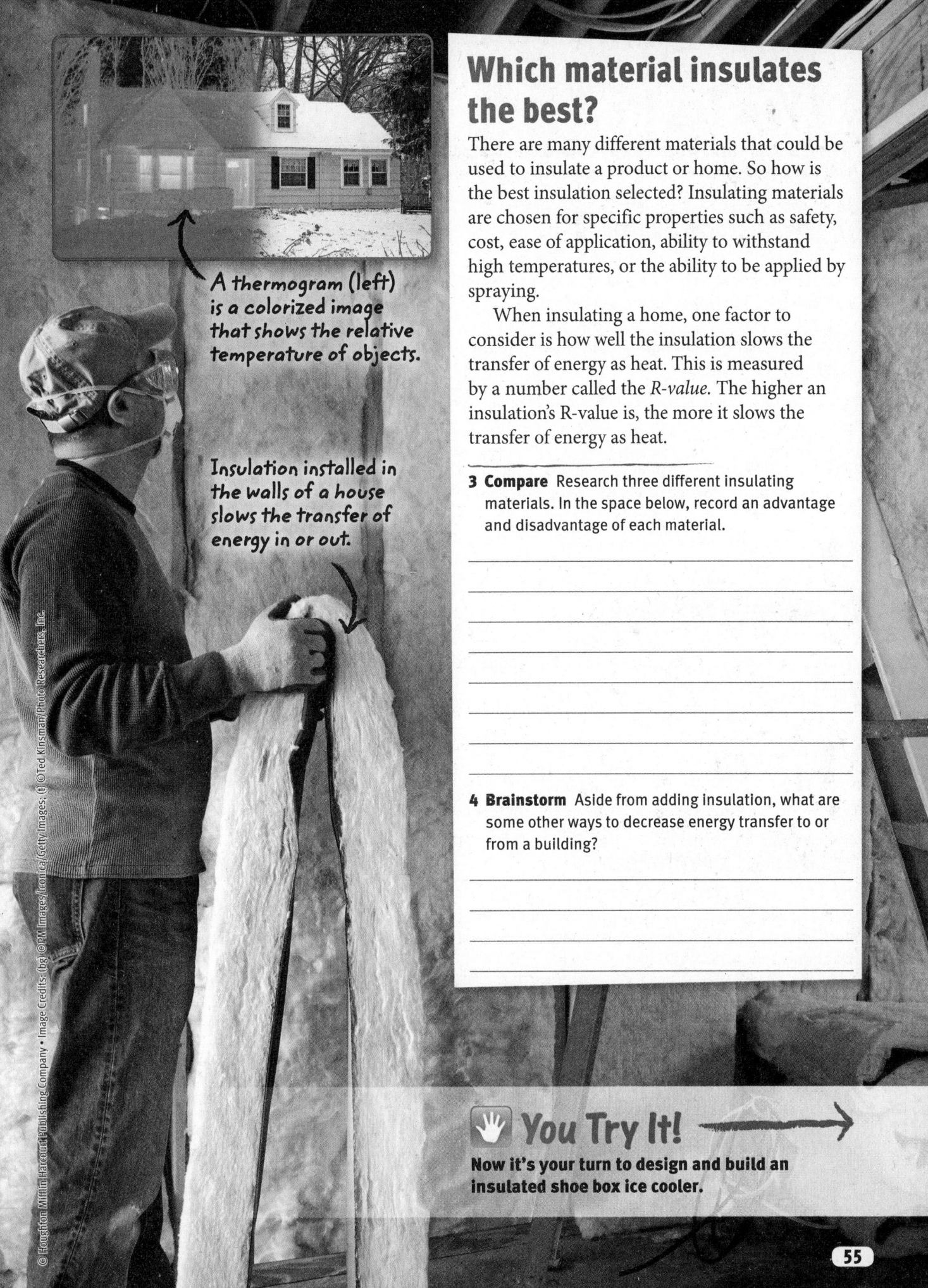

A thermogram (left) is a colorized image that shows the relative temperature of objects.

Insulation installed in the walls of a house slows the transfer of energy in or out.

Which material insulates the best?

There are many different materials that could be used to insulate a product or home. So how is the best insulation selected? Insulating materials are chosen for specific properties such as safety, cost, ease of application, ability to withstand high temperatures, or the ability to be applied by spraying.

When insulating a home, one factor to consider is how well the insulation slows the transfer of energy as heat. This is measured by a number called the *R-value*. The higher an insulation's R-value is, the more it slows the transfer of energy as heat.

3 Compare Research three different insulating materials. In the space below, record an advantage and disadvantage of each material.

_____

_____

_____

_____

_____

_____

_____

_____

4 Brainstorm Aside from adding insulation, what are some other ways to decrease energy transfer to or from a building?

_____

_____

_____

_____

👋 You Try It! ⟶

Now it's your turn to design and build an insulated shoe box ice cooler.

 You Try It!

Now it's your turn to design and build an insulated cooler that will keep an ice cube frozen for an entire class period.

① Brainstorm Solutions

You Will Need

✓ balance

✓ duct tape or packing tape

✓ ice cube

✓ insulation material

✓ plastic bag or waterproof container

✓ shoe box, empty

Brainstorm ideas to construct an insulated shoe box cooler that will keep an ice cube frozen for a class period.

A What insulation materials could you put into the empty shoe box to prevent the transfer of energy as heat?

_____

_____

B What waterproof container will you place under or around the ice cube so water doesn't affect the insulation as the ice cube melts?

_____

_____

② Select a Solution

Which materials and design offer the best promise for success? Why?

_____

_____

_____

_____

③ Design a Prototype

In the space below, draw a prototype of your insulated cooler. Be sure to include all the parts you will need and show how they will be connected.

(4) Build a Prototype

Now build your insulated cooler. What parts, if any, did you have to revise as you were building the prototype?

_____

_____

_____

_____

(5) Test and Evaluate

A At the beginning of a class period, find the mass of an ice cube. Record your result below.

_____

B Place the ice cube in your cooler and close it. At the end of the class period, open the cooler and observe the ice cube. Find the ice cube's mass and record your result below.

_____

C Was part of the ice still frozen? Calculate the fraction of the ice cube that remained frozen.

_____

(6) Communicate Results

A Did your cooler provide effective insulation? Explain.

_____

_____

_____

B Is there anything you could have done to increase the amount of ice remaining?

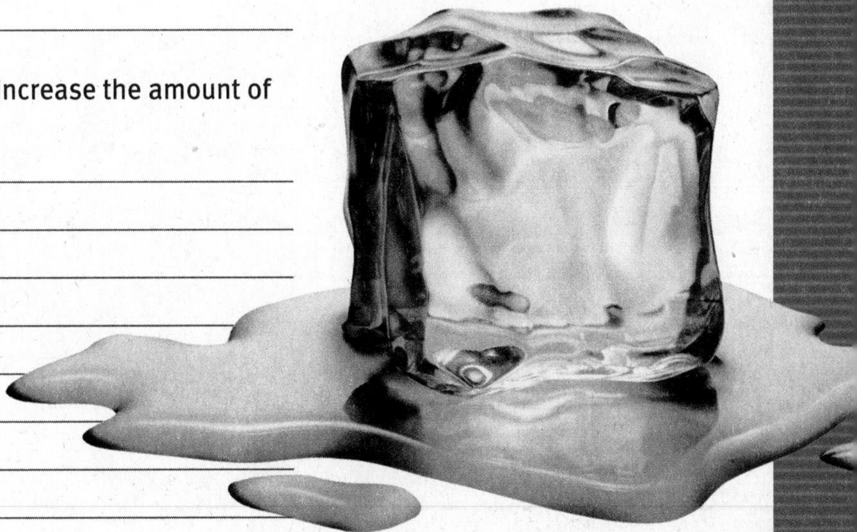

_____

_____

_____

_____

_____

_____

_____

_____

_____

Pure Substances and Mixtures

ESSENTIAL QUESTION

How do pure substances and mixtures compare?

By the end of this lesson, you should be able to distinguish between pure substances and mixtures.

Seawater is a unique mixture that contains many dissolved substances. One such substance, called calcium carbonate, is used by these stony coral to build their hard skeletons.

S8P1.a Pure substances and mixtures

S8P1.d Chemical and physical changes in substances

Lesson Labs

Quick Labs
• Observing Mixtures
• Identifying Elements and Compounds
Exploration Lab
• Investigating Separating Mixtures

Engage Your Brain

1 Predict Check T or F to show whether you think each statement is true or false.

T F

☐ ☐ Atoms combine in different ways to make up all of the substances you encounter every day.

☐ ☐ Saltwater can be separated into salt and water.

☐ ☐ A mixture of soil has the same chemical composition throughout.

2 Apply Think of a substance that does not dissolve in water. Draw a sketch below that shows what happens when this substance is added to water.

Active Reading

3 Synthesize Many English words have their roots in other languages. Use the Greek words below to make an educated guess about the meanings of the words *homogeneous* and *heterogeneous*.

Greek word	Meaning
genus	type
homos	same
heteros	different

Example sentence
Saltwater is homogeneous throughout.

homogeneous:

_____

_____

Example sentence
A heterogeneous mixture of rocks varies from handful to handful.

heterogeneous:

_____

_____

Vocabulary Terms

• atom
• element
• compound
• mixture

• pure substance
• heterogeneous
• homogeneous

4 Identify This list contains the key terms you'll learn in this lesson. As you read, circle the defnition of each term.

A Great Combination

How can matter be classified?

What kinds of food could you make with the ingredients shown below? You could eat slices of tomato as a snack. Or, you could combine tomato slices with lettuce to make a salad. Combine more ingredients, such as bread and cheese, and you have a sandwich. Just as these meals are made up of simpler foods, matter is made up of basic "ingredients" known as *atoms*. **Atoms** are the smallest unit of an element that maintains the properties of that element. Atoms, like the foods shown here, can be combined in different ways to produce different substances.

The substances you encounter every day can be classified into one of the three major classes of matter: *elements, compounds,* and *mixtures*. Atoms are the basic building blocks for all three types of matter. Elements, compounds, and mixtures differ in the way that atoms are combined.

Active Reading 5 **Compare** What do elements, compounds, and mixtures have in common?

_____

_____

Think Outside the Book Inquiry

6 **Predict** If you have ever baked a cake or bread, you know that the ingredients that combine to make it taste different from the baked food. Why do you think that is?

Just as these ingredients combine to make a tasty sandwich, atoms are the basic "ingredients" that make up matter.

Matter Can Be Classified into Elements, Compounds, and Mixtures

You can think of atoms as the building blocks of matter. Like these toy blocks, atoms can be connected in different ways. The models below show how atoms make up elements and compounds. Elements and compounds, in turn, make up mixtures.

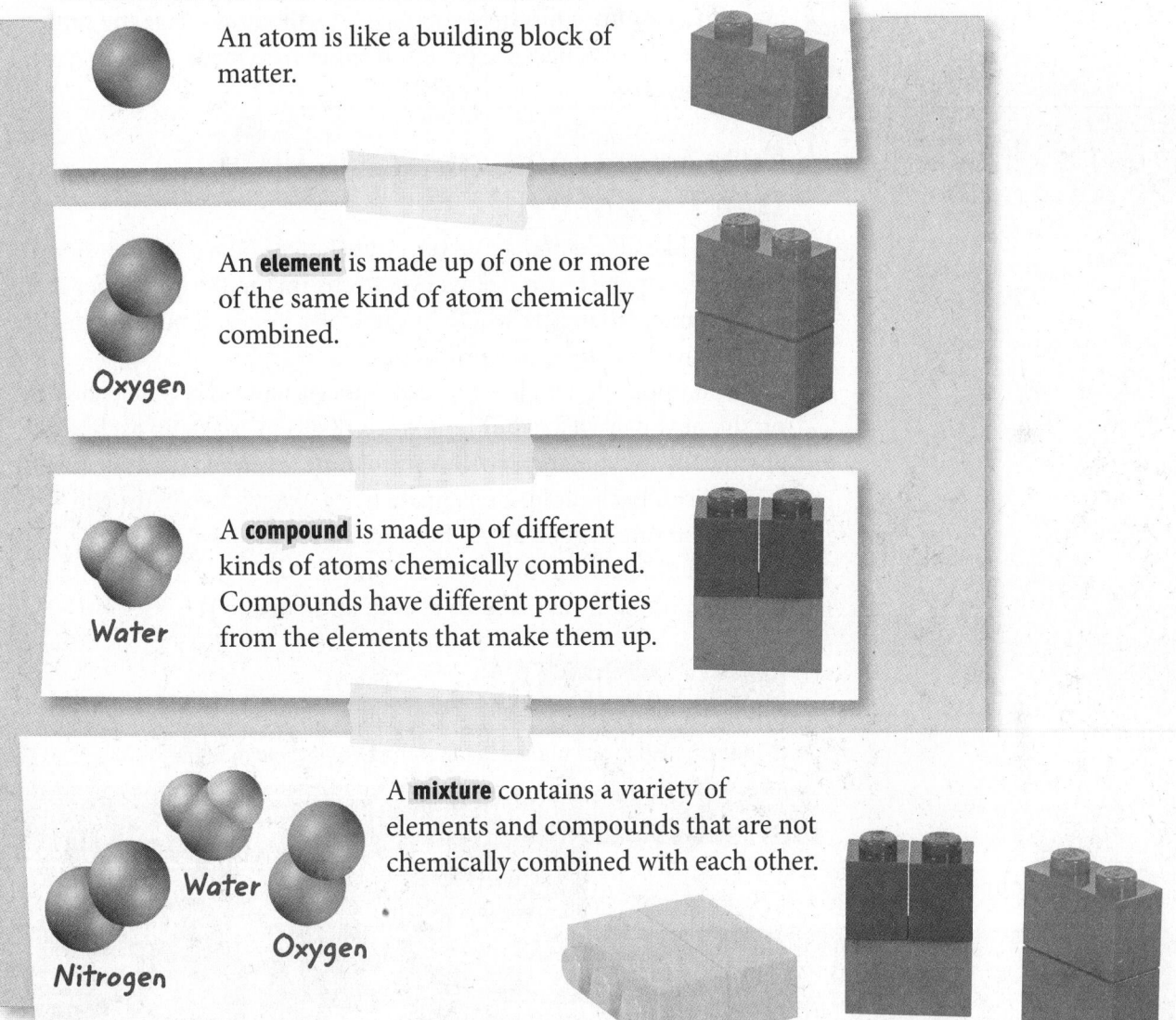

An atom is like a building block of matter.

An **element** is made up of one or more of the same kind of atom chemically combined.

Oxygen

A **compound** is made up of different kinds of atoms chemically combined. Compounds have different properties from the elements that make them up.

Water

A **mixture** contains a variety of elements and compounds that are not chemically combined with each other.

Nitrogen   Water   Oxygen

Visualize It!

7 Analyze Why are the spheres representing nitrogen and oxygen different colors?

_____

_____

_____

_____

Pure Genius

What are pure substances?

Elements and compounds are **pure substances**. A pure substance is a substance that has definite physical and chemical properties such as appearance, melting point, and reactivity. No matter the amount of a pure substance you have, it will always have the same properties. This is because pure substances are made up of one type of particle.

Pure Substances Are Made Up of One Type of Particle

Copper, like all elements, is a pure substance. Take a look at the element copper, shown below. The atoms that make up copper are all the same. No matter where in the world you find pure copper, it will always have the same properties.

Compounds are also pure substances. Consider water, shown on the next page. Two different kinds of atoms make up each chemically combined particle, or *molecule*. Every water molecule is identical. Each molecule is made up of exactly two hydrogen atoms and one oxygen atom. Because water is a pure substance, we can define certain properties of water. For example, at standard pressure, water always freezes at 0 °C and boils at 100 °C.

Visualize It!

8 Identify Fill in the blanks to label the two particle models.

A Copper _____

9 Explain Copper is an element. How do these images of copper illustrate this?

_____
_____
_____
_____

Pure Substances Cannot Be Formed or Broken Down by Physical Changes

Physical changes such as melting, freezing, cutting, or smashing do not change the identity of pure substances. For example, if you cut copper pipe into short pieces, the material is still copper. And if you freeze liquid water, the particles that make up the ice remain the same: two hydrogen atoms combined with one oxygen atom.

The chemical bonds that hold atoms together cannot be broken easily. To break or form chemical bonds, a chemical change is required. For example, when an electric current is passed through water, a chemical change takes place. The atoms that make up the compound break apart into two elements: hydrogen and oxygen. When a pure substance undergoes a chemical change, it is no longer that same substance. A chemical change changes the identity of the substance. Individual atoms cannot be broken down into smaller parts by normal physical or chemical changes.

Active Reading **11 Identify** What happens when a pure substance undergoes a chemical change?

_____

_____

_____

_____

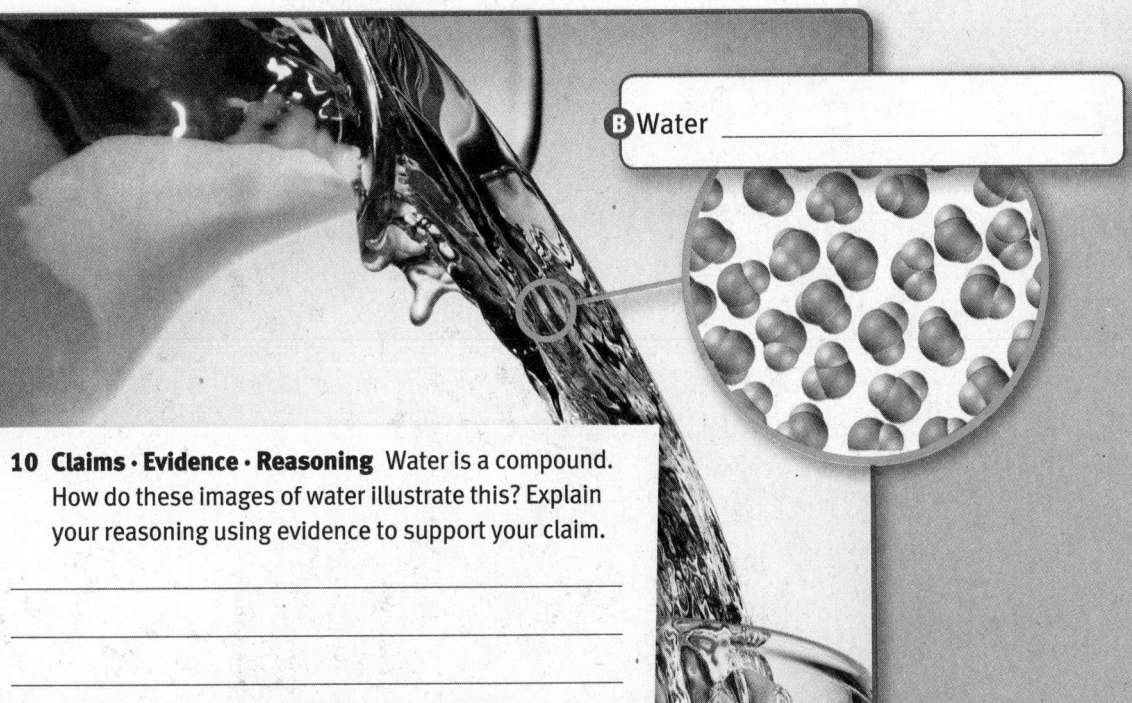

B Water _____

10 Claims · Evidence · Reasoning Water is a compound. How do these images of water illustrate this? Explain your reasoning using evidence to support your claim.

_____

_____

_____

Classified Information

Active Reading

12 Identify As you read, underline the ways in which elements are organized on the periodic table.

How can elements be classified?

Differences in physical and chemical properties allow us to classify elements. By knowing the category to which an element belongs, you can predict some of its properties. Elements are broadly classified as metals, nonmetals, or metalloids. Most metals are shiny, conduct heat and electricity well, and can be shaped into thin sheets and wires. Nonmetals are not shiny and do not conduct heat or electricity well. Metalloids have some properties of both metals and nonmetals.

There are over 100 elements known to exist. Each element has a place in an arrangement called the periodic table of the elements. The periodic table is a useful tool that can help you to identify elements that have similar properties. Metals, nonmetals, and metalloids occupy different regions in the periodic table. Metals start at the left and make up most of the elements in the periodic table. Nonmetals are at the right and are often shaded with a color different from that of the metals. Not surprisingly, the metalloids lie between the metals and nonmetals. In many instances, you can even predict which elements combine with others to form compounds based on their positions in the periodic table.

Aluminum, like many metals, can be formed into a thin foil.

Charcoal, made mostly of carbon atoms, is brittle and dull like many other nonmetals.

How can compounds be classified?

You are surrounded by compounds. Compounds make up the food you eat, the school supplies you use, and the clothes you wear—even you! There are so many compounds that it would be very difficult to list or describe them all. Fortunately, these compounds can be grouped into a few basic categories by their properties.

By Their pH

Compounds can be classified as acidic, basic, or neutral by measuring a special value known as *pH*. Acids have a pH value below 7. Vinegar contains acetic acid, which gives a sharp, sour taste to salad dressings. Bases, on the other hand, have pH values greater than 7. Baking soda is an example of a basic compound. Bases have a slippery feel and a bitter taste. Neutral compounds, such as pure water and table salt, have a pH value of 7. A type of paper called litmus paper can be used to test whether a compound is an acid or a base. Blue litmus paper turns red in the presence of an acid. Red litmus paper turns blue in the presence of a base. Although some foods are acidic or basic, you should NEVER taste, smell, or touch a chemical to classify them. Many acids and bases can damage your body or clothing.

Visualize It!

13 Classify Read about some of the ways in which compounds can be classified. Then fill in the blanks to complete the photo captions.

Baking soda is an example of a(n) _____

The compounds that make up plastic are _____ because they contain carbon and hydrogen

As Organic or Inorganic

You may have heard of organically-grown foods. But in chemistry, the word *organic* refers to compounds that contain carbon and hydrogen. Organic compounds are found in most foods. They can also be found in synthetic goods. For example, gasoline contains a number of organic compounds, such as octane and heptane.

By Their Role in the Body

Organic compounds that are made by living things are called biochemicals. Biochemicals are divided into four categories: carbohydrates, lipids, proteins, and nucleic acids. *Carbohydrates* are used as a source of energy and include sugars, starches, and fiber. *Lipids* are biochemicals that store excess energy in the body and make up cell membranes. Lipids include fats, oils, and waxes. *Proteins* are one of the most abundant types of compounds in your body. They regulate chemical activities of the body and build and repair body structures. *Nucleic acids* such as DNA and RNA contain genetic information and help the body build proteins.

Your body gets _____ such as sugars, starches, and fiber, from many of the foods you eat.

Mix and Match

What are mixtures?

Imagine that you roll out some dough, add tomato sauce, and sprinkle some cheese on top. Then you add green peppers, mushrooms, and pepperoni. What have you just made? A pizza, of course! But that's not all. You have also created a mixture.

A mixture is a combination of two or more substances that are combined physically but not chemically. When two or more materials are put together, they form a mixture if they do not change chemically to form a new substance. For example, cheese and tomato sauce do not react when they are combined to make a pizza. They keep their original identities and properties. So, a pizza is a mixture.

Mixtures Are Made Up of More Than One Type of Particle

Unlike elements and compounds, mixtures are not pure substances. Mixtures contain more than one type of substance. Each substance in a mixture has the same chemical makeup it had before the mixture formed.

Unlike pure substances, mixtures do not have definite properties. Granite from different parts of the world could contain different minerals in different ratios. Pizzas made by different people could have different toppings. Mixtures do not have defined properties because they do not have a defined chemical makeup.

14 Describe This student is going to make and separate a mixture of sand and salt. Complete these captions to describe what is taking place in each photo.

Ⓐ Sand and salt are poured into a single beaker. The result is a mixture because

_____

_____

_____

_____

Mixtures Can Be Separated by Physical Changes

You don't like mushrooms on your pizza? Just pick them off. This change is a physical change of the mixture because the identities of the substances do not change. But not all mixtures are as easy to separate as a pizza. You cannot just pick salt out of a salt water mixture. One way to separate the salt from the water is to heat the mixture until the water evaporates. The salt is left behind. Other ways to separate mixtures are shown at the right and below.

A magnet can separate a mixture of aluminum nails and iron nails.

Active Reading **15 Devise** How could you separate a mixture of rocks and sand?

_____

_____

_____

A machine called a centrifuge separates mixtures by the densities of the components. It can be used to separate the different parts of blood.

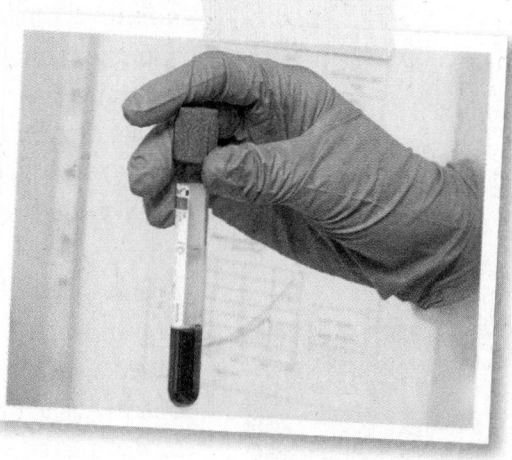

B When water is added to the sand-salt mixture,

_____

_____

_____

_____

C When the liquid is poured through a filter,

_____

_____

_____

_____

D The remaining salt water is heated until

_____

_____

_____

_____

A Simple Solution

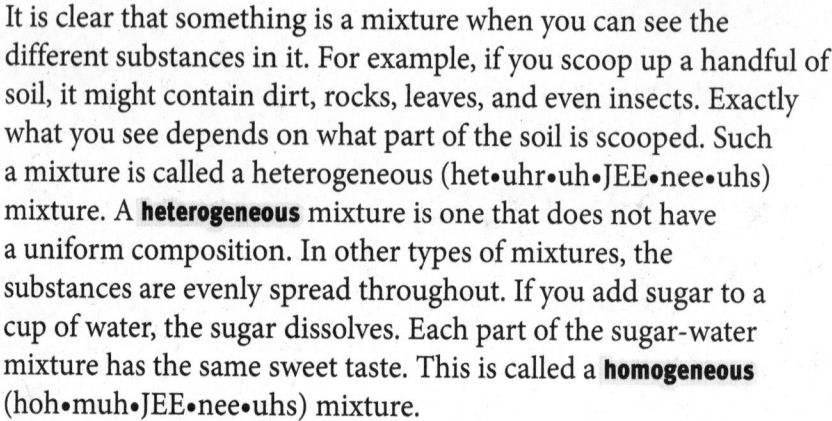

A snow globe contains a suspension.

How can mixtures be classified?

Active Reading

16 Identify As you read, underline the everyday examples of mixtures on this page.

It is clear that something is a mixture when you can see the different substances in it. For example, if you scoop up a handful of soil, it might contain dirt, rocks, leaves, and even insects. Exactly what you see depends on what part of the soil is scooped. Such a mixture is called a heterogeneous (het•uhr•uh•JEE•nee•uhs) mixture. A **heterogeneous** mixture is one that does not have a uniform composition. In other types of mixtures, the substances are evenly spread throughout. If you add sugar to a cup of water, the sugar dissolves. Each part of the sugar-water mixture has the same sweet taste. This is called a **homogeneous** (hoh•muh•JEE•nee•uhs) mixture.

As Suspensions

The snow globe (above) contains a type of heterogeneous mixture called a *suspension*. Suspensions are mixtures in which the particles of a material are spread throughout a liquid or gas but are too large to stay mixed without being stirred or shaken. If a suspension is allowed to sit, the particles will settle out.

As Solutions

Tea is a solution.

Tea is an example of a type of homogeneous mixture known as a *solution*. In a solution, one substance is dissolved in another substance. When you make tea, some of the compounds inside the tea leaves dissolve in the hot water. These compounds give your tea its unique color and taste. Many familiar solutions are liquids. However, solutions may also be gases or solids. Air is an example of a gaseous solution. Alloys, such as brass and steel, are solid solutions in which substances are dissolved in metals.

As Colloids

Gelatin is a colloid.

Colloids are a third type of mixture that falls somewhere between suspensions and solutions. As in a suspension, the particles in a colloid are spread throughout a liquid or gas. Unlike the particles in a suspension, colloid particles are small and do not settle out quickly. Milk and gelatin are colloids. Colloids look homogeneous, but we consider them to be heterogeneous.

17 Summarize Complete the graphic organizer below by filling in the blanks with terms from this lesson. Then add definitions or sketches of each term inside the appropriate box.

Classifying Matter

Matter
Definition:

Matter is anything that has mass and takes up space. Matter is made up of building blocks called atoms.

Pure Substances
Definition:

Sketch:

Elements
Sketch:

Definition:

Sketch:

Homogeneous
Definition:

Other Mixtures

Suspensions
Sketch:

Colloids
Definition:

Definition:

Role Models

How can models be used to differentiate between elements, compounds, and mixtures?

Elements differ from compounds even though both consist of only one type of particle, making them pure substances. Pure substances differ from mixtures even though both may appear to be uniform in appearance. The differences that distinguish elements, compounds, and mixtures lie at the level of the particles that make them up. Since these particles are so small, you cannot observe these differences directly. However, you can use models to represent what you cannot see. Models can illustrate the differences in the types and variety of particles in a substance that allow you to classify the substance as an element, compound, or mixture.

Several different types of models can be used to represent the particles in a substance. Most models represent an atom as an object such as a circle or sphere. Atoms of different elements are often shown in different colors. If atoms are bonded together, they are shown connected to one another in the model. Some models are two-dimensional illustrations on a computer screen or on paper, while others are three-dimensional physical models that can be rotated and viewed from all sides.

18 Analyze What information shown in models 1 and 3 is absent in model 2?

_____

_____

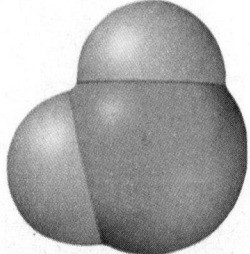
Two-dimensional illustration of a water molecule

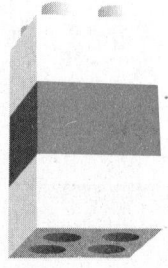
Three-dimensional block model of a water molecule

Three-dimensional ball-and-stick model of a water molecule

The models shown below represent elements, compounds, and mixtures and were made using items from a toolbox. Each nut, bolt, and washer represents a single atom.

19 Classify Indicate on the chart whether you would classify each model as representing an element, compound, or mixture.

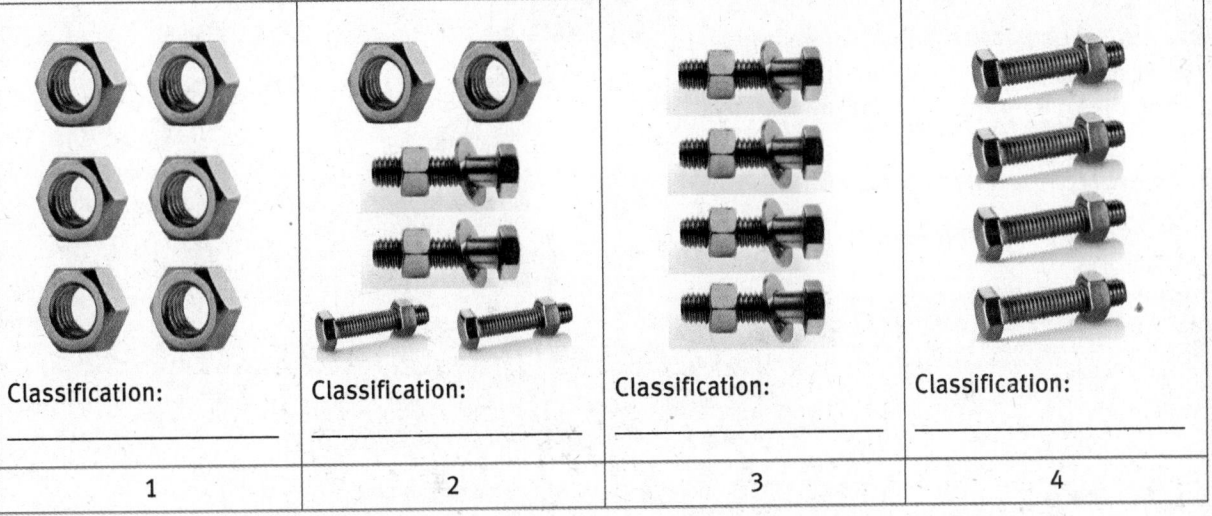

Classification: _____	Classification: _____	Classification: _____	Classification: _____
1	2	3	4

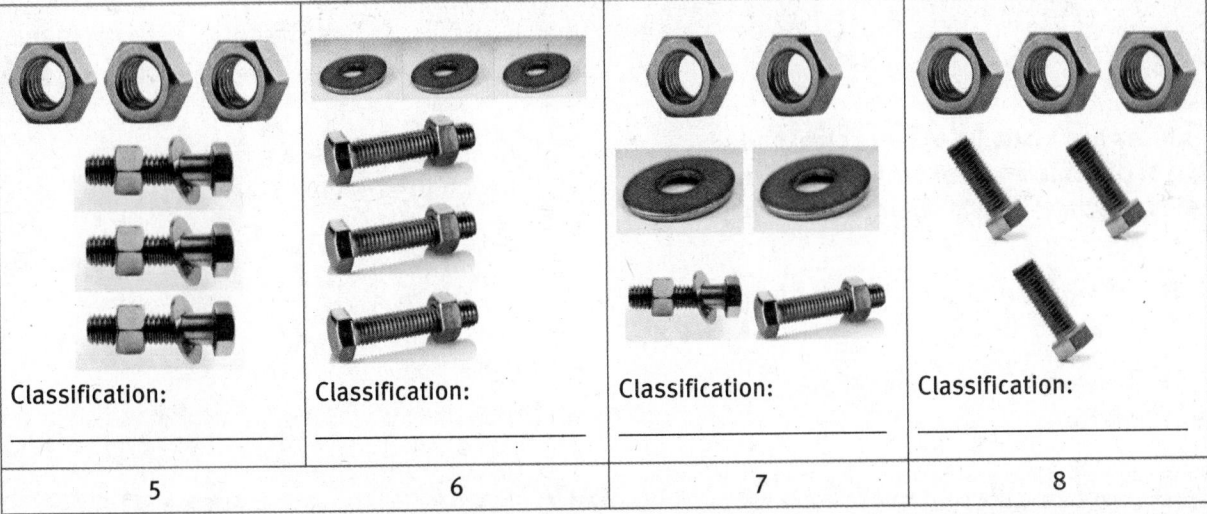

Classification: _____	Classification: _____	Classification: _____	Classification: _____
5	6	7	8

20 Model A model of a pure substance consists of 20% bolts, 40% washers, and 40% nuts. Another model of a mixture contains the same percentages of the same parts. Draw a sketch to show each model.

21 Evaluate How well does the use of nuts, bolts, and washers work in creating models to represent elements, compounds, and mixtures? Are there drawbacks?

_____

_____

Visual Summary

To complete this summary, circle the correct word or phrase. Then use the key below to check your answers. You can use this page to review the main concepts of the lesson.

Pure substances are made up of a single type of particle and cannot be formed or broken down by physical changes.

22 Water is a pure substance / mixture.

23 Water is a(n) element / compound.

Water molecules

Pure Substances and Mixtures

Mixtures are made up of more than one type of particle and can be separated into their component parts by physical changes.

24 Saltwater and sand can be separated with a magnet / filter.

25 Saltwater is a homogeneous / heterogeneous mixture.

Answers: 22 pure substance; 23 compound; 24 filter; 25 homogeneous

---

26 **Predict** Why do you think that the particles of a suspension settle out but the particles of a colloid do not? Explain your reasoning.

Lesson Review

Vocabulary

Fill in the blanks with the term that best completes the following sentences.

1 The basic building blocks of matter are called

_____

2 A(n) _____ is a substance that is made up of a single kind of atom.

3 Elements and compounds are two types of

_____

4 A(n) _____ is a combination of substances that are combined physically but not chemically.

Key Concepts

5 Identify What kind of mixture is a solution? A suspension? A colloid?

_____
_____
_____
_____

6 Apply Fish give off the compound ammonia, which has a pH above 7. To which class of compounds does ammonia belong?

_____
_____

7 Compare Fill in the following table with properties of elements and compounds.

How are elements and compounds similar?	How are elements and compounds different?

Use this drawing to answer the following question.

8 Identify What type of mixture is this salad dressing?

_____
_____

Critical Thinking

9 Explain Could a mixture be made up of only elements and no compounds? Explain your reasoning.

_____
_____
_____
_____
_____

10 Synthesize Describe a procedure to separate a mixture of sugar, black pepper, and pebbles.

_____
_____
_____
_____
_____
_____
_____
_____
_____
_____

My Notes

States of Matter

ESSENTIAL QUESTION

How do particles in solids, liquids, gases, and plasmas move?

By the end of this lesson, you should be able to model the motion of particles in solids, liquids, gases, and plasmas.

All four states of matter are present in this Arctic landscape.

 S8P1.b Thermal energy and movement of particles

Lesson Labs

Quick Labs
- Changing Volumes
- Can Crusher

Engage Your Brain

1 Describe Fill in the blank with a word or phrase that you think correctly completes the following sentences.

________________ is an example of a solid.

________________ is an example of a gas.

Unlike solids, gases can ________________

____

2 Identify Unscramble the letters below to find several liquids. Write your words on the blank lines.

TWRAE ________________

EICJU ________________

RIVAENG ________________

LIKM ________________

PSAOMOH ________________

Active Reading

3 Apply Use context clues to write your own definitions for the words *definite* and *occupy*.

Example sentence
Solid is the state of matter that has a definite shape and volume.

definite:

____

____

Example sentence
A larger container will allow a gas to occupy more space.

occupy:

____

____

Vocabulary Terms

- **solid**
- **liquid**
- **gas**
- **electron**
- **ion**
- **ionization**
- **plasma**

4 Identify As you read, place a question mark next to any words that you don't understand. When you finish reading the lesson, go back and review the text that you marked. If the information is still confusing, consult a classmate or a teacher.

Particles in Motion

How do particles move in solids, liquids, gases, and plasma?

All matter is made of particles that are in constant motion. This idea is the basis for the *kinetic theory of matter*. How much the particles move and how often they bump into each other determine the state of matter of the substance. This view of a movie theater helps to illustrate the differences between the particle motion in each of the four states of matter.

In Solids, Particles Vibrate in Place

A **solid** has a definite volume and shape. The particles in a solid are close together and do not move freely. The particles vibrate but are fixed in place. Often, the particles in a solid are packed together to form a regular pattern like the one shown at the right.

For most materials, the particles in a solid are closer together than the particles in a liquid. For example, the atoms in solid steel are closer together than the atoms in liquid steel. Water is an important exception to this rule. The molecules that make up ice actually have more space between them than the molecules in liquid water do.

Particles in a solid

5 Describe How are particles in a solid like people sitting in a movie theater?

_____

_____

_____

_____

_____

In Liquids, Particles Slide Past One Another

A **liquid** has a definite volume but not a definite shape. Particles in a liquid, shown at the right, have more kinetic energy than particles in a solid do. The particles are attracted to one another and are close together. However, particles in a liquid are not fixed in place and can move from one place to another.

Particles in a liquid

6 Describe How are particles in a liquid like people in a movie theater lobby?

_____

_____

_____

In Gases, Particles Move Freely

A **gas** does not have a definite volume or shape. Particles in a gas have more kinetic energy than particles in a liquid or solid. As you can see in the model at the right, gas particles are very far apart. This space can increase or decrease with changes in temperature or pressure.

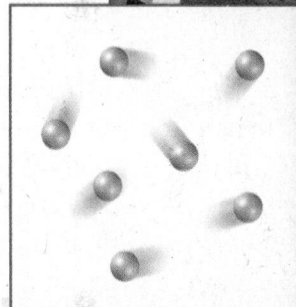
Particles in a gas

7 Describe How are particles in a gas like people outside of a movie theater?

_____

_____

_____

In Plasmas, Particles Move Freely

Plasma is a state of matter that forms when added heat energy causes gas particles to lose electrons. An **electron** is a particle found in an atom and has a negative charge. Gas particles are neutral and have no charge, but when they lose electrons during the change to the plasma state, they become positively charged. Particles in plasmas have the highest kinetic energies.

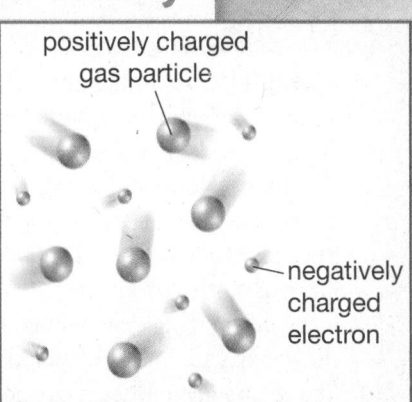
positively charged gas particle

negatively charged electron

Particles in a plasma

Shape up!

How does particle motion affect the properties of solids, liquids, gases, and plasmas?

Imagine what you would see if you put a few ice cubes into a pan on a hot stove. The hard blocks of ice would melt to form liquid water. If the pan is hot enough, the water would boil, giving off steam. Ice, liquid water, and the gaseous water in steam are all made up of the same water molecules. Yet ice looks and behaves differently than liquid water or steam does. These observed differences can be explained using the kinetic theory of matter.

Active Reading **8 Identify** Underline words or phrases that describe the properties of solids, liquids, gases, and plasmas.

Solids Have a Definite Volume and Shape

The fish tank at the right contains a small toy castle. When the castle was added to the glass container, the castle kept its original size and shape. The castle, like all solids has a definite shape and volume. The container does not change these properties of the toy. The particles in a solid are in fixed positions and are close together. Although the particles vibrate, they cannot move from one part of the solid to another part. As a result, a solid cannot easily change in shape or volume. If you force the particles apart, you can change the shape of a solid by breaking it into pieces. However, each of those pieces will still be a solid and have its own definite shape.

Think Outside the Book (Inquiry)

9 Model Think about the general shape and behavior of particles in solids, liquids, and gases within a container. What objects could be used as a model of particles? How could you model a container for your particles? Gather the materials and make your model. How does your model of solid, liquid, and gas particles compare to the real particles?

Liquids Have a Definite Volume but Can Change Shape

Unlike the solid toy castle, the water in this fish tank does not have a definite shape. The water has taken the shape of the fish tank. If you poured this same water into a round fishbowl, the water would take the shape of that container. However, the water would have the same volume as it did before. It would still take up the same amount of space. Like water, all liquids have a definite volume but no definite shape. The particles in a liquid are close together, but they are not tightly attached to one another as the particles in a solid are. Instead, particles in liquids can slide past one another. As a result, liquids can flow. Instead of having a rigid form, the particles in a liquid move and fill the bottom of the container they are in.

Gases Can Change in Volume and Shape

The small bubbles in this fish tank are filled with gas. Gases do not have a definite volume or shape. The particles in a gas are very far apart compared to the particles in a solid or a liquid. The amount of space between the particles in a gas can change more easily. If a rigid container has a certain amount of air inside and more air is pumped in, the volume of the gas does not change. The gas will still fill the entire container. Instead, the particles will become closer together. If the container is opened, the particles will spread out and mix with the air in the atmosphere.

Plasmas Can Change in Volume and Shape

Like gases, plasmas take on the shape and volume of their container. Unlike gases, plasmas are not electrically neutral. Plasmas form when neutral atoms in a gas undergo **ionization**, a process in which atoms lose or gain electrons to become electrically charged particles called ions. An **ion** is an atom that has lost or gained one or more electrons. The plasma state is created inside the fluorescent light bulb on the fish tank when an electric current is passed through the bulb. Energy from the electric current causes ionization of argon gas present in the bulb. When this happens, argon goes from the gaseous state to the plasma state. You observe light as a result of this plasma state. An example of a natural plasma is the display known as the northern lights.

Visualize It!

10 Apply Identify substances A, B, C, and D as a solid, liquid, gas, or plasma.

_____

_____

C
D

Icicles grow as water drips down them and then freezes, sticking to the ice that is already there. Freezing is an example of a change of state.

What happens when substances change state?

Ice, liquid water, and water vapor are different states of the same substance. As liquid water turns into ice or water vapor, the water molecules themselves do not change. What changes are the motion of the molecules and the amount of space between them.

The Motion of the Particles Changes

The particles of a material even a solid, are always in motion. As a solid is heated, its particles gain energy and vibrate faster. If the vibrations are fast enough, the particles break loose and slide past one another. The process in which a solid becomes a liquid is known as *melting*. As the temperature of a liquid is lowered, its particles lose energy. Eventually, the particles move slowly enough for the attractions between them to cause the liquid to become a solid. This process is called *freezing*. Because water freezes at 0 °C, you may associate freezing with cold temperatures. But some materials are frozen at room temperature or above. For example, an aluminum can is an example of frozen aluminum. It will not melt until it reaches a temperature above 660 °C! The table below shows types of state changes.

When a material loses or gains energy, one of two things can happen: its temperature can change or its state can change. Both do not happen at the same time. The energy that is added or removed during a change of state is used to break or form the attractions between particles. The temperature of boiling water stays at 100 °C until all of the liquid has become a gas.

11 Apply Complete the table below with examples of state changes.

State change	Result	Example
Melting	A solid becomes a liquid.	
Freezing	A liquid becomes a solid.	
Boiling	A liquid becomes a gas (throughout).	
Evaporation	A liquid becomes a gas (at the liquid's surface).	A puddle dries out.
Condensation	A gas becomes a liquid.	
Sublimation	A solid becomes a gas.	Dry ice becomes a gas at room temperature.
Deposition	A gas becomes a solid.	Frost forms on a cold windowpane.
Ionization	A gas becomes a plasma.	

Making Glass

You can see through it, drink water from it, and create objects of art with it. It's glass, a material that has been crafted by humans for about 5,000 years! Read on to see how a few simple ingredients can become a beautiful work of art.

Glass Blowing

Glass blowing is the technique of shaping glass by blowing air into a blob of molten glass at the end of a tube. The *blowpipe* is the long, hollow tube that the glass blower uses to shape the molten glass. By blowing air through the blowpipe, a glass blower expands the open space inside the glass. This process is similar to inflating a balloon.

Glass from Sand?

Glass is made by heating a mixture of sand, soda ash, limestone, and other ingredients. Colored glass is made by adding small amounts of metal compounds. The mixture is melted in a roaring hot furnace at about 1,600 °C. Once the mixture melts, the molten glass can be shaped and allowed to cool into the solid state.

Extend

Inquiry

12 Describe In your own words, describe the glass-blowing process.

13 Investigate People once thought that old glass windows are thicker at the bottom because the solid glass had flowed to the bottom over time. Research this theory and report your findings.

14 Investigate Research the various methods of making glass objects. Present your findings by doing one of the following:
- make a poster
- write a short essay
- draw a graphic novel

Visual Summary

To complete this summary, check the box that indicates true or false. Then use the key below to check your answers. You can use this page to review the main concepts of the lesson.

The particles in solids vibrate in place.

15   T   F   □   □   Solids can easily change in volume.

The particles in plasma move freely.

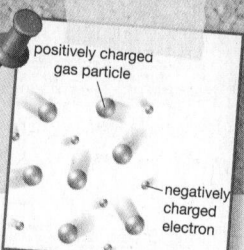

positively charged gas particle

negatively charged electron

16   T   F   □   □   The particles in plasma have the highest kinetic energies.

States of Matter

The particles in liquids slide past each other.

17   T   F   □   □   Liquids take the shape of their container.

The particles in gases move freely.

18   T   F   □   □   When the distance between gas particles increases, the volume of the gas increases.

Answers: 15 F; 16 T; 17 T; 18 T

19 Describe What happens to the kinetic energy of the particles of a substance as the substance changes from a liquid to a gas? Explain your reasoning.

Lesson Review

Vocabulary

Draw a line to connect the following terms to the description of their particle motion.

1 solid

2 plasma

3 liquid

4 gas

A particles are close together and locked in place

B particles are far apart and can move freely

C particles are close together and can slide past each other

D particles are charged, far apart, and move freely

Key Concepts

5 Define What is the kinetic theory of matter?

_____

_____

_____

_____

6 Analyze What happens to the temperature of a substance while it is changing state? Explain.

_____

_____

_____

_____

7 Analyze What could you do to change the volume of a gas?

_____

_____

_____

Critical Thinking

8 Apply Can a tank of oxygen gas ever be half empty? Explain your reasoning.

_____

_____

_____

_____

Use this drawing to answer the following questions.

9 Predict This jar contains helium gas. What would happen if the lid of this jar was removed?

_____

_____

_____

_____

10 Explain How are the helium atoms in this model different from real helium atoms?

_____

_____

_____

_____

_____

11 Claims · Evidence · Reasoning A rock does not visibly vibrate, yet a student claims that the particles making up the rock are constantly in motion. Do you agree with the student's claim? Explain your reasoning.

_____

_____

_____

_____

_____

_____

My Notes

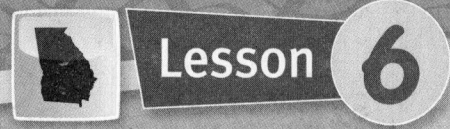

Lesson **6**

Changes of State

ESSENTIAL QUESTION

What happens when matter changes state?

By the end of this lesson, you should be able to describe changes of state in terms of the attraction and motion of particles.

Two changes of state happen at the hot springs in Yellowstone National Park. Very hot liquid water changes to invisible water vapor, or gas, above the surface of the spring. Then the water vapor changes back into a liquid as it cools in the air. This liquid water can be seen as fog.

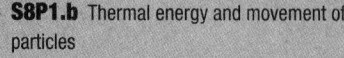 **S8P1.b** Thermal energy and movement of particles

© Houghton Mifflin Harcourt Publishing Company • Image Credits: (bg) ©Robert Glusic/Corbis

✋ **Lesson Labs**

Quick Labs
• Investigating Conservation of Mass
• Modeling Particle Motion
• Boiling Water Without Heating It

Exploration Lab
• Changes of State

Engage Your Brain

1 Identify Unscramble the letters of each word below to find objects in your classroom that are solids. Write the words on the blank lines.

PCLINE

_____

SKED

_____

OSBOK

_____

ODRO

_____

2 Describe Write your own caption for this photo.

_____

_____

_____

Active Reading

3 Apply Use context clues to write your own definitions for the words *converted* and *constantly*.

Example sentence
When an ice cube melts, a solid is <u>converted</u> to a liquid.

converted:

_____

_____

Example sentence
The particles that make up matter are <u>constantly</u> in motion.

constantly:

_____

_____

Vocabulary Terms
- freezing
- melting
- evaporation
- boiling
- condensation
- sublimation
- deposition
- neutralization

4 Identify This list contains the vocabulary terms you'll learn in this lesson. As you read, circle the definition of each term.

The Fact of the Matte

What happens when matter changes state?

Eating ice cream on a hot summer day can be messy business. Faster than you can lick it, the ice cream melts and drips down your hand. As ice cream melts, it goes through a change of state. The four states of matter are solid, liquid, gas, and plasma.

Energy Is Gained and Lost

To change a substance from one state to another, energy must be added or removed. When a substance gains or loses energy, its temperature changes or its state changes. These two changes do not happen at the same time; the temperature remains constant until the change of state is complete. In the graph below, notice that the temperature of a solid remains the same until all of the solid has melted into a liquid. Also, the temperature of a liquid remains the same until all of the liquid changes to a gas.

Active Reading

5 Identify As you read, underline the four states of matter.

Solid wax becomes liquid when the warmth of the flame causes a change of state.

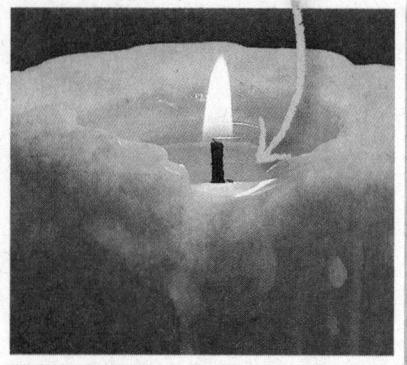

Visualize It!

6 Apply Use the graph to determine which point— A, B, or C—represents a candle melting. Circle the correct letter.

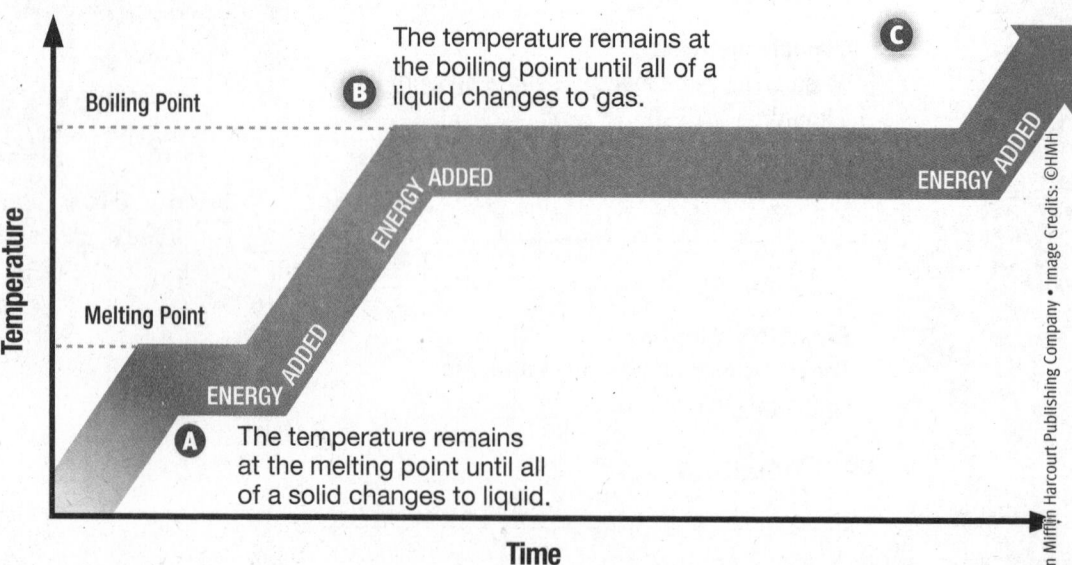

The temperature remains at the boiling point until all of a liquid changes to gas.

B

Boiling Point

ENERGY ADDED

A The temperature remains at the melting point until all of a solid changes to liquid.

ENERGY ADDED

Melting Point

C

ENERGY ADDED

Temperature

Time

Particle Motion Changes

All matter is made of tiny particles that are in constant motion. During a change of state, the motion of the particles changes. Particles can break away from each other and gain more freedom to move. This happens when a solid changes to a liquid, or a liquid changes to a gas. Particles can also attract each other more strongly, and have less freedom to move. This happens when gas changes to a liquid, or a liquid changes to a solid.

Energy Is Conserved

During a change of state, a material must gain energy from the environment or lose energy to the environment, but the total amount of energy is conserved. Look at the diagram of the water cycle below. Water is converted from liquid water to water vapor, to solid snow, and back to liquid. Each change of state represents a transfer of energy either into or out of the water cycle from the surrounding environment, but energy is never created or destroyed.

 **Visualize It!**

7 Analyze Determine whether water particles will have more or less freedom to move at each stage, A, B, and C. Write *more freedom* or *less freedom* in each box.

Loss of Energy

Loss of Energy

B

Gain of Energy

C

A

Gain of Energy

8 Categorize Identify whether each picture below shows a (1) gain of energy or a (2) loss of energy for the substance. Write the appropriate number in the box at the bottom of each picture.

An ice cube melts.

A puddle dries up.

A lake freezes.

Solid Facts

How do solids and liquids change states?

Particles in a liquid can slide past each other, but particles in a solid can only move enough to vibrate. Removing energy from a liquid can cause it to change to a solid as the particles stop sliding past each other. Adding energy to a solid can cause it to change to a liquid as particles begin sliding past each other.

By Freezing

The change in state in which a liquid becomes a solid is called **freezing**. When a liquid is cooled, its particles have less energy than they did before. The particles slow down, and the attractions between particles increase. Eventually, the particles lock into the fixed arrangement of a typical solid. The temperature at which a liquid changes into a solid is the liquid's *freezing point*. Different substances have different freezing points. For example, the freezing point of water is 0 °C. When energy is removed at 0 °C, water converts to its frozen state—ice. The freezing point of the element mercury is –38.8 °C. At 0 °C, mercury is still a liquid.

9 Predict In which sample of water do the water particles have more energy: 5 grams (g) of ice cubes at –10 °C, or 5 g of liquid water at 20 °C? Explain your reasoning.

_____

_____

_____

_____

_____

_____

Visualize It!

10 Identify In the box below each picture, write the state of the substance shown.

Solids can change to liquids.
Liquids can change to solids.

A _____   B _____

The freezing point of water is 0 °C (32 °F). Liquid water changes to solid ice at this temperature. You can see this change taking place in the waterfall.

© Houghton Mifflin Harcourt Publishing Company • Image Credits: (bg) ©ION/amanaimagesRF/Getty Images

By Melting

Particles in a solid have an ordered arrangement. When a solid is warmed, its particles have more energy than they did before. The particles speed up, and the attraction between the particles decreases. Eventually the particles are able to slide past one another. This change of state from a solid to a liquid is called **melting**. The temperature at which a solid changes to a liquid is called the *melting point*. Melting is the reverse of freezing. Water freezes and melts at 0 °C. Mercury freezes and melts at −38.8 °C.

Think about a melting snowman. Energy from the sun is added to the solid snow. The particles in the snow begin to move faster. When the temperature of the snow reaches 0° C, the added energy of the particles will overcome some of the attractions that hold the particles in place. The snow starts to melt. As the sun continues to shine on the snowman, even more attractions are broken. Eventually, all the snow turns to liquid water.

Active Reading **11 Apply** Describe what happens to water particles when ice melts.

_____

_____

_____

_____

_____

Inquiry

12 Infer Both the freezing temperature and the melting temperature of water are the same (0 °C). Explain why a substance like water freezes and melts at the same temperature.

_____

_____

_____

_____

Bubbling Over

How do liquids and gases change state?

Particles in a gas have a great deal of energy. Removing enough energy from a gas causes a gas to change into a liquid or a solid. Adding enough energy to a liquid or a solid causes it to change into a gas. The process by which a liquid or a solid changes to a gas is *vaporization*.

By Evaporation or Boiling

As a liquid is warmed, its particles gain energy. Some particles gain enough energy that they escape from the surface of the liquid and become a gas. This process is called **evaporation**. Evaporation occurs slowly at a range of temperatures, but it happens more quickly at higher temperatures.

A rapid change from a liquid to a gas, or vapor, is called **boiling**. This change takes place throughout a liquid, not just at the surface. As a liquid is warmed to a high enough temperature, bubbles form. The specific temperature at which this occurs in a liquid is called the *boiling point*. As air pressure changes at different elevations above sea level, so does the boiling point of liquids. The greater the air pressure, the higher the boiling point of a liquid.

---

13 Predict What would happen to the boiling point of water at 8,000 m above sea level, where air pressure is lower? Explain your reasoning.

_____

_____

_____

The boiling point of water is 100 °C (212 °F) at sea level.

👁 **Visualize It!**

14 Identify In the box below each picture, write the state of the substance shown.

Liquids change to gases.
Gases change to liquids.

A

B

By Condensation

Particles in a gas have very little attraction to one another. As a gas is cooled its particles lose energy. The attraction between particles overcomes the speed of their motion, and a liquid forms. This change of state from a gas to a liquid is called **condensation**. Condensation is the reverse of evaporation.

Grass is often wet in early morning because gaseous water vapor in the air condenses on the cool grass. Water droplets form on the outside of a cold glass of lemonade when water vapor in the warm air condenses on the cool glass.

Look at the photo below of contrail lines left by jet planes. Water vapor and soot form when fuel burns in jet engines. The gaseous water vapor condenses as tiny liquid water droplets. The water droplets then freeze into ice crystals on the soot particles to form a contrail. The word *contrail* is short for condensation trail.

15 Apply Indicate whether the change of state in each process causes particles to (A) have more freedom or (B) have less freedom. Write the appropriate letter next to each process.

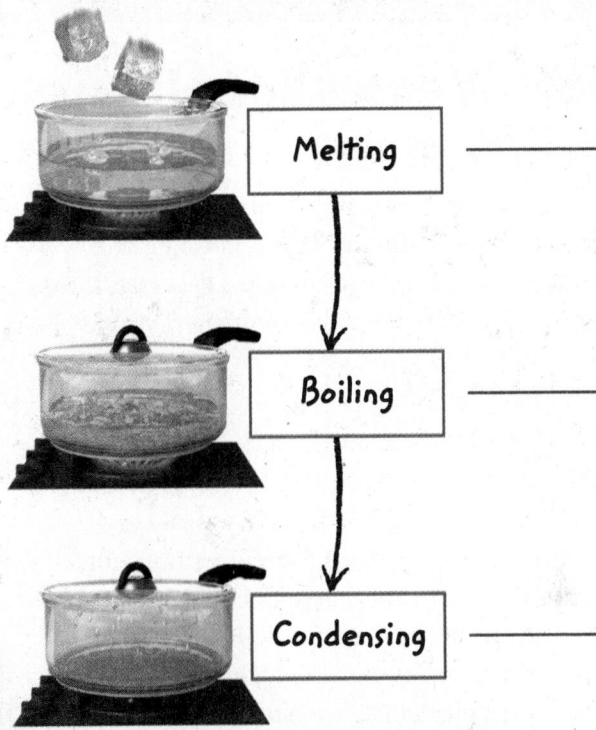

Melting _____

Boiling _____

Condensing _____

Visualize It!

16 Compare How are the planes' contrail lines similar to clouds?

_____

_____

_____

_____

_____

The dramatic effect of contrails is the result of condensation and freezing.

In a Flash

How do gases and plasmas change state?

Under conditions of high energy input, some gases can transition to the plasma state. For this to happen, particles in these gases must lose electrons as a result of this high energy input.

By Ionization

You have seen a substance in the plasma state anytime you have looked up at the sky during a thunderstorm. Air consists primarily of nitrogen molecules (N_2). These neutral molecules normally exist in the gas state in air. However, when a thunderstorm develops, nitrogen atoms in the molecules can lose electrons. This loss of electrons, known as ionization, results in the transition of air molecules to the plasma state. You cannot see the actual plasma-forming process, although you can see when a column of air in the plasma state conducts an electric charge. You see this as lightning. Lightning results from a column of super-heated air particles sometimes called a plasma path stretching from one cloud to another. You observe lightning whenever static electric charge buildup in clouds is discharged along this plasma path.

17 Explain Why does air in the plasma state conduct electric current but air in the gas state does not?

_____

_____

_____

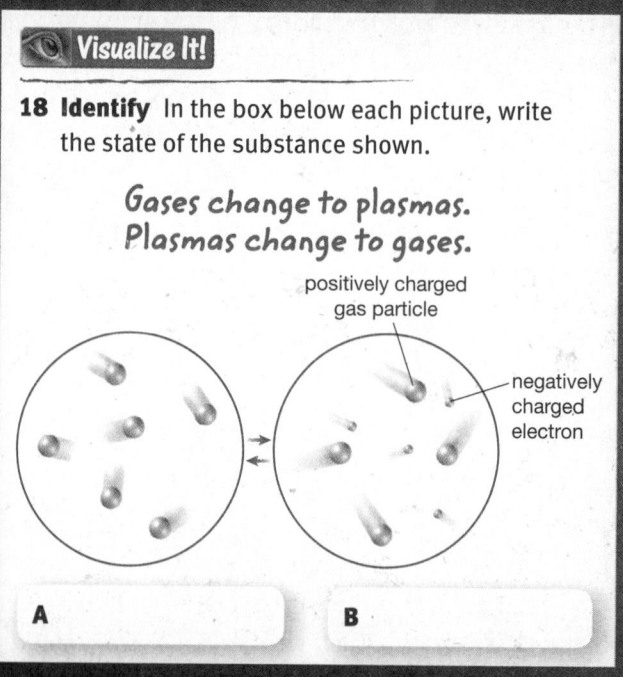

Visualize It!

18 Identify In the box below each picture, write the state of the substance shown.

Gases change to plasmas.
Plasmas change to gases.

positively charged gas particle

negatively charged electron

A

B

© Houghton Mifflin Harcourt Publishing Company • Image Credits: DeepDesertPhoto/RooM/Getty Images

By Neutralization

Plasmas change back to the gaseous state through the process of neutralization. **Neutralization** is the gain or loss of electrons by an ion to become electrically neutral. Before neutralization, plasmas are good conductors of electricity. Following neutralization, particles in the gaseous state no longer have the ability to conduct electricity. Plasmas are also very sensitive to magnetic fields. For these reasons, certain types of devices involve plasmas rather than gases in their design.

For example, engineers have used the electrical and magnetic properties of plasmas to develop plasma screen TVs and computer monitors. Other human-made plasmas include fluorescent light bulbs and neon signs. These plasmas are produced from argon or neon gas sealed in glass tubes and subjected to electric current. Ionization of the neutral gas molecules results in electrically conductive plasmas inside the bulbs. Some of the electrical energy absorbed by the plasma during this process is emitted as light. In all of these devices, shutting off the source of electrical energy results in the plasma changing back to a neutral gas state.

---

19 Design If you were an engineer designing a plasma display device, would you select a gas for your design that formed a plasma at a high temperature or at a low temperature? Explain your reasoning.

_____

_____

_____

Into Thin Air

How do solids and gases change state?

Under the right conditions, some solids and gases can change state without ever becoming a liquid. The substance must gain or lose a great deal of energy for this to occur.

By Sublimation

Have you ever received a package of food shipped in dry ice to keep it frozen? If so, you may have noticed that the ice disappears without leaving a puddle of liquid. Dry ice is frozen carbon dioxide (CO_2). It changes from its solid state directly into a gas. The change from a solid state directly into a gas is called **sublimation**. As the particles of solid dry ice gain energy their motion completely overcomes the attraction between the particles, and the particles escape into the air as gas.

Dry ice is extremely cold, about −80 °C, and at room temperature, 25 °C, the air provides the energy for it to sublimate. A fog is observed as water vapor condenses when it comes in contact with cold CO_2 gas.

Snow and ice formed by water sublimate at below-freezing temperatures. To see sublimation in action, hang wet clothes outside on a day that temperatures are below freezing. First the water in the clothes freezes, and then the solid ice sublimates into the air.

No liquid is visible in the bowl as the solid CO_2 disappears. It sublimates from a solid directly to an invisible gas.

Think Outside the Book

20 Research With a partner, find another substance that can sublimate. Describe the conditions under which sublimation occurs.

By Deposition

In physical science, **deposition** is the change in state from a gas directly to a solid. Deposition is the process by which ice crystals form in clouds. The photo at the right shows deposition of invisible water vapor into ice crystals on a cold window.

When conditions are right, deposition occurs when the particles of a gas lose energy. Attraction between particles locks the particles into the rigid structure of a solid. No liquid is formed in the process.

Active Reading **21 Compare** Explain how sublimation and deposition are alike and how they are different.

_____

_____

_____

_____

Ice crystals form on a cold window when water vapor in the air is converted to ice by the process of deposition.

22 Relate Complete Column 1 and Column 2 to identify opposite processes. In the third column, indicate whether the process in Column 1 or Column 2 is the result of a gain in energy.

Column 1	Column 2	
The opposite of...	is	Gain in Energy
deposition		
	condensation	Column 1
melting		
	neutralization	

Conserve

What happens to matter when a change of state occurs?

When matter changes from one state to another, it remains the same kind of matter. Its physical state changes, but its chemical identity does not. For example, an ice cube and the puddle it forms when it melts are both made up of water.

Energy and Motion of Particles Change

You might ask, "What *does* change as a result of a change of state?" The answer is that the energy of the particles, the movement of the particles, and the distance between them change. You can create a model to illustrate the relationships among these changes in all four states of matter.

Active Reading

23 Identify As you read, underline the ways particles of matter are affected by a change of state.

Visualize It!

24 Model Complete the diagram below to show changes in the particles of a substance undergoing state changes. Be sure to address both the movement of particles and the distances between particles in your model.

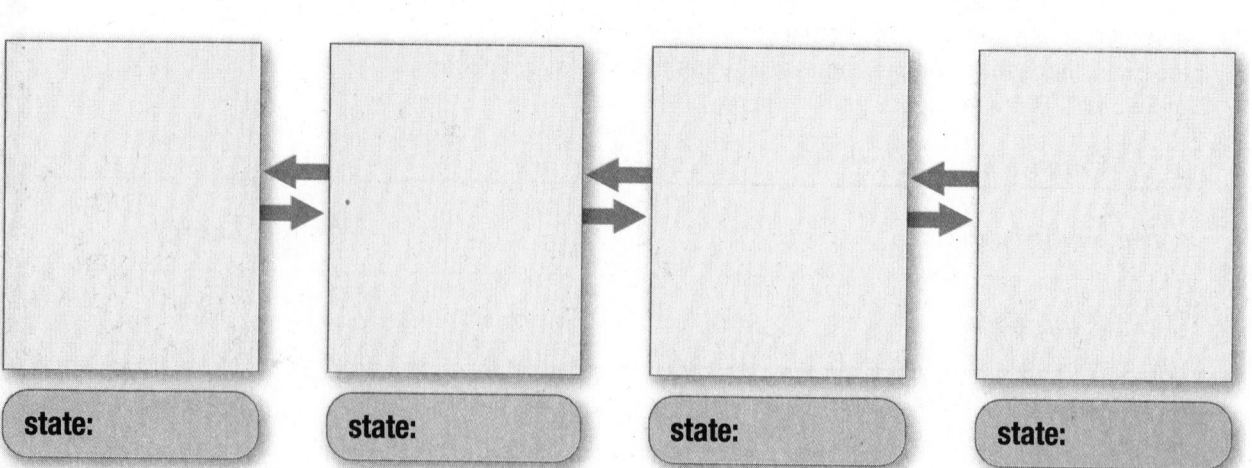

Increasing energy added to substance

state: state: state: state:

Increasing energy removed from substance

Mass Is Conserved

What happens to the *amount* of matter in a change of state? Suppose you do an experiment. You put ice cubes in a sealed container so that the container plus the ice has a total mass of 100 g. You warm the ice to the melting point. It becomes liquid water. Then you continue to warm the water to the boiling point so that it becomes a gas. After each step, you measure the mass of the water. You find no difference in the mass. The sealed container at each state has a mass of 100 g. You know that the mass of the container itself cannot change. So you can conclude that the gaseous water vapor has the same mass as the liquid water and the solid ice. The mass of a substance does not change when its state changes. Each state contains the same amount of matter.

Think about the particles of water in the closed container. They do not disappear. Even the particles that escape from the liquid state stay in the container as gas. Because the number of particles in the container stays the same, the amount of matter is conserved.

water   ice

Mass is conserved when a change of state occurs.

![Visualize It!] **Visualize It!**

25 Apply A flask of water is sealed with a balloon and heated to various temperatures on a hot plate. Fill in the missing information below.

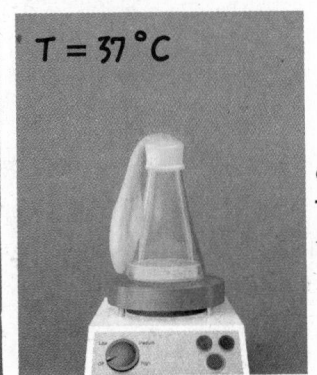

T = 37 °C

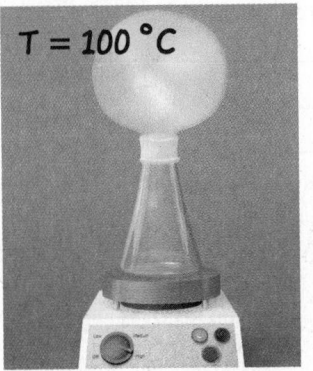

T = 100 °C

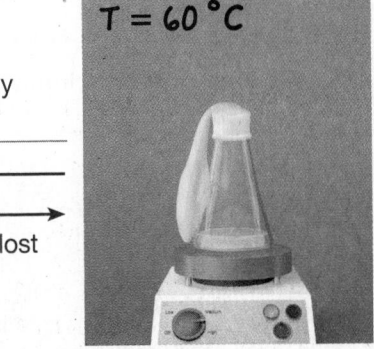

T = 60 °C

energy gained →

B energy ←

C energy ←
_____

energy lost →

A m = _____

m = 52 g

D m = _____

26 Claims · Evidence · Reasoning Explain how the system of the flask and the balloon illustrates the conservation of mass. Use evidence to support your reasoning.

_____

_____

_____

Visual Summary

To complete this summary, fill in the blanks with the correct word or phrase. Then use the key below to check your answers. You can use this page to review the main concepts of the lesson.

Changes of State

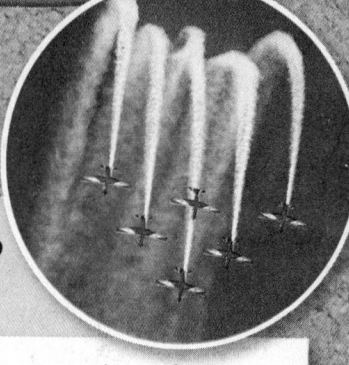

A solid can change to a liquid or gas.

27 The change from a solid to a liquid is called _____

28 The change of a solid directly to a gas is called _____

A gas can change to a solid, a liquid, or a plasma.

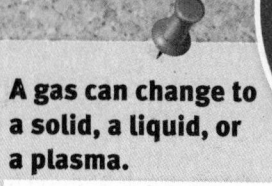

29 Water vapor changes directly to ice by _____

30 _____ is the process in which water vapor changes to a liquid.

31 _____ is the process by which a gas changes to a plasma.

A liquid can change to a gas or a solid.

32 Ice is formed from liquid water during the process of _____

33 Two ways that liquid water can become a gas are by _____

Mass is conserved when a change of state occurs.

34 The amount of mass _____ _____ during a change of state.

Answers: 27 melting; 28 sublimation; 29 deposition; 30 Condensation; 31 Ionization; 32 freezing; 33 boiling and evaporation; 34 stays the same

35 **Predict** What would happen to the amount of matter on Earth if mass were not conserved during changes of state? Explain your reasoning.

Lesson Review

Vocabulary

Draw a line to connect the following terms to their definitions.

1 freezing

2 evaporation

3 neutralization

4 sublimation

5 melting

A change of state from solid to liquid

B change of state from liquid to gas

C change of state from solid to gas

D change of state from liquid to solid

E change of state from plasma to gas

Key Concepts

6 Describe What happens to particles when a substance gains energy and changes state?

_____

_____

_____

7 Explain What happens to the energy that is lost when water freezes?

_____

_____

8 Compare How does the movement of particles in a stick of butter differ from the movement of particles in a dish of melted butter? Explain your reasoning.

_____

_____

_____

9 Identify As water is cooled, at what temperature do its particles become fixed in place?

_____

_____

_____

Critical Thinking

Use this drawing to answer the following questions.

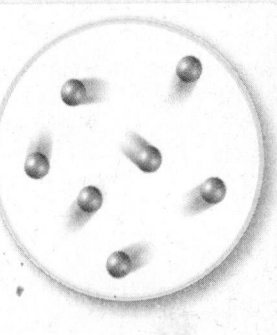

10 Relate The drawing represents the movement of particles in a substance. What changes of state can this substance undergo?

_____

_____

11 Describe What processes will the substance in the drawing undergo when those changes of state occur? Explain.

_____

_____

_____

_____

_____

12 Compare How do evaporation and boiling differ?

_____

_____

_____

_____

13 Apply The boiling point of a substance in City A is found to be 145 °C. The boiling point of the same substance in City B is 141 °C. Which city, A or B, is at a higher elevation? How do you know?

_____

_____

_____

_____

My Notes

Unit 1

Lesson 1
ESSENTIAL QUESTION
What properties define matter?

Relate mass, weight, volume, and density to one another.

Lesson 2
ESSENTIAL QUESTION
What are physical and chemical properties of matter?

Classify and compare substances based on their physical and chemical properties.

Lesson 3
ESSENTIAL QUESTION
What are physical and chemical changes of matter?

Distinguish between physical and chemical changes of matter.

Lesson 4
ESSENTIAL QUESTION
How do pure substances and mixtures compare?

Distinguish between pure substances and mixtures.

Lesson 5
ESSENTIAL QUESTION
How do particles in solids, liquids, gases, and plasmas move?

Model the motion of particles in solids, liquids, gases, and plasmas.

Lesson 6
ESSENTIAL QUESTION
What happens when matter changes state?

Describe changes of state in terms of the attraction and motion of particles.

Connect ESSENTIAL QUESTIONS
Lessons 4 and 6

1 Synthesize How can understanding changes of state help you to separate a saltwater solution?

_____

_____

_____

_____

_____

_____

Think Outside the Book

2 Synthesize Choose one of these activities to help synthesize what you have learned in this unit.

☐ Using what you learned in lessons 1, 2, 3, and 4, explain how matter can be classified by its physical and chemical properties by creating an informative brochure. Include examples of both pure substances and mixtures.

☐ Using what you learned in lessons 5 and 6, create a presentation that describes the particle movement in a substance as it changes from a solid, to a liquid, to a gas, to a plasma, and then back to a solid.

Unit 1 Review

Name _____

Vocabulary

Check the box to show whether each statement is true or false.

T	F	
☐	☐	**1** <u>Matter</u> is anything that has mass and takes up space.
☐	☐	**2** An <u>element</u> is a substance that is made up of one type of atom.
☐	☐	**3** <u>Evaporation</u> is the change of state from a gas to a liquid.
☐	☐	**4** A <u>solid</u> has a definite volume and shape.
☐	☐	**5** A <u>physical property</u> can be measured without changing the identity of the substance.

Key Concepts

Read each question below, and circle the best answer.

6 One chemical property that can be measured in a substance is its reactivity with water. What is another chemical property?

A density

B combustibility

C malleability

D solubility

7 Matter is made up of particles. Which of the following statements is true about these particles?

A The particles that make up solids do not move.

B The particles that make up liquids do not move.

C The particles that make up all matter are constantly in motion.

D Only the particles that make up gases and plasmas are constantly in motion.

8 Two balloons are inflated to an equal volume. Balloon 2 is placed in the freezer for 20 minutes.

Balloon 1   Balloon 2

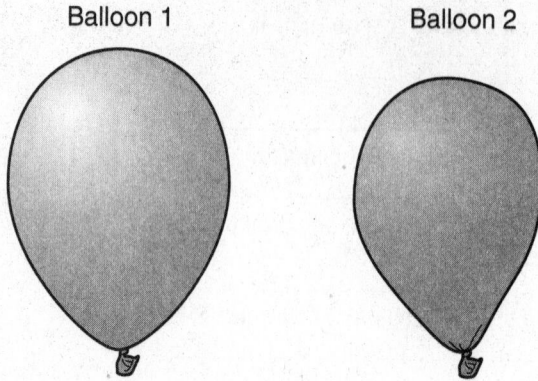

Why would freezing a balloon produce the results shown in Balloon 2?

A Increased kinetic energy decreases the attraction between particles inside the balloon.

B Increased kinetic energy increases the attraction between particles inside the balloon.

C Decreased kinetic energy decreases the attraction between particles inside the balloon.

D Decreased kinetic energy increases the attraction between particles inside the balloon.

9 Which of the following statements describes a plasma?

A A plasma has both a definite shape and a definite volume.

B A plasma has neither a definite shape nor a definite volume.

C A plasma has a definite shape but not a definite volume.

D A plasma has a definite volume but not a definite shape.

10 A water molecule is made up of one oxygen atom and two hydrogen atoms. Why is water considered a pure substance?

A Water can be broken down by physical means.

B Water can be combined with other substances by physical means.

C Each water molecule is identical.

D Water molecules are made up of different types of atoms.

11 A beaker containing a certain substance has heat applied to it. The particles that make up the substance begin to move farther apart from each other.

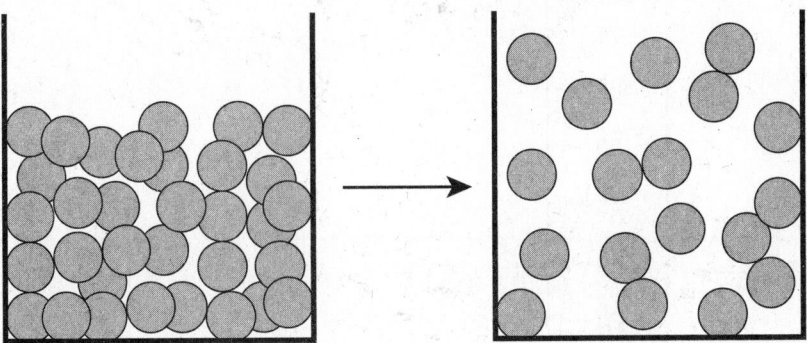

What change of state could be occurring to the substance in the beaker?

A The substance is changing from a plasma to a gas.

B The substance is changing from a gas to a solid.

C The substance is changing from a liquid to a solid.

D The substance is changing from a liquid to a gas.

12 The law of conservation of mass states that mass cannot be created or destroyed. To what type of change does this law apply?

A physical changes only

B chemical changes only

C both physical and chemical changes

D only mass that is not undergoing change

13 A beaker containing ice and water is placed on a warm hotplate. Will the ice in the beaker undergo a physical or chemical change?

A a physical change because it will change state

B a chemical change because it will change state

C a physical change because it will form a new substance

D a chemical change because it will form a new substance

14 What is the boiling point of water?

A 0° C

B 32° C

C 100° C

D 212° C

15 A rock is dropped into a graduated cylinder filled with 35 mL of water.

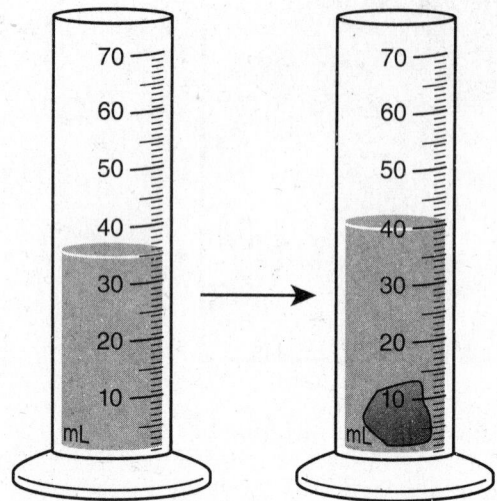

What is the volume of the rock? (Hint: 1 mL water = 1 cm^3)

A 40 cm^3

B 14 cm^3

C 5 cm^3

D 35 cm^3

16 The instrument below is used to measure an object.

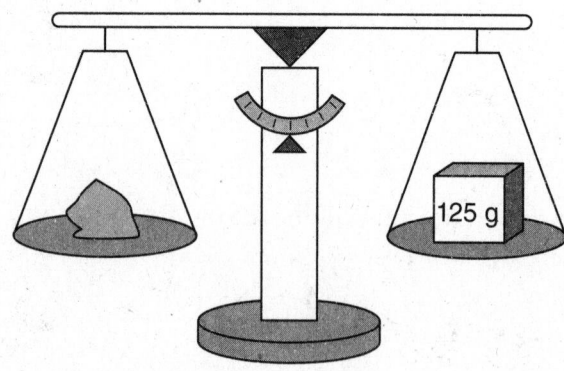

What is the instrument measuring?

A gravity

B weight

C density

D mass

Name _____

17 The diagram below shows a chemical reaction.

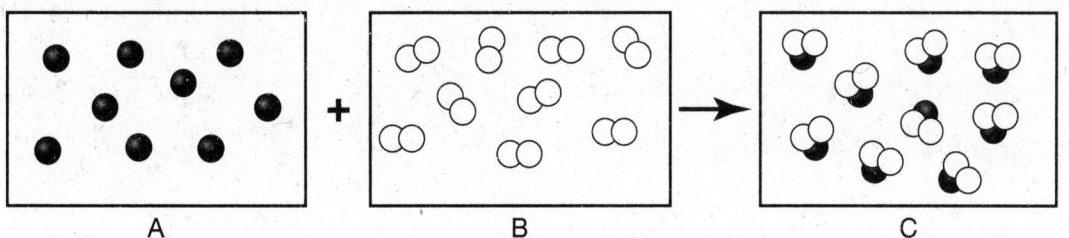

What is being formed in the box labeled C?

A a compound   **C** a mixture

B an element   **D** an atom

Critical Thinking

Answer the following questions in the space provided.

18 In the space below, sketch the particles in a solution, a suspension, and a colloid.

Give an example of a solution, a suspension, and a colloid.

Solution: _____

Suspension: _____

Colloid: _____

19 A sample liquid is heated in a closed container until it changes to a gas. What happens to the size of the particles in the sample?

_____

What happens to the number of particles in the sample?

_____

What happens to the average speed of the particles?

_____

20 Describe the difference between a chemical change and a physical change.

_____

_____

What are three examples of physical changes?

_____

_____

_____

What are three signs that a chemical change has taken place?

_____

_____

_____

How does temperature affect chemical changes?

_____

_____

Connect ESSENTIAL QUESTIONS
Lessons 1 and 2

Answer the following question in the space provided.

21 An unknown substance has a volume of 2 cm³ and a mass of 38.6 grams. What is the density of the sample? _____

Material	Density (g/cm³)
water	1.0
aluminum	2.7
iron	7.9
silver	10.5
gold	19.3

Use the chart above to find the identity of the unknown sample: _____

List three other physical properties that could be used to identify this sample.

_____

_____

_____

UNIT 2
Energy

ghton Mifflin Harcourt Publishing Company • Image Credits: (bkgd) ©Alfred Pasieka/Photo Researchers, Inc.; (br) ©David Hoffman Photo Library/Alamy

Big Idea

Energy exists in different forms and can change from one form to another, but energy is always conserved.

S8P2., S8P2.b, S8P2.c, S8P2.d

A thermogram is a special type of image that shows the relative temperatures of objects.

Sealing windows keeps the warmth inside.

What do you think?

See all the red areas in this thermogram? These areas show where energy (in the form of heat) is escaping through gaps around windows and doors. Why is it important to reduce this loss of energy from a home? As you explore the unit, gather evidence to help you state and support claims to answer this question.

Unit 2
Energy

CITIZEN SCIENCE

Saving Energy

Humans use many sources of energy in our everyday lives. For example, we need electricity to see at night, fuel to keep our cars running, and food to nourish our bodies. But we need to be careful in our use of energy resources. And you can help!

① Ask A Question

How can individuals avoid wasting energy resources at home?

Make a list of all the sources of energy, such as electricity or natural gas, used in your home. Then, write down what those energy sources are used for, and estimate how much your family uses them each week. For example: "We use natural gas for cooking on our stove approximately three hours each week." Can your family reduce energy consumption in any areas? Work with your family to develop your ideas.

Using a programmable thermostat can help conserve energy.

② Think About It

A What is one source of energy used in your home?

_____

B Where is energy used most often in your school?

_____
_____
_____

C Where is energy used most often in your home?

_____
_____

D What are some possible areas in the home and at school where energy usage can be easily reduced?

_____
_____
_____
_____
_____

③ Apply Your Knowledge

A Choose some of the places you identified in your home. Develop strategies for reducing the amount of energy your family uses in those areas.

Area	Strategy

B Apply the strategies you listed above. Track how your energy usage changes as you conserve energy. Examine your utility bill if you have access to it.

_____
_____
_____

Solar panels can convert energy from the sun into a form that can be used in a home.

Take It Home

As a class, create an energy conservation plan for your school. Implement it in your class and track how much energy you have saved. Share your results with your school. See *ScienceSaurus®* for more information about conservation energy.

Introduction to Energy

© Houghton Mifflin Harcourt Publishing Company • Image Credits: (bg) ©Thinkstock/Getty Images

ESSENTIAL QUESTION

What is energy?

By the end of this lesson, you should be able to describe how energy is conserved through transformation between different forms.

The chemical energy contained in fireworks is transformed into sound, light, and energy as heat when the fireworks shells explode.

S8P2.b Transformation between kinetic and potential energy

S8P2.c Energy transformations in a system

✋ **Lesson Labs**

Quick Labs
• Setting Objects in Motion
• Conservation of Energy
• Bungee Jumping

S.T.E.M. Lab
• Designing a Simple Device

 Engage Your Brain

1 Predict Check T or F to show whether you think each statement is true or false.

T   **F**

☐   ☐   Energy can change from one form to another.

☐   ☐   An object can have only one type of energy at a time.

☐   ☐   If an object has energy, it must be moving.

☐   ☐   All energy travels in waves.

2 Describe Write a caption for this picture that includes the concept of sound energy.

_____

_____

 Active Reading

3 Apply The phrase *conservation of energy* has an everyday meaning. We speak of trying to conserve, or save, energy for environmental reasons. It also refers to a law of nature. Use context clues to write your own definition for the meaning of the *law of conservation of energy*.

Example sentence
According to the <u>law of conservation of energy</u>, when a rolling ball slows, the energy of the ball does not disappear. Instead, it changes to energy as heat generated from moving across the ground.

law of conservation of energy:

_____

_____

_____

Vocabulary Terms

• **energy**
• **kinetic energy**
• **potential energy**
• **mechanical energy**
• **energy transformation**
• **law of conservation of energy**

4 Apply As you learn the definition of each vocabulary term in this lesson, create your own definition or sketch to help you remember the meaning of the term.

Get Energized!

What are two types of energy?

In science, **energy** is the ability to cause change. Energy takes many different forms and has many different effects. There are two general types of energy: kinetic energy and potential energy.

Kinetic Energy

Kinetic energy (kih•NET•ik EN•er•jee) is the energy of an object that is due to motion. All moving objects have kinetic energy. The amount of kinetic energy an object has depends on its mass and its speed. Kinetic energy increases as mass increases. Imagine that a bowling ball and a soccer ball roll across the floor at the same speed. The bowling ball has more kinetic energy than the soccer ball has because the bowling ball has a greater mass.

Kinetic energy also increases as speed increases. If two bowling balls with the same mass roll across the floor at different speeds, the faster ball will have the greater kinetic energy.

Active Reading

5 Identify As you read this page and the next, underline the factors that affect an object's kinetic and potential energy.

As the skater moves up the ramp, he gains height but loses speed. Some of his kinetic energy is converted back to potential energy. The rest of it is transferred as heat due to friction. **D**

At the bottom of the ramp, the skater's kinetic energy is at its peak because he is going the fastest. His potential energy is at its lowest because he is closer to the ground than at any other point on the ramp. **C**

Potential Energy

Potential energy (puh•TEN•shuhl EN•er•jee) is the energy that an object has due to its position, condition, or chemical composition. A ball held above the ground has potential energy because the force of gravity can pull it to the ground. Potential energy that is the result of an object's position is called gravitational potential energy. Gravitational potential energy increases as the object's height or mass increases.

A change in condition can also affect potential energy. For example, stretching a rubber band increases its potential energy.

Chemical potential energy depends on chemical composition. As bonds break and new bonds form between atoms during a chemical change, energy can be released.

Can objects have potential and kinetic energy at the same time?

An object can have both kinetic and potential energy. For example, the skater in the picture below has kinetic energy as he moves down the ramp. He has potential energy due to his position on the ramp. A flying bird has kinetic energy because of its speed, mass, and potential energy due to its height from the ground.

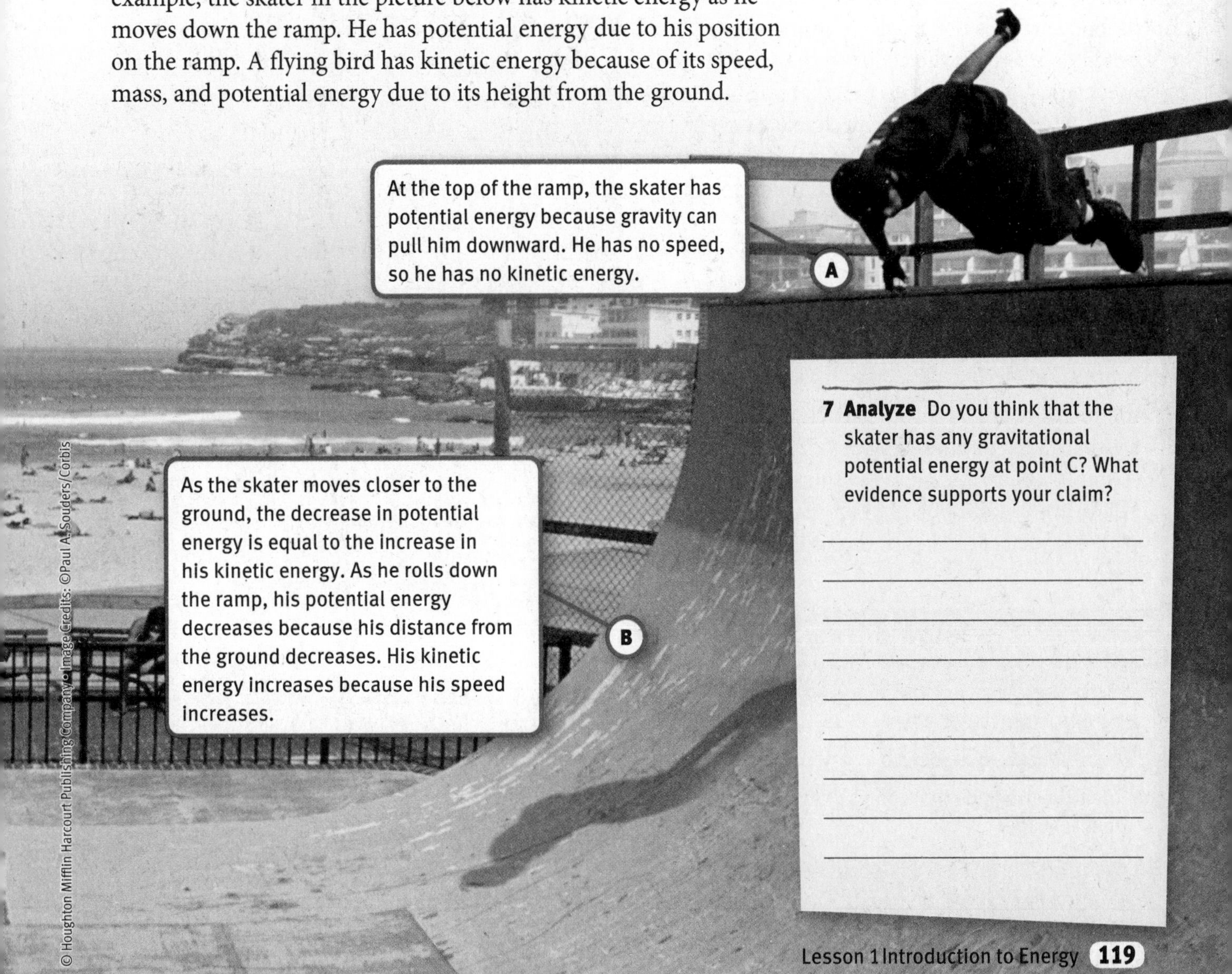

Think Outside the Book Inquiry

6 Diagram Think of another situation that shows kinetic and potential energy. Draw a sketch of and write a description explaining the situation in terms of potential and kinetic energy.

At the top of the ramp, the skater has potential energy because gravity can pull him downward. He has no speed, so he has no kinetic energy.

A

As the skater moves closer to the ground, the decrease in potential energy is equal to the increase in his kinetic energy. As he rolls down the ramp, his potential energy decreases because his distance from the ground decreases. His kinetic energy increases because his speed increases.

B

7 Analyze Do you think that the skater has any gravitational potential energy at point C? What evidence supports your claim?

_____

_____

_____

_____

_____

_____

_____

_____

_____

_____

© Houghton Mifflin Harcourt Publishing Company • Image Credits: ©Paul A. Souders/Corbis

In Perfect Form

What forms can energy take?

Kinetic energy and potential energy are two types of energy that can come in many different forms. Some common forms of energy include mechanical, sound, electromagnetic, electrical, chemical, thermal, and nuclear energy. Energy is expressed in joules (J) (JOOLZ).

Mechanical Energy

Mechanical energy is the sum of an object's kinetic energy and potential energy. Remember that kinetic energy is the energy of motion, and potential energy is the energy of position. So mechanical energy is the energy of position and motion. A moving car has mechanical energy. An object's mechanical energy can be all potential energy, all kinetic energy, or a combination of potential and kinetic energy.

Sound Energy

Sound energy is kinetic energy caused by the vibration of particles in a medium such as steel, water, or air. As the particles vibrate, they transfer the sound energy to other particles. The sound a guitar makes is caused by the vibrations of its strings transferring energy to the air around it. You hear the sound because special structures in your ears detect the vibrations of the particles in the air.

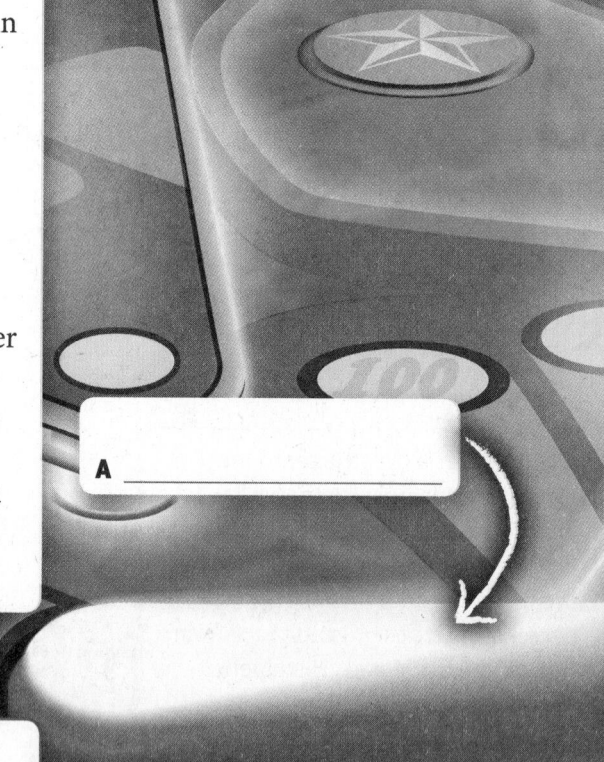

A _____

8 Identify Label the three forms of energy represented in this image.

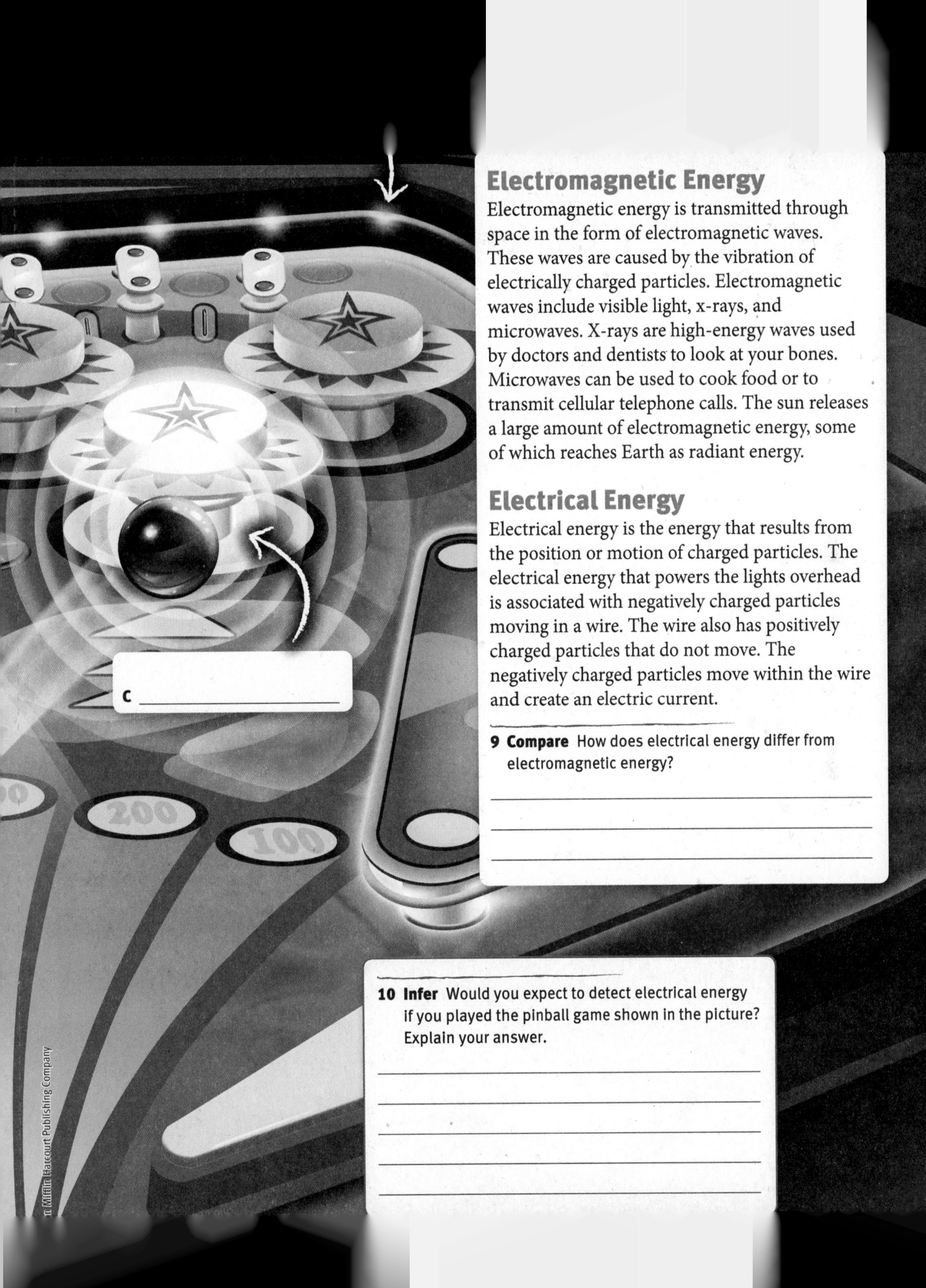

Electromagnetic Energy

Electromagnetic energy is transmitted through space in the form of electromagnetic waves. These waves are caused by the vibration of electrically charged particles. Electromagnetic waves include visible light, x-rays, and microwaves. X-rays are high-energy waves used by doctors and dentists to look at your bones. Microwaves can be used to cook food or to transmit cellular telephone calls. The sun releases a large amount of electromagnetic energy, some of which reaches Earth as radiant energy.

Electrical Energy

Electrical energy is the energy that results from the position or motion of charged particles. The electrical energy that powers the lights overhead is associated with negatively charged particles moving in a wire. The wire also has positively charged particles that do not move. The negatively charged particles move within the wire and create an electric current.

9 Compare How does electrical energy differ from electromagnetic energy?

_____

_____

_____

10 Infer Would you expect to detect electrical energy if you played the pinball game shown in the picture? Explain your answer.

_____

_____

_____

_____

_____

C _____

11 Identify As you read, underline
the source of energy in a
chemical reaction.

Chemical Energy

Chemical energy is a form of potential energy. The amount of chemical energy in a molecule depends on the kinds of atoms and their arrangement. During a chemical change, bonds between these atoms break, and new bonds form. The foods you eat, batteries, and matches are sources of chemical energy.

Thermal Energy

The thermal energy of an object is the kinetic energy of its particles. Particles move faster at higher temperatures than at lower temperatures. The faster the molecules in an object move, the more thermal energy the object has. Also, the more particles an object has, the more thermal energy it has. Heat is the energy transferred from an object at a higher temperature to an object at a lower temperature.

Nuclear Energy

The nucleus of an atom is the source of nuclear energy. When an atom's nucleus breaks apart, or when the nuclei of two small atoms join together, energy is released. The energy given off by the sun comes from nuclear energy. In the sun, hydrogen nuclei join to make a helium nucleus. This reaction gives off a huge amount of energy. The sun's light and heat come from these reactions. Without nuclear energy from the sun, life would not exist on Earth.

12 Synthesize Why is the chemical energy of a battery potential energy and not kinetic energy?

_____

_____

_____

_____

_____

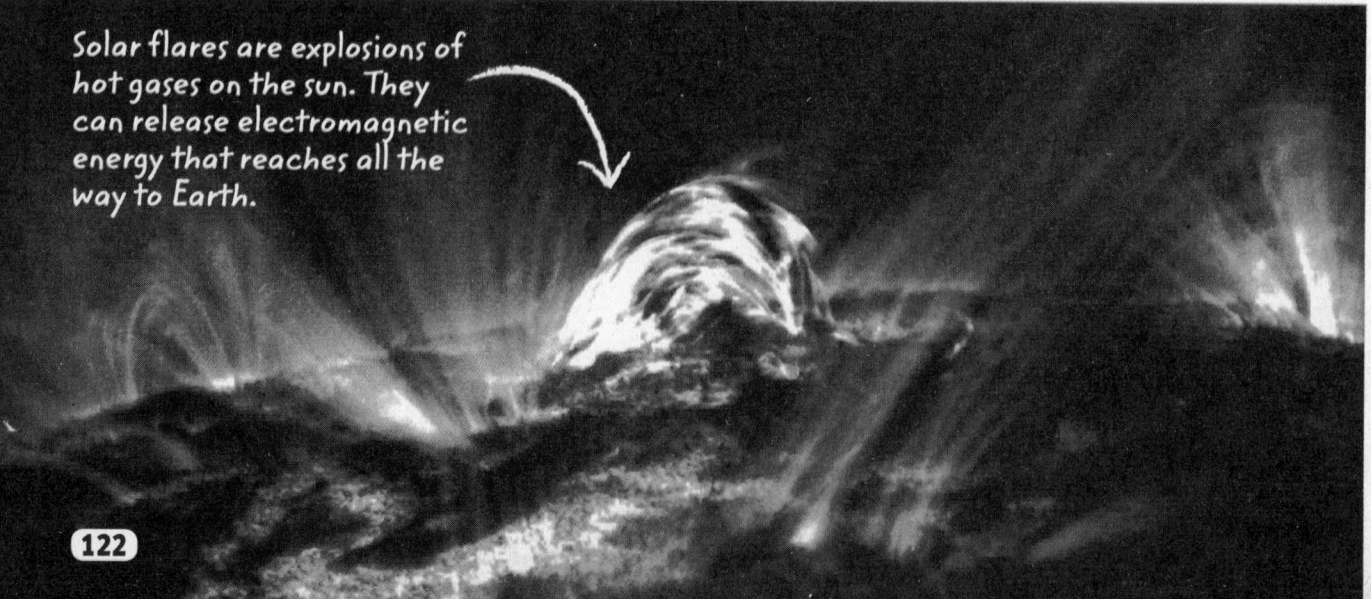

Solar flares are explosions of hot gases on the sun. They can release electromagnetic energy that reaches all the way to Earth.

Space Weather and Technology

SOCIETY AND TECHNOLOGY

Every time you turn on a TV or use a cell phone, you may be affected by the "weather" in space. Space weather includes any activity happening in space that might affect Earth's environment, such as solar flares. A solar flare can release a million times more energy than the largest earthquake. It is an intense release of electromagnetic energy as a burst of radiation.

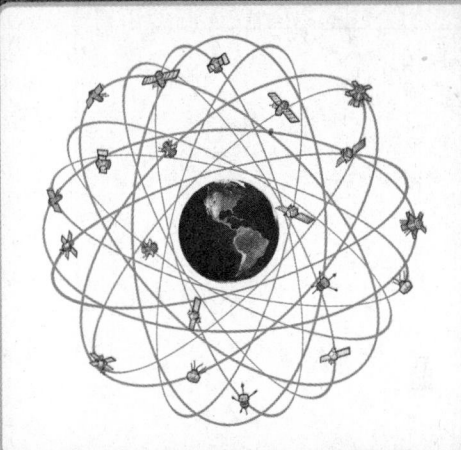

Space Weather Can Damage Satellites
Many of the satellites orbiting Earth provide phone service. Damage from space weather can interrupt phone communications.

Space Weather Can Affect Navigation
Space weather can also cause navigation errors by interrupting satellite signals to Global Positioning System (GPS) receivers.

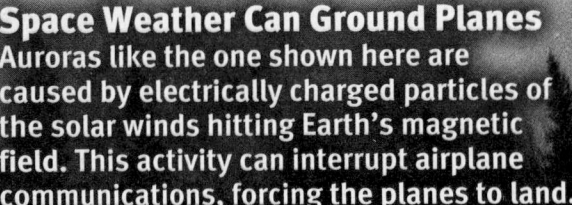

Space Weather Can Ground Planes
Auroras like the one shown here are caused by electrically charged particles of the solar winds hitting Earth's magnetic field. This activity can interrupt airplane communications, forcing the planes to land.

Extend

Inquiry

13 Identify What type of energy is monitored by scientists forecasting future space weather?

14 Infer Why is space weather a bigger concern now than it was in the past?

15 Research How do scientists forecast space weather? Why?

Transformers

What is an energy transformation?

An **energy transformation** (EN•er•jee trans•fohr•MAY•shuhn) takes place when energy changes from one form into another form. Any form of energy can change into any other form of energy. Often, one form of energy changes into more than one form. When you rub your hands together, you hear a sound, and your hands get warm. The mechanical energy of your moving hands was transformed into both sound energy and energy as heat.

Another example of an energy transformation is when chemical energy is converted in the body. Why is eating breakfast so important? Eating breakfast gives your body the energy needed to help you start your day. Chemical potential energy is stored in the food you eat. Your body breaks down the components of the food to access the energy stored in them. Some of this energy is then changed to the kinetic energy that allows you to move and play. Some of the chemical energy is converted into energy as heat that keeps your body warm.

 **Visualize It!**

Some examples of energy transformation are illustrated in this flashlight. Follow the captions to learn how energy is transformed into the light energy that you rely on when you turn on a flashlight.

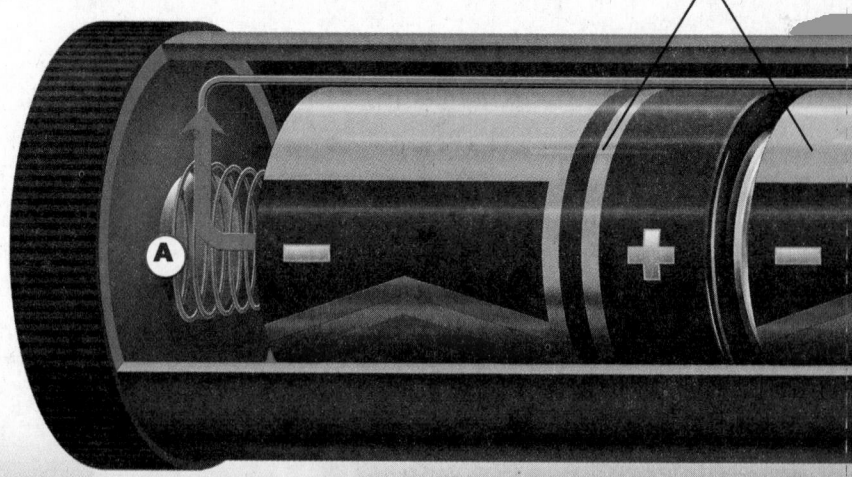

Batteries

(A) The chemical energy from the batteries is transformed into electrical energy.

16 Describe Give two examples of other devices in which the chemical energy in a battery is transformed into electrical energy.

_____

_____

_____

Is energy conserved?

A closed system is a group of objects that transfers energy only to one another. For example, a roller coaster can be considered a closed system if it includes everything involved, such as the track, the cars, and the air around them. Energy is conserved in all closed systems. The **law of conservation of energy** states that energy cannot be created or destroyed. It can only change forms. All of the different forms of energy in a closed system always add up to the same total amount of energy. It does not matter how many energy transformations take place.

For example, on a roller coaster some mechanical energy gets transformed into sound and energy as heat energy as the roller coaster goes down a hill. The total of the coaster's mechanical energy at the bottom of the hill, the extra energy as heat, and the sound energy is the same total amount of energy as the original amount of mechanical energy. In other words, total energy is conserved.

Active Reading **17 Relate** How are energy transformations related to the law of conservation of energy?

_____

_____

_____

_____

Think Outside the Book

18 Apply Have you ever thought about how cell phones work? What form of energy is used to power a cell phone? What form of energy do you use from a cell phone? Can you think of any other forms of energy that may be used inside of a cell phone? Explain your reasoning.

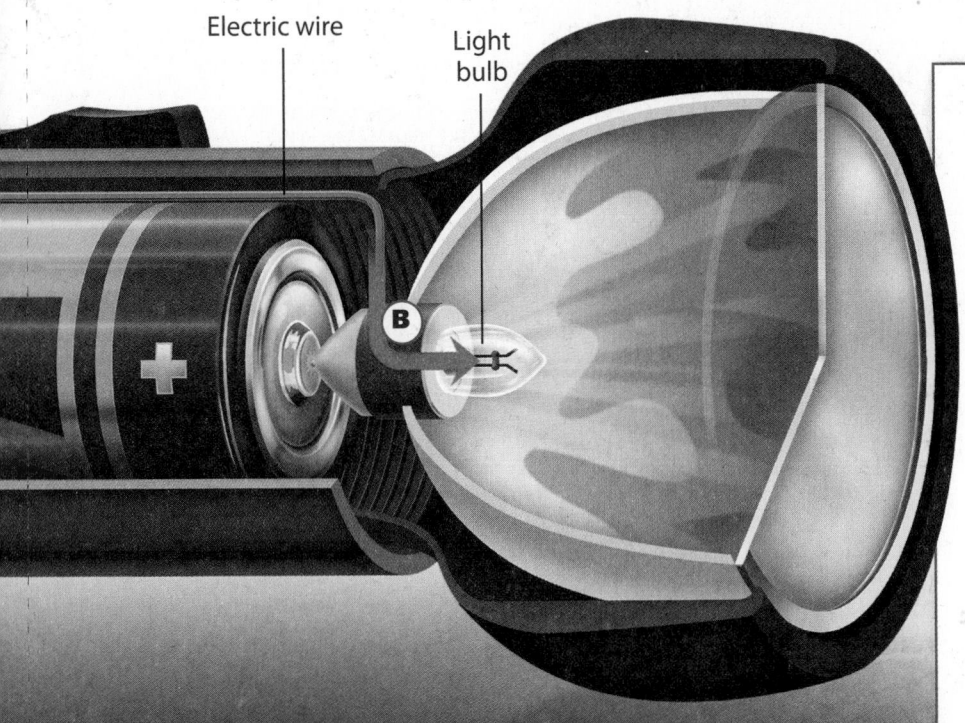

Electric wire

Light bulb

B The electrical energy in the wire is transformed into light in the light bulb. Some of the electrical energy is also transformed into energy as heat.

19 Describe Give another example of electrical energy being transformed into light.

_____

_____

_____

_____

_____

_____

Visual Summary

To complete this summary, circle the correct word. Then use the key below to check your answers. You can use this page to review the main concepts of the lesson.

Energy is the ability to cause change; it cannot be created or destroyed.

20 The total energy in a closed system remains the same / changes as energy changes forms.

Potential energy results from an object's position, composition, or condition, and kinetic energy results from an object's motion.

21 A basketball that is balanced on the rim of a basketball hoop has potential energy / kinetic energy.

22 A basketball that is rolling across a floor has potential energy / kinetic energy.

Energy transformation takes place when energy changes from one form to another.

23 When a candle is burned, some chemical energy is transformed into nuclear energy / energy as heat.

Answers: 20 remains the same; 21 potential energy; 22 kinetic energy; 23 energy as heat.

24 Claims • Evidence • Reasoning Identify and give examples of at least three types of energy you see being used as you look around your classroom. For each example, state evidence to support your claim and explain your reasoning.

Lesson Review

Vocabulary

Draw a line to connect the following terms to their definitions.

1 kinetic energy   **A** energy of position

2 mechanical energy   **B** sum of energy of motion and energy of position

3 potential energy   **C** energy of motion

Key Concepts

4 Describe What happens to the kinetic energy of a snowball as it rolls across the lawn at a constant speed and gains mass?

_____

_____

5 Relate How is the sun related to nuclear energy, electromagnetic energy, and energy as heat?

_____

_____

_____

_____

_____

_____

6 Apply When a person uses an iron to remove the wrinkles from a shirt, why does heat travel from the iron to the shirt?

_____

_____

_____

7 Explain What determines the amount of chemical energy a substance has?

_____

_____

_____

_____

_____

Critical Thinking

Use the picture below to answer the following questions.

8 Identify Name at least three types of energy associated with the microwave.

_____

_____

_____

9 Hypothesize How is electromagnetic energy from the microwave transformed into energy as heat?

_____

_____

_____

10 Infer Explain the law of conservation of energy.

_____

_____

_____

_____

_____

_____

_____

My Notes

Lesson 2

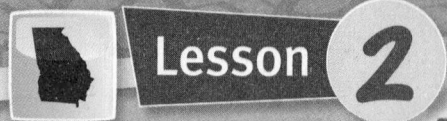

Temperature

ESSENTIAL QUESTION

How is temperature related to kinetic energy?

By the end of this lesson, you should be able to relate the temperature of a substance to the kinetic energy of its particles.

What does it mean to be hot or cold? You can tell that this environment is cold because there is ice and because the person is in a hat and coat.

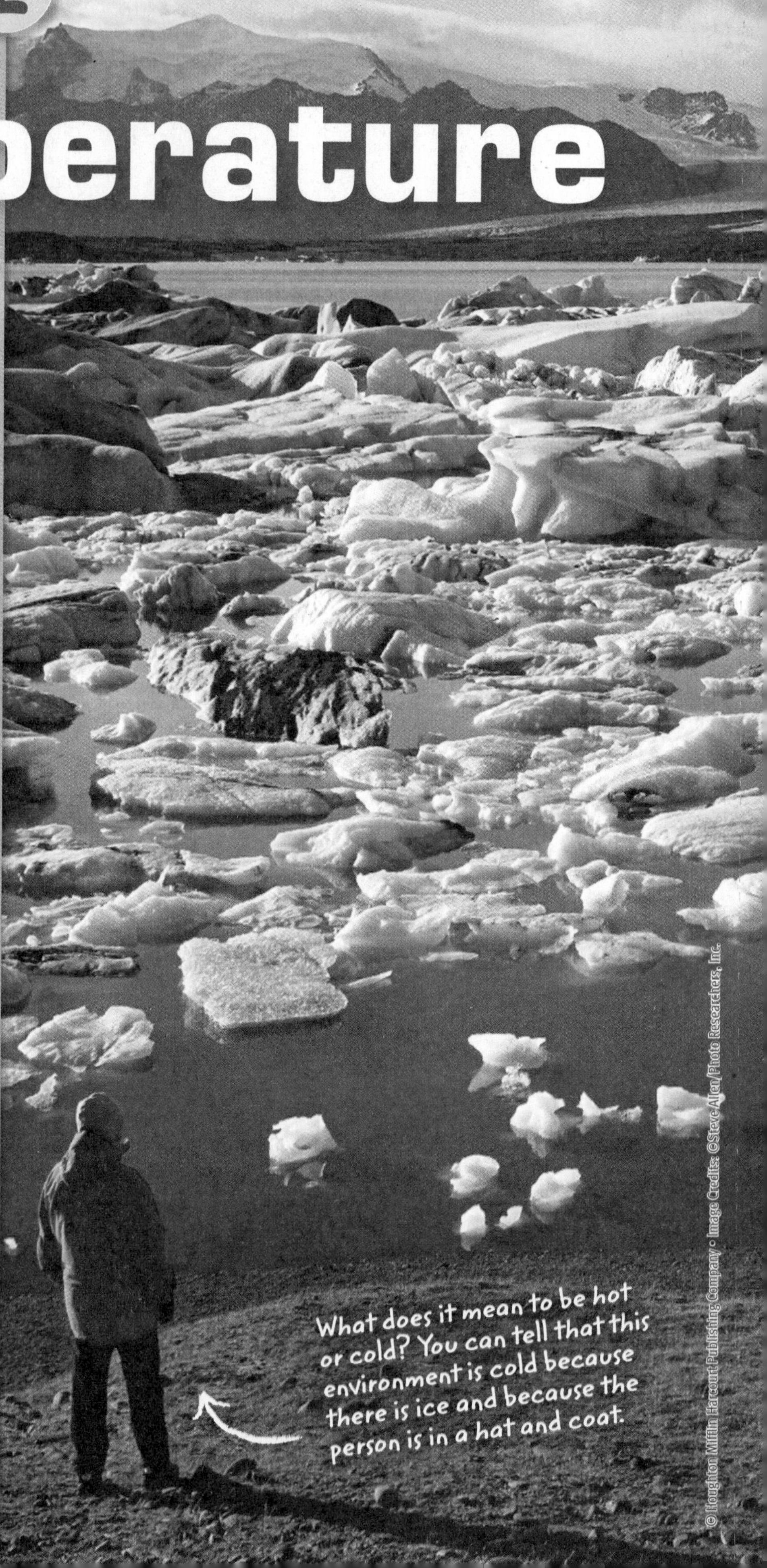

S8P2.d Heat transfer and molecular motion

Engage Your Brain

1 Predict Check T or F to show whether you think each statement is true or false.

T F

☐ ☐ Solids and liquids are made of particles, but gases are made of air, which is not made of particles.

☐ ☐ Kinetic energy is the energy of motion.

☐ ☐ Kinetic energy depends on mass and speed.

2 Illustrate Think about a time when you were very cold. Then draw a picture of a time when you were very hot. Write a caption about the differences between the two situations.

 Active Reading

3 Synthesize Many English words have their roots in other languages. Use the Greek words below to make an educated guess about the meaning of the word *thermometer*. A context sentence is provided for help. Then, write a sentence using the word correctly.

Greek word	Meaning
thermos	warm
metron	to measure

Example sentence
This <u>thermometer</u> indicates that it is 72 °F in this room.

Define thermometer:

_____

_____

Sentence with thermometer:

_____

_____

Vocabulary Terms

• kinetic theory of matter
• temperature
• degree
• thermometer

4 Identify This list contains the key terms you'll learn in this lesson. As you read, circle the definition of each term.

Particle Party

What is the kinetic theory of matter?

All matter is made of small particles. These particles are always moving, even if it doesn't look like they are. The **kinetic theory of matter** states that all of the particles that make up matter are constantly in motion. Because the particles are in motion, they have kinetic energy. The faster the particles are moving, the more kinetic energy they have.

While the particles of matter are constantly moving, the particles move in different directions and at different speeds. This motion is random. Therefore, the individual particles of matter have different amounts of kinetic energy. The average kinetic energy of all these particles takes into account their different random movements. As seen in this picture, solids, liquids, and gases have different average kinetic energies.

This bridge is a solid, so its particles are close together and vibrate.

In this hot pool, the liquid particles are moving around.

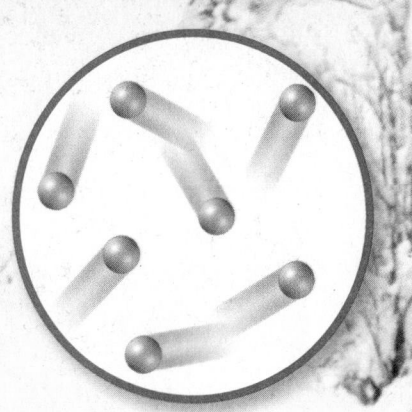

The particles in the gas in the air are far apart and moving quickly.

The particles in this cold river water are moving freely.

How do particles move in solids, liquids, gases, and plasmas?

The kinetic theory of matter explains the motion of particles in solids, liquids, gases, and plasmas.

- The particles in a solid, such as concrete, are not free to move around very much. They vibrate back and forth in the same position and are held tightly together by forces of attraction.
- The particles in a liquid, such as water in a pool, move much more freely than particles in a solid. They are constantly sliding around and tumbling over each other as they move.
- In a gas, such as the air around you, particles are far apart and move around at high speeds. Particles collide with one another, but otherwise they do not interact much.
- In a plasma, such as in stars, particles are very far apart and can move around at extremely high speeds. Particles rarely collide with one another but instead interact though electricity and magnetism.

Active Reading **5 Describe** In your own words, describe the difference between the movement of particles in liquids and the movement of particles in gases.

_____

_____

_____

_____

Visualize It!

6 Illustrate Locate another solid, liquid, or gas in this photo. Sketch a representation of the particles that make up the solid, liquid, or gas. Make sure to indicate how fast you think the particles might be moving based on temperature. Then, write a caption describing the particle movement.

_____

_____

_____

_____

Mercury Rising

How does temperature relate to kinetic energy?

Temperature (TEM•per•uh•chur) is a measure of the average kinetic energy of all the particles in an object. In the picture on the previous page, the particle diagrams for two different liquids are shown. For the colder liquid, the particles are moving slower. For the warmer liquid, the particles are moving faster. If an iron is hot, the particles in the solid are vibrating very fast and have a high average kinetic energy. If the iron has a low temperature, the particles in the solid are vibrating more slowly and have a lower average kinetic energy.

Absolute zero is the temperature at which the motion of particles stops. It is not possible to actually reach absolute zero, though temperatures very close to absolute zero have been reached in laboratories.

How is temperature measured?

Suppose you hear on the radio that the temperature outside is 30 degrees. Do you need to wear a warm coat to spend the day outside? The answer depends on the temperature scale being used. There are three common temperature scales, all of which measure the average kinetic energy of particles. These scales are called Celsius, Fahrenheit, and Kelvin. However, 30 degrees on one scale is quite different from 30 degrees on the other scales.

To establish a temperature scale, two known values and the number of units between the values are needed. The freezing and boiling points of pure water are often used as the standard values. These points are always the same under the same conditions, and they are easy to reproduce. In the Celsius and Fahrenheit scales, temperature is measured in units called degrees. **Degrees** (°) are equally spaced units between two points. The space between degrees can vary from scale to scale. In the Kelvin scale, no degree sign is used. Instead, the unit is just called a kelvin. Temperature is measured using an instrument called a **thermometer**.

Active Reading **7 Explain** How does a substance's temperature change when the average kinetic energy of its particles increases? When it decreases?

_____

_____

_____

Think Outside the Book Inquiry

8 Produce Write a story about someone who travels from one extreme temperature to another. Make sure to talk about how your character adjusts to the change in temperature. How are the character's daily activities or decisions affected?

Celsius Scale

The temperature scale most commonly used around the world, and often used by scientists, is the Celsius (SEL•see•uhs) scale (°C). This scale was developed in the 1740s by Anders Celsius. On the Celsius scale, pure water freezes at 0 °C and boils at 100 °C, so there are 100 degrees—100 equal units—between these two temperatures.

Fahrenheit Scale

The scale used most commonly in the United States for measuring temperature is the Fahrenheit scale (°F). It was developed in the early 1700s by Gabriel Fahrenheit. On the Fahrenheit scale, pure water freezes at 32 °F and boils at 212 °F. Thus, there are 180 degrees—180 equal units—between the freezing point and the boiling point of water.

Kelvin Scale

A temperature scale used commonly by physicists is the Kelvin scale. This scale was not developed until the 20th century. The equal units in the Kelvin scale are called kelvins, not degrees. On the kelvin scale, pure water freezes at 273 K and boils at 373 K. There are 100 kelvins—100 equal units—between these two temperatures. The lowest temperature on the Kelvin scale is absolute zero, or 0 K.

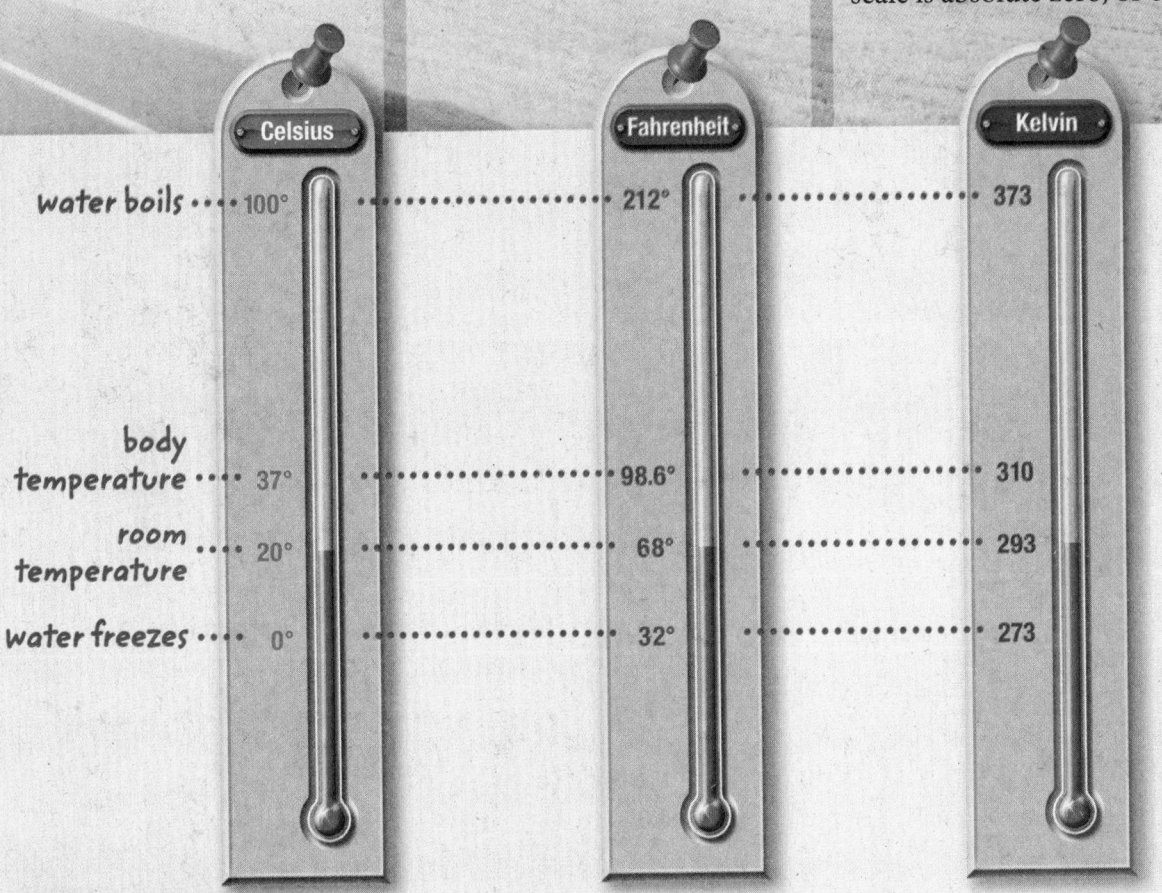

	Celsius	Fahrenheit	Kelvin
water boils	100°	212°	373
body temperature	37°	98.6°	310
room temperature	20°	68°	293
water freezes	0°	32°	273

Visualize It!

9 Identify What is body temperature in the Celsius scale? In the Fahrenheit scale? In the Kelvin scale?

_____

_____

10 Apply The water in swimming pools is typically about 80 °F. Mark this temperature on the Fahrenheit thermometer above. Estimate what temperature this is in the Celsius and Kelvin scales.

_____

_____

Visual Summary

To complete this summary, fill in the blanks with the correct word. Then use the key below to check your answers. You can use this page to review the main concepts of the lesson.

Temperature

All of the particles that make up matter are constantly in motion.

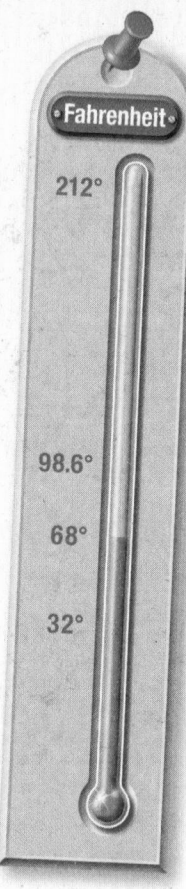

Temperature is a measure of the average kinetic energy of all the particles in an object. Temperature is measured using one of three scales: Celsius, Fahrenheit, or Kelvin.

Fahrenheit

212°

98.6°

68°

32°

11 The particles in a hot liquid move _____ than the particles in a cold liquid.

12 Temperature is measured using a _____.

13 Infer If a puddle of water is frozen, do particles in the ice have kinetic energy? Explain your reasoning.

Lesson Review

Vocabulary

For each pair of terms, write a sentence using both words that demonstrates the definition of each word.

1 Kinetic theory of matter and temperature

_____

_____

_____

_____

_____

2 Thermometer and degree

_____

_____

_____

_____

_____

Key Concepts

3 Relate Describe the relationship between temperature and kinetic energy.

_____

_____

_____

4 Apply Particles in a warmer substance have a _____ average kinetic energy than particles in the substance when it is cooler.

5 Identify What are the three scales used to measure temperature? What are the units of each scale?

_____

_____

_____

_____

Critical Thinking

Use the art below to answer the following questions.

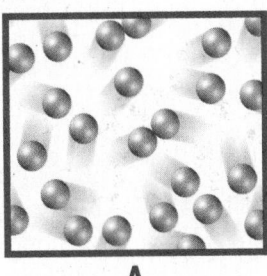
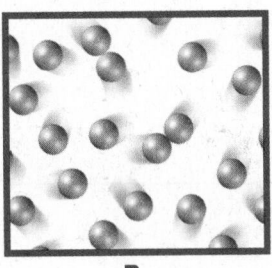

A   B

6 Observe Which illustration represents the substance at a higher temperature? Explain.

_____

_____

_____

7 Claims • Evidence • Reasoning What would happen to the particles in illustration A if the substance were chilled? What would happen if the particles in illustration B were warmed? State the reasoning behind each of your claims.

_____

_____

_____

_____

_____

8 Apply Using your knowledge of the difference between the three different temperature scales, what do you think would happen if a human's body temperature was 98.6 °C? Why do doctors worry more about a fever of a couple of degrees Celsius than a fever of a couple of degrees Fahrenheit?

_____

_____

_____

_____

_____

My Notes

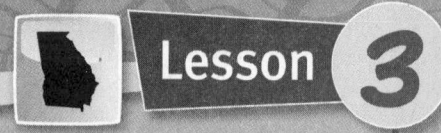
Thermal Energy and Heat

ESSENTIAL QUESTION

What is the relationship between heat and temperature?

By the end of this lesson, you should be able to analyze the relationship between heat, temperature, and thermal energy.

The Afar Depression, in Eastern Africa, is one of the hottest places on Earth. In the summer, temperatures average over 38 °C (100 °F)!

 S8P2.c Energy transformations in a system

S8P2.d Heat transfer and molecular motion

✋ **Lesson Labs**

Quick Labs
• Simple Heat Engine
• Observing the Transfer of Energy
• Exploring Thermal Conductivity

Field Lab
• Building a Solar Cooker

🧠 Engage Your Brain

1 Describe Fill in the blanks with the words that you think correctly complete the following sentences.

When you put your hands on a cold object, like a glass of ice water, your hands become _____ The glass of water becomes _____ if you leave your hands on it for a long time. If you leave the glass of ice water out in the sun, the ice will start to _____

2 Describe Write your own caption for this photo.

_____
_____
_____
_____

📖 Active Reading

3 Apply Many scientific words, such as *conductor*, also have everyday meanings. Use context clues to write your own definition for each meaning of the word *conductor*.

Example sentence
That school's band is very good because its <u>conductor</u> is a great teacher.

conductor:

_____
_____

Example sentence
That metal spoon is a good <u>conductor</u>, so it will get hot if you put it into boiling soup.

conductor:

_____
_____

Vocabulary Terms

• thermal energy   • conductor
• heat   • insulator
• calorie   • convection
• conduction   • radiation

4 Apply As you learn the definition of each vocabulary term in this lesson, create your own definition or sketch to help you remember the meaning of the term.

What is thermal energy?

Thermal energy is the total kinetic energy of all particles in a substance. In the SI system, thermal energy is measured in joules (J). Remember that temperature is not energy, but it does give a measure of the average kinetic energy of all the particles in a substance. If you have two identical glasses of water and one is at a higher temperature than the other, the particles in the hotter water have a higher average kinetic energy. The water at a higher temperature will have a higher amount of thermal energy.

What is the difference between thermal energy and temperature?

Temperature and thermal energy are different from each other. Temperature is related to the average kinetic energy of particles, while thermal energy is the total kinetic energy of all the particles. A glass of water can have the same temperature as Lake Superior, but the lake has much more thermal energy because the lake contains many more water molecules.

After you put ice cubes into a pitcher of lemonade, energy is transferred from the warmer lemonade to the colder ice. The lemonade's thermal energy decreases and the ice's thermal energy increases. Because the particles in the lemonade have transferred some of their energy to the particles in the ice, the average kinetic energy of the particles in the lemonade decreases. Thus, the temperature of the lemonade decreases.

Active Reading 5 **Explain** What are two factors that determine the thermal energy of a substance?

_____

_____

There are more water molecules in this lake than in the glass of water on the right.

Houghton Mifflin Harcourt Publishing Company • Image Credits: ©John Warden/SuperStock

Under Where?

There are fewer water molecules in this glass than in the lake.

6 Apply For each object pair in the table below, circle the object that has more thermal energy. Assume that both objects are at the same temperature.

bowl of soup	small balloon	tiger
pot of soup	large balloon	house cat

Heat It Up!

What is heat?

You might think of the word *heat* as having to do with things that feel hot. But heat also has to do with things that feel cold. Heat causes objects to feel hot or cold or to get hot or cold under the right conditions. You probably use the word *heat* every day to mean different things. However, in science, **heat** is the energy transferred from an object at a higher temperature to an object at a lower temperature.

When two objects at different temperatures come into contact, energy is always transferred from the object that has the higher temperature to the object that has the lower temperature. Energy in the form of heat always flows from hot to cold. For example, if you put an ice cube into a glass of water, energy is transferred from the warmer water to the colder ice cube.

Energy in the form of heat flows from the warm drinks to the cold ice. The ice melts.

7 Apply For each object pair in the table below, draw an arrow in the direction in which energy in the form of heat would flow.

Object 1	Direction of heat flow	Object 2
metal rod		fire
hat		snowman
ice cube		glass of warm water

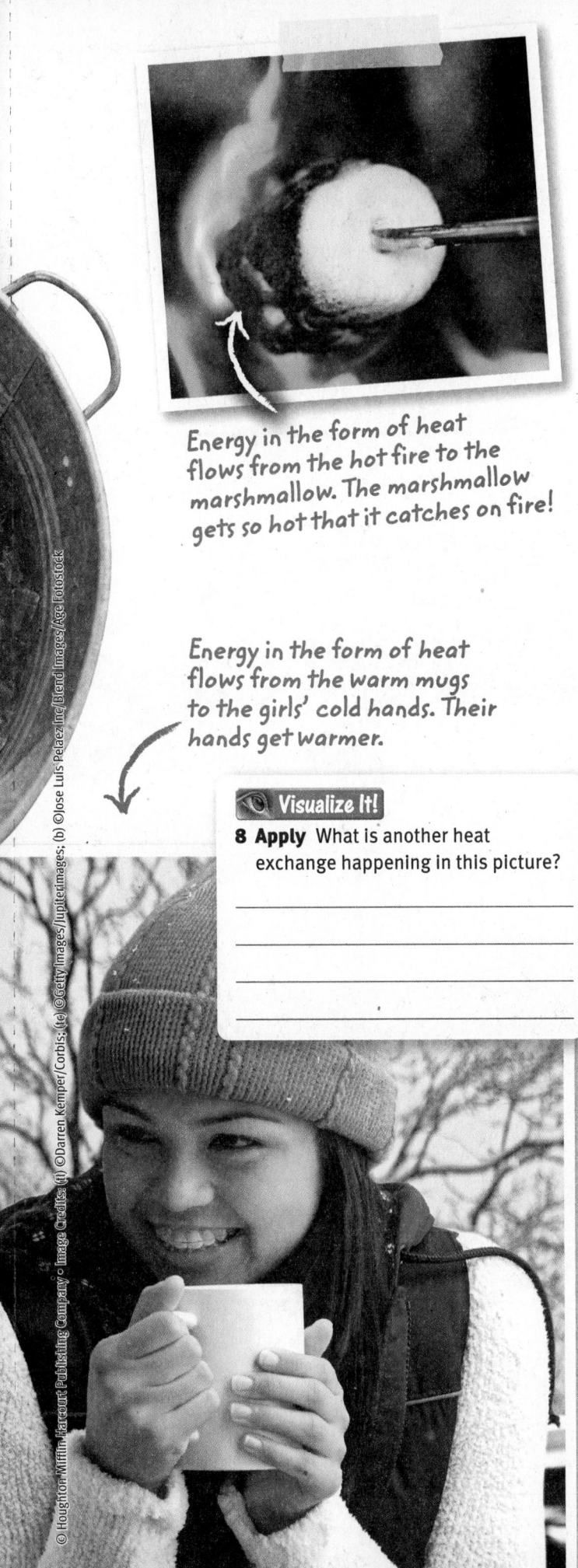

Energy in the form of heat flows from the hot fire to the marshmallow. The marshmallow gets so hot that it catches on fire!

Energy in the form of heat flows from the warm mugs to the girls' cold hands. Their hands get warmer.

Visualize It!

8 Apply What is another heat exchange happening in this picture?

_____

_____

_____

_____

How is heat measured?

Heat is measured in two ways. One way is the calorie (cal). One **calorie** is equal to the amount of energy needed to raise the temperature of 1 g of water by 1 °C. Heat can also be measured in joules (J) because heat is a form of energy. One calorie is equal to 4.18 J.

You probably think of calories in terms of food. However, in nutrition, one Calorie—written with a capital C—is actually one kilocalorie, or 1,000 calories. This means that one Calorie (Cal) contains enough energy to raise the temperature of 1 kg of water by 1 °C. Each Calorie in food contains 1,000 cal of energy.

To find out how many Calories are in an apple, the apple is burned inside an instrument called a calorimeter. A thermometer measures the increase in temperature, which is used to calculate how much energy is released. This amount is the number of Calories.

How is heat related to thermal energy?

Adding or removing heat from a substance will affect its temperature and thermal energy. Heat, however, is not the same as thermal energy and temperature. These are properties of a substance. Heat is the energy involved when these properties change.

Think of what happens when two objects at different temperatures come into contact. Energy as heat flows from the object at the higher temperature to the object at the lower temperature. When both objects come to the same temperature, no more energy as heat flows. Just because the temperature of the two objects is the same does not mean they have the same thermal energy. One object may be larger than the other and thus have more particles in motion.

Active Reading 9 Claims • Evidence • Reasoning
What will happen if two objects at different temperatures come into contact? Describe evidence that you could gather to support your claim.

_____

_____

_____

_____

© Houghton Mifflin Harcourt Publishing Company • Image Credits: (t) ©Darren Kemper/Corbis; (tc) ©Getty Images/Jupiterimages; (b) ©Jose Luis Pelaez Inc/Blend Images/Age Fotostock

How can heat affect the state of an object?

The matter that makes up a frozen juice bar is the same whether the juice bar is frozen or has melted. The matter is just in a different form, or state. Remember that the kinetic theory of matter states that the particles that make up matter move around at different speeds. The state of a substance depends on the speed of its particles. Adding energy in the form of heat to a substance may result in a change of state. The added energy may cause the bonds between particles to break. This is what allows the state to change. Adding energy in the form of heat to a chunk of glacier may cause the ice to melt into water. Removing energy in the form of heat from a substance may also result in a change of state.

Active Reading **11 Predict** What are two ways to change the state of a substance?

_____

_____

Think Outside the Book **Inquiry**

10 Compare Have you ever needed to touch a very hot object? What did you use to touch it without burning yourself? Make a list. Have you ever needed to protect yourself from being cold? What sorts of things did you use? Make a list. Now, looking at the two lists, what do the things have in common?

Image Credits: ©Arcticphoto /Alamy

© Houghton Mifflin Harcourt Publishing Company

Some of this ice is changing state. It is melting into water.

How do polar bears stay warm?

Keep Your Cool

© Houghton Mifflin Harcourt Publishing Company • Image Credits: ©Andrew Syred/Photo Researchers, Inc.

What is conduction?

There are three main ways to transfer energy as heat: conduction, convection, and radiation. **Conduction** is the transfer of energy as heat from one substance to another through direct contact. It occurs any time that objects at different temperatures come into contact with each other. The average kinetic energy of particles in the warmer object is greater than the average kinetic energy of the particles in the cooler object. As the particles collide, some of the kinetic energy of the particles in the warmer object is transferred to the cooler object. As long as the objects are in contact, conduction continues until the temperatures of the objects are equal.

Conduction can also occur within a single object. In this case, energy in the form of heat is transferred from the warmer part of the object to the cooler part of the object. Imagine you put a metal spoon into a cup of hot cocoa. Energy will be conducted from the warm end of the spoon to the cool end until the temperature of the entire spoon is the same.

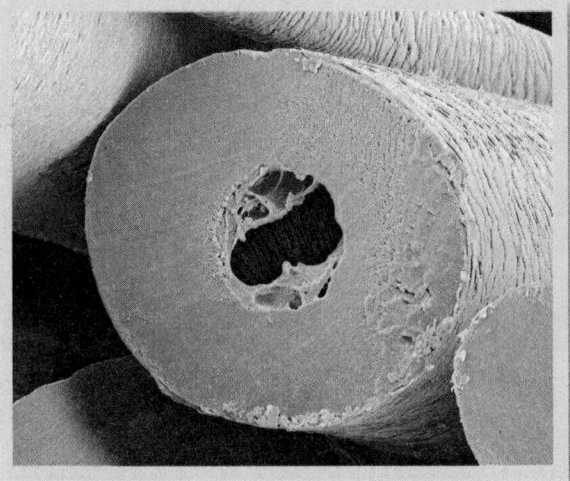

This is a photo of polar bear hair magnified about 350 times! Notice that it is hollow inside. The air inside is a good insulator.

Conductors

Some materials transfer the kinetic energy of particles better than others. A **conductor** is a material that transfers heat very well. Metals are typically good conductors. You know that when one end of a metal object gets hot, the other end quickly becomes hot as well. Consider pots or pans that have metal handles. A metal handle becomes too hot to touch soon after the pan is placed on a hot stove.

Insulators

An **insulator** (IN•suh•lay•ter) is a material that is a poor conductor of heat. Some examples of insulators are wood, paper, and plastic foam. Plastic foam is a good insulator because it contains many small spaces that are filled with air. A plastic foam cup will not easily transfer energy in the form of heat by conduction. That is why plastic foam is often used to keep hot drinks hot. Think about the metal pan handle mentioned above. It can be dangerous to have handles get hot so quickly. Instead, pot handles are often made of an insulator, such as wood or plastic. Although a plastic handle will also get hot when the pot is on the stove, it takes a much longer time for it to get hot than it would for a metal handle.

12 Classify Decide whether each object below is a conductor or an insulator. Then check the correct box.

Flannel shirt	☐ Conductor ☐ Insulator
Iron skillet	☐ Conductor ☐ Insulator
Copper pipe	☐ Conductor ☐ Insulator
Oven mitt	☐ Conductor ☐ Insulator

What is convection?

Energy in the form of heat can also be transferred through the movement of gases or liquids. **Convection** (kuhn•VEK•shuhn) is the transfer of energy as heat by the movement of a liquid or gas. In most substances, as temperature increases, the density of the liquid or gas decreases. Convection occurs when a cooler, denser mass of a gas or liquid replaces a warmer, less dense mass of a gas or liquid by pushing it upward.

When you boil water in a pot, the water moves in roughly circular patterns because of convection. The water at the bottom of the pot gets hot because there is a source of heat at the bottom. As the water heats, it becomes less dense. The warmer water rises through the denser, cooler water above it. At the surface, the warm water begins to cool. The particles move closer together, making the water denser. The cooler water then sinks back to the bottom, is heated again, and the cycle repeats. This cycle causes a circular motion of liquids or gases. The motion is due to density differences that result from temperature differences. The motion is called a *convection current*.

What is radiation?

Radiation is another way in which heat can be transferred. **Radiation** is the transfer of energy by electromagnetic waves. Some examples of electromagnetic waves include visible light, microwaves, and infrared light. The sun is the most significant source of radiation that you experience on a daily basis. However, all objects—even you—emit radiation and release energy.

When radiation is emitted from one object and then absorbed by another, the result is often a transfer of heat. Like conduction and convection, radiation can transfer heat from warmer to cooler objects. However, radiation differs from conduction and convection in a very significant way. Radiation can travel through empty space, as it does when it moves from the sun to Earth.

Active Reading

13 Identify As you read, underline examples of heat transfer.

This pot of boiling water shows how convection currents move.

14 Classify Fill in the blanks in the chart below.

Example	Conduction, Convection, or Radiation
When you put some food in the microwave, it gets hot.	
	Conduction
A heater on the first floor of the school makes the air on the second floor warm.	

Practical Uses of Radiation

Do you think that you could cook your food using the energy from the sun? Using a device called a solar cooker, you could! A solar cooker works by concentrating the radiation from the sun into a small area using mirrors. Solar cookers aren't just fun to use—they also help some people eat clean food!

In a refugee camp
This woman, who lives in a refugee camp in Sudan, is making tea with water that she boiled in a solar cooker. For many people living far from electricity or a source of clean water, a solar cooker provides a cheap and portable way to sterilize their water. This helps to prevent disease.

As a hobby
This woman demonstrates how her solar cooker works. Many people like to use solar cookers because they do not require any fuel. They also do not release any emissions that are harmful to the planet.

Extend

Inquiry

15 Identify Two examples of radiation are shown in the photos above. What is the source of the radiation in the examples?

16 Relate Research other places throughout the world where solar cookers are being used.

17 Produce Explain how solar cookers are useful to society by doing one of the following:
• Make a solar cooker and demonstrate how it works.
• Write a story about a family who uses a solar cooker to stay healthy and safe.

Visual Summary

To complete this summary, circle the correct word or phrase. Then use the key below to check your answers. You can use this page to review the main concepts of the lesson.

Thermal energy is the total kinetic energy of all particles in a substance.

18 If two objects are at the same temperature, the one with more / fewer / the same amount of particles will have a higher thermal energy.

Heat is the energy transferred from an object at a higher temperature to an object at a lower temperature.

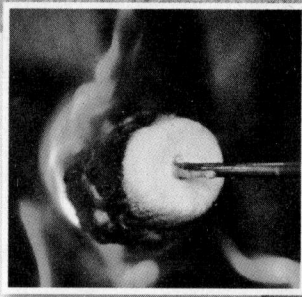

19 Heat always flows from cold to hot / hot to cold / left to right.

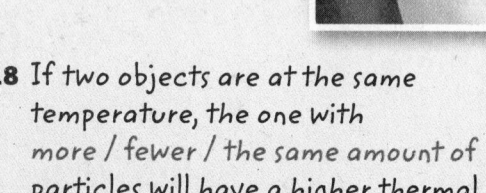

Heat

Heat can change the state of a substance.

20 Adding heat to an object causes bonds between particles to form / break / combine. This is what allows the state change.

There are three main ways to transfer energy as heat: conduction, convection, and radiation.

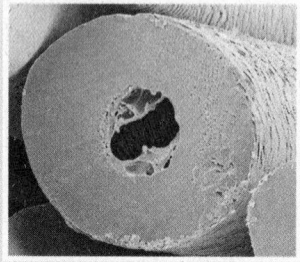

conduction

convection

radiation

21 Conduction is the transfer of energy from a warmer object to a cooler object through a gas / empty space / direct contact.

22 Energy from the sun travels to Earth through conduction / convection / radiation.

Answers: 18 more; 19 hot to cold; 20 break; 21 direct contact; 22 radiation

23 **Conclude** Suppose you are outside on a hot day and you move into the shade of a tree. Which form of energy transfer are you avoiding? Explain your reasoning.

Lesson Review

Vocabulary

In your own words, define the following terms.

1 heat

_____

_____

_____

2 thermal energy

_____

_____

_____

3 conduction

_____

_____

_____

4 convection

_____

_____

_____

5 radiation

_____

_____

_____

Key Concepts

6 Compare What is the difference between heat and temperature?

_____

_____

_____

_____

7 Predict If two objects at different temperatures are in contact with each other, what happens to their temperatures?

_____

_____

_____

_____

Use this photo to answer the following questions.

8 Classify Which type of energy transfer is occurring at each lettered area?

A _____

B _____

C _____

Critical Thinking

9 Synthesize Describe the relationships among temperature, heat, and thermal energy.

_____

_____

_____

_____

_____

10 Synthesize Do you think that solids can undergo convection? Explain your reasoning.

_____

_____

_____

_____

_____

_____

My Notes

Planning an Investigation

Scientists ask many questions and develop hypotheses about the natural world. They conduct investigations to help answer these questions. A scientist must plan an investigation carefully. The investigation should gather information that might support or disprove the hypothesis.

Tutorial

Use the following steps to help plan an investigation.

(1) Write a hypothesis.
The hypothesis should offer an explanation for the question that you are asking. The hypothesis must also be testable. If it is not testable, rewrite the hypothesis.

(2) Identify and list the possible variables in your experiment.
Select the independent variable and the dependent variable. In your investigation, you will change the independent variable to see any effect it may have on the dependent variable.

(3) List the materials that you will need to perform the experiment.
This list should also include equipment that you need for safety.

(4) Determine the method you will use to test your hypothesis.
Clearly describe the steps you will follow. If you change any part of the procedure while you are conducting the investigation, record the change. Another scientist should be able to follow your procedure to repeat your investigation.

(5) Analyze the results.
Your data and observations from all of your experiments should be recorded carefully and clearly to maintain credibility. Record how you analyze your results so others can review your work and spot any problems or errors in your analysis.

(6) Draw conclusions.
Describe what the results of the investigation show. Tell whether the results support your hypothesis.

You Try It!

You are a member of a research team that is trying to design and test a solar balloon. A solar balloon is an object filled with air that rises when exposed to radiant energy from the sun. They rise because of differences in density between the air inside and outside of the balloon. To begin your project, do research on solar balloon design. Then consider the following question to investigate: Does the color of a solar balloon affect its ability to rise?

1 Forming a Hypothesis Write down your hypothesis. How does your hypothesis explain or answer your question? Is your hypothesis testable?

_____
_____
_____
_____

2 Identifying Variables List the possible variables in this experiment. Identify dependent variables and independent variables.

_____
_____
_____
_____

3 Selecting Materials What materials will you need to test this variable? What might happen if you select inappropriate materials?

_____
_____
_____
_____

4 Testing Your Hypothesis What will your system look like? Will it support your testing? You may sketch the system on a separate page.

_____
_____
_____
_____

5 Maintaining Accurate Records What steps will you need to follow in order to test your hypothesis? What kinds of measurements will you collect? What kind of graphic organizer will you use to record your information?

_____
_____
_____
_____

6 Drawing Conclusions What conclusions can you draw from your data? How can you explain your results in terms of changes to molecular motion taking place inside your test balloons? Was radiation, conduction, and/or convection involved? Explain.

_____
_____
_____

Take It Home

Look closely at objects and materials in your home. Write a list of things that help to prevent the transfer of energy as heat. Design an investigation using one or more of these items to learn more about the job they do. Record your observations. Evaluate your results to see if they might point to a further investigation or an improvement to a product. Present your results in a pamphlet.

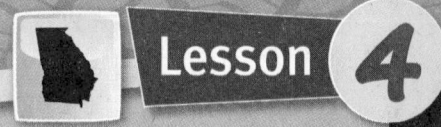

Effects of Energy Transfer

ESSENTIAL QUESTION

How does the use of energy resources affect the environment?

By the end of this lesson, you should be able to recognize how the production and use of different types of energy resources can have environmental consequences.

This power generation plant transforms the heat released from burning coal into electrical energy. Unfiltered smoke from the plant causes air pollution.

Lesson Labs

Quick Labs
- Modeling Renewable Energy
- Designing a Vehicle Using Alternative Energy

Exploration Lab
- Sustainable Resource Management

Engage Your Brain

1 Identify In the space below, list as many sources of energy as you can think of. Circle the sources you use most often during a typical day.

_____

_____

_____

_____

_____

_____

_____

_____

2 Describe Write your own caption for this photo of a polluted city.

_____

_____

_____

Active Reading

3 Synthesize You can often define an unknown word if you know the meaning of its word parts. Use the word parts and sentence below to make an educated guess about the meaning of *renewable*.

Word part	Meaning
re-	again, back
new	having been recently made
-able	capable of

Example sentence
Sunlight is classified as a <u>renewable</u> resource because it is constantly replaced.

renewable: _____

_____

_____

Vocabulary Terms
- **renewable resource**
- **nonrenewable resource**
- **fossil fuel**

4 Apply As you learn the definition of each vocabulary term in this lesson, create your own definition or sketch to help you remember the meaning of the term.

Check the Source!

5 Identify As you read, underline ways in which humans use energy.

Solar panels can help people harness the energy from the sun to use at home!

How do people use energy?

Recall that energy is the capacity to do work. Any work that you do or that you observe around you requires energy. Humans use energy to heat and cool their homes and provide light. Factories use energy to produce everything from toothpicks to airplanes. Energy is required to produce and prepare the food that you eat and beverages that you drink. Vehicles that move you from one place to another require energy. Where does all the energy you use come from?

What are sources of energy?

The sun is Earth's main source of energy. When it reaches Earth, the sun's energy can be stored in various ways, such as in green plants. Useful chemical energy is sometimes stored in minerals. Earth's internal heat, or geothermal energy, is another energy source. An *energy source* is an available source of stored energy that humans can use.

Visualize It!

6 Identify List all of the examples of objects that use energy in this room.

_____

_____

_____

_____

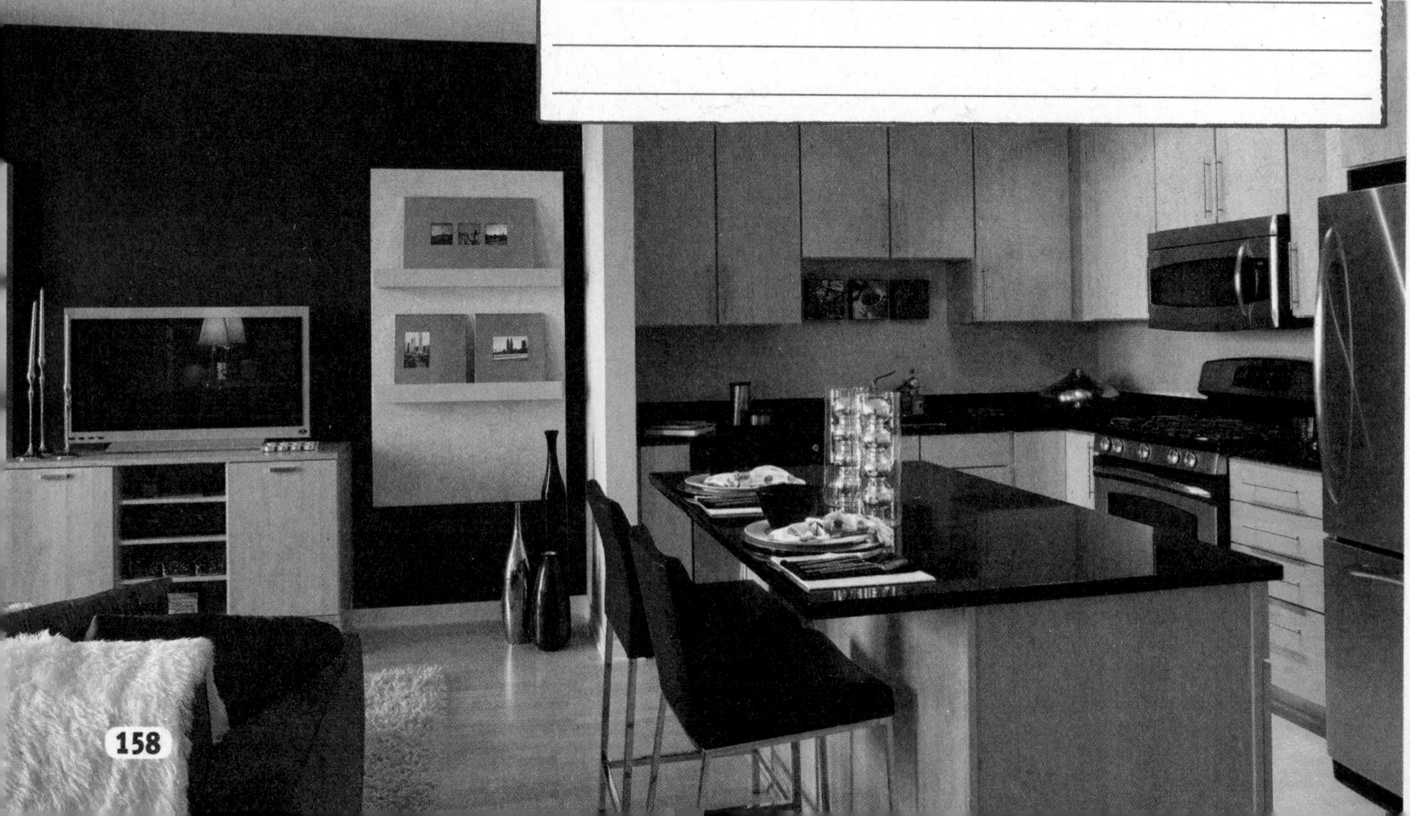

Renewable Energy Sources

A **renewable resource** is an energy source that can be easily reproduced or replaced by nature. Renewable resources are replaced at a rate equal to or greater than the rate that they are used. For example, sunlight and wind are continually available. Humans can use these resources to produce energy without using them up. Other renewable resources, such as trees or crops, are destroyed as they are used. They are renewable because they grow back in a relatively short time.

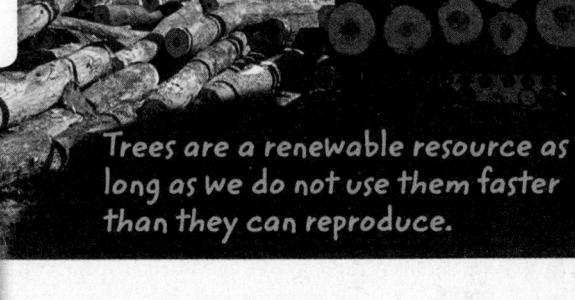

Trees are a renewable resource as long as we do not use them faster than they can reproduce.

Gasoline is nonrenewable. Its chemical energy comes from organisms that died millions of years ago.

Nonrenewable Energy Sources

A **nonrenewable resource** is an energy source that cannot be produced, grown, or restored as fast as it is used. For example, energy-rich minerals, such as uranium, are nonrenewable because they no longer form. Coal, petroleum, and natural gas are found deep below Earth's surface. They formed over millions of years, so there is a fixed amount of these resources currently available. Humans are using them much more quickly than they can form, so they will eventually run out if we continue to use them at the same rate.

7 Compare Fill in the Venn diagram to compare and contrast characteristics of renewable and nonrenewable energy sources.

Renewable Energy Source | Both | Nonrenewable Energy Source

Running Out of Gas!

What are some fossil fuels?

Fossil fuels are energy resources made from carbon-rich plant and animal remains. Heat and pressure from layers of sediment converted the remains to coal, petroleum, or natural gas. Fossil fuels are nonrenewable because they take millions of years to form. Burning fossil fuels produces carbon dioxide, a greenhouse gas, as well as harmful acids and other forms of pollution.

 **Active Reading**

8 Synthesize What environmental effects are shared by all fossil fuels?

_____

_____

Coal

Coal is a sedimentary rock formed from the remains of dead plants at the bottom of ancient swamps. Coal mining can involve removing soil and rocks or creating deep mines. These processes can destroy landscapes and pollute water supplies.

Natural Gas

Some fossil fuels are gases that became trapped in rock formations. Methane (CH_4) is the main component of natural gas. About half of the homes in the United States use natural gas for heating. Natural gas burns more cleanly than other fossil fuels. However, it still produces carbon dioxide. Methane can sometimes leak into the atmosphere from wells, storage tanks, and pipelines.

Petroleum

Petroleum means "rock oil." It formed from the remains of single-celled aquatic organisms that lived long ago. Petroleum is mined on land or under the ocean. It is then separated into fuels such as gasoline, diesel, and jet fuel. Transporting oil by pipeline, ship, or truck can result in spills that pollute the soil and harm wildlife. Pollutants produced by burning petroleum can react with sunlight to produce smog, a foglike layer of air pollution.

Visualize It!

9 Analyze Use the diagrams below to describe how plant and animal remains can become buried and form natural gas or petroleum (oil) after millions of years of heat and pressure.

_____

_____

_____

_____

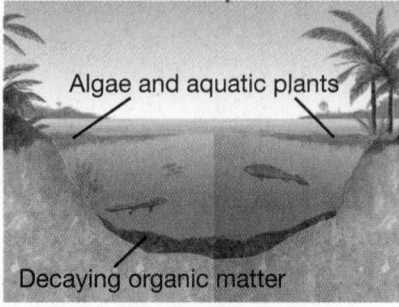

Algae and aquatic plants

Decaying organic matter

Mud

Decaying organic matter

Rock

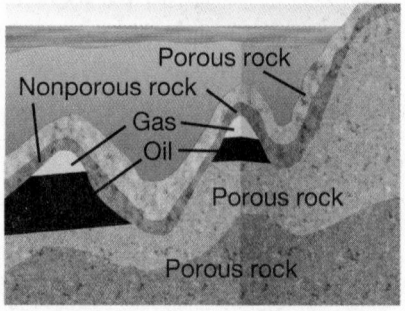

Porous rock

Nonporous rock

Gas

Oil

Porous rock

Porous rock

What transformations do fossil fuels undergo?

First, raw fossil fuels are obtained by drilling or mining. Then, the fossil fuels are transported, converted into useful forms, stored, and eventually burned for energy. Each transformation can potentially affect the environment in negative ways.

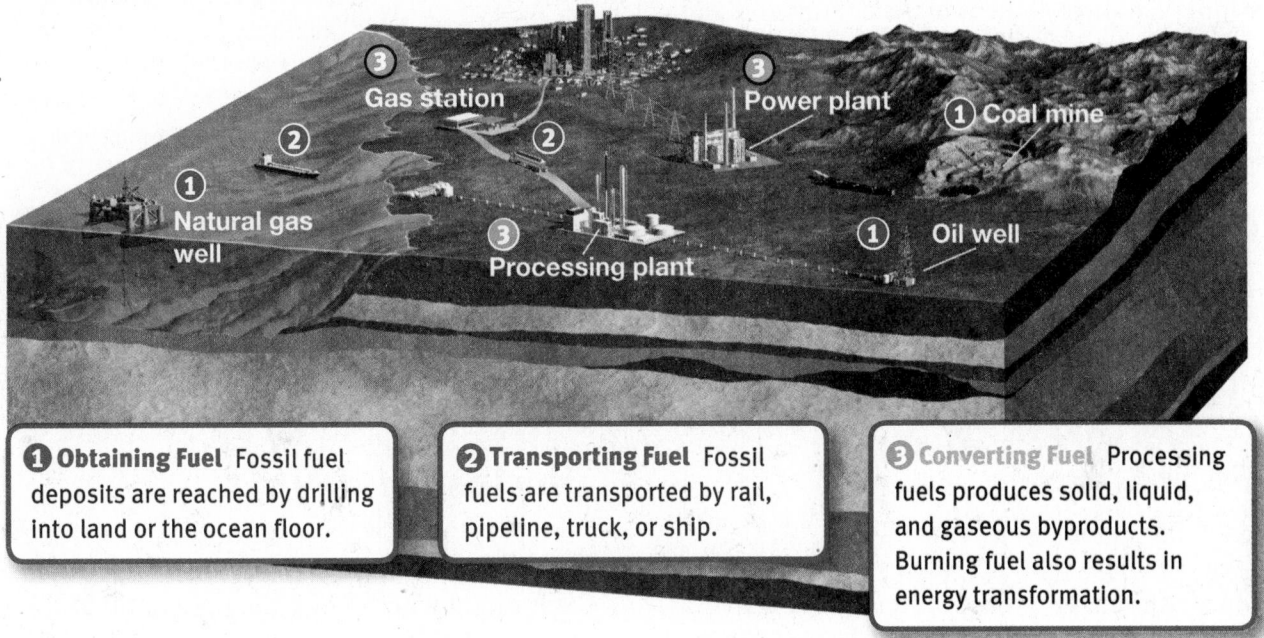

Gas station

Power plant

① Coal mine

③

②

③

②

① Natural gas well

① Oil well

③ Processing plant

❶ Obtaining Fuel Fossil fuel deposits are reached by drilling into land or the ocean floor.

❷ Transporting Fuel Fossil fuels are transported by rail, pipeline, truck, or ship.

❸ Converting Fuel Processing fuels produces solid, liquid, and gaseous byproducts. Burning fuel also results in energy transformation.

Visualize It!

10 Apply Study the three photos of the environmental consequences of obtaining, transporting, and using fossil fuels. Write captions for the second and third photographs.

Mining fossil fuels from the ocean floor can disrupt marine habitats.

(A) _____
_____
_____
_____

(B) _____
_____
_____
_____

Nature's Storehouse

What are some alternative sources of energy?

More than three-fourths of the energy used in the United States comes from fossil fuels. These fuels will eventually run out if we keep using them. An alternative energy source is a resource that can be used in place of fossil fuels. Most of these sources are renewable. Using these sources can *conserve*, or save, fossil fuels.

Think Outside the Book

12 **Research** Choose one of these alternative energy sources. Research ways in which the energy from your source is distributed to users. Prepare a brochure explaining your energy source.

Active Reading

11 **Identify** As you read the cards on this page and the next two pages, underline whether each source is renewable or nonrenewable.

Solar Energy

Renewable energy from the sun can be converted into electrical energy. Solar panels absorb the energy from the sun for our use. In some areas, solar collectors use energy from the sun to produce steam. The steam runs generators to produce electrical energy.

Solar energy is free and clean, but the technologies to transform it into electrical energy aren't widely used. Also, sunlight does not fall evenly over Earth.

These portable solar panels can charge batteries on the go!

Nuclear Energy

Converting nuclear energy into electrical energy is a complex process with a powerful payoff. Splitting the nuclei of a kilogram of uranium atoms releases thousands of times more energy than burning the same mass of coal.

Nuclear energy is nonrenewable because minerals in Earth's crust cannot be replaced. Nuclear power plants do not produce carbon dioxide, but they do produce harmful radioactive wastes that must be safely stored.

Nuclear power plants must be carefully designed to prevent harmful radiation from leaking into the environment.

Hydroelectric Energy

Energy from water is one of the most widely used alternative energy sources. Water in fast-moving rivers or flowing downhill through dams turns generators that generate electrical energy.

Hydroelectric energy is powered by the water cycle, so it is a renewable resource. However, it can only be produced by large volumes of falling water. Flooding land to produce reservoirs can destroy habitats. Dams can also disrupt migratory paths of fish and create erosion problems.

Water flowing through a failed dam could threaten thousands of people living downstream.

To capture more wind, turbines may be 20 stories tall with blades 60 meters (200 ft) in length.

Wind Energy

Blowing wind causes the blades of wind turbines to turn. The blades are connected to a shaft that turns a generator, converting wind energy into electrical energy.

Wind energy is renewable and it doesn't cause any pollution. However, it depends on steady, strong winds that are found only in certain places. Wind farms can also create noise pollution and threaten birds and bats that fly too close to the giant turning blades.

13 Summarize Use the table to list advantages and disadvantages of each alternative energy source.

Energy source	Advantages	Disadvantages
Solar		
Nuclear		
Hydroelectric		
Wind		

Geothermal Energy

Geothermal energy is extracted from heat stored within Earth. This energy source is available near hot springs, geysers, or active volcanoes. Water or steam heated by geothermal energy can be used to heat buildings directly or to generate electrical energy.

Geothermal energy is renewable, but it is found only in specific areas on Earth. Some of these areas are protected within national parks.

Energy from Burning Biomass

Biomass includes living or recently dead organic material that can be used as fuel. Examples include trees, crops, or decaying organic matter. Some types of biomass are directly burned for fuel. Others, such as corn, are first converted into fuels such as methane or alcohol.

Energy from biomass is renewable. Using organic waste as an energy source is useful. However, burning biomass or its fuels releases carbon dioxide into the environment.

A nearby processing plant captures the geothermal energy from its natural source, an underground hot zone in Iceland.

Gasoline burns cleaner when it is mixed with ethanol made from corn. Growing corn absorbs carbon dioxide from the air.

14 Summarize Use the table to list advantages and disadvantages of geothermal and biomass energy sources.

Energy source	Advantages	Disadvantages
Geothermal		
Biomass		

Inquiry

15 Claims • Evidence • Reasoning
Which of the alternative energy sources do you think would have the least impact on the environment? Use evidence to support your claim and explain your reasoning.

© Houghton Mifflin Harcourt Publishing Company • Image Credits: (bkgd) ©Neale Clark/Robert Harding World Imagery/Getty Images; (inset) ©Photodisc/Getty Images

Acid Rain

Burning fossil fuels produces the gases sulfur dioxide and nitrogen oxides. Acid rain forms when these gases combine with water in the air and then fall to Earth as rain. The acids have harmful effects on plants, aquatic animals, and human-made objects, such as buildings.

Effect on Aquatic Organisms

Acid rain falling into rivers and lakes changes the acidity of the water. Fish and other aquatic life forms can become deformed or die.

Effect on Materials

The acids in acid rain react with metals and with substances in marble and stone. The surface becomes weakened and wears away, as shown on this statue.

Effect on Trees

Acid rain damages leaves and causes substances toxic to trees to be released from the soil in which the trees live.

Extend

Inquiry

16 Predict Develop a prediction about where the effects of acid rain would be the most pronounced. Explain the reasoning you used to develop your prediction.

17 Assemble Gather more information about acid rain and organize this information in a poster or illustrated report. Present your poster to your class.

18 Research Identify an area that has been affected by acid rain. What effects are clearly visible? How might those effects be reduced?

Visual Summary

To complete this summary, fill in the blank for each statement. Then, use the key below to check your answers. You can use this page to review the main concepts of the lesson.

Energy sources may be renewable or nonrenewable.

19 _____ resources are those that are easily replaced in nature.

Obtaining, transporting, and burning fossil fuels has many environmental consequences.

20 Spills that endanger animals sometimes occur while transporting _____

Energy and the Environment

Alternative energy sources have the potential to replace fossil fuels.

21 Sources of renewable alternative energy include wind, solar, hydroelectric, _____ , and _____

Answers: 19 renewable; 20 oil; 21 biomass, geothermal

22 **Debate** What are some arguments for and against the use of alternative energy sources rather than fossil fuels? Describe evidence that supports each argument.

Lesson Review

Vocabulary

Circle the terms that best complete the following sentences.

1 An example of a renewable energy resource is *uranium/wind/natural gas.*

2 An example of a nonrenewable energy resource is *the sun/biomass/coal.*

3 Fossil fuels include petroleum, coal, and *natural gas/biomass/geothermal.*

Key Concepts

4 Explain How might a renewable energy source become nonrenewable?

_____

_____

_____

_____

_____

5 Differentiate Compare the environmental consequences related to obtaining the three major types of fossil fuels.

_____

_____

_____

_____

_____

_____

6 Summarize Why are wind, hydroelectric, and geothermal energy resources not suitable for providing energy worldwide?

_____

_____

_____

_____

_____

_____

_____

Critical Thinking

Use this table to answer the following questions.

The Role of Renewable Energy Resources in the Nation's Energy Supply

U.S. Energy Supply		Renewable Energy	
petroleum	37%	biomass	50%
natural gas	25%	hydropower	35%
coal	21%	wind	9%
nuclear electric power	9%	geothermal	5%
renewable energy	8%	solar	1%

Source: U.S. Energy Information Administration

7 Analyze What percentage of the total energy supply was provided by fossil fuels?

_____

_____

8 Analyze Which renewable resource had the highest percentage of use?

_____

_____

9 Recommend Which alternative energy source do you think should be developed in the future? Explain your reasoning.

_____

_____

_____

_____

_____

10 Evaluate What factors will be important in deciding the future use of energy resources?

_____

_____

_____

_____

_____

_____

_____

My Notes

Unit 2 [Big Idea] Energy exists in different forms and can change from one form to another, but energy is always conserved.

Lesson 1
ESSENTIAL QUESTION
What is energy?

Describe how energy is conserved through transformation between different forms.

Lesson 3
ESSENTIAL QUESTION
What is the relationship between heat and temperature?

Analyze the relationship between heat, temperature, and thermal energy.

Lesson 2
ESSENTIAL QUESTION
How is temperature related to kinetic energy?

Relate the temperature of a substance to the kinetic energy of its particles.

Lesson 4
ESSENTIAL QUESTION
How does the use of energy resources affect the environment?

Recognize how the production and use of different types of energy resources can have environmental consequences.

[Connect] ESSENTIAL QUESTIONS
Lessons 1 and 3

1 Synthesize Give an example of an energy transformation that results in a temperature change.

_____

_____

_____

_____

_____

_____

Think Outside the Book

2 Synthesize Choose one of these activities to help synthesize what you have learned in this unit.

☐ Using what you learned in lessons 1, 2, and 3, explain the movement of particles in a cold glass as energy is transferred to it from warm hands by making a poster presentation. Include captions and labels.

☐ Using what you learned in lessons 1 and 4, describe the energy conversions related to the use of renewable and nonrenewable energy resources by creating a brochure.

Image Credits: (tl) ©Thinkstock/Getty Images; (tr) ©Carsten Peter/National Geographic/Getty Images; (bl) ©Steve Allen/Photo Researchers, Inc.; (br) ©Mark Green/Taxi/Getty Images

Unit 2 Review

Name _____

Vocabulary

Check the box to show whether each statement is true or false.

T	F	
☐	☐	**1** A <u>fossil fuel</u> is a renewable resource formed from the remains of ancient organisms.
☐	☐	**2** <u>Mechanical energy</u> is the sum of an object's kinetic and potential energy.
☐	☐	**3** A <u>renewable resource</u> forms at a rate that is much slower than the rate in which the resource is used.
☐	☐	**4** The <u>kinetic theory of matter</u> states that all of the particles that make up matter are in a fixed position.
☐	☐	**5** <u>Heat</u> is the energy transferred from an object at a higher temperature to an object at a lower temperature.

Key Concepts

Read each question below, and circle the best answer.

6 How could two objects have the same temperature but different thermal energies?

A One object could have more heat.

B One object could have more calories.

C One object could have more particles and lesser total kinetic energy.

D One object could have more particles and greater total kinetic energy.

7 What is any energy resource that can be used in place of fossil fuels called?

A alternative energy   **C** nuclear energy

B solar energy   **D** biomass energy

8 Energy exists in different forms. Which of the following forms of energy best describes the energy stored in food?

A electromagnetic energy   **C** sound energy

B mechanical energy   **D** chemical energy

9 A mass hanging from a spring moves up and down. The mass stops moving temporarily each time the spring is extended to its fullest at Position 2 and each time it returns to its tight coil at Position 4.

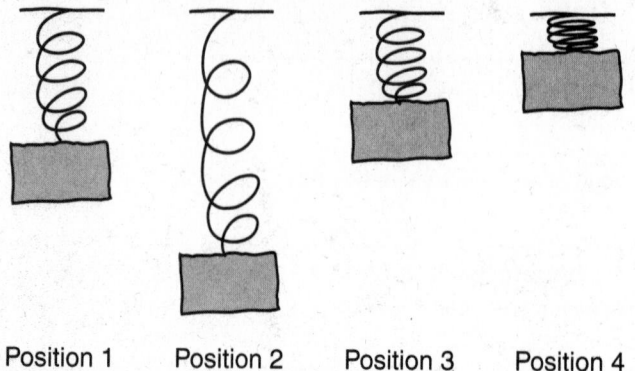

Position 1   Position 2   Position 3   Position 4

Which answer choice best describes the type of energy the spring has at Position 1?

A potential energy

B kinetic energy

C both potential energy and kinetic energy

D neither potential energy or kinetic energy

10 Which of the following is the transfer of energy as heat by the movement of a liquid or gas?

A conduction

B convection

C emission

D radiation

11 Which of the following terms means the amount of energy needed to raise the temperature of 1 gram of water by 1 degree Celsius?

A heat

B temperature

C thermal energy

D calorie

12 A student collects and records the following data throughout the day.

Time	Temperature (°C)
9 a.m.	12
11 a.m.	14
3 p.m.	16
5 p.m.	13

What instrument did the student use to collect these data?

A barometer

B scale

C thermometer

D balance

13 What is the difference between a conductor and an insulator?

A Wood is a good conductor but not a good insulator.

B Metal is a good insulator but not a good conductor.

C A conductor transmits energy very well while an insulator does not.

D An insulator transmits energy very well while a conductor does not.

Critical Thinking

Answer the following questions in the space provided.

14 Describe the law of conservation of energy.

_____

_____

_____

Give two examples of energy being transformed from one type to another.

_____

_____

_____

_____

15 Three thermometers are lined up side by side.

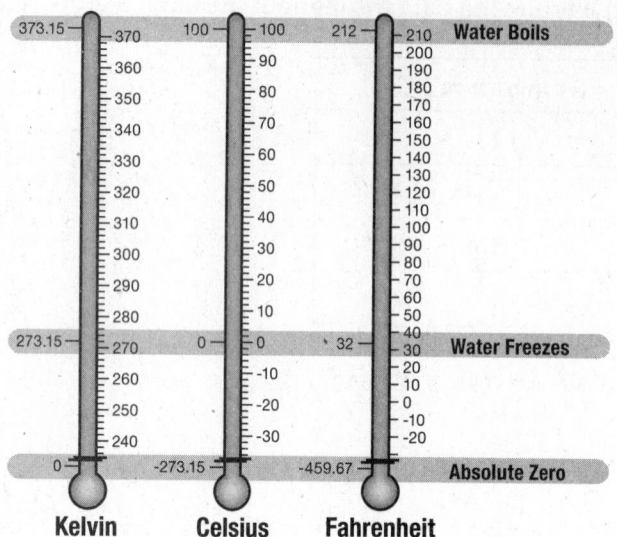

If the temperature outside is 60°F, what is the approximate temperature on the Celsius scale? _____ What is the temperature on the Kelvin scale? _____

If the air temperature drops to 30°F during the night, how has the kinetic energy of the air particles changed?

_____

Connect ESSENTIAL QUESTIONS

Lessons 2 and 3

Answer the following question in the space provided.

16 An ice cube sits in an open container of water placed outside on a sunny day.

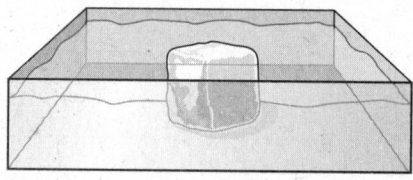

The warmer water contacting the ice cube transfers energy to the ice cube through what process? _____

Use the set-up shown in the diagram to give two examples of how adding energy as heat to a system may result in a change of state.

_____

Compare the speeds of particles in the ice, water, and air.

_____

_____

Atoms and the Periodic Table

Big Idea

The atomic structure of an element determines the properties of the element and determines how the element interacts with other elements.

S8P1., S8P1.e

At room temperature, gold is a solid. But at very high temperatures, solid gold becomes a liquid that flows.

What do you think?

Gold is a shiny metal. Water is a clear liquid. Although they have different properties, both are made up of atoms. How can different substances have different properties? What do all substances have in common? As you explore the unit, gather evidence to help you state and support claims to answer these questions.

Unit 3
Atoms and the Periodic Table

Matter Up Close

Matter is anything that has mass and takes up space. All things, large and small, on Earth are made up of matter! Atoms are the smallest parts of the matter you see. You can't see atoms with your eyes alone.

Fly, about 7×10^{-3} m
The eye of a fly has been magnified so that you can see more detail. Magnification allows us to see things we cannot see with the human eye alone.

Grain of salt, about 5×10^{-4} m

This seasoning and preservative can be harvested from seawater.

Table salt

Rhinovirus, about 3×10^{-8} m

Watch out for this virus—it causes the common cold.

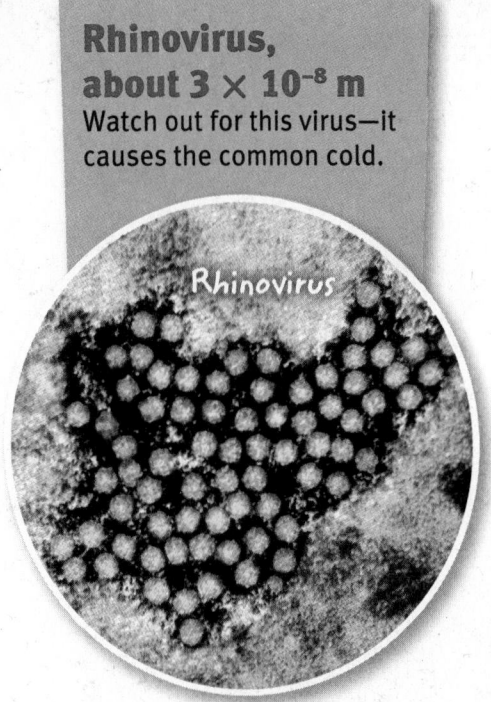

Rhinovirus

Helium atom, about 3×10^{-11} m

Atoms are so small that they cannot be viewed with traditional microscopes. Often, they are represented by models such as this one.

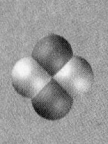

Object	Width
Grain of salt	5×10^{-4} m (or 0.0005 m)
Rhinovirus	3×10^{-8} m (or 0.00000003 m)
Helium atom	3×10^{-11} m (or 0.00000000003 m)

 **Size Is Relative**

By looking at ratios of sizes, you can compare the relative sizes of objects. How many times greater is the size of a grain of salt than a rhinovirus particle? You can write a ratio to find the answer:

$$\frac{\text{grain of salt}}{\text{rhinovirus}} = \frac{0.0005 \text{ m}}{0.00000003 \text{ m}} \approx 17,000$$

A grain of salt is about 17,000 times the size of a rhinovirus.

A Determine how many times greater a rhinovirus is than a helium atom.

B Measure the width of one of your textbooks to the nearest millimeter. How many helium atoms could you line up across the book?

See **ScienceSaurus**® for more information about atoms.

Lesson 1

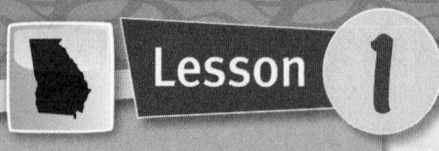

The Atom

ESSENTIAL QUESTION

How do we know what parts make up the atom?

By the end of this lesson, you should be able to describe how the development of the atomic theory has led to the modern understanding of the atom and its parts.

S8P1.e Structure and properties of atoms and simple molecules

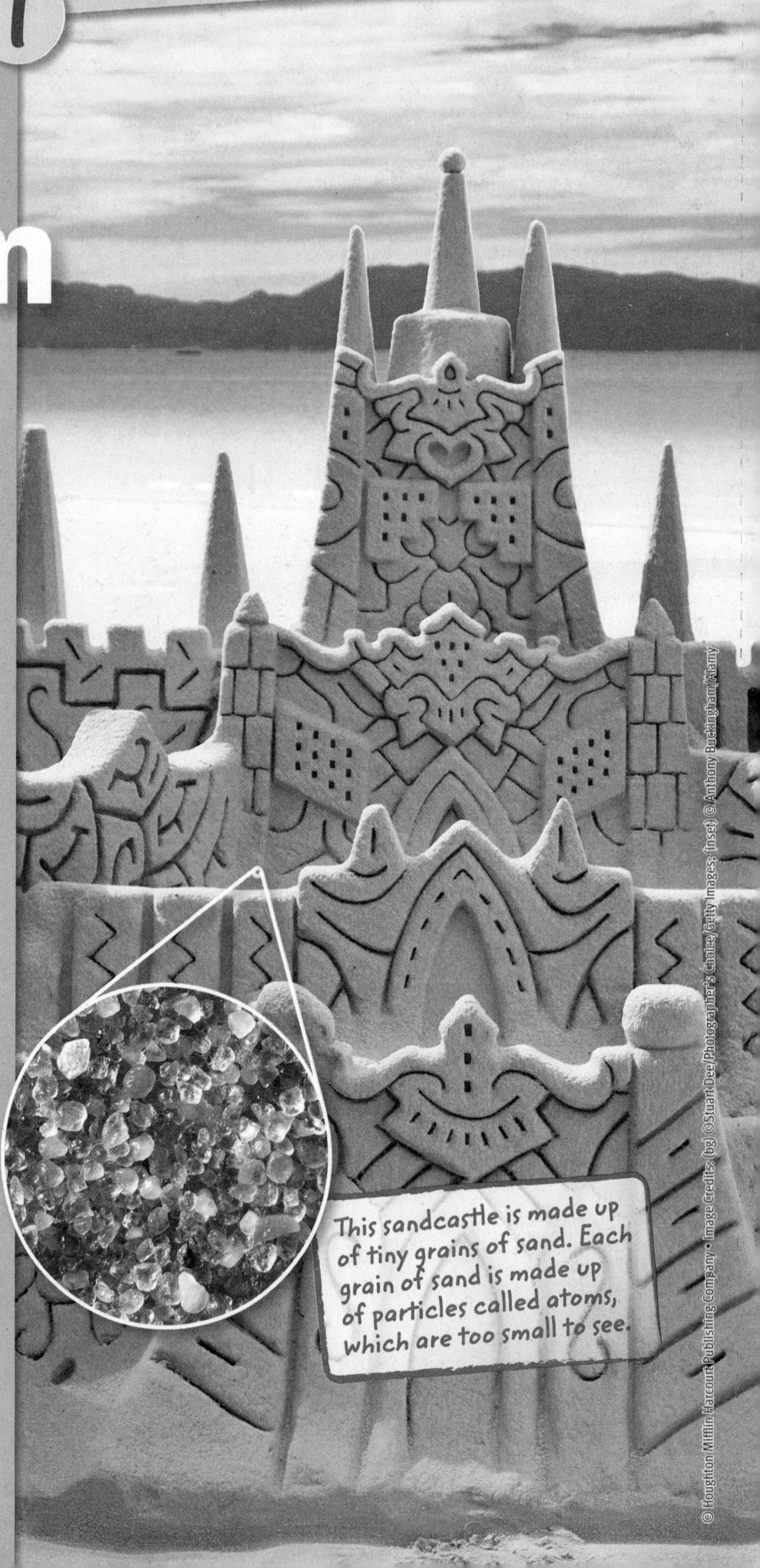
This sandcastle is made up of tiny grains of sand. Each grain of sand is made up of particles called atoms, which are too small to see.

Engage Your Brain

1 Identify Read over the following vocabulary terms. In the spaces provided, place a + if you know the term well, a ~ if you have heard the term but are not sure what it means, and a ? if you are unfamiliar with the term. Then, write a sentence that includes the word you are most familiar with.

_____ atom

_____ electron

_____ neutron

_____ proton

_____ nucleus

Sentence using known word:

_____

_____

2 Compare Use the figure below to answer the questions. Check T or F to show whether you think each statement is true or false.

T	F	
☐	☐	Electrons move in orbits in the same way planets orbit the sun.
☐	☐	If this were a model of the atom, the nucleus would be in the same place as the sun.

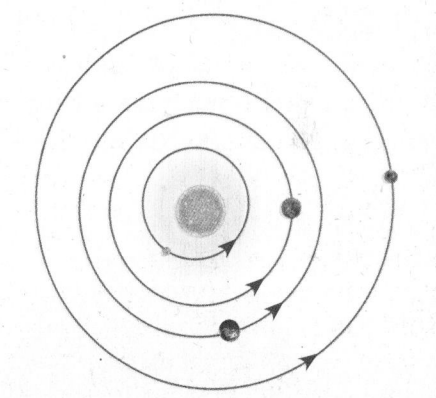

Active Reading

3 Apply Use context clues to write your own definition for the words *theory* and *revise*.

Example sentence
The scientist developed a <u>theory</u> to explain the structure of the atom.

theory:

_____

_____

Example sentence
As scientists learned new information about atoms, they had to <u>revise</u> the model of the atom.

revise:

_____

_____

Vocabulary Terms

- atom
- electron
- nucleus
- proton

- neutron
- electron cloud
- atomic number
- mass number

4 Apply As you learn the definition of each vocabulary term in this lesson, create your own definition or sketch to help you remember the meaning of the term.

As a Matter of Fact

What makes up matter?

Imagine that you are cutting fabric to make a quilt. You cut a piece of fabric in half. Then, you cut each half in half again. Could you keep cutting the pieces in half forever? Around 400 BCE, a Greek philosopher named Democritus (dih·MAHK·rih·tuhs) thought that you would eventually end up with a particle that could not be cut. He called this particle *atomos*, a Greek word meaning "not able to be divided." Aristotle (AIR·ih·staht'l), another Greek philosopher, disagreed. He did not believe that such a particle could make up all substances found in nature.

Neither Democritus nor Aristotle did experiments to test their ideas. It would be centuries before scientists tested these hypotheses. Within the past 200 years, scientists have come to agree that matter is made up of small particles. Democritus's term *atom* is used to describe these particles.

Active Reading

5 Describe Who was Democritus?

_____

_____

_____

_____

There is a limit to how small you can cut a piece of fabric. Even the smallest piece of fabric you can cut is made up of a huge number of particles of many different elements.

Atoms

An **atom** is the smallest particle into which an element can be divided and still be the same element. People used to think that atoms could not be divided into anything simpler. Scientists now know that atoms are made of even smaller particles. But the atom is still considered to be the basic unit of matter because it is the smallest unit that has the chemical properties of an element.

You cannot see individual atoms. But they make up everything you do see. The food you eat and the water you drink are made of atoms. Plants, such as moss, are made of atoms. Even things you cannot see are made of atoms. The air you breathe is made of atoms. There are many types of atoms that combine in different ways to make all substances.

You can use a light microscope to see the cells that make up a tiny moss leaf. But you cannot see the atoms that make up the substances in the cells. Atoms are so small that you cannot see them with an ordinary microscope. Only powerful instruments can make images of atoms. How small are atoms? Think about a penny. A penny contains about 2×10^{22}, or 20,000,000,000,000,000,000,000 atoms of copper and zinc. That's almost 3,000 billion times more atoms than there are people living on Earth!

Moss

Atoms are much smaller than the cells in living things.

© Houghton Mifflin Harcourt Publishing Company • Image Credits: (t) ©photoalto/Photolibrary New York; (c) ©Nuridsany et Perenno/Photo Researchers, Inc.; (b) ©MCT /Landov

Visualize It! Inquiry

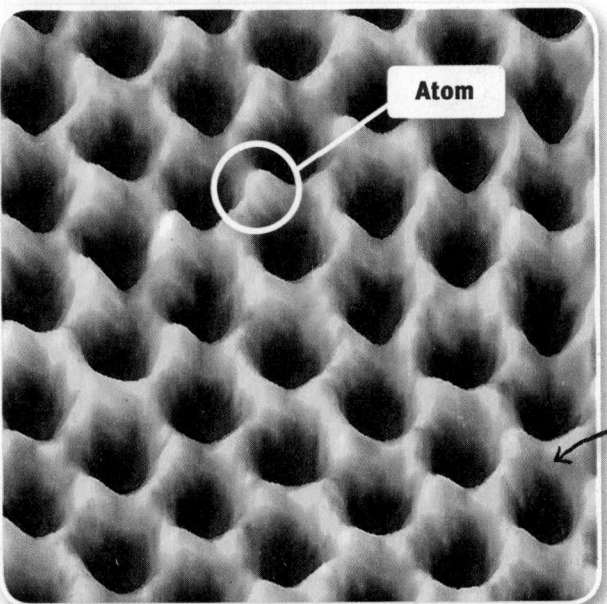

Atom

This image shows how carbon atoms are connected in a substance. It was taken with a special type of electron microscope.

6 Analyze What can you infer about atoms from this image? What can't you infer from the image?

_____

_____

_____

_____

_____

_____

Something Old, Something New

Who developed the atomic theory?

In 1808, a British chemist named John Dalton published an atomic theory. This was the start of the modern theory of the atom. Dalton's theory could explain most observations of matter at that time. Over time, scientists learned more about atoms. The atomic theory was revised as scientists discovered new information.

John Dalton

Active Reading **7 Identify** As you read, underline the four main ideas of Dalton's theory of the atom.

Unlike the ideas of Democritus and Aristotle, John Dalton's theory was based on evidence from experiments. Dalton's theory stated that all matter is made up of atoms. He also thought that atoms cannot be created, divided, or destroyed.

Dalton's theory also stated that all atoms of a certain element are identical. But they are different from atoms of all other elements. For example, every atom of carbon is the same as every other atom of carbon. However, every atom of carbon is different from any atom of oxygen. Dalton also thought that atoms join with other atoms to make new substances. For example, an oxygen atom combines with two hydrogen atoms to form water. Every substance is made up of atoms combined in certain ways.

J. J. Thomson

J. J. Thomson's experiments provided evidence that atoms are made up of even smaller particles. He found particles within the atom that have a negative charge. These negatively charged particles later became known as **electrons**. Thomson thought that an atom was a positive sphere with the electrons mixed through it, as shown below.

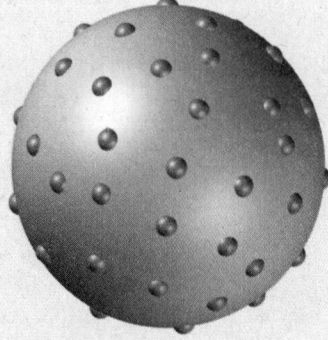

1897

1808

8 Model Describe how you would show J. J. Thomson's model of the atom using small beads and clay.

_____
_____
_____
_____
_____

Ernest Rutherford

In 1909, Ernest Rutherford conducted an experiment to study the parts of the atom. His experiment suggested that atoms have a **nucleus**—a small, dense center that has a positive charge and is surrounded by moving electrons. Rutherford later found that the nucleus is made up of smaller particles. He called the positively charged particles in the nucleus **protons**.

Niels Bohr

Niels Bohr made observations that led to a new theory of how the electrons in the atom behaved. Bohr agreed that an atom has a positive nucleus surrounded by electrons. In his model, electrons move around the nucleus in circular paths. Each path is a certain distance from the nucleus. Bohr's model helped scientists predict the chemical properties of elements. However, scientists have since made observations that could not be explained by Bohr's model. The model of the atom has been revised to explain these observations.

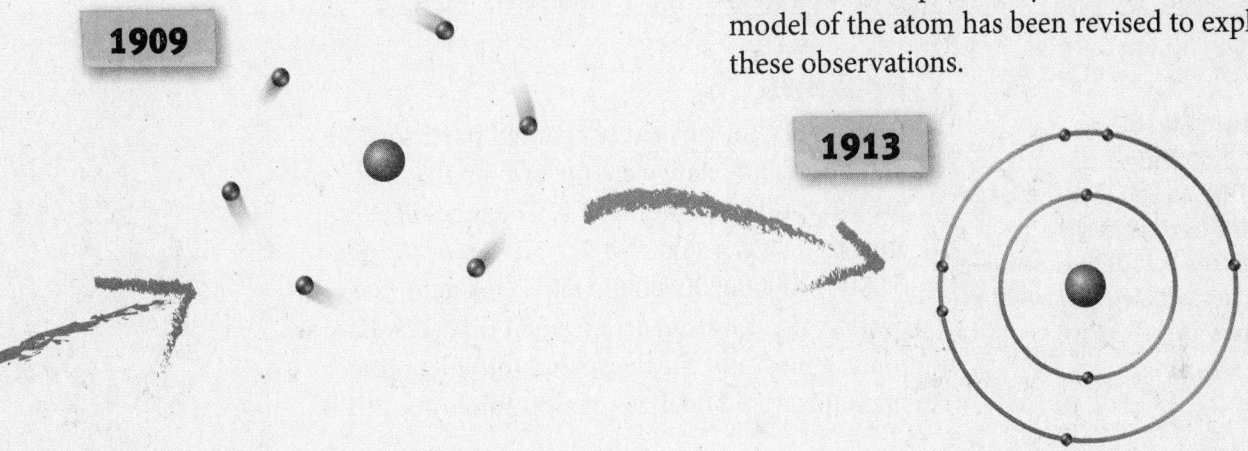

1909

1913

What is the current atomic theory?

Modern atomic theory is based on the work of many scientists. It keeps Dalton's ideas that atoms are the basic unit of matter and that the atoms of each element are unique. The experiments of Thomson and Rutherford showed that atoms are made up of electrons and protons. James Chadwick was Rutherford's student. In 1932, Chadwick discovered that the nucleus contains uncharged particles called **neutrons**. In the current atomic theory, electrons do not move in circular paths around the nucleus as Bohr thought. Instead, the current theory suggests that electrons move within an area around the nucleus called the **electron cloud**.

9 Analyze Today's model of the atom looks different from the models that came before it. Why has the model of the atom changed?

_____

_____

_____

_____

Up and Atom!

What are the parts of an atom?

This model of an atom shows where protons, neutrons, and electrons are found within the atom. Protons and neutrons are found in the center of the electron cloud. The particles in this model are not shown in their correct proportions. If they were, the protons and neutrons would be too small to see.

Active Reading

10 Identify As you read this page and the next, underline the sentences that define the three types of particles that make up an atom.

Protons

Protons are the positively charged particles of atoms. The relative charge of a single proton is often written as 1+. The mass of a proton is very small—1.7×10^{-24} g, or 0.0000000000000000000000017 g. The masses of particles in the atom are so small that scientists made a new unit for them: the unified atomic mass unit (u). The mass of a proton is about 1 u.

Neutrons

Neutrons are particles that have no electric charge. They are a little more massive than protons are. But the mass of a neutron is still very close to 1 u. Atoms usually have at least as many neutrons as they have protons.

Together, protons and neutrons form the nucleus of the atom. The nucleus is located at the center of an atom. This model of a beryllium atom shows that the nucleus of this atom is made up of four protons and five neutrons. Because each proton has a 1+ charge, the overall charge of this nucleus is 4+. (Remember: neutrons have no electric charge.) The volume of the nucleus is very small compared to the rest of the atom. But protons and neutrons are the most massive particles in an atom. So the nucleus is very dense. If it were possible to have a nucleus the volume of a grape, that nucleus would have a mass greater than 9 million metric tons!

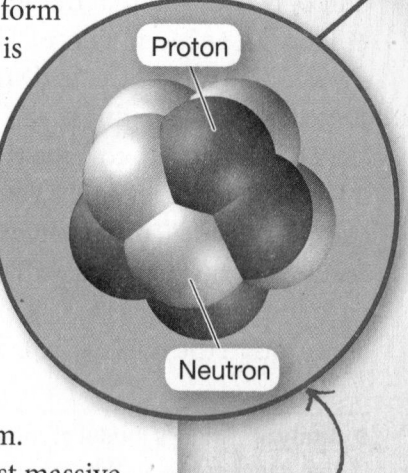

Proton

Neutron

Nucleus

The Electron Cloud

The negatively charged particles of the atom are called electrons. Electrons move around the nucleus very quickly. Scientists have found that it is not possible to determine both their exact positions and speed at the same time. This is why we picture the electrons as being in an electron cloud around the nucleus.

Compared with protons and neutrons, electrons have very little mass. It takes more than 1,800 electrons to equal the mass of 1 proton. The mass of an electron is so small that it is usually thought of as almost 0 u.

The charge of a single electron is represented as 1−. The charges of protons and electrons are opposite but equal. The number of protons in an atom equals the number of electrons. So the atom has a net, or overall, charge of 0. For example, this beryllium atom contains four electrons. The combined charge of the electrons is 4−. But remember that the charge of the nucleus is 4+.

$$(4+) + (4-) = 0$$

The net charge of the atom is 0.

An atom can lose or gain electrons. When this happens, we refer to the atom as an *ion*. Ions have a net charge that is not 0.

11 Summarize Complete the following table with information about the parts of the atom.

Part of the atom	Location in the atom	Electric charge	Relative mass
Proton			Slightly less massive than a neutron
	Nucleus		
		1−	

Take a Number!

How can we describe atoms?

Think of all the substances you see and touch every day. Are all of these substances the same? No. The substances that make up this book are quite different from the substances in the air you are breathing. If all atoms are composed of the same particles, how can there be so many different types of substances? Different combinations of protons, neutrons, and electrons produce atoms with different properties. The number of each kind of particle within an atom determines its unique properties. In turn, these different atoms combine to form the different substances all around us.

By Atomic Number

The number of protons distinguishes the atoms of one element from the atoms of another. For example, every hydrogen atom contains one proton. And every carbon atom has exactly six protons in its nucleus.

The number of protons in the nucleus of an atom is the **atomic number** of that atom. Hydrogen has an atomic number of 1 because each of its atoms contains just one proton. Carbon has an atomic number of 6 because each of its atoms contains six protons.

Active Reading **12 Compare** How are two atoms of the same element alike? Explain your reasoning.

_____

_____

_____

_____

_____

_____

Think Outside the Book Inquiry

13 Apply Research how scientists make new types of atoms using particle accelerators. Choose one element that has been made by scientists. Create a brochure that describes its properties and how it was made.

© Houghton Mifflin Harcourt Publishing Company • Image Credits: ©Yana Paskova/Getty Images

By Mass Number

The atoms of a certain element always have the same number of protons. But they may not always have the same number of neutrons. For example, all chlorine atoms have 17 protons. But some chlorine atoms have 18 neutrons. Other chlorine atoms have 20 neutrons. These two types of chlorine atoms are called isotopes. *Isotopes* are atoms of the same element that have different numbers of neutrons. Some elements have many isotopes, and other elements have just a few.

The total number of protons and neutrons in an atom's nucleus is its **mass number**. Different isotopes of chlorine have different mass numbers. What is the mass number of a chlorine atom that contains 18 neutrons?

$$17 + 18 = 35$$

The mass number of this atom is 35.

---

14 Calculate Use this model of a helium atom to find its atomic number and mass number.

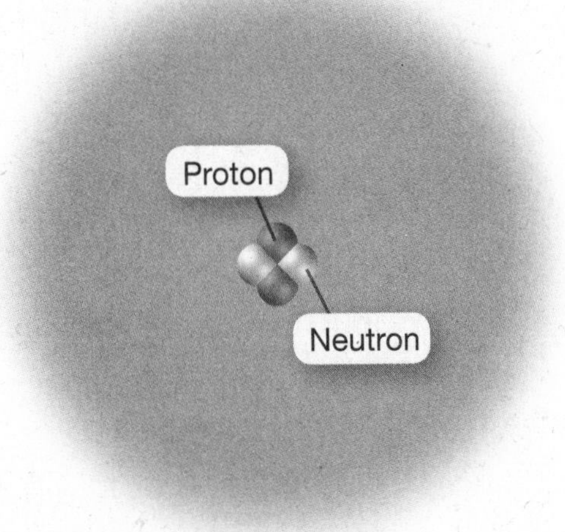

Proton

Neutron

Atomic number: ☐

Mass number: ☐

The helium in these balloons is less massive than an equal volume of the nitrogen in the air, so the balloons float.

Visual Summary

To complete this summary, check the box that indicates true or false. Then, use the key below to check your answers. You can use this page to review the main concepts of the lesson.

The Atom

An atom is the smallest particle of an element. All substances are made up of atoms.

T F
15 ☐ ☐ You can use a light microscope to see the atoms in fabric.

Atomic theory has changed over time as scientists learned more about the particles that make up matter.

T F
16 ☐ ☐ According to current atomic theory, electrons are in fixed locations.

Atoms contain a positively charged nucleus surrounded by a negatively charged electron cloud.

T F
17 ☐ ☐ The nucleus contains neutrons and electrons.

Atomic number and mass number are used to describe atoms.

T F
18 ☐ ☐ Every atom of the same element has the same atomic number.

Answers: 15 False; 16 False; 17 False; 18 True

19 Claims • Evidence • Reasoning Do you think the current model for the atom will continue to change over time? Why or why not? Use evidence to support your claim, and explain your reasoning.

Lesson Review

Vocabulary

Draw a line to connect the following terms to their definitions.

1 atom

2 proton

3 neutron

A a positively charged atomic particle

B an uncharged atomic particle

C the smallest particle of an element that has the chemical properties of that element

Key Concepts

4 Compare Compare the charges and masses of protons, neutrons, and electrons.

_____

_____

_____

_____

_____

5 Explain How can atoms make up all of the substances around you? Explain your reasoning.

_____

_____

_____

6 Compare How does the current model of the atom differ from J. J. Thomson's model?

_____

_____

_____

_____

7 Calculate What is the atomic number of a sodium atom that has 11 protons and 12 neutrons?

Critical Thinking

Use this diagram to answer the following questions.

8 Analyze The red sphere represents a proton. What is the atomic number of this atom? Explain how you found the atomic number.

_____

_____

_____

9 Apply What is the mass number of an isotope of this atom that has 2 neutrons?

_____

10 Analyze Where are the nucleus and the electrons located in this atom?

_____

_____

_____

_____

11 Infer If atoms are made of smaller parts such as electrons, why are atoms considered the basic unit of matter?

_____

_____

_____

_____

My Notes

Lesson 2

The Periodic Table

ESSENTIAL QUESTION

How are elements arranged on the periodic table?

By the end of this lesson, you should be able to describe the relationship between the arrangement of elements on the periodic table and the properties of those elements.

In this market, similar foods are arranged in groups. Can you identify some of the properties each group shares?

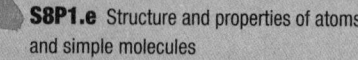
S8P1.e Structure and properties of atoms and simple molecules

Engage Your Brain

1 Describe Write a word or phrase beginning with each letter of the word GOLD that describes the properties of these gold coins.

G _____

O _____

L _____

D _____

2 Describe As you will learn in this lesson, elements are arranged by their properties on the periodic table. What other objects are often arranged by their properties?

_____

_____

_____

_____

_____

Active Reading

3 Apply Many scientific words, such as *table*, also have everyday meanings. Use context clues to write your own definition for each meaning of the word *table*.

Example sentence
The books are on the <u>table</u>.

table:

_____

_____

Example sentence
A data <u>table</u> is a useful way to organize information.

table:

_____

_____

Vocabulary Terms

- periodic table
- chemical symbol
- average atomic mass
- metal
- nonmetal
- metalloid
- group
- period

4 Apply As you learn the definition of each vocabulary term in this lesson, create your own definition or sketch to help you remember the meaning of the term.

Get Organized!

What are elements?

People have long sought to find the basic substances of matter. It was once believed that fire, wind, earth, and water, in various combinations, made up all objects. By the 1860s, however, scientists considered there to be at least 60 different basic substances, or elements. They saw that many of these elements shared certain physical and chemical properties and began classifying them. Knowing what you know about the properties of matter, try classifying the elements below.

Bismuth

Sulfur

Chlorine

Visualize It!

5 Identify Observe the appearance of these six elements. Create two or three categories that group the elements by similar properties. Below each element, write the name of the category in which the element belongs.

Mercury

Copper

Bromine

How are the elements organized?

Around this time, a Russian chemist named Dmitri Mendeleev (dih•MEE•tree men•duh•LAY•uhf) began thinking about how he could organize the elements based on their properties. To help him decide how to arrange the elements, Mendeleev made a set of element cards. Each card listed the mass of an atom of each element as well as some of the element's properties. Mendeleev arranged the cards in various ways, looking for a pattern to emerge. When he arranged the element cards in order of increasing atomic mass, the properties of those elements occurred in a *periodic,* or regularly repeating, pattern. For this reason, Mendeleev's arrangement of the elements became known as the **periodic table**. Mendeleev used the periodic pattern in his table to predict elements that had not yet been discovered.

In the early 1900s, British scientist Henry Moseley showed how Mendeleev's periodic table could be rearranged. After determining the numbers of protons in the atoms of the elements, he arranged the elements on the table in order of increasing number of protons, or *atomic number.* Moseley's new arrangement of the elements corrected some of the flaws in Mendeleev's table.

The periodic table is a useful tool to scientists because it makes clear many patterns among the elements' properties. The periodic table is like a map or a calendar of the elements.

Active Reading

6 Explain How did Henry Moseley revise Mendeleev's periodic table?

_____

_____

_____

_____

_____

7 Apply What are you doing this week? Fill in the calendar with activities or plans you have for this week and next. Do any events occur periodically? Explain.

_____

_____

_____

What does the periodic table have in common with a calendar? They both show a periodic pattern. On a calendar, the days of the week repeat in the same order every 7 days.

Sunday	Monday	Tuesday	Wednesday	Thursday	Friday	Saturday

The Periodic Table of Elements

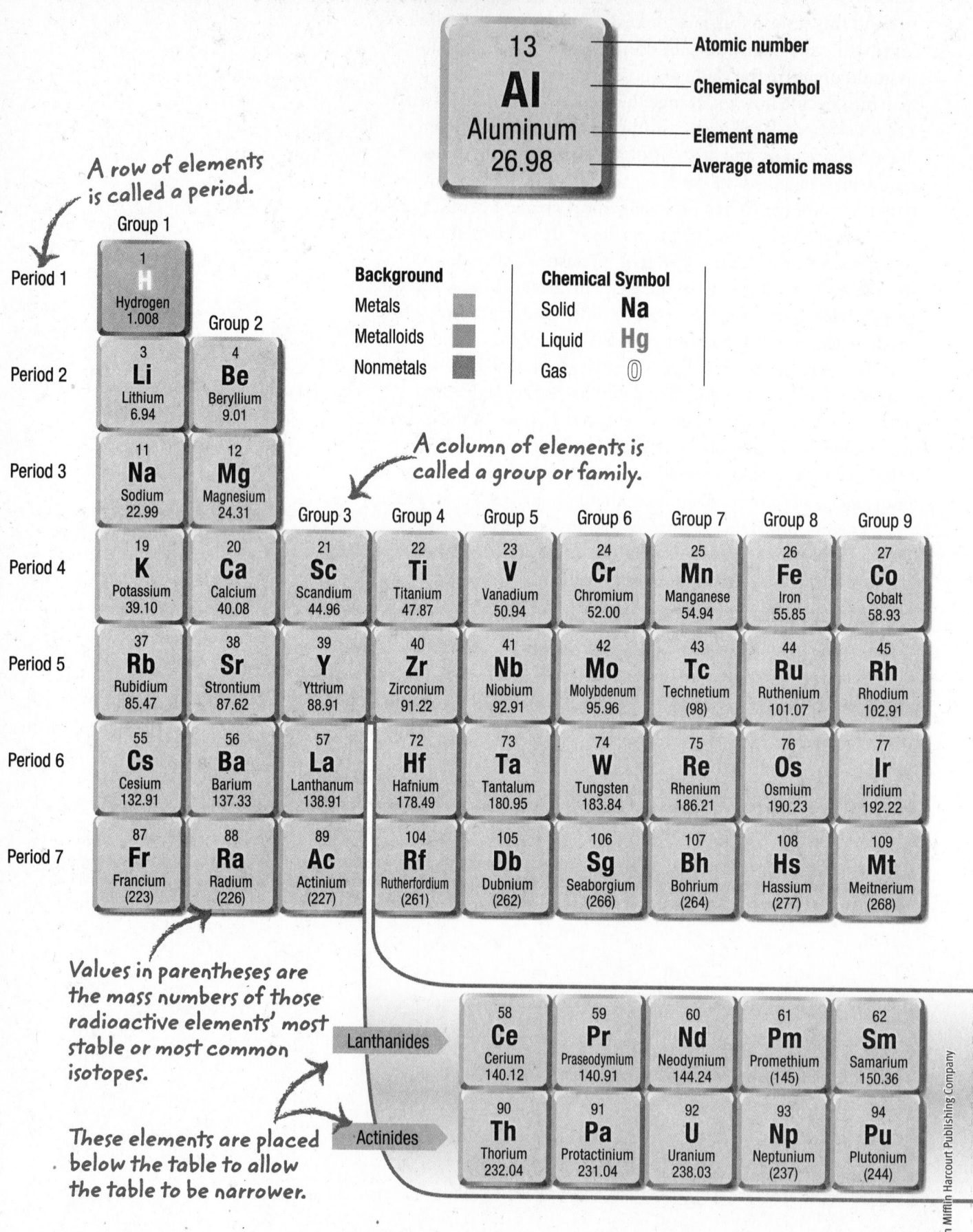

		Atomic number
13	Al	Chemical symbol
	Aluminum	Element name
	26.98	Average atomic mass

A row of elements is called a period.

Background
Metals
Metalloids
Nonmetals

Chemical Symbol
Solid   Na
Liquid   Hg
Gas   ⓞ

A column of elements is called a group or family.

Group 1

Period 1	1 H Hydrogen 1.008

Group 2

| Period 2 | 3 Li Lithium 6.94 | 4 Be Beryllium 9.01 |

| Period 3 | 11 Na Sodium 22.99 | 12 Mg Magnesium 24.31 |

			Group 3	Group 4	Group 5	Group 6	Group 7	Group 8	Group 9
Period 4	19 K Potassium 39.10	20 Ca Calcium 40.08	21 Sc Scandium 44.96	22 Ti Titanium 47.87	23 V Vanadium 50.94	24 Cr Chromium 52.00	25 Mn Manganese 54.94	26 Fe Iron 55.85	27 Co Cobalt 58.93
Period 5	37 Rb Rubidium 85.47	38 Sr Strontium 87.62	39 Y Yttrium 88.91	40 Zr Zirconium 91.22	41 Nb Niobium 92.91	42 Mo Molybdenum 95.96	43 Tc Technetium (98)	44 Ru Ruthenium 101.07	45 Rh Rhodium 102.91
Period 6	55 Cs Cesium 132.91	56 Ba Barium 137.33	57 La Lanthanum 138.91	72 Hf Hafnium 178.49	73 Ta Tantalum 180.95	74 W Tungsten 183.84	75 Re Rhenium 186.21	76 Os Osmium 190.23	77 Ir Iridium 192.22
Period 7	87 Fr Francium (223)	88 Ra Radium (226)	89 Ac Actinium (227)	104 Rf Rutherfordium (261)	105 Db Dubnium (262)	106 Sg Seaborgium (266)	107 Bh Bohrium (264)	108 Hs Hassium (277)	109 Mt Meitnerium (268)

Values in parentheses are the mass numbers of those radioactive elements' most stable or most common isotopes.

These elements are placed below the table to allow the table to be narrower.

Lanthanides

58 Ce Cerium 140.12	59 Pr Praseodymium 140.91	60 Nd Neodymium 144.24	61 Pm Promethium (145)	62 Sm Samarium 150.36

Actinides

90 Th Thorium 232.04	91 Pa Protactinium 231.04	92 U Uranium 238.03	93 Np Neptunium (237)	94 Pu Plutonium (244)

Visualize It!

8 Analyze According to the periodic table, how many elements are a liquid at room temperature?

_____

9 Analyze According to the periodic table, how many elements are metalloids?

_____

The zigzag line separates metals from nonmetals.

			Group 13	Group 14	Group 15	Group 16	Group 17	Group 18
								2 **He** Helium 4.003
			5 **B** Boron 10.81	6 **C** Carbon 12.01	7 **N** Nitrogen 14.01	8 **O** Oxygen 16.00	9 **F** Fluorine 19.00	10 **Ne** Neon 20.18
Group 10	Group 11	Group 12	13 **Al** Aluminum 26.98	14 **Si** Silicon 28.09	15 **P** Phosphorus 30.97	16 **S** Sulfur 32.06	17 **Cl** Chlorine 35.45	18 **Ar** Argon 39.95
28 **Ni** Nickel 58.69	29 **Cu** Copper 63.55	30 **Zn** Zinc 65.38	31 **Ga** Gallium 69.72	32 **Ge** Germanium 72.63	33 **As** Arsenic 74.92	34 **Se** Selenium 78.96	35 **Br** Bromine 79.90	36 **Kr** Krypton 83.80
46 **Pd** Palladium 106.42	47 **Ag** Silver 107.87	48 **Cd** Cadmium 112.41	49 **In** Indium 114.82	50 **Sn** Tin 118.71	51 **Sb** Antimony 121.76	52 **Te** Tellurium 127.60	53 **I** Iodine 126.90	54 **Xe** Xenon 131.29
78 **Pt** Platinum 195.08	79 **Au** Gold 196.97	80 **Hg** Mercury 200.59	81 **Tl** Thallium 204.38	82 **Pb** Lead 207.2	83 **Bi** Bismuth 208.98	84 **Po** Polonium (209)	85 **At** Astatine (210)	86 **Rn** Radon (222)
110 **Ds** Darmstadtium (271)	111 **Rg** Roentgenium (272)	112 **Cn** Copernicium (285)	113 **Nh** Nihonium (286)	114 **Fl** Flerovium (289)	115 **Mc** Moscovium (289)	116 **Lv** Livermorium (293)	117 **Ts** Tennessine (294)	118 **Og** Oganesson (294)

63 **Eu** Europium 151.96	64 **Gd** Gadolinium 157.25	65 **Tb** Terbium 158.93	66 **Dy** Dysprosium 162.50	67 **Ho** Holmium 164.93	68 **Er** Erbium 167.26	69 **Tm** Thulium 168.93	70 **Yb** Ytterbium 173.05	71 **Lu** Lutetium 174.97
95 **Am** Americium (243)	96 **Cm** Curium (247)	97 **Bk** Berkelium (247)	98 **Cf** Californium (251)	99 **Es** Einsteinium (252)	100 **Fm** Fermium (257)	101 **Md** Mendelevium (258)	102 **No** Nobelium (259)	103 **Lr** Lawrencium (262)

Ma**K**ing Arrangements

What information is contained in each square on the periodic table?

The periodic table is not simply a list of element names. The table contains useful information about each of the elements. The periodic table is usually shown as a grid of squares. Each square contains an element's chemical name, atomic number, chemical symbol, and average atomic mass.

Atomic Number

The number at the top of the square is the atomic number. The atomic number is the number of protons in the nucleus of an atom of that element. All atoms of an element have the same atomic number. For example, every aluminum atom has 13 protons in its nucleus. So the atomic number of aluminum is 13.

Chemical Symbol

The **chemical symbol** is an abbreviation for the element's name. The first letter is always capitalized. Any other letter is always lowercase. For most elements, the chemical symbol is a one- or two-letter symbol. However, some elements have temporary three-letter symbols. These elements will receive a permanent one- or two-letter symbol once it has been reviewed by an international committee of scientists.

13
Al
Aluminum
26.98

Chemical Name

The names of the elements come from many sources. Some elements, such as mendelevium, are named after scientists. Others, such as californium, are named after places.

Average Atomic Mass

All atoms of a given element contain the same number of protons. But the number of neutrons in those atoms can vary. So different atoms of an element can have different masses. The **average atomic mass** of an atom is the weighted average of the masses of all the naturally occurring isotopes of that element. A weighted average accounts for the percentages of each isotope. The unit for atomic mass is u.

Active Reading

10 Apply What is the average atomic mass of aluminum?

_____

How are the elements arranged on the periodic table?

Have you ever noticed how items in a grocery store are arranged? Each aisle contains a different kind of product. Within an aisle, similar products are grouped together on shelves. Because the items are arranged in categories, it is easy to find your favorite brand of cereal. Similarly, the elements are arranged in a certain order on the periodic table. If you understand how the periodic table is organized, you can easily find and compare elements.

Metals, Nonmetals, and Metalloids Are Found in Three Distinct Regions

Elements on the periodic table can be classified into three major categories: metals, nonmetals, and metalloids. The zigzag line on the periodic table can help you identify where these three classes of elements are located. Except for hydrogen, the elements to the left of the zigzag line are metals. **Metals** are elements that are shiny and conduct heat and electricity well. Most metals are solid at room temperature. Many metals are *malleable*, or able to be formed into different shapes. Some metals are *ductile*, meaning that they can be made into wires. The elements to the right of the zigzag line are nonmetals. **Nonmetals** are poor conductors of heat and electricity. Nonmetals are often dull and brittle. Metalloids border the zigzag line on the periodic table. **Metalloids** are elements that have some properties of metals and some properties of nonmetals. Some metalloids are used to make semiconductor chips in computers.

11 Identify Fill in the blanks below with the word *metal, nonmetal,* or *metalloid.*

Iron is a good conductor of thermal energy.

Silicon has some properties of metals and some properties of nonmetals. Silicon is used in solar panels.

Graphite is brittle, meaning that it breaks easily. Graphite is made of carbon.

Elements in Each Column Have Similar Properties

The periodic table groups elements with similar properties together. Each vertical column of elements (from top to bottom) on the periodic table is called a **group**. Elements in the same group often have similar physical and chemical properties. For this reason, a group is sometimes called a *family*.

The properties of elements in a group are similar because the atoms of these elements have the same number of *valence electrons*. Valence electrons are found in the outermost portion of the electron cloud of an atom. Because they are far from the the attractive force of the nucleus, valence electrons are able to participate in chemical bonding. The number of valence electrons helps determine what kind of chemical reactions the atom can undergo. For example, all of the atoms of elements in Group 1 have a single valence electron. These elements are very reactive. The atoms of elements in Group 18 have a full set of valence electrons. The elements in Group 18 are all unreactive gases.

Active Reading 12 **Claims • Evidence • Reasoning** Make a claim about why elements within a group have similar chemical properties. Explain your reasoning.

_____

_____

_____

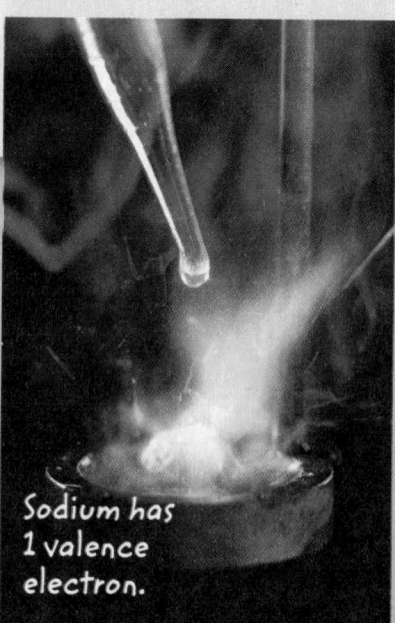

Just as this family is made up of members that have similar characteristics, families in the periodic table are made up of elements that have similar properties.

Groups of Elements Have Similar Properties

Observe the similarities of elements found in Group 1 and in Group 18.

Alkali metals, found in Group 1, share the property of reactivity with water.

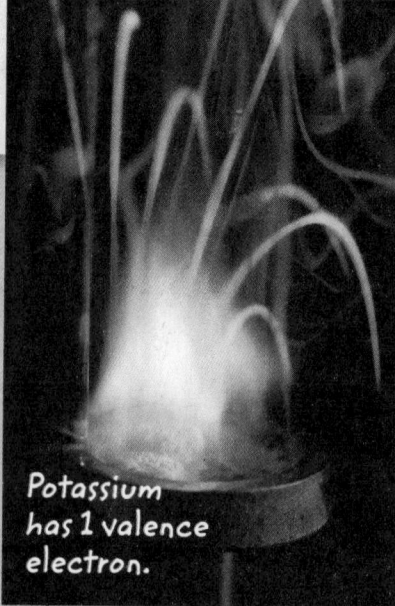

Sodium has 1 valence electron.

Potassium has 1 valence electron.

Elements in Each Row Follow Periodic Trends

Each horizontal row of elements (from left to right) on the periodic table is called a **period**. The physical and chemical properties of elements change in predictable ways from one end of the period to the other. For example, within any given period on the periodic table, atomic size decreases as you move from left to right. The densities of elements also follow a pattern. Within a period, elements at the left and right sides of the table are the least dense, and the elements in the middle are the most dense. The element osmium has the highest known density, and it is located at the center of the table. Chemists cannot predict the exact size or density of an atom of elements based on that of another. However, these trends are a valuable tool in predicting the properties of different substances.

Elements Are Arranged in Order of Increasing Atomic Number

As you move from left to right within a period, the atomic number of each element increases by one. Once you've reached the end of the period, the pattern resumes on the next period. You might have noticed that two rows of elements are set apart from the rest of the periodic table. These rows, the lanthanides and actinides, are placed below the table to allow it to be narrower. These elements are also arranged in order of increasing atomic number.

© Houghton Mifflin Harcourt Publishing Company • Image Credits: (l) ©Charles D. Winters/Photo Researchers, Inc.; (r) ©Charles D. Winters/Photo Researchers, Inc.

Noble gases, found in Group 18, glow brightly when an electric current is passed through them.

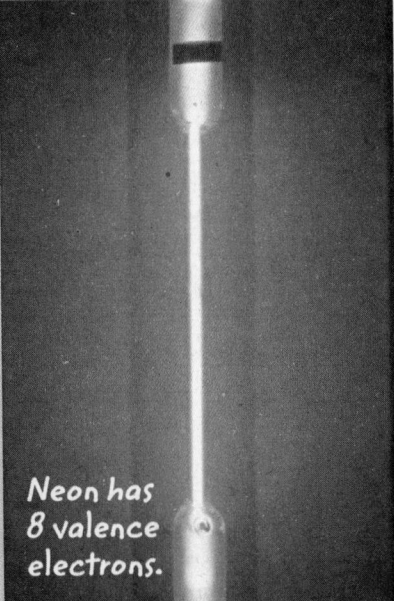

Neon has 8 valence electrons.

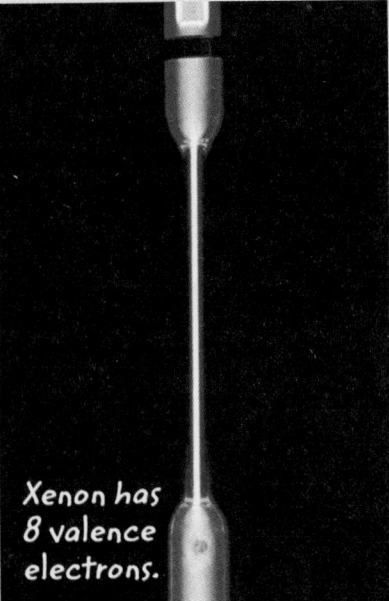

Xenon has 8 valence electrons.

Active Reading

13 Describe How do elements change as you move from left to right across the periodic table? Underline the patterns that are described on this page.

14 Analyze List three other elements that have 1 valence electron. (Hint: Refer to the periodic table.)

_____

_____

_____

15 Analyze List three other elements that have 8 valence electrons. (Hint: Refer to the periodic table.)

_____

_____

_____

How can the periodic table be used to predict an element's characteristics?

An element's position on the periodic table reveals information about its structure and properties. At the time when the periodic table was being developed, many elements were still unknown. However, Mendeleev was able to use his early arrangements of the elements to predict the existence of some elements that had not yet been discovered. He was even able to predict the characteristics of some unknown elements. Years later, when those elements were discovered, they fit into the table just as Mendeleev and others had predicted.

Scientists continue to use the periodic table to understand the characteristics of known elements and explore the possibility of new ones.

Hydrogen has 1 proton and 1 electron. It fits at the top left of the periodic table.

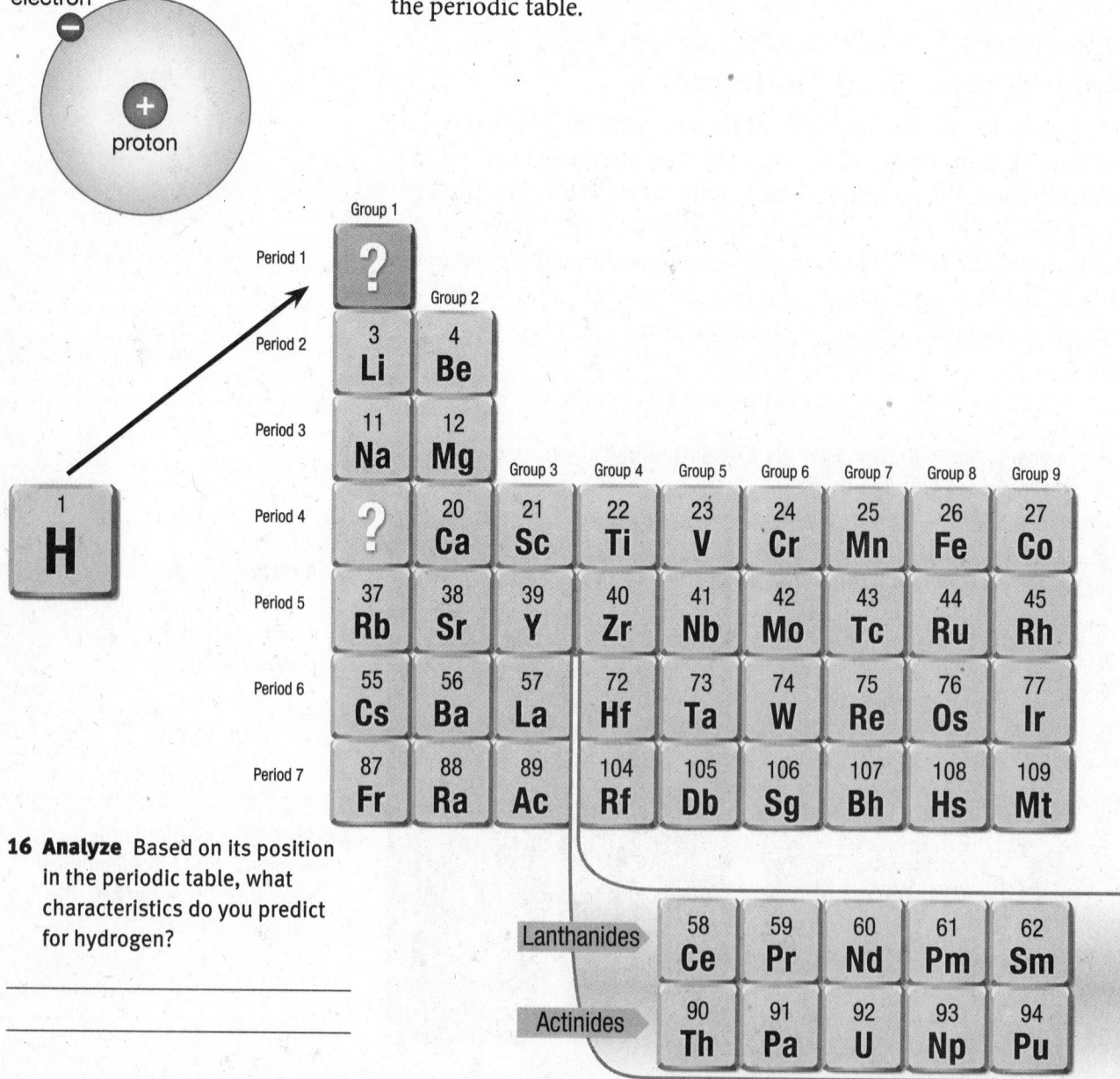

electron

proton

16 Analyze Based on its position in the periodic table, what characteristics do you predict for hydrogen?

_____

_____

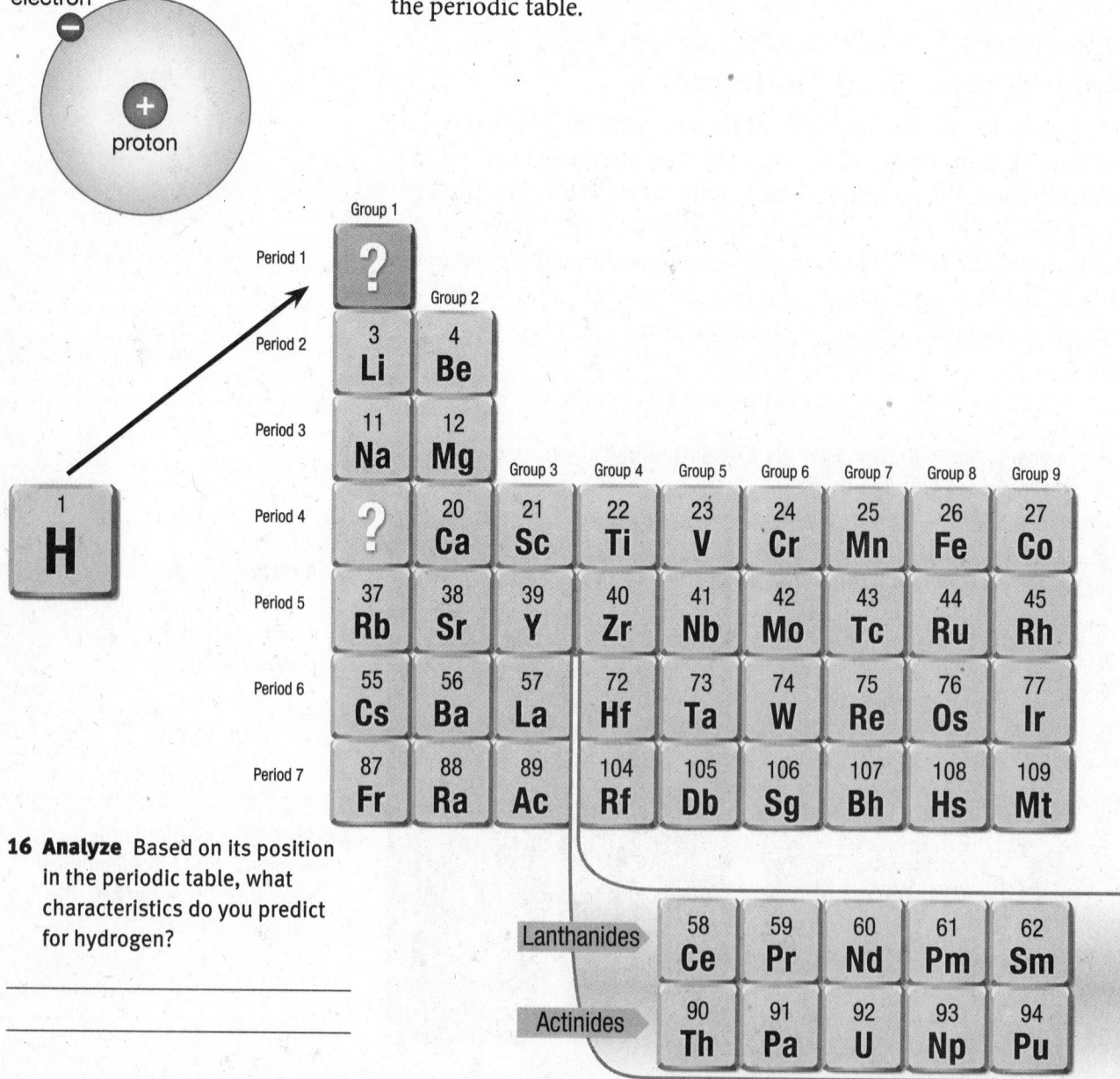

Visualize It!

17 Explain Can you fill in the gaps in this periodic table? Use the information given about the four elements below to predict where each fits. Identify the atomic number of each element and explain your reasoning.

Potassium, K, is a very reactive metal because it only has one valence electron.

Atomic number: ☐

Explain your reasoning:

_____

_____

Neon, Ne, has a full set of valence electrons and is the smallest atom in the period.

Atomic number: ☐

Explain your reasoning:

_____

_____

Iodine, I, is a highly reactive nonmetal.

Atomic number: ☐

Explain your reasoning:

_____

_____

Silicon, Si, has properties of both metals and nonmetals.

Atomic number: ☐

Explain your reasoning:

_____

			Group 13	Group 14	Group 15	Group 16	Group 17	Group 18
								2 He
			5 B	6 C	7 N	8 O	9 F	?
			13 Al	?	15 P	16 S	17 Cl	18 Ar
Group 10	Group 11	Group 12						
28 Ni	29 Cu	30 Zn	31 Ga	32 Ge	33 As	34 Se	35 Br	36 Kr
46 Pd	47 Ag	48 Cd	49 In	50 Sn	51 Sb	52 Te	?	54 Xe
78 Pt	79 Au	80 Hg	81 Tl	82 Pb	83 Bi	84 Po	85 At	86 Rn
110 Ds	111 Rg	112 Cn	113 Nh	114 Fl	115 Mc	116 Lv	117 Ts	118 Og

63 Eu	64 Gd	65 Tb	66 Dy	67 Ho	68 Er	69 Tm	70 Yb	71 Lu
95 Am	96 Cm	97 Bk	98 Cf	99 Es	100 Fm	101 Md	102 No	103 Lr

Think Outside the Book Inquiry

18 Apply Select one of the four elements you have just placed on the periodic table. Draw a model of the element showing the number of protons, neutrons, and electrons. How does the model of this atom compare to other atoms in the same period? How does it compare to other atoms in the same group?

Visual Summary

To complete this summary, fill in the blanks with the correct word or phrase. Then use the key below to check your answers. You can use this page to review the main concepts of the lesson.

The periodic table arranges elements in columns and rows.

19 Elements in the same

_____

have similar properties.

20 Rows on the periodic table are known as

_____

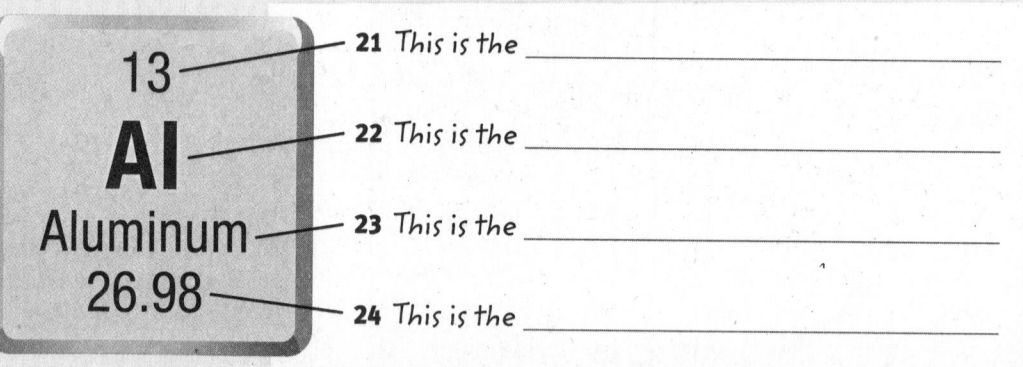

The Periodic Table

The periodic table contains information about each element.

13	**21** This is the _____
Al	**22** This is the _____
Aluminum	**23** This is the _____
26.98	**24** This is the _____

Answers: 19 group; 20 periods; 21 atomic number; 22 chemical symbol; 23 chemical name; 24 average atomic mass

25 Describe Some elements are highly unstable and break apart within seconds, making them difficult to study. How can the periodic table help scientists infer the properties of these elements?

Lesson Review

Vocabulary

Draw a line to connect the following terms to their definitions.

1 metal

2 nonmetal

3 metalloid

A an element that has properties of both metals and nonmetals

B an element that is shiny and that conducts heat and electricity well

C an element that conducts heat and electricity poorly

Key Concepts

4 Identify Elements in the same _____ on the periodic table have the same number of valence electrons.

5 Identify Properties of elements within a _____ on the periodic table change in a predictable way from one side of the table to the other.

6 Describe What is the purpose of the zigzag line on the periodic table?

_____

_____

_____

7 Apply Thorium (Th) has an average atomic mass of 232.04 u and an atomic number of 90. In the space below, draw a square from the periodic table to represent thorium.

Critical Thinking

Use this graphic to answer the following questions.

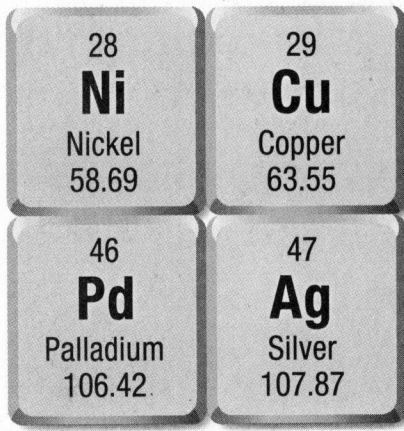

8 Infer What can you infer about copper and silver based on their position relative to each other? Support your claim with evidence.

_____

_____

_____

9 Apply How does the nucleus of a copper atom compare to the nucleus of a nickel atom?

_____

_____

_____

10 Explain Explain how chemists can state with certainty that no one will discover an element that would appear on the periodic table between sulfur (S) and chlorine (Cl).

_____

_____

_____

_____

_____

_____

_____

My Notes

Electrons and Chemical Bonding

ESSENTIAL QUESTION

How do atoms interact with each other?

By the end of this lesson, you should be able to use atomic models to predict whether atoms can form bonds.

A special type of light microscope can help us see these needle-like sodium carbonate crystals. The way the sodium, carbon, and oxygen atoms are joined by chemical bonds determines the structure of the crystals.

S8P1.e Structure and properties of atoms and simple molecules

Lesson Labs

Quick Labs
• What's in a Change?
• Sharing Electrons

S.T.E.M. Lab
• Build a Bohr Model

Engage Your Brain

1 Predict Check T or F to show whether you think each statement is true or false.

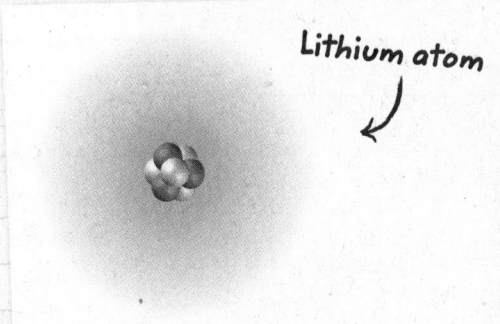
Lithium atom

T	F	
☐	☐	The nucleus of an atom does not change when the atom undergoes a chemical reaction.
☐	☐	An atom does not react with other atoms if it has the same number of protons as it has electrons.
☐	☐	All of an atom's electrons can interact with the electrons of other atoms to form bonds.

2 Describe Fill in the blank with the word or phrase that you think correctly completes the following sentences. Use the model of a lithium atom shown above.

The _____

represents the location of the electrons.

The _____

is represented by the red and silver spheres.

Active Reading

3 Apply Many scientific words, such as *bond*, also have everyday meanings. Use context clues to write your own definition for each meaning of the word *bond*.

Example sentence
Zach used glue to form a <u>bond</u> between the broken parts of the chair.

bond:

_____

_____

Example sentence
A chemical <u>bond</u> can form between two atoms.

bond:

_____

_____

Vocabulary Terms

• chemical bond
• valence electron

4 Identify As you read, create a reference card for each vocabulary term. On one side of the card, write the term and its meaning. On the other side, draw an image that illustrates or makes a connection to the term. These cards can be used as bookmarks in the text so that you can refer to them while studying.

Bound to Change

How do atoms join together?

There are only 26 letters in the alphabet. Yet you could combine these letters in different ways to form nearly a million words. Similarly, atoms of a limited number of elements join together in different ways to form the many substances around you. Some substances, such as water, are made up of only a few atoms. Other substances, such as DNA, can contain billions of atoms. A huge variety of substances are possible because atoms join together by forming chemical bonds. A **chemical bond** is an interaction that holds atoms or ions together.

A group of atoms that are held together by chemical bonds is called a *molecule*. Look at the model of a water molecule below. Every water molecule is made of one oxygen atom bonded to two hydrogen atoms. The chemical bonds hold the atoms together.

 **Active Reading** 5 **Describe** What are chemical bonds?

_____

_____

_____

 **Visualize It!**

6 Identify Draw arrows that point to the location of the chemical bonds in the water molecule. (Hint: The oxygen atom is red, and the hydrogen atoms are blue.)

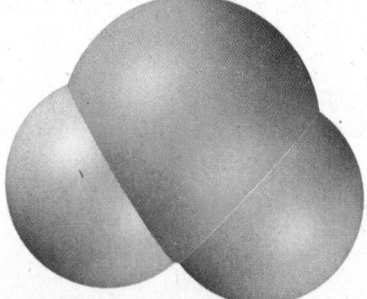

Water molecule

All water molecules are the same. They are made up of two hydrogen atoms bonded to one oxygen atom.

What happens to atoms during chemical changes?

Chemical changes change the identity of substances. However, a chemical change does not create or destroy atoms. Instead, the atoms are rearranged to make new substances with different properties. The changing colors of leaves in fall is due to chemical changes. Leaves contain pigments of different colors including green, red, and yellow. Usually leaves appear green because they contain a larger amount of green pigment. In the fall, the atoms that make up the green pigment are rearranged to form new, colorless substances. You can see the red and yellow pigments because they do not break down as easily.

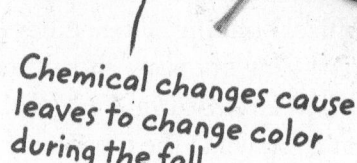

Chemical changes cause leaves to change color during the fall.

Atoms Are Rearranged

In order for atoms to be rearranged, chemical bonds have to be formed or broken. The models below show how hydrogen gas and chlorine gas undergo a chemical change to make hydrogen chloride. Initially, there are bonds between the hydrogen atoms and bonds between the chlorine atoms. These bonds break. A new bond forms between each chlorine atom and hydrogen atom. The atoms that make up hydrogen gas and chlorine gas do not change their identity. Instead, the atoms are simply rearranged to form hydrogen chloride.

7 Analyze Label each hydrogen atom with an "H" and each chlorine atom with a "Cl."

8 Apply How many of each type of atom are there on each side of the arrow?

H: _____ Cl: _____

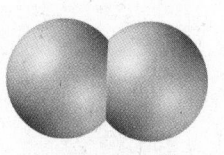

In a hydrogen molecule, two hydrogen atoms are connected by a bond.

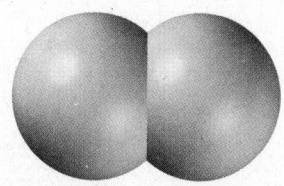

In a chlorine molecule, two chlorine atoms are connected by a bond.

A hydrogen chloride molecule forms when a bond is made between a hydrogen atom and a chlorine atom.

9 Analyze What evidence from this model shows that atoms are not created or destroyed by this chemical change?

_____

_____

A Model Atom

What do different atom models show?

Because atoms are too small to observe directly, scientists often use models of the atom to show how atoms behave. They use different models depending on what they need to study. For example, the way a model shows electrons is important because electrons are involved in chemical bonding. Three different models used to represent atoms are shown at the right.

The *electron cloud model* of a hydrogen atom is shown at the top. This model shows how electrons are found in a region around the nucleus. It helps show the general locations of the different parts of the atom. But it does not show the number of electrons.

The *Bohr model* of the hydrogen atom is shown in the middle. This atom model shows the number of electrons in an atom. The electrons are shown as dots placed in rings around the nucleus. Bohr models do not show the true arrangement of electrons in the atom. Each ring represents an energy level, not a physical location in the atom. However, showing the electrons in energy levels helps predict how and why atoms form chemical bonds.

The *space-filling model* of a molecule is shown at the bottom. In this type of model, atoms are represented as solid spheres. The spheres do not show the parts that make up the atoms. But this model clearly shows how the atoms are connected to each other.

When you taste a banana flavor, you are sensing certain molecules.

Visualize It!

10 Describe Write a caption for each model describing what it shows.

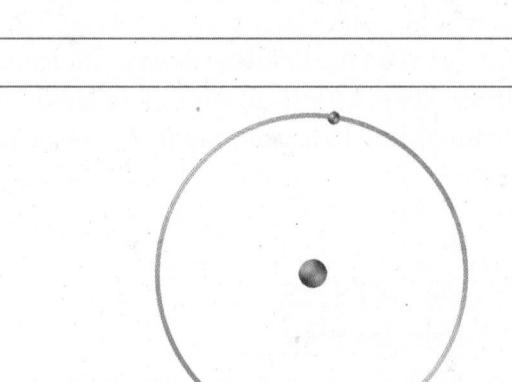

_____

_____

_____

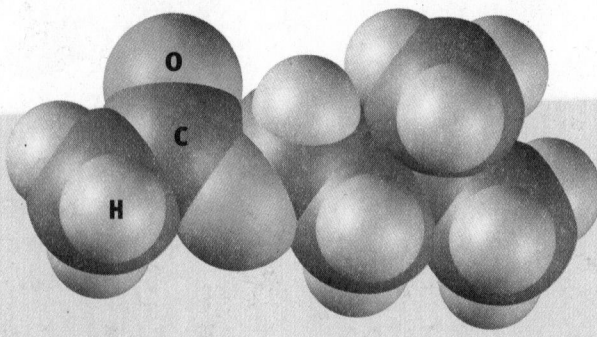

O

C

H

This model uses spheres to show the 3-D arrangement of atoms in one of the molecules that gives bananas their flavor.

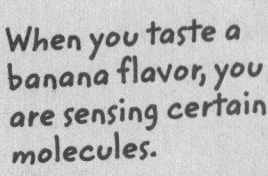

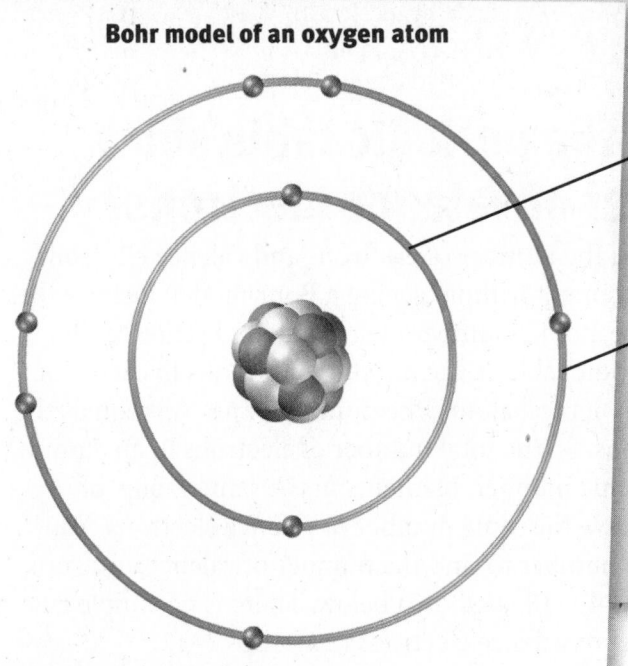

Bohr model of an oxygen atom

The first energy level can hold up to two electrons. This level is filled first.

The second energy level can hold up to eight electrons. Larger atoms have more energy levels, which can hold more electrons.

What are valence electrons?

Active Reading **11 Identify** As you read, underline the maximum number of electrons that can be in the first energy level of an atom.

Bohr models show electrons in energy levels. Each energy level can hold a specific number of electrons. The first energy level can hold up to two electrons and is filled first. The second energy level can hold up to eight electrons. Many atoms have additional energy levels. Electrons are usually not added to higher energy levels until the lower ones are filled. The energy level furthest from the nucleus is called the *outermost energy level.* Electrons found in the outermost energy level of an atom are called **valence electrons.** Different atoms might have different numbers of valence electrons.

The Bohr model above shows how the electrons in an oxygen atom are arranged in energy levels. An oxygen atom has eight electrons—two electrons in the first energy level and six electrons in the second energy level. In the oxygen atom, the second energy level is the outermost energy level. So, oxygen has six valence electrons.

Visualize It!

12 Apply A fluorine atom has nine electrons. Draw a model to determine how many valence electrons the atom has.

Step 1

(F)

A. Add two electrons to the first energy level.

B. How many electrons still need to be added?

_____

Step 2

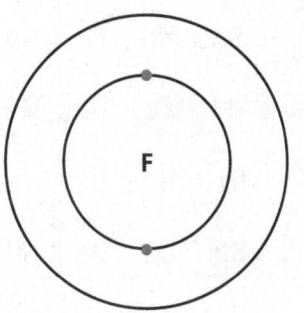

A. Add the remaining electrons to the second energy level.

B. How many valence electrons does fluorine have?

_____

Fill It Up!

How does the periodic table show the number of valence electrons?

You can determine the number of electrons and valence electrons in an atom of an element without seeing a Bohr model. Just use the periodic table. The atomic number of an element, listed in each square of the periodic table, is the number of protons in each atom of that element. In neutral atoms, the number of protons equals the number of electrons. So the total number of electrons in an atom is equal to the atomic number. Elements in the same group, or vertical column, have the same number of valence electrons. You can use the group number to find the number of valence electrons in Groups 1, 2, and 13–18, as shown below. There is no simple rule to find the number of valence electrons in Groups 3–12.

The atoms of elements in the last group of the periodic table, Group 18, have full outermost energy levels. Helium (He) has two valence electrons in its first and only energy level. All of the atoms of the other elements in Group 18 have eight valence electrons. These atoms are unreactive and do not tend to form bonds. They rarely participate in chemical changes. Almost all atoms of other elements readily form chemical bonds.

Visualize It!

Group 1 atoms have one valence electron. Group 2 atoms have two valence electrons.

Atoms of elements in Groups 13–18 have the same number of valence electrons as the last digit in their group number. For example, all atoms of the elements in Group 16 have six valence electrons. Helium atoms have two valence electrons.

1	2	3	4	5	6	7	8	9	10	11	12	13	14	15	16	17	18
1 H	2																2 He
3 Li	4 Be											5 B	6 C	7 N	8 O	9 F	10 Ne
11 Na	12 Mg	3	4	5	6	7	8	9	10	11	12	13 Al	14 Si	15 P	16 S	17 Cl	18 Ar
19 K	20 Ca	21 Sc	22 Ti	23 V	24 Cr	25 Mn	26 Fe	27 Co	28 Ni	29 Cu	30 Zn	31 Ga	32 Ge	33 As	34 Se	35 Br	36 Kr
37 Rb	38 Sr	39 Y	40 Zr	41 Nb	42 Mo	43 Tc	44 Ru	45 Rh	46 Pd	47 Ag	48 Cd	49 In	50 Sn	51 Sb	52 Te	53 I	54 Xe
55 Cs	56 Ba	57 La	72 Hf	73 Ta	74 W	75 Re	76 Os	77 Ir	78 Pt	79 Au	80 Hg	81 Tl	82 Pb	83 Bi	84 Po	85 At	86 Rn
87 Fr	88 Ra	89 Ac	104 Rf	105 Db	106 Sg	107 Bh	108 Hs	109 Mt	110 Ds	111 Rg	112 Cn	113 Nh	114 Fl	115 Mc	116 Lv	117 Ts	118 Og

13 Apply How many valence electrons do nitrogen (N) and phosphorus (P) have?

N:_____   P:_____

Why do atoms form bonds?

An atom tends to form bonds if its outermost energy level is not full. Atoms that have fewer than eight valence electrons, except for helium, do not have a full outermost energy level. These atoms gain, lose, or share valence electrons to form bonds.

Forming bonds allows atoms to fill their outermost energy level. For example, a chlorine atom has seven valence electrons. It needs one more electron to have a full outermost energy level. A chlorine atom can gain one electron from a sodium atom. When this happens, the chlorine atom becomes a negative ion. An *ion* is a charged particle that forms when an atom loses or gains an electron. The sodium atom that loses the electron becomes a positive ion. The ions formed by chlorine and sodium both have eight valence electrons. They have full outermost energy levels. Bonds hold the negative and positive ions together. The resulting substance is sodium chloride, also known as table salt.

Think Outside the Book Inquiry

14 Research Some of the molecules in our bodies can be composed of hundreds, thousands, or even millions of atoms. Research one molecule that is found in our bodies. Identify the atoms that form bonds in the molecule. Then, create a model of this molecule.

Visualize It!

15 Compare In the space below each Bohr model, write the number of valence electrons that each atom has.

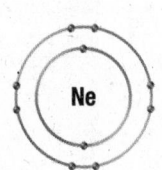

Has _____ valence electrons

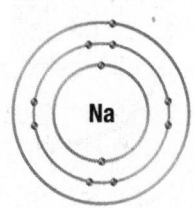

Has _____ valence electrons

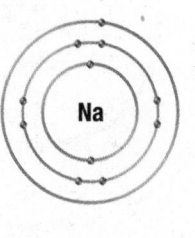

Has _____ valence electrons

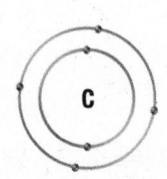

Has _____ valence electrons

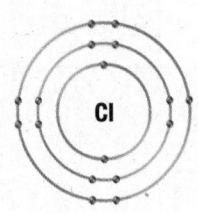

Has _____ valence electrons

Has _____ valence electrons

Table salt, NaCl, is made of sodium and chloride ions that are bonded together.

16 Classify Circle the atoms that are likely to form chemical bonds with other atoms.

© Houghton Mifflin Harcourt Publishing Company • Image Credits: ©HMH

Visual Summary

To complete this summary, check the box that indicates true or false. Then, use the key below to check your answers. You can use this page to review the main concepts of the lesson.

Electrons and Chemical Bonding

A chemical bond is an interaction that holds two atoms together.

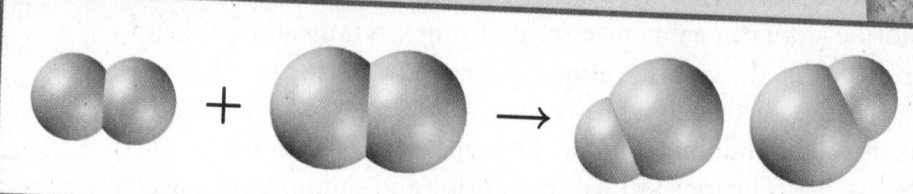

    T   F
17 ☐ ☐ *Atoms are rearranged during a chemical change when bonds break and form.*

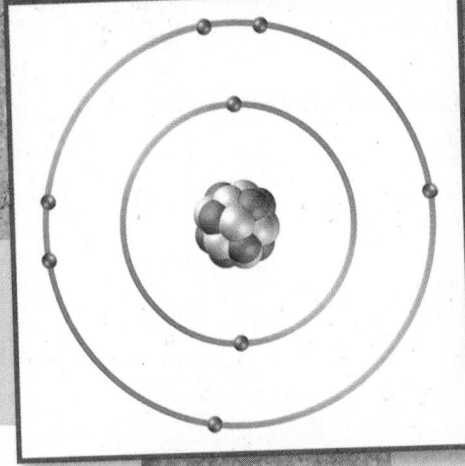

A Bohr model shows the number of electrons in each energy level of an atom.

    T   F
18 ☐ ☐ *A Bohr model is the best choice to show how atoms are arranged in molecules.*

Valence electrons are the electrons in the outermost energy level of an atom.

    T   F
19 ☐ ☐ *The atom above is reactive because its outermost energy level is not full.*

Answers: 17 True; 18 False; 19 True

20 Claims • Evidence • Reasoning Why are atoms of lithium, sodium, and potassium almost never found alone in nature? Explain your reasoning.

Vocabulary

Circle the term that best completes each of the following sentences.

1 A chemical bond joins *atoms / electrons* together in a water molecule.

2 The four valence electrons of a carbon atom are in its *innermost / outermost* energy level.

Key Concepts

3 Relate Which of the following can happen during a chemical change?

  A Atoms change into new types of atoms.

  B Bonds break, and new bonds form.

  C Nuclei of atoms break apart and combine.

  D All of the electrons in the atom are lost.

4 Explain What are the three ways in which an atom can form bonds with other atoms?

_____

_____

_____

5 Identify Sulfur (S) is in Group 16 of the periodic table. How many valence electrons does an atom of sulfur have?

_____

6 Model Find beryllium (Be) on the periodic table. In the space below, draw a Bohr model of a beryllium atom.

Critical Thinking

Use this model of a nitrogen atom to answer the following questions.

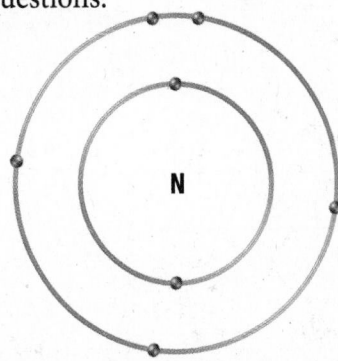

7 Analyze How many valence electrons do nitrogen atoms have?

_____

8 Infer A nitrogen atom will bond with three hydrogen atoms. Draw a model showing the resulting molecule.

9 Distinguish How would a Bohr model of a neon atom differ from the model of nitrogen above?

_____

_____

_____

_____

_____

My Notes

Wayne Rossi

METAL ARTISAN

Wayne Rossi works where art and science meet. Using a torch, he shapes pieces of steel into amazing works of art. The torch produces a flame that results from burning a combination of oxygen and acetylene. This action causes the steel to change from a solid to a liquid along the torch line. The change in matter results in the steel softening and separating into two pieces. Mr. Rossi uses the metal's change of state from solid to liquid to make his sculptures. In its liquid state, the steel can be easily cut or reshaped. Mr. Rossi brings art to his work as he imagines an interesting sculpture, envisions the cuts he needs, and guides the torch precisely to where he wants the cuts.

After he has cut out all of the pieces, Mr. Rossi uses more science to join the pieces together into the final sculpture. He joins them by welding, or melting metals together, and then letting them cool down and harden in place. When they harden, the metal pieces form one mass, and they are more strongly bonded to each other than if they were bolted together. Often, a third melted metal is added to help strengthen the bond. The end result is a nearly indestructible work of art!

Welding requires both precision and safety precautions.

The reddish color is from a chemical change that forms rust when rain and air react with the metal.

JOB BOARD

Sheet Metal Worker

What You'll Do: Set up and operate a shop that uses sheet metal. You may also manufacture, maintain, and repair metal products.

Where You Might Work: In a heating, air conditioning, and refrigeration shop. For a railroad cars and tracks manufacturer, sign manufacturer, or aircraft manufacturer. With an oil company, in construction, or various factories.

Education: High school diploma or equivalent

Other Job Requirements: You should be attentive to detail. You should also be able to read blueprints, take accurate measurements, and have knowledge of computerized saws, scissors, compressors, and lasers.

Geochemist

What You'll Do: Use physical and inorganic chemistry to study Earth's features related to rocks, minerals, fluids, and gases. Collect and analyze soil samples. Study the effects of Earth's movements. Write technical reports.

Where You Might Work: At a geochemical company, engineering firm, petroleum company, mining company, university, or environmental consulting firm.

Education: A master's or doctorate

Other Job Requirements: You need a strong background in math, science, chemistry, and geology. You must be willing to work outdoors in all types of weather and to collaborate with a team.

PEOPLE IN SCIENCE NEWS

MIMI So

Rough gemstones are cut and polished into beautiful jewels.

The Science Behind Jewelry

When you look at an interesting necklace, do you think to yourself, "There's a scientist at work"? Perhaps you should! For jewelry designer Mimi So, every day at work includes a little science.

She uses her knowledge of stone size, hardness, color, grade, and cut to choose a gemstone for a piece of jewelry. Then she considers the hardness, melting point, color, and malleability of the metal she would like to use. For example, Mimi says that emeralds are soft and fragile. She explains that a platinum setting would be too hard and could damage the emerald. Therefore, emeralds are usually set in a softer metal, such as 18-karat gold.

Mimi So has a Bachelor's of Fine Arts and a Gemologist Certification. Another option for jewelry-making training is to go to gemology school to gain the needed technical knowledge.

Lesson 4

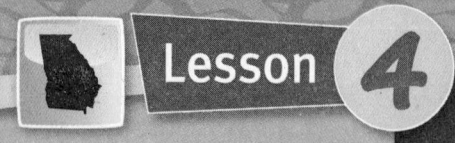

Ionic, Covalent, and Metallic Bonding

ESSENTIAL QUESTION

How can atoms join together?

By the end of this lesson, you should be able to describe the interactions between atoms in ionic, covalent, and metallic bonding.

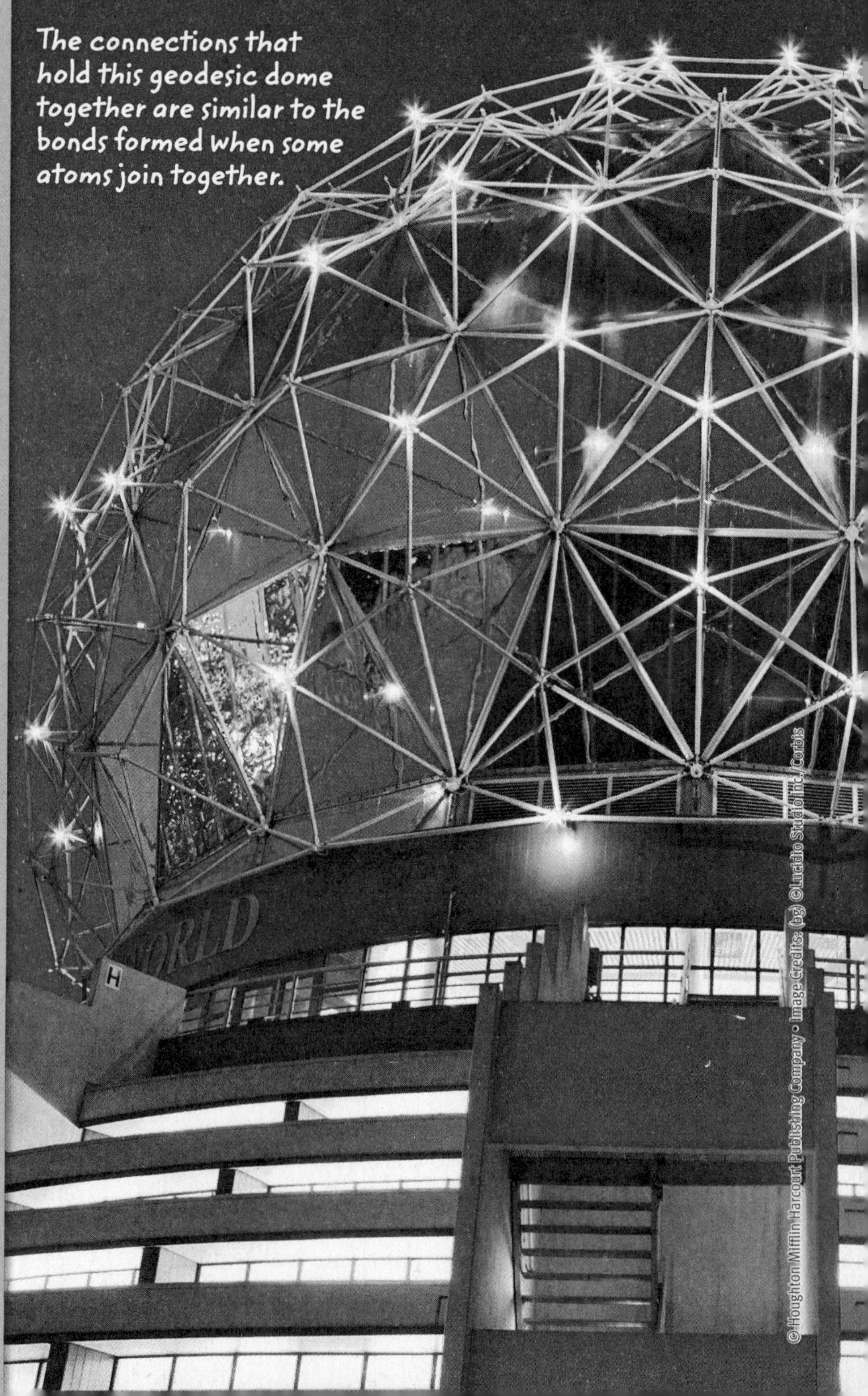

The connections that hold this geodesic dome together are similar to the bonds formed when some atoms join together.

Lesson Labs

Quick Labs
- Growing Crystals
- Modeling Bonding

Exploration Lab
- Chemical Bonds

Engage Your Brain

1 Predict Check T or F to show whether you think each statement is true or false.

T   F

☐   ☐   Metals are good conductors of electric current.

☐   ☐   An ion is always a negatively charged particle.

☐   ☐   Some atoms bond by sharing electrons.

☐   ☐   Metallic bonds are the strongest type of bond.

2 Describe Write a short description that explains how the pieces of a puzzle can stay together without the use of glue or tape.

_____

_____

_____

Active Reading

3 Synthesize You can often define an unknown term if you know the meaning of its word parts. Use the word parts and sentence below to make an educated guess about the meaning of the term *covalent bond*.

Word part	Meaning
co-	with or together
-valence	outermost level of electrons

Example sentence
The two atoms were joined by a <u>covalent bond</u>.

covalent bond:

_____

_____

Vocabulary Terms

- ion
- ionic bond
- covalent bond
- molecule
- metallic bond

4 Apply As you learn the definition of each vocabulary term in this lesson, create your own definition or sketch to help you remember the meaning of the term.

Opposites Attract

What is an ion?

An atom has a neutral charge because it has an equal number of electrons and protons. An **ion** is a particle with a positive or negative charge. An ion forms when an atom gains or loses electrons from its outermost energy level. When atoms join together, the number of protons in each atom does not change, but the valence electrons can move from one atom to another.

If an atom gains at least one electron, it then has more electrons than protons. The resulting ion has an overall negative charge. If an atom loses at least one electron, it then has fewer electrons than protons. The resulting ion has an overall positive charge.

Active Reading **5 Identify** Explain the difference between a positive and a negative ion.

_____

_____

_____

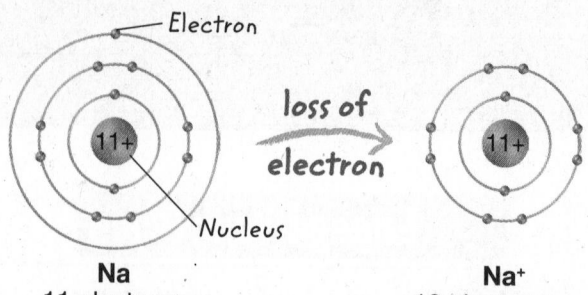

Na
11 electrons
(no charge)

loss of electron

Na⁺
10 electrons
(1+ total charge)

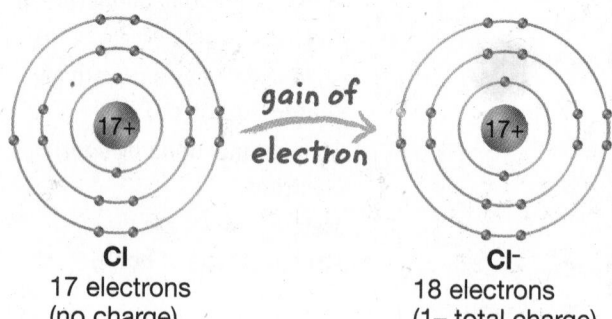

Cl
17 electrons
(no charge)

gain of electron

Cl⁻
18 electrons
(1– total charge)

How does an ionic bond form?

Chemical bonds hold two or more atoms or ions together. An **ionic bond** is a force that brings oppositely charged ions together. Ionic bonds form when electrons are transferred from a metal atom to a nonmetal atom. In the process of ionic bonding, valence electrons move from the outermost energy level of the metal atom to the outermost energy level of the nonmetal atom. The outermost energy level of each atom is filled as a result of ionic bonds forming.

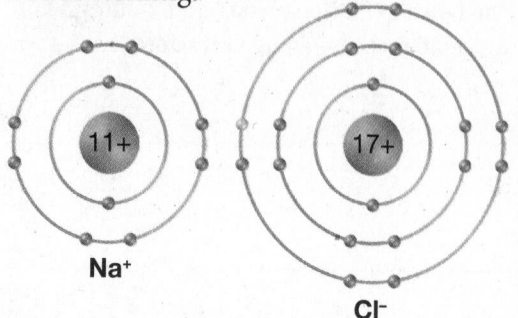

Na⁺

Cl⁻

The electron transfer from a sodium atom to a chlorine atom creates an ionic bond, forming the compound sodium chloride (NaCl), also known as table salt.

Calcite ($CaCO_3$) is held together by ionic bonds. Calcite is a common mineral found in rock.

© Houghton Mifflin Harcourt Publishing Company • Image Credits: ©Maurice Nimmo/Corbis Documentary/Getty Images

What properties do most ionic compounds share?

When an ionic bond forms, the number of electrons lost by the metal atom is equal to the number of electrons gained by the nonmetal atom. The compound formed is neutral because the charges of the ions cancel each other. Most ionic compounds have similar physical properties.

Crystal Lattice Structure

When you pour table salt into your hand, you can see tiny crystals. When ions bond, they form a repeating three-dimensional pattern called a *crystal lattice*. Each ion has many oppositely charged ions around it, and every ion is held firmly in place with strong bonds. It takes a lot of energy to separate these ions from one another. So most ionic compounds have high melting and boiling points.

Electrical Conductivity

Solid ionic compounds are poor conductors of electric current because the ions are held tightly in place. Electric charges cannot pass through an ionic solid. Melting an ionic solid, however, allows the individual ions to move around. Melted ionic compounds can conduct an electric current. Ionic compounds dissolved in water can also conduct an electric current.

Brittleness

The crystals of ionic compounds are hard and brittle. They are more likely to break than bend. Striking a crystal of an ionic compound with a hammer will likely shatter the crystals in many places.

Solubility in Water

Solubility is the ability to dissolve in liquid. Most ionic compounds, such as table salt (NaCl), dissolve in water. When salt is added to water, water molecules attract the positive and negative salt ions. Water molecules surround each ion and move the ions apart from each other. The separated ions dissolve in water.

Salt deposits along the shore of the Dead Sea contain ionic compounds such as NaCl.

Visualize It!

6 Describe What properties of ionic bonds are illustrated by the images on this page? Explain your reasoning.

_____

_____

_____

_____

_____

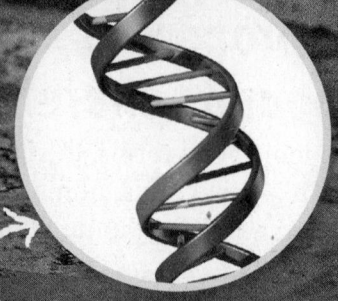

Let's Share!

DNA is a molecule found in all living things. The atoms in each strand of a DNA molecule are held together by covalent bonds.

What is a covalent bond?

Most things around you, such as water, sugar, oxygen, and wood, are held together by covalent bonds. A **covalent bond** forms when atoms share one or more pairs of electrons. When two nonmetal atoms bond, a large amount of energy is needed for either atom to lose an electron. So, instead of transferring electrons, these atoms bond by sharing valence electrons, as shown in the diagram at the right. The shared electrons fill empty spaces in the outermost energy level of each atom in a covalent bond.

What is a molecule?

When atoms join together with covalent bonds, they form a type of particle called a molecule. A **molecule** is a group of atoms held together by chemical bonds. Most molecules, such as the water molecule shown, are made up of atoms of two or more elements. Molecules that contain atoms of more than one element are called *covalent compounds*.

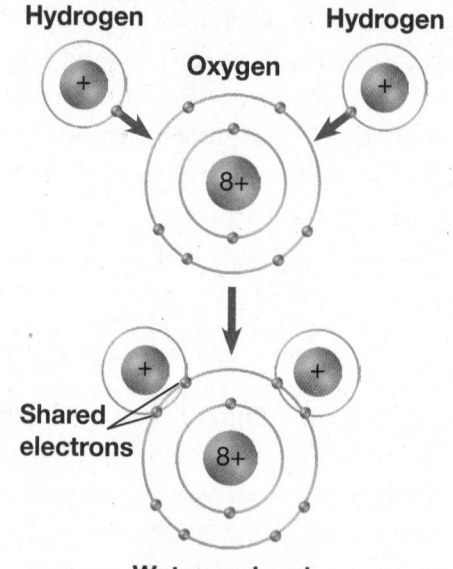

Water molecule

A water molecule forms when two hydrogen atoms and an oxygen atom share electrons.

---

7 Compare In the table below, list the differences between ionic and covalent bonds.

Ionic bonds	Covalent bonds

What properties do most covalent compounds share?

The covalent bonds that hold the atoms of some molecules together are strong, but the force holding those molecules close to one another is weak. This characteristic leads to common physical properties for most compounds held together by covalent bonds.

8 Identify As you read, underline the difference between covalent bonds and the forces holding molecules close to each other.

Some covalent compounds, such as wax, do not dissolve easily in water.

Other covalent compounds, such as this purple dye, are soluble in water.

Low Solubility in Water

Some covalent compounds dissolve in water while others do not. Wax molecules have a stronger attraction to other wax molecules than they do to water molecules. This is why wax does not dissolve in water. A lava lamp depends on the low solubility of wax for its flowing "blob" effect. The blobs of covalently bonded wax molecules stay separate from the water as they rise and fall inside the lamp, making interesting shapes.

Low Melting and Boiling Points

When a covalent compound melts or boils, the covalent bonds holding the molecules together do not break as ionic bonds in an ionic compound do. Instead, one molecule separates from another. Because molecules separate easily from other molecules, they tend to have lower melting and boiling points than ionic compounds.

Poor Electrical Conductivity

Most covalent compounds are poor conductors of electric current in both solid and liquid form. Unlike ions, which are charged, molecules are neutral. So, even in a liquid in which molecules can move around, the compound cannot conduct electric current. However, some covalent compounds that can dissolve in water do break up into ions. Those covalent compounds are usually able to conduct electric current.

Think Outside the Book Inquiry

9 Infer With a classmate, discuss why oil and vinegar do not mix. How might this example relate to covalent bonding?

Free to Move

How does a metallic bond form?

Active Reading 10 **Identify** As you read, underline the characteristics of electrons in a metallic bond.

How can a sculptor change the shape of a metal without breaking it? Metal can be shaped because of the nature of the bonds that form between metal atoms. A **metallic bond** forms between metal atoms when their outermost energy levels overlap. Metallic bonding is weak compared to ionic or covalent bonding.

Positively charged metal ions form when metal atoms temporarily lose electrons. The positive ions are held in a crystal structure and do not move.

Because the outermost energy levels of metal atoms overlap, electrons move freely in all directions throughout the metal. You can think of a metal as being made up of positive metal ions that have enough valence electrons "swimming" around to hold the ions together. The moving electrons maintain the metallic bonds when the shape of the metal changes. So, metal objects can be bent without being broken.

This artist is able to form his sculptures in many different shapes because of the nature of metallic bonds.

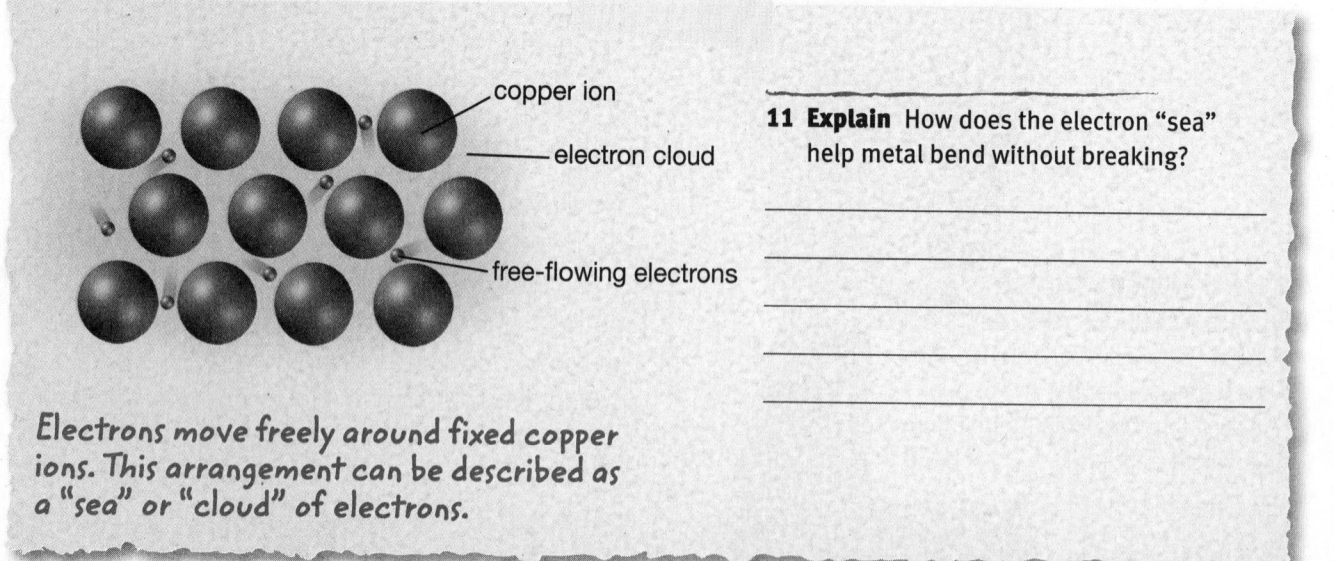

copper ion

electron cloud

free-flowing electrons

Electrons move freely around fixed copper ions. This arrangement can be described as a "sea" or "cloud" of electrons.

11 Explain How does the electron "sea" help metal bend without breaking?

_____
_____
_____
_____
_____

What properties do most metals share?

About 80 percent of the elements in the periodic table are metals. The metallic bonds that hold these metals together give the metals their properties.

Good Electrical Conductors

Because the electrons in a metal can move freely, most metals are good conductors of electric current. For example, when you turn on a lamp, electrons move through the copper wire that connects the light bulb in the lamp to the electrical outlet. The electrons that move are the valence electrons in the copper atoms. These electrons are free to move because the electrons are not connected to any one atom.

The metal base conducts electric current to light the light bulb.

Malleable and Ductile

Due to their free-moving electrons, metals have two properties that allow them to be reshaped. *Malleability* [mal•ee•uh•BIL•ih•tee] is the ability of metal to be hammered into sheets. The metal aluminum can be pounded into thin sheets of aluminum foil. *Ductility* is the ability to be formed into long, thin wires. The metal copper, for example, can be made into wires.

Copper made into long, thin wire is used to conduct electric current.

12 Compare Fill in the Venn diagram to compare and contrast ionic compounds and metals.

Ionic Compounds

transfer of electrons between atoms

Both

Metals

malleable

Visual Summary

To complete this summary, circle the correct word. Then, use the key below to check your answers. You can use this page to review the main concepts of the lesson.

Ionic, Covalent, and Metallic Bonding

A covalent bond forms when atoms share one or more pairs of electrons.

14 In general, covalent compounds have low/high boiling points.

An ionic bond forms between oppositely charged ions.

13 Ionic bonds usually form between a positively charged metal ion and a negatively charged metal/nonmetal ion.

A metallic bond is formed by the attraction between positive metal ions and the free electrons around them.

15 Metals can/cannot be reshaped without breaking.

Answers: 13 nonmetal; 14 low; 15 can

16 Summarize List the similarities and differences between ionic, covalent, and metallic bonds.

Lesson Review

Vocabulary

Draw a line to connect the following terms to their definitions.

1 molecule

2 ion

3 covalent bond

A forms when an atom gains or loses one or more electrons

B group of atoms held together by chemical bonds

C bond formed by atoms sharing electrons

Key Concepts

4 Explain Describe the role of electrons in the formation of a covalent bond.

5 Identify How is the position of electrons involved in metallic bonding different from the position of electrons that form ionic and covalent bonds?

6 List Name the physical properties that many ionic compounds share.

7 Compare Using Bohr models of atoms, illustrate how ionic bonding differs from covalent bonding.

Critical Thinking

Use this table to answer the following questions.

Property	Unknown substance
solubility in water	not soluble
melting point	45 °C
electrical conductivity	poor conductor

8 Identify Is the substance in the chart a metal or a covalent compound? Explain.

9 Infer Is the substance described in the chart above held together by metallic, covalent, or ionic bonds? Explain.

10 Infer Why might metallic bonding be weak compared to ionic and covalent bonding?

11 Claims • Evidence • Reasoning Which type of bond does the phrase "opposites attract" apply to best? Explain your reasoning.

My Notes

Unit 3 〈 Big Idea 〉 The atomic structure of an element determines the properties of the element and determines how the element interacts with other elements.

Lesson 1

ESSENTIAL QUESTION
How do we know what parts make up the atom?

Describe how the development of the atomic theory has led to the modern understanding of the atom and its parts.

Lesson 3

ESSENTIAL QUESTION
How do atoms interact with each other?

Use atomic models to predict whether atoms can form bonds.

Lesson 2

ESSENTIAL QUESTION
How are elements arranged on the periodic table?

Describe the relationship between the arrangement of elements on the periodic table and the properties of those elements.

Lesson 4

ESSENTIAL QUESTION
How can atoms join together?

Describe the interactions between atoms in ionic, covalent, and metallic bonding.

Connect ESSENTIAL QUESTIONS
Lessons 2 and 3

1 Synthesize How is chemical bonding related to the organization of the periodic table?

_____

_____

_____

_____

_____

_____

Think Outside the Book

2 Synthesize Choose one of these activities to help synthesize what you have learned in this unit.

☐ Using what you learned in lessons 1 and 2, explain how the structure of the atom is related to the periodic table by making a poster presentation. Include captions and labels.

☐ Using what you learned in lessons 3 and 4, explain how chemical bonding differs in ionic, covalent, and metallic bonding. Include spherical models to show how atoms are connected together.

Name _____

Vocabulary

Fill in each blank with the term that best completes the following sentences.

1 A(n) _____ is a bond that forms when electrons are transferred from one atom to another.

2 A(n) _____ is an interaction that holds two atoms together.

3 A(n) _____ is the smallest particle of an element that has the chemical properties of that element.

4 A(n) _____ is a bond that forms when atoms share one or more pairs of electrons.

5 A(n) _____ is a negatively-charged subatomic particle.

Key Concepts

Read each question below, and circle the best answer.

6 Which of the following is a property of metals?

A low melting point

B good electrical conductor

C good thermal insulator

D cannot bend without breaking

7 The chart below gives the atomic number and mass number of two elements.

	Element A	Element B
Atomic number	10	9
Mass number	20	19

How many protons does Element B have?

A 10

B 20

C 9

D 19

8 The diagram below is one model of an atom.

Atom

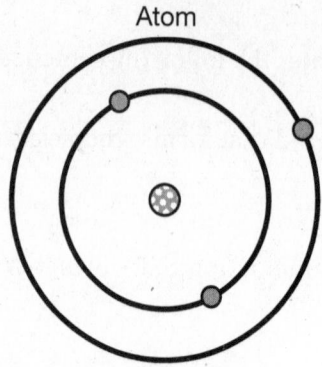

By whom was this model of an atom proposed?

A Thomson   **C** Rutherford

B Dalton   **D** Bohr

9 In a neutral atom, the number of electrons equals the number of what other part?

A protons   **C** nuclei

B neutrons   **D** energy levels

10 Below is a square that represents one element of the periodic table.

> 20
> **Ca**
> Calcium
> 40.078

What information is in this square of the periodic table, from top to bottom?

A average atomic mass, chemical symbol, chemical name, atomic number

B atomic number, chemical symbol, chemical name, average atomic mass

C average atomic mass, chemical symbol, chemical name, proton number

D atomic number, chemical symbol, chemical name, proton number

11 What must happen for an ion to form?

A An atom must gain or lose an electron.

B An atom must gain or lose a proton.

C An atom must gain or lose a neutron.

D An atom must gain or lose a nucleus.

12 The periodic table is arranged in columns and rows. What are the columns and the rows of the periodic table called?

A periods and energy levels   **C** atomic numbers and periods

B groups and periods   **D** groups and atomic numbers

13 The diagram below shows how atomic theory has changed over time.

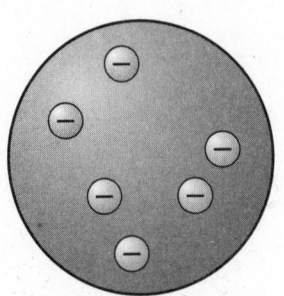
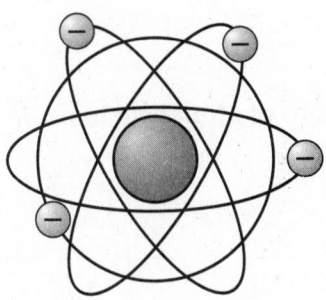
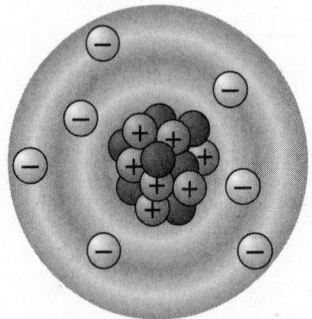

Thomson's model of atom   Rutherford's model of atom   Current model of atom

How is the current understanding of atomic structure different from both Thomson's model and Rutherford's model?

A Electrons move only in the current model of the atom.

B Electrons are fixed only in the current model of the atom.

C Electrons travel in orbits only in the current model of the atom.

D Electrons move within an electron cloud only in the current model of the atom.

Critical Thinking

Answer the following questions in the space provided.

14 List three properties of metals that nonmetals typically do not have.

_____

_____

Describe where metals and nonmetals are found on the periodic table.

_____

_____

What are elements that have some properties of metals and some properties of nonmetals called? _____

Unit 3 Review continued

15 Fluorine has 7 valence electrons. What type of bond is likely to form between two atoms of fluorine? _____

Draw two atoms of fluorine showing the bond that forms between them.

How does the number of valence electrons of an atom help to determine whether an atom is likely to form bonds?

_____

_____

Connect **ESSENTIAL QUESTIONS**
Lessons 1 and 3

Answer the following question in the space provided.

16 In the space below, draw a Bohr model of an atom.

Label the valence electrons. How many valence electrons does this atom have? _____

What element does your atom represent? Explain.

_____

_____

Bohr models do not correctly show the location of electrons in an atom. Explain why they are still useful to predict bonding of atoms.

_____

_____

_____

Interactions of Matter

A controlled release of energy is used at a nuclear power plant to meet many of our energy needs.

Big Idea

In chemical reactions, matter and energy are conserved, while in nuclear reactions, matter is converted into energy.

S8P1., S8P1.b, S8P1.f

Batteries—our most common "mini" energy source—supply power for toys and other devices.

What do you think?

Interactions of matter occur on both large and small scales. What interactions of matter have you observed in your daily life? Look for information in this unit that provides evidence to support your claim.

Unit 4
Interactions of Matter

Medical Metamorphosis

The study of chemistry has helped transform and improve medical science for the better health of humans worldwide. Scientists work to discover new ways to help people live healthier, longer lives.

1889–1911
Marie Curie proposed the use of radium to relieve suffering and established a radioactivity laboratory. Curie, along with her husband, won the Nobel Prize in Physics in 1903. She won a second Nobel Prize in Chemistry in 1911 for her work in radioactivity.

1931–1939
The son of former Alabama slaves, **Percy Julian** was one of the first African Americans to earn a Ph.D. in chemistry. His work in discovering the chemical properties of plant steroids led to the development of medicinal steroids.

1951–1953
In 1953, **James Watson and Francis Crick** proposed that DNA consisted of the now familiar double-helical structure. This led to breakthroughs in genetic diseases and in crime scene identifications.

1991
Richard R. Ernst won the Nobel Prize for his work in the development of high-resolution nuclear magnetic resonance (NMR) spectroscopy. Physicians use an NMR imaging (MRI) machine to scan patients for serious internal injuries.

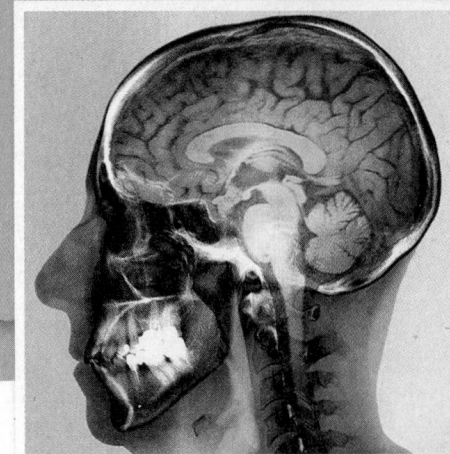

Take It Home

1 Think About It
With an adult, talk about personal experiences with medical breakthroughs related to chemistry. Friends or family members may be living with a genetic disease. Sometimes patients are diagnosed using MRI technology.

2 Ask Some Questions
Conduct Internet research to learn more about Percy Julian's life and work.

A Name two medicinal uses for plant steroids and one nonmedicinal use.

_____

_____

_____

_____

_____

B How is Julian's work still being carried out?

_____

_____

3 Make a Plan
Investigate a career in the medical field. Find out the steps to becoming a doctor, pharmacist, dentist, nurse, or other health-care professional. Make notes about your findings.

_____

_____

_____

_____

See **ScienceSaurus**® for more information about society and research.

Chemical Reactions

ESSENTIAL QUESTION

How are chemical reactions modeled?

By the end of this lesson, you should be able to use balanced chemical equations to model chemical reactions.

A chemical reaction that releases light energy occurs inside lightning bugs.

S8P1.f Conservation of matter in chemical reactions

✋ **Lesson Labs**

Quick Labs
• Breaking Bonds in a Chemical Reaction
• Catalysts and Chemical Reactions

Exploration Lab
• Change of Pace

Engage Your Brain

1 Identify Unscramble the letters below to find two types of energy that can be released when chemical reactions occur. Write your words on the blank lines.

GLITH _____

DSNUO _____

2 Describe Write your own caption to the photo below. Describe what kind of changes have happened to the ship and anchor.

_____
_____
_____
_____

Active Reading

3 Synthesize You can often define an unknown word if you know the meaning of its word parts. Use the word parts and sentence below to make an educated guess about the meaning of the word *exothermic*.

Word part	Meaning
exo-	go out, exit
therm-	heat

Example sentence
<u>Exothermic</u> reactions can sometimes quickly release so much heat that they can melt iron.

exothermic:

_____
_____
_____

Vocabulary Terms
• chemical reaction
• chemical formula
• chemical equation
• reactant
• product
• law of conservation of mass
• endothermic reaction
• exothermic reaction
• law of conservation of energy

4 Identify This list contains the vocabulary terms you'll learn in this lesson. As you read, circle the definition of each term.

Change It Up!

What are the signs of a chemical reaction?

Have you seen leaves change color in the fall or smelled sour milk? The changes in leaves and milk are caused by chemical reactions. A **chemical reaction** is the process in which atoms are rearranged to produce new substances. During a chemical reaction, the bonds that hold atoms together may be formed or broken. The properties of the substances produced in a chemical reaction are different than the properties of the original substances. So, a change in properties is a sign that a chemical reaction may have happened. For example, a solid substance called a *precipitate* may form in a solution. A color change, a change in odor, precipitate formation, and the appearance of gas bubbles are all evidence of a chemical reaction.

 **Visualize It!**

5 Identify In each blank box, identify the evidence that a chemical reaction has taken place.

B
_____
_____

A black column forms when sugar reacts with sulfuric acid.

A yellow liquid and a colorless liquid react to form a red precipitate.

C
_____
_____

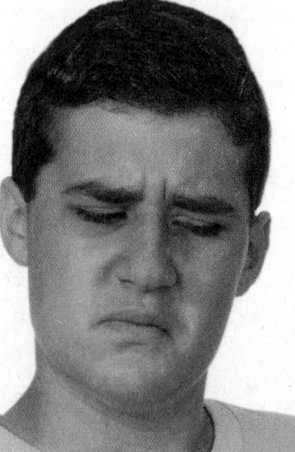

New substances that smell bad are produced when milk turns sour.

A
_____
_____

Gas bubbles form when baking soda and vinegar react.

D
_____
_____

How are chemical reactions modeled?

You can describe the substances before and after a reaction by their properties. You can also use symbols to identify the substances. Each element has its own chemical symbol. For example, H is the symbol for hydrogen, and O is the symbol for oxygen. You can use the periodic table to find the chemical symbol for any element. A **chemical formula** uses chemical symbols and numbers to represent a given substance. The chemical symbols in a chemical formula tell you what elements make up a substance. The numbers written below and to the right of chemical symbols are called *subscripts*. Subscripts tell you how many of each type of atom are in a molecule. For example, the chemical formula for water is H_2O. The subscript 2 tells you that there are two atoms of hydrogen in each water molecule. There is no subscript on O, so each molecule of water contains only one oxygen atom.

6 Identify Circle the subscript in the chemical formula below.

H_2O

A water molecule has two hydrogen (H) atoms and one oxygen (O) atom.

With Chemical Equations

To model reactions, chemical formulas can be joined together in an equation. A **chemical equation** is an expression that uses symbols to show the relationship between the starting substances and the substances that are produced by a chemical reaction. The chemical equation below shows that carbon and oxygen react to form carbon dioxide. The chemical formulas of carbon and oxygen are written to the left of the arrow. The chemical formula of carbon dioxide is written to the right of the arrow. Plus signs separate the chemical formulas of multiple products or reactants.

Visualize It!

Reactants are the substances that participate in a chemical reaction. Their chemical formulas are written on the left.

Products are the substances formed in a reaction. Their chemical formulas are written on the right.

$$C + O_2 \longrightarrow CO_2$$

An arrow known as a *yields sign* points from reactants to products.

7 Analyze Atoms of which elements are involved in this reaction?

8 Apply How many atoms of each element are in one molecule of the product?

A Balancing Act

How do chemical equations show the law of conservation of mass?

The **law of conservation of mass** states that matter is neither created nor destroyed in ordinary physical and chemical changes. Mass is conserved because the mass of products in a reaction is equal to the mass of reactants. In addition, matter is conserved because the same numbers and kinds of atoms are present in the products and reactants. When writing a chemical equation, you must be sure that the reactants and products contain the same number of atoms of each element. This is called *balancing the equation*.

You use coefficients to balance an equation. A *coefficient* is a number that is placed in front of a chemical formula. For example, $3H_2O$ represents three water molecules. The number 3 is the coefficient. For an equation to be balanced, all atoms must be counted. So, you must multiply the subscript of each element in a formula by the formula's coefficient. There are a total of six hydrogen atoms and three oxygen atoms in $3H_2O$. Only coefficients—not subscripts—can be changed when balancing equations. Changing the subscripts in the chemical formula of a compound would change the identity of that compound. For example, H_2O_2 represents the compound hydrogen peroxide, not water.

Active Reading 9 **Compare** What is the difference between a coefficient and a subscript?

_____

_____

_____

_____

_____

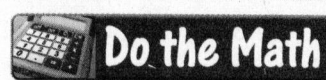

Do the Math **Sample Problem**

Follow these steps to write a balanced chemical equation.

Identify

A Count the atoms of each element in the reactants and in the product. You can see that there are more oxygen atoms in the reactants than in the product.

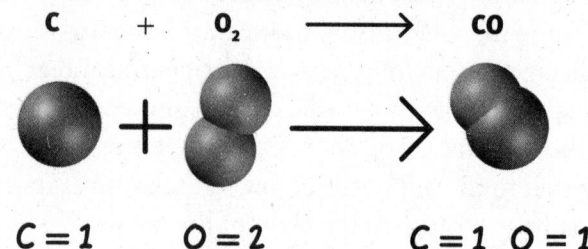

$$C \quad + \quad O_2 \quad \longrightarrow \quad CO$$

$$C = 1 \qquad O = 2 \qquad C = 1 \quad O = 1$$

Solve

B To balance the number of oxygen atoms, place the coefficient 2 in front of CO. Now the number of oxygen atoms in the reactants is the same as in the product. Next, the number of carbon atoms needs to be balanced. Place the coefficient 2 in front of C. Finally, be sure to double-check your work!

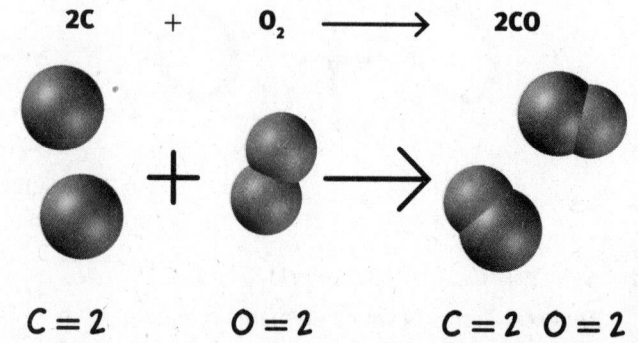

$$2C \quad + \quad O_2 \quad \longrightarrow \quad 2CO$$

$$C = 2 \qquad O = 2 \qquad C = 2 \quad O = 2$$

Do the Math You Try It

10 Analyze The data table shows results of an experiment combining baking soda and vinegar inside a closed flask. What evidence indicates a reaction occurred?

_____

_____

	Substance	Mass(g)
Reactants	Baking Soda	21
	Vinegar	15
Products	Sodium acetate	20
	Water	5
	Carbon dioxide	11

Solve

A The balanced equation for this reaction is shown below. Verify that this equation is balanced and explain how you made your verification.

vinegar + baking soda ⟶ sodium acetate + water + carbon dioxide

$$CH_3COOH + NaHCO_3 \longrightarrow NaC_2H_3O_2 + H_2O + CO_2$$

_____

_____

Explain

B State a claim about the conservation of both mass and matter in this reaction. Use evidence from the data table to support your claim.

_____

_____

Combining baking soda with vinegar results in a chemical reaction. Carbon dioxide gas is released during the reaction and can be trapped in a balloon attached to the reaction flask.

Think Outside the Book Inquiry

11 Apply Research hydrogen-powered vehicles. Create a poster that describes the advantages and disadvantages of vehicles that use hydrogen as a fuel. Be sure to include a balanced chemical equation to represent the use of hydrogen fuel.

Energy, Energy

Plants absorb energy when they carry out photosynthesis.

What happens to energy during chemical reactions?

Changes in energy are a part of all chemical reactions. Chemical reactions can either release energy or absorb energy. Energy is needed to break chemical bonds in the reactants. As new bonds form in the products, the reactants release energy. Reactions are described by the overall change in energy between the products and reactants.

Energy Can Be Absorbed

A chemical reaction that requires an input of energy is called an **endothermic reaction**. The energy taken in during an endothermic reaction is absorbed from the surroundings, usually as heat. This is why endothermic reaction mixtures often feel cold.

Photosynthesis is an example of an endothermic process that absorbs light energy. In photosynthesis, plants use energy from the sun to change carbon dioxide and water to oxygen and the sugar glucose. Overall, more energy is absorbed during photosynthesis than is released to the surroundings. Some of the absorbed energy is stored in the products: oxygen and glucose.

Energy Can Be Released

A chemical reaction in which energy is released to the surroundings is called an **exothermic reaction**. Exothermic reactions can give off energy in several forms. For example, you feel warmth and see a glow when a candle burns. Burning is an exothermic reaction. The products of the reaction are lower in energy than the reactants. Some of the energy in the bonds of the reactants changes to energy as heat and light. Exothermic reaction mixtures often feel warm when heat is released to the surroundings.

Burning a candle releases energy as heat and light.

12 **Describe** Name three everyday exothermic chemical reactions. Provide evidence to support your reasoning.

_____

_____

_____

Energy Is Always Conserved

The **law of conservation of energy** states that energy cannot be created or destroyed. However, energy can change form. The total amount of energy does not change in endothermic or exothermic reactions. For example, light energy from the sun changes into energy stored in chemical bonds during photosynthesis.

Methane (CH_4) burns when it reacts with oxygen (O_2). This reaction produces carbon dioxide (CO_2) and water (H_2O), as shown below. The reaction of methane and oxygen is exothermic. Burning methane releases energy as heat and light into the surroundings. This energy was first stored in the chemical bonds of the reactants. The energy that was stored in the bonds of the reactants is equal to the energy released plus the energy stored in the bonds of the products. The total amount of all of the types of energy is the same before and after every chemical reaction.

13 Describe What happens to the energy absorbed during an endothermic reaction?

_____
_____
_____
_____
_____

Exothermic Reaction of Methane and Oxygen

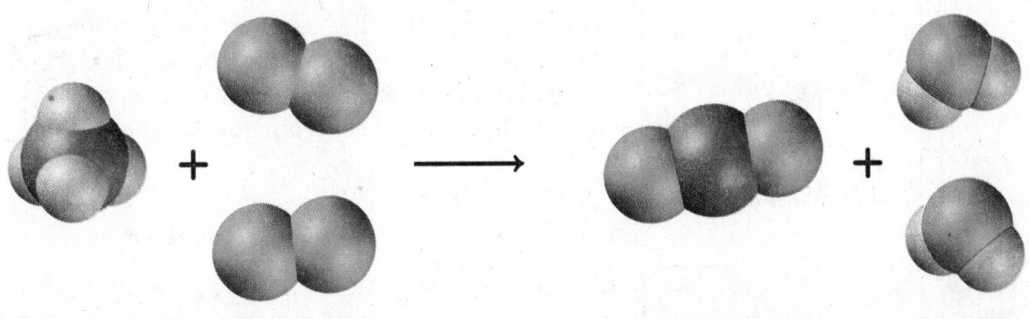

Stored energy of reactants   =   Stored energy of products and released energy

14 Compare Complete the Venn diagram to compare endothermic and exothermic reactions.

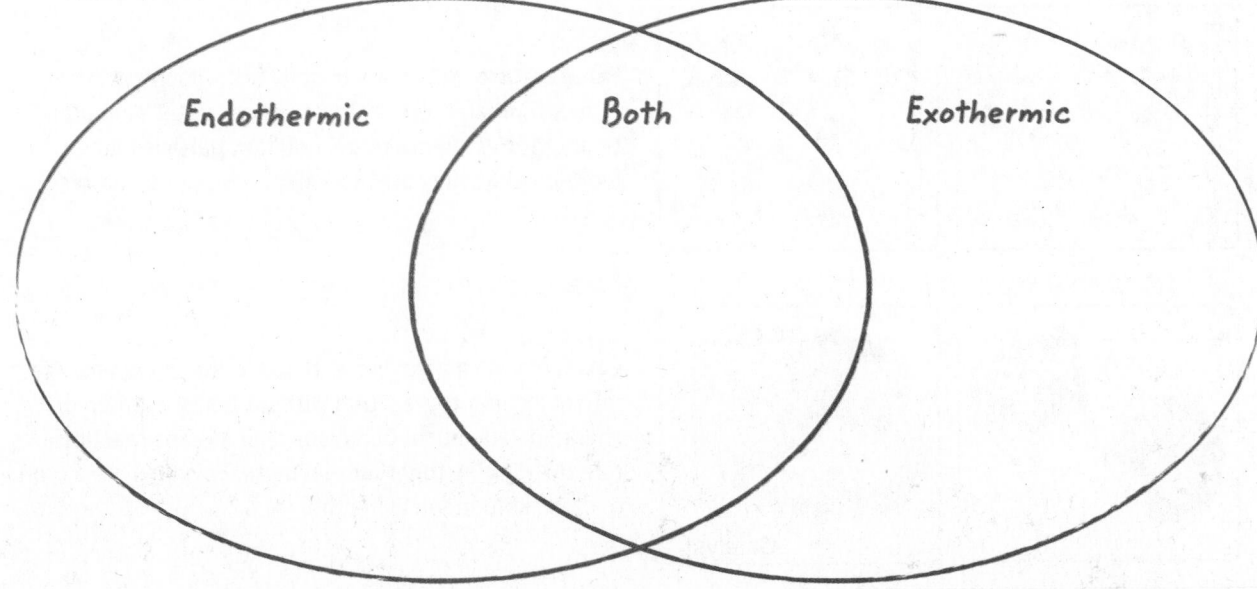

Endothermic   Both   Exothermic

The Need for Speed

Active Reading

15 Identify As you read, underline factors that affect reaction rate.

What affects the rates of reactions?

Some chemical reactions occur in less than a second. Others may take days. The rate of a reaction describes how fast the reaction occurs. For a reaction to occur, particles of the reactants must collide. Reaction rates are affected by how often the particles collide. Factors that affect reaction rates include concentration, surface area, temperature, and the presence of a catalyst.

Changing the Rate of Reaction

Decreased Rate	Increased Rate	Factors That Affect Reaction Rates
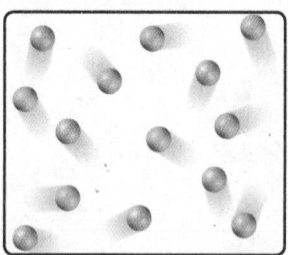	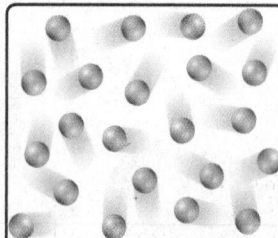	**Concentration** At higher concentrations, there are more reactants in a given volume. The reactants are more likely to collide and react. The reaction rate is higher when reactant concentration is higher.
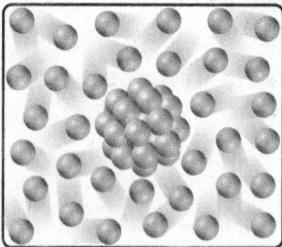	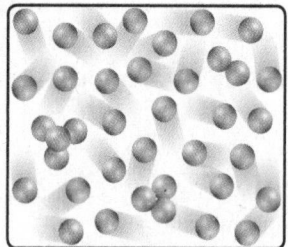	**Surface Area** The reaction rate increases when more reactant particles are exposed to one another. Crushing or grinding solids increases their surface area and the reaction rate.
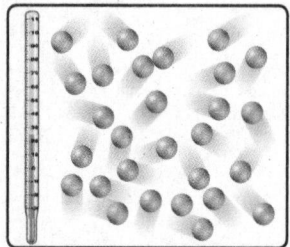	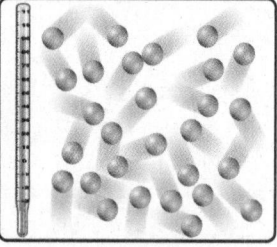	**Temperature** Reactions usually occur faster at higher temperatures. Particles move faster at higher temperatures. Because the reactant particles move more quickly, they are more likely to collide and react.
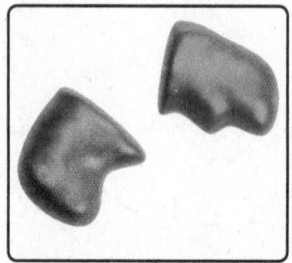	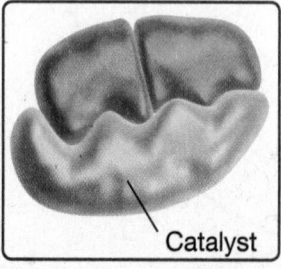 Catalyst	**Catalysts** A catalyst is a substance that increases the rate of a chemical reaction without being used up or changed very much. Catalysts can increase reaction rate by bringing together reactants. Enzymes are a type of catalyst found in living things.

Enzymes

Enzymes that increase the rates of reactions keep your body going. They help digest food so your body has the energy it needs. They also help build the molecules your body needs to grow.

Energy

All living things need energy to function. This energy is released when food molecules break down. Enzymes speed up reactions so energy is readily available.

Medical Conditions

Problems with enzymes can cause medical conditions or changes in the body. Albinism, a lack of pigment, occurs when a certain enzyme in animals does not work the way it should work.

Cleaners

Enzymes are not only found in living things. They can be used outside of the body, too. The enzymes in some cleaners help break down substances such as grease.

Extend

Inquiry

16 Describe Explain how enzymes affect reactions.

17 Claims · Evidence · Reasoning Lactose intolerance is a condition that occurs when people are unable to digest milk. Investigate and make a claim about the cause of lactose intolerance. Summarize the evidence supporting your claim.

18 Design Create a project that explains how lactose intolerance affects people and why it occurs. Present your project as a written report, a poster, or an oral report.

Visual Summary

To complete this summary, fill in the blanks with the correct word or phrase. Then, use the key below to check your answers. You can use this page to review the main concepts of the lesson.

Bonds are broken and formed during chemical reactions to produce new substances.

A chemical equation uses symbols to show the relationship between the products and the reactants.

$$C + O_2 \longrightarrow CO_2$$

19 One sign of a chemical reaction is the formation of a solid _____

20 A balanced chemical equation shows that chemical reactions follow the law of conservation of _____

Chemical Reactions

Exothermic reactions release energy to the surroundings, and endothermic reactions absorb energy from the surroundings.

Reaction rate is affected by reactant concentration, temperature, surface area, and catalysts.

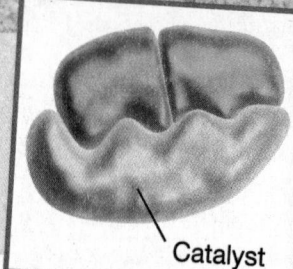

Catalyst

21 The total amount of energy before and after a chemical reaction is

_____

22 A _____ is not changed much by a chemical reaction.

23 The rate of reaction is _____ at higher temperatures because particles collide more often.

Answers: 19 precipitate; 20 mass; 21 the same; 22 catalyst; 23 faster

24 **Design** Write a procedure for how you would measure the effect of reactant concentration on the reaction rate.

Lesson Review

Vocabulary

Draw a line to connect the following terms to their definitions.

1 reactant

2 product

A a substance that is produced by a chemical reaction

B a substance that participates in a chemical reaction

Key Concepts

3 Describe What happens to the atoms in the reactants during a chemical reaction? What evidence supports your claim?

_____
_____
_____

4 Explain How does a balanced chemical equation show that mass is never lost or gained in a chemical reaction?

_____
_____
_____
_____
_____

5 Relate Describe four ways you could increase the rate of a chemical reaction.

_____
_____
_____
_____

6 Compare How do exothermic and endothermic reactions differ?

_____
_____
_____

Critical Thinking

Use this diagram to answer the following questions.

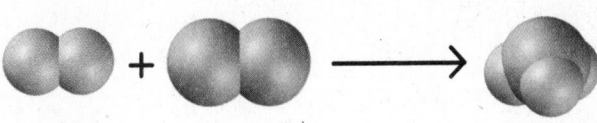

7 Model The reactants in the above reaction are hydrogen (H_2) and nitrogen (N_2). The product is ammonia (NH_3). In the space below, write a balanced chemical equation that represents the reaction.

8 Analyze This reaction releases energy as heat. Explain whether the reaction is exothermic or endothermic and whether it obeys the law of conservation of energy.

_____
_____
_____
_____
_____

9 Evaluate Two colorless solutions are mixed together. Bubbles form as the solution is stirred. Make a claim about a possible cause for this result and support your reasoning with evidence.

_____
_____
_____
_____

10 Apply The chemical formula of glucose is $C_6H_{12}O_6$. What are the names of the elements in glucose, and how many atoms of each element are present in a glucose molecule?

_____
_____

My Notes

Organic Chemistry

ESSENTIAL QUESTION

How does carbon form molecules?

By the end of this lesson, you should be able to describe how carbon forms many of the molecules essential to modern materials and living things.

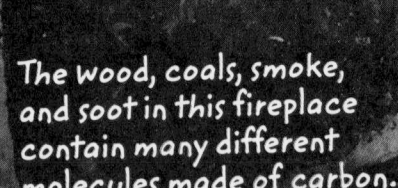

The wood, coals, smoke, and soot in this fireplace contain many different molecules made of carbon.

Lesson 2

© Houghton Mifflin Harcourt Publishing Company • Image Credits: ©mediithouse/Alamy

256 Unit 4 Interactions of Matter

Lesson Labs

Quick Labs
- Natural vs. Synthetic Fibers
- Investigate Organic Molecules

Exploration Lab
- Investigate Carbon Bonding

Engage Your Brain

1 Identify Unscramble the letters below to find materials that are made from organic compounds. Write your words on the blank lines.

LSTACPI EPPI _____

CHRTSA _____

ODOW _____

TTNCOO _____

TBLAEEEGVS _____

2 Predict Make a list of five objects in your classroom. Predict which of these objects are made of organic compounds.

_____

_____

_____

_____

Active Reading

3 Synthesize Many English words have their roots in other languages. Use the Greek words below to make an educated guess about the meaning of the word *polymer*.

Greek word	Meaning
polys	many
meros	a part

Example sentence:
Starch is a <u>polymer</u>.

polymer:

_____

_____

Vocabulary Terms

- organic compound
- carbohydrate
- hydrocarbon
- polymer
- organic acid

4 Identify As you read, place a question mark next to any words that you don't understand. When you finish reading the lesson, go back and review the text that you marked. If the information is still confusing, consult a classmate or a teacher.

© Houghton Mifflin Harcourt Publishing Company • Image Credits: ©mirfuse/Alamy

C is for Carbon

Why does carbon form many different compounds?

Take a look around you. Nearly everything that you see contains carbon in one form or another. Most atoms can form bonds with other types of atoms. Carbon has the ability to form bonds with other types of atoms, and bonds with other carbon atoms, too. The structure of a carbon atom allows it to form molecules in a wide range of sizes and shapes. Let's begin our exploration by taking a closer look at a carbon atom.

A Carbon Atom Has Four Valence Electrons

Active Reading 5 **Identify** As you read, underline the location of a valence electron in a carbon atom.

The secret to carbon's ability to form a wide variety of molecules lies in the arrangement of its electrons. A carbon atom has a total of six electrons arranged in two energy levels around its nucleus. Two of these electrons are in an inner level. The four electrons in the outer level form bonds with other atoms, and are called *valence* electrons (VAY•luhns ee•LEK•trahnz).

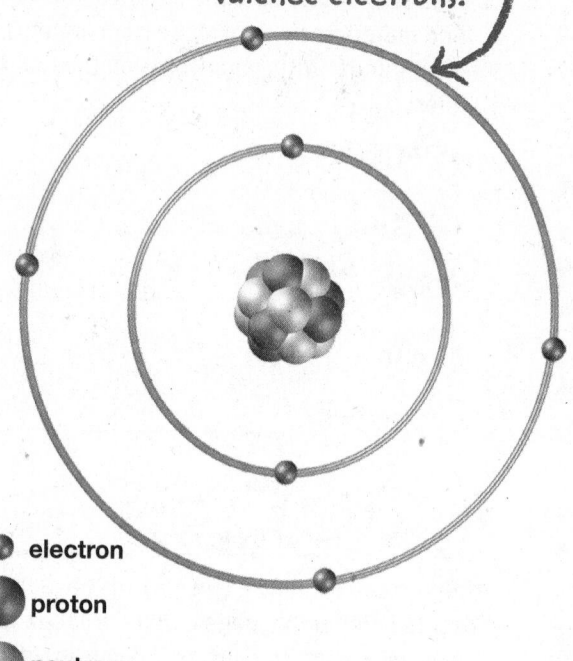

A carbon atom has four electrons in its outermost level. These are called valence electrons.

- electron
- proton
- neutron

Visualize It!

6 **Identify** Locate and circle the bonds in the molecule below.

```
    H
    |
H - C - H
    |
    H
```

A Carbon Atom Can Bond With Multiple Atoms

Bonds between two atoms always form in pairs of electrons. Sometimes one atom supplies both electrons in the pair. Sometimes each atom in a bond provides one electron to the pair. Carbon atoms form bonds by sharing their valence electrons with other atoms. Because carbon has four valence electrons, it can form bonds with up to four other atoms at the same time.

How does carbon form molecules?

Molecules are groups of atoms joined together by bonds. Carbon forms molecules by bonding with other carbon atoms and with atoms of other elements. Most molecules that do not contain carbon have only a few atoms, but molecules that contain carbon can involve hundreds or even thousands of atoms.

Carbon Can Form Single, Double, and Triple Bonds

A bond between two atoms that is made up of only two electrons is a single bond. Carbon can form up to four single bonds at one time. Carbon atoms also form double and triple bonds. A double bond is made up of two pairs of electrons (four electrons in total). A carbon atom can form a maximum of two double bonds. A triple bond is made up of three pairs of electrons (six electrons in total), so a carbon atom cannot form more than one triple bond. A single bond is represented by one short line between two atoms. A double bond is represented by two lines and a triple bond by three lines.

Carbon Molecules Can Form Chains

A carbon atom can form up to four bonds with other carbon atoms at the same time. This ability to form bonds with other carbon atoms makes it possible for long chains of carbon atoms to form. These chains can spread in a straight line, or they can branch off into other directions. The branches may also contain chains, which add to the size of the molecule.

Visualize It!

7 Identify Circle the triple bond in the diagram below.

$$H-C-C-C-H$$ (with H above and below each C)

$$H_2C=CH_2$$ (drawn as two C's double bonded with H's)

$$H-C\equiv C-H$$

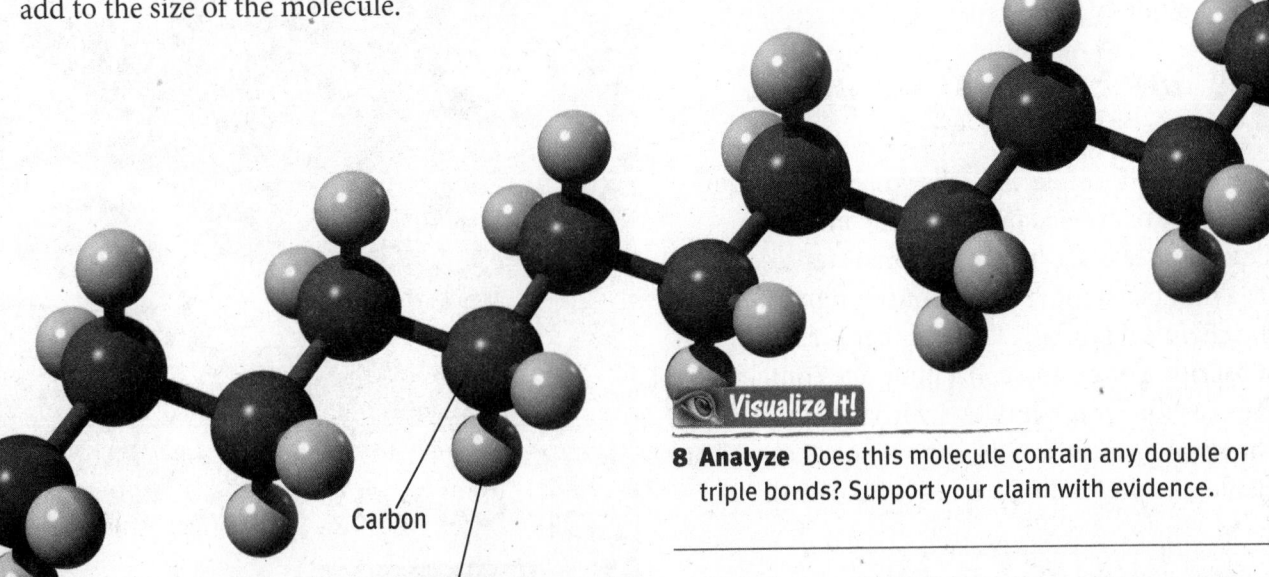

Carbon

Hydrogen

In this model of a straight-chain carbon molecule, each carbon is connected to at least one other carbon.

Visualize It!

8 Analyze Does this molecule contain any double or triple bonds? Support your claim with evidence.

_____

_____

_____

_____

The Secret Formula

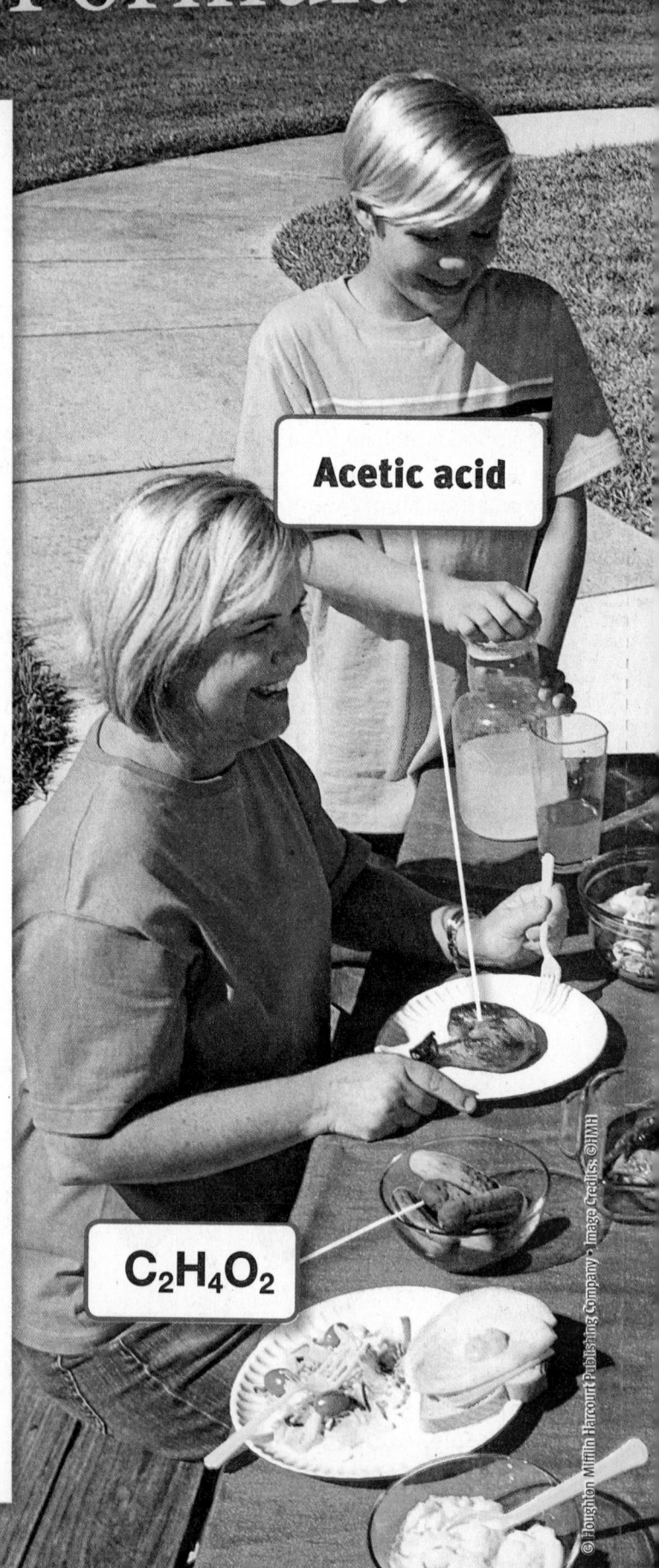

Acetic acid

$C_2H_4O_2$

What information does a chemical formula contain?

Molecules can be composed of many atoms, and their names can be complex. A chemical formula is an easier way to identify a molecule accurately. A chemical formula is a combination of letters and numbers that have specific meanings.

The Types of Atoms in the Molecule

The letters in a chemical formula identify the types of atoms in the molecule. Chemical formulas use the same one- and two-letter combinations that are used to identify elements in the periodic table. For example, a C in a chemical formula tells you that the molecule includes at least one carbon atom. An H tells you that the formula includes at least one hydrogen atom. Using chemical symbols lets you show the composition of a molecule quickly.

The Number of Each Type of Atom in the Molecule

A chemical formula also tells you how many of each type of atom is present in the molecule. The number of each type of atom is represented by a number written at the bottom right of the chemical symbol. This number is called a subscript. For example, if a molecule contains four carbon atoms and ten hydrogen atoms, the chemical formula is C_4H_{10}. If only one atom of an element is present, no subscript is needed.

9 Apply Write the chemical formula for a compound that contains 5 carbon atoms, 12 hydrogen atoms, and 1 oxygen atom. The symbol for oxygen is O.

_____

© Houghton Mifflin Harcourt Publishing Company • Image Credits: ©HMH

Nearly every food on this table contains vinegar. Vinegar's sour taste is caused by acetic acid, an organic compound. This image shows the different ways that acetic acid can be identified.

$$H_3C-\overset{\overset{\displaystyle O}{\|}}{C}-OH$$

Visualize It!

11 Apply The simplified structural formula of acetic acid is shown below. Write the full structural formula for this compound.

$$H_3C-\overset{\overset{\displaystyle O}{\|}}{C}-OH$$

What are the types of structural formulas?

A chemical formula tells you the types and numbers of atoms in a molecule but not how they are bonded together. A structural formula shows how atoms are connected. There are two types of structural formulas: full and simplified.

Active Reading 10 **Identify** As you read, underline the characteristics of the full structural formula and the simplified structural formula.

Full Structural Formulas

A full structural formula shows all of the bonds between the atoms of a molecule. For example, methanol (METH•uh•nawl) has the chemical formula CH_4O. The formula shows that methanol is composed of one carbon atom, four hydrogen atoms, and one oxygen atom. How are these atoms bonded to form a molecule of methanol?

If we draw the bonds between each atom, we will see the full structure of methanol:

$$H-\overset{\overset{\displaystyle H}{|}}{\underset{\underset{\displaystyle H}{|}}{C}}-O-H$$

Now we can see that the carbon and oxygen atoms are connected by a single bond. We can also see how the hydrogen atoms are arranged around the carbon and oxygen atoms.

Simplified Structural Formulas

Sometimes we need to see how atoms relate to one another within a molecule but do not need to see every bond. Then we can use a simplified structural formula. The atoms bonded to each central carbon atom are grouped together. The simplified structural formula for methanol is shown below.

$$H_3COH$$

You can now see how the hydrogen atoms are arranged around the carbon atom and the oxygen atom.

It's All Organic

Where are organic compounds found?

Organic compounds serve many different purposes and are found in both non-living and living things. An **organic compound** (ohr•GAN•ik KAHM•pownd) is a chemical compound that is composed of carbon, hydrogen, and possibly other elements.

In Nonliving Things

Many of the nonliving things we use every day are made of organic compounds. The nylon used to make fishing line, the special materials used to make waterproof backpacks, and the fuel used for heating our homes are made up of organic molecules. In many cases, organic compounds in nonliving things were originally in living things. For example, the paper in a newspaper contains organic compounds that came from trees.

In Living Things

Active Reading 12 **Identify** As you read, underline the two main roles of organic molecules in living things.

Living things are also made up of organic compounds. Many organic molecules are found in the human body, other animals, trees, and plants. Organic compounds provide energy and structure for living things to grow and change.

Visualize It!

13 Identify List two nonliving and two living things in the photograph that contain carbon compounds.

Nonliving:

_____

_____

Living:

_____

_____

What other elements make up organic compounds?

Organic compounds are usually composed of mostly carbon and hydrogen. But they can also include other elements. These elements include fluorine, chlorine, oxygen, phosphorus, nitrogen, and sulfur. Plastic pipes used for plumbing are made of an organic compound that includes chlorine. An organic compound that includes fluorine is used to make nonstick surfaces on cookware. Nitrogen is found in the nucleic acids that make up DNA.

Periodic Table of Elements

The periodic table lists all the chemical elements that are currently known. The table contains 18 groups of elements—a portion of groups 13–18 is shown below.

14 Identify Each highlighted element below is found in an organic compound. Based on your reading, identify the item that contains each element.

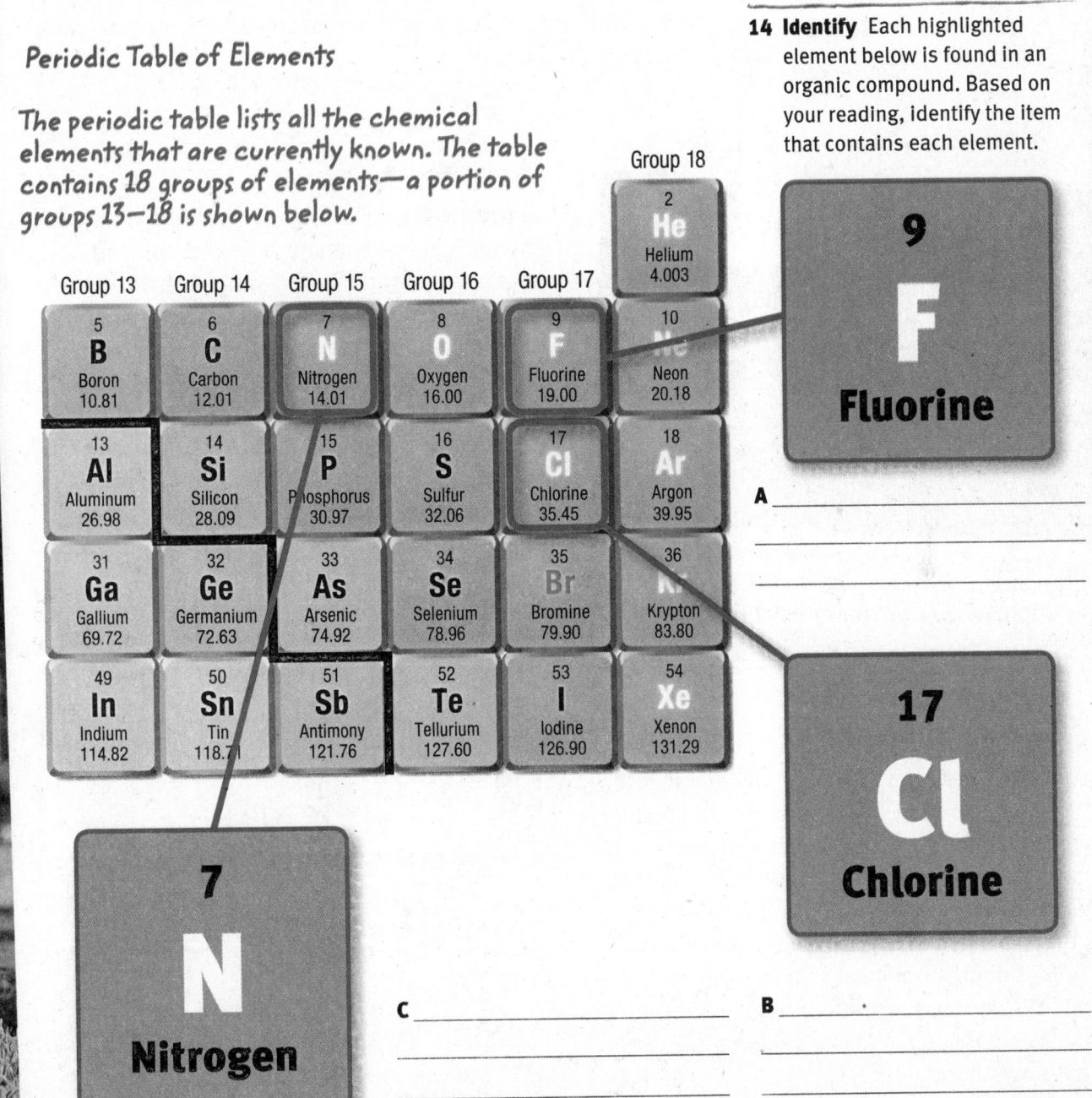

A _____

_____

_____

B _____

_____

C _____

_____

Shhh...It's Classified!

How are organic compounds classified?

Active Reading

15 Identify As you read this page and the next, underline the characteristics of each type of organic compound.

With so many different types of organic compounds, chemists need a way to keep them organized. Chemists classify these compounds based on their composition and structure. Three of the classes of organic compounds are hydrocarbons, organic acids, and carbohydrates.

Butane

The wax in the candles and the butane in the lighter are both made of hydrocarbons.

Hydrocarbons

A **hydrocarbon** (HY•druh•kar•buhn) is an organic compound that contains only carbon atoms and hydrogen atoms. The simplest hydrocarbon is methane, CH_4. It has just one carbon atom bonded to four hydrogen atoms. However, not all hydrocarbons are this small—some hydrocarbons have more than 20 carbon atoms! Most long-chain hydrocarbons are found in oils and waxes. Their high energy content makes them ideal fuels.

Citric acid

These citrus fruits get their tangy taste from citric acid, which is an organic acid.

Organic Acids

An **organic acid** is an organic compound that has acidic properties. All organic acids contain carbon, hydrogen, oxygen, and sometimes other atoms. Organic acids are identified by a group of atoms called a *carboxyl* (kar•BAHK•suhl) group, COOH. In a carboxyl group, one oxygen atom is double-bonded to a carbon atom. The other oxygen in the group is single-bonded to the same carbon atom and a hydrogen atom. Organic acids are essential for life.

Sucrose

Sugars are the simplest forms of carbohydrates.

Carbohydrates

A **carbohydrate** (kar•boh•HY•drayt) is a neutral organic compound containing carbon, hydrogen, and oxygen. Carbohydrates often contain two hydrogen atoms for every one oxygen atom. Many of the foods we eat contain carbohydrates. Carbohydrates are one of nature's energy stores. Living things break down carbohydrates and use the energy released to grow and reproduce.

Carbohydrates can be simple or complex. Simple carbohydrates are found in foods like fruit, vegetables, and milk. The sugars in the photo above contain sucrose, a simple carbohydrate found in sugar cane and sugar beets. Complex carbohydrates are long chains of sugar molecules. Plants make complex carbohydrates to store energy and for support.

Think Outside the Book

16 **Synthesize** Candle wax belongs to a class of organic compounds called lipids. Look up the relationship between lipids and organic acids. Share your findings with the class.

17 **Apply** Determine whether each structure below represents a hydrocarbon, an organic acid, or a carbohydrate. The first one has been done for you.

organic acid

A _____

B _____

© Houghton Mifflin Harcourt Publishing Company • Image Credits: ©HMH

What other structures can organic compounds form?

The carbon atom's unique bonding properties allow it to form more than just straight or branched chains. For example, a chain of carbon atoms can curl around and attach to itself to form a ring. Or the same small unit of atoms can repeat over and over again to form what is called a *polymer*. Many compounds that we encounter every day contain rings or are polymers.

Rings

Active Reading **18 Identify** As you read, underline examples of organic compounds that contain rings.

A ring of carbon atoms can form from three or more carbon atoms. Some molecules include rings formed from six carbon atoms that are connected by alternating double and single bonds. These compounds are called *aromatic compounds*. Many aromatic compounds have distinctive odors. Examples of aromatic compounds include benzene, vanillin, and aspirin.

Polymers

Polymers (PAHL•uh•merz) are molecules composed of the same repeating small groups of atoms joined together in long chains. The repeating groups are called *monomers* (MAHN•uh•merz). Some molecules essential for life, such as fats and nucleic acids, are polymers. Complex carbohydrates, such as cellulose, are polymers of sugars. Some people think the words *plastic* and *polymer* mean the same thing, but not every polymer is a plastic. Plastics are solid, flexible polymers made from petroleum and used in many products.

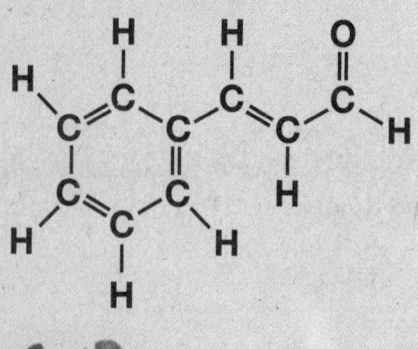

Cinnamaldehyde is the aromatic compound that gives cinnamon its distinctive aroma.

Visualize It!

19 Apply The structure below is a portion of a plastic called polyvinyl chloride (PVC). Place square brackets around one of its monomers.

$$-C-C-C-C-C-C-$$

Technology Can Be Organic

Flat-panel screens are common on many electronic devices today. Many of these screens use organic compounds in a device called an organic light-emitting diode (OLED). An OLED display doesn't need to be lit from behind, so the screens can be thinner and lighter, making them very useful for portable devices. These panels also require less energy than liquid crystal display (LCD) screens.

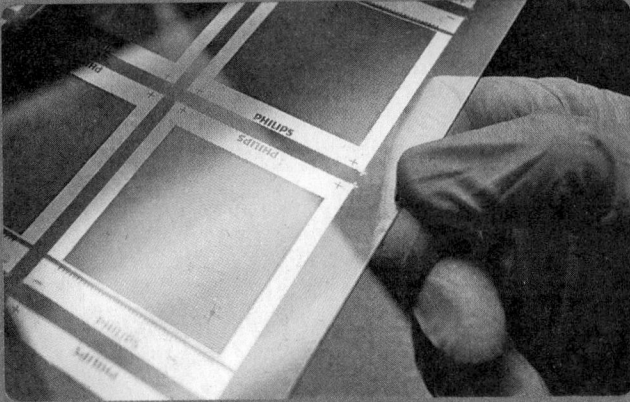

OLED Panels Are Versatile

One of the advantages of OLED panels is that they do not have to be flat to work properly. Technology companies are beginning to design products with curved and folding screens to take advantage of this unique property of OLEDs.

How OLED Panels Are Made

The OLED panels are made of several layers of material that conduct electric current. Some organic layers are composed of small organic molecules, while others are composed of polymers. When a current passes through the organic layers, light is emitted.

Extend

Inquiry

20 Explain Why are organic compounds used in electronic displays?

21 Predict How might the increasing use of OLED technology help reduce energy consumption? Explain your reasoning.

22 Research Use the Internet to discover different applications for OLED technology and create a poster display with your findings.

Visual Summary

To complete this summary, fill in the correct word or phrase. Then, use the key below to check your answers. You can use this page to review the main concepts of the lesson.

A carbon atom can form bonds with up to four other atoms at the same time.

23 A carbon atom forms bonds with its _____ electrons.

Carbon atoms can form long chains, branched chains, rings, and polymers.

Organic Chemistry

Classes of organic compounds include hydrocarbons, organic acids, and carbohydrates.

Organic compounds are found in both living and nonliving things.

24 Plants and animals use organic compounds for _____ and _____

25 The double bond in a carboxyl group is located between a(n) _____ atom and a carbon atom.

Answers: 23 valence; 24 energy, structure; 25 oxygen

26 **Claims · Evidence · Reasoning** Make a claim about how carbon is able to form so many different types of compounds. Support your claim with evidence and explain your reasoning.

Lesson Review

Vocabulary

Draw a line to connect the following terms to their definitions.

1 organic acid

2 hydrocarbon

3 polymer

4 carbohydrate

A an organic compound that contains only carbon and hydrogen

B a large molecule composed of smaller repeating units

C an organic compound that behaves like an acid

D a neutral organic compound that contains carbon, oxygen, and hydrogen

Key Concepts

5 Explain Why are the valence electrons of carbon important?

_____

_____

_____

_____

_____

6 Distinguish Do hydrocarbons differ structurally from carbohydrates? Make a claim and use evidence to support your reasoning.

_____

_____

_____

_____

7 Relate How are monomers related to polymers?

_____

_____

_____

Critical Thinking

Use this chemical structure to answer the following questions.

8 Categorize What types of bonds are present in this molecule?

_____

_____

9 Analyze What elements are present in this molecule?

_____

_____

10 Solve What is the chemical formula of this organic compound?

_____

_____

11 Debate Can aromatic compounds belong to other classes of compounds? Explain your answer.

_____

_____

_____

_____

_____

12 Apply How does a carbon atom's ability to form bonds with other carbon atoms allow it to form large molecules?

_____

_____

_____

My Notes

Shirley Ann Jackson

PHYSICIST AND EDUCATOR

How can you make contributions to many areas of science all at once? One way is to promote the study of science by others. This is precisely what physicist Dr. Shirley Ann Jackson does as the president of Rensselaer Polytechnic Institute in Troy, New York.

Earlier in her career, she was a research scientist, investigating the electrical and optical properties of matter. Engineers used her research to help develop products for the telecommunications industry. She later became a professor of physics at Rutgers University in New Jersey.

In 1995, President Bill Clinton appointed Dr. Jackson to chair the U.S. Nuclear Regulatory Commission (NRC). The NRC is responsible for promoting the safe use of nuclear energy. At the NRC, Dr. Jackson used her knowledge of how the particles that make up matter interact and can generate energy. She also used her leadership skills. She helped to start the International Nuclear Regulators Association. This group made it easier for officials from many nations to discuss issues of nuclear safety.

Dr. Jackson's interest in science started when she observed bees in her backyard. She is still studying the world around her, making careful observations, and taking actions based on what she learns. These steps for learning were the foundation for all her later contributions to science. As a student, Dr. Jackson learned the same things about matter and energy that you are learning.

Nuclear power plant

Language Arts Connection

Research how nuclear energy is generated, what it can be used for, and what concerns surround it. Write a summary report to the government outlining the risks and benefits of using nuclear energy.

JOB BOARD

Chemical Technician

What You'll Do: Help chemists and chemical engineers in laboratory tests, observe solids, liquids, and gases for research or development of new products. You might handle hazardous chemicals or toxic materials.

Where You Might Work: Mostly indoors in laboratories or manufacturing plants, but may do some research outdoors.

Education: An associate's degree in applied science or science-related technology, specialized technical training, or a bachelor's degree in chemistry, biology, or forensic science is needed.

Other Job Requirements: You need to follow written steps of procedures and to accurately record measurements and observations. You need to understand the proper handling of hazardous materials.

Chef

What You'll Do: Prepare, season, and cook food, keep a clean kitchen, supervise kitchen staff, and buy supplies and equipment.

Where You Might Work: Restaurants, hotels, the military, schools, and in your own kitchen as a private caterer.

Education: Many chefs gain on-the-job training without formal culinary school training. However, you can also learn cooking skills at culinary institutes and earn a two-year or four-year degree.

Other Job Requirements: Your job will require you to be on your feet for many hours and lift heavy equipment and boxes of food.

PEOPLE IN SCIENCE NEWS

Andy Goldsworthy

Changing Matter Is Art

Andy Goldsworthy is interested in how matter changes over time. He is inspired by the changes that occur in nature. As a sculptor, he uses materials found in nature, like snow, ice, twigs, and leaves. Many of his sculptures do not last for very long, but these materials show the changing state of matter. For example, for one of his art projects, he made 13 large snowballs in the winter and placed them in cold storage. In the middle of summer, he placed the snowballs around London. It took five days for the snowballs to melt. During that time they were reminders of a wider world of nature. Movement, change, light, growth, and decay are factors that affect his pieces. Because his work is constantly changing, Goldsworthy takes photographs of his sculptures.

Nuclear Reactions

ESSENTIAL QUESTION

How do nuclear reactions differ from chemical reactions?

By the end of this lesson, you should be able to distinguish nuclear reactions from chemical reactions and compare the types of nuclear reactions.

S8P1.b Thermal energy and movement of particles

Nuclear reactions are the source of energy of all of the stars in the universe.

Engage Your Brain

1 Identify Fill in the blank with the words or phrases that you think correctly completes the following sentence. Use the model to help you.

Helium

The nucleus of this atom contains two

_____ and

two _____

2 Relate List three things that you think of when you hear the word *radioactivity*.

_____

_____

_____

_____

_____

_____

Active Reading

3 Synthesize Many English words have their roots in other languages. Use the Latin words below to make an educated guess about the meaning of the words *fission* and *fusion*.

Latin word	Meaning
fissus	to split
fusus	to melt

Example sentence:
The nuclei of large atoms undergo <u>fission</u> in nuclear power plants.

fission:

_____

_____

Example sentence:
In stars, small atoms undergo <u>fusion</u> to form larger atoms.

fusion:

_____

_____

Vocabulary Terms

• nuclear reaction
• isotope
• radioactive decay
• nuclear fission
• nuclear fusion

4 Identify This list contains the vocabulary terms you'll learn in this lesson. As you read, circle the definition of each term.

New Identity

What happens during a nuclear reaction?

In 1896, French physicist Henri Becquerel (ahn•REE beh•KREL) made a discovery. He was studying minerals that released energy after being exposed to sunlight. The released energy produced images on photographic plates. During cloudy weather, Becquerel stored his materials in a drawer. When he developed the photographic plate, he was surprised to see that even without sunlight, one of the minerals left an image on the plate. Becquerel inferred that the image was made by energy given off by uranium, an element in the mineral. Marie and Pierre Curie began their studies of uranium in Becquerel's lab. Their research led to the discovery of two new elements: polonium and radium. These elements also gave off energy on their own. This energy was released as the result of a nuclear reaction. A **nuclear reaction** is a change that affects the nucleus of an atom. Nuclear reactions differ from chemical reactions in several ways.

Henri Becquerel discovered that energy released from uranium ore produced an image on a photographic plate, even in the dark.

Some Mass Changes to Energy

One difference is that chemical reactions do not change the mass of atoms. However, nuclear reactions do change the mass of atoms by a very small amount. This mass changes into the energy that is released during the reaction. The amount of energy produced from a certain mass can be calculated. Energy (E) is equal to mass (m) times the speed of light (c) squared.

$$E = mc^2$$

The speed of light is equal to 3.00×10^8 m/s. So, a small amount of mass can change into a large amount of energy. All nuclear reactions release energy. However, only some chemical reactions release energy.

Active Reading **5 Summarize** What happens to the mass of atoms during a nuclear reaction?

_____

_____

_____

© Houghton Mifflin Harcourt Publishing Company • Image Credits: (t) ©SPL/Photo Researchers, Inc.; (b) ©Harry Taylor/Dorling Kindersley/Getty Images

The Nucleus Changes

Another difference between chemical and nuclear reactions is that chemical reactions do not change the nucleus of atoms, but nuclear reactions do. Each atom of an element has the same number of protons in its nucleus. Nuclear reactions can change the identity of atoms by changing the number of protons in the nucleus. For example, a nuclear reaction that decreases the number of protons can change a beryllium atom into a lithium atom. On the other hand, nuclear reactions that change the number of neutrons do not change an atom into a new element.

Atoms with the same number of protons but different numbers of neutrons are called **isotopes**. For example, isotopes of lithium must have three protons but can have different numbers of neutrons. So, isotopes of the same element have different mass numbers. The mass number is added to the end of the name of an element to identify isotopes, such as lithium-6 and lithium-7.

Active Reading

6 Compare As you read, underline what happens during a nuclear reaction that does not happen during a chemical reaction.

Visualize It!

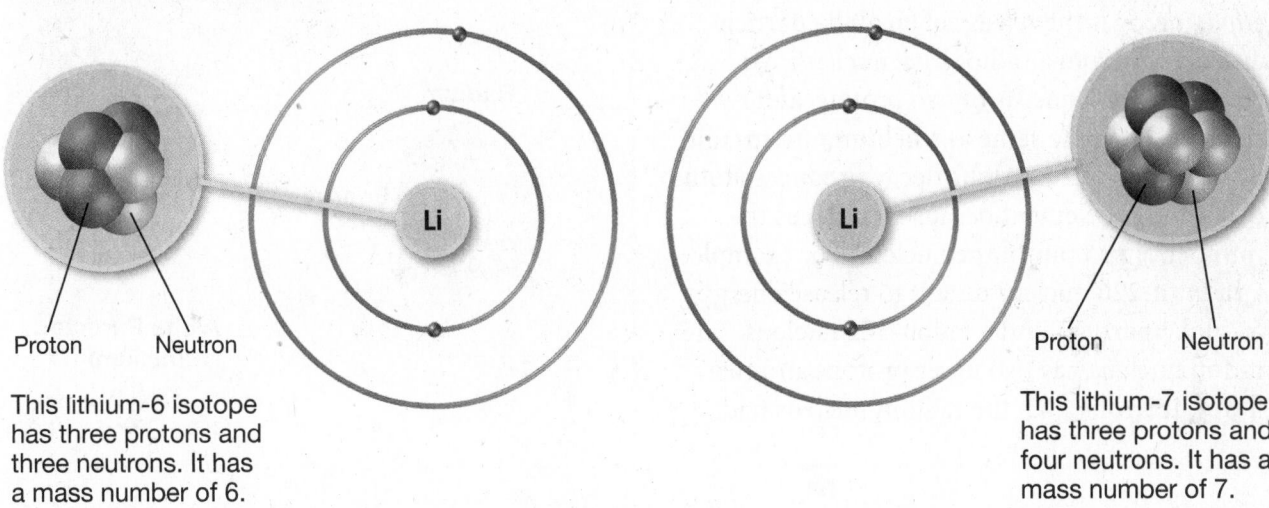

Proton   Neutron

This lithium-6 isotope has three protons and three neutrons. It has a mass number of 6.

Proton   Neutron

This lithium-7 isotope has three protons and four neutrons. It has a mass number of 7.

7 Model Draw an isotope of beryllium-9 that has two more particles in the nucleus than the beryllium-7 isotope below. Label the protons and neutrons in your model.

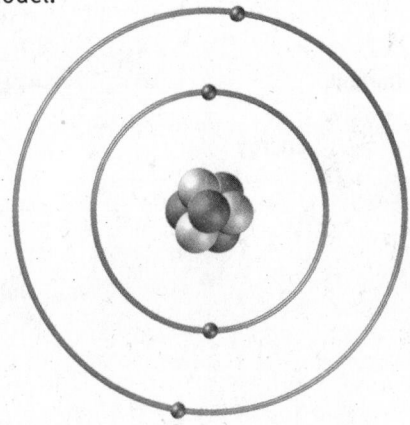

Just Passing Through

What are the types of radioactive decay?

![Active Reading]

8 Identify As you read this page and the next, underline the products of each type of radioactive decay.

The nuclei of some isotopes are not stable. Unstable nuclei undergo radioactive decay. **Radioactive decay** is a nuclear reaction in which an unstable nucleus can give off energy and, sometimes, particles. The particles and energy given off are called *nuclear radiation*. Unstable nuclei continue to decay until they form stable nuclei. Three kinds of radioactive decay are alpha decay, beta decay, and gamma decay.

Alpha Decay

Alpha decay is the release of an alpha particle and energy from a radioactive nucleus. An alpha particle consists of two protons and two neutrons. It is the same as a helium nucleus and has a charge of 2+. Alpha decay produces atoms of a different element because it reduces the number of protons in the nucleus. For example, a radium-226 nucleus decays to release energy, an alpha particle, and a radon-222 nucleus. The radon nucleus has two fewer protons and two fewer neutrons than the radium nucleus had.

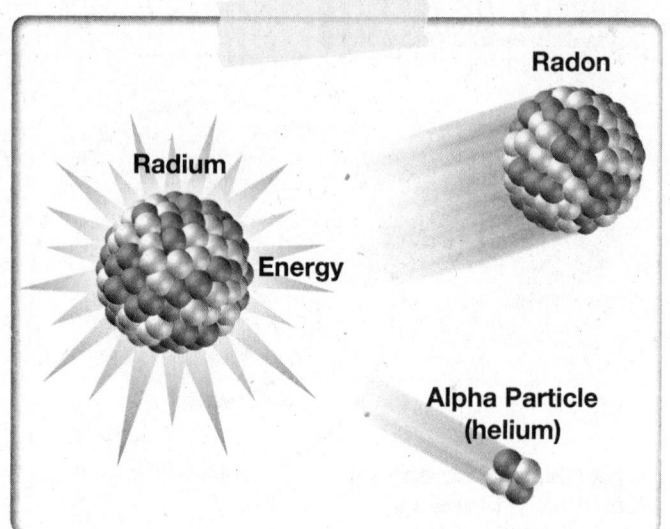

Beta Decay

A beta particle and energy are released during *beta decay*. There are two types of beta particles: positrons and electrons. Both particles have a mass of almost zero. Positrons have a charge of 1+. Electrons have a charge of 1−. A proton can break apart into a neutron and a positron that is released. A neutron can break apart into a proton and an electron that is released. Beta decay changes a nucleus into that of a different element. The atomic number increases when electrons are released. For example, carbon-14 decays to form nitrogen-14 and an electron. The atomic number decreases when positrons are released.

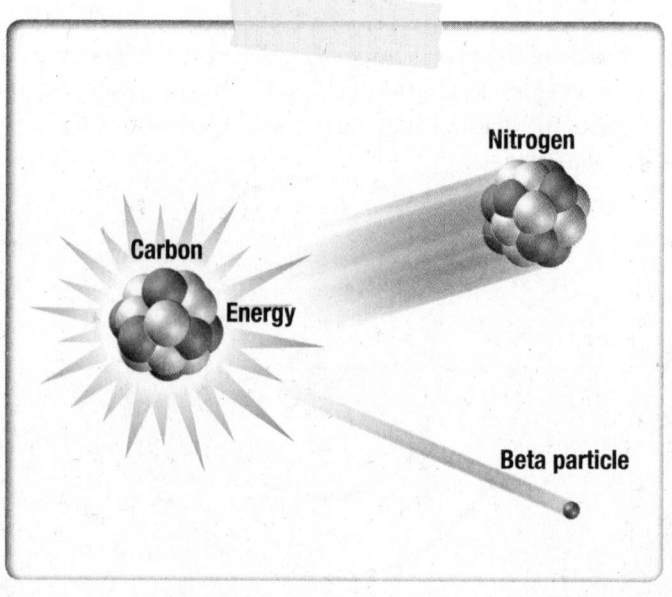

Gamma Decay

Gamma rays are released during *gamma decay*. Gamma rays are high-energy radiation and have no mass and no charge. Gamma decay alone does not change the number of particles in the nucleus. Therefore, it does not form a different element or isotope. Some of the energy released during alpha decay and beta decay is in the form of gamma rays.

How does radioactive decay affect matter?

These three forms of decay affect matter differently because the radiation they produce has different masses, charges, and energy. The model below shows their ability to penetrate, or go through, matter. Even though alpha particles do not penetrate deeply, they can still damage living cells. They can break apart chemical bonds when they hit substances. Beta particles can also break bonds in the molecules in cells and cause illness. Gamma rays have the greatest penetrating power. They can pass through tissues in the body. They can also remove electrons from atoms, which can damage cells and weaken metals. Large doses of gamma radiation lead to radiation sickness. People with radiation sickness may experience fatigue, vomiting, hair loss, and other symptoms. Long-term exposure to radiation increases the risk of cancer.

Active Reading

9 Identify What are two effects of too much exposure to radiation?

_____

_____

_____

_____

Visualize It!

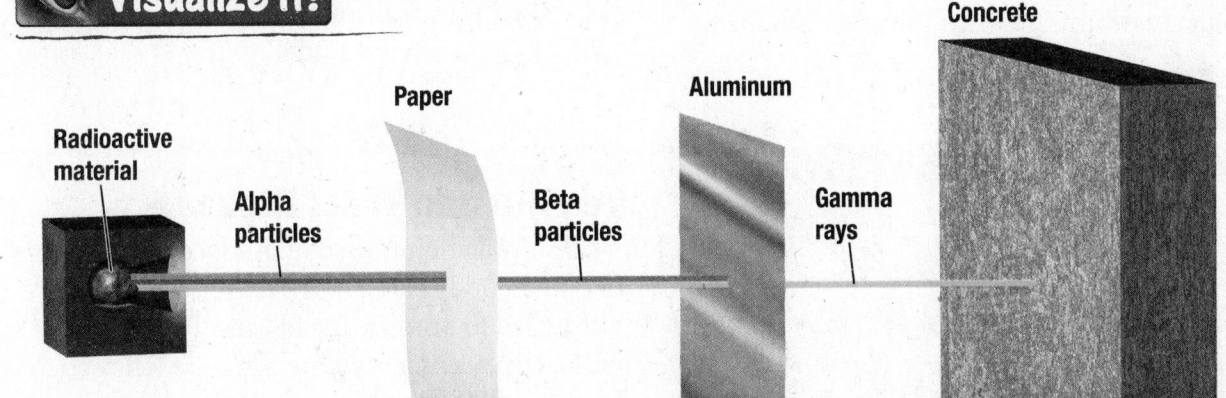

Alpha particles have the largest mass and charge. They lose energy quickly when they go through matter. They cannot pass through paper or cloth.

Beta particles have a very small mass and a small charge. They can penetrate more than alpha particles. They can pass through paper or cloth but not thin metal.

Gamma rays easily pass through most matter. They are high in energy and have no mass or charge. Only dense, thick material blocks them.

10 Claims · Evidence · Reasoning Which types of nuclear radiation can pass through a T-shirt? State evidence to support your claim. _____

© Houghton Mifflin Harcourt Publishing Company

How is radioactive decay used?

What do smoke detectors and sterile bandages have in common? They are both technologies that use radioactive decay. Many smoke detectors contain a small amount of the radioactive element americium. This element emits alpha particles that are used to detect smoke. Gamma rays are used to kill bacteria on bandages. Radioactive isotopes are used in other ways, too. Radioactive decay is used to test the thickness of metal sheets and to find leaks in pipes. Even scientists and doctors use radioactive decay.

To Date Remains

Different elements decay at different rates. Some decay in seconds. Others decay over billions of years. Scientists use radioactive isotopes to determine the age of artifacts, remains, and fossils. Geologists often want to know the age of rocks that formed millions of years ago. They can find the age of some rocks by measuring an element in the rocks that decays very slowly. Carbon decays more quickly. Scientists use carbon to date the remains of animals that died less than 50,000 years ago. Scientists need a very small sample of bone to measure carbon isotopes. They measure the number of isotopes in the bone sample to determine when the organism died.

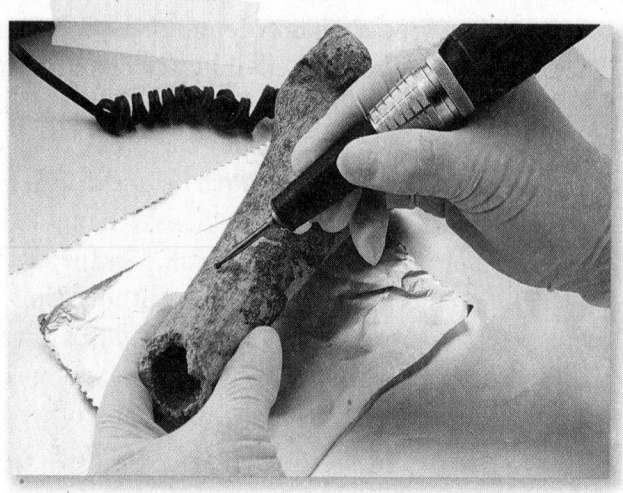

Only a small sample of bone is needed to date the bone using radioactive decay.

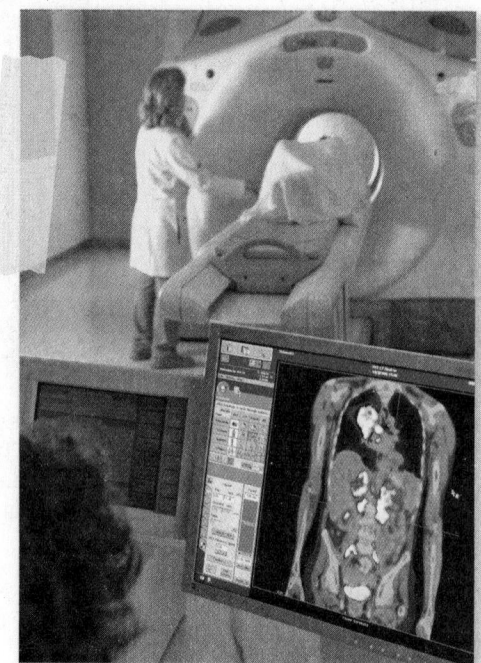

Beta decay can be used to make images of the organs inside the body.

To Find and Treat Disease

Nuclear radiation is used to produce images of human body parts. Radioactive tracers are often used to produce the images. Tracers are radioactive elements whose paths are followed as they decay. A special instrument is used to detect radiation from the tracer. Radioactive decay is also used to treat certain diseases. Radioactive material inserted into a tumor can kill the cancer cells that make up the tumor.

Radioactive Decay in Medicine

Medical technologies that involve radioactive decay are used to detect and treat cancer. Many methods use tracers that decay quickly inside the body. Tracers are monitored as they move through the patient's body to the organ of interest.

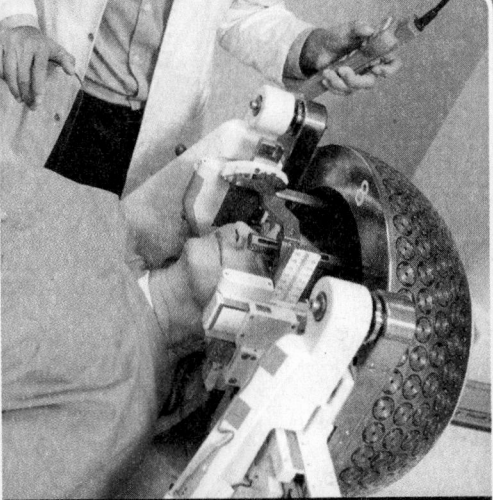

PET Scans

Positron emission tomography (PET) is often used to study brain activity. Areas of the brain that are more active than others absorb more of the radioactive tracer. Tumors are more active than other areas.

Gamma Knife

A gamma knife is a medical device that can be used to destroy brain tumors. Instead of cutting into the patient, it delivers doses of gamma rays to very precise areas. The radiation destroys the tumor tissue.

Radioactive Tracers

Radioactive tracers can be used to detect cancer. A radioactive isotope of technetium helps doctors find tumors in bones. The tracer is absorbed by bone cells and builds up in bone tumors. Tumors show up as bright spots in images because they give off more radiation than other body parts.

Extend

Inquiry

12 Infer Why is it important that radioactive tracers decay quickly?

13 Research Investigate another medical technology that uses nuclear radiation to detect or treat cancer. Make a claim about how nuclear radiation makes cancer detection or treatment possible. Summarize evidence to support your claim and explain your reasoning.

14 Distinguish X-ray images are made by passing x-rays through the body to develop film that is sensitive to x-rays. The x-rays are produced by a machine. In what way are x-ray images different from the images taken using radioactive tracers?

Breaking Up

What is nuclear fission?

Some atoms have very large, unstable nuclei. The nuclear reaction in which a large, unstable nucleus breaks into two smaller nuclei is called **nuclear fission**. The smaller nuclei are more stable than the larger nucleus was. Nuclear fission also releases neutrons and a large amount of energy. Like alpha decay and beta decay, fission changes the nucleus of the atom that breaks apart.

The nuclei of some plutonium and uranium isotopes undergo nuclear fission naturally. Other isotopes can be forced to undergo nuclear fission by striking them with neutrons. The model below shows one of the fission reactions that can happen when a neutron hits a uranium-235 nucleus. Nuclei of the atoms krypton-91 and barium-142 form. Three neutrons are released. A small amount of the mass of the uranium nucleus changes to energy.

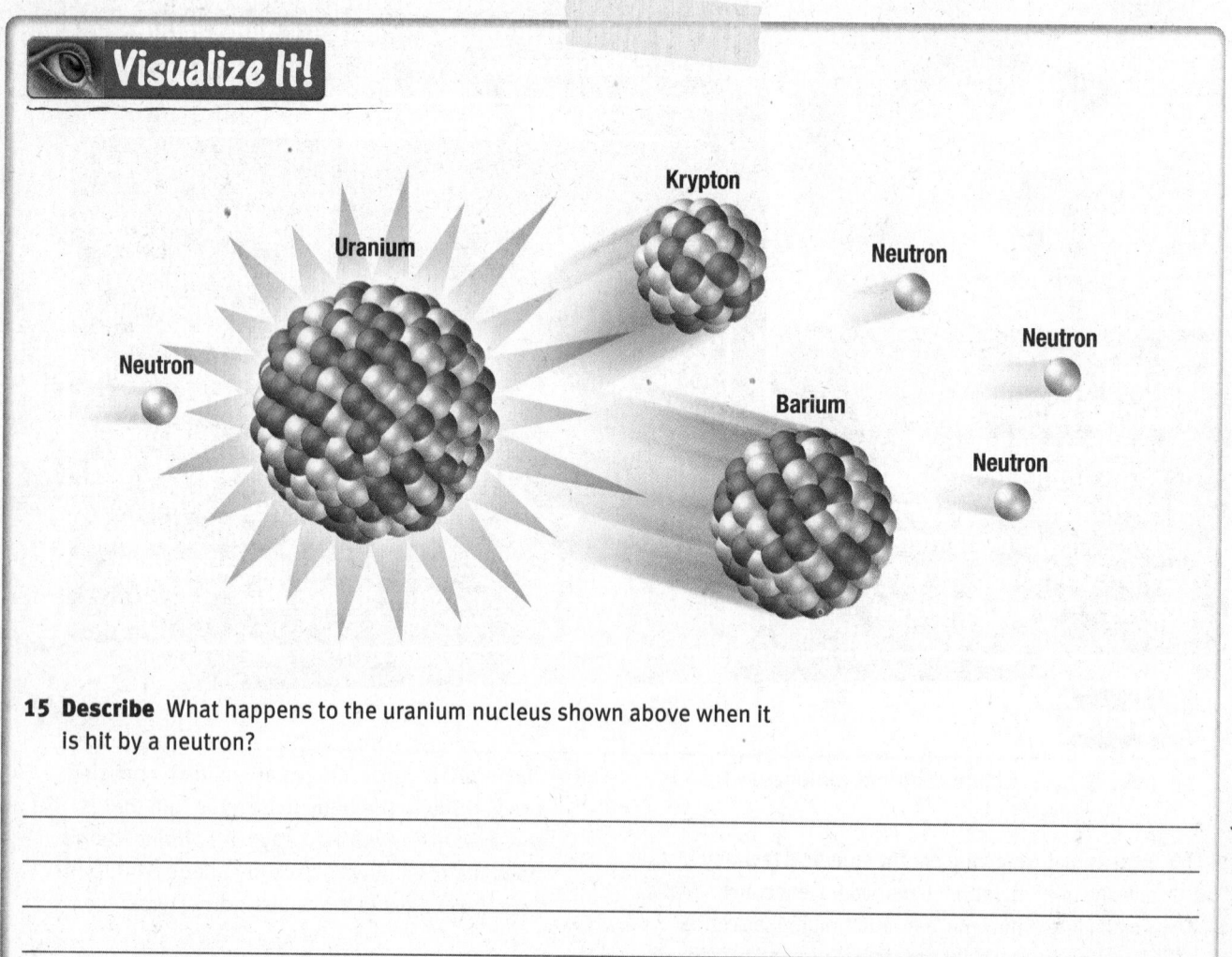

Visualize It!

Krypton

Uranium

Neutron

Neutron

Neutron

Barium

Neutron

15 Describe What happens to the uranium nucleus shown above when it is hit by a neutron?

_____

_____

_____

_____

How are mass and energy conserved?

Suppose you could measure the mass of the two nuclei and three neutrons released during this fission reaction. You would find that their total mass is slightly less than the mass of the uranium nucleus and neutron. Where is the missing mass? In a fission reaction, the missing mass was transformed into energy. The amount of energy given off by single fission reaction is small. But a large amount of energy is produced by the fission of many atoms.

What is the source of nuclear power?

Uranium-235 is the fuel used in nuclear power plants. Neutrons are released when a uranium nucleus splits apart. Some of these neutrons then hit other uranium nuclei. These uranium nuclei split apart, too. With each fission reaction, more neutrons are produced that can cause more fission reactions. More and more energy and neutrons are given off. This continuous series of fission reactions is known as a *nuclear chain reaction*.

An uncontrolled chain reaction gives off huge amounts of energy very quickly. The nuclear explosions of atomic bombs are the result of uncontrolled chain reactions. But chain reactions can be controlled. Nuclear power plants turn the energy released by these controlled reactions into electrical energy.

Do the Math You Try It

17 Graph Make a bar graph of the number of neutrons released by the reactions at each of the three stages of the chain reaction below. Add a bar to show the predicted number of neutrons released at the fourth stage if two neutrons from each fission reaction hit another nucleus.

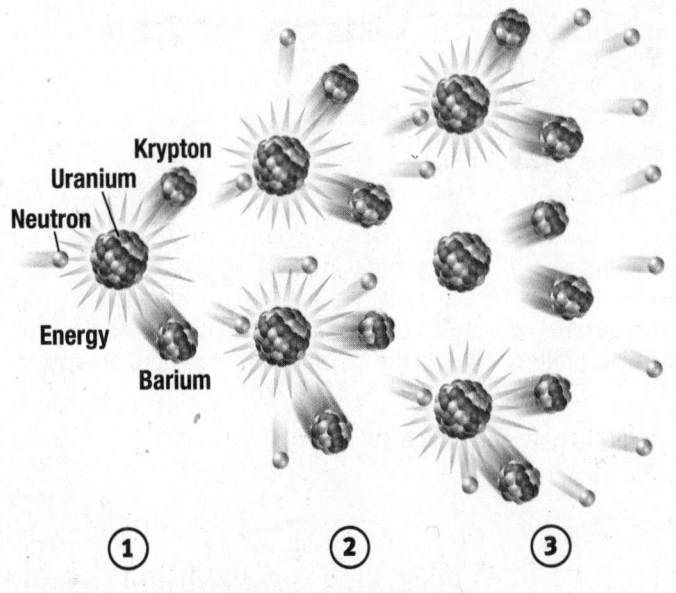

Nuclear Chain Reaction

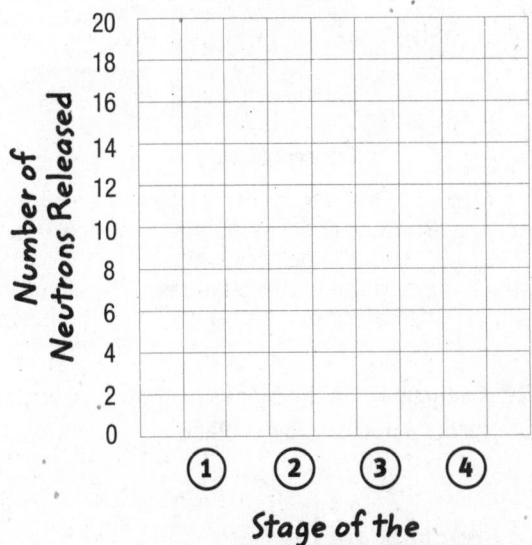

Number of Neutrons Released

Stage of the Nuclear Chain Reaction

Active Reading

16 Explain Where does the energy that is released by a fission reaction come from?

_____

_____

_____

_____

How do nuclear power plants work?

Active Reading 18 **Identify** As you read, underline what control rods do.

A small amount of uranium fuel can release a large amount of energy. In a nuclear power plant, the energy released during a controlled chain reaction is used to generate electrical energy. To control the chain reaction, engineers must keep many of the released neutrons from hitting other uranium nuclei. Control rods absorb these neutrons. They limit the number of neutrons that are available to continue the chain reaction. The diagram below shows how a nuclear power plant changes nuclear energy from fission reactions into electrical energy.

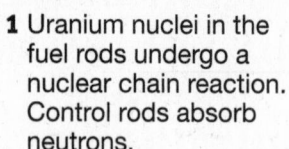 **Visualize It!**

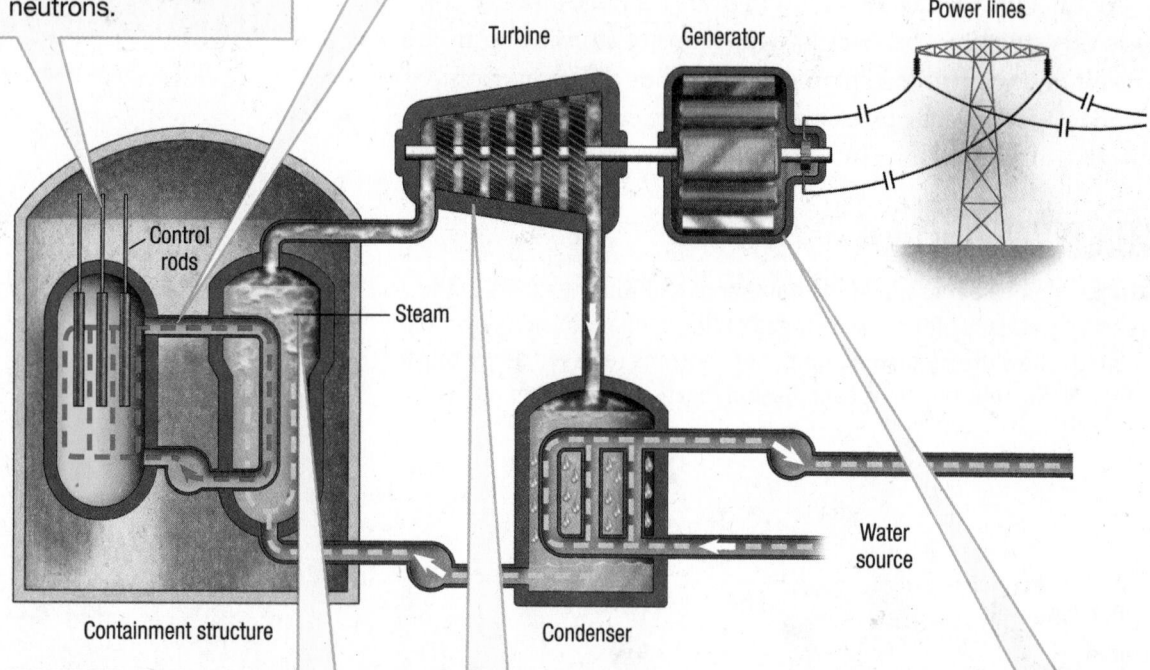

1 Uranium nuclei in the fuel rods undergo a nuclear chain reaction. Control rods absorb neutrons.

2 Energy is released during the chain reaction and is transferred to a coolant.

3 Water absorbs energy from the hot coolant, and the water changes to steam.

4 The thermal energy of the steam turns a turbine. The turbine now has mechanical energy.

5 The turbine is attached to an electrical generator. The generator changes the mechanical energy of the turbine into electrical energy.

Turbine Generator Power lines

Control rods

Steam

Water source

Containment structure Condenser

19 **Analyze** Fill in the blanks to show how nuclear energy changes into electrical energy inside a nuclear power plant.

 nuclear energy _____  _____  electrical energy

The Nucleus Changes

Another difference between chemical and nuclear reactions is that chemical reactions do not change the nucleus of atoms, but nuclear reactions do. Each atom of an element has the same number of protons in its nucleus. Nuclear reactions can change the identity of atoms by changing the number of protons in the nucleus. For example, a nuclear reaction that decreases the number of protons can change a beryllium atom into a lithium atom. On the other hand, nuclear reactions that change the number of neutrons do not change an atom into a new element.

Atoms with the same number of protons but different numbers of neutrons are called **isotopes**. For example, isotopes of lithium must have three protons but can have different numbers of neutrons. So, isotopes of the same element have different mass numbers. The mass number is added to the end of the name of an element to identify isotopes, such as lithium-6 and lithium-7.

Active Reading

6 **Compare** As you read, underline what happens during a nuclear reaction that does not happen during a chemical reaction.

Visualize It!

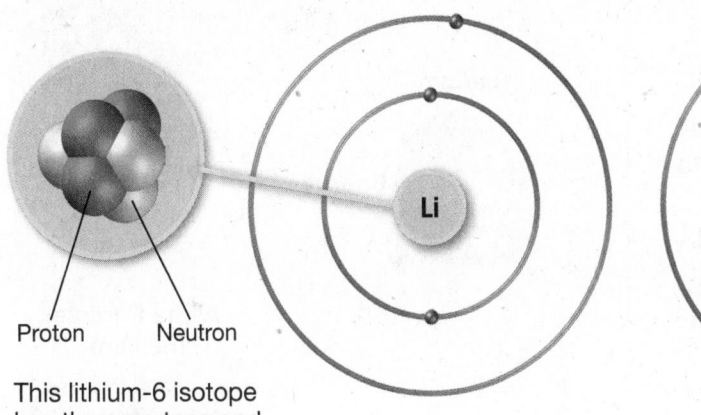

Proton   Neutron

This lithium-6 isotope has three protons and three neutrons. It has a mass number of 6.

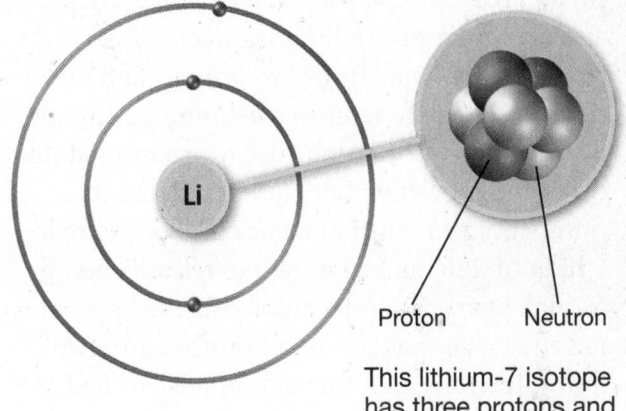

Proton   Neutron

This lithium-7 isotope has three protons and four neutrons. It has a mass number of 7.

7 **Model** Draw an isotope of beryllium-9 that has two more particles in the nucleus than the beryllium-7 isotope below. Label the protons and neutrons in your model.

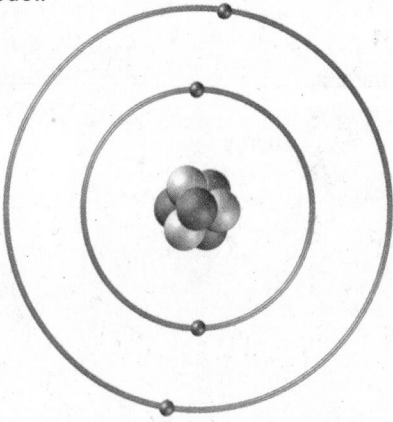

Just Passing Through

What are the types of radioactive decay?

The nuclei of some isotopes are not stable. Unstable nuclei undergo radioactive decay. **Radioactive decay** is a nuclear reaction in which an unstable nucleus can give off energy and, sometimes, particles. The particles and energy given off are called *nuclear radiation*. Unstable nuclei continue to decay until they form stable nuclei. Three kinds of radioactive decay are alpha decay, beta decay, and gamma decay.

Active Reading

8 Identify As you read this page and the next, underline the products of each type of radioactive decay.

Alpha Decay

Alpha decay is the release of an alpha particle and energy from a radioactive nucleus. An alpha particle consists of two protons and two neutrons. It is the same as a helium nucleus and has a charge of 2+. Alpha decay produces atoms of a different element because it reduces the number of protons in the nucleus. For example, a radium-226 nucleus decays to release energy, an alpha particle, and a radon-222 nucleus. The radon nucleus has two fewer protons and two fewer neutrons than the radium nucleus had.

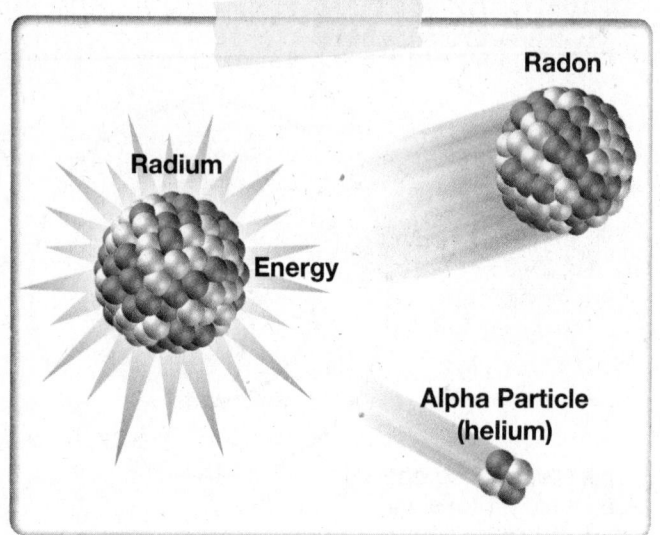

Beta Decay

A beta particle and energy are released during *beta decay*. There are two types of beta particles: positrons and electrons. Both particles have a mass of almost zero. Positrons have a charge of 1+. Electrons have a charge of 1−. A proton can break apart into a neutron and a positron that is released. A neutron can break apart into a proton and an electron that is released. Beta decay changes a nucleus into that of a different element. The atomic number increases when electrons are released. For example, carbon-14 decays to form nitrogen-14 and an electron. The atomic number decreases when positrons are released.

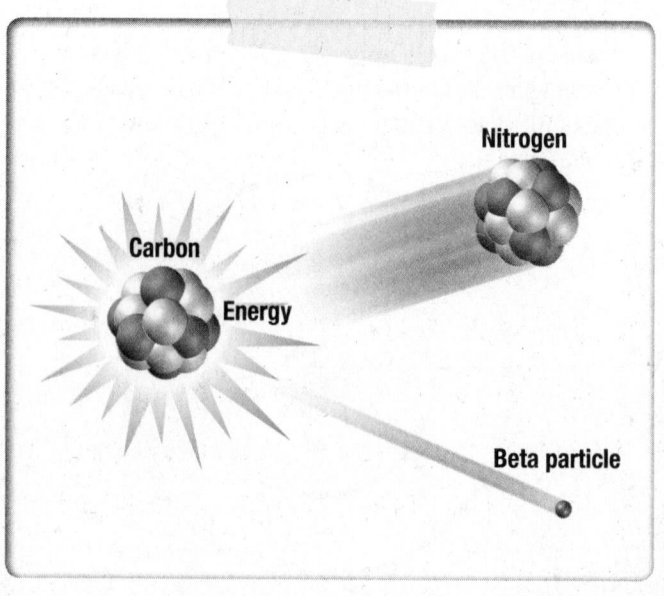

How can we evaluate nuclear power?

The way nuclear power plants generate electrical energy is similar to the way power plants that burn fossil fuels generate electrical energy. However, the fuels used by each type of power plant are different. Nuclear power has different advantages and different disadvantages than other energy sources. You can make informed decisions about the energy sources you use by knowing their advantages and disadvantages.

Think Outside the Book   Inquiry

20 **Debate** In small teams, debate whether nuclear fission should be used to provide energy. As you argue your position, state evidence to support it and explain your reasoning.

A modern nuclear power plant uses a small amount of fuel to produce large amounts of electricity.

By Its Advantages

Nuclear fission produces a large amount of energy from a small amount of fuel. The cost of fuel for nuclear power plants is less than for fossil fuel power plants. So, the electricity provided by nuclear power plants is often cheaper.

Burning fossil fuels produces greenhouse gases. It also produces other air pollutants that can cause acid rain and smog. Unlike fossil fuels, nuclear energy does not pollute the air or produce greenhouse gases. There have been few accidents involving nuclear power plants because they have high safety standards.

Nuclear waste must be stored safely until it is much less radioactive.

By Its Disadvantages

Although there have been few nuclear accidents, explosions from nuclear power plants are still a risk. An explosion can send large amounts of radioactive materials into the atmosphere. Smaller accidents may cause radioactive materials to leak into the environment. Living things that are exposed to radioactive materials in the environment may be harmed.

Another disadvantage of nuclear energy is that it is not renewable. Supplies of uranium are limited and could be used up some day.

Also, some of the products of the fission of uranium are radioactive. The radioactive waste produced by nuclear power plants could give off high levels of radiation for thousands of years. The waste must be handled and stored safely until it gives off less nuclear radiation.

Superstars!

Fusion reactions in the sun give off energy as heat and light that reaches Earth.

What is fusion?

The energy given off by the sun and other stars comes from nuclear fusion. **Nuclear fusion** is the process by which nuclei of small atoms combine to form a new, more massive nucleus. At the sun, hydrogen nuclei undergo fusion to form helium nuclei. This reaction is possible because the particles comprising the sun are in a plasma state. This state is characterized by extremely high temperatures and pressures. Fusion requires such conditions in order for hydrogen atoms to lose their electrons to form positively charged hydrogen nuclei, and to have enough energy to collide and fuse together. At the sun, fusion of hydrogen produces beta particles in addition to helium.

21 Describe A company wants to make an animated film showing fusion at the sun. Write a brief explanation about what the animation should show.

_____

_____

👁 Visualize It!

22 Summarize Use the table to record the number of each type of particle present before and after the fusion reaction of four hydrogen nuclei.

Particle	Before	After
proton	4	
neutron	0	
beta particle	0	

Hydrogen

Hydrogen

Hydrogen

Hydrogen

Helium

Energy

Beta particle (positron)
Charge: 1+

Beta particle (positron)
Charge: 1+

How can we evaluate power from fusion?

For years, scientists have tried to create the kind of fusion reactions that occur in stars. The goal of these scientists is to develop a source of clean and unlimited energy. Some scientists think that fusion will be the energy source of the future. Others think that fusion will never be a usable source of energy. You can evaluate potential technologies by their challenges and potential benefits.

Active Reading

23 Identify As you read, underline the reason scientists are trying to produce fusion reactions on Earth.

By Its Challenges

The conditions needed to shift matter into the plasma state so that fusion reactions can occur are challenging to produce on Earth. Scientists have been able to keep fusion reactions going for only a few seconds. Fusion reactions are also difficult to contain. Hydrogen fusion takes place only at temperatures of millions of degrees Celsius. To produce these temperatures requires a large input of energy, which is very expensive. In addition, there is no known material that can sustain this high reaction temperature. Special fusion reactors like the one shown at the right are needed to contain the reactions. Currently, more energy is needed to produce the conditions needed for fusion than can be produced by the fusion reaction itself.

Reactors like this one are used to study fusion reactions.

The hydrogen fuel needed for fusion can be obtained from ocean water.

By Its Potential Benefits

Researchers are exploring ways to use fusion to generate energy because of its potential benefits. The hydrogen fuel needed is readily available. Hydrogen is an element that makes up the water in Earth's oceans. It is not renewable, but it is available in almost unlimited amounts.

Radioactive waste and greenhouse gases are not a problem with fusion. The helium that is produced is not reactive and is not radioactive. Also, the hydrogen isotopes used in fusion reactions do not produce high levels of radiation. An accident at a fusion reactor would release little nuclear radiation into the environment.

Visual Summary

To complete this summary, circle the correct word or phrase. Then, use the key below to check your answers. You can use this page to review the main concepts of the lesson.

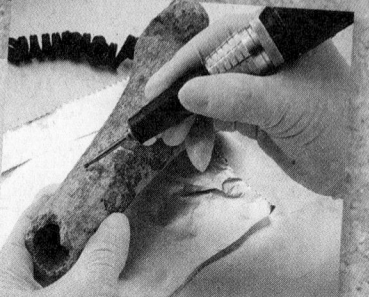

During nuclear reactions, the nuclei of atoms change, and a small amount of mass changes into energy.

Nuclear Reactions

24 Isotopes of an element have different numbers of protons / neutrons.

25 The type of radiation with the most penetrating power is alpha particles / beta particles / gamma rays.

During nuclear fission, a large unstable nucleus splits to produce two smaller nuclei and energy.

26 The energy released during fission comes from mass / chemical energy.

27 The neutrons / smaller nuclei released during fission can cause additional fission reactions.

During nuclear fusion, two small nuclei combine to produce a more massive nucleus and energy.

Answers: 24 neutrons; 25 gamma rays; 26 mass 27 neutrons; 28 the sun

28 Nuclear fusion is the source of energy in nuclear power plants / the sun.

29 **Analyze** In what ways can a nucleus change during a nuclear reaction? Explain your reasoning.

Lesson Review

Vocabulary

Draw a line to connect the following terms to their definitions.

1 nuclear reaction

2 radioactive decay

3 nuclear fission

4 nuclear fusion

A the process by which small nuclei combine to form a larger nucleus

B the process by which one large nucleus splits into two nuclei

C the process by which an unstable nucleus gives off nuclear radiation

D a change that affects the nucleus of an atom

Key Concepts

5 **Explain** How is a nuclear reaction different from a chemical reaction?

_____

_____

_____

_____

6 **Describe** What types of atoms release nuclear radiation?

_____

_____

7 **Explain** How are nuclear chain reactions controlled in nuclear power plants?

_____

_____

_____

8 **Analyze** Why are the products of nuclear fusion slightly less massive than the reactants?

_____

_____

Critical Thinking

9 **Claims · Evidence · Reasoning** Would fusion be a better energy source than fission? Make a claim and support it with evidence.

_____

_____

_____

_____

_____

10 **Conclude** One nucleus contains 31 protons and 40 neutrons. Another nucleus contains 31 protons and 41 neutrons. What can you conclude about the identity of these nuclei? Explain your reasoning.

_____

_____

11 **Infer** Why can the effects of radioactive decay on the body be useful and harmful?

_____

_____

_____

_____

Use this model to answer the following question.

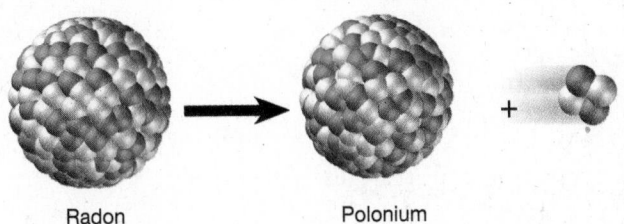

Radon   Polonium

12 **Analyze** What decay process is shown? Explain.

_____

_____

_____

My Notes

Unit 4 | Big Idea

In chemical reactions matter and energy are conserved, while in nuclear reactions matter is converted into energy.

Lesson 1

ESSENTIAL QUESTION
How are chemical reactions modeled?

Use balanced chemical equations to model chemical reactions.

Lesson 2

ESSENTIAL QUESTION
How does carbon form molecules?

Describe how carbon forms many of the molecules essential to modern materials and living things.

Lesson 3

ESSENTIAL QUESTION
How do nuclear reactions differ from chemical reactions?

Distinguish nuclear reactions from chemical reactions, and compare the types of nuclear reactions.

Think Outside the Book

2 Synthesize Choose one of these activities to help synthesize what you have learned in this unit.

☐ Using what you learned in lessons 1 and 2, illustrate different ways to model a molecule of methane by creating a diagram. Your diagram should include a chemical formula, a full structural formula, and a molecular model.

☐ Using what you learned in lessons 1 and 3, describe the law of conservation of mass and the law of conservation of energy by making a poster presentation. Be sure to mention both chemical reactions and nuclear reactions.

Connect ESSENTIAL QUESTIONS
Lessons 1 and 3

1 Compare How do nuclear reactions differ from chemical reactions?

_____

_____

_____

_____

Name _____

Vocabulary

Check the box to show whether each statement is true or false.

T	F	
☐	☐	**1** In a <u>chemical reaction</u>, atoms are rearranged and bonds can be broken or formed.
☐	☐	**2** <u>Nuclear fission</u> is the process by which the nuclei of smaller atoms combine to form a new, more massive nucleus.
☐	☐	**3** A <u>nuclear reaction</u> changes the number of electrons in the nucleus.
☐	☐	**4** An <u>endothermic reaction</u> releases energy.
☐	☐	**5** A <u>hydrocarbon</u> is any substance that contains oxygen and carbon.

Key Concepts

Read each question below, and circle the best answer.

6 What is an atom that has the same number of protons as other atoms of the same element but a different number of neutrons?

A catalyst

C reactant

B isotope

D product

7 Which of the following can speed up the rate of a chemical reaction?

A removing a catalyst

B lowering the reactant concentration

C lowering the temperature

D breaking up a reactant into smaller pieces

8 What is a limitation to using nuclear fusion for energy?

A Nuclear fusion produces a large amount of radioactive waste.

B The hydrogen fuel needed for the reaction is hard to collect.

C The atoms needed in nuclear fusion reactions are too small to use.

D Creating the proper pressure and temperature conditions on Earth is difficult.

9 The chemical formula of glucose is shown below.

$$C_6H_{12}O_6$$

How many atoms of carbon are in one molecule of glucose?

A 1

C 12

B 6

D 24

10 Carbon, hydrogen, and oxygen are always found in what type of molecule?

A hydrocarbon

B carbohydrate

C acid

D polymer

11 A chemical reaction is shown below.

$$Fe + H_2O \rightarrow Fe_3O_4 + H_2$$

What are the products in the equation?

A Fe_3O_4 only

B Fe only

C Fe and H_2O

D Fe_3O_4 and H_2

12 Which of the following occurrences indicates that a chemical reaction has taken place?

A An odor is produced by burning a sugar cube.

B A puddle is produced by melting an ice cube.

C A loud noise is produced by crushing a can.

D A shard of glass is produced by breaking a bottle.

13 Which of the following is an example of an exothermic chemical reaction?

    A photosynthesis

    B burning wood

    C melting ice cubes

    D boiling water

Critical Thinking

Answer the following questions in the space provided.

14 The diagram below shows a nuclear reaction.

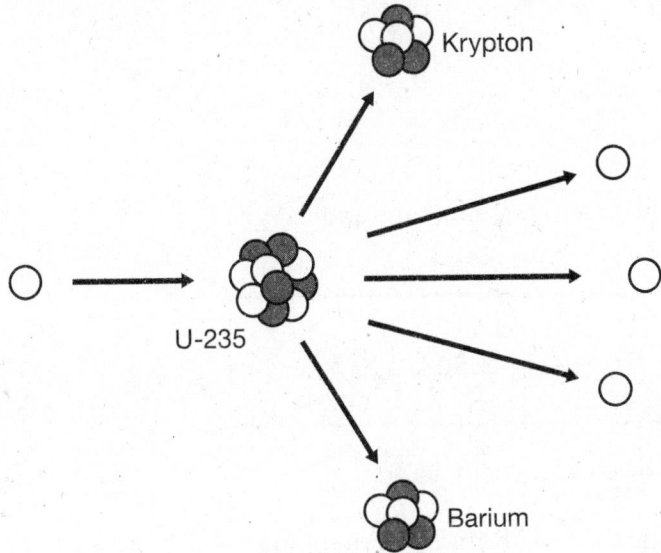

    Does the diagram show an example of nuclear fission or fusion? Explain.

_____

_____

    Using the diagram, explain how a nuclear chain reaction could occur.

_____

_____

_____

15 What are the three types of radioactive decay?

_____

What is one way in which radioactive decay is used to benefit society?

_____

_____

_____

In your opinion, do the risks of using radioactive decay outweigh the benefits? Explain.

_____

_____

_____

Connect ESSENTIAL QUESTIONS
Lessons 1 and 2

Answer the following question in the space provided.

16 The following chemical equation shows the reaction of methane and oxygen to form carbon dioxide and water.

$$CH_4 + 2O_2 \rightarrow CO_2 + H_2O$$

Balance the above reaction by writing in the correct coefficient(s).

How does a balanced equation demonstrate the law of conservation of mass?

_____

_____

What molecule in the above equation is a hydrocarbon?

_____

Draw a full structural formula for the hydrocarbon that you listed above.

Motion and Forces

The parachute helps slow the shuttle down.

Houghton Mifflin Harcourt Publishing Company • Image Credits: (bkgd) ©Gary I. Rothstein/epa/Corbis; (br) ©Eliot J. Schechter/Getty Images

Big Idea

Unbalanced forces cause changes in the motion of objects, and these changes can be predicted and described.

S8P3., S8P3.a, S8P3.b, S8P3.c, S8P5.a

What do you think?

How do you change the direction in which an object is moving? What allows the shuttle to slow down or the rocket to lift off? As you explore the unit, gather evidence to help you state and support claims to answer these questions.

Unit 5
Motion and Forces

CITIZEN SCIENCE
What's in a Vane?

For hundreds of years, people have used the wind to do work, such as grind flour and pump water.

① Define The Problem

We need electricity to do work, such as power the lights and appliances that we use daily. As our need for electricity grows, many people are becoming more interested in new ways to generate electricity. Have you heard of using windmills to generate electricity?

A windmill vane, or sail, is a large structure that is attached to a rotating axle. The vane catches the wind and turns around. This turning motion can be used to generate electricity.

② Think About It

Designing a windmill vane

What characteristics of a windmill vane help it to catch the most wind? Create two different designs for windmill vanes that you can test to see which characteristics are the most beneficial.

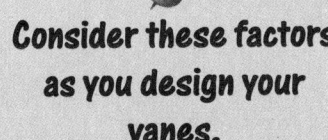

Consider these factors as you design your vanes.

☐ the size of the vanes

☐ the shape of the vanes

☐ materials used to build the vanes

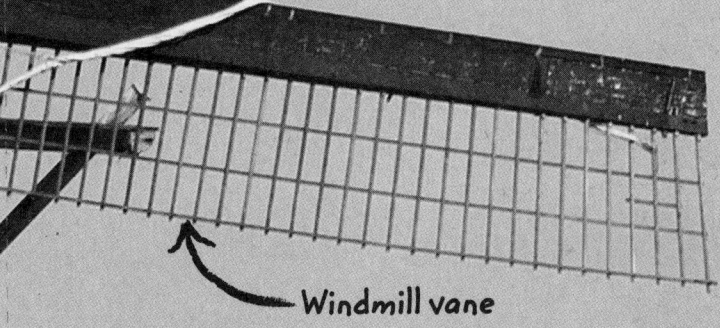

— Windmill vane

③ Plan and Test Your Design

A Your windmill designs should feature four windmill vanes attached to a straw or wooden spindle. The straw or spindle will be the axle. You should mount your axle so that it can spin freely. In the space below, sketch two designs that you would like to test.

B In the space below, identify what you will use as a wind source and the variables you must control.

_____
_____
_____
_____
_____
_____

C Conduct your test and briefly state your findings below.

_____
_____
_____
_____
_____

Take It Home

With the help of an adult, research windmills that are used to generate electricity for homes. Study the different designs and decide which would be best for your family. See *ScienceSaurus*® for more information about wind.

Motion and Speed

ESSENTIAL QUESTION

How are distance, time, and speed related?

By the end of this lesson, you should be able to analyze how distance, time, and speed are related.

 S8P3.a Speed, distance, velocity, and acceleration

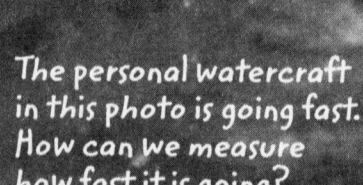

The personal watercraft in this photo is going fast. How can we measure how fast it is going?

Lesson Labs

Quick Labs
• Investigate Changing Positions
• Create a Distance-Time Graph

S.T.E.M. Lab
• Investigate Average Speed

Engage Your Brain

1 Predict Circle the correct words in the paragraph below to make true statements.

A dog usually moves faster than a bug. That means that if I watch them move for one minute, then the dog would have traveled a *greater*/ *smaller* distance than the bug. However, a car usually goes *faster*/*slower* than a dog. If the car and the dog both traveled to the end of the road, then the *car*/*dog* would get there first.

2 Explain Draw or sketch something that you might see move. Write a caption that answers the following questions: How would you describe its motion? Is it moving at a constant speed, or does it speed up and slow down?

 **Active Reading**

3 Define Fill in the blank with the word that best completes the following sentences.

If an object changes its position, then it is

_____

The speed of a car describes

_____

_____

Vocabulary Terms

• position   • speed
• reference point • vector
• motion   • velocity

4 Apply As you learn the definition of each vocabulary term in this lesson, make your own definition or sketch to help you remember the meaning of the term.

Location, location,

How can you describe the location of an object?

Have you ever gotten lost while looking for a specific place? If so, you probably know that the description of the location can be very important. Imagine that you are trying to describe your location to a friend. How would you explain where you are? You need two pieces of information: a position and a reference point.

With a Position

Position describes the location of an object. Often, you describe where something is by comparing its position with where you currently are. For example, you might say that a classmate sitting next to you is two desks to your right, or that a mailbox is two blocks south of where you live. Each time you identify the position of an object, you are comparing the location of the object with the location of another object or place.

With a Reference Point

When you describe a position by comparing it to the location of another object or place, you are using a reference point. A **reference point** is a location to which you compare other locations. In the example above of a mailbox that is two blocks south of where you live, the reference point is "where you live."

Imagine that you are at a zoo with some friends. If you are using the map to the right, you could describe your destination using different reference points. Using yourself as the reference point, you might say that the red panda house is one block east and three blocks north of your current location. Or you might say the red panda house is one block north and one block east of the fountain. In this example, the fountain is your reference point.

Active Reading 5 **Apply** How would you describe where this question is located on the page? Give two different answers using two different reference points.

_____

_____

_____

_____

location

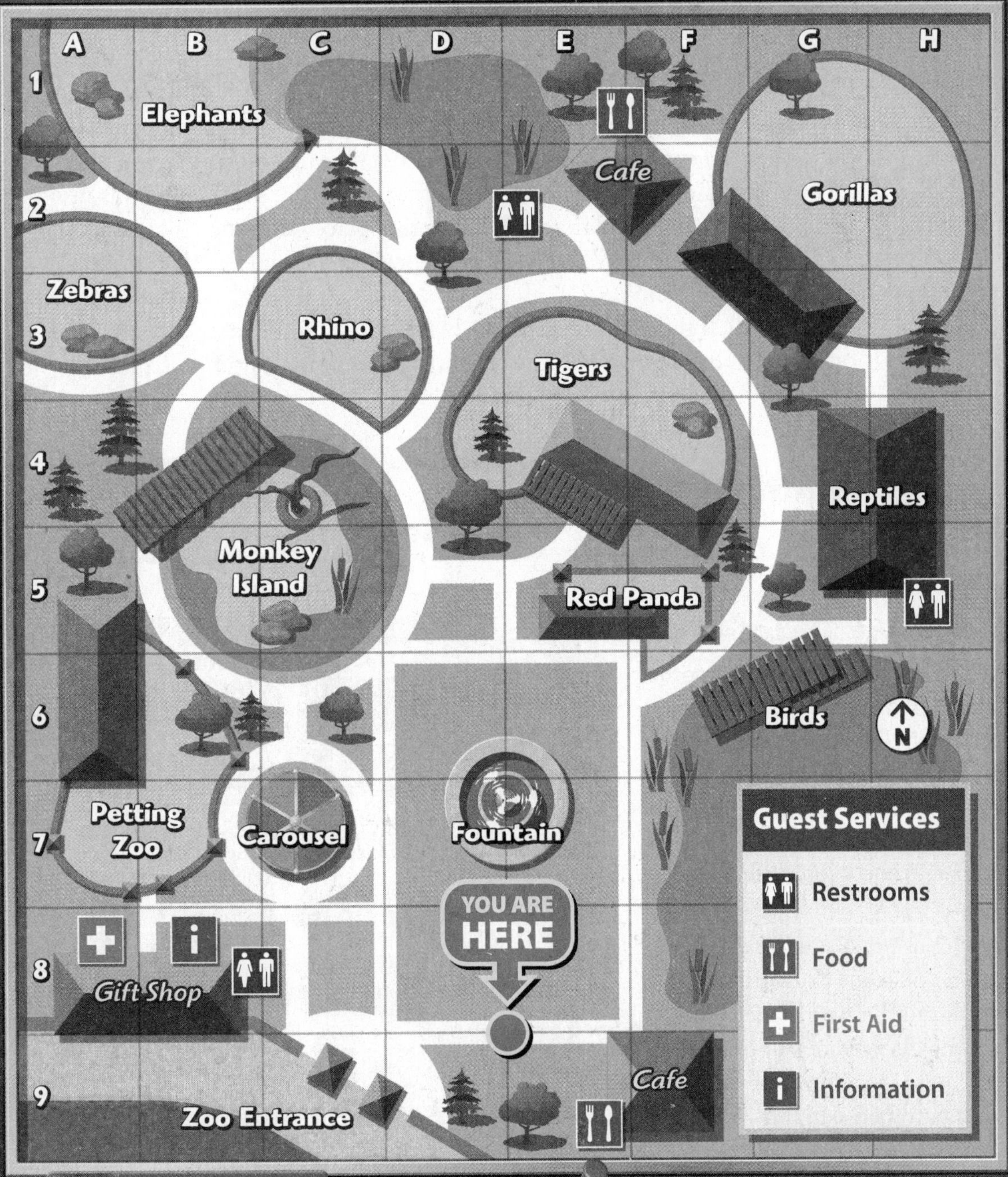

ZOO MAP

	A	B	C	D	E	F	G	H
1		Elephants						
2					Cafe		Gorillas	
3	Zebras		Rhino					
4					Tigers		Reptiles	
5		Monkey Island			Red Panda			
6						Birds	N ↑	
7	Petting Zoo	Carousel		Fountain				
8	Gift Shop			YOU ARE HERE				
9	Zoo Entrance				Cafe			

Guest Services

- 🚻 Restrooms
- 🍴 Food
- ✚ First Aid
- ℹ Information

Visualize It!

6 Apply One of your friends is at the southeast corner of Monkey Island. He would like to meet you. How would you describe your location to him?

_____

_____

_____

7 Apply You need to go visit the first aid station. How would you describe how to get there?

_____

_____

_____

_____

MOVE It!

What is motion?

An object moves, or is in motion, when it changes its position relative to a reference point. **Motion** is a change in position over time. If you were to watch the biker pictured to the right, you would see him move. If you were not able to watch him, you might still know something about his motion. If you saw that he was in one place at one time and a different place later, you would know that he had moved. A change in position is evidence that motion has happened.

If the biker returned to his starting point, you might not know that he had moved. The starting and ending positions cannot tell you everything about motion.

How is distance measured?

Suppose you walk from one building to another building that is several blocks away. If you could walk in a straight line, you might end up 500 meters from where you started. The actual distance you travel, however, would depend on the exact path you take. If you take a route that has many turns, the distance you travel might be 900 meters or more.

The way you measure distance depends on the information you want. Sometimes you want to know the straight-line distance between two positions, or the displacement. Sometimes, however, you might need to know the total length of a certain path between those positions.

When measuring any distances, scientists use a standard unit of measurement. The standard unit of length is the meter (m), which is about 3.3 feet. Longer distances can be measured in kilometers (km), and shorter distances in centimeters (cm). In the United States, distance is often measured in miles (mi), feet (ft), or inches (in).

The distance from point A to point B depends on the path you take.

Visualize It!

8 Illustrate Draw a sample path on the maze that is a different distance than the one in red but still goes from the start point, "A," to the finish point, "B."

This biker is in motion.

What is speed?

A change in an object's position tells you that motion took place, but it does not tell you how quickly the object changed position. The **speed** of an object is a measure of how far something moves in a given amount of time. In other words, speed measures how quickly or slowly the object changes position. In the same amount of time, a faster object would move farther than a slower moving object would.

What is average speed?

The speed of an object is rarely constant. For example, the biker in the photo above may travel quickly when he begins a race but may slow down as he gets tired at the end of the race. *Average speed* is a way to calculate the speed of an object that may not always be moving at a constant speed. Instead of describing the speed of an object at an exact moment in time, average speed describes the speed over a stretch of time.

Active Reading **9 Compare** What is the difference between speed and average speed?

_____

_____

_____

© Houghton Mifflin Harcourt Publishing Company • Image Credits: ©Wave Royalty Free/age fotostock

Think Outside the Book Inquiry

10 Analyze Research the top speeds of a cheetah, a race car, and a speed boat. How do they rank in order of speed? Make a poster showing which is fastest and which is slowest. How do the speeds of the fastest human runners compare to the speeds you found?

Speed It Up!

How is average speed calculated?

Speed can be calculated by dividing the distance an object travels by the time it takes to cover the distance. Speed is shown in the formula as the letter *s*, distance as the letter *d*, and time as the letter *t*. The formula shows how distance, time, and speed are related. If two objects travel the same distance, the object that took a shorter amount of time will have the greater speed. An object with a greater speed will travel a longer distance in the same amount of time than an object with a lower speed will.

 Active Reading

11 Identify As you read, underline sentences that relate distance and time.

> **The following equation can be used to find average speed:**
>
> $$\text{average speed} = \frac{\text{distance}}{\text{time}}$$
>
> $$s = \frac{d}{t}$$

The standard unit for speed is meters per second (m/s). Speed can also be given in kilometers per hour (km/h). In the United States, speeds are often given in miles per hour (mi/h or mph). One mile per hour is equal to 0.45 m/s.

 Do the Math **Sample Problem**

A penguin swimming underwater goes 20 meters in 8 seconds. What is its average speed?

Identify

A. What do you know? $d = 20$ m, $t = 8$ s

B. What do you want to find out? average speed

Plan

C. Draw and label a sketch: ⊢——20 m——⊣
                                        8 sec

D. Write the formula: $s = d/t$

E. Substitute into the formula: $s = \frac{20\text{ m}}{8\text{ s}}$

Solve

F. Calculate and simplify: $s = \frac{20\text{ m}}{8\text{ s}} = 2.5$ m/s

G. Check that your units agree: Unit is m/s. Unit of speed is distance/time. Units agree.

Answer: 2.5 m/s

Do the Math · You Try It

12 Calculate This runner completed a 100-meter race with a time of 13.75 seconds. What was her average speed?

Identify

A. What do you know?

B. What do you want to find out?

Plan

C. Draw and label a sketch:

D. Write the formula:

E. Substitute into the formula:

Solve

F. Calculate and simplify:

G. Check that your units agree:

Answer:

Fast Graphs

How is constant speed graphed?

A convenient way to show the motion of an object is by using a graph that plots the distance the object has traveled against time. This type of graph is called a distance-time graph. You can use it to see how both distance and speed change with time.

How far away the object is from a reference point is plotted on the *y*-axis. So the *y*-axis expresses distance in units such as meters, centimeters, or kilometers. Time is plotted on the *x*-axis, and can display units such as seconds, minutes, or hours. If an object moves at a constant speed, the graph is a straight line.

You can use a distance-time graph to determine the average speed of an object. The slope, or steepness, of the line is equal to the average speed of the object. You calculate the average speed for a time interval by dividing the change in distance by the change in time for that time interval.

Suppose that an ostrich is running at a constant speed. The distance-time graph of its motion is shown below. To calculate the speed of the ostrich, choose two data points from the graph below and calculate the slope of the line. The calculation of the slope is shown below. Since we know that the slope of a line on a distance-time graph is its average speed, then we know that the ostrich's speed is 14 m/s.

How can you calculate slope?

$$slope = \frac{change\ in\ y}{change\ in\ x}$$

$$= \frac{140\ m - 70\ m}{10\ s - 5\ s}$$

$$= \frac{70\ m}{5\ s}$$

$$= 14\ m/s$$

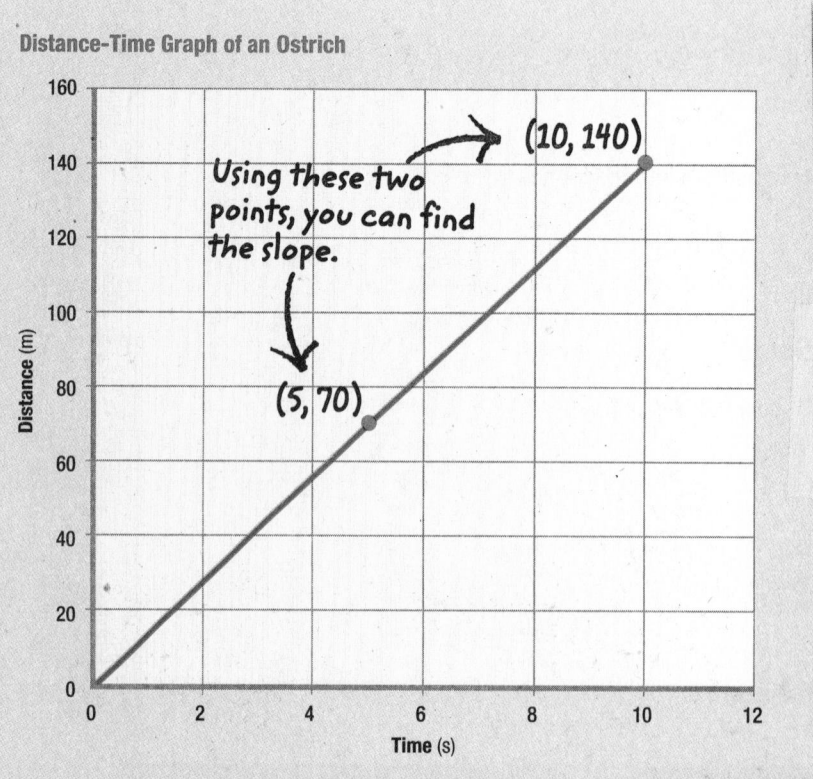

Distance-Time Graph of an Ostrich

Using these two points, you can find the slope.

(10, 140)

(5, 70)

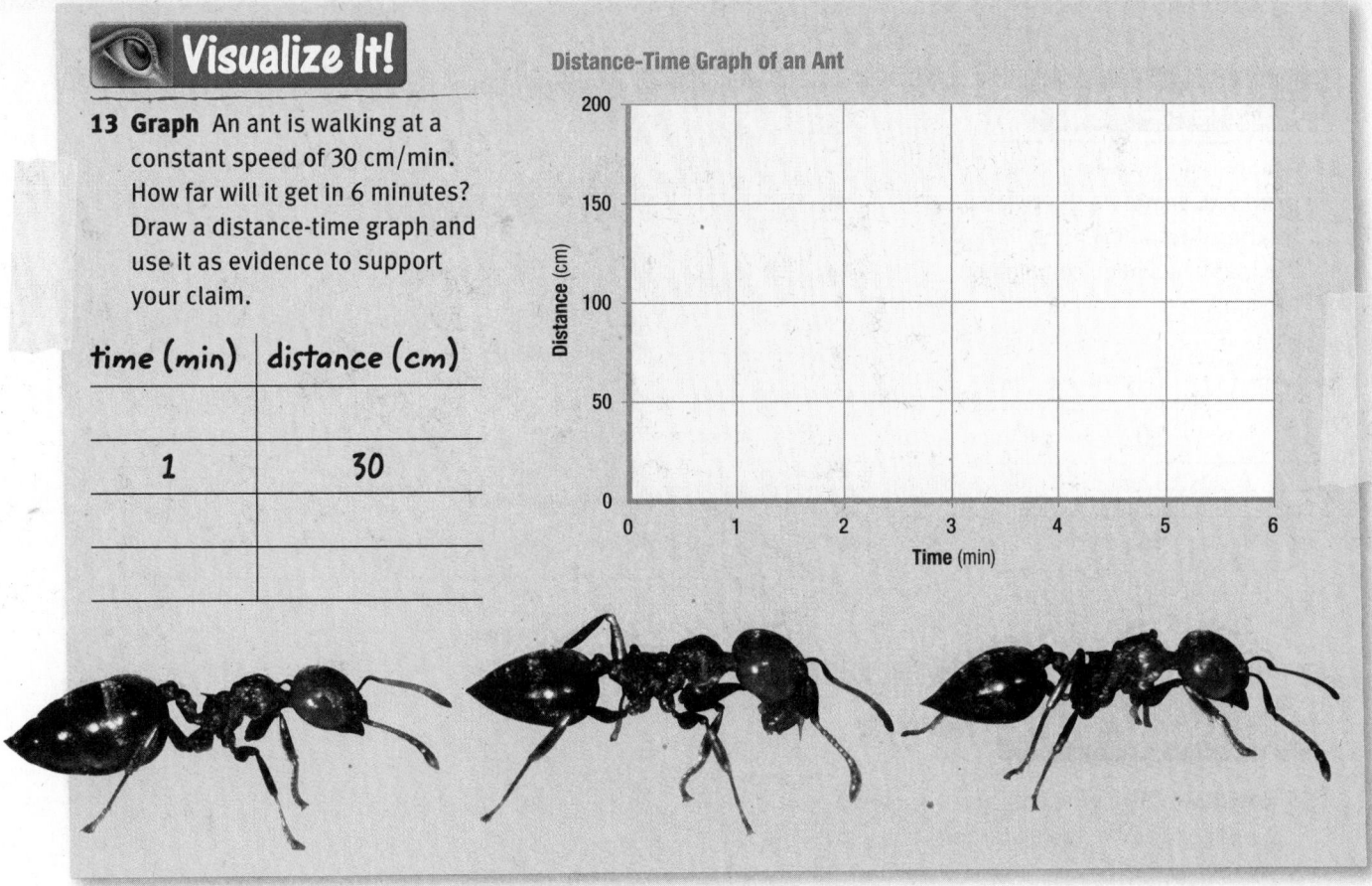

Visualize It!

13 Graph An ant is walking at a constant speed of 30 cm/min. How far will it get in 6 minutes? Draw a distance-time graph and use it as evidence to support your claim.

time (min)	distance (cm)
1	30

Distance-Time Graph of an Ant

How are changing speeds graphed?

Some distance-time graphs show the motion of an object with a changing speed. In these distance-time graphs, the change in the slope of a line indicates that the object has either sped up, slowed down, or stopped.

As an object moves, the distance it travels increases with time. The motion can be seen as a climbing line on the graph. The slope of the line indicates speed. Steeper lines show intervals where the speed is greater than intervals with less steep lines. If the line gets steeper, the object is speeding up. If the line gets less steep, the object is slowing. If the line becomes flat, or horizontal, the object is not moving. In this interval, the speed is zero meters per second.

For objects that change speed, you can calculate speed for a specific interval of time. You would choose two points close together on the graph. Or, you can calculate the average speed over a long interval of time. You would choose two points far apart on the graph to calculate an average over a long interval of time.

Active Reading **14 Analyze** If a line on a distance-time graph becomes steeper, what has happened to the speed of the object? What if it becomes a flat horizontal line? Explain your reasoning.

_____

_____

_____

Distance-Time Graph of an All-Terrain Vehicle

15 Graph Using the data table provided, complete the graph for the all-terrain vehicle. Part of the graph has been completed for you.

Time (s)	Distance (m)
1	10
3	10
4	30
5	50

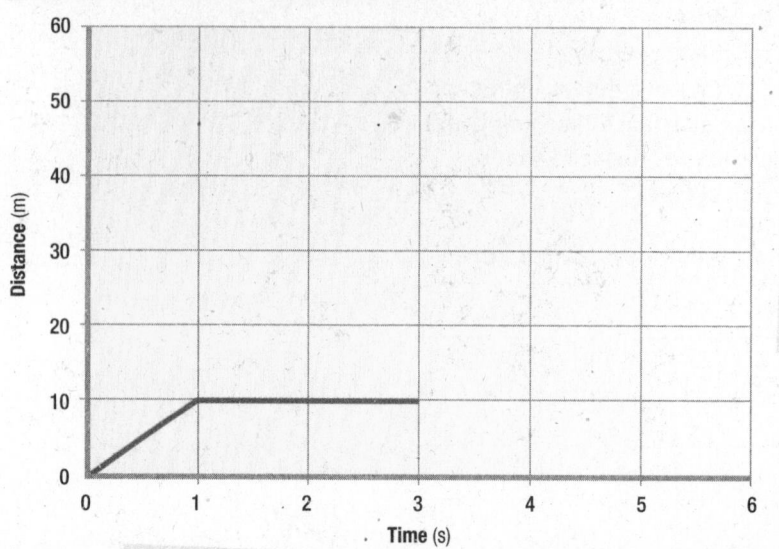

 Do the Math **You Try It**

16 Calculate Using the data given above, calculate the average speed of the all-terrain vehicle over the entire five seconds.

Identify

A. What do you know?

B. What do you want to find out?

Plan

C. Draw and label a sketch:

D. Write the formula:

E. Substitute into the formula:

Solve

F. Calculate and simplify:

G. Check that your units agree:

Answer:

What would the distance-time graph of this ATV's motion look like?

Follow Directions

What is velocity?

Suppose that two birds start from the same place and fly at 10 km/h for 5 minutes. Why might they not end up at the same place? Because the birds were flying in different directions! There are times when the direction of motion must be included in a measurement. A **vector** is a quantity that has both size and direction.

In the example above, the birds' speeds were the same, but their velocities were different. **Velocity** [vuh•LAHS•ih•tee] is speed in a specific direction. If a police officer gives a speeding ticket for a car traveling 100 km/h, the ticket does not list a velocity. But it would list a velocity if it described the car traveling south at 100 km/h.

These chair lifts have opposite velocities because they are going at the same speed but in opposite directions.

Because velocity includes direction, it is possible for two objects to have the same speed but different velocities. In the picture to the right, the chair lifts are going the same speed but in opposite directions: some riders are going up the mountain while others are going down the mountain.

Average velocity is calculated in a different way than average speed. Average speed depends on the total distance traveled along a path. Average velocity depends on the straight-line distance from the starting point to the final point, or the displacement. A chair lift might carry you up the mountain at an average speed of 5 km/h, giving you an average velocity of 5 km/h north. After a round-trip ride, your average traveling speed would still be 5 km/h. Your average velocity, however, would be 0 km/h because you ended up exactly where you started.

17 Compare Fill in the Venn diagram to compare and contrast speed and velocity.

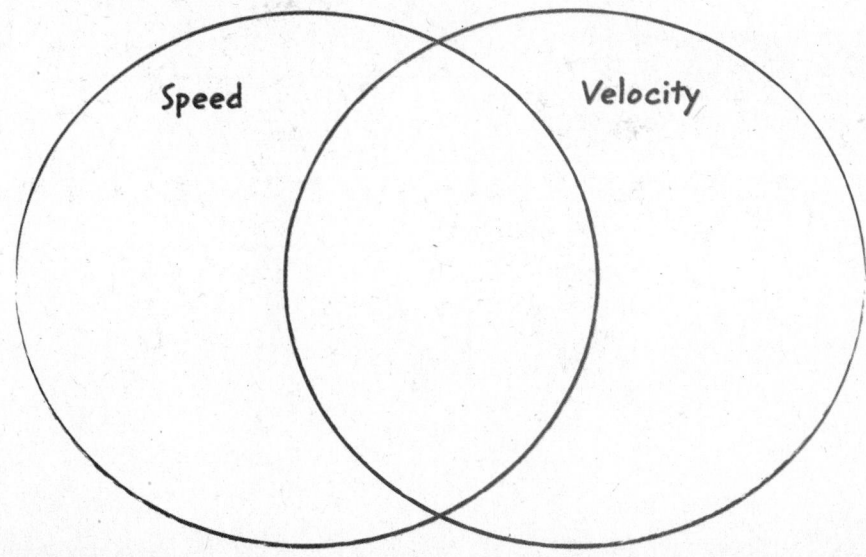

Speed   Velocity

Visual Summary

To complete this summary, check the box that indicates true or false. Then use the key below to check your answers. You can use this page to review the main concepts of the lesson.

Motion is a change in position over time.

YOU ARE HERE

	T	F	
18	☐	☐	A reference point is a location to which you compare other locations.
19	☐	☐	Distance traveled does not depend on the path you take.

Speed measures how far something moves in a given amount of time.

$$s = \frac{d}{t}$$

	T	F	
20	☐	☐	To calculate speed, you first need to find the mass of an object.
21	☐	☐	Average speed is a way to describe the speed of an object that may not always be moving at a constant speed.

Motion and Speed

A distance-time graph plots the distance traveled by an object and the time it takes to travel that distance.

	T	F	
22	☐	☐	In the graph at the right, the object is moving at a constant speed.

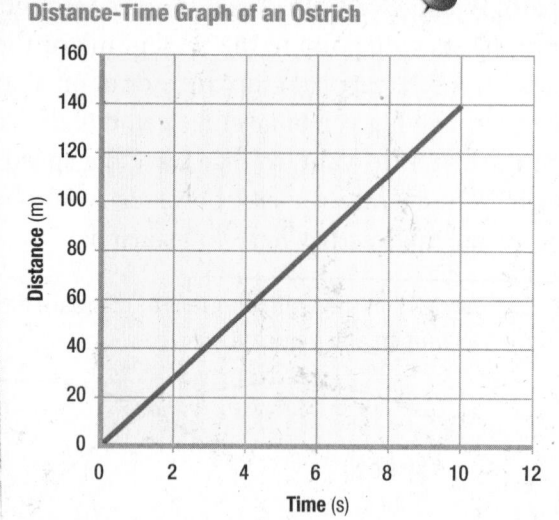

Distance-Time Graph of an Ostrich

23 Claims · Evidence · Reasoning

Amy and Ellie left school at the same time. Amy lives farther away than Ellie, but she and Ellie arrived at their homes at the same time. Which girl walked faster? What evidence supports your claim?

Lesson Review

Vocabulary

Draw a line to connect the following terms to their definitions.

1 velocity

2 reference point

3 speed

4 position

A describes the location of an object

B speed in a specific direction

C a location to which you compare other locations

D a measure of how far something moves in a given amount of time

Key Concepts

5 Describe What information do you need to describe an object's location?

_____

_____

6 Predict How would decreasing the time it takes you to run a certain distance affect your speed?

_____

_____

_____

_____

7 Calculate Juan lives 100 m away from Bill. What is Juan's average speed if he reaches Bill's home in 50 s?

_____

_____

_____

_____

_____

8 Describe What do you need to know to describe the velocity of an object?

_____

_____

_____

Use this graph to answer the following questions.

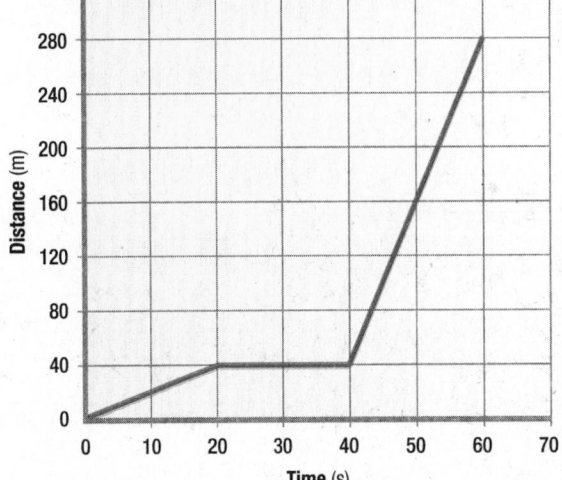

Distance-Time Graph of a Zebra

9 Analyze When is the zebra in motion? When is it not moving?

In motion: _____

Not moving: _____

10 Calculate What is the average speed of the zebra during the time between 0 s and 40 s?

_____

_____

_____

_____

Critical Thinking

11 Apply Look around you to find an object in motion. Describe the object's motion by discussing its position and direction of motion in relation to a reference point. Then explain how you could determine the object's speed.

_____

_____

_____

_____

_____

My Notes

S8P3.a Speed, distance, velocity, and acceleration

Interpreting Graphs

A visual display, such as a graph or table, is a useful way to show data that you have collected in an experiment. The ability to interpret graphs is a necessary skill in science, and it is also important in everyday life. You will come across various types of graphs in newspaper articles, medical reports, and, of course, textbooks. Understanding a report or article's message often depends heavily on your ability to read and interpret different types of graphs.

Tutorial

Ask yourself the following questions when studying a graph.

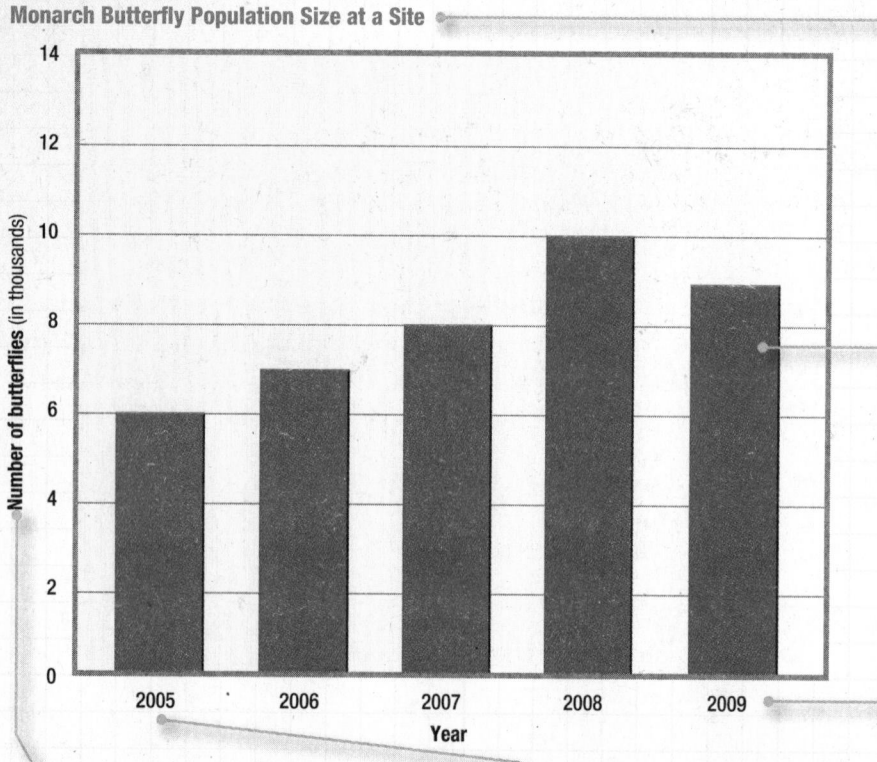

Monarch Butterfly Population Size at a Site

What is the title of the graph? Reading the title can tell you the subject or main idea of the graph. The subject here is monarch butterfly population.

What type of graph is it? Bar graphs, like the one here, are useful for comparing categories or total values. The lengths of the bars are proportional to the value they represent.

Do you notice any trends in the graph? After you understand what the graph is about, look for patterns. For example, here the monarch butterfly population increased each year from 2005 to 2008. But in 2009, the monarch butterfly population decreased.

What are the labels and headings in the graph? What is on each axis of the graph? Here, the vertical axis shows the population in thousands. Each bar represents a different year from 2005 to 2009. So from 2005 to 2009, the monarch butterfly population ranged from 6,000 to 10,000.

Can you describe the data in the graph? Data can be numbers or text. Analyze the information you read at specific data points. For example, the graph here tells us that there were 6,000 monarch butterflies in 2005.

You Try It!

A member of your research group has made the graph shown below about an object in motion. Study the graph, then answer the questions that follow.

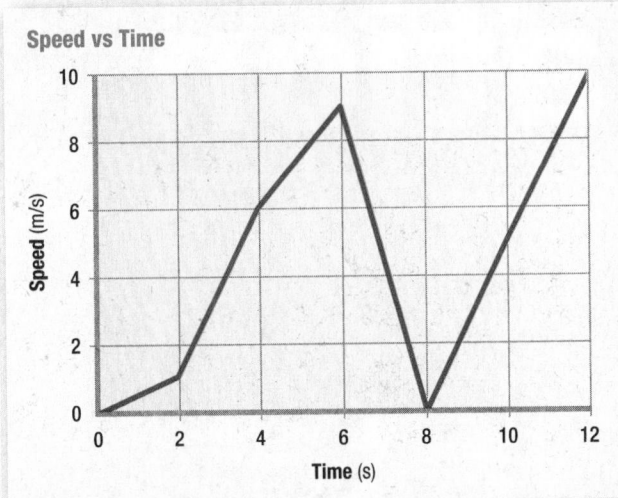

Speed vs Time

3 Using Graphs Use the graph to answer the following questions.

A What is the approximate speed of the object at 5 seconds?

_____

B During what time interval is the object slowing down? Explain how you can tell.

_____

_____

_____

1 Interpreting Graphs Study the graph shown above. Identify the title of this graph, the *x*-axis, the *y*-axis, and the type of graph.

A title of graph _____

B *x*-axis _____

C *y*-axis _____

D type of graph _____

C At what time or times was the speed of the object about 4 m/s?

_____

_____

4 Communicating Results In a short paragraph, describe the motion of the object.

_____

_____

2 Identify Study the graph shown above and record the speed at the indicated times.

Time (s)	Speed (m/s)
2	
4	
6	
8	
10	

_____

_____

_____

_____

_____

Take It Home

Find a newspaper or magazine article that has a graph. What type of graph is it? Study the graph and determine its main message. Bring the graph to class and be prepared to discuss your interpretation of the graph.

Lesson 2

Acceleration

ESSENTIAL QUESTION

How does motion change?

By the end of this lesson, you should be able to analyze how acceleration is related to time and velocity.

S8P3.a Speed, distance, velocity, and acceleration

The riders on this roller coaster are constantly changing direction and speed.

© Houghton Mifflin Harcourt Publishing Company • Image Credits: ©Chad Slattery/Stone/Getty Images

Lesson Labs

Quick Labs
- Acceleration and Slope
- Mass and Acceleration

S.T.E.M. Lab
- Investigate Acceleration

Engage Your Brain

1 Predict Check T or F to show whether you think each statement is true or false.

T F

☐ ☐ A car taking a turn at a constant speed is accelerating.

☐ ☐ If an object has low acceleration, it isn't moving very fast.

☐ ☐ An accelerating car is always gaining speed.

2 Identify The names of the two things that can change when something accelerates are scrambled together below. Unscramble them!

P E D S E

_____

C D E I I N O R T

_____

Active Reading

3 Synthesize You can often define an unknown word if you know the meaning of its word parts. Use the word parts and sentence below to make an educated guess about the meaning of the word *centripetal*.

Word part	Meaning
centri-	center
pet-	tend toward

Example Sentence:
Josephina felt the <u>centripetal</u> force as she spun around on the carnival ride.

centripetal:
_____
_____
_____

Vocabulary Terms

- acceleration
- centripetal acceleration

4 Distinguish As you read, draw pictures or make a chart to help remember the relationship between distance, velocity, and acceleration.

How do we measure changing velocity?

Imagine riding a bike as in the images below. You start off not moving at all, then move slowly, and then faster and faster each second. Your velocity is changing. You are accelerating.

Active Reading **5 Identify** Underline the two components of a vector.

Acceleration Measures a Change in Velocity

Just as velocity measures a rate of change in position, acceleration measures a rate of change in velocity. **Acceleration** (ack•SELL•uh•ray•shuhn) is the rate at which velocity changes. Velocity is a vector, having both a magnitude and direction, and if either of these change, then the velocity changes. So, an object accelerates if its speed, its direction of motion, or both change.

Keep in mind that acceleration depends not only on how much velocity changes, but also on how much time that change takes. A small change in velocity can still be a large acceleration if the change happens quickly, and a large change in velocity can be a small acceleration if it happens slowly. Increasing your speed by 5 m/s in 5 s is a smaller acceleration than to do the same in 1 s.

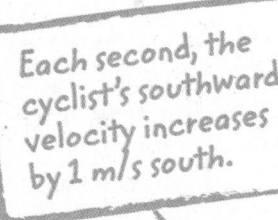

Each second, the cyclist's southward velocity increases by 1 m/s south.

1 m/s   2 m/s   3 m/s   4 m/s   5 m/s

South →

Speed

How is average acceleration calculated?

Acceleration is a change in velocity as compared with the time it takes to make the change. You can find the average acceleration experienced by an accelerating object using the following equation.

$$\text{average acceleration} = \frac{(\text{final velocity} - \text{starting velocity})}{\text{time}}$$

Velocity is expressed in meters per second (m/s) and time is measured in seconds (s). So acceleration is measured in meters per second per second, or meters per second squared (m/s^2).

As an example, consider an object that starts off moving at 8 m/s west, and then 16 s later is moving at 48 m/s west. The average acceleration of this object is found by the following equation.

$$a = \frac{(48 \text{ m/s} - 8 \text{ m/s})}{16 \text{ s}}$$
$$a = 2.5 \text{ m/s}^2 \text{ west}$$

© Houghton Mifflin Harcourt Publishing Company • Image Credits: (bkgd) ©Tim Graham/Getty Images

Active Reading

6 Identify Underline the units of acceleration.

This formula is often abbreviated as

$$a = \frac{(v_2 - v_1)}{t}$$

Visualize It!

7 Claims · Evidence · Reasoning What is the change in velocity of the cyclist below as he travels from point *B* to point *C*? What is his acceleration from point *B* to point *C*? Provide evidence to support your claim. Explain your reasoning.

8 Calculate Find the average acceleration of the cyclist moving from point *A* to point *B*, and over the whole trip (from point *A* to point *D*).

The cyclist is riding at 4 m/s. One second later, at the bottom of the hill, he is riding at 8 m/s. After going up a small incline, he has slowed to 7 m/s.

A 4 m/s
t = 0 s

B 8 m/s
t = 1 s

C 8 m/s
t = 2 s

D 7 m/s
t = 3 s

What a Drag!

How can accelerating objects change velocity?

Like velocity, acceleration is a vector, with a magnitude and a direction.

Accelerating Objects Change Speed

Although the word *acceleration* is commonly used to mean an increasing speed, in scientific use, the word applies to both increases and decreases in speed.

When you slide down a hill, you go from a small velocity to a large one. An increase in velocity like this is called *positive acceleration*. When a race car slows down, it goes from a high velocity to a low velocity. A decrease in velocity like this is called *negative acceleration*.

What is the acceleration when an object decreases speed? Because the initial velocity is larger than the final velocity, the term $(v_2 - v_1)$ will be negative. So the acceleration $a = \dfrac{(v_2 - v_1)}{t}$ will be a negative.

When acceleration and velocity (rate of motion) are in the same direction, the speed will increase. When acceleration and velocity are in opposing directions, the acceleration works against the initial motion in that direction, and the speed will decrease.

Active Reading

9 Identify Underline the term for an increase in velocity and the term for a decrease in velocity.

The parachute dragging on the air slows the car down, causing a negative acceleration.

Sliding down a hill causes a positive acceleration.

Accelerating Objects Change Direction

An object changing direction of motion experiences acceleration even when it does not speed up or slow down. Think about a car that makes a sharp left turn. The direction of velocity changes from "forward" to "left." This change in velocity is an acceleration, even if the speed does not change. As the car finishes the turn, the acceleration drops to zero.

What happens, however, when an object is *always* turning? An object traveling in a circular motion is always changing its direction, so it always experiences acceleration. Acceleration in circular motion is known as **centripetal acceleration**. (sehn•TRIP•ih•tahl ack•SELL•uh•ray•shuhn)

A skater rounding a curve experiences centripetal acceleration.

Inquiry

10 Conclude An acceleration in the direction of motion increases speed, and an acceleration opposite to the direction of motion decreases speed. What direction is the acceleration in centripetal acceleration, where speed does not change but direction does? Describe an example as evidence and reasoning to support your claim.

_____

_____

_____

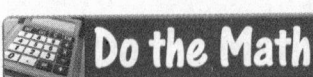
Do the Math

11 Calculate The horse is galloping at 13 m/s. Five seconds later, after climbing the hill, the horse is moving at 5.5 m/s. Find the acceleration that describes this change in velocity.

$$a = \frac{(v_2 - v_1)}{t}$$

5.5 m/s
5 seconds

Running uphill is tough to do without slowing down!

13 m/s
0 seconds

Visual Summary

To complete this summary, complete the statements below by filling in the blanks. You can use this page to review the main concepts of the lesson.

Acceleration

Acceleration measures a change in velocity.

 0:03  0:11

1 m/s   5 m/s

12 The formula for calculating average acceleration is

_____

Acceleration can be a change in speed or a change in direction of motion.

13 When acceleration and velocity are in the same direction, the speed will _____

14 When acceleration and velocity are in opposing directions, the speed will _____

15 Objects traveling in _____ motion experience centripetal acceleration.

Answers: 12 $a = \dfrac{(v_2 - v_1)}{t}$; 13 increase; 14 decrease; 15 circular

16 Synthesize Explain why a moving object cannot come to a stop instantaneously (in zero seconds). Hint: Think about the acceleration that would be required.

Lesson Review

Vocabulary

Fill in the blank with the term that best completes the following sentences.

1 Acceleration is a change in _____

2 _____ occurs when an object travels in a curved path.

3 A decrease in the magnitude of velocity is called _____

4 An increase in the magnitude of velocity is called _____

Key Concepts

5 State The units for acceleration are

_____

6 Label In the equation $a = \dfrac{(v_2 - v_1)}{t}$, what do v_1 and v_2 represent?

_____

_____

7 Calculate What is the acceleration experienced by a car that takes 10 s to reach 27 m/s from rest?

8 Identify Acceleration can be a change in speed or _____

9 Identify A helicopter flying west begins experiencing an acceleration of 3 m/s² east. Will the magnitude of its velocity increase or decrease?

_____

_____

Critical Thinking

10 Model Describe a situation when you might travel at a high velocity, but with low acceleration.

_____

_____

_____

Use this graph to answer the following questions. Assume Jenny's direction did not change.

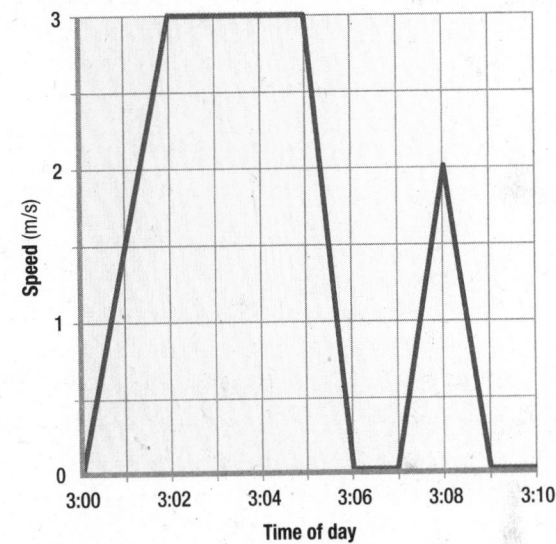

Jenny's Bike Ride

11 Analyze During what intervals was Jenny negatively accelerating?

_____

_____

12 Analyze During what intervals was Jenny positively accelerating?

_____

_____

13 Analyze During what intervals was Jenny not accelerating at all?

_____

_____

_____

My Notes

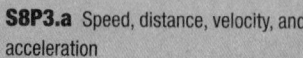

Forces

ESSENTIAL QUESTION

How do forces affect motion?

By the end of this lesson, you should be able to describe different types of forces and explain the effect force has on motion.

Even though this skydiver is not touching the ground, a force is still being exerted on him by Earth.

S8P3.a Speed, distance, velocity, and acceleration

S8P3.b Newton's Laws of Motion

S8P3.c Force, acceleration, and inertia

S8P5.a Fields and forces

Lesson Labs

Quick Labs
• Net Force
• First Law of Skateboarding

S.T.E.M. Lab
• Newton's Laws of Motion

 **Engage Your Brain**

1 Illustrate Draw a diagram showing how forces act on a ball tossed into the air.

2 Describe Write a caption for this photo.

 Active Reading

3 Apply Many scientific words, such as *net*, also have everyday meanings. Use context clues to write your own definition for each meaning of the word *net*.

Example sentence
The fisherman scooped his catch out of the water with a net.

net:

_____

_____

Example sentence
Subtract the mass of the container from the total mass of the substance and the container to determine the net mass of the substance.

net:

_____

_____

Vocabulary Terms
• force   • inertia
• net force

4 Apply As you learn the definition of each vocabulary term in this lesson, create your own definition or sketch to help you remember the meaning of the term.

A Tour de Forces

What is a force, and how does it act on an object?

You have probably heard the word *force* used in conversation. People say, "Don't force the issue," or "Our team is a force to be reckoned with." Scientists also use the word *force*. What exactly is a force, as it is used in science?

A Force Is a Push or a Pull

 **Active Reading** **5 Identify** As you read, underline the unit that is used to express force.

In science, a **force** is simply a push or a pull. All forces have both a size and a direction. A force can cause an object to change its speed or direction. When you see a change in an object's motion, one or more forces caused the change. The unit used to express force is the newton (N). You will learn how to calculate force a little later in this lesson.

Forces exist only when there is an object for them to act on. However, forces do not always cause an object to move. When you sit in a chair, the chair does not move. Your downward force on the chair is balanced by the upward force from the floor.

Visualize It!

6 Identify Draw arrows to represent the pushing forces in the image at left and the pulling forces in the image at right.

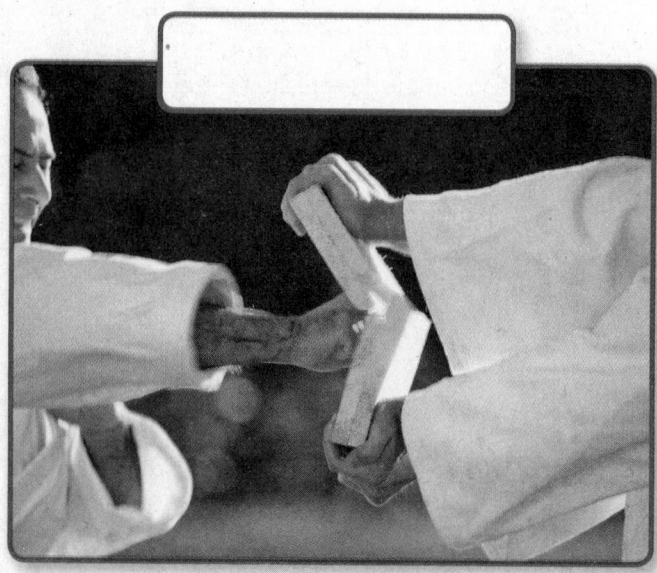

A Force Can Act Directly on an Object

It is not always easy to tell what is exerting a force or what is being acted on by a force. When one object touches or bumps into another object, we say that the objects are in contact with each other. A force exerted during contact between objects is a contact force. Friction is an example of a contact force between two surfaces. Suppose you slide a book across your desk. The amount of friction between the surface of the desk and the book cover determines how easily the book moves. Car tires rely on friction to keep a moving car from sliding off a road. Cars may slide on icy roads because ice lowers the force of friction on the tires.

A Force Can Act on an Object from a Distance

Forces can also act at a distance. One force that acts at a distance is called gravity. When you jump, gravity pulls you back to the ground even though you are not touching Earth. Magnetic force is another example of a force that can act at a distance. Magnetic force can be a push or a pull. A magnet can hold paper to a metal refrigerator door. The magnet touches the paper, not the metal, so the magnetic force is acting on the refrigerator door at a distance. Magnetic force also acts at a distance when the like poles of two magnets push each other apart. A magnetic levitation train floats because magnetic forces push the train away from its track.

Visualize It!

7 Identify The arrows in the picture below represent contact and distance forces. Label each arrow with a "C" if it is a contact force or "D" if it is a distance force.

In the Balance

What happens when multiple forces act on an object?

Usually, more than one force is acting on an object. The combination of all the forces acting on an object is called the **net force**. How do you determine net force? The answer depends on the directions of the forces involved.

When forces act in the same direction, you simply add them together to determine the net force. For example, when forces of 1 N and 2 N act in the same direction on an object, the net force is 1 N + 2 N = 3 N. When forces act in opposite directions, you subtract the smaller force from the larger force to determine the net force: 2 N – 1 N = 1 N.

Active Reading

8 Identify As you read, underline how one determines net force.

Visualize It!

9 Calculate Calculate the net force acting on the appliance box and use it to determine if the box will move.

_____

_____

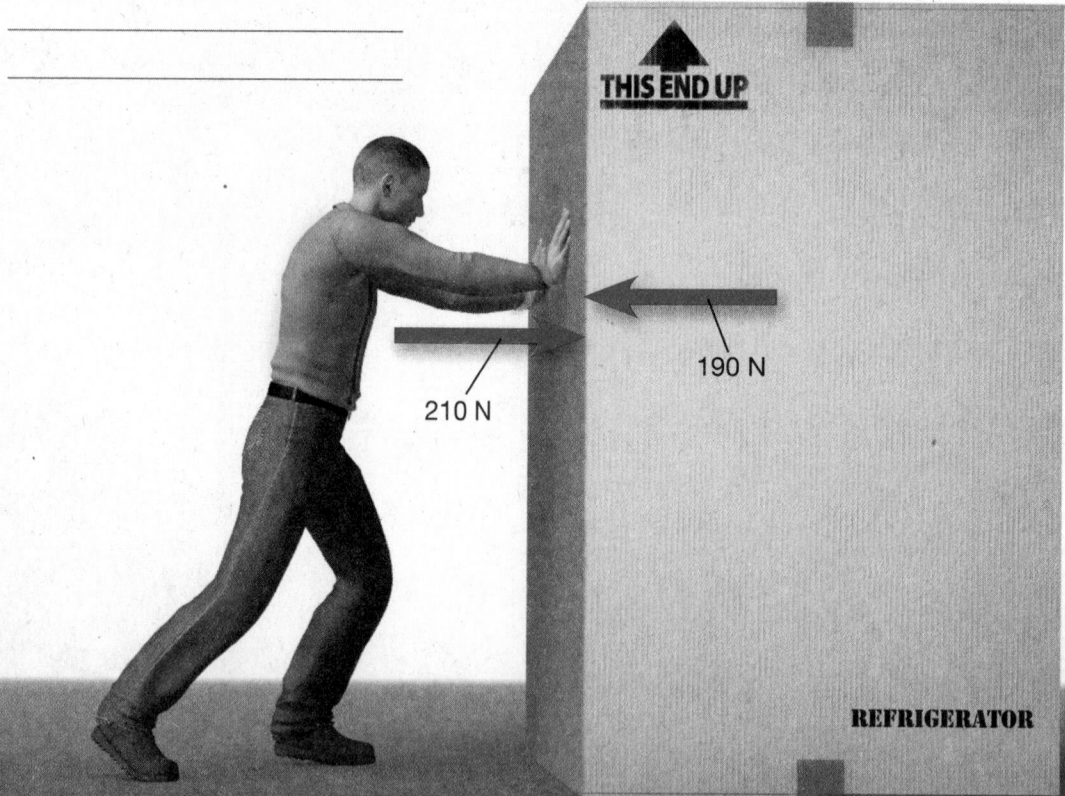

210 N

190 N

THIS END UP

REFRIGERATOR

The Forces Can Be Balanced

When the forces on an object produce a net force of 0 N, the forces are balanced. Balanced forces will not cause a change in the motion of a moving object or cause a nonmoving object to start moving. Many objects around you have only balanced forces acting on them. A light hanging from the ceiling does not move, because the force of gravity pulling downward on the light is balanced by the force of the chain pulling the light upward.

The Forces Can Be Unbalanced

When the net force on an object is not 0 N, the forces are unbalanced. Unbalanced forces produce a change in the object's motion. It could be a change in its speed or direction or both. This change in motion is called acceleration. The acceleration is always in the direction of the net force. For example, when a big dog and a small dog play with a tug toy, the bigger dog pulls with greater force, so the acceleration is in the direction of the bigger dog.

 **Visualize It!**

10 **Apply** The arrows in the first image show that the forces on the rope are balanced. Draw arrows on the second image to show how the forces on the rope are unbalanced.

These two tug-of-war teams are pulling on the rope with equal force to produce a net force of 0 N. The rope does not move.

One of these teams is pulling on the rope with more force. The rope moves in the direction of the stronger team.

What is Newton's First Law of Motion?

Force and motion are related. In the 1680s, British scientist Sir Isaac Newton explained this relationship between force and motion with three laws of motion.

Newton's first law describes the motion of an object that has a net force of 0 N acting on it. The law states: *An object at rest stays at rest, and an object in motion stays in motion at the same speed and direction, unless it experiences an unbalanced force.* Let's look at the two parts of this law more closely.

An Object at Rest Stays at Rest

Active Reading **11 Identify** As you read, underline examples of objects affected by inertia.

Newton's first law is also called the law of inertia. **Inertia** (ih•NER•shuh) is the tendency of all objects to resist a change in motion. An object will not move until a force makes it move. So a chair will not slide across the floor unless a force pushes the chair, and a golf ball will not leave the tee until a force pushes it off.

Visualize It!

12 Explain Do the dishes on a table have inertia? Provide evidence from the illustrations below. Explain your reasoning.

_____

_____

_____

An Object in Motion Stays in Motion

Now let's look at the second part of Newton's first law of motion. It states that an object in motion stays in motion at the same speed and direction, or velocity, unless it experiences an unbalanced force. Think about coming to a sudden stop while riding in a car. The car stops because the brakes apply friction to the wheel, making the forces acting on the car unbalanced. You keep moving forward until your seat belt applies an unbalanced force on you. This force stops your forward motion.

Both parts of the law are really stating the same thing. After all, an object at rest has a velocity—its velocity is zero!

© Houghton Mifflin Harcourt Publishing Company • Image Credits: (bg) ©Fstop/Photodisc/Getty Images

Think Outside the Book Inquiry

13 **Claims · Evidence · Reasoning**
Create a model that demonstrates the concept of inertia. Clearly state Newton's first law. Summarize how your model supports the law. Explain your reasoning.

When this car was in motion, the test dummy was moving forward at the same velocity as the car. When the car hit the barrier and stopped, the dummy kept moving until it, too, was acted on by a net backward force.

FO4305OZ02

0001768

👁 **Visualize It!**

14 **Infer** What forces acted on the test dummy to stop its forward motion?

_____

_____

_____

_____

_____

What is Newton's Second Law of Motion?

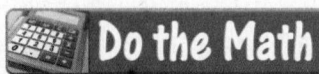

15 Identify As you read, underline Newton's second law of motion.

When an unbalanced force acts on an object, the object accelerates. Newton's second law describes this motion. The law states: *The acceleration of an object depends on the mass of the object and the amount of force applied.*

In other words, objects that have different masses will have different accelerations if the same amount of force is used. Imagine pushing a shopping cart. When the cart is empty, you need only a small force to accelerate it. But if the cart is full of groceries, the same amount of force causes a much smaller acceleration.

Force Equals Mass Times Acceleration

Newton's second law links force, mass, and acceleration. We can express this relationship using the equation $F = ma$, where F stands for applied force, m stands for mass, and a stands for acceleration. This equation tells us that a given force applied to a large mass will result in a small acceleration. When the same force is applied to a smaller mass, the acceleration will be larger.

Do the Math Sample Problem

These players train by pushing a massive object. If the players push with a force of 150 N, and the object has a mass of 75 kg, what is the object's acceleration? One newton is equal to $1 \text{ kg} \cdot \text{m/s}^2$.

Use Newton's law:

$$F = ma$$
$$150 \text{ kg} \cdot \text{m/s}^2 = (75 \text{ kg})(a)$$
$$a = \frac{150}{75} \text{ m/s}^2$$
$$a = 2.0 \text{ m/s}^2$$

You Try It

16 Calculate For a more difficult training session, the mass to be pushed is increased to 160 kg. If the players still push with a force of 150 N, what is the acceleration of the object?

Use Newton's law:

$$F = ma$$
$$150 \text{ N} =$$

© Houghton Mifflin Harcourt Publishing Company • Image Credits: (l) ©HMH; (r) ©HMH

How is the law of force and acceleration applied to everyday situations?

The law of force and acceleration indicates that an object with greater mass requires a larger force in order to accelerate the object. For example, you know that a strong adult can lift a heavier object than a small child can. This is because the adult has larger muscles and can exert more force.

Engineers use the law of force and acceleration when they design engines for vehicles and construction equipment. The larger the vehicle, the more powerful the engine that will be needed in order to make the vehicle move.

Visualize It!

17 Explain Look at the picture to the right. The truck is out of gas. The truck has a mass of 1500 kg and is loaded with 1000 kg of furniture. The man must apply 82 N of force for 60 seconds to bring the truck from rest to a velocity of 2.0 m/s. If the man had first unloaded half of the furniture (500 kg), only 66 N of force for 60 seconds would be needed to reach the same velocity. If he had unloaded all of the furniture, only 50 N of force for 60 seconds would be needed to reach the same velocity. Calculate the acceleration of the loaded truck, half-loaded truck, and empty truck.

A

B Plot the data above in the space below.

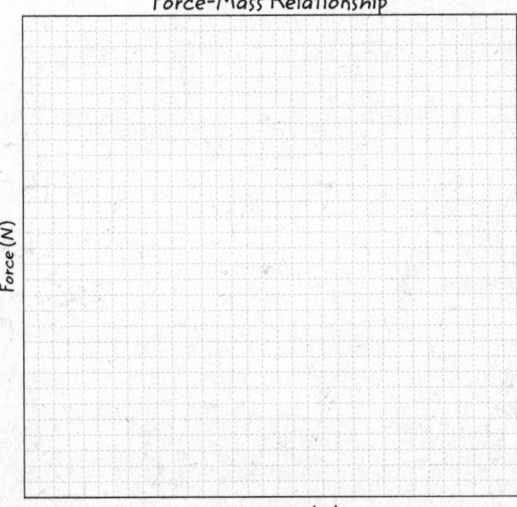

Force-Mass Relationship

Force (N)

Truck mass (kg)

C How does the amount of force needed to accelerate an object relate to the object's mass? State your claim and use the graph as evidence to support it.

What is Newton's Third Law of Motion?

Newton also devised a third law of motion. The law states: *Whenever one object exerts a force on a second object, the second object exerts an equal and opposite force on the first.*

So when you push against a wall, Newton's law tells you that the wall is actually pushing back against you.

Objects Exert Force on Each Other

Newton's third law also can be stated as: All forces act in pairs. Whenever one object exerts a force on a second object, the second object exerts an equal and opposite force on the first. There are action forces and reaction forces. Action and reaction forces are present even when there is no motion. For example, you exert a force on a chair when you sit on it. Your weight pushing down on the chair is the action force. The reaction force is the force exerted by the chair that pushes up on your body.

Forces in Pairs Have Equal Size but Opposite Directions

When an object pushes against another object, the second object pushes back equally hard, in the opposite direction. In the pool below, the swimmer's feet push against the wall as he moves forward. This push is the action force. The wall also exerts a force on the swimmer. This is the reaction force, and it moves the swimmer forward. The forces do not act on the same object. Read on to find out why the swimmer moves but the wall does not!

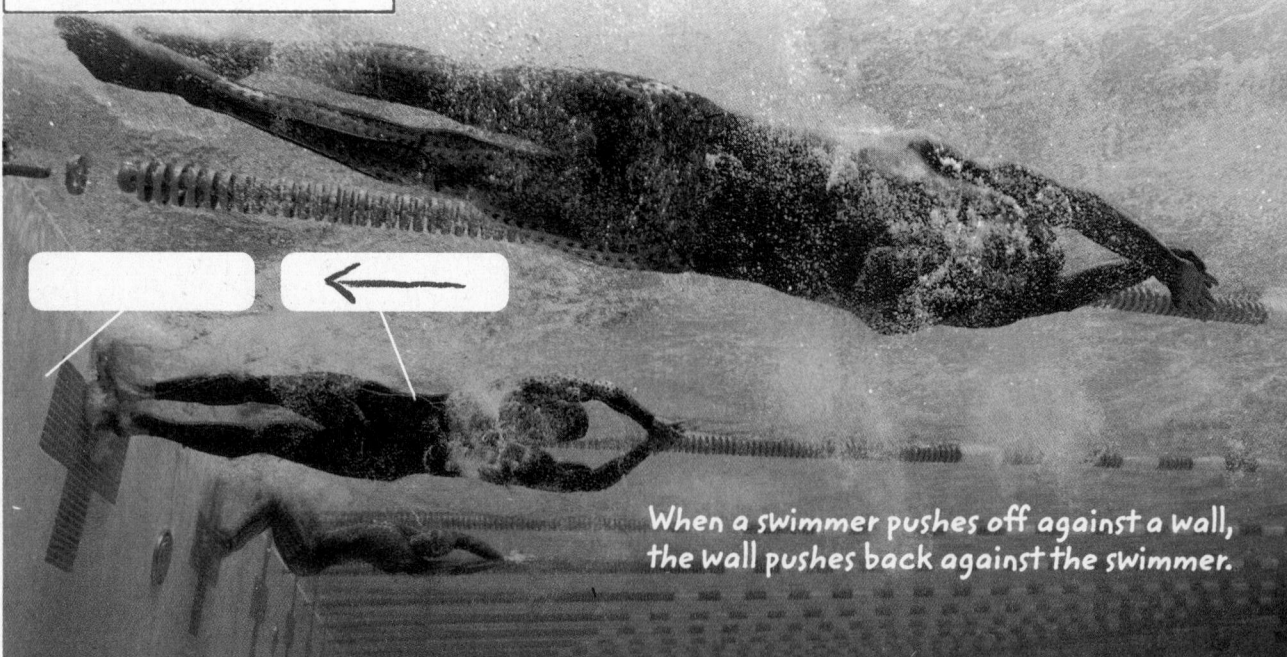

> **Visualize It!**
>
> **18 Apply** The arrow below represents the action force exerted by the swimmer. Draw an arrow that represents the reaction force.

When a swimmer pushes off against a wall, the wall pushes back against the swimmer.

Forces Acting in Pairs Can Have Unequal Effects

Even though action and reaction forces are equal in size, their effects are often different. Gravitation is a force pair between two objects. If you drop a ball, gravity in an action force pulls the ball toward Earth. But the reaction force pulls Earth toward the ball! It's easy to see the effect of the action force. Why don't you see the effect of the reaction force—Earth being pulled upward? Newton's second law answers this question. The force on the ball is the same size as the force on Earth. However, Earth has much more mass than the ball. So Earth's acceleration is much smaller than that of the ball!

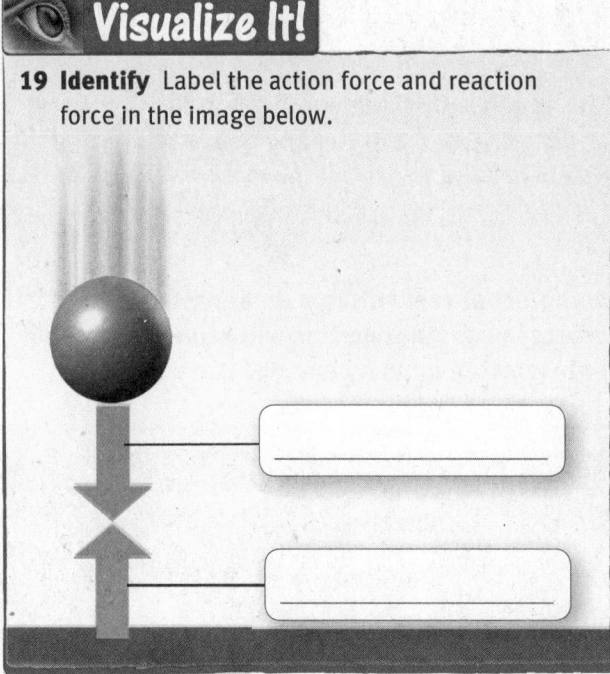

Visualize It!

19 Identify Label the action force and reaction force in the image below.

Forces Can Act in Multiple Pairs

An object can have multiple forces acting on it at once. When this happens, each force is part of a force pair. For example, when a baseball bat hits a baseball, the bat does not fly backward. A force is exerted on the ball by the bat. The bat does not fly backward, because the player's hands are exerting another force on the bat. What then keeps the player's hands from flying backward when the bat hits the ball? The bones and muscles in the player's arms exert a force on the hands. As you can see, a simple activity such as playing baseball involves the action of many forces at the same time.

20 Claims · Evidence · Reasoning. Can Earth's gravitational field exert a force on objects not in contact with Earth? Use evidence and Newton's laws of motion to support your claim.

_____

_____

Visual Summary

To complete this summary, fill in the blanks with the correct word or phrase. Then use the key below to check your answers. You can use this page to review the main concepts of the lesson.

Forces

An object at rest will remain at rest and an object in constant motion will remain in motion unless acted upon by an unbalanced force.

21 Newton's first law is also called the law of _____

When an unbalanced force acts on an object, the object moves with accelerated motion.

22 In the formula F = ma, m stands for _____

Whenever one object exerts a force on a second object, the second object exerts an equal and opposite force on the first.

23 Forces in the same pair have equal size but opposite_____

24 Synthesize A car designer is designing a new model of a popular car. He wants to use the same engine as in the old model, but improve the new car's acceleration. Use Newton's second law to explain how to improve the car's acceleration without redesigning the engine.

Lesson Review

Vocabulary

Draw a line to connect the following terms to their definitions.

1 force

2 inertia

3 newton

A resistance of an object to a change in motion

B the unit that expresses force

C a push or a pull

Key Concepts

4 Describe What is the action force and the reaction force when you sit down on a chair?

_____

_____

_____

_____

_____

_____

5 Summarize How do you determine net force?

_____

_____

_____

_____

_____

6 Explain How do tests with crash dummies, seat belts, and air bags illustrate Newton's first law of motion?

_____

_____

_____

_____

_____

Critical Thinking

Use this photo to answer the following questions.

7 Identify This rock, known as Balanced Rock, sits on a thin spike of rock in a canyon in Idaho. Explain the forces that keep the rock balanced on its tiny pedestal.

_____

_____

_____

8 Calculate Balanced Rock has a mass of about 36,000 kg. If the acceleration due to gravity is 9.8 m/s^2, what is the force that the rock is exerting on its pedestal?

_____

_____

_____

_____

9 Infer What would happen to the moon if Earth stopped exerting the force of gravity on it?

_____

_____

_____

My Notes

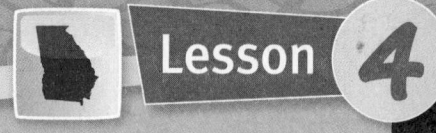
Gravity and Motion

ESSENTIAL QUESTION

How do objects move under the influence of gravity?

By the end of this lesson, you should be able to describe the effect that gravity, including Earth's gravity, has on matter.

Overcoming the force of gravity is hard to do for very long!

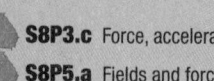 **S8P3.c** Force, acceleration, and inertia

S8P5.a Fields and forces

Engage Your Brain

1 Predict Check *T* or *F* to show whether you think each statement is true or false.

T F

☐ ☐ Earth's gravity makes heavy objects fall faster than light objects.

☐ ☐ A person would weigh the same on other planets as on Earth.

☐ ☐ Planets are round because of gravity.

2 Infer List some ways houses would be built differently if gravity were much stronger or much weaker.

_____

_____

_____

_____

_____

Active Reading

3 Predict What do you think the phrase *free fall* might mean? Write your own definition. After reading the lesson, see how close you were!

_____

_____

_____

_____

Vocabulary Terms

- gravity
- free fall
- orbit

4 Apply This list contains the key terms you'll learn in this section. As you read, underline the definition of each term.

Down to EARTH

Gravity pulls the skydiver, his clothes, and his parachute toward the Earth, all with the same acceleration.

This stop-action photo shows that when there is no air resistance, a feather and a billiard ball fall at the same rate.

Active Reading

5 Analyze Does Earth's gravity accelerate all masses at the same rate? Provide evidence and reasoning to support your claim.

_____

_____

What is gravity?

If you watch video of astronauts on the moon, you see them wearing big, bulky spacesuits and yet jumping lightly. Why is leaping on the moon easier than on Earth? The answer is gravity. **Gravity** is a force of attraction between objects due to their mass. Gravity is a noncontact force that acts between two objects at any distance apart. Even when a skydiver is far above the ground, Earth's gravity acts to pull him downward.

Gravity Is An Attractive Force

Earth's gravity pulls everything toward Earth's center. It pulls, but it does not push, so it is called an attractive force.

You feel the force due to Earth's gravity as the heaviness of your body, or your weight. Weight is a force, and it depends on mass. Greater mass results in greater weight. This force of gravity between Earth and an object is equal to the mass of the object m multiplied by a factor due to gravity g.

$$F = mg$$

On Earth, g is about 9.8 m/s^2. The units are the same as the units for acceleration. Does this mean that Earth's gravity accelerates all objects in the same way? The surprising answer is yes.

Suppose you dropped a heavy object and a light object at the same time. Which would hit the ground first? Sometimes an object experiences a lot of air resistance and falls slowly or flutters to the ground. But if you could take away air resistance, all objects would fall with the same acceleration. When gravity is the only force affecting the fall, a light object and a heavy object hit the ground at the same time.

Acceleration depends on both force and mass. The heavier object experiences a greater force, or weight. But the heavier object is also harder to accelerate, because it has more mass. The two effects cancel, and the acceleration due to gravity is the same for all masses.

Gravity Affects Mass Equally

All matter has mass. Gravity is a result of mass, so all matter is affected by gravity. Every object exerts a gravitational pull on every other object. Your pencil and shoes are gravitationally attracted to each other, each to your textbook, all three to your chair, and so on. So why don't objects pull each other into a big pile? The gravitational forces between these objects are too small. Other forces, such as friction, are strong enough to balance the gravitational pulls and prevent changes in motion. Gravity is not a very powerful force—you overcome the attraction of Earth's entire mass on your body every time you stand up!

However, when enough mass gathers together, its effect can be large. Gravity caused Earth and other planets to become round. All parts of the planet pulled each other toward the center of mass, resulting in a sphere.

Some astronomical bodies do not have enough mass to pull themselves into spheres. Small moons and asteroids can maintain a lumpy shape, but larger moons such as Earth's have enough mass to form a sphere.

Gravity also acts over great distances. It determines the motion of celestial bodies. The paths of planets, the sun, and other stars are determined by gravity. Even the motion of our galaxy through the universe is due to gravity.

Galaxies, made up of billions of stars, have characteristic shapes and motions that are due to gravity.

Deimos, one of the moons of Mars, is only about 15 km at its longest stretch. Deimos does not have enough mass to form a sphere.

Visualize It!

6 Claims · Evidence · Reasoning
Use the diagram below to explain how the moon's path in its orbit around Earth is evidence of a gravitational field that acts over distances. Clearly state your reasoning.

_____

_____

Earth's moon has a diameter of more than 3,400 km. It has more than enough mass to pull itself into a sphere.

≈3,400 km

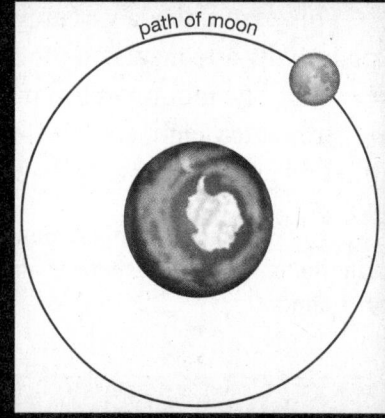

path of moon

A WEIGHTY Issue

What determines the force of gravity?

The law of universal gravitation relates gravitational force, mass, and distance. It states that all objects attract each other through gravitational force. The strength of the force depends on the masses involved and distance between them.

Gravity Depends on Distance

The gravitational force between two objects increases as the distance between their centers decreases. This means that objects far apart have a weaker attraction than objects close together. If two objects move closer, the attraction between them increases. For example, you can't feel the sun's gravity because it is so far away, but if you were able to stand on the surface of the sun, you would find it impossible to move due to the gravity!

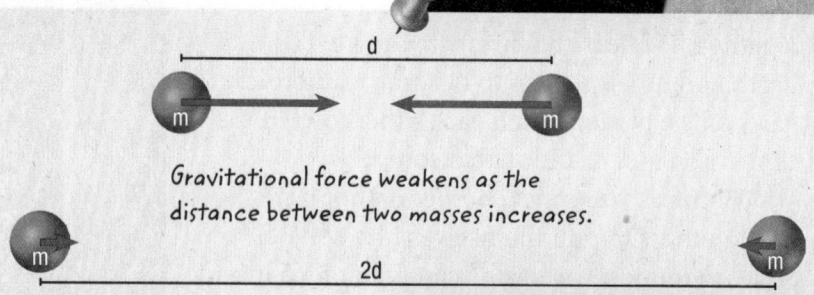

Gravitational force weakens as the distance between two masses increases.

Active Reading **7 Explain** How does distance affect gravitational force?

_____

_____

Gravity Depends on Mass

The gravitational force between two objects increases with the mass of each object. This means that objects with greater mass have more attraction between them. A cow has more mass than a cat, so there is more attraction between the Earth and the cow, and the cow weighs more.

This part of the law of universal gravitation explains why astronauts on the moon bounce when they walk. The moon has less mass than Earth, so the astronauts weigh less. The force of each step pushes an astronaut higher than it would on Earth.

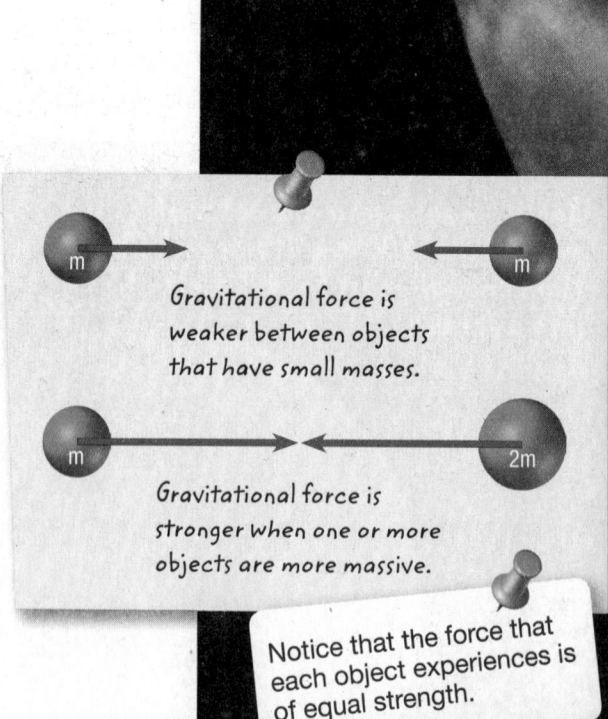

Gravitational force is weaker between objects that have small masses.

Gravitational force is stronger when one or more objects are more massive.

Active Reading **8 Explain** How does mass affect gravitational force? Use evidence and reasoning to support your claim.

_____

_____

Notice that the force that each object experiences is of equal strength.

Finding Gravity in Strange Places

The gravity of the moon is less than that of Earth, because the moon has much less mass than Earth.

Weight ≠

The moon does not pull as hard on an astronaut, so the force of her weight on the scale is less. The astronaut weighs less on the moon than on Earth.

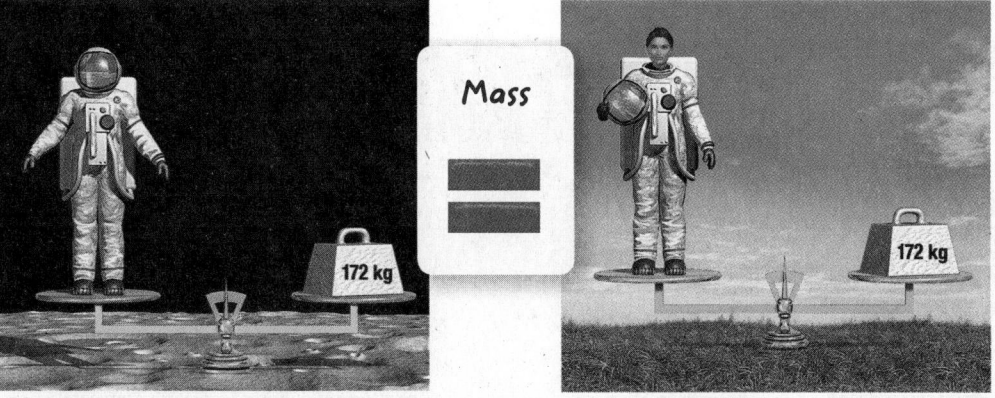

Mass =

The astronaut has the same mass on the moon and Earth.

9 List This table lists the weights of a 80 kg person on different planets. List these planets in decreasing order of mass.

_____
_____
_____
_____

Planet	Weight of 80 kg
Venus	710 N
Earth	784 N
Mars	297 N
Jupiter	1983 N

10 Justify The weight of 80 kg of mass on Mercury is 296 N, almost identical to the weight of the same mass on Mars! But Mercury has much less mass than Mars! Explain how this can be. (What else could affect gravitational force?)

_____
_____
_____
_____
_____

Don't Bring Me DOWN

How does gravity keep objects in orbit?

Something is in **free fall** when gravity is pulling it down and no other forces are acting on it. An object is in **orbit** when it travels around another object in space. When a satellite or spacecraft orbits Earth, it is moving forward. But it is also in free fall. The combination of the forward motion and downward motion due to gravity combine to cause orbiting.

A spacecraft in orbit is always falling, but never hits the ground! This happens because of forward motion. As the object falls, it moves forward far enough that the planet curves away under it, so it has exactly that much farther to fall. It never actually gets closer to Earth. In order to move forward far enough to counteract the fall, objects in orbit must travel very fast—as much as 8 kilometers per second!

Active Reading

11 Identify When is an object in free fall?

_____

_____

_____

_____

How Does a Satellite Stay in Orbit?

The satellite moves forward at a constant speed. If there were no gravity, the satellite would follow the path of the green line.

The satellite is in free fall because gravity pulls it toward Earth. The satellite would move straight down if it were not traveling forward.

12 Claims • Evidence • Reasoning Does Earth's gravitational field affect objects in space? State your claim. Summarize evidence to support your claim. Explain your reasoning.

_____

_____

_____

_____

_____

The discovery of the planet Neptune (above) was predicted by observing the effect that its gravity had on the motions of the planet Uranus.

The path of the satellite follows the curve of Earth's surface. Following a path around Earth is known as orbiting.

Gravity Can Make Objects Move in Circles

Besides spacecraft and satellites, many other objects in the universe are in orbit. The moon orbits Earth. Planets orbit the sun. Many stars orbit large masses in the center of galaxies. These objects travel along circular or elliptical paths. As an object moves along a curve, it changes direction constantly. The change in motion is due to an unbalanced force. The direction of the force must change constantly to produce curved motion. The force must be directed inward, toward the center of the curve or circle.

Gravity provides the force that keeps objects in orbit. This force pulls one object into a path that curves around another object. Gravitational force is directed inward. For example, this inward force pulls the moon toward Earth and constantly changes the moon's motion.

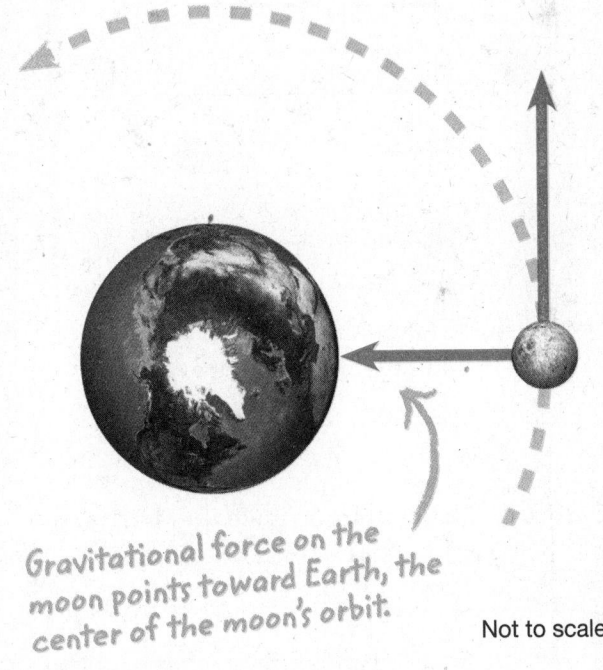

Gravitational force on the moon points toward Earth, the center of the moon's orbit.

Not to scale

13 **Model** Imagine tying a string to a ball and twirling it around you. How is this similar to the moon orbiting Earth? In this example, what is providing the constantly changing, inward force?

_____

_____

_____

_____

_____

Visual Summary

To complete this summary, read the statements in the boxes below. Circle any that are true. Cross out any that are false, and correct the statement so that it is true. You can use this page to review the main concepts of the lesson.

Gravity and Motion

Gravity is an attractive force that exists between all objects with mass.

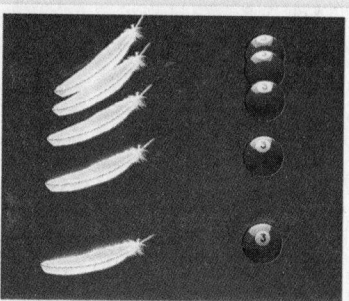

14 The acceleration due to gravity is the same for all falling objects when there is no air resistance.

_____

_____

Gravity depends on mass and distance.

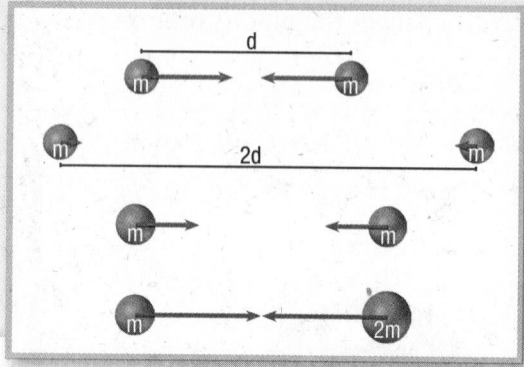

15 Gravitational force is stronger between objects with more mass.

_____

_____

16 Gravitational force is weaker between objects that are closer together.

_____

_____

Gravity keeps objects in orbit.

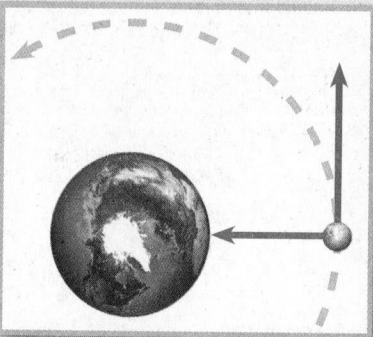

17 The moon does not fall to Earth because of friction.

_____

_____

Answers: 14 True; 15 True; 16 False, gravity is stronger when objects are closer; 17 False, the moon does not fall to Earth because of its forward motion.

18 Justify If Earth were replaced by an object with the same mass but much smaller in size, would the moon continue to orbit the new object, fall into it, or fly off into space? Why?

Lesson Review

Vocabulary

Fill in the blanks with the term that best completes the following sentences.

1 _____ is a force that attracts all matter to each other.

2 When the only force affecting an object is gravity, that object is in _____

3 An object traveling around another object in space is in _____

Key Concepts

4 Relate The gravitational attraction between two objects will _____ if one object acquires more mass.

5 Relate The gravitational attraction between two objects will _____ if the objects move farther apart.

6 Explain Why are large astronomical bodies such as planets and stars round?

_____

_____

_____

7 Identify What two motions combine to produce an orbit?

_____

_____

_____

_____

8 Distinguish Explain the difference between mass and weight.

_____

_____

_____

_____

_____

Critical Thinking

9 Infer The weight of an object on a planet depends not only on its mass, but also on its distance from the planet's center. This table lists the weight of 80 kg on each planet in the solar system. Uranus has more than 14 times as much mass as Earth, yet the gravitational force is less. Explain how this could be.

_____

_____

_____

_____

Planet	Weight of 80 kg
Mercury	296 N
Venus	710 N
Earth	784 N
Mars	297 N
Jupiter	1983 N
Saturn	838 N
Uranus	708 N
Neptune	859 N

10 Apply Why don't satellites in orbit fall to the ground? Why don't they fly off into space?

_____

_____

_____

_____

_____

My Notes

Steve Okamoto

ROLLER COASTER DESIGNER

A day in the life of a roller coaster designer is filled with twists and turns—just ask designer Steve Okamoto. As a kid, he became interested in roller coasters after a trip to Disneyland. To become a product designer, Steve studied subjects like math and science. He later earned a degree in product design that involved studying mechanical engineering and studio art.

Before he starts designing roller coasters, Steve has to think about all of the parts of a roller coaster and how it will fit in the amusement park. It's like putting together a huge puzzle. Different parts of the puzzle include the safety equipment needed, what the roller coaster will be made out of, and how the track will fit in next to other rides.

He also has to think about what visitors to the park will want to see and experience in a roller coaster ride.

As he is designing a roller coaster, Steve's math and science background comes in handy. For example, in order to make sure that a roller coaster's cars make it up each hill, he has to calculate the speed and acceleration of the cars on each part of the track. To create the curves, loops, and dips of the roller coaster track, he uses his knowledge of physics and geometry.

Acceleration from the downhill run provides the speed for the next climb.

JOB BOARD

Machinists

What You'll Do: Use machine tools, such as lathes, milling machines, and machining centers, to produce new metal parts.

Where You Might Work: Machine shops and manufacturing plants in industries including the automotive and aerospace industries.

Education: In high school, you should take math courses, especially trigonometry, and, if available, courses in blueprint reading, metalworking, and drafting. After high school, most people acquire their skills in an apprenticeship program. This gives a person a mix of classroom and on-the-job training.

Bicycle Mechanic

What You'll Do: Repair and maintain different kinds of bikes, from children's bikes to expensive road bikes.

Where You Might Work: Independent bicycle shops or large chain stores that carry bicycles; certain sporting events like Olympic and national trials.

Education: Some high schools and trade schools have shop classes that teach bicycle repair. Most bicycle mechanics get on-the-job training. To work as a mechanic at national and international cycling events, you will have to earn a bicycle mechanic's license.

PEOPLE IN SCIENCE NEWS

Mike Hensler

The Surf Chair

As a Daytona Beach lifeguard, Mike Hensler realized that the beach was almost impossible for someone in a wheelchair. Although he had never invented a machine before, Hensler decided to build a wheelchair that could be driven across sand without getting stuck. He began spending many evenings in his driveway with a pile of lawn-chair parts, designing the chair by trial and error.

The result looks very different from a conventional wheelchair. With huge rubber wheels and a thick frame of white PVC pipe, the Surf Chair not only moves easily over sandy terrain but also is weather resistant and easy to clean. The newest models of the Surf Chair come with optional attachments, such as a variety of umbrellas, detachable armrests and footrests, and even places to attach fishing rods.

Lesson 5

Fluids and Pressure

ESSENTIAL QUESTION

What happens when fluids exert pressure?

By the end of this lesson, you should be able to explain why fluids exert pressure and how the resulting pressure causes motion and the buoyant force.

The water in the river is a fluid. The air used to inflate the raft is also a fluid.

© Houghton Mifflin Harcourt Publishing Company • Image Credits: (bg) ©Henry Georgi/Corbis

---

Lesson Labs

Quick Labs
- Pressure Differences
- Finding the Buoyant Force

Field Lab
- Pressure in Fluids

Engage Your Brain

1 Describe Fill in the blank with the word that you think correctly completes the following sentences.

A cork will _____ on top of water.

A rock will _____ in water.

An object that sinks in water is more

_____ than water.

2 Describe Write your own caption to this photo. Include a description of the liquid's properties.

_____
_____
_____
_____

Active Reading

3 Apply Many scientific words, such as *pressure*, also have everyday meanings. Use context clues to write your own definition for each meaning of the word *pressure*.

Example sentence
Damien felt a lot of <u>pressure</u> because he knew the team was relying on him to hit a home run.

pressure:

_____
_____

Example sentence
When Jodie applied <u>pressure</u> to the clay, it started to flatten.

pressure:

_____
_____

Vocabulary Terms

- fluid
- pressure
- pascal
- atmospheric pressure
- buoyant force
- Archimedes' principle

4 Identify As you read, create a reference card for each vocabulary term. On one side of the card, write the term and its meaning. On the other side, draw an image that illustrates or makes a connection to the term. These cards can be used as bookmarks in the text so that you can refer to them while studying.

Feel the Pressure!

What are fluids?

Active Reading 5 Identify As you read, underline the characteristics of a fluid.

Can you think of a similarity between a container of water and a container of air? Water and air both take the shape of the container they are put into. Liquids and gases, like air, are fluids. A **fluid** is any material that can flow and that takes the shape of its container. A fluid can flow because its particles easily move past each other.

The water flows and takes the shape of the river channel.

Why do fluids exert pressure?

All fluids exert pressure. So, what is pressure? **Pressure** is the measure of how much force is acting on a given area. Any force exerted over an area, such as your body weight pushing down on the ground, creates pressure. When you pump up a bicycle tire, you push air into the tire. And like all matter, air is made of tiny particles that are constantly moving. Inside the tire, the air particles bump against one another and against the walls of the tire. The bumping of particles creates a force on the tire. The particles move in all directions and act on every part of the tire.

The air in the balloon exerts pressure on the balloon. As more air is added to the balloon, more pressure is exerted.

Visualize It!

6 Analyze Describe how the gas particles inside the balloon exert pressure on the balloon.

_____

_____

_____

© Houghton Mifflin Harcourt Publishing Company • Image Credits: (t) ©Philip and Karen Smith/Iconica/Getty Images; (b) ©HMH

How is pressure calculated?

Pressure can be calculated by using the following equation:

$$pressure = \frac{force}{area}$$

The SI unit for pressure is the **pascal**. One pascal (1 Pa) is the force of one newton exerted over an area of one square meter (1 N/m²). This equation can be used to find the pressure exerted by fluids as well as other materials.

As you can see from the equation, a greater force results in greater pressure. Pressure also depends on the area over which the force is exerted. A greater area results in less pressure.

Water inside is exerting pressure on the tank in all directions.

 Do the Math

Sample Problem

Calculate the pressure that water exerts on the bottom of a fish tank. The water presses down on the bottom with a force of 2,000 N, and the area of the bottom of the tank is 0.4 m².

Identify

A What do you know? area $= 0.4$ m², force $= 2,000$ N

B What do you want to find? pressure

Plan

C Write the formula: $pressure = \frac{force}{area}$

D Substitute the given values into the formula: $pressure = \frac{2,000\ N}{0.4\ m^2}$

Solve

E Divide: $\frac{2,000\ N}{0.4\ m^2} = 5,000\ N/m^2$

F Check that your units agree: *A pascal is a N/m², so the units are correct.*

Answer: 5,000 Pa

You Try It

7 Calculate Calculate the pressure that the air outside exerts on a window pane that is 1.5 m². The force with which the air pushes on the window is 150,000 N.

Identify

A What do you know?

B What do you want to find?

Plan

C Write the formula:

D Substitute the given values into the formula:

Solve

E Divide:

F Check that your units agree:

Answer:

Under Pressure

What are two familiar fluids that exert pressure?

All matter exerts pressure when it exerts force over an area. The atmosphere and water are two familiar fluids that exert pressure.

Active Reading **8 Identify** As you read, underline the similarities between air pressure and water pressure.

As altitude decreases, pressure increases.

The Atmosphere

The atmosphere is the layer of nitrogen, oxygen, and other gases that surrounds Earth. Gravity pulls these gases toward Earth's center, which results in the atmosphere having weight. The pressure caused by the weight of the atmosphere is called **atmospheric pressure**. Atmospheric pressure is exerted on everything on Earth, including you. Atmospheric pressure is usually expressed in kilopascals (kPa). A kilopascal is equal to 1,000 pascals.

Water

Gravity pulls water toward Earth's center just as it pulls the atmosphere. The weight of water causes pressure on objects under its surface. In addition to the weight of water above it, anything under water, such as a scuba diver, also has the weight of the air above the water pushing down on it. As a result, the total pressure under water is the sum of the pressures of the atmosphere and the water above.

As water depth increases, pressure increases.

Think Outside the Book Inquiry

9 Claims · Evidence · Reasoning In a small group, research the connection between Earth's gravity and the pressure of fluids. Clearly state how fluids may behave differently on the moon or on other planets. Summarize the evidence to support your claim. Explain your reasoning.

10 Identify Match each pressure with where it is found. Write the pressure 40 kPa, 100 kPa, or 130 kPa in the appropriate box.

A

B

C

How does depth affect fluid pressure?

Imagine a meteoroid heading toward Earth. At the top of the atmosphere, the pressure is close to 0 kPa. As the meteoroid falls, it passes Mt. Everest, the highest point on Earth. The pressure the atmosphere exerts on the meteoroid is about 33 kPa. As the meteoroid hits the ground at sea level, the atmospheric pressure is about 101 kPa. Notice that as the meteoroid travels deeper into the atmosphere, the pressure increases. The increase occurs because at a lower elevation, there is more atmosphere being pulled down by Earth's gravity. The greater weight of the air exerts a greater force, so the pressure is higher.

Water pressure also increases as depth increases. Imagine a diver on the surface of the ocean. Here, only the atmospheric pressure, or 101 kPa, acts on the diver. When the diver is 10 meters below the surface, the total pressure is about 202 kPa. At the deepest part of the ocean, the heaviest layer of both air and water press down with the greatest amount of force on the diver. This is where pressure is greatest.

11 Infer Is it more difficult to breathe at the top of Mt. Everest than on the beach? Support your claim with evidence and reasoning.

_____
_____
_____
_____
_____
_____
_____

Thar She Blows!

This whale exhales air explosively through its blowhole before taking another breath. The exhaled air forms a stream of air and water vapor.

What are some examples of fluid motion due to pressure?

When you drink through a straw, you remove some of the air in the straw. Because there is less air inside the straw, the pressure in the straw is reduced. However, the atmospheric pressure on the surface of the liquid outside of the straw remains the same. So, there is a difference between the pressure inside the straw and the pressure outside the straw. The outside pressure forces the liquid up the straw and into your mouth. So, just by drinking through a straw, you can observe an important property of fluids: At any given altitude, fluids flow from areas of higher pressure to areas of lower pressure.

Fluid Motion and Breathing

When you take a deep breath, fluid flows from higher to lower pressure. As you inhale, your lungs expand. This expansion lowers the pressure in your lungs. The pressure in your lungs is now lower than the air pressure outside your lungs. Air flows into your lungs—from higher to lower pressure. When your lungs are filled, the pressure inside your lungs increases. When you exhale, the air in your lungs flows out from a region of higher pressure to a region of lower pressure.

Active Reading **12 Describe** In your own words, describe the movement of air when you inhale.

_____
_____
_____
_____

13 Explain Is greater pressure exerted inside the whale's body or outside the blowhole? Explain your reasoning.

_____
_____
_____
_____

© Houghton Mifflin Harcourt Publishing Company • Image Credits: ©Francois Gohier/Photo Researchers, Inc.

Fluid Motion and Weather

At any given altitude in the atmosphere, there are areas of higher pressure and areas of lower pressure. Air moves from areas of higher pressure to areas of lower pressure. The movement of the air is known as wind.

Some of the damaging winds caused by tornadoes are the result of pressure differences. There is a great difference between the very low air pressure inside a tornado and the higher air pressure outside a tornado. This difference causes air to rush into the center of the tornado.

 Visualize It!

14 Analyze Write *low pressure* or *high pressure* in each of the blank boxes.

A

B

A tornado acts like a giant vacuum cleaner. Objects are pushed toward the center of the tornado and sucked inside. The tornado can even carry them away.

Sink or Swim?

What causes buoyant force?

When an object is immersed in fluid, pressure is exerted on all sides of the object. The pressure that the fluid exerts against the bottom of an object is the buoyant force. **Buoyant force** (BOY•uhnt FOHRS) is an upward force that fluids exert on all matter.

How is buoyant force calculated?

Archimedes was a Greek mathematician who lived in the third century BCE. He described buoyant force. **Archimedes' principle** (ar•kuh•MEE•deez PRIN•suh•puhl) states that the buoyant force acting on an object in a fluid is an upward force equal to the weight of fluid that the object displaces. Imagine that you lower a brick into a glass of water. As the brick sinks, the water level rises. The volume of water that must be moved to make room for the brick is equal to the volume of the brick. And the weight of that water is the buoyant force.

The buoyant force acting on this iceberg pushes it up, so that part of it is out of the water.

👁 Visualize It!

15 Apply Which part of the iceberg displaces water equal in weight to the buoyant force? Support your claim with evidence and reasoning.

_____

_____

Mifflin Harcourt Publishing Company • Image Credits: ©Ralph A. Clevenger/Corbis

What can happen as a result of weight and buoyant force?

Imagine that you use a straw to push an ice cube under water. Then you release the ice cube. Will it sink or pop back up to the surface? This depends on its weight and the buoyant force.

Some Objects Float

An object in a fluid will float if the object's weight is equal to the buoyant force. In this case, the buoyant force pushing the object up is the same as the force pushing the object down. If the object and the fluid have the same density, the object will float suspended under the surface of the fluid. If the object is less dense than the fluid, it will float at the surface, and will be only partly submerged.

Some Objects Sink

An object in a fluid will sink if the object's weight is greater than the buoyant force. The object's weight will be greater than the buoyant force if the object is denser than the fluid.

Some Objects Are Buoyed Up

If the buoyant force on an object is greater than the object's weight, the object is buoyed up. This means that an object moves upward in a fluid until the buoyant force equals the object's weight, causing the object to float. This principle explains why an ice cube pops to the surface when it is pushed to the bottom of a glass of water.

Active Reading

16 Identify As you read, underline the relationships between weight and buoyant force that cause an object to float, sink, or be buoyed up.

Visualize It!

17 Predict Examine each of the three pictures below and determine whether the object shown floats, sinks, or is buoyed up when submerged in water.

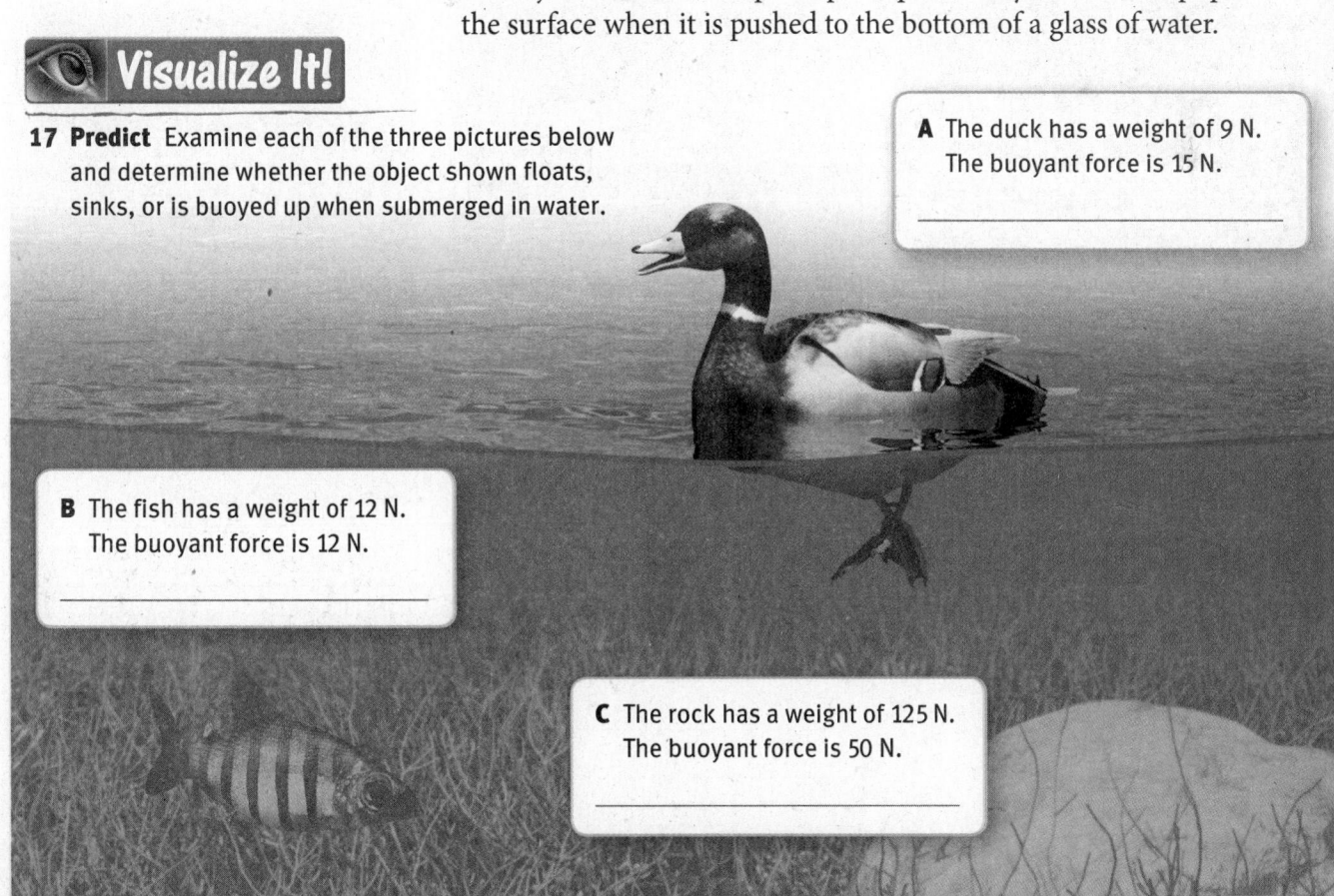

A The duck has a weight of 9 N. The buoyant force is 15 N.

_____

B The fish has a weight of 12 N. The buoyant force is 12 N.

_____

C The rock has a weight of 125 N. The buoyant force is 50 N.

_____

What affects the density of an object?

The density of an object is related to its ability to sink or float. Sometimes it is possible to change the density of an object to control whether it sinks or floats. Density is related to mass and volume. This relationship can be expressed in a mathematical formula.

$$density = \frac{mass}{volume}$$

Active Reading 18 **Describe** If an object's density is decreasing but its mass stays constant, what must be true of the object's volume?

_____

_____

A submarine rises to the surface when its density is less than that of water.

Its Mass

A submarine can travel both on the surface of the ocean and under water. Submarines have large ballast tanks that can be opened to allow seawater to flow in. As water is added, the submarine's mass increases, but its volume stays the same. The submarine's overall density increases so that it sinks below the surface. Adding more water allows the submarine to dive deeper. When the submarine needs to rise, air is added to its tanks and the water is blown out. The submarine's mass decreases as water is expelled, and so the density also decreases. The submarine rises to the surface.

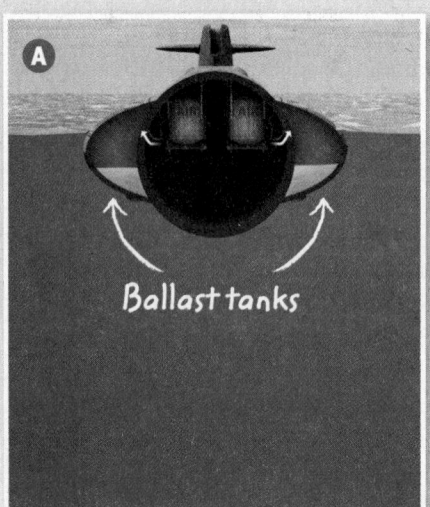

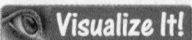

When a submarine's tanks are mostly filled with air, the submarine floats on the surface.

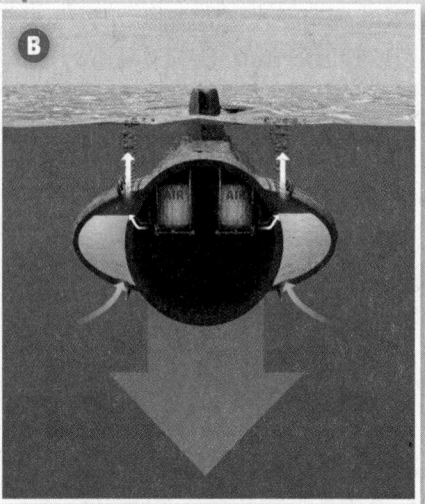

As water fills the tanks from below and air escapes from the top, a submarine sinks.

As air is pumped into the tanks to force the water out, a submarine buoys up to the surface.

Visualize It!

19 **Analyze** Explain how the density of the submarine changes in each image.

_____

_____

_____

_____

_____

_____

_____

Its Volume

Steel is almost eight times denser than water. Yet huge steel ships cruise the oceans with ease. How is this possible? It all depends on the shape of the ship. What if a ship were just a big block of steel? If you put that block into water, the block would sink because it is denser than water. So ships are built with a hollow shape. The amount of steel in the ship is the same as in the block. But the hollow shape increases the overall volume of the ship. An increase in the ship's volume leads to a decrease in its density. Ships float because their overall density is less than the density of water.

Like a submarine, some fish adjust their density to stay at a certain depth in the water. Most bony fish have an organ called a *swim bladder*. This organ is filled with gases. The inflated swim bladder increases the fish's volume, which decreases the fish's overall density. By adjusting the volume of gas in its swim bladder, the fish can move to different depths.

This fish uses its swim bladder to change its volume so that it can float at different depths in water.

20 Predict Each row of the table below shows the density of an object and the density of a fluid. Predict whether each object will sink or float on the surface of the fluid. Write your prediction, *sink* or *float,* in the table.

Object and its density	Fluid and its density	Prediction
cork, 0.24 g/cm³	water, 1.0 g/cm³	
penny, 8.96 g/cm³	mercury, 13.53 g/cm³	
boiled egg, 1.02 g/cm³	cooking oil, 0.93 g/cm³	
ice cube, 0.92 g/cm³	vinegar, 1.01 g/cm³	

21 Identify Placing the egg in which fluid would give a different result?

_____

_____

Visual Summary

To complete this summary, fill in the blanks with the correct word. Then use the key below to check your answers. You can use this page to review the main concepts of the lesson.

Pressure is the amount of force exerted on a given area.

Fluids and Pressure

22 Gases are one type of _____ because they flow and take the shape of their container.

Fluids flow from higher pressure areas to lower pressure areas.

23 The force of _____ causes atmospheric pressure by pulling down on the air.

Archimedes' principle explains buoyant force.

24 An object that has a weight greater than the buoyant force will _____

25 The mass of an object divided by its volume is its _____

26 Design Imagine you want to design a toy boat from a block of clay. What would you need to consider to make sure that your boat can float?

Lesson Review

Vocabulary

Draw a line to connect the following terms to their definitions.

1 pascal

2 fluid

3 pressure

A the amount of force exerted per unit area of a surface

B the SI unit of pressure

C a material that can flow and takes the shape of its container

Key Concepts

4 Compare A pebble sinks in water. A twig floats on top of the water. Compare the densities of the water, the pebble and the twig.

_____

_____

5 Describe Explain why atmospheric pressure changes as atmospheric depth changes.

_____

_____

_____

6 Define What does Archimedes' principle state?

_____

_____

_____

_____

7 Calculate An object exerts 140 N of force on a surface that has an area of 2.0 m². How much pressure does the object exert?

_____

8 Apply Describe the motion of air particles inside an inflated balloon.

_____

_____

_____

Critical Thinking

Use this photo to answer the following questions.

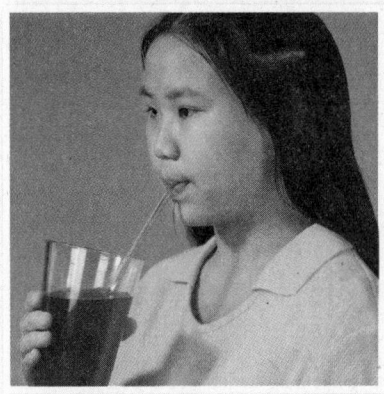

9 Analyze What two properties show that the drink is a fluid?

_____

_____

_____

10 Apply Explain how drinking through a straw illustrates fluid flowing from high-pressure to low-pressure areas.

_____

_____

_____

_____

_____

11 Evaluate Your friend tells you that all heavy objects sink in water. Do you agree or disagree? Explain your answer in terms of buoyant force.

_____

_____

_____

_____

_____

My Notes

Unit 5 [Big Idea]

Unbalanced forces cause changes in the motion of objects, and these changes can be predicted and described.

Lesson 1

ESSENTIAL QUESTION
How are distance, time, and speed related?

Analyze how distance, time, and speed are related.

Lesson 2

ESSENTIAL QUESTION
How does motion change?

Analyze how acceleration is related to time and velocity.

Lesson 3

ESSENTIAL QUESTION
How do forces affect motion?

Describe different types of forces and explain the effect force has on motion.

Lesson 4

ESSENTIAL QUESTION
How do objects move under the influence of gravity?

Describe the effect that gravity, including Earth's gravity, has on matter.

Lesson 5

ESSENTIAL QUESTION
What happens when fluids exert pressure?

Explain why fluids exert pressure and how the resulting pressure causes motion and the buoyant force.

Connect ESSENTIAL QUESTIONS
Lessons 2 and 3

1 Synthesize How is force related to acceleration and gravity? Provide evidence and reasoning to support your claim.

_____

_____

_____

_____

Think Outside the Book

2 Synthesize Choose one of these activities to help synthesize what you have learned in this unit.

☐ Using what you learned in lessons 1–4, create a brochure to explain how objects can exert forces on each other even when the objects are not in direct contact. Give specific examples as evidence. Explain your reasoning.

☐ Using what you learned in lessons 3–5, make a poster presentation describing the forces acting on a falling skydiver with an open parachute.

Vocabulary

Fill in each blank with the term that best completes the following sentences.

1 The _____ of an object describes the speed and the direction in which it is going.

2 The change in the velocity of an object is defined as its _____.

3 An object that is traveling around another body in space is in _____ around that body.

4 The _____ on an object is the combination of all the forces acting on the object.

5 The _____ is the upward force that fluids exert on all matter.

Key Concepts

Read each question below, and circle the best answer.

6 An airplane leaves New York to fly to Los Angeles. It travels 3,850 km in 5.5 hours. What is the average speed of the airplane?

A 700 km

B 700 hours

C 700 km/hour

D 700 hours/km

7 The law of universal gravitation says all bodies attract each other. If you drop a cup, it falls to Earth. Why doesn't the gravitational attraction between your hand and the cup keep the cup from falling?

A The law of universal gravitation only applies to planets in space.

B There is a gravitational attraction between you and the cup, but Earth's gravity is stronger, so Earth's gravity pulls the cup down.

C The gravitational attraction between you and the cup is so strong that the force pushes the cup down.

D There is no gravitational attraction between you and the cup, so Earth's gravity pulls the cup down.

8 This distance-time graph shows the speeds of four toy cars.

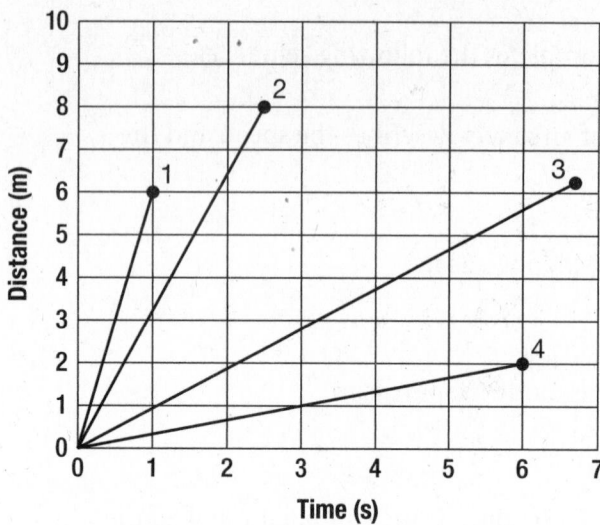

Which car is the fastest?

A Car 1

C Car 3

B Car 2

D Car 4

9 The diagram below shows the forces acting on a sneaker. As the force F is applied, the sneaker does not move.

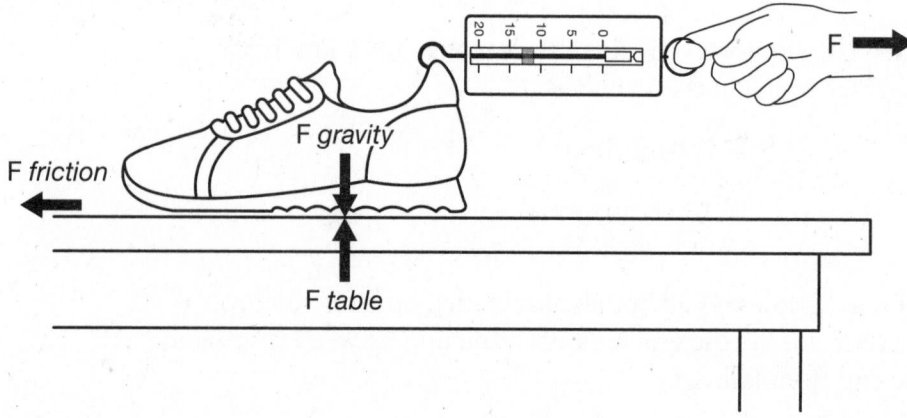

Which statement below correctly describes the forces?

A The net force is acting in an upward direction.

B The net force is acting to the left.

C The net force is moving to the right.

D The net force is zero and all the forces are balanced.

10 The diagram below shows a satellite in orbit around Earth. It is orbiting in the direction shown and is pulled toward Earth by gravity.

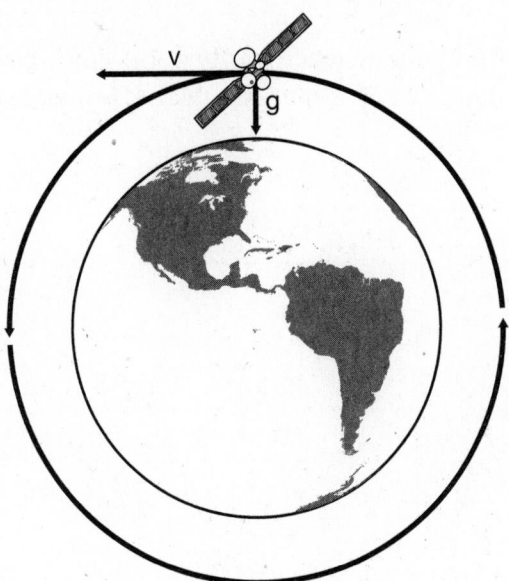

What would happen if Earth's gravity suddenly disappeared?

A The satellite would continue to orbit Earth.

B The satellite would fall to Earth.

C The satellite would move into space in a straight line.

D The satellite would stop moving.

11 Julia is in a car with her father. The car is undergoing centripetal acceleration. What is happening to the car?

A The car is changing direction at a constant speed.

B The car is changing direction and speeding up.

C The car is stopping suddenly.

D The car is slowing down.

12 Rajiv made a model of a boat. When he places it in water, it sinks. According to Archimedes' principle, why does the boat sink?

A The boat is too small.

B The buoyant force is less than the boat's weight.

C The buoyant force is equal to the boat's weight.

D The buoyant force is greater than the boat's weight.

Critical Thinking

Answer the following questions in the space provided.

13 Marek is trying to push a box of sports equipment across the floor. The arrow on the box is a vector representing the force that Marek exerts. Marek is unable to move the box.

Explain the relative magnitudes of the various forces acting on the box. Use evidence from the diagram and reasoning to support your claims.

_____

_____

_____

14 What does the formula $F = ma$ mean, and which of Newton's three laws does it describe?

_____

_____

_____

Connect ESSENTIAL QUESTIONS
Lessons 1 and 2

Answer the following question in the space provided.

15 What is the difference between the speed of an object, the velocity of an object, and the acceleration of an object?

_____

_____

_____

UNIT 6
Work, Energy, and Machines

Big Idea

Energy is transferred when a force moves an object.

S8P2., S8P2.a, S8P2.b, S8P2.c

Machines are found everywhere—even in the skate park.

What do you think?

Machines make work and play easier. How are skateboards made out of simple machines? What are the two basic parts of this skateboard? As you explore the unit, gather evidence to help you state and support claims to answer these questions.

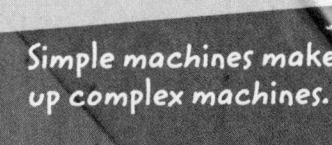

Simple machines make up complex machines.

© Houghton Mifflin Harcourt Publishing Company • Image Credits: (bg) ©Chase Jarvis/Corbis; (inset) ©HMH

379

Unit 6

Work, Energy, and Machines

CITIZEN SCIENCE

A Day at the Races

Both simple and complex machines can make work easier and play more exciting. Creating a small-scale downhill racing machine is a fun way to learn about simple machines.

1 Think about It

A Investigate some ways to create a small-scale downhill racer with everyday objects. Make notes about your research.

B Most downhill racers will have two axles and four wheels. Define *axle* and *wheel* below and explain what function each would serve in a racer.

C Check out the recycling bin in your school, classroom, or home. Can you use any recyclable materials to make a downhill racer? (Safety note: Some materials are toxic or dangerous. Before you touch anything, ask your teacher.)

② Ask a Question

What are some ways that you could make a downhill racer go faster? Do some research and write notes below.

_____
_____
_____
_____
_____

The downhill racer is traveling over 20 mph! Do you think the driver is frightened or exhilarated?

③ Make a Plan

Draw a sketch of a small-scale downhill racer that you would make. Label it, and note if any of the parts are reused or recyclable.

Take It Home

With an adult, make the small-scale downhill racer you designed. Challenge the adult to design and help you make a different downhill racer. Conduct a race to find out which racer was faster. Think about how the design may affect speed. See *ScienceSaurus*® for more information about speed.

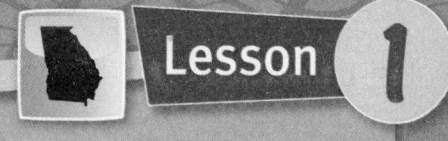

Lesson 1

Work, Energy, and Power

ESSENTIAL QUESTION

How is work related to energy?

By the end of this lesson, you should be able to relate work to energy and power.

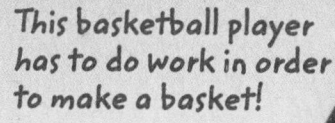

This basketball player has to do work in order to make a basket!

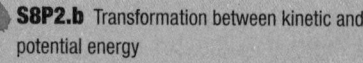

S8P2.b Transformation between kinetic and potential energy

S8P2.c Energy transformations in a system

Lesson Labs

Quick Labs
• Investigating Work
• Calculating Power

STEM Lab
• Using Water to Do Work

Engage Your Brain

1 Identify Circle the correct words in the paragraph below to make true statements.

Max, Jorge, and Wendy are in a race. They push identical rolling carts for the same distance. Max finishes the race first, so he did *more / the same / less* work than Jorge. Wendy finishes the race second, so she has *more / the same / less* power than Max.

2 Illustrate What do you think of when you hear the word *work*? Draw a picture of yourself doing work. Then write a caption describing what you are doing.

_____

_____

Active Reading

3 Apply Many scientific words, such as *work* and *power*, also have everyday meanings. Use context clues to write your own definition for each meaning of the words *work* and *power*.

Example sentence
My mom always waves goodbye before leaving for <u>work</u>.

work:

_____

_____

_____

Example sentence
The team coach has the <u>power</u> to decide when to meet for practice.

power:

_____

_____

Vocabulary Terms

• work   • power
• energy

4 Apply As you learn the definition of each vocabulary term in this lesson, create your own definition or sketch to help you remember the meaning of the term.

Work It Out

What is work?

What comes to mind when you think of work? Most people say they are working when they do anything that requires a physical or mental effort. But in physical science, **work** is the use of force to move an object some distance in the direction of the force. In scientific terms, you do work only when you exert a force on an object and move it. If you want to do work, you have to use force to move something.

Work is done only by the part of the force that is in the same direction as the motion. Imagine that you pull a sled through the snow. You pull the rope up at an angle while you pull the sled forward. Only the part of your force pulling the sled forward is doing work. The upward part of your force is not doing work, because the sled is not moving upward.

Active Reading 5 **Summarize** How does the scientific definition of work differ from the familiar definition?

_____

_____

How is work calculated?

Work is a measure of how much force is applied to move an object through a certain distance. You can calculate the work a force does if you know the size of the force applied to an object and the distance through which the force acts. The distance involved is the distance the object moved. You can calculate work using the following formula:

$$\text{work} = \text{force} \times \text{distance}$$
$$W = F \times d$$

Force can be expressed in newtons, and distance can be expressed in meters. When you multiply a force in newtons by a distance in meters, the product is a unit called the *newton-meter* (N•m), or the *joule*. The joule (J) is the standard unit used to express work. One joule of work is done when a force of one newton moves an object one meter. To get an idea of how much a joule of work is, lift an apple (which weighs about one newton) from your foot to your waist (about one meter).

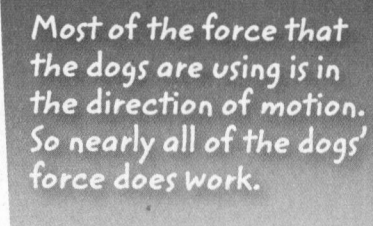

Most of the force that the dogs are using is in the direction of motion. So nearly all of the dogs' force does work.

© Houghton Mifflin Harcourt Publishing Company • Image Credits: (bkgd) ©Radius Images/Corbis; (b) ©Bert Scharpmann/Corbis

Do the Math

Sample Problem

A boy pulls a sled 22 m. The force that he applies in the direction of motion is 20 N. How much work does he do?

Identify

A. What do you know? force = 20 N, distance = 22 m

B. What do you want to find out? work

Plan

C. Draw and label a sketch:

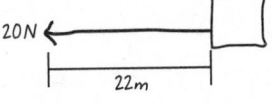

$20 N$ ← $22m$

D. Write the formula: $W = F \times d$

E. Substitute into the formula: $W = 20\,N \times 22\,m$

Solve

F. Calculate and simplify: $W = 20\,N \times 22\,m$
$$= 440\,N \times m$$
$$= 440\,J$$

G. Check that your units agree: Unit is J.

Unit of work is J.

Units agree.

Answer: 440 J

You Try It

6 Calculate A team of dogs pulls a sled 15 m using a force of 200 N. How much work did the dogs do?

Identify

A. What do you know?

B. What do you want to find out?

Plan

C. Draw and label a sketch:

D. Write the formula:

E. Substitute into the formula:

Solve

F. Calculate and simplify:

G. Check that your units agree:

Answer:

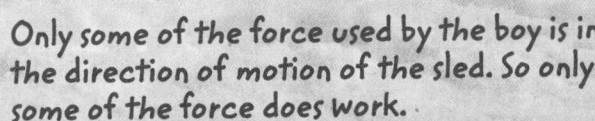

Only some of the force used by the boy is in the direction of motion of the sled. So only some of the force does work.

Energizing

How are work and energy related?

"It's important to conserve energy!" your teacher might say as she turns off the classroom lights when everyone leaves. "I'm all out of energy," you might say when you just ran outside for a long time. What does the word *energy* actually mean? And what does it have to do with work?

Energy Is the Ability to Do Work

You might think of energy as the ability to cause a change. But now that you know more about work, you can learn more about energy. **Energy** is the ability to do work. This means that energy is the ability to apply force to cause movement in the direction of the force. For example, when a dog pulls a sled, the dog is using energy. When you do work by swinging a tennis racket and hitting a ball, you are using energy. The work done by energy doesn't have to be visible, however. For example, when energy is transferred to an object in the form of heat, the particles in the object move faster even though the object itself does not move. Work and energy are so related that they are both expressed in the same unit, the *joule*. You can think of work as a transfer of energy. In fact, energy is transferred every time work is done.

7 **Identify** As you read this page and the next, underline examples of energy provided in the text.

Active Reading

8 **Apply** Can you think of another example of energy doing work? Fill out the table below with your own idea.

Example of energy	Description of work
the energy transferred to a bowling ball	The bowler does work because a force is applied to the bowling ball that makes it move through a distance.

© Houghton Mifflin Harcourt Publishing Company • Image Credits: (bkgd) ©Stockbyte/Alamy

Work Transfers Energy

When a person does work on an object, he or she can transfer energy to that object. For example, you may know that wind turbines are a way to produce clean and renewable energy. But how is work involved? The wind does work moving the blades so that they spin. The wind has the capacity to do this work because of the energy of its motion. Inside the turbines, more energy transfers occur so that the energy of the blades is transformed into electrical energy that can be used at home.

A carnival game can be an example of work transferring energy. The goal of the game is to hit a target with a ball. You do work on the ball as you throw with your arm. When you change the position and speed of the ball, you transfer energy to the ball. The ball then does work on the target and you win a prize.

9 Synthesize The wind does work on the wind turbines below. Describe how the work is done. Explain your reasoning.

_____

_____

_____

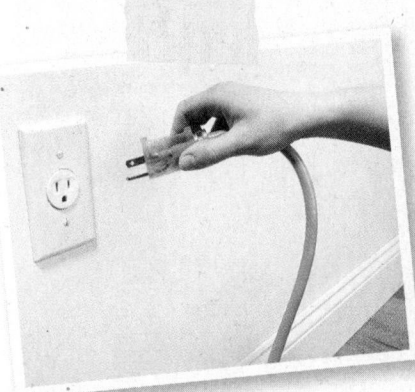

Work is done inside wind turbines to transform mechanical energy from the wind into electrical energy.

Think Outside the Book (Inquiry)

10 Design Imagine that you work for a wind turbine company. Your company would like to provide tours of the wind farms to students and tourists. Make an advertising brochure that explains what wind turbines do and why people might be interested in learning more about them.

Superpower

What is power?

The word *power* has several common meanings. It is used to mean a source of energy, as in a power plant, or strength, as in a powerful engine. When you talk about a powerful swimmer, for example, you would probably say that the swimmer is very strong or very fast. However, if you use the scientific definition of power, you would instead say that a powerful swimmer is one who does the work of moving herself through the water in a short time.

Power is the rate at which work is done. For example, when two cranes lift the same crate the same height, they do the same amount of work. The one that lifts the crate the fastest is the more powerful crane. Because work is also a measure of energy transfer, you can also think of power as the rate at which energy is converted from one form to another.

A crane's power depends on how quickly it lifts a crate.

This is an incandescent light bulb.

 Do the Math   **Sample Problem**

Here's an example of how to find the power used by an incandescent light bulb. A light bulb uses 600 J of energy in 6 s. What is the power of the light bulb?

To calculate power, divide energy by time.

$$P = \frac{E}{t}$$

$$P = \frac{600 \text{ J}}{6 \text{ s}}$$

$$P = \frac{100 \text{ J}}{s}$$

Unit is J/s. Unit for power is W, which is also J/s. Units agree.

$$P = 100 \text{ W}$$

How is power calculated?

Because power is a measure of how much energy is transferred in a given time, power can be calculated from energy and time. Sometimes you know that energy is being transferred, but you cannot directly measure the work being done. For example, you know that a TV uses energy. But there is no way to measure all of the work that every part of the TV does. To calculate the TV's power, divide the amount of energy used by the time it is used.

$$power = \frac{energy}{time}$$

$$P = \frac{E}{t}$$

Remember that energy is expressed in joules. So power is often expressed in joules per second. One joule of energy transferred in one second is equal to one *watt* (W). The watt is the unit of measurement for power. You have probably heard the term *watt* used in connection with light bulbs. A 60-watt light bulb requires 60 joules of energy every second to shine at its rated brightness.

Active Reading

11 Apply What two things would you need to know to calculate the power of a microwave oven?

_____

_____

You Try It

12 Calculate A compact fluorescent light bulb, called a CFL, is advertised as being just as bright as an incandescent 100 W light bulb but using less energy. The CFL uses only 156 J of energy in 6 s. What is the power of this CFL bulb?

13 Analyze Why might someone buy a more expensive CFL instead of an incandescent light bulb?

_____

_____

_____

A compact fluorescent light bulb uses less energy each second than an equally bright incandescent light bulb.

Visual Summary

To complete this summary, fill in the blanks with the correct word or phrase. Then, use the key below to check your answers. You can use this page to review the main concepts of the lesson.

Work is the use of force to move an object a distance.

14 Work is force multiplied by
_____

15 Work is done only by the part of the force that acts in the _____ as the motion of an object.

Energy is the ability to do work.

16 _____ transfers energy.

Work, Energy, and Power

Power is the rate at which energy is transferred.

17 Power is _____ divided by time.

18 Power is typically expressed in _____

19 Claims • Evidence • Reasoning Ben and Andy each pushed an empty grocery cart. Ben used twice the force, but they both did the same amount of work. How is this possible? State your claim. Summarize evidence to support your claim and explain your reasoning.

Lesson Review

Vocabulary

Fill in the blanks with the term that best completes the following sentences.

1 The joule is the standard unit of measurement

for both _____ and _____

2 The watt is the standard unit of measurement

for _____.

Key Concepts

3 Apply If you push very hard on an object but it doesn't move, have you done any work? Why or why not?

_____

_____

_____

4 Describe What two factors do you need to know to calculate how much work was done in any situation? Explain your reasoning.

_____

_____

5 Relate Explain the relationship between power, energy, and time.

_____

_____

_____

6 Calculate If an electric hair dryer uses 2,400 J of energy in 2 s, what is its power? Use the space below to solve this problem.

Critical Thinking

Use the photo below to answer the following questions.

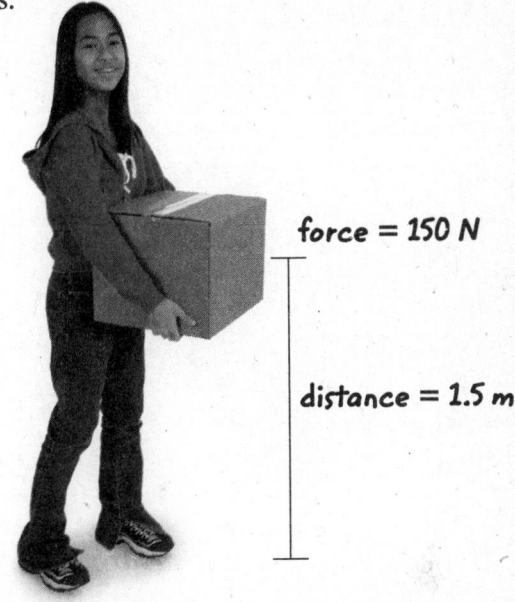

force = 150 N

distance = 1.5 m

7 Apply Is this girl doing any work while she stands still and holds the box? Why or why not?

_____

_____

8 Calculate When the girl lifted the box from the floor, did she do any work? If so, how much work did she do?

9 Synthesize Think of an activity that involves work. Write about how the work is transferring energy and where the transferred energy goes.

_____

_____

_____

My Notes

Kinetic and Potential Energy

ESSENTIAL QUESTION

What are kinetic and potential energy?

By the end of this lesson, you should be able to calculate kinetic and potential energy and know how these two types of energy are related.

S8P2.a Kinetic and potential energy

S8P2.b Transformation between kinetic and potential energy

S8P2.c Energy transformations in a system

Climbing a hill requires a lot of energy but it makes the ride back down fun.

Lesson Labs

Quick Labs
• Investigate Potential Energy
• Identify Potential and Kinetic Energy
Exploration Lab
• Mechanical Energy

Engage Your Brain

1 Predict Check T or F to show whether you think each statement is true or false.

T	F	
☐	☐	Objects that are sitting still have kinetic energy.
☐	☐	The kinetic energy of an object depends on how much space the object takes up.
☐	☐	The gravitational potential energy of an object depends on its height above a surface.

2 Analyze If the baseball and the plastic ball were moving at the same speed, which ball would hit a bat harder? Why?

_____
_____
_____
_____

Active Reading

3 Synthesize Many English words have their roots in other languages. Use the Greek word below to make an educated guess about the meaning of the term *kinetic energy*.

Greek word	Meaning
kinetos	moving

Example sentence:
The harder the football is thrown, the more <u>kinetic energy</u> it has.

kinetic energy:

_____
_____

Vocabulary Terms

• kinetic energy
• potential energy
• mechanical energy

4 Identify As you read, create a reference card for each vocabulary term. On one side of the card, write the term and its meaning. On the other side, draw an image that illustrates or makes a connection to the term. These cards can be used as bookmarks in the text so that you can refer to them while studying.

On the Move

What is kinetic energy?

Energy is the ability to do work. There are different forms of energy. One form that you can find all around you is kinetic energy. **Kinetic energy** is the energy of motion. Every moving object has kinetic energy. For example, a hammer has kinetic energy as it moves toward a nail. When the hammer hits the nail, energy is transferred. Work is done when movement occurs in the direction of the force, and the nail is driven into a board.

The Energy of Motion

Active Reading **5 Identify** As you read, underline two factors that affect an object's kinetic energy.

What determines the amount of kinetic energy that an object has? The faster an object moves, the more kinetic energy it has. So kinetic energy depends, in part, on speed. Kinetic energy also depends on mass. If two objects move at the same speed, then the one that has more mass will have more kinetic energy. Imagine a bike and a car that are moving at the same speed. The car has more kinetic energy than the bike has because the car has more mass.

Visualize It!

6 Apply How does the rider's ability to stop the bike change as the bike moves down a steep hill? Explain your reasoning.

_____

_____

The bike at the top of the hill is not moving. It does not have kinetic energy. The bike that is going down the hill has kinetic energy. As the bike moves faster, its kinetic energy increases.

How is the kinetic energy of an object calculated?

An object's kinetic energy is related to its mass and speed. The speed of an object is the distance that it travels in a unit of time. The following equation shows how kinetic energy is calculated.

$$\text{kinetic energy} = \frac{1}{2}mv^2$$

The letter m is the object's mass, and the letter v is the object's speed. When the mass is expressed in kilograms and the speed in meters per second, kinetic energy is expressed in *joules* (J).

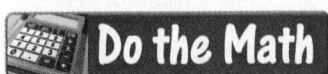 **Do the Math**

Sample Problem

A foal has a mass of 100 kg and is moving at 8 m/s along the beach. What is its kinetic energy?

Identify

A. What do you know? The mass, m, is 100 kg.

The speed, v, is 8 m/s.

B. What do you want to find? kinetic energy

Plan

C. Write the formula: $KE = \frac{1}{2}mv^2$

D. Substitute into the formula: $KE = \frac{1}{2}(100 \text{ kg})(8 \text{ m/s})^2$

Solve

E. Multiply: $KE = \frac{1}{2}(100 \text{ kg})(64 \text{ m}^2/\text{s}^2) = 3{,}200 \text{ kg} \cdot \text{m}^2/\text{s}^2 = 3{,}200 \text{ J}$

Answer: 3,200 J

m	v	KE
800 kg	10 m/s	
800 kg	15 m/s	
800 kg	20 m/s	

You Try It

7 Calculate Complete the tables. Then, draw two graphs using the information from the tables. The first graph should show how kinetic energy changes as velocity changes. The second graph should show how kinetic energy changes as mass changes.

m	v	KE
800 kg	10 m/s	
900 kg	10 m/s	
1000 kg	10 m/s	

It Could Change

What is potential energy?

Some energy is stored energy, or potential energy. **Potential energy** is the energy an object has because of its position, condition, or chemical composition. Like kinetic energy, potential energy is the ability to do work. For example, an object has *elastic potential energy* when it has been stretched or compressed. Elastic potential energy is stored in a stretched spring or rubber band. An object has *gravitational potential energy* due to its position above the ground. An object held above the ground has the potential to fall. The higher the object is above the ground, the greater its gravitational potential energy. Potential energy that depends on an object's position is referred to as *mechanical potential energy.* But there are other types of potential energy that do not depend on an object's position. For example, a substance stores *chemical potential energy* as a result of its chemical bonds. Some of that energy can be released during chemical reactions.

Visualize It!

9 Identify Fill in the type of potential energy that is illustrated in each image.

Fruit can provide energy to your body.

A _____

The boulder is high above the ground.

B _____

The archer pulls back on the string and bends the bow's limbs.

C _____

How is the gravitational potential energy of an object calculated?

The following equation describes an object's gravitational potential energy.

> gravitational potential energy = mgh

The letter *m* represents the object's mass expressed in kilograms. The letter *g* represents the acceleration due to Earth's gravity, which is 9.8 m/s^2. The letter *h* is the object's height from the ground in meters. The height is a measure of how far the object can fall. Like kinetic energy, potential energy is expressed in units of joules.

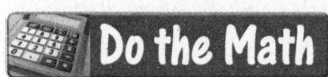 **Do the Math**

Sample Problem

The cat has a mass of 4 kg and is 1.5 m above the ground. What is the gravitational potential energy of the cat?

Identify

A. What do you know? mass = 4 kg, height = 1.5 m, acceleration due to gravity = 9.8 m/s^2

B. What do you want to find? gravitational potential energy

Plan

C. Write the formula: *GPE = mgh*

D. Substitute the given values into the formula:

GPE = (4 kg)(9.8 m/s^2)(1.5 m)

Solve

E. Multiply: *PE = (4 kg)(9.8 m/s^2)(1.5 m) = 58.8 kg • m^2/s^2 = 58.8 J*

Answer: 58.8 J

You Try It

10 Calculate Three books are on different shelves. Calculate the gravitational potential energy of each book based on its mass and its height above the floor.

Object	m	h	PE
picture book	0.2 kg	2 m	
picture book	0.2 kg	3 m	
textbook	1.5 kg	4 m	

It All Adds Up!

How is the mechanical energy of an object calculated?

A moving object can have both kinetic and potential energy. **Mechanical energy** is the energy possessed by an object due to its motion and position. For example, a thrown baseball has kinetic energy. It also has potential energy because it is above the ground. The sum of the ball's kinetic energy and mechanical potential energy is its mechanical energy. You can use the following equation to find mechanical energy.

$$\text{mechanical energy} = KE + PE$$

If the object's only potential energy is gravitational potential energy, you can use the following equation to find mechanical energy.

$$ME = \frac{1}{2}mv^2 + mgh$$

Visualize It!

12 Compare Circle the position of the ball when its gravitational potential energy is greatest.

The mechanical energy of the ball is the sum of its kinetic energy and potential energy.

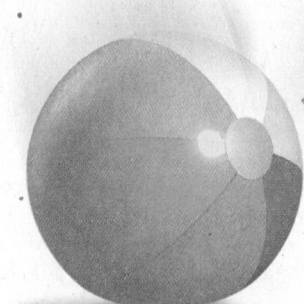

13 Analyze When does the ball have zero gravitational potential energy? Explain your reasoning.

_____

_____

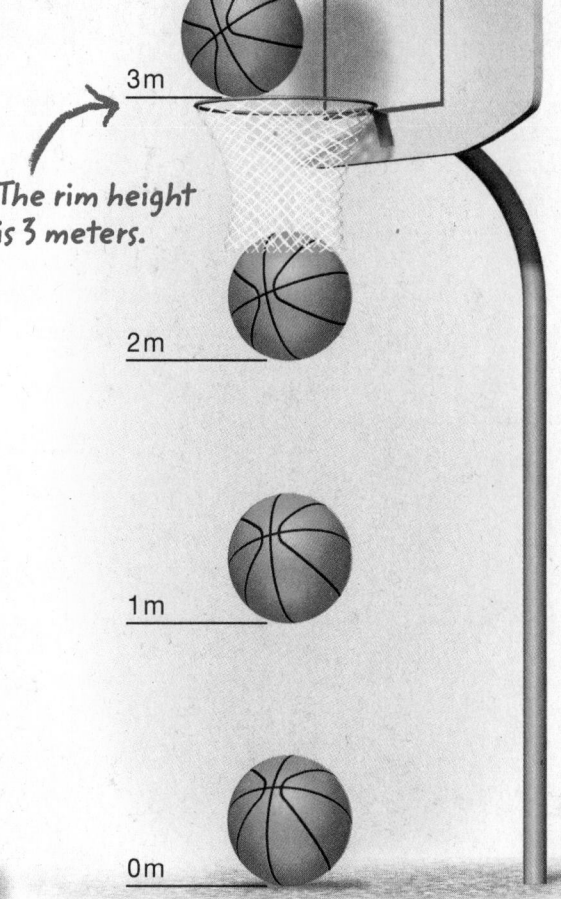

The rim height is 3 meters.

3m

2m

1m

0m

Do the Math · You Try It

14 Calculate When the basketball is at its maximum height of 3 meters, it is not moving. The table below lists the KE and GPE for the basketball at heights of 3 m, 2 m, 1 m, and 0 m. Write the missing values for KE and GPE in the table. Then find the mechanical energy for each height.

Height	KE	GPE	ME
3.0 m		18 J	
2.0 m	6 J	12 J	
1.0 m	12 J	6 J	
0 m	18 J		

15 Graph Use the data above to plot and label two lines representing the kinetic energy and the gravitational potential energy of the basketball.

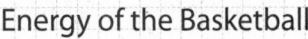
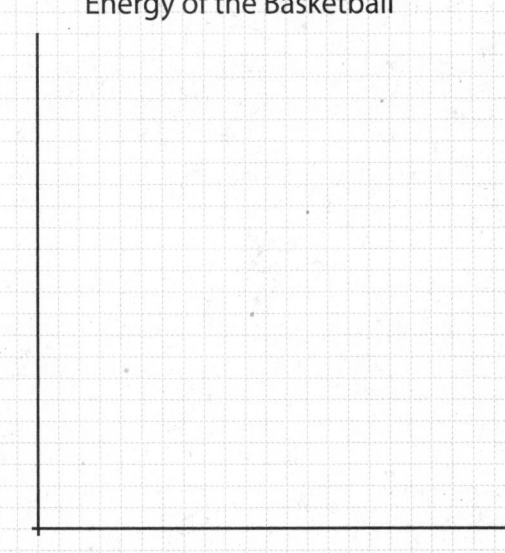

Energy of the Basketball

Energy (J)

Height above floor (m)

16 Analyze What is the relationship between the kinetic energy and the gravitational potential energy of the basketball?

_____

_____

Visual Summary

To complete this summary, fill in the blanks with the correct word. Then, use the key below to check your answers. You can use this page to review the main concepts of the lesson.

Kinetic and Potential Energy

All moving objects have kinetic energy.

$$\text{kinetic energy} = \frac{1}{2}mv^2$$

17 Kinetic energy depends on an object's mass and _____

Mechanical energy is kinetic energy plus potential energy due to position.

$$\text{mechanical energy} = KE + PE$$

Potential energy is stored energy.

$$\text{gravitational potential energy} = mgh$$

18 Potential energy can be gravitational, _____, or elastic.

19 The formula $ME = \frac{1}{2}mv^2 + mgh$ can be used to calculate mechanical energy if the only potential energy is _____ potential energy.

Answers: 17 speed; 18 chemical; 19 gravitational.

20 Claims · Evidence · Reasoning A skydiver jumps out of a plane. Describe how gravitational potential energy changes as the skydiver falls. State how the skydiver's kinetic energy changes when the parachute opens. Summarize evidence to support your claim and explain your reasoning.

Lesson Review

Vocabulary

In your own words, define the following terms.

1 kinetic energy

_____

_____

2 potential energy

_____

_____

3 mechanical energy

_____

_____

Key Concepts

4 Relate Describe the relationship between a moving object's mass and its kinetic energy.

_____

_____

_____

_____

5 Identify What are two factors that determine an object's gravitational potential energy?

_____

_____

_____

6 Analyze A passenger plane is flying above the ground. Describe the two components of its mechanical energy.

_____

_____

_____

_____

_____

Critical Thinking

7 Evaluate Can an object's mechanical energy be equal to its gravitational potential energy? Explain.

_____

_____

_____

_____

Use this graph to answer the following questions.

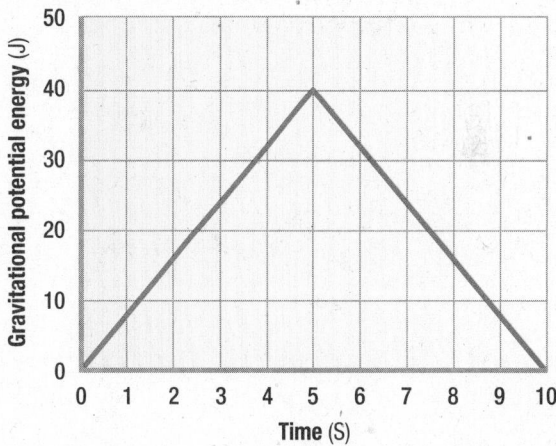

Gravitational Potential Energy over Time

8 Apply The graph shows the gravitational potential energy of a radio-controlled toy helicopter. Describe the motion of the toy.

_____

_____

_____

_____

9 Calculate At 2.5 seconds, the helicopter has a kinetic energy of 20 J. What is its mechanical energy at that time?

_____

_____

_____

My Notes

S.T.E.M. Engineering & Technology

Engineering Design Process

Skills
Identify a need
Conduct research
✓ Brainstorm solutions
✓ Select a solution
✓ Design a prototype
✓ Build a prototype
✓ Test and evaluate
✓ Redesign to improve
✓ Communicate results

Objectives

- Build a simple machine.
- Evaluate the design using mechanical advantage.

Testing a Simple Machine

Simple machines are devices that change the way work is done. Some simple machines allow us to lift objects using less force over a longer distance. Others help us to move something faster or farther when we exert a greater force over a shorter distance. Still other machines allow us to change the direction of force. The six types of simple machines are shown below.

Six simple machines

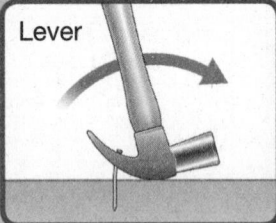
Lever

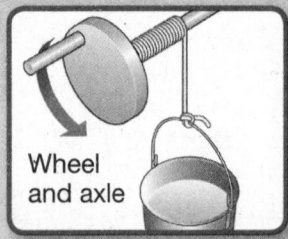
Wheel and axle

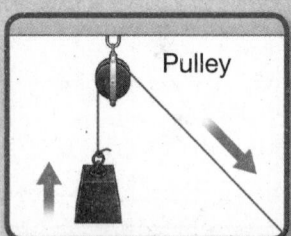
Pulley

Inclined plane

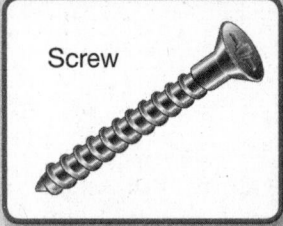
Screw

Wedge

1 Brainstorm What simple machines are found in your home?

_____

_____

_____

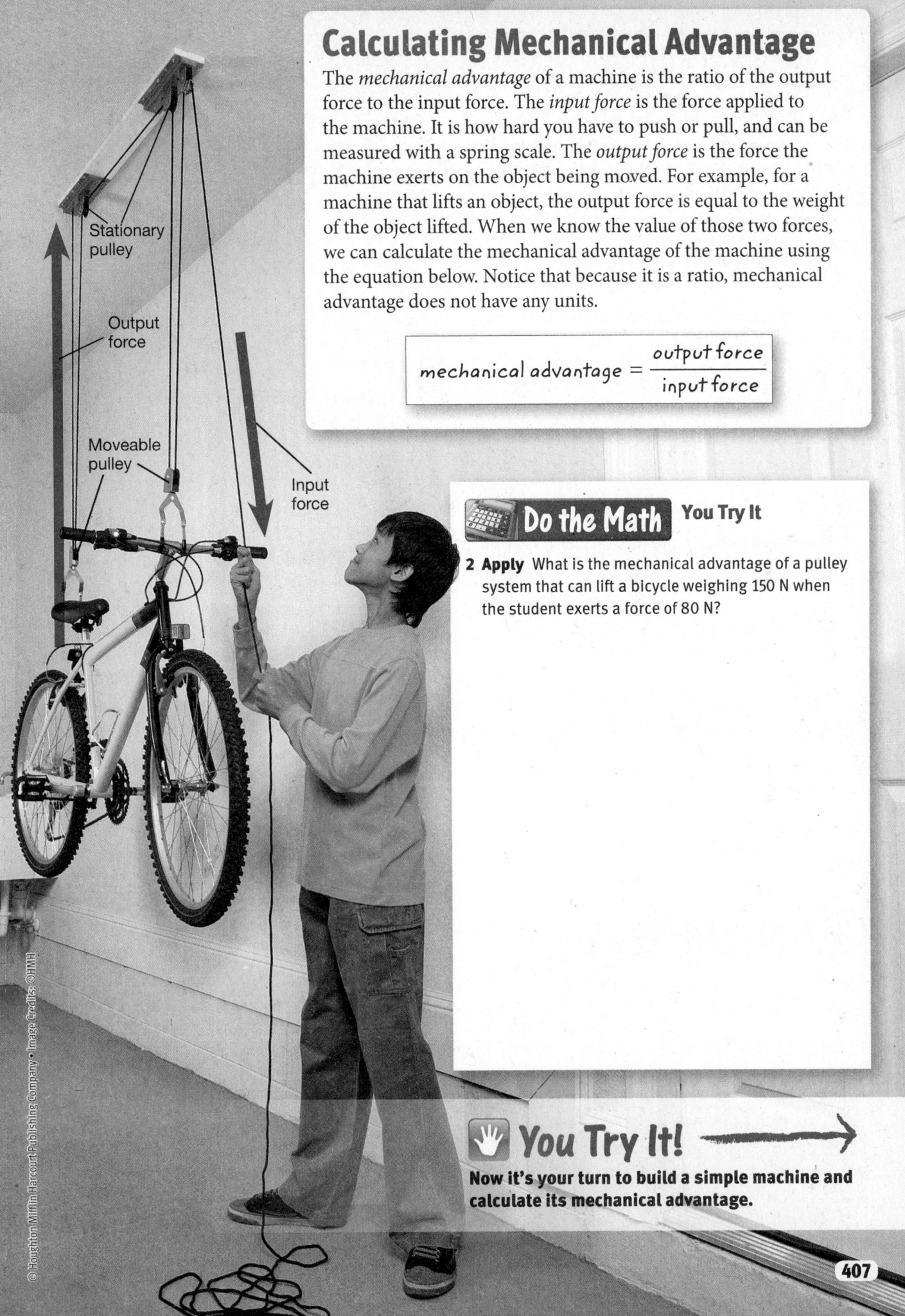

Calculating Mechanical Advantage

The *mechanical advantage* of a machine is the ratio of the output force to the input force. The *input force* is the force applied to the machine. It is how hard you have to push or pull, and can be measured with a spring scale. The *output force* is the force the machine exerts on the object being moved. For example, for a machine that lifts an object, the output force is equal to the weight of the object lifted. When we know the value of those two forces, we can calculate the mechanical advantage of the machine using the equation below. Notice that because it is a ratio, mechanical advantage does not have any units.

$$\text{mechanical advantage} = \frac{\text{output force}}{\text{input force}}$$

Stationary pulley

Output force

Moveable pulley

Input force

Do the Math You Try It

2 Apply What is the mechanical advantage of a pulley system that can lift a bicycle weighing 150 N when the student exerts a force of 80 N?

✋ **You Try It!** ——→

Now it's your turn to build a simple machine and calculate its mechanical advantage.

 You Try It!

Now it's your turn to build a simple machine that can lift an object and to calculate the machine's mechanical advantage.

① Brainstorm Solutions

Brainstorm ideas for a simple machine to lift a mass against gravity.

A Which simple machine or machines could accomplish this task?

_____

_____

_____

B How could you measure the force of gravity on the mass?

_____

_____

_____

_____

C How could you measure the input force?

_____

_____

_____

_____

② Select a Solution

Which of your ideas seems to offer the best promise for success?

_____

_____

_____

_____

_____

You Will Need

✔ blocks or stands

✔ board, wooden

✔ dowel, wooden

✔ duct tape or masking tape

✔ mass, 200 g to 1,000 g

✔ meterstick or ruler

✔ pulley

✔ spring scale, calibrated in newtons

✔ string

✔ wheel and axle

③ Design a Prototype

In the space below, draw a prototype of your simple machine. Be sure to include and label all the parts you will need and show how they will be connected. Show where on the machine you will measure the input force.

④ Build a Prototype

Now build your lifting device. Were there any parts you had to revise as you were building the prototype?

_____

_____

_____

⑤ Test and Evaluate

What is the output force (the weight in newtons that was lifted)? What is the input force needed to raise the mass? Calculate the mechanical advantage of your machine.

Output force:

_____

Input force:

_____

Mechanical advantage =

⑥ Redesign to Improve

A How could you redesign your machine to increase its mechanical advantage?

_____

_____

B Make a change and take measurements to see if the mechanical advantage has increased. How many revisions did you have to make to see an increase in mechanical advantage?

_____

_____

⑦ Communicate Results

What is the largest mechanical advantage that you measured? As the mechanical advantage increased, did you notice any change in function of the machine? Why do you think that was the case?

_____

_____

_____

_____

Machines

ESSENTIAL QUESTION

How do simple machines work?

By the end of this lesson, you should be able to describe different types of simple machines and to calculate the mechanical advantages and efficiencies of various simple machines.

Machines come in all shapes and sizes. This huge Ferris wheel contains a type of simple machine known as a wheel and axle.

 Lesson Labs

Quick Labs
• Mechanical Efficiency
• Investigate Pulleys

S.T.E.M. Lab
• Compound Machines

Engage Your Brain

1 Identify Unscramble the letters below to find the names of some simple machines. Write your words on the blank lines.

VEERL _____

EGDWE _____

YPLLUE _____

HELWE DAN EXAL _____

2 Compare How is using the stairs similar to and different from using a ramp to get into a building?

_____
_____
_____
_____
_____
_____
_____
_____
_____

Active Reading

3 Apply Use context clues to write your own definition for the phrases *input force* and *output force*.

Example sentence
An <u>input force</u> was applied to the pedal to make it move.

input force:

_____
_____

Example sentence
The <u>output force</u> of the pedal made the gear of the bike turn.

output force:

_____
_____

Vocabulary Terms

• machine
• mechanical advantage
• mechanical efficiency
• lever
• fulcrum
• wheel and axle
• pulley
• inclined plane

4 Identify As you read, create a reference card for each vocabulary term. On one side of the card, write the term and its meaning. On the other side, draw an image that illustrates or makes a connection to the term. These cards can be used as bookmarks in the text so that you can refer to them while studying.

© Houghton Mifflin Harcourt Publishing Company • Image Credits: © Steve Allen/Brand X Pictures/Getty Images

Simply Easier

What do simple machines do?

5 Identify As you read, underline the types of simple machines.

What do you think of as a machine—maybe a car or a computer? A **machine** is any device that helps people do work by changing the way work is done. The machines that make up other machines are called *simple machines*. The six types of simple machines are *levers, wheels and axles, pulleys, inclined planes, wedges,* and *screws*.

Change the Way Work Is Done

The wheelbarrow and rake shown below contain simple machines. They change the way you do work. Work is the use of force to move an object some distance. The force you apply to a machine through a distance is called the *input force*. The work that you do on a machine is called *work input*. You do work on a wheelbarrow when you lift the handles. You pull up on the handles to make them move. The wheelbarrow does work on the leaves. The work done by the machine on an object is called *work output*. The *output force* is the force a machine exerts on an object. The wheelbarrow exerts an output force on the leaves to lift them up.

6 Identify The person raking leaves applies an input force to the handle of the rake. The output force is applied to the leaves. Label the input force and the output force on the rake.

Machines, such as a wheelbarrow and rake, make yard work easier.

Output force

Input force

A _____

B _____

Change the Size of a Force and the Distance

Machines make tasks easier without decreasing the amount of work done. Work is equal to force times distance. If you apply less force with a machine, you apply that force through a longer distance. So the amount of work done remains the same. A ramp is an example of a machine that can change the magnitude, or size, of the force needed to move an object. You apply less force when you push a box up a ramp than when you lift the box. However, you apply the force through a longer distance. The amount of work you do is the same as when you lift the box to the same height, if friction is ignored. Other machines increase the amount of force needed, but you apply the force over a shorter distance.

The work done on the box is equal to the input force needed to lift the box times the height to which the box is lifted.

Less force is applied through a longer distance when the box is pushed up a ramp. But the work done on the box is the same.

7 Summarize Complete the table below by filling in the word *larger, smaller,* or *same* to compare lifting the box with pushing it up the ramp.

	Lifting box	Using ramp
Force applied	larger	smaller
Distance through which force is applied		
Work done		

Change the Direction of a Force

Some machines change the way you do work by changing the direction of a force. For example, you apply a downward force when you pull on the rope to raise a flag. The rope runs over a pulley at the top of the flagpole. The rope exerts an upward force on the flag, and the flag goes up. The direction of the force you applied has changed. But the magnitude of force and distance through which you apply the force are the same.

The pulley on the flagpole changed only the direction of the force. However, other machines can change the direction of a force, the magnitude of the force, and the distance through which the force is applied.

Pulling down on the rope pulls up the flag.

Input force

Input and Output

What is mechanical advantage?

Machines change force by different amounts. A machine's **mechanical advantage** is the number of times the machine multiplies the input force. It is a way of comparing the input force with the output force. Ignoring friction, you can calculate mechanical advantage, MA, of any machine by dividing the output force by the input force.

$$\text{mechanical advantage} = \frac{\text{output force}}{\text{input force}}$$

The bottle opener, pulley, and hammer shown below have different mechanical advantages. A machine that has a mechanical advantage greater than one multiplies the input force, producing greater output force. A machine that has a mechanical advantage equal to one changes only the direction of the force. A machine that has a mechanical advantage less than one requires greater input force, but the output force is applied through a longer distance.

Active Reading

8 Identify As you read, underline what happens when the mechanical advantage of a machine is equal to one.

Do the Math

Sample Problem

The bottle opener changes the input force of 1 N to an output force of 2 N. Calculate the mechanical advantage of the bottle opener.

$$MA = \frac{\text{output force}}{\text{input force}}$$
$$= 2\,N / 1\,N$$
$$= 2$$

You Try It

9 Calculate The pulley changes the direction of a 5 N input force. The output force is equal to the input force. Calculate the mechanical advantage.

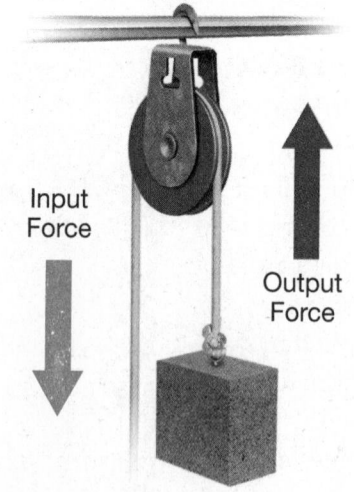

$MA = $ _____

$\quad = $ _____

$\quad = $ _____

You Try It

10 Calculate The input force applied on the hammer is 6 N. The output force applied to the nail is 2 N. Calculate the mechanical advantage.

$MA = $ _____

$\quad = $ _____

$\quad = $ _____

What is mechanical efficiency?

Ideally, the work a machine does on an object is the same as the work that you put into it. But even when the mechanical advantage is greater than one, the work input is greater than the work output because some work is done to overcome friction. **Mechanical efficiency** is a comparison of a machine's work output with the work input. Mechanical efficiency, ME, is equal to the work output divided by the work input, expressed as a percentage.

$$\text{mechanical efficiency} = \frac{\text{work output}}{\text{work input}} \times 100\%$$

 **Do the Math**

Sample Problem

Suppose 5,000 J of work is put into a go-cart engine. The work output of the engine is 1,250 J. What is the mechanical efficiency of the engine?

$$ME = \frac{\text{work output}}{\text{work input}} \times 100\%$$

$$= \frac{1,250\ J}{5,000\ J} \times 100\%$$

$$= 25\%$$

What Happens to Input Work

Work output 25%

Unusable work 75%

Only 25% of work that goes into the engine is used to move the go-cart.

You Try It!

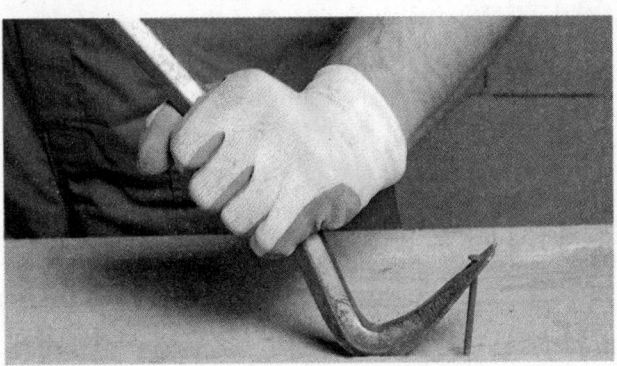

11 Calculate A person does 500 J of work on a crowbar. The crowbar does 475 J of work on a nail. What is the mechanical efficiency of the crowbar?

12 Graph Draw and label a pie graph that shows the percentages of work output and unusable work.

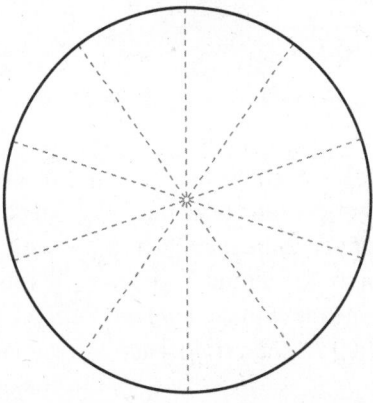

Gaining Leverage

What are the classes of levers?

What do hammers, seesaws, and baseball bats have in common? They are all levers. A **lever** is a simple machine that has a bar that pivots at a fixed point. This fixed point is called a **fulcrum**. Levers are used to apply a force to move an object. The force of the object is called the load.

Ideal mechanical advantage is the mechanical advantage of a simple machine that does not take friction into account. In other words, ideal mechanical advantage is the mechanical advantage of a machine that is 100% efficient. The ideal mechanical advantage of a lever is equal to the distance from input force to fulcrum (d_{input}) divided by the distance from output force to fulcrum (d_{output}).

$$\text{ideal mechanical advantage} = \frac{d_{input}}{d_{output}}$$

First-Class Levers

There are three classes of levers that differ based on the positions of the fulcrum, the load, and the input force. A seesaw is an example of a *first-class lever*. In a first-class lever, the fulcrum is between the input force and the load. First-class levers always change the direction of the input force. They may also increase the force or the distance through which the force is applied. The ideal mechanical advantage of first-class levers can be greater than one, equal to one, or less than one, depending on the location of the fulcrum.

Active Reading **13 Describe** Where is the fulcrum located in a first-class lever?

_____

_____

Visualize It!

14 Illustrate In box C, draw and label a first-class lever that has an ideal mechanical advantage less than one.

A

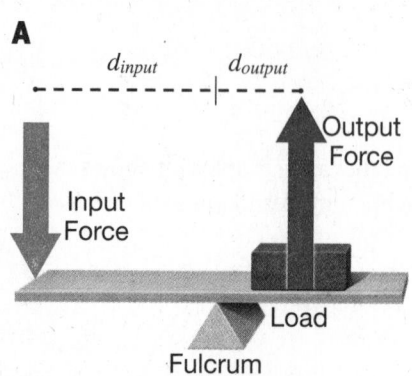

This lever has a mechanical advantage greater than one. The fulcrum is closer to the load than to the input force. The output force is larger than the input force, but it is applied through a shorter distance.

B

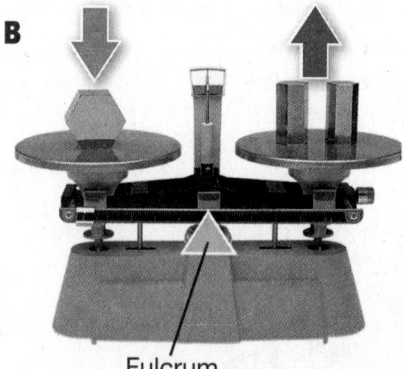

This balance is a lever that has a mechanical advantage equal to one. The fulcrum is exactly in the middle of the lever. The direction of the force is changed, but the distance and magnitude of the input force and output force are the same.

C

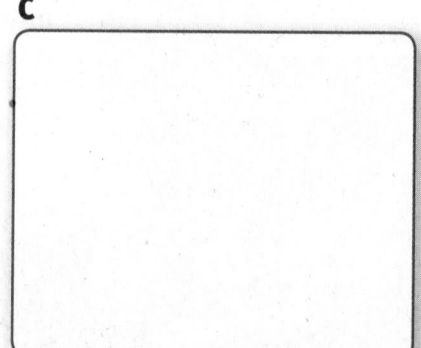

This lever has a mechanical advantage of less than one. The fulcrum is closer to the input force than to the load. The output force is less than the input force, but it is applied through a longer distance.

© Houghton Mifflin Harcourt Publishing Company • Image Credits: ©HMH

Second-Class Levers

In a *second-class lever,* the load is between the fulcrum and the input force. Second-class levers do not change the direction of the input force. They allow you to apply less force than the load. But you must exert the input force through a greater distance. The ideal mechanical advantage for a second-class lever is always greater than one. Wheelbarrows, bottle-cap openers, and staplers are second-class levers. A stapler pivots at one end when you push on the other end. The output force of the stapler drives the staple into the paper. The output force is applied between where you push and where the stapler pivots.

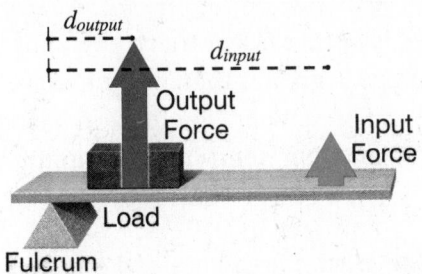

The load is between the fulcrum and input force in a stapler.

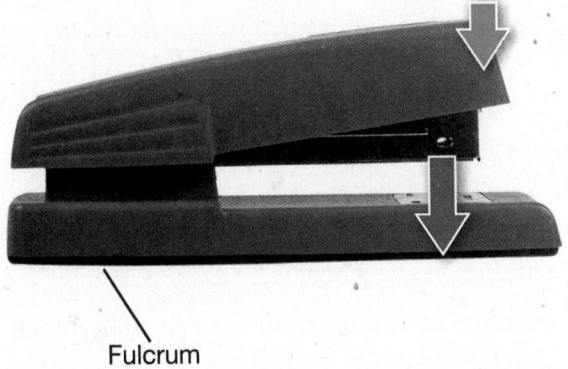

Third-Class Levers

In a *third-class lever,* the input force is between the fulcrum and the load. Like second-class levers, third-class levers do not change the direction of the input force. The mechanical advantage for a third-class lever is always less than one. The output force is less than the input force. But the output force is applied through a longer distance. Hammers and baseball bats are examples of third-class levers. When you swing a baseball bat, the fulcrum is at the base of the handle. The output force is at the end of the bat where it hits the ball. A bat applies a force to the ball in the same direction as you swing the bat. Your hands move a much shorter distance than the end of the bat moves when you swing.

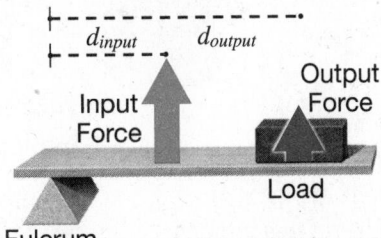

The input force is between the fulcrum and the load in a baseball bat.

 **You Try It!**

15 Calculate The input force of a third-class lever is 5 cm away from the fulcrum. The output force is 20 cm away from the fulcrum. What is the ideal mechanical advantage of the lever?

16 Model Draw and label a diagram of the lever described in question 15. Make sure to show the correct relative distances of the input and output forces from the fulcrum.

Turn, Turn, Turn

What is a wheel and axle?

A **wheel and axle** is a simple machine that is made of a wheel connected to a smaller cylindrical object, the axle. Doorknobs, tires, and screwdrivers are machines that contain wheels and axles.

The ideal mechanical advantage of a wheel and axle equals the radius corresponding to the input force divided by the radius corresponding to the output force.

$$\text{ideal mechanical advantage} = \frac{radius_{input}}{radius_{output}}$$

The radius of the wheel is always larger than the radius of the axle. The mechanical advantage is greater than one when the input force is applied to the wheel, such as when you turn on a faucet. The mechanical advantage is less than one when the input force is applied to the axle, such as when a Ferris wheel is turned.

Active Reading **17 Describe** When does a wheel and axle have a mechanical advantage greater than one?

_____

_____

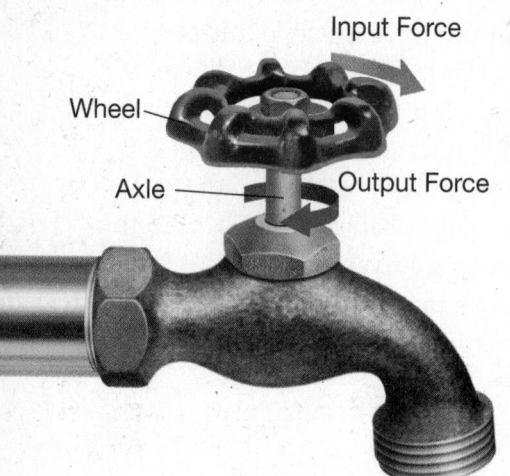

Input Force

Wheel

Axle

Output Force

The axle of this faucet turns when an input force is applied to the wheel. The axle rotates through a shorter distance than the wheel does. So the output force is larger than the input force.

Do the Math

Sample Problem

The faucet has a wheel radius of 5 cm and an axle radius of 1 cm. What is its ideal mechanical advantage?

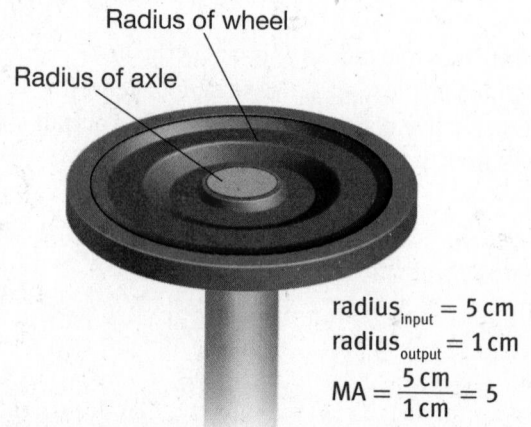

Radius of wheel

Radius of axle

$radius_{input} = 5\,cm$

$radius_{output} = 1\,cm$

$MA = \dfrac{5\,cm}{1\,cm} = 5$

You Try It!

The wheel of a Ferris wheel turns when a force is applied to the axle. The radius of its axle is 1 m. The radius of the wheel is 20 m.

18 Identify What is the radius corresponding to the input force and the output force?

$radius_{input}$: _____

$radius_{output}$: _____

19 Calculate What is the ideal mechanical advantage of the Ferris wheel?

What are the types of pulleys?

When you open window blinds by pulling on a cord, you're using a pulley. A **pulley** is a simple machine that has a grooved wheel that holds a rope or a cable. A load is attached to one end of the rope, and an input force is applied to the other end. There are three different types of pulleys.

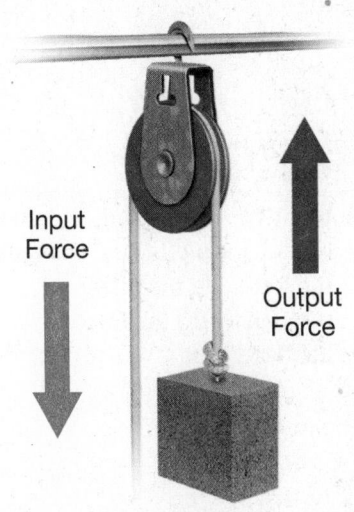

Input Force

Output Force

Fixed Pulleys

The pulley at the top of a flagpole is a *fixed pulley*. A fixed pulley is attached to something that does not move. It allows you to pull down on the rope to lift the load up. The wheel of the pulley turns and changes the direction of the force. Fixed pulleys do not change the size of the force. The size of the output force is the same as the size of the input force. Therefore, a fixed pulley has an ideal mechanical advantage of one.

Movable Pulleys

Unlike a fixed pulley, the wheel of a *movable pulley* is attached to the object being moved. One end of the rope is fixed. You can pull on the other end of the rope to make the wheel and load move along the rope. A movable pulley moves up with the load as the load is lifted. A movable pulley does not change the direction of a force, but does increase the force. The ideal mechanical advantage of all movable pulleys is two. They also increase the distance through which the input force must be applied. The rope must be pulled twice the distance that the load is moved.

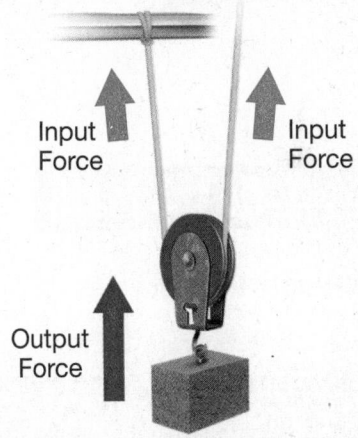

Input Force   Input Force

Output Force

Block and Tackle Pulleys

A *block and tackle pulley* is a pulley system made by combining a fixed pulley and a movable pulley. Cranes at construction sites use block and tackle pulleys to lift heavy objects. Block and tackle pulleys change the direction of the force and increase the force. The ideal mechanical advantage of a block and tackle pulley depends on the number of rope segments. The ideal mechanical advantage of a block and tackle with four rope segments is four. It multiplies your input force by four. But you have to pull the rope four times as far.

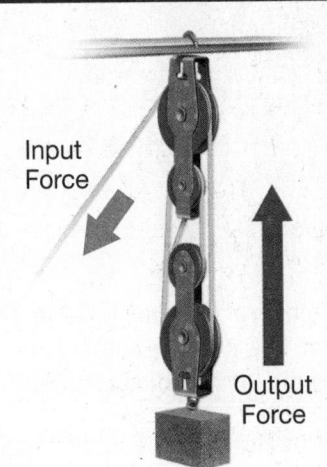

Input Force

Output Force

20 Identify Which type(s) of pulley could you use to increase your output force?

_____

_____

So Inclined

 **Active Reading**

21 Identify As you read, underline how an inclined plane changes the force and the distance through which the force is applied.

What are inclined planes?

Why is pushing furniture up a ramp easier than lifting the furniture? When you push something up a ramp, you are using a machine called an *inclined plane*. An **inclined plane** is a simple machine that is a straight, slanted surface. A smaller input force is needed to move an object using an inclined plane than is needed to lift the object. However, the force must be applied through a longer distance. So, the amount of work done on the object is the same. The ideal mechanical advantage of an inclined plane can be calculated by dividing the length of the incline by the height that the load is lifted.

$$\text{ideal mechanical advantage} = \frac{length}{height}$$

 **Do the Math**

Sample Problem

Length   Height

The length of the ramp is 4.2 m. The height of the ramp is 1.2 m. How does the output force on the chair compare to the input force applied to the chair?

$$\text{ideal mechanical advantage} =$$
$$\frac{length}{height} = \frac{4.2\ m}{1.2\ m} = 3.5$$

The output force on the chair is 3.5 times the input force.

You Try It!

22 Illustrate Use the grid below to draw and label a diagram of an inclined plane that has a length of 6 meters and an ideal mechanical advantage of 3. Use the squares to approximate the length. (Hint: In the space below, use the mechanical advantage to calculate the height.)

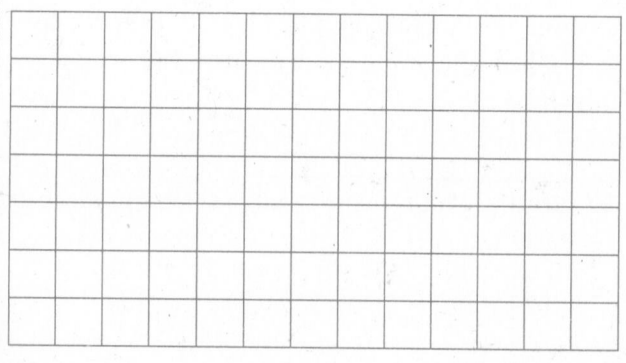

What are wedges?

Sculptors use chisels to break rock and wood. Chisels, ax heads, and knife blades are wedges. A *wedge* is a pair of inclined planes that move. They have one thick end and one thin end. Wedges are used to cut and split objects. For example, a sculptor applies an input force to the thick end of a chisel. The thin end of the chisel exerts an outward force that splits open the object. The output force of the wedge is greater than the input force, but the output force is applied through a shorter distance. The longer and thinner the wedge is, the greater its ideal mechanical advantage. So a longer chisel has a greater mechanical advantage than a shorter chisel that is the same width at the thick end.

Wedges have two sloped sides and help split objects.

What are screws?

Screws are often used to hold wood together. A *screw* is an inclined plane that is wrapped in a spiral around a cylinder. Think of wrapping a long triangular piece of paper around a pencil, as shown below. The ridges formed by the paper are like the threads of a screw. When a screw is turned, a small force is applied through the distance along the inclined plane of the screw. The screw applies a large force through the short distance it is pushed.

Imagine unwinding the inclined plane of a screw. You would see that the plane is very long and has a gentle slope. The longer an inclined plane is compared with its height, the greater its ideal mechanical advantage. Similarly, the longer the spiral on a screw is and the closer together the threads are, the greater the screw's mechanical advantage.

The threads of a screw are made by wrapping an inclined plane around a cylinder.

Think Outside the Book Inquiry

23 Apply Make a list of simple machines you use every day. In a small group, try to classify all the machines identified by the group members.

Visual Summary

To complete this summary, check the box that indicates true or false. Then, use the key below to check your answers. You can use this page to review the main concepts of the lesson.

Machines

Mechanical efficiency is a way to compare a machine's work output with work input.

The six types of simple machines:

- levers
- wheel and axles
- pulleys
- inclined planes
- wedges
- screws

	T	F	
24	☐	☐	Mechanical advantage is calculated by dividing the output force by the input force and multiplying by 100.
25	☐	☐	Friction causes the real mechanical advantage of a ramp to be less than the ideal mechanical advantage.

	T	F	
26	☐	☐	The location of the fulcrum differs for first-class levers, second-class levers, and third-class levers.
27	☐	☐	Types of pulleys include fixed pulleys, movable pulleys, and wheel and axles.
28	☐	☐	Using ramps, wedges, and screws reduces the amount of work that is done.

Answers: 24 False; 25 True; 26 True; 27 False; 28 False

29 Claims · Evidence · Reasoning A third-class lever has an ideal mechanical advantage of less than one. Explain why it is useful for some tasks, and identify two examples of third-class levers. Summarize evidence to support your claim and explain your reasoning.

Lesson Review

Vocabulary

Draw a line to connect the following terms to their definitions.

1 machine

A a simple machine that has a grooved wheel that holds a rope

2 lever

B a simple machine consisting of two circular objects of different sizes

3 wheel and axle

C a simple machine that is a straight, slanted surface

4 pulley

D a device that helps people do work by changing the way work is done

5 inclined plane

E a simple machine that has a bar that pivots at a fixed point

Key Concepts

6 Explain In what two ways can machines change the way work is done?

_____
_____
_____
_____

7 Identify What equation would you use to calculate the ideal mechanical advantage of a wheel and axle if the input force is applied to the axle? Explain your reasoning.

_____
_____
_____

8 Solve A stone block is pushed up a ramp that is 120 m long and 20 m high. What is the ideal mechanical advantage of the ramp?

_____
_____

Critical Thinking

9 Apply A person does 50 J of work to lift a crate using a pulley. The pulley's work output is 42 J. What is the pulley's mechanical efficiency?

_____
_____

Use this drawing to answer the following questions.

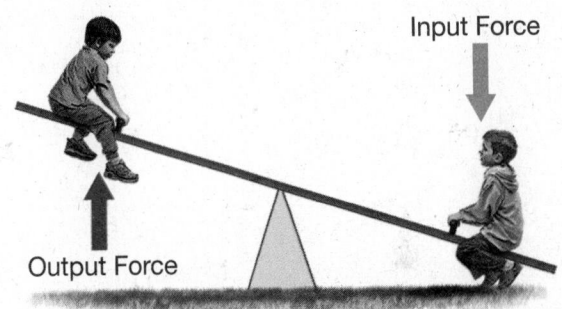

Input Force

Output Force

10 Classify What type of lever is the seesaw? Explain your reasoning.

_____
_____
_____

11 Calculate The input force is 245 N, and the output force is 245 N. Calculate the ideal mechanical advantage of the seesaw.

_____
_____

12 Predict The boy applying the input force moves so that he is 1.5 m from the fulcrum. The seesaw applies an output force to the other boy, who is 2 m from the fulcrum. What is the new ideal mechanical advantage?

_____
_____
_____
_____

My Notes

Lesson 1

ESSENTIAL QUESTION
How is work related to energy?

Relate work to energy and power.

Lesson 2

ESSENTIAL QUESTION
What are kinetic and potential energy?

Calculate kinetic and potential energy and know how these two types of energy are related.

Lesson 3

ESSENTIAL QUESTION
How do simple machines work?

Describe different types of simple machines, and calculate the mechanical advantages and efficiencies of various simple machines.

Connect ESSENTIAL QUESTIONS
Lessons 1 and 2

1 **Synthesize** What happens when you lift a basket of laundry and move it to the washing machine? Explain in terms of work, potential energy, kinetic energy, and power.

_____

_____

_____

_____

_____

_____

Think Outside the Book

2 **Synthesize** Choose one of these activities to help synthesize what you have learned in this unit.

☐ Using what you learned in lessons 1 and 2, create a poster presentation to explain what happens when you wind up a music box and release the key. Illustrate the events in terms of energy.

☐ Using what you learned in lessons 1 and 3, in an informative brochure, describe a machine that you have used recently. Explain how the machine helped you do work.

Unit 6 Review

Name _____

Vocabulary

Fill in each blank with the term that best completes the following sentences.

1 _____ is the use of force to move an object in the direction of the force.

2 The stored energy that an object has due to its position, condition, or chemical composition is called _____ .

3 A(n) _____ is a device that helps people do work by changing the way work is done.

4 A machine's _____ is the ratio of the machine's output force to its input force.

5 A(n) _____ is a simple machine that consists of a solid bar that pivots at a fixed point.

Key Concepts

Read each question below, and circle the best answer.

6 Which of the following is an example of the conversion of kinetic energy into gravitational potential energy?

A a person parachuting out of an airplane

B a car racing around an oval track

C a person skiing down a hill

D a person walking up a hill

7 Which is an example of a wedge?

A knife   **C** ramp

B hammer   **D** screw

8 A ramp is an example of which type of simple machine?

A a lever   **C** an inclined plane

B a wheel and axle   **D** a block and tackle pulley

9 The diagram below shows a swinging pendulum. During every swing, the pendulum's speed and position change. Three positions during the swing are identified as Position 1, Position 2, and Position 3.

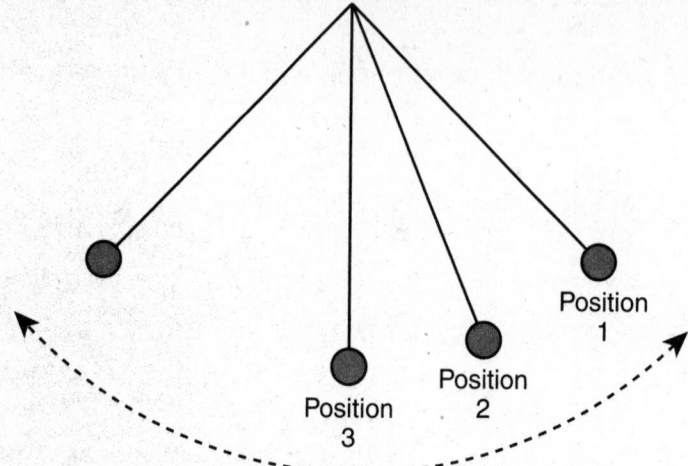

Ignoring the effects of friction or air resistance, at which point would the pendulum have the greatest amount of mechanical energy?

A Position 1

C Position 3

B Position 2

D Mechanical energy does not change.

10 Below is a diagram of a weight on a spring. When the weight is pulled down and then released, the spring compresses and expands. Each position indicates a different point in time.

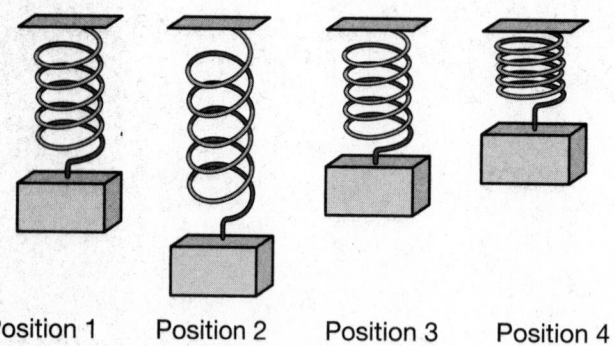

Position 1   Position 2   Position 3   Position 4

Which of the following statements is true?

A In all four positions, mechanical energy is 0 J.

B The elastic potential energy of the spring at Position 2 is converted to kinetic energy.

C The chemical potential energy of the spring is greatest at Position 4.

D In all four positions, the gravitational potential energy of the spring is the same.

11 A bottle opener is an example of a second-class lever.

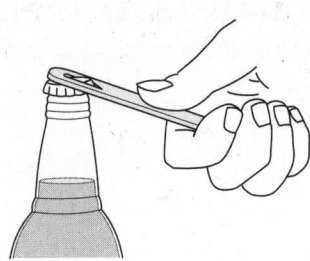

Which of the following statements is true about
second-class levers?

A The input force is between the output force and the fulcrum.

B The fulcrum is between the input force and the output force.

C The output force is between the input force and the fulcrum.

D The input force and output force move in opposite directions.

12 All moving objects have kinetic energy. The four vehicles in the diagram below

are all moving at the same speed along a road.

Which of the following statements is correct?

A The motorcycle has the most kinetic energy because it is the vehicle with the least mass.

B All the vehicles have the same kinetic energy because they are moving at the same speed.

C The delivery truck has the greatest kinetic energy because its mass is greater than that of the other vehicles.

D The delivery truck has the greatest kinetic energy because it has the most tires in contact with the pavement.

13 A faucet is an example of a simple machine, a wheel and axle. The faucet wheel has a radius of 5 cm. The axle has a radius of 0.5 cm. The input force is applied to the faucet wheel. What is the mechanical advantage of this simple machine?

A 0.1   **C** 5

B 1   **D** 10

Critical Thinking

Answer the following questions in the space provided.

14 What is mechanical efficiency, and how is it calculated?

_____

_____

_____

_____

15 Work is defined as the use of force to move an object in the direction of that force and is equal to the force times the distance the object moved. How do energy and power relate to work?

_____

_____

_____

_____

Connect **ESSENTIAL QUESTIONS**
Lessons 2 and 3

Answer the following question in the space provided.

16 Explain how an inclined plane makes loading a piano into a truck easier. Refer to the changing potential energy and kinetic energy of the piano as it (a) sits on the ground, (b) is being moved into the truck, and (c) sits in the truck.

_____

_____

_____

_____

_____

Electricity and Magnetism

Lightning is the discharge of static electricity that builds up in clouds during a storm.

© Houghton Mifflin Harcourt Publishing Company • Image Credits: (bg) ©A. T. Willett/Alamy; (Inset) ©Mark Burnett/Photo Researchers, Inc.

Big Idea

An electric current can produce a magnetic field, and a magnetic field can produce an electric current.

S8P5., S8P5.a, S8P5.b, S8P5.c

What do you think?

How can static electricity generate an electrical force to make your hair stand on end? As you explore the unit, gather evidence to help you state and support your claim.

This Van de Graaff generator makes a safe but hair-raising demonstration.

CITIZEN SCIENCE

Be Lightning Safe

Lightning can be an impressive display, but it is also very dangerous. Lightning strikes carry a great deal of energy that can split apart trees, damage property, and start fires. People can be injured or killed if they are struck by lightning.

① Define the Problem

Research how people can protect themselves from lightning while participating in outdoor activities.

A What are some signs that lightning may occur?

_____

_____

_____

B Where and for how long should people take shelter from lightning?

_____

_____

_____

To be safe from lightning, people should wait out a storm by going inside a school building that is completely enclosed.

Game Canceled due to severe weather

② Ask Some Questions

A Where is your school's lightning-safety plan posted?

_____

_____

B Are students and teachers aware of your school's plan for lightning safety?

_____

_____

C What is your school's current policy for canceling outdoor events when there is a risk of lightning?

_____

_____

_____

D Is your school's current plan for lightning safety adequate?

_____

_____

③ Make a Plan

A What are two ways in which your school's lightning-safety plan could be improved?

_____

_____

_____

_____

B Describe two steps that you could take to promote your improved lightning-safety plan at your school.

_____

_____

_____

_____

Take It Home

With an adult, make a lightning-safety plan for your family. And, discuss the weather conditions that would cause you to put your plan into action. See *ScienceSaurus®* for more information about weather.

Electric Charge and Static Electricity

ESSENTIAL QUESTION

What makes something electrically charged?

By the end of this lesson, you should be able to describe electric charges in objects and distinguish between electrical conductors and insulators.

A Van de Graaff generator contains a metal dome that becomes electrically charged when turned on. Touching the dome has caused this student to become electrically charged.

S8P5.a Fields and forces

S8P5.b Conductors and insulators

S8P5.c Strength of electric and magnetic forces

Engage Your Brain

1 Predict Check T or F to show whether you think each statement is true or false.

T	F	
☐	☐	Electrons have a negative charge.
☐	☐	Objects with like charges attract each other.
☐	☐	Copper is an electrical conductor.
☐	☐	Objects must be touching to exert an electric force on each other.

2 Describe Write your own caption describing what is happening to this student's hair.

_____

_____

_____

_____

Active Reading

3 Synthesize Many scientific words, such as *charge*, also have everyday meanings. Use context clues to write your own definition for each meaning of the word *charge*.

Example sentence
The <u>charge</u> for entry to the zoo goes up every year.

charge:

_____

_____

Example sentence
When Andre touched the doorknob, the <u>charge</u> gave him a shock.

charge:

_____

_____

Vocabulary Terms
• electric charge
• electric field
• static electricity
• electrical conductor
• electrical insulator
• semiconductor

4 Identify As you read, create a reference card for each vocabulary term. On one side of the card, write the term and its meaning. On the other side, draw an image that illustrates or makes a connection to the term. These cards can be used as bookmarks in the text so that you can refer to them while studying.

Opposites Attract

What is electric charge?

Have you ever touched a doorknob and felt a shock? Have you ever seen clothes cling to each other after they are taken from a dryer? Both of these events are due to a fundamental property of matter called *electric charge*. **Electric charge** is a property that leads to electromagnetic interactions between the particles that make up matter. An object can have a positive (+) charge, a negative (−) charge, or no charge. An object that has no charge is *neutral*.

The diagram below shows charges within an atom. All atoms have a dense center called a *nucleus*. The nucleus contains two types of particles: *protons* and *neutrons*. A proton has a charge of 1+. A neutron has no charge. *Electrons* are a third type of particle and are found outside the nucleus. An electron has a charge of 1−. When an atom has the same number of protons as electrons, the atom has no overall charge. This is because the charges of its protons and electrons add up to zero. However, atoms can lose or gain electrons. When this happens, the atom has an overall positive or negative charge and is called an *ion*. Positively charged ions have more protons than electrons. Negatively charged ions have fewer protons than electrons. The overall charge of an object is the sum of the charges of its atoms.

5 Apply An atom gains an additional electron. What is the overall charge of the ion that is formed? _____

Pieces of paper cling to a ruler due to the electric charge of the ruler.

Visualize It!

6 Label Complete the diagram by labeling the nucleus and an electron.

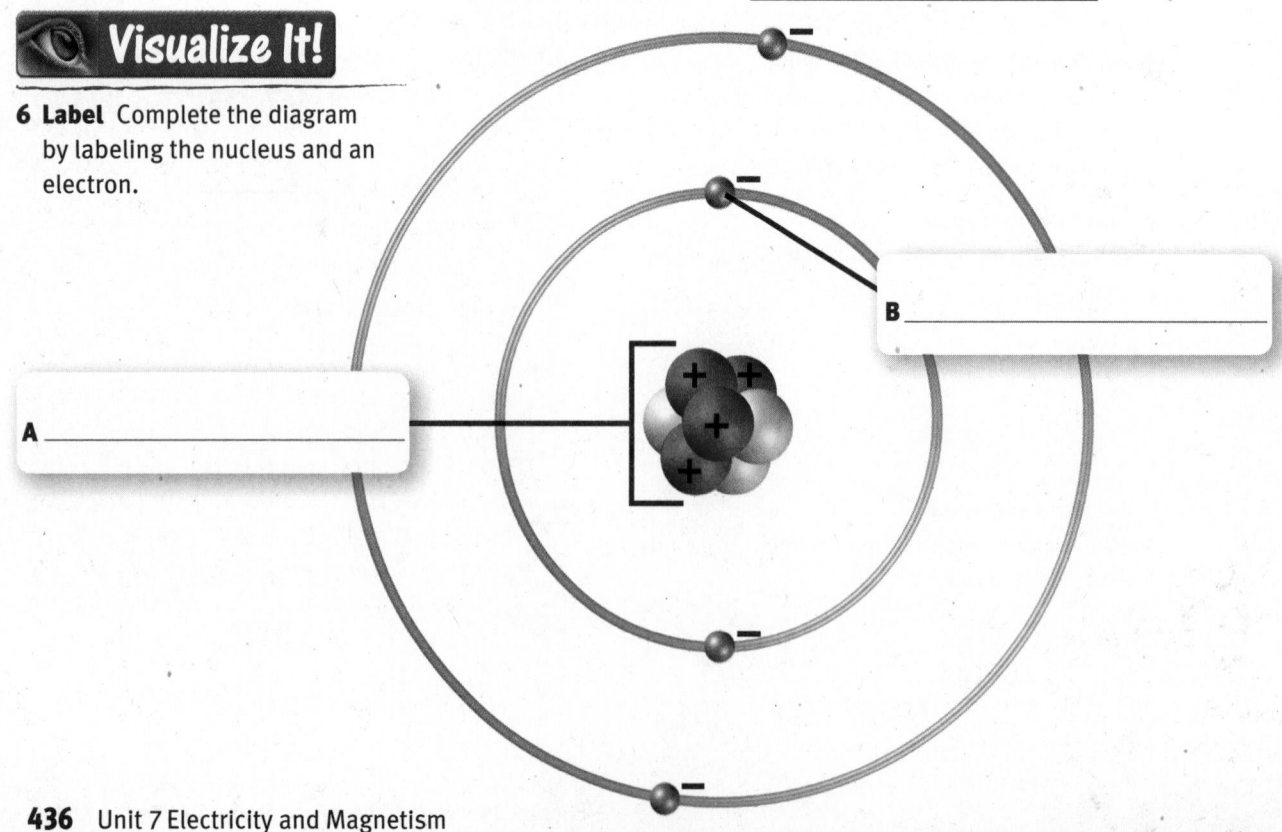

A _____

B _____

What affects the electric force between two objects?

Any two charged objects exert a force on each other called an *electric force*. Like gravity, electric force acts between objects even when they do not touch. But gravity always pulls objects together. Unlike gravity, the electric force can either pull objects together or push them apart. How strongly the electric force pushes or pulls depends on the charge of each object and how close together the objects are.

The area surrounding a charge where electrical force can be detected is called the **electric field.** A charged object placed anywhere in the electric field will be affected by the charge.

Charge

If objects have like charges, they repel each other. The objects exert an electric force that pushes them apart. The balls in the diagram A at the right both have a positive charge. The arrows show the electric force acting on each ball.

Two objects with unlike charges attract each other. So an object with a positive charge and an object with a negative charge are attracted. Each object exerts a force on the other, pulling the objects together.

The amount of charge on each object also affects the strength of the electric force between them. The greater an object's charge is, the greater the electric force is.

Distance

The distance between two objects affects the size of the electric force, too. As charged objects move farther apart, they attract or repel each other less strongly.

Active Reading **7 Explain** Can two charged objects push or pull each other even when they are not touching? Explain your reasoning and give an example.

_____
_____
_____
_____

8 Analyze Label diagrams B and C with the missing charge signs. Then add a caption below each diagram to describe the forces between the objects.

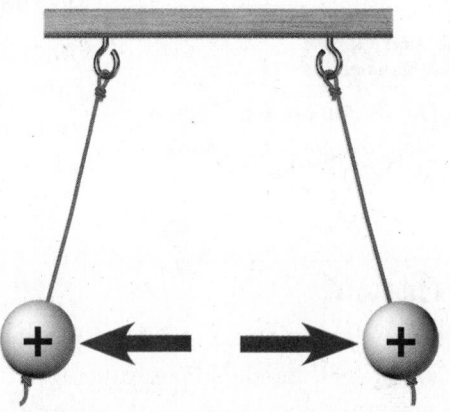

A The balls have like positive charges. They push each other apart.

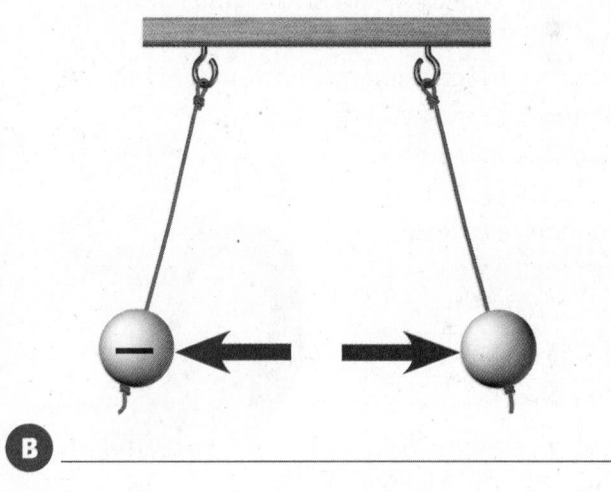

B _____
_____

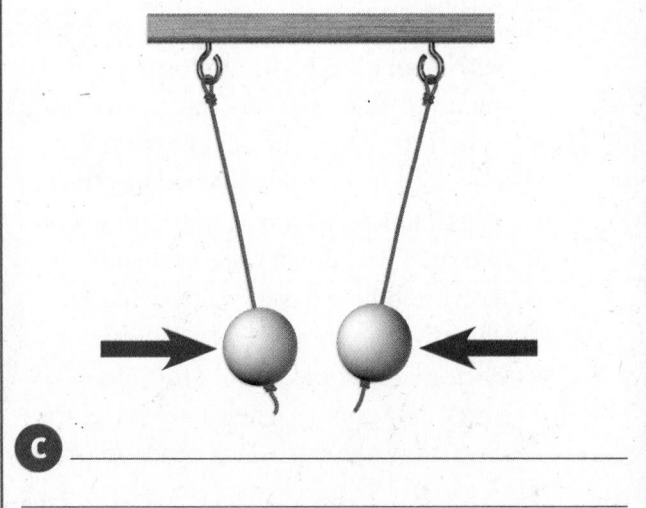

C _____
_____

What a *Shock!*

How can an object become charged?

Objects become charged when their atoms gain or lose electrons. Three ways that objects can gain or lose electrons are by friction, contact, or induction.

📖 **Active Reading**

9 Identify As you read, underline examples of objects becoming charged.

By Friction

Charging by friction occurs when two objects are rubbed together, causing a transfer of electrons between the objects. For example, rubbing a balloon on your hair moves electrons from your hair to the balloon. Your hair becomes positively charged, and the balloon becomes negatively charged. Similarly, when you rub your shoes on a carpet on a dry day, you may become charged. If you then touch a metal object such as a doorknob, you may feel a shock from the sudden release of electric charge.

By Contact

If a charged object and an uncharged object touch each other, the charged object can transfer some of its charge to the area it touches. This student is touching the dome of a *Van de Graaff generator*. The generator places a charge on its dome. An uncharged object that touches the dome becomes charged by contact. This student's hair is standing on end because the charged hairs repel each other.

By Induction

Induction is a way of rearranging the charges within an object without touching it. For example, this ruler has a negative charge. When the ruler is brought near the metal knob, it repels electrons in the metal. Electrons move away from the ruler and down the metal rod. The knob now has a positive charge. The thin pieces of metal foil at the bottom of the metal rod now have a negative charge. Their like charges cause them to push each other apart.

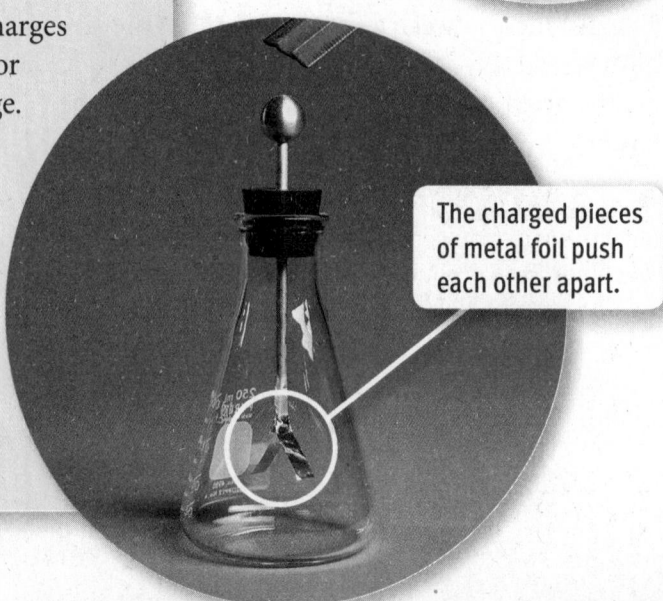

The charged pieces of metal foil push each other apart.

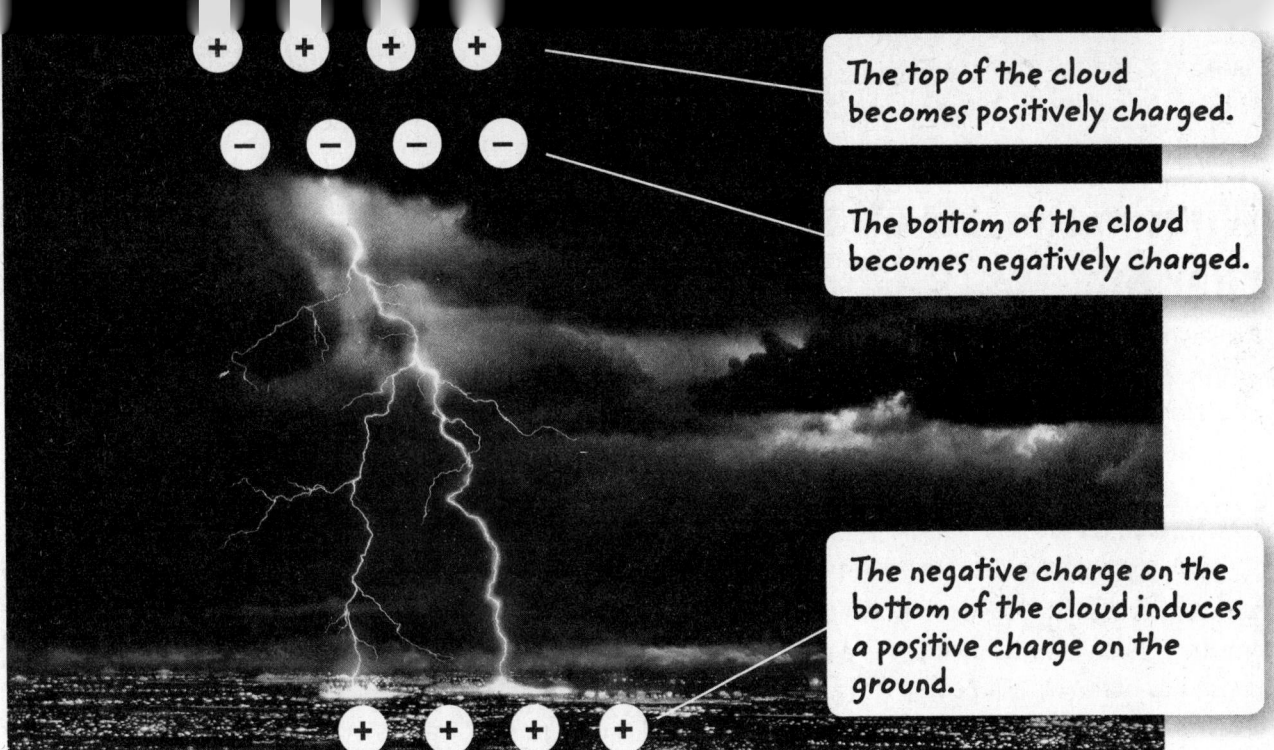

The top of the cloud becomes positively charged.

The bottom of the cloud becomes negatively charged.

The negative charge on the bottom of the cloud induces a positive charge on the ground.

What is static electricity?

After you take your clothes out of the dryer, they sometimes are stuck together. They stick together because of static electricity. **Static electricity** is the buildup of electric charge on an object. When something is static, it is not moving. Static electricity is the extra positive or negative charge that builds up on an object until it eventually moves elsewhere.

The Buildup of Charge on an Object

For an object to have static electricity, charge must build up on the object. For example, static electricity can build up inside storm clouds. The top of the cloud becomes positively charged. The bottom of the cloud becomes negatively charged. The negative charge in the bottom of the cloud can cause the ground to become positively charged by induction.

Charges that build up as static electricity eventually leave the object. This loss of charges is known as *electric discharge*. Electric discharge may happen slowly or quickly. Lightning is an example of rapid electric discharge. Lightning can occur between clouds. It can also occur between the negative part of the cloud and the positively charged ground. When lightning strikes, charged particles move toward places with opposite charge.

Active Reading **10 Analyze** During a lightning storm, what can cause the ground to become positively charged?

_____

_____

© Houghton Mifflin Harcourt Publishing Company • Image Credits: © Rob Matheson/Corbis

Think Outside the Book Inquiry

11 Apply Think of an everyday example of an object becoming charged. Draw and label a diagram that shows how charges moved. (Hint: You may need to use reference materials to learn more about the process you have chosen.)

Charging Ahead

What materials affect the flow of charge?

Have you ever noticed that electrical cords are often made from both metal and plastic? Different materials are used because electric charges move through some materials more easily than they move through others.

Conductors

An **electrical conductor** is a material through which charges can move freely. Many electrical conductors are metals. Copper is a metal that is used to make wires because it is an excellent electrical conductor. When an electrically charged plastic ruler touches a metal conductor, the charge it transfers to the metal can move freely through the metal.

Insulators

An **electrical insulator** is a material through which charges cannot move easily. The electrons are tightly held in the atoms of the insulator. Plastic, rubber, glass, and dry air are all good electrical insulators. Plastic is often used to coat wires because electric charges cannot move through the plastic easily. This stops the charges from leaving the wire and prevents you from being shocked when you touch the lamp cord.

Visualize It!

12 Identify What is the purpose of the material surrounding the metal inside the lamp cord?

_____

_____

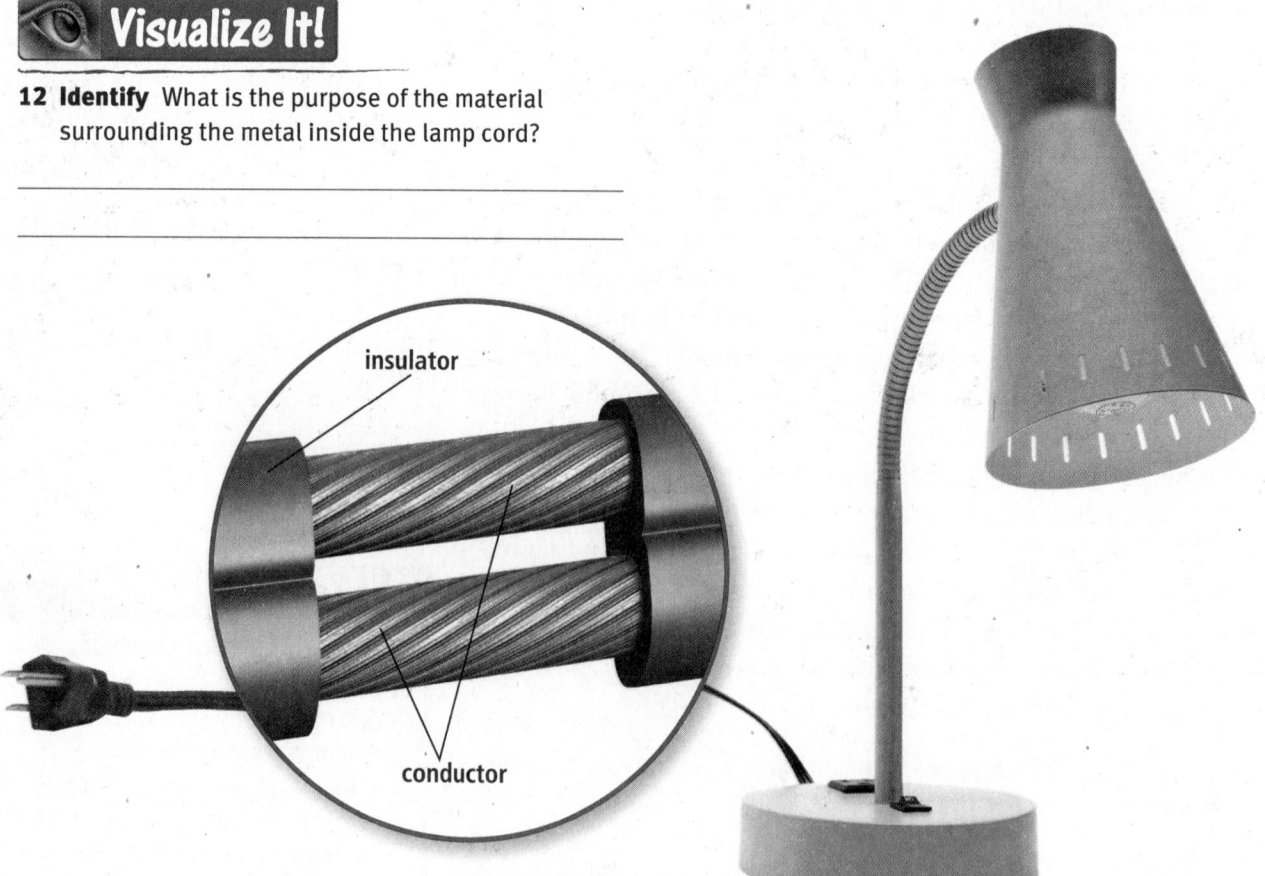

insulator

conductor

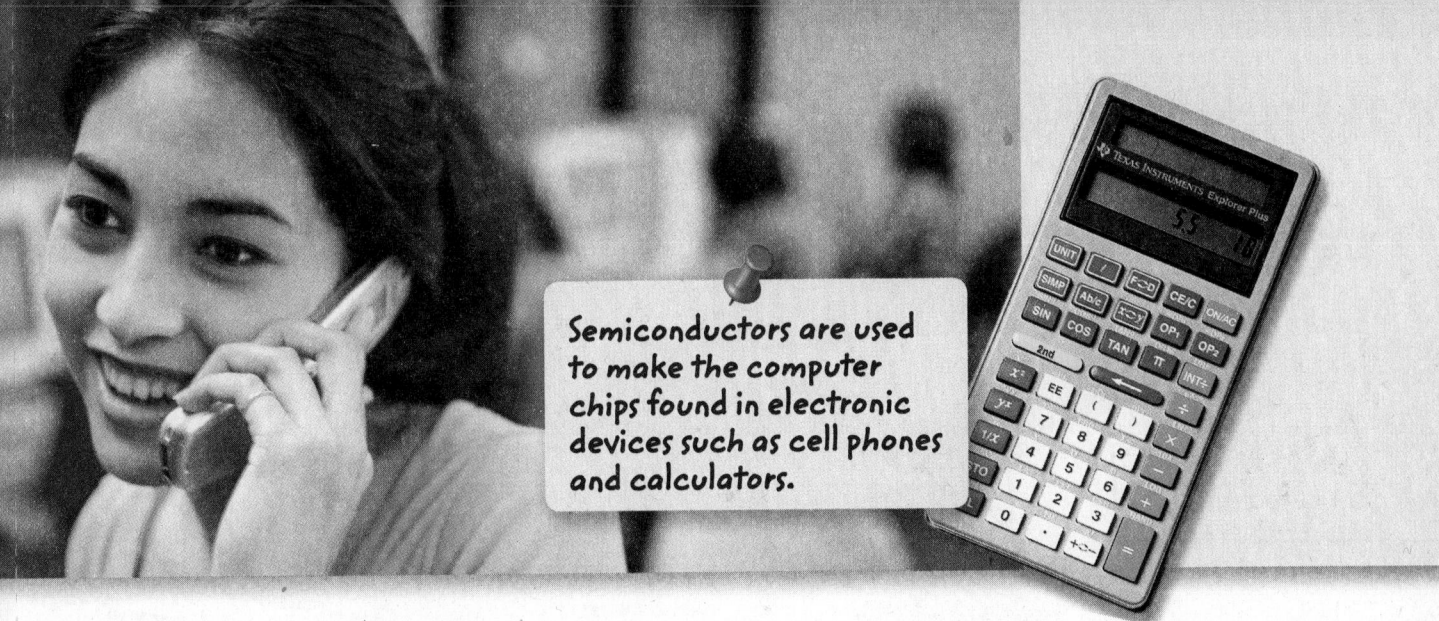

Semiconductors are used to make the computer chips found in electronic devices such as cell phones and calculators.

Semiconductors

Semiconductors are a special class of materials that conduct electric charge better than electrical insulators but not as well as electrical conductors. Their properties allow them to be used to control the flow of charge. Electrical devices use semiconductors to process electrical signals in many different ways. Silicon is the basis of many kinds of semiconductors. It is used to make computer chips found in electronic devices such as the ones shown above.

13 Summarize Fill in the table at the right to summarize what you have learned about conductors, insulators, and semiconductors.

	Example	Effect on the movement of charges
Conductor		
Insulator		
Semiconductor		

How is charge conserved?

All objects contain positive charges from the protons and negative charges from the electrons within their atoms. A neutral object becomes negatively charged when it gains one or more electrons and then has more negative charges than positive charges. Where do these electrons come from? They might come from a second object that loses the electrons and becomes positively charged. So electrons are not really lost. Charging objects involves moving electrons from one object to another. The total amount of charge always stays the same. This principle is called the conservation of charge.

Active Reading **14 Describe** What happens to the charge lost by an object? Support your claim with evidence.

_____

_____

Visual Summary

To complete this summary, fill in the blanks with the correct word. Then use the key below to check your answers. You can use this page to review the main concepts of the lesson.

Electric Charge and Static Electricity

Like charges repel each other, while unlike charges attract each other.

15 An object that has a positive charge equal to its negative charge is _____

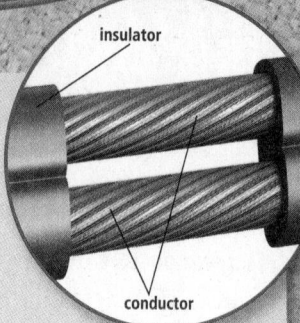

insulator

conductor

Electrical conductors allow electric charges to move freely, while electrical insulators do not.

17 A _____ is a material whose conductivity is between that of an electrical conductor and an electrical insulator.

Objects can become charged by friction, contact, or induction.

16 _____ is the buildup of electric charges on an object.

Electric charge is always conserved.

18 The electrons lost by one object are _____ by another.

19 Claims • Evidence • Reasoning Suppose an electrically charged ruler transfers some of its charge by contact to a tiny plastic sphere. Will the ruler and the sphere attract or repel afterwards? Explain your reasoning.

Lesson Review

Vocabulary

Draw a line to connect the following terms to their definitions.

1 electric charge

2 electrical conductor

3 electrical insulator

A a material that allows electrons to flow easily

B a material that does not allow electrons to flow easily

C property that leads to electromagnetic interactions

Key Concepts

4 Explain Describe electric discharge.

_____

_____

_____

_____

_____

5 Compare What properties of semiconductors make them useful in electronic devices?

_____

_____

_____

_____

_____

6 Predict Two objects have unlike charges. How would the electric force between the two objects change as they are moved apart?

_____

_____

_____

_____

_____

_____

Critical Thinking

Use this diagram to answer the following questions.

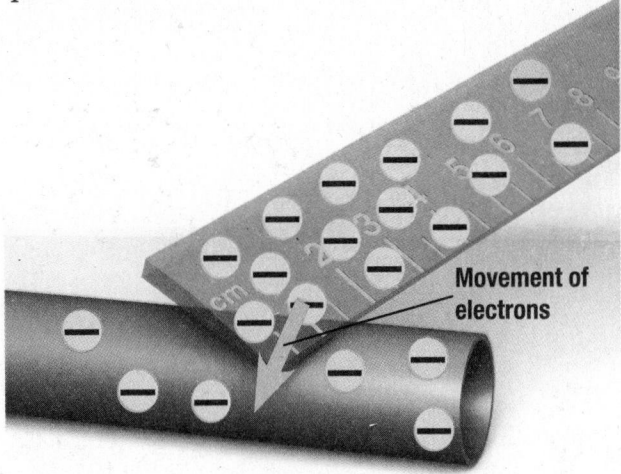

Movement of electrons

Not to scale

7 Analyze Describe how charge is transferred from the ruler to the metal rod.

_____

_____

_____

_____

_____

8 Describe Explain how this transfer observes the conservation of charge.

_____

_____

_____

_____

_____

_____

9 Evaluate A student places two charged objects near each other. The objects repel each other. The student concludes that the objects must both be negative. Do you agree? Explain.

_____

_____

_____

_____

My Notes

Electric Current

ESSENTIAL QUESTION

What flows through an electric wire?

By the end of this lesson, you should be able to describe how electric charges flow as electric current.

Electric current sent over wires from power plants supplies this city with energy for lights and other uses.

Lesson Labs

Quick Labs
• Investigate Electric Current
• Lemon Battery

S.T.E.M. Lab
• Voltage, Current, and Resistance

Engage Your Brain

1 Identify Unscramble the letters below to find terms related to electric current. Write your words on the blank lines.

SGARCHE _____

EGATOVL _____

EERPAM _____

EIRW _____

2 Describe Describe what makes this electric sign light up when it is in use.

_____

_____

_____

_____

Active Reading

3 Apply Many scientific words such as *resistance* also have everyday meanings. Use context clues to write your own definition for the word *resistance*.

Example sentence
John's request to go to the movies met with <u>resistance</u> from his friends.

resistance:

_____

_____

Example sentence
The composition of a wire determines its electrical <u>resistance</u>.

resistance:

_____

_____

_____

Vocabulary Terms

• electric current   • resistance
• voltage

4 Identify As you read, place a question mark next to any words that you do not understand. When you finish reading the lesson, go back and review the text that you marked. If the information is still confusing, consult a classmate or a teacher.

Current Events

What is an electric current?

When you watch TV, use a computer, or even turn on a light bulb, you depend on moving charges to provide the electrical energy that powers them. *Electrical energy* is the energy of electric charges. In most devices that use electrical energy, the electric charges flow through wires. The rate of flow of electric charges is called **electric current**.

How is electric current measured?

To understand an electric current, think of people entering the seating area for a sporting event through turnstiles. A counter in each turnstile records the number of people who enter. The number of people who pass through a turnstile each minute describes the rate of flow of people into the stadium. Similarly, an electric current describes the rate of flow of charges, such as the slow flow of many electrons through a wire. Electric current is the amount of charge that passes a location in the wire every second. Electric current is expressed in units called *amperes* (AM•pirz), which is often shortened to "amps." The symbol for ampere is A. A wire with a current of 2 A has twice as much charge passing by each second as a wire with a current of 1 A.

Active Reading

5 Identify As you read, underline the units used to express electric current.

Visualize It!

6 Identify How can you express the rate of flow of people into a stadium? How can you express the rate of flow of charges through a wire?

_____

_____

_____

_____

What are two kinds of current?

Two kinds of electric current are *direct current* (DC) and *alternating current* (AC). Both kinds of current carry electrical energy. They differ in the way that the charges move.

Direct Current (DC)

In direct current, charges always flow in the same direction. The electric current generated by batteries is DC. Some everyday devices that use DC from batteries are flashlights, cars, and cameras.

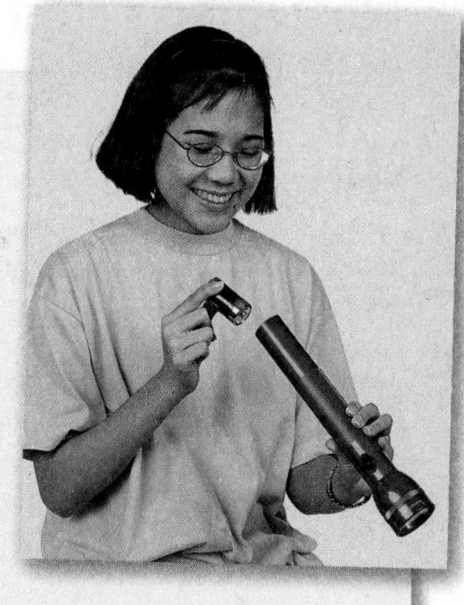

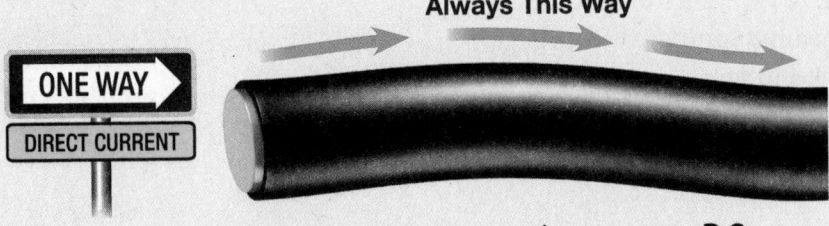

Charges move in one direction in DC.

Alternating Current (AC)

In alternating current, charges repeatedly shift from flowing in one direction to flowing in the reverse direction. The current *alternates* direction. The electric current from outlets in your home is AC. So, most household appliances run on alternating current. In the United States, the alternating current reverses direction and then returns back to the original direction 60 times each second.

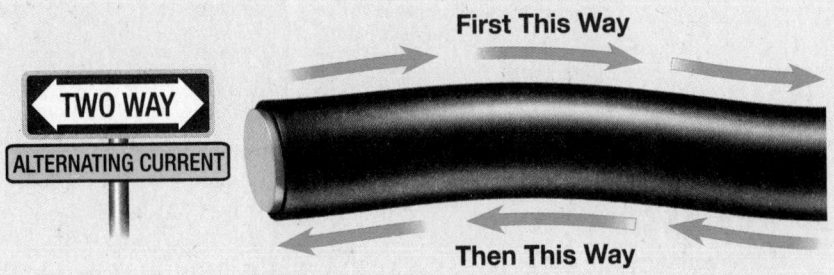

Charges repeatedly change direction in AC.

 **Active Reading**

7 Explain What alternates in alternating current?

_____

_____

You've Got *Potential*

What affects electric current?

Two factors that can affect the current in a wire are *voltage* and *resistance*.

Voltage

Compare the two drink containers below. If you pour lemonade from a full container, your glass fills quickly. If the container is nearly empty, the flow of lemonade is weaker. The lemonade in the full container exerts more pressure due to its weight, causing a higher rate of flow. This pressure can be compared to voltage. **Voltage** is the amount of work required to move each unit of charge between two points. Just as higher pressure produces a higher rate of flow of lemonade, higher voltage produces a higher rate of flow of electric charges in a given wire. Voltage is expressed in units of volts (V). Voltage is sometimes called *electric potential* because it is a measure of the electric potential energy per unit charge.

Visualize It!

8 Analyze How does the flow of the lemonade coming out of these containers relate to current and voltage?

_____

_____

_____

_____

_____

_____

© Houghton Mifflin Harcourt Publishing Company • Image Credits: (l) ©HMH; (r) ©MHM

Resistance

Think about the difference between walking around your room and walking around in waist-deep water. The water resists your movement more than the air, so you have to work harder to walk through water. If you walked in waist-deep mud, you would have to work even harder. Similarly, some materials do not allow electric charges to move freely. The opposition to the flow of electric charge is called **resistance**. Resistance is expressed in ohms (Ω, the Greek letter *omega*). Higher resistance at the same voltage results in lower current.

Think Outside the Book Inquiry

9 Apply In a small group, create a skit that illustrates the idea of electrical resistance. Be sure to compare high resistance and low resistance.

What affects electrical resistance?

A material's composition affects its resistance. Some metals, such as silver and copper, have low resistance and are very good electrical conductors. Other metals, such as iron and nickel, have a higher resistance. Electrical insulators such as plastic have such a high resistance that electric charges cannot flow in them at all. Other factors that affect the resistance of a wire are thickness, length, and temperature.

- A thin wire has higher resistance than a thicker wire.
- A long wire has higher resistance than a shorter wire.
- A hot wire has higher resistance than a cooler wire.

Conductors with low resistance, such as copper, are used to make wires. But conductors with high resistance are also useful. For example, an alloy of nickel and chromium is used in heating coils. Its high resistance causes the wire to heat up when it carries electric current.

Like lemonade in a drinking straw, electric charges move more easily through a short, wide pathway than through a long, narrow one.

Visualize It!

10 Predict For each pair of images, place a check mark in the box that shows the material that has higher electrical resistance.

Composition Wires made from different materials have different uses in electronic devices.	Pure copper	Nickel and chromium alloy
Thickness A three-way light bulb contains a thin filament and a thick filament. Charges move through one filament or the other or both to produce different brightness levels.	Thin filament	Thick filament
Temperature The electrical resistance of this heating element changes as its temperature increases.		

Visual Summary

To complete this summary, fill in the blanks with the correct word or phrase. Then use the key below to check your answers. You can use this page to review the main concepts of the lesson.

Electric current is the rate of flow of electric charges.

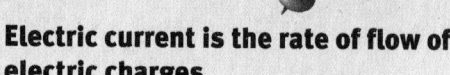

First This Way

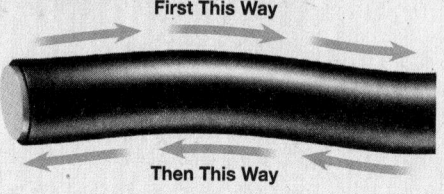

Then This Way

11 In _____ current, the flow of charge changes direction and then reverses back to the original direction.

The opposition to the flow of electric charges is called resistance.

13 Four factors that determine the resistance of a wire are

_____

_____

_____

_____

Voltage is the amount of work to move an electric charge between two points.

12 If the voltage applied to a given wire increases, its current will

_____

Electric Current

Answers: 11 alternating; 12 increase
13 composition, temperature, length, and thickness

14 Analyze What might happen if a wire in an electronic device is replaced with a thinner, longer wire? Explain your reasoning.

© Houghton Mifflin Harcourt Publishing Company • Image Credits: (t) ©HMH; (b) ©HMH

Lesson Review

Vocabulary

Draw a line to connect the following terms to their definitions.

1 electric current

2 voltage

3 resistance

A the opposition to the flow of electric charges

B the rate of flow of electric charges

C the amount of work required to move each unit of electric charge between two points

Key Concepts

4 Compare How does direct current differ from alternating current?

_____

_____

_____

_____

_____

5 Summarize Describe how resistance affects electric current.

_____

_____

_____

_____

_____

6 Apply What happens to the electric current in a wire as voltage is increased?

_____

_____

_____

7 Apply List two everyday devices that use DC and two everyday devices that use AC.

_____

_____

_____

_____

Critical Thinking

Use the diagram to answer the following questions.

Electrical Resistance of Various Materials

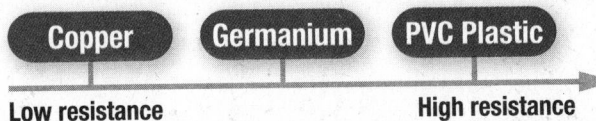

Copper   Germanium   PVC Plastic

Low resistance   High resistance

8 Claims · Evidence · Reasoning Make a claim about which material is likely to slow the flow of electric charges the most. Explain your reasoning.

_____

_____

_____

9 Infer A certain voltage is applied to a copper wire and to a germanium wire of the same thickness and length. How will the current in the two wires compare?

_____

_____

_____

_____

_____

10 Compare How do the currents produced by a 1.5 V flashlight battery and a 12 V car battery compare if the resistance is the same?

_____

_____

_____

_____

11 Infer What does it mean to say that the electric current from a wall socket is "120 V AC?"

_____

_____

_____

My Notes

Electric Circuits

ESSENTIAL QUESTION

How do electric circuits work?

By the end of this lesson, you should be able to describe basic electric circuits and how to use electricity safely.

Microscopic electric circuits inside these computer chips carry electric charges that can power computers, video games, and home appliances.

Lesson Labs

Quick Labs
- Compare Parallel and Series Circuits
- Compare Materials for Use in Fuses

Exploration
- Model the Electric Circuits in a Room

Engage Your Brain

1 Predict Check T or F to show whether you think each statement is true or false.

T	F	
☐	☐	A circuit must form a closed loop to have an electric current.
☐	☐	Electricity is dangerous only when it is labeled as high voltage.
☐	☐	Every electric circuit must have an energy source.

2 Describe Write a caption explaining how these light bulbs are connected.

_____
_____
_____
_____

Active Reading

3 Apply Many scientific words, such as *current*, also have everyday meanings. Use context clues to write your own definition for each meaning of the word *current*.

Example sentence
The magazine covered <u>current</u> events.

current:
_____
_____

Example sentence
The circuit had an electric <u>current</u> in it.

current:
_____
_____

Vocabulary Terms
- electric circuit
- series circuit
- parallel circuit

4 Apply As you learn the definition of each vocabulary term in this lesson, create your own definition or sketch to help you remember the meaning of the term.

A Complete Circuit

What are the parts of an electric circuit?

Think about a running track. It forms a loop. The spot where you start running around the track is the same as the spot where you end. This kind of closed loop is called a circuit. Like a track, an electric circuit also forms a loop. An **electric circuit** is a complete, closed path through which electric charges can flow. All electric circuits contain three basic parts: an energy source, an electrical conductor, and a load.

Energy Source

The energy source converts some type of energy, such as chemical energy, into electrical energy. One common household energy source is a battery. A battery changes chemical energy stored inside the battery into electrical energy. A solar cell is an energy source that changes light energy into electrical energy.

Inside a power plant, a form of energy such as chemical or nuclear energy is changed into mechanical energy. Electric generators in the power plant change the mechanical energy into electrical energy. Power transmission lines deliver this energy to wall outlets in homes, schools, and other buildings.

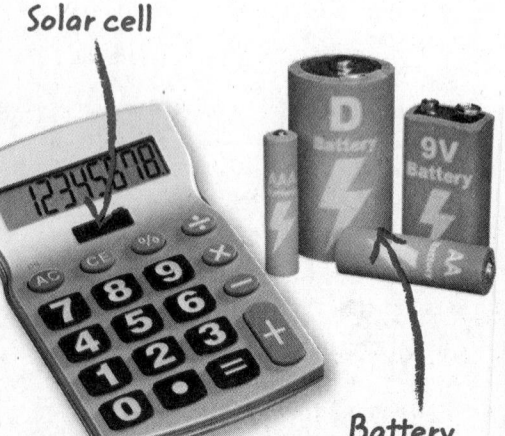

Solar cell

Battery

Power plant

Electrical Conductor

Materials in which electric charges can move easily are called *electrical conductors.* Most metals are good conductors of electric current. Electric wires are often made of copper. Copper is a metal that is a good conductor and is inexpensive compared to many other metals. Conducting wires connect all the parts of an electric circuit.

To protect people from harmful electrical shocks, copper wire is often covered with an insulator. An *electrical insulator* is a material, such as glass, plastic, or rubber, through which electric charges cannot move easily.

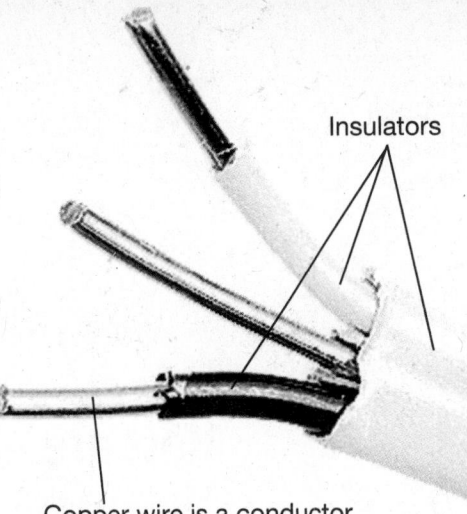

Insulators

Copper wire is a conductor.

Load

A complete circuit also includes a *load,* a device that uses electrical energy to operate. The conductor connects the energy source to the load. Examples of loads include light bulbs, radios, computers, and electric motors. The load converts electrical energy into other forms of energy. A light bulb, for example, converts electrical energy into light and energy as heat. A doorbell produces sound waves, energy that is transmitted through the air to your ear. A cell phone converts electrical energy into electromagnetic waves that carry information.

👁 **Visualize It!**

7 Identify List the devices in the photograph that could be a load in an electric circuit.

_____
_____
_____
_____
_____
_____
_____
_____

Around and Around

How are electric circuits modeled?

![Active Reading]

8 Identify As you read, underline the descriptions of symbols used in circuit diagrams.

To make an electric circuit, you need only three basic parts: an energy source, an electrical conductor, and a load. Most electric circuits, however, have more than one load. A circuit in your home might connect a desk lamp, clock radio, computer, and TV set. The circuit may even include devices in more than one room. Circuits can be complex. A single computer chip can have many millions of parts. One tool that can be used to model electric circuits is a circuit diagram.

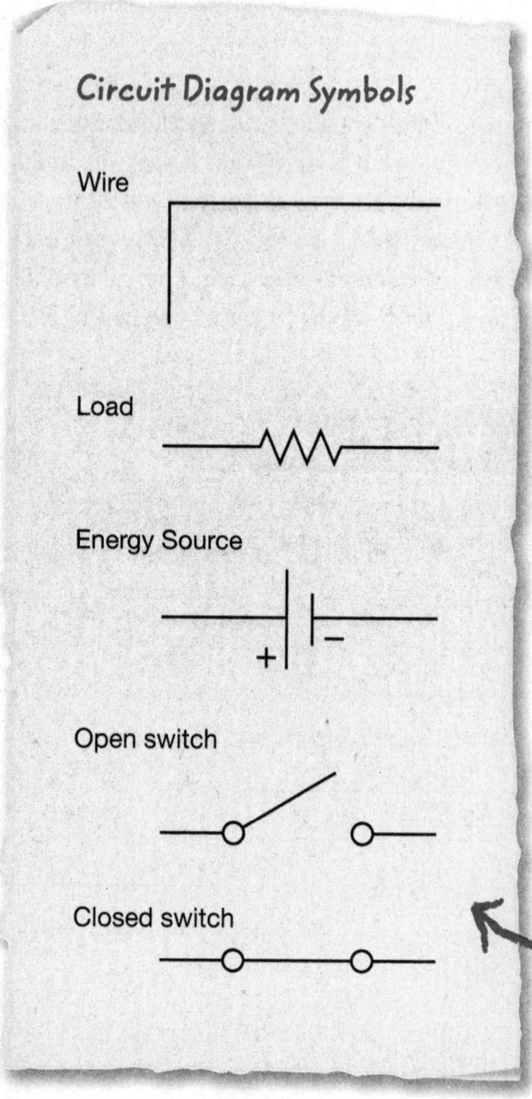

With Circuit Diagrams

A circuit diagram helps engineers and electricians design and install electric circuits so that they function correctly and safely. Sometimes, special software is used to create complex circuit designs on computers. A diagram for an electric circuit shows all the parts in the complete circuit and the relationships among the different parts. The chart at the left shows how each part of a circuit can be represented in a circuit diagram. The energy source can be represented by two parallel lines of different length. A wire or other conductor is shown as a line. A load is represented by a zigzag line segment. A small circle shows where two wires are connected. A straight line between two circles shows an on-off switch. When the line of the switch symbol is slanted up, the switch is open. When the line for the switch symbol connects two dots, the switch is closed.

Circuit Diagram Symbols

Wire

Load

Energy Source

Open switch

Closed switch

Symbols are put together to show the arrangement of parts in a circuit. A circuit diagram is like a road map for the moving charges.

How does current stop and start?

Electric charges move continuously in the closed loop of an electric circuit. What do you do if you want the charges to stop flowing? You open the switch! A switch is a device that turns electrical devices on and off. A switch is usually made of a piece of conducting material that can move. When the switch is open, the circuit is open. That means it does not form a closed loop, so charges cannot flow. When you turn a light switch on, the switch closes the circuit. Charges flow through the light bulb. If you turn a light switch off, the switch opens the circuit, and the charges stop flowing.

9 Apply Does an open light switch turn a light off or on? Explain your reasoning.

_____

_____

_____

_____

_____

Visualize It!

10 Identify Label the parts in this circuit diagram. Then draw a switch to match the circuit shown in the photograph.

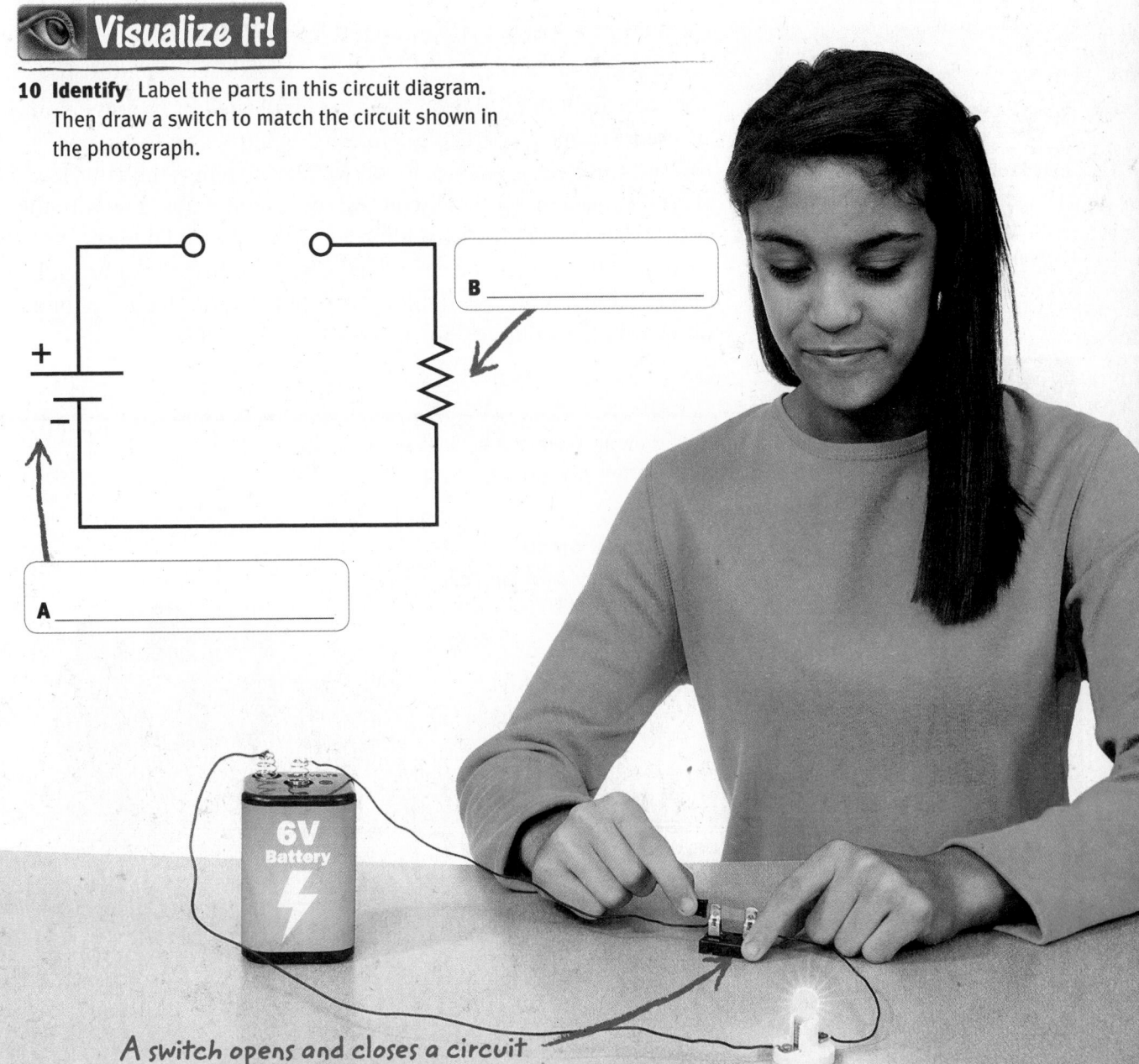

A switch opens and closes a circuit to turn a light bulb off and on.

© Houghton Mifflin Harcourt Publishing Company • Image Credits: ©HMH

All Together?

How do series circuits and parallel circuits differ?

Most electric circuits have more than one load. Simple electric circuits that contain one energy source and more than one load are classified as either a series circuit or a parallel circuit.

In Series Circuits, Charges Follow a Single Path

The three light bulbs shown below are connected in a series circuit. In a **series circuit**, all parts are connected in a row that forms one path for the electric charges to follow. The current is the same for all of the loads in a series circuit. All three light bulbs glow with the same brightness. However, adding a fourth bulb would lower the current in the circuit and cause all the bulbs to become dimmer. If one bulb burns out, the circuit is open and electric charges cannot flow through the circuit. So all of the bulbs go out.

Active Reading

11 Identify As you read this page and the next, underline what happens if you add a bulb to a series circuit and to a parallel circuit.

Visualize It!

12 Apply In these two circuit illustrations, draw an *X* over the bulbs that would not glow if the bulb closest to the battery burned out.

Series circuit
with battery and switch

The bulbs are connected to one another in a single loop.

In Parallel Circuits, Charges Follow Multiple Paths

Think about what would happen if all of the lights in your home were connected in series. If you needed to turn on a light in your room, all other lights in the house would have to be turned on, too! Instead of being wired in series, circuits in buildings are wired in parallel. In a **parallel circuit**, electric charges have more than one path that they can follow. Loads in a parallel circuit are connected side by side. In the parallel circuit shown below, any bulb can burn out without opening the circuit.

Unlike the loads in a series circuit, the loads in a parallel circuit can have different currents. However, each load in a parallel circuit experiences the same voltage. For example, if three bulbs were hooked up to a 12-volt battery, each would have the full voltage of the battery. Each light bulb would glow at the same brightness no matter how many more bulbs were added to the circuit.

13 Compare In the table below, list the features of series and parallel circuits.

Series circuits	Parallel circuits

Parallel circuit with battery and switch

The bulbs are connected side by side.

Safety First!

How can I use electricity safely?

You use many electrical devices every day. It is important to remember that electrical energy can be hazardous if it is not used correctly. Electric circuits in buildings have built-in safeguards to keep people safe. You can stay safe if you are careful to avoid electrical dangers and pay attention to warning signs and labels.

By Avoiding Exposure to Current

Pure water is a poor conductor of electric current. But water usually has substances such as salt dissolved in it. These substances make water a better conductor. This is especially true of fluids inside your body. The water in your body is a good conductor of electric current. This is why you should avoid exposure to current. Even small currents can cause severe burns, shock, and even death. A current can prevent you from breathing and stop your heart.

Following basic safety precautions will protect you from exposure to electric current. Never use electrical devices around water. Do not use any appliance if its power cord is worn or damaged. Always pay attention to warning signs near places with high-voltage transmission lines. You do not actually have to touch some high-voltage wires to receive a deadly shock. Even coming near high-voltage wires can do serious harm to your body.

Active Reading

14 Identify As you read, underline the reason that electric currents can be harmful to people.

A damaged cord exposes the metal wires that conduct electric charges.

Stay away from places where there is high-voltage electrical equipment.

DANGER
High Voltage
Trespassers may
be electrocuted

By Using Electrical Safety Devices

Damage to wires can cause a "short circuit," in which charges do not pass through all the loads. When this happens, current increases and wires can get hot enough to start a fire.

Fuses, circuit breakers, and ground fault circuit interrupters (GFCIs) are safety devices that act like switches. When the current is too high in a fuse, a metal strip that is part of the circuit heats up and melts. Circuit breakers are switches that open when the current reaches a certain level. A GFCI is a type of circuit breaker. GFCIs are often built into outlets that are used near water, such as in a kitchen or bathroom.

Fuses

When the current is too high in the fuse, the metal strip melts and opens the circuit.

Ground fault circuit interrupter (GFCI)

Active Reading **15 Identify** Name three safety devices that you might find in electric circuits at home.

_____

_____

The lightning rod attached to the top of this building helps to protect it from a lightning strike.

By Taking Precautions during a Lightning Storm

When lightning strikes, electric charges can travel between a cloud and the ground. Lightning often strikes objects that are taller than their surroundings, such as skyscrapers, trees, barns, or even a person in an open field. During a thunderstorm, be sure to stay away from trees and other tall objects. The best place to seek shelter during a thunderstorm is indoors.

Many buildings have lightning rods. These are metal rods at the highest part of the building. The rod is connected to the ground by a thick conducting wire. The rod and wire protect the building by *grounding* it, or providing a path that allows charges to flow into the ground.

16 Infer What would happen if there were no electrical path from the top of the building to the ground?

_____

_____

Visual Summary

To complete this summary, fill in the blanks with the correct word or phrase. Then, use the key below to check your answers. You can use this page to review the main concepts of the lesson.

Electric Circuits

An electric circuit has three basic parts: an energy source, an electric conductor, and a load.

17 Batteries are an example of an _____ in an electric circuit.

18 To open and close a circuit, a _____ can be used.

Circuits can be connected in series or in parallel.

19 When one of several bulbs in a series circuit burns out, the other bulbs _____

20 When one of several bulbs in a parallel circuit burns out, the other bulbs _____

Taking precautions when using electricity and during a lightning storm can keep you safe from electrical dangers.

21 This outlet contains a GFCI, which acts as a _____ to protect people from short circuits.

Answers: 17 energy source; 18 switch; 19 go out; 20 stay lit; 21 circuit breaker

22 Synthesize Compare the function of a switch in an electric circuit to the function of a water faucet. How are they alike and how are they different? Explain your reasoning.

Lesson Review

Vocabulary

Draw a line to connect the following terms to their definitions.

1 series circuit

2 parallel circuit

A a circuit with two or more paths for charges

B a circuit with a single path for charges

Key Concepts

3 Explain Why is an energy source needed in order to have a working electric circuit?

_____

_____

_____

_____

4 Compare Describe the difference between a closed circuit and an open circuit.

_____

_____

_____

_____

5 Apply Why does removing one bulb from a string of lights in a series circuit cause all the lights to go out?

_____

_____

_____

_____

6 Describe How does a lightning rod protect a building from lightning damage?

_____

_____

_____

_____

Critical Thinking

Use this drawing to answer the following questions.

Energy source

7 Identify Circuits can be either series or parallel. What type of circuit is shown above?

_____

_____

8 Infer Imagine that a circuit breaker opened the circuit every time that you operated the light, coffee maker, and microwave at the same time. What could be causing this?

_____

_____

_____

_____

9 Claims · Evidence · Reasoning What electrical safety device could be used in this kitchen to decreases risk of electric shock? Support your claim with evidence.

_____

_____

_____

_____

_____

_____

My Notes

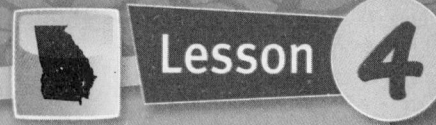
Magnets and Magnetism

ESSENTIAL QUESTION

What is magnetism?

By the end of this lesson, you should be able to describe magnets and magnetic fields and explain their properties.

 S8P5.a Fields and forces

S8P5.c Strength of electric and magnetic forces

When cows are grazing, they may eat pieces of metal, such as nails. Farmers can feed the cows a smooth magnet to attract such objects. This prevents the objects from moving farther through the cow's system and causing damage.

Engage Your Brain

1 Predict Check Yes or No to show whether you think the object would be attracted to a magnet.

Yes	No	
☐	☐	A paper clip
☐	☐	A plastic water bottle
☐	☐	A piece of notepaper
☐	☐	Another magnet
☐	☐	Aluminum foil
☐	☐	A penny

2 Describe Write your own caption for this photo of a cow magnet.

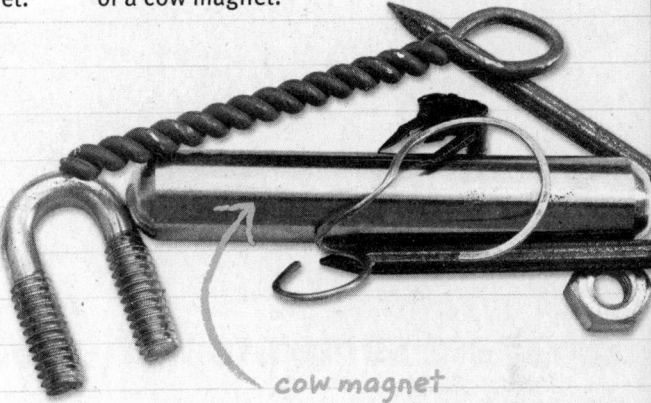

cow magnet

_____

_____

_____

 ## Active Reading

3 Apply Many scientific words, such as *field*, also have everyday meanings. Use context clues to write your own definition for each meaning of the word *field*.

Example sentence
The farm animals in the <u>field</u> are eating grass and clover.

field:

_____

_____

Example sentence
The magnet attracted all the pins that were within its magnetic <u>field</u>.

field:

_____

_____

Vocabulary Terms
- **magnet**
- **magnetic force**
- **magnetic pole**
- **magnetic field**

4 Identify As you read, place a question mark next to any words you don't understand. When you finish reading the lesson, go back and review the text that you marked. If the information is still confusing, consult a classmate or a teacher.

Stuck on You

What are some properties of magnets?

Have you wondered what a magnet is and why all materials are not magnets? The ancient Greeks discovered a mineral, called *magnetite* (MAG•nih•tyt), that would attract things made of iron. Today, we use the term **magnet** to describe any material that attracts iron or objects made of iron. Many magnets are made of iron, nickel, cobalt, or mixtures of these metals.

Magnetic Forces

When you bring two magnets together, they exert a push or pull called a **magnetic force** on each other. This force results from spinning electric charges in the magnets. The force can either push the magnets apart or pull them together. Magnetic force is one of only three forces in nature that can act at a distance—electrostatic force and gravity are the other two.

Magnetic force explains why, when you hold a magnet close enough to a paper clip, the paper clip will start to move toward the magnet. You have probably noticed that either end of a magnet can pull on a paper clip. So why is it that when you place two magnets near each other, sometimes they pull together and sometimes they push each other apart?

Active Reading **6 State** Name two things magnetic force can do.

_____

_____

Inquiry

5 Infer What might be an advantage to making a magnet horseshoe-shaped?

_____

_____

_____

_____

_____

_____

Magnetic Poles

Two magnets can push each other apart because of their ends, or **magnetic poles**. Every magnet has a north pole and a south pole. If you place the north poles of two magnets together, they will repel, or push away. If you place the north pole and the south pole of two magnets near each other, they will attract, or come together. The saying "opposites attract" applies well to magnets.

Magnetic Fields

The area surrounding a magnet where magnetic forces can be detected is called the **magnetic field**. A magnetic object placed anywhere in the magnetic field will be affected by the magnet.

As you can see in the illustration below, the magnetic field is arranged in lines. Notice that the magnetic field lines enter the magnet at the south pole and exit at the north pole. The magnetic field is strongest near the poles. The greater the distance from the poles, the weaker the magnetic field.

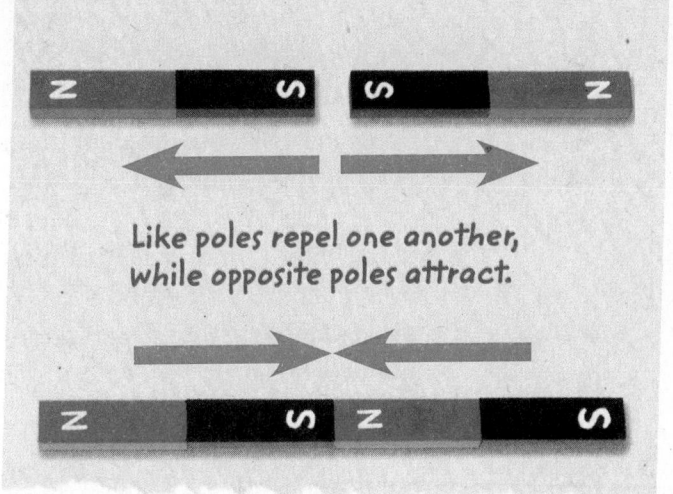

Like poles repel one another, while opposite poles attract.

Visualize It!

7 Diagram Draw an *X* on the illustration below to show one location in which a magnetic object would be attracted to the magnet. Draw an *O* to show one location in which a magnetic object would not be attracted to the magnet.

8 Relate Two magnets that are not in contact with each other can still exert a force on each other. How does the diagram below explain this ability?

_____

_____

_____

_____

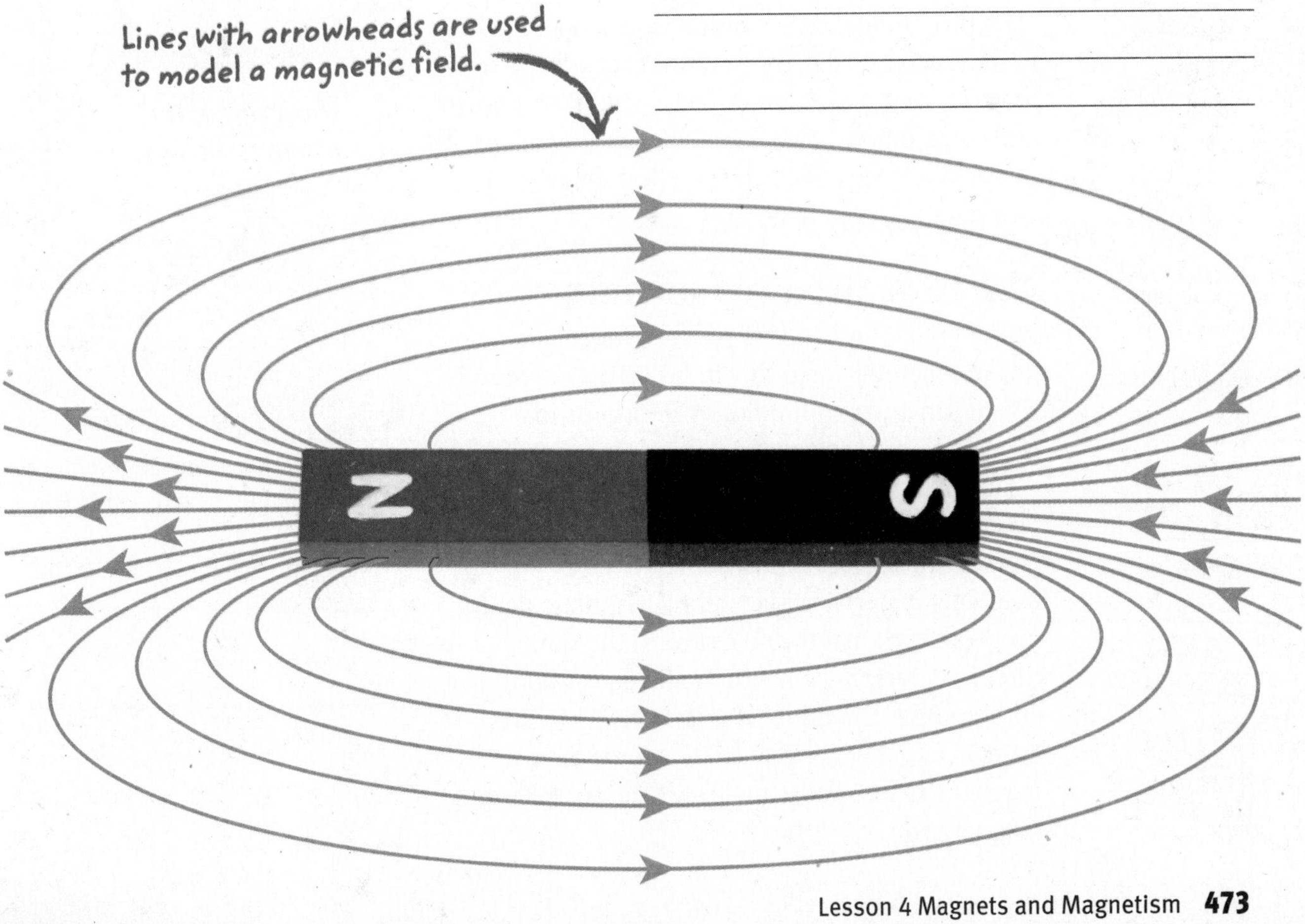

Lines with arrowheads are used to model a magnetic field.

When Everything Lines Up

What causes magnetism?

Some materials are magnetic. Some are not. For example, you know that a magnet can pick up some metal objects such as paper clips and iron nails. But it cannot pick up paper, plastic, or even pennies or aluminum foil. What causes the difference? Whether a material is magnetic or not depends on the material's atoms.

The Type of Atom

All matter is made of atoms. Electrons are negatively charged particles of atoms. As an electron moves in an atom, it makes, or induces, a magnetic field. The electron will then have a north and a south magnetic pole. In most atoms, such as copper and aluminum, the magnetic fields of the individual electrons cancel each other out. These materials are not magnetic.

But the magnetic fields of the electrons in iron, nickel, and cobalt atoms do not completely cancel each other out. As a result, atoms of these materials have small magnetic fields. These materials are magnetic.

If you were to cut a magnet into two pieces, each piece would be a magnet with a north and a south pole. And if you were to break those two magnets into pieces, each would still have a north and a south pole. It does not matter how many pieces you make. Even the smallest magnet has two poles.

The Formation of Domains

In materials such as iron, nickel, and cobalt, groups of atoms form tiny areas called *domains*. The north and south poles of the atoms in a domain line up and make a strong magnetic field.

Domains are like tiny magnets within an object. The domains in an object determine whether the object is magnetic. When a magnetic material is placed in a magnetic field, most of the domains point toward the same direction, forming a magnetic field around the entire object. In other materials, there are no domains to line up because the atoms have no magnetic fields. These materials cannot become magnetized.

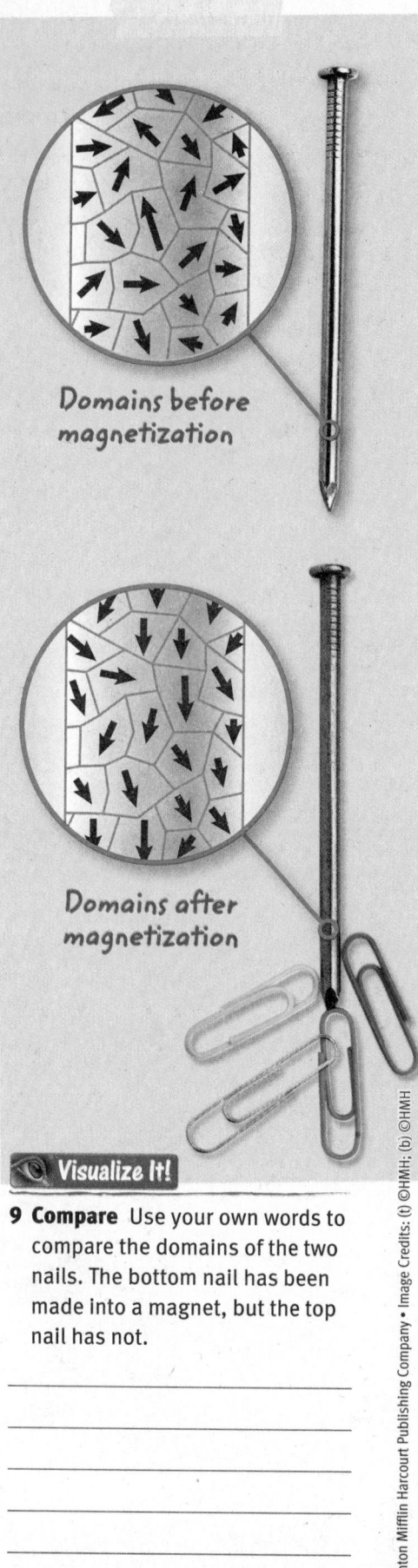

Domains before magnetization

Domains after magnetization

Visualize It!

9 Compare Use your own words to compare the domains of the two nails. The bottom nail has been made into a magnet, but the top nail has not.

_____

_____

_____

_____

_____

What are some types of magnets?

There are different types of magnets. Some materials are naturally magnetic, such as the mineral magnetite. Some materials can be turned into either permanent or temporary magnets.

Ferromagnets

A material that can be turned into a magnet is called *ferromagnetic* (fehr•oh•mag•NET•ik). Natural materials such as iron, nickel, cobalt, or mixtures of these materials have strong magnetic properties. They are considered ferromagnets.

A ferromagnetic material can be turned into a permanent magnet when placed in a strong magnetic field. Permanent magnets are difficult to make, but they keep their magnetic properties longer. Magnets can be made into various shapes such as bar magnets, disc magnets, and horseshoe magnets.

Electromagnets

Strong magnets are used to pick up metals in scrap yards, as shown in the photo below. To get a magnet powerful enough to do this, an *electromagnet* is used. An electromagnet is an iron core wrapped with electrical wire. When an electric current is in the wire, a magnetic field forms. When the current is turned off, the magnetic field stops. The strength of an electromagnet depends on the strength of the electric current.

Temporary Magnets

Some materials, such as soft iron, can be made into magnets temporarily when placed in a strong magnetic field. The material's domains line up, and the material is magnetized. You can make a temporary magnet by rubbing one pole of a strong magnet in one direction on a magnetic material, for example, a pair of scissors. The domains line up in the scissors, and it becomes a temporary magnet. Over time, the domains will lose their alignment. Banging or dropping a temporary magnet can also make it lose its magnetism.

This electromagnet uses electricity to produce a magnetic field.

© Houghton Mifflin Harcourt Publishing Company • Image Credits: (t) ©HMH; (c) ©HMH; (b) ©Photolibrary

Think Outside the Book Inquiry

10 Design Plan an investigation to find out how the strength of a temporary magnet is affected by the number of times you rub the object with a permanent magnet.

Polar Opposites

How is Earth like a giant magnet?

Earth acts like a giant magnet. Like a magnet, Earth has a magnetic field. Earth also has a north magnetic pole and a south magnetic pole. Earth's magnetic poles can attract another magnet, such as the needle of a compass.

It Has a Magnetic Field

Active Reading **11 Identify** As you read, underline the text that explains why Earth has a magnetic field.

As early as the 1600s, scientists hypothesized that Earth has a magnetic field. This was before the properties of magnets were understood. Scientists now think that Earth's inner structure produces its magnetic field. Earth has an inner core and an outer core. The inner core is made of solid metals. The outer core is made of liquid iron and nickel, which are ferromagnetic. As Earth rotates, the liquid outer core moves. Charged particles, including electrons, move in the liquid and form a magnetic field. The constant rotation keeps Earth magnetized. Earth's magnetic field is strongest near its poles.

Inquiry

12 Infer Earth's magnetic poles do not stay in the same place. After reading about what causes Earth's magnetic field, write a possible explanation for why Earth's magnetic poles move. Explain your reasoning.

_____

_____

_____

_____

_____

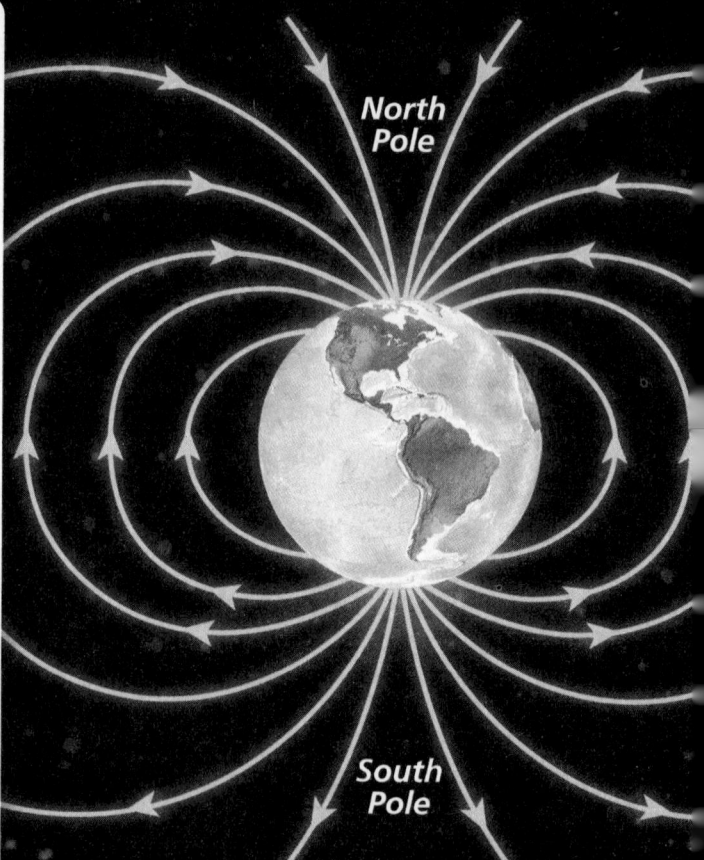

Like a magnet, Earth has magnetic poles and a magnetic field. Some animals may use Earth's magnetic field to navigate.

It Has Magnetic Poles

Earth's magnetic poles are not the same as Earth's geographic poles. The geographic poles mark the ends of Earth's axis. The geographic poles are near, but not exactly at, the magnetic poles. Navigators on airplanes and ships must take this small difference into account.

How can the north end of a compass point to the north magnetic pole? A compass needle is a magnet. If like poles repel, why do they not repel each other? The "north" pole of a magnet gets its name because it points toward Earth's geographic North Pole. A better term for the north pole of a magnet would be a "north-seeking" pole. Using these terms, the magnetic pole near Earth's North Pole is considered the south pole of a magnet. Likewise, the magnetic pole near Earth's South Pole is considered the north pole of a magnet.

13 Illustrate Draw a bar magnet on the image of Earth to show Earth's magnetic poles.

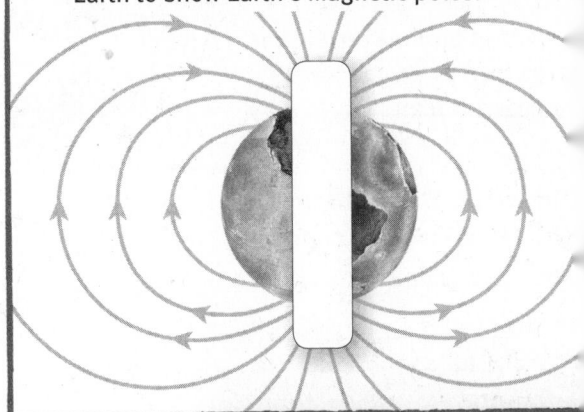

What is an aurora?

The beautiful displays of light that can be seen at northern or southern latitudes are related to Earth's magnetic field. The sun ejects charged particles. When they reach Earth, they are guided by its magnetic field. They enter Earth's upper atmosphere near the magnetic poles. There, the charged particles interact with atoms in the air, causing the atoms to emit visible light. This glow is called an *aurora*. In the Northern Hemisphere, an aurora is called an aurora borealis (bohr•ee•AL•is). In the Southern Hemisphere, it is called an aurora australis (aw•STRAY•lis).

This photo shows an aurora streaming across the night sky in Manitoba, Canada.

Visual Summary

To complete this summary, fill in each blank with the correct word or phrase. Then, use the key below to check your answers. You can use this page to review the main concepts of the lesson.

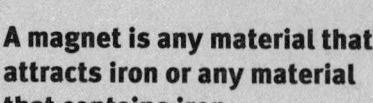

Magnets and Magnetism

A magnet is any material that attracts iron or any material that contains iron.

14 Magnetic materials exert _____ and have magnetic _____ and _____.

15 If the _____ of a material are lined up, the object will be magnetic.

There are different types of magnets.

16 A material such as iron is _____.

17 A(n) _____ is a magnet produced by electricity.

18 An object can become a(n) _____ magnet by rubbing the object with the end of a magnet.

Earth acts like a magnet because it has properties similar to those of magnets.

19 Earth has a _____ and north and south _____.

20 **Claims · Evidence · Reasoning** How can a compass be used to find north? Explain your reasoning.

Lesson Review

Vocabulary

Draw a line to connect the following terms to their definitions.

1 magnet

2 magnetic force

3 magnetic pole

4 magnetic field

A a magnet's push or pull

B the end of a magnet where the force is the strongest

C the lines of force surrounding a magnet

D a metal object that attracts iron or nickel

Key Concepts

5 List What are three properties of a magnet?

_____

_____

6 Explain How are magnetic objects able to be affected by each other even when not in contact with each other?

_____

_____

7 Identify List three types of magnets.

_____

_____

8 Describe How is Earth like a magnet?

_____

_____

9 Describe How do auroras form?

_____

_____

_____

Critical Thinking

Use this drawing to answer the following question.

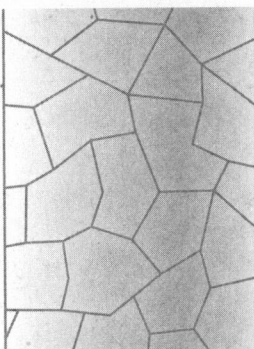 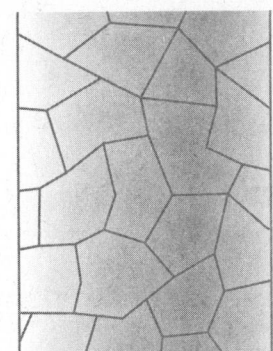

10 Illustrate The metal on the left has been magnetized, and the metal on the right has not. Draw the arrows in the domains of both.

11 Contrast What is the difference between the geographic North Pole and the magnetic north pole?

_____

_____

12 Explain If opposite poles repel each other, why does the north end of a compass point to the North Pole? Explain your reasoning.

_____

_____

_____

13 Apply Food manufacturers want to prevent small bits of metal from entering their product. How might magnets be used?

_____

_____

_____

My Notes

Engineering Design Process

Skills
Identify a need
Conduct research
✓ Brainstorm solutions
✓ Select a solution
✓ Design a prototype
✓ Build a prototype
✓ Test and evaluate
✓ Redesign to improve
✓ Communicate results

Objectives

• Design an electric circuit to provide an answer to a problem.

• Test and modify a prototype circuit to achieve the desired result.

Building an Electric Circuit

Electric circuits are an essential part of many devices and technologies. Automobiles, televisions, digital watches, music players, cell phones, computers, and sports scoreboards all function, in part, because of carefully designed circuits.

An electric circuit is simply a path for electric charges to follow. A *series circuit* has only a single path for the charges to follow. A *parallel circuit* has two or more paths for electric charges to follow. A parallel circuit has the advantage that if one device is disconnected from the circuit, charges can still flow to the other devices in the circuit. For example, if a parallel circuit contains several light bulb lamps and one bulb burns out, the light bulbs on the other paths remain lit.

In this activity, you will make an electric circuit of conducting wires, batteries, lamps, and switches. A switch can form a break in the circuit to stop the flow of electric charges and turn a device, such as a lamp, on and off.

This robotic device contains a number of electric circuits.

1 Infer Do you think the lights in your home are wired in series circuits or parallel circuits? Explain.

_____

_____

_____

_____

_____

Modeling an Electric Circuit

Sketching a complex circuit could take a lot of time and expertise. Circuits are often drawn using simple symbols so that models or plans are easier to create and easier to read. You can use symbols like the ones shown below to show parts of a circuit such as wire, lamps, and switches.

2 Apply Compare the series circuit diagram shown on the left to the art of a series circuit on the right. Then, label the symbols in the circuit diagram with *wire*, *lamp*, or *energy source*.

closed switch

3 Apply Complete this parallel circuit diagram by drawing in the symbols for the missing switch and energy source.

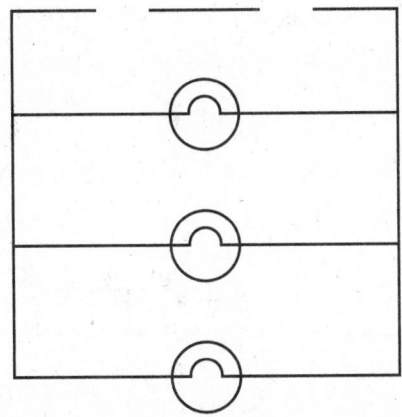

4 Explain What will happen if a light bulb is unscrewed from a lamp in the series circuit? What will happen if a light bulb is unscrewed from a lamp in the parallel circuit?

_____

_____

_____

 You Try It!  ⟶

Now it's your turn to model and build a simple electric circuit.

 You Try It!

Now it's your turn to model and build a simple electric circuit with three light bulb lamps and three switches.

(1) Brainstorm Solutions

Brainstorm ideas for a simple circuit that lights up three light bulbs. The setup must include three switches so that one switch controls only one lamp, one switch controls two lamps, and one switch controls all three lamps.

You Will Need

✔ batteries

✔ battery holders

✔ masking tape or duct tape

✔ small lamp bulbs, 1.5 V (3)

✔ small lamp bulb holders (3)

✔ switches (3)

✔ wires

A How will you decide whether to build a series circuit or a parallel circuit?

_____

_____

_____

B How can a switch turn on or off only one or two lamps in a three-lamp circuit?

_____

_____

_____

(2) Select a Solution

Which of your ideas seems to offer the best promise for success?

_____

_____

(3) Design a Prototype

In the space below, draw a circuit diagram for your three-lamp prototype. Be sure to include all the parts you will need, and show how they will be connected.

(4) Build a Prototype

Now assemble your three-lamp circuit with the switches in place. Are there some parts of your design that cannot be assembled as you had predicted? What parts did you have to revise?

_____

_____

_____

(5) Test and Evaluate

Open and close the switches and see what happens. Did one switch turn all the lamps on and off? Did the other two switches control only one or two lamps as predicted? If not, what parts of your setup could you revise?

_____

_____

(6) Redesign to Improve

Keep making revisions until your switches control only the specified number of lamps. What kinds of revisions did you have to make?

_____

_____

(7) Communicate Results

In the space below, sketch a diagram of the successful circuit.

Electromagnetism

ESSENTIAL QUESTION

What is electromagnetism?

By the end of this lesson, you should be able to describe the relationship between electricity and magnetism and how this relationship affects our world.

When the strings on this guitar vibrate, small magnets in the pickups convert the vibrations into electrical signals.

pickups

S8P5.a Fields and forces

S8P5.c Strength of electric and magnetic forces

Engage Your Brain

1 Predict Check T or F to show whether you think each statement is true or false.

T   F

☐   ☐   A moving magnetic field can produce electricity.

☐   ☐   Electricity can produce a magnetic field.

☐   ☐   Electricity and magnetism are the same thing.

2 Describe An electromagnet is a magnet produced from electric current. Describe what is happening in the photo.

_____

_____

Active Reading

3 Apply Many scientific words, such as *induction*, also have everyday meanings. Use context clues to write your own definition for each meaning of *induction*.

Example sentence
There was a party after the baseball star's <u>induction</u> into the Hall of Fame.

induction:

_____

_____

Example sentence
<u>Induction</u> occurs when a wire moving near a magnet gains an electric current.

induction:

_____

_____

Vocabulary Terms

- electromagnetism
- solenoid
- electromagnet
- electric motor
- electromagnetic induction
- transformer
- electric generator

4 Apply As you learn the definition of each vocabulary term in this lesson, create your own definition or sketch to help you remember the meaning of the term.

MAGNETIC ATTRACTION

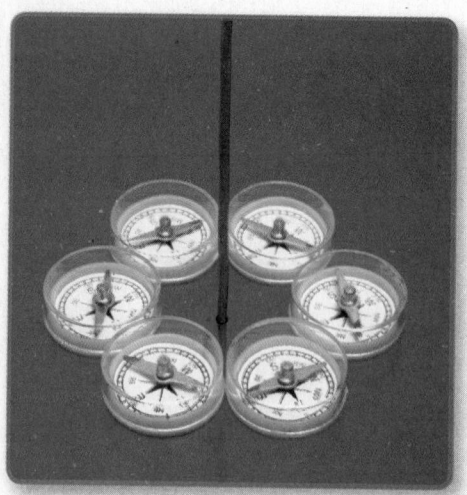

The compasses show that an electric current produces a circular magnetic field around the wire.

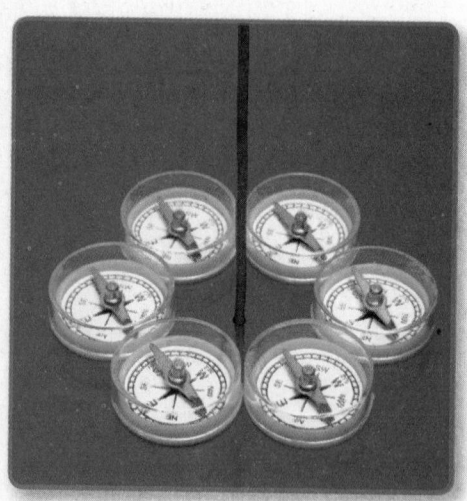

When the current is turned off, the needles align with Earth's magnetic field.

What is electromagnetism?

Electromagnetism is a relationship between electricity and magnetism. **Electromagnetism** results when electric currents and magnetic fields interact with each other.

The Interaction Between Magnets and Electricity

In 1820, physicist Hans Christian Oersted of Denmark made an interesting discovery by accident. He discovered that there is a connection between electricity and magnetism. No one at the time knew that electricity and magnetism were related. One day while preparing for a lecture, he brought a compass close to a wire carrying an electric current. Oersted was surprised to see the compass needle move. A compass needle is a magnet. It usually points north because of Earth's magnetic field. However, the compass moved because it was affected by a magnetic field other than Earth's.

Magnetism Produced by Electricity

Active Reading 5 **Identify** As you read, underline what caused Oersted's compass needle to move.

Oersted hypothesized that it was the electric current in the wire that had produced the magnetic field. He then did more experiments with electricity and magnetism. He found that when the wire is carrying a current, a magnetic field is produced around the wire. You can see this in the photograph on the top left. When the current is turned off, as shown in the bottom photograph, the magnetic field disappears. The compasses again point north.

Oersted found that the direction of the electric current also affects the magnetic field. Current in one direction caused a compass needle to move clockwise. Current in the other direction caused the compass needle to move counterclockwise. Oersted's hypothesis was confirmed.

How can you make a magnet using current?

An electric current in a single loop of wire produces a weak magnetic field. You can make a more powerful magnet by making a solenoid or an electromagnet.

With a Solenoid

A coil of wire that carries an electric current, and therefore produces a magnetic field, is called a **solenoid** (SOH•luh•noyd). The more loops, the stronger the magnetic field. A solenoid's magnetic field acts like a bar magnet. Increasing the number of loops or the current increases the strength of the magnetic field.

With an Electromagnet

Wrapping a solenoid around an iron core makes an **electromagnet**. An electromagnet combines the magnetic field of the solenoid with the magnetic field of the magnetized iron core. This combination creates a more powerful magnetic field than the solenoid alone. You can make it stronger by adding loops to the solenoid or increasing the current.

Active Reading **6 Solve** What benefit is gained by the addition of the iron core in an electromagnet?

_____

_____

_____

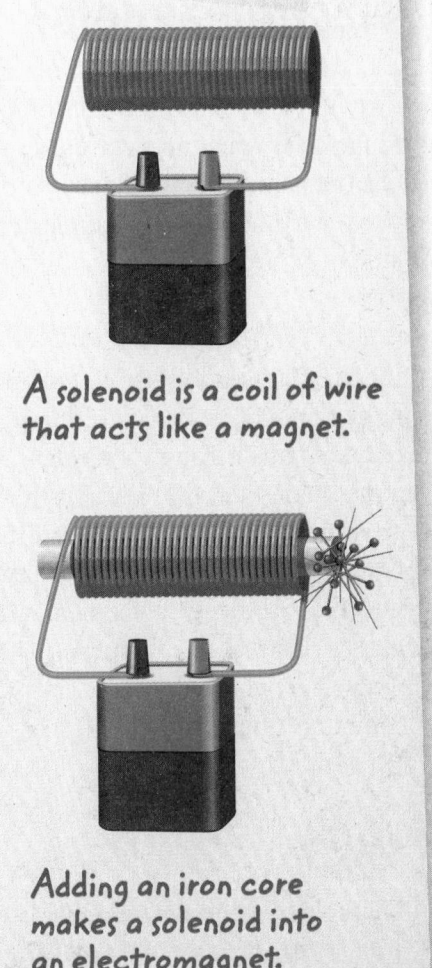

A solenoid is a coil of wire that acts like a magnet.

Adding an iron core makes a solenoid into an electromagnet.

Electromagnets lift this maglev train off the tracks and move it forward.

What are some uses for electromagnets?

Electromagnets are used in many devices that you may use every day. A solenoid around an iron piston makes a doorbell ring. Huge electromagnets are used in industry to move metal. Small electromagnets drive electric motors in objects from hair dryers to speakers. Physicists use electromagnets in "atom smashers" to study the tiny particles and high energies that make up an atom.

To Lift Metal Objects

Electromagnets are useful for lifting and moving large metal objects containing iron. When current runs through the solenoid coils, it creates a magnetic field that attracts the metal objects. Turning off the current turns off the magnetic field so that the metal can be easily dropped in a new place. Powerful electromagnets can raise a maglev train above its track. Just as poles of a bar magnet repel each other, electromagnets in the train and track repel each other when the electric current is turned on.

To Measure Current

A *galvanometer* (gal•vuh•NAHM•ih•ter) is a device that measures the strength and direction of an electric current in a wire. A galvanometer contains an electromagnet between the poles of a permanent magnet, such as a horseshoe magnet. When current is applied to the electromagnet, the two magnetic fields interact and cause the electromagnet to turn. The indicator, attached to the electromagnet, moves to one side of the zero on the scale, indicating the strength and direction of the current. The parts of a simple galvanometer are shown below.

7 Infer What is one advantage of using an electromagnet to move loads of metal?

_____

_____

Industrial electromagnets can lift tons of metal.

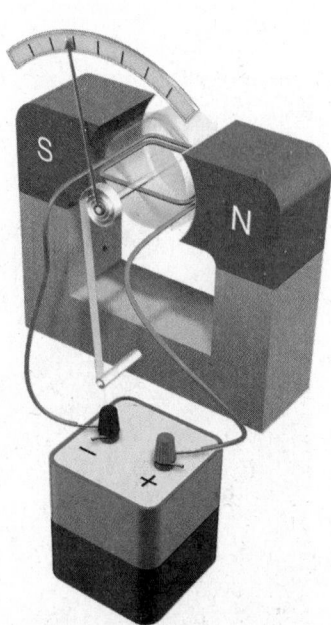

The indicator on a galvanometer shows current direction and strength.

Why It Matters

HEALTH WATCH

A Look Inside

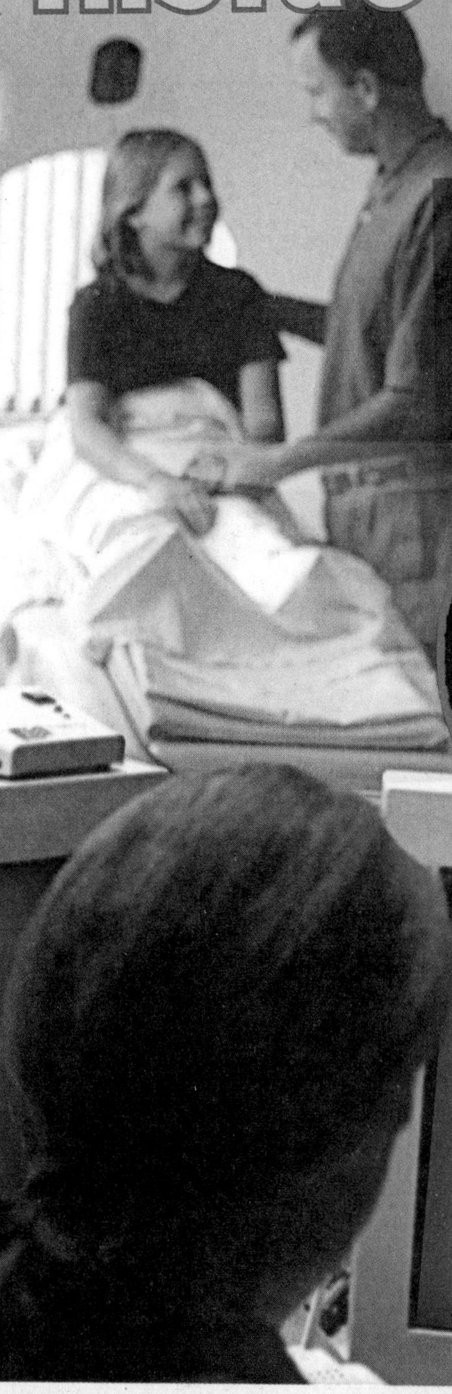

Magnetic resonance imaging (MRI) machines use powerful electromagnets and radio waves to "see" inside the body. The MRI scans they produce contain much more detail than x-ray images, and they can be used to diagnose a wide variety of conditions.

Some MRI scans can help scientists understand how the brain works. The brain scan pictured here shows the eyes and the folds of the brain as seen from above.

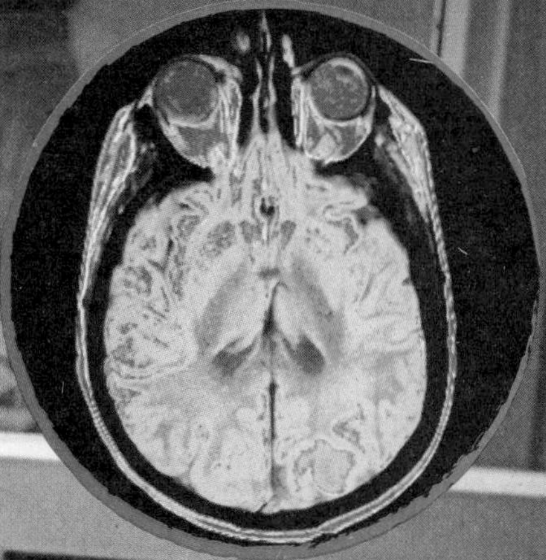

Super Cool

In most MRI machines, the solenoid coils of an electromagnet are kept at temperatures around −452 °F (−269 °C). It takes little energy for current to flow at that temperature, so the machines can produce a strong magnetic field.

Getting a Scan

Doctors use MRI scans to diagnose many conditions, including broken bones and strained tendons. Because MRI machines use powerful electromagnets, no metal objects or magnetic credit cards are allowed in the MRI room.

Extend

Inquiry

8 Explain Why are the electromagnets in MRIs kept at very low temperatures?

9 Infer Why are electromagnets, rather than permanent magnets, used in MRIs?

10 Research Investigate *magnetoencephalography* (mag•nee•toh•en•sef•uh•LAHG•ruh•fee), or MEG. Write about one way in which it is being used.

LET'S MOTOR!

How do motors work?

One of the most common places to find an electromagnet is in a motor. An **electric motor** changes electrical energy into mechanical energy. Some electric motors run on direct current (DC), while others are designed to use alternating current (AC). Electric motors range in size from large motors, used to power a Ferris wheel, to small motors used in computer cooling fans. Almost every time a device uses electricity to make something move, there is a motor involved.

👁 **Visualize It!**

11 List Make a list of all the items in this photo that you think might use motors.

_____

_____

_____

_____

Motors Use Electromagnets

Electric motors are very similar to galvanometers. The main difference is that, in a motor, the electromagnet is made to rotate all the way around instead of back and forth in the magnetic field.

A simple motor has a coil or loop of wire called an armature (AR•muh•chur) mounted between the poles of a magnet. The armature becomes an electromagnet when current passes through it. The armature rotates because its poles are pushed and pulled by the opposite poles of the magnet. The armature turns until its north pole is opposite the magnet's south pole. Then, a device called a commutator reverses the direction of the current in the wire, causing the armature to complete its turn.

Visualize It!

Current in the armature causes the magnet to exert force on the armature, making it rotate.

Permanent magnet

Battery

Brush

N

Armature

Commutator

Brush

S

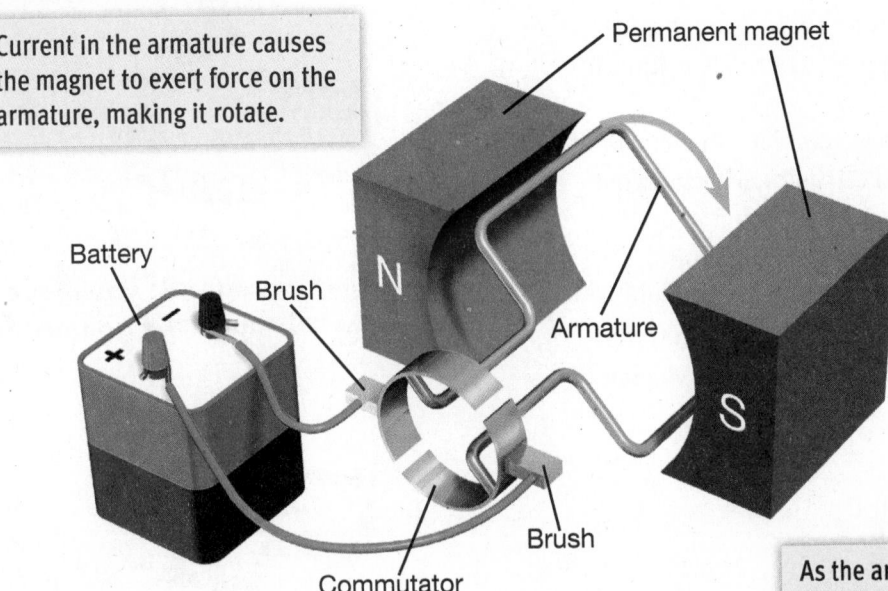

As the armature rotates, the commutator causes the current to change direction. This reverses the direction of force and keeps the armature rotating.

12 Compare Analyze the illustration of the motor, and compare it to the galvanometer on the previous spread. Explain how they are alike.

_____

_____

_____

_____

_____

_____

A NEW GENERATION

What are some uses for induction?

Electric current can produce a magnetic field. In the early 1830s, scientists wondered if the opposite is true. Can a magnetic field create an electric current? English scientist Michael Faraday showed that it could. He connected a galvanometer to a wire coil. When he moved a magnet back and forth inside the coil, the galvanometer needle moved, indicating current. American physicist Joseph Henry made a similar discovery.

Using a magnetic field to create an electric current in a wire is called **electromagnetic induction**. When electric charges move through a wire, the wire carries a current. Magnetic force from a magnet moving inside a coil of wire can make the electric charges in the wire move. When the magnet stops moving inside the coil, the electric current stops.

 **Visualize It!**

13 State What are two ways to increase the current in the wire?

_____

_____

_____

_____

14 Claims • Evidence • Reasoning What would happen to the current if the magnet and coil were not moving? Explain your reasoning.

_____

_____

_____

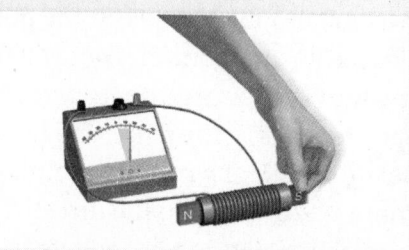

An electric current is induced when you move a magnet through a coil of wire.

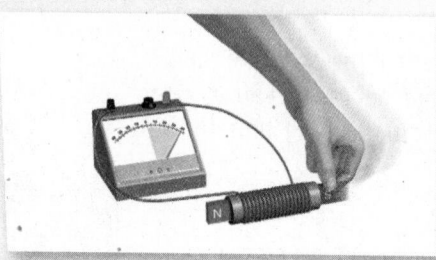

The current increases if you move the magnet through the coil faster.

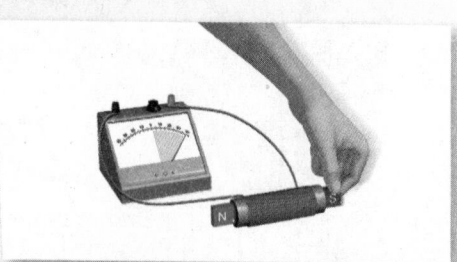

The current also increases if you add more loops of wire.

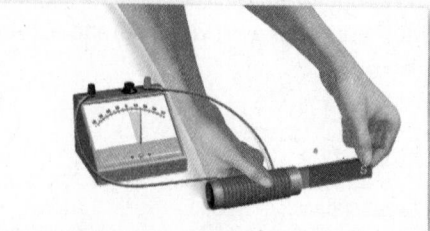

The current can also be induced by reversing the motion—moving the coil over the magnet.

To Change Voltage

An important device that relies on electromagnetic induction is a transformer. **Transformers** use induction to increase or decrease the voltage of alternating current. For example, transformers on power lines increase voltage to send it miles away and then decrease it for a single home. Most transformers are iron "rings" with two coils of wire. The current in the wire on the primary side makes an electromagnet. Because the current alternates, the magnetic field changes. This induces a current in the wire on the secondary side.

Active Reading

15 Identify As you read, underline the sentence that explains the purpose of transformers.

Step-Up Transformer

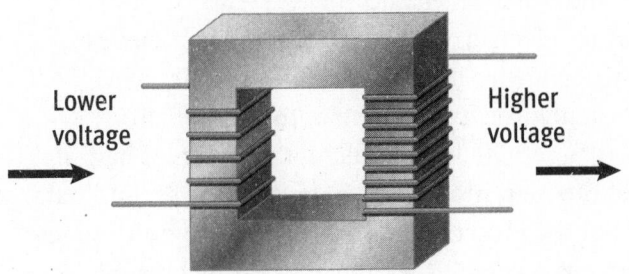

Lower voltage

Higher voltage

In a step-up transformer, there are more turns of wire on the secondary side.

Step-Down Transformer

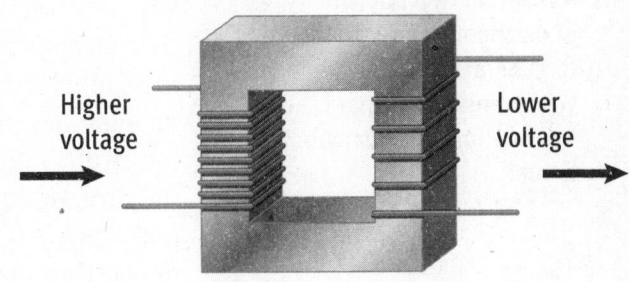

Higher voltage

Lower voltage

In a step-down transformer, there are more turns of wire on the primary side.

Do the Math

Sample Problem

Imagine the voltage on the primary side of a step-down transformer is 300 volts and the wire has 1,200 turns. The wire on the secondary side has 720 turns. What is the voltage on the secondary side?

The number of volts to wire turns on a transformer coil can be expressed as a ratio. This ratio is equal for both sides of the transformer. Cross-multiply to find the answer to the problem.

$$\frac{300 \text{ volts}}{1{,}200 \text{ turns}} = \frac{X \text{ volts}}{720 \text{ turns}}$$

$$300 \times 720 = 216{,}000$$

$$216{,}000 \,/\, 1{,}200 = 180$$

$$X = 180$$

Answer: 180 volts

You Try It

16 Calculate The voltage on the primary side of a step-down transformer is 500 volts, and the wire has 1,500 turns. The wire on the secondary side has 600 turns. What is the voltage on the secondary side?

To Generate Electricity

Did you know that most of the electricity you use every day comes from electromagnetic induction? **Electric generators** use induction to change mechanical energy into electrical energy. You can think of electric generators as being the "opposite" of electric motors.

In all different types of power plants, mechanical energy is used to rotate turbines. In some power plants turbines turn magnets inside coils of wire, generating electricity. Many power plants use rising steam to turn the turbines. The steam is produced from burning fossil fuels or using nuclear reactions to heat water. Other sources of mechanical energy to turn turbines are blowing wind, falling water, and ocean tides and waves.

Generators induce electric current when a magnet moves in a coil of wire or when a wire moves between the poles of a magnet. In a simple generator, a wire loop at the end of a rod moves through the magnetic field of a magnet. In the first half of the turn, one side of the loop moves downward. In the second half of the turn, the part of the loop that was moving down now moves upward, and the current reverses, creating alternating current.

Active Reading **18 Summarize** How does the function of a generator relate to the function of a motor?

_____

_____

Generating Electricity

A generator induces electric current in wire that is moving in a magnetic field. A crank would be used to turn the wire in this generator.

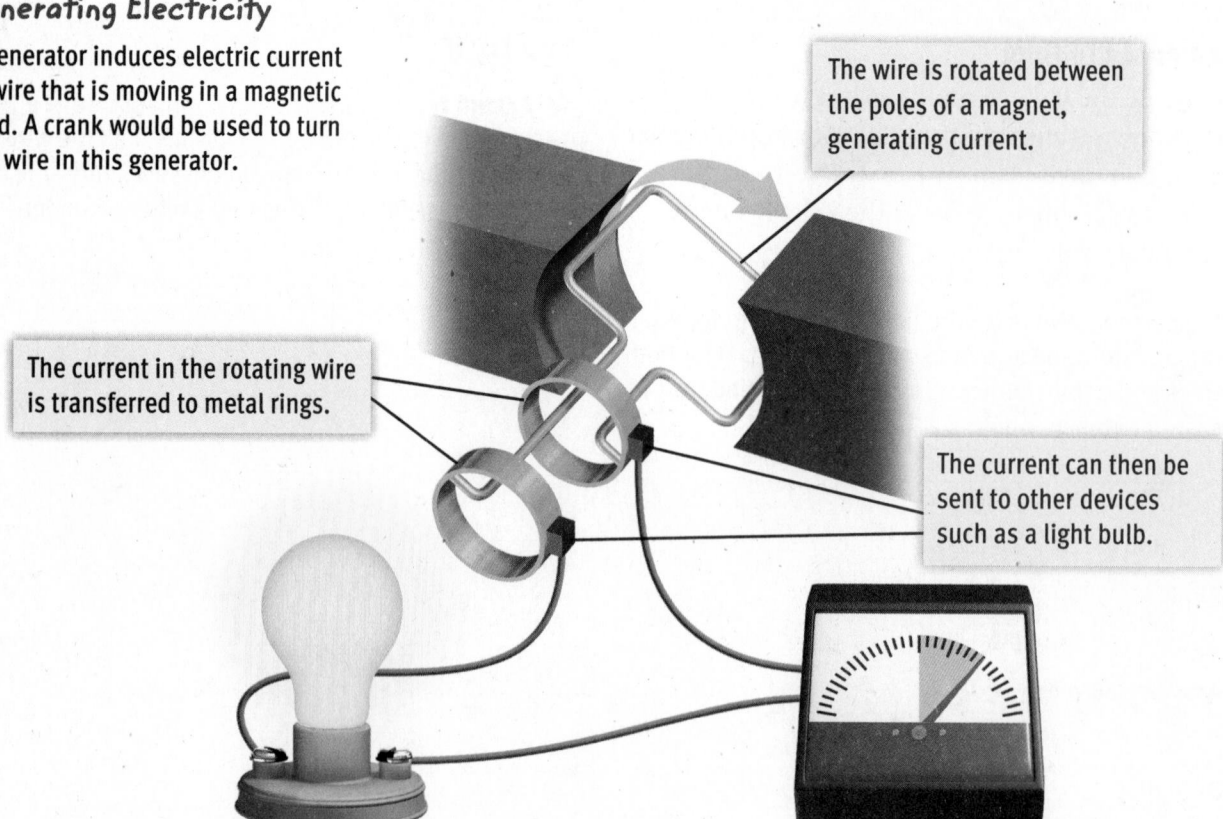

The wire is rotated between the poles of a magnet, generating current.

The current in the rotating wire is transferred to metal rings.

The current can then be sent to other devices such as a light bulb.

19 Diagram Fill in the chart below to help you organize the key concepts from this lesson.

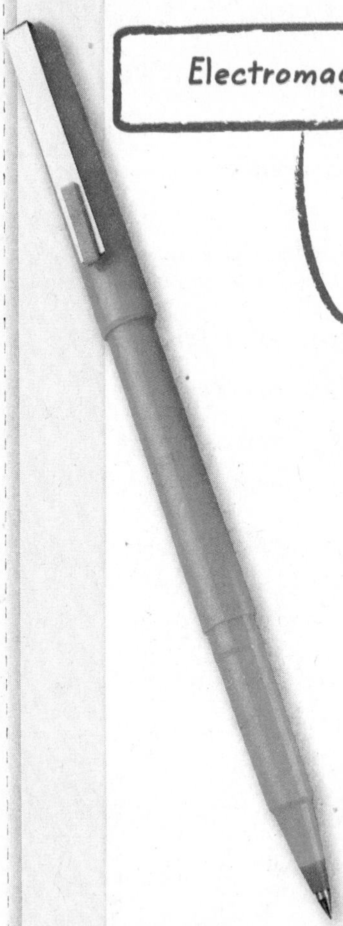

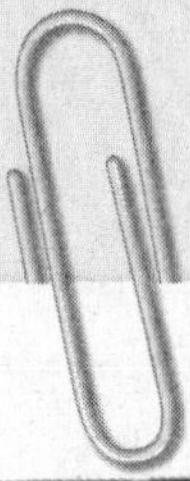

Electromagnetism → Definition:
_____
_____

Uses:
    maglev train
    motor
_____
_____
_____
_____
_____
_____
_____

Electromagnetic induction → Definition:
_____
_____

Uses:
_____
_____
_____
_____
_____
_____

Visual Summary

To complete this summary, check the box that indicates true or false. Then, use the key below to check your answers. You can use this page to review the main concepts of the lesson.

Electromagnetism results from the interaction of electric currents and magnetic fields.

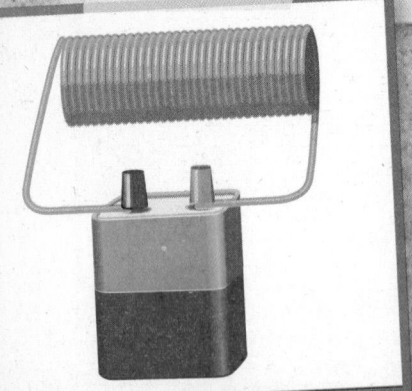

	T	F	
20	☐	☐	Solenoids are magnetic.
21	☐	☐	The strength of an electromagnet decreases when you increase the current.
22	☐	☐	You can increase the number of coils to make an electromagnet stronger.
23	☐	☐	Electromagnets are used to lift heavy metal items.
24	☐	☐	Motors use electromagnets to produce movement.

Electromagnetism

Electromagnetic induction is electric current that results from magnetism.

	T	F	
25	☐	☐	Generators use induction to produce electricity.
26	☐	☐	Transformers detect electric current.

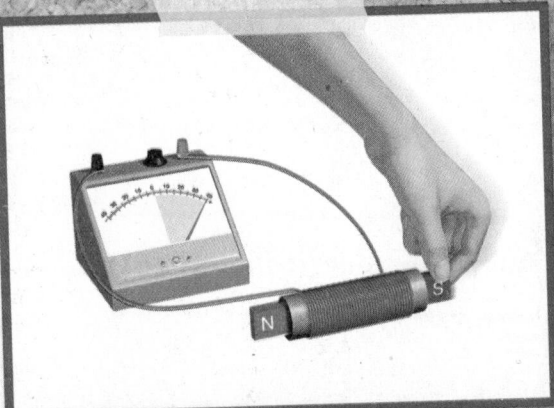

Answers: 20 True; 21 False; 22 True; 23 True; 24 True; 25 True; 26 False

27 **Synthesize** Describe how you could use a motor in reverse to generate electricity. Use evidence to support your claim.

Lesson Review

Vocabulary

Fill in the blank with the term that best completes the following sentences.

1 A(n) _____ is a coil of wire that produces a magnetic field when it carries an electric current.

2 A(n) _____ changes mechanical energy into electrical energy by means of electromagnetic induction.

3 A(n) _____ changes electrical energy into mechanical energy.

Key Concepts

4 Relate How do electricity and magnetism interact?

_____

_____

_____

5 Describe Describe how turning off the electric current in an industrial electromagnet affects its magnetic field.

_____

_____

6 Predict What effect would increasing the number of loops in a coil of wire have on an electromagnet?

_____

_____

_____

7 Summarize How can a magnetic field be used to create an electric current?

_____

_____

_____

8 Identify List three everyday devices that could not have been developed without the discovery of electromagnetism.

_____

Critical Thinking

9 Predict If Faraday had used a more powerful battery in his experiments with electromagnetic induction, what effect would this have had on his galvanometer's measurements of current when the battery was fully connected? Explain your reasoning.

_____

_____

_____

_____

Use the diagram to answer the following questions.

10 Illustrate Draw how the coils would look on a step-up transformer.

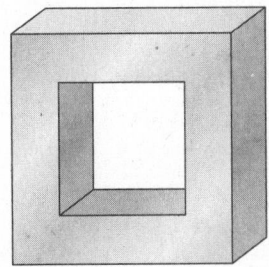

11 Identify On which side would the voltage be higher?

_____

_____

_____

12 Describe How would the illustration look if it were showing a step-down transformer?

_____

_____

_____

_____

My Notes

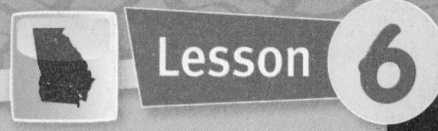

Electronic Technology

ESSENTIAL QUESTION

What are electronics, and how have they changed?

By the end of this lesson, you should be able to describe what electronic devices do and how they change as technology changes.

This microchip is small enough to fit inside the mandibles of an ant!

Lesson Labs

Quick Labs
- The Speed of a Simple Computer
- Investigate Satellite Imaging

Engage Your Brain

1 Predict Check T or F to show whether you think each statement is true or false.

T	F	
☐	☐	Electrical devices and electronic devices are the same.
☐	☐	Electronic technology affects the way people work, play, and communicate.
☐	☐	Codes, which used to be an important part of communication between humans, are no longer used.

2 List Make a list of as many electronic devices as you can think of.

____

____

____

____

____

____

____

____

Active Reading

3 Apply Many scientific words, such as *digit*, also have everyday meanings. Use context clues to write your own definition for each meaning of *digit*.

Example sentence
She wore a ring on the fourth digit of her left hand.

digit:

____

____

____

Example sentence
I made a mistake when I wrote the last digit of the phone number.

digit:

____

____

____

Vocabulary Terms

- **electronic device**
- **digital signal**
- **integrated circuit**
- **computer**
- **analog signal**

4 Apply As you learn the definition of each vocabulary term in this lesson, write down your own definition or make a sketch to help you remember the meaning of the term.

Speaking in Code

What are electronics?

Electronic devices like computers are not the same as electrical devices like toasters. Both use electrical energy. But electronic devices can perform more sophisticated tasks than electrical devices can. **Electronic devices** are able to control the flow of electrons using *integrated circuits*. An **integrated circuit** is a single, tiny chip of specially treated silicon containing many circuit parts. Integrated circuits carry out instructions, or programs, by controlling current.

A TV remote control is an example of an electronic device. Imagine that you push a button on the remote control to change the channel. A signal goes to integrated circuits inside the remote control. The circuits process the information and send an infrared signal to the TV. The signal tells the TV to change channels.

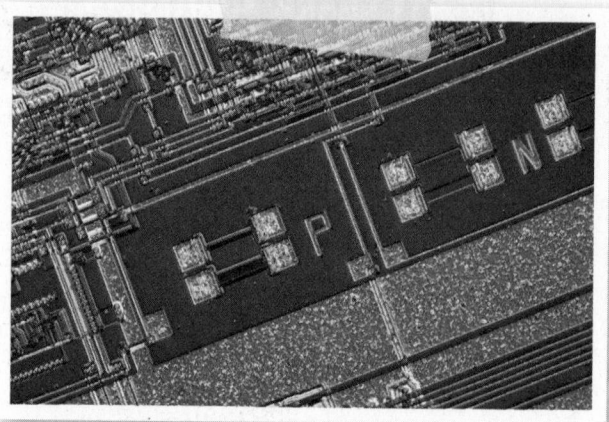

Integrated circuits, or microchips, are tiny silicon-based chips that can process information.

Visualize It!

5. Distinguish Pick one electronic device and one electrical device from the photo and explain how they are different.

_____

_____

_____

_____

_____

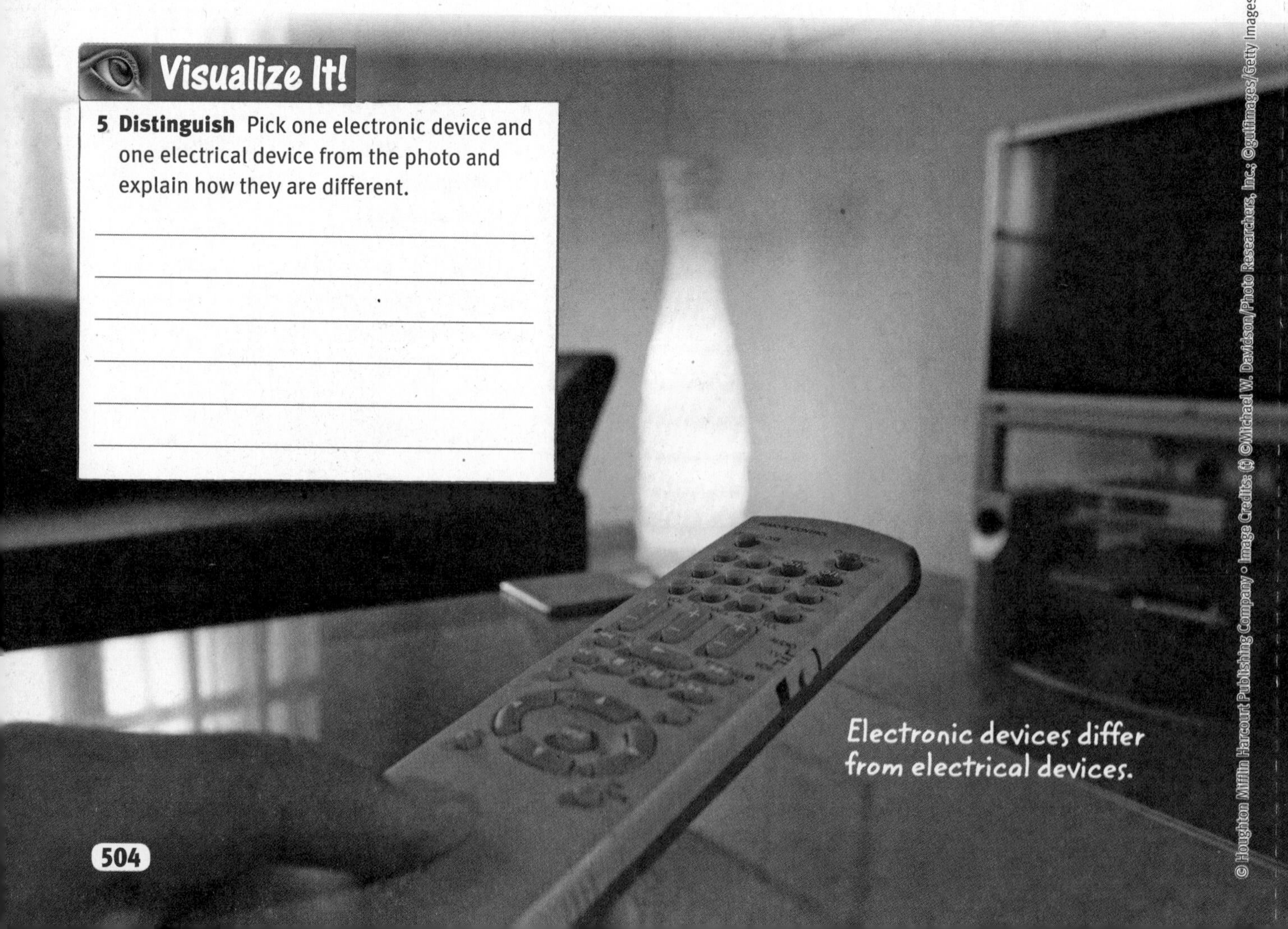

Electronic devices differ from electrical devices.

How can information be coded?

A signal is a pattern that contains coded information. For example, when you speak, information is coded in the pattern of sounds you make. Your voice is the carrier of the signal, and a listener interprets it. Morse code is a signal that uses dashes and dots to represent letters of the alphabet. People used to send telegraph messages in Morse code using wires as the carrier. Electronics also use coded signals. The two kinds of signals they use are *analog signals* and *digital signals*.

As an Analog Signal

Signals that change continuously in a given range are called **analog signals**. For example, a dimmer switch sends an analog electrical signal to a light fixture. You slide a dimmer switch up or down in one continuous motion. As you move the switch up or down, the amount of electric current supplied to the lighting goes up or down. If you move the switch just a little bit, the lighting changes just a little bit. A record also produces an analog signal. A record needle moves up and down continuously as it moves over a record's grooves. The up-and-down movements are turned into sound waves by the record player. As the record groove changes, the sound changes.

Visualize It!

6 Identify What are the carriers of the analog signals in the examples shown below?

_____

_____

Morse Code

A	B	C	D
•—	—•••	—•—•	—••
E	F	G	H
•	••—•	——•	••••
I	J	K	L
••	•———	—•—	•—••
M	N	O	P
——	—•	———	•——•
Q	R	S	T
——•—	•—•	•••	—
U	V	W	X
••—	•••—	•——	—••—
	Y	Z	
	—•——	——••	

Think Outside the Book Inquiry

7 Apply With a classmate, come up with a carrier that you can use to send Morse code. Then use the Morse code chart to send each other a short message.

A dimmer switch is an example of a device that sends an analog signal.

Records are used to store analog signals, which can be accessed using a record player.

© Houghton Mifflin Harcourt Publishing Company • Image Credits: (l) ©Tetra Images/Alamy Images; (r) ©HMH

Lesson 6 Electronic Technology **505**

CDs and DVDs use digital signals.

As a Digital Signal

Unlike an analog signal, such as the one used by the dimmer switch, a digital signal does not change continuously. A **digital signal** is a sequence of separate values. Like a regular light switch, it goes back and forth between on or off. Information in a digital signal is represented using a pattern called the *binary code* (BY•nuh•ree KOHD). Binary means "two." The digital binary code is made up of the two digits 1 and 0. In computers and other digital electronics, digital signals are carried by a series of on-off electric pulses. A 1 is encoded as a pulse. A 0 is encoded as no pulse.

An analog signal, like music, can be converted to a digital signal and stored on a compact disc (CD). The flat, reflecting layer of a CD is called the *land*. Data is recorded on the land in a spiral-shaped series of bumps called *pits*. Inside a computer or CD player, a laser shines light on a spinning CD. Pits are read as dark areas because they reflect light differently than the land does. The patterns of light and dark are interpreted as a digital signal that can be converted into your favorite song.

Active Reading **8 Compare** How do digital signals differ from analog signals? Support your claim with evidence.

_____

_____

Binary Code

The binary code for the numbers 1 through 16 is shown below.

9. Predict What is the binary code for 17?

Number		Binary Code
0	=	0
1	=	1
2	=	10
3	=	11
4	=	100
5	=	101
6	=	110
7	=	111
8	=	1000
9	=	1001
10	=	1010
11	=	1011
12	=	1100
13	=	1101
14	=	1110
15	=	1111
16	=	10000
17	=	

Think of how much information a computer can process. And it's all processed using only two digits!

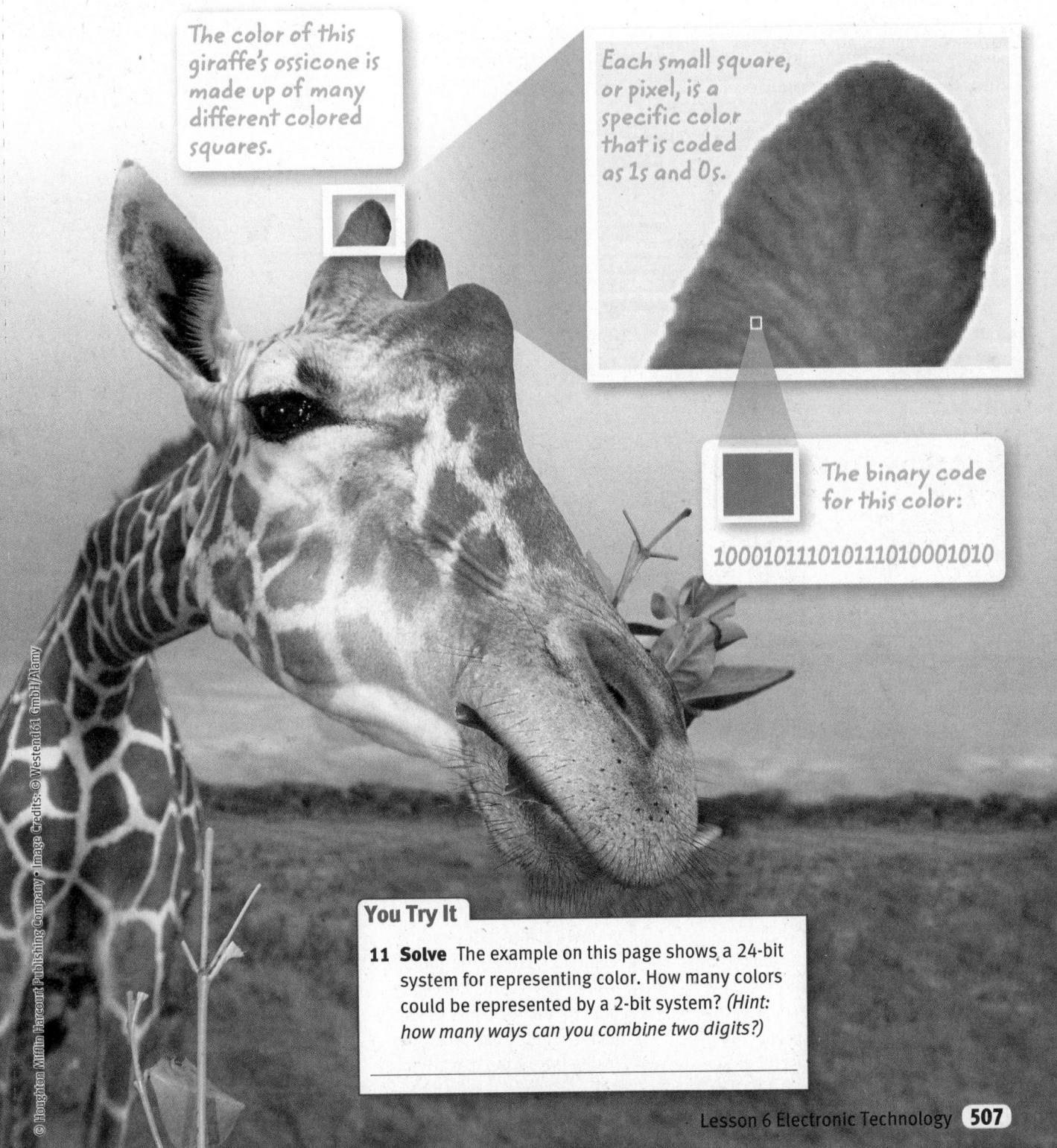

Do the Math

Digital images, like this picture of a giraffe, are created using digital signals. The lens of a digital camera focuses light onto a computer chip inside the camera. The chip stores digital data about the light in binary code.

You Try It

10 Calculate In computer terms, a *bit* is a binary digit, either a one or a zero. A *byte* is a string of 8 bits, and there are 1,000,000 bytes in a megabyte (MB). Suppose you are sending a picture that is 2.6 MB. How many 1s and 0s (bits) is that? *(Hint: Use multiplication.)*

The color of this giraffe's ossicone is made up of many different colored squares.

Each small square, or pixel, is a specific color that is coded as 1s and 0s.

The binary code for this color:

100010111010111010001010

You Try It

11 Solve The example on this page shows a 24-bit system for representing color. How many colors could be represented by a 2-bit system? *(Hint: how many ways can you combine two digits?)*

The Incredible

How have computers changed?

A **computer** is any electronic device that performs tasks by following instructions given to it. Computers receive information, called *input*, through keyboards, touchscreens, or other devices. The input can be processed through a central processor or stored in memory. Computers output information through monitors, printers, or other devices.

Computers have changed greatly over time, as shown below. Today's computers include *smartphones*, cell phones that have functions such as Internet access, cameras, and built-in applications.

👁 Visualize It!

12 Sequence Read the timeline at the bottom of the page. Write a letter and year on each photo to match it to its description. Write a label for each photo. Two have been completed for you.

B 1945
ENIAC, the first general-purpose computer

1800		1945	

Ⓐ In 1801, French weaver Joseph Marie Jacquard invented wooden punch cards to program which pattern a loom would weave. The presence of a hole meant the loom needle could go through, and the absence of a hole meant it could not, similar to the 1s and 0s of modern software.

Ⓑ In 1945, engineers completed one of the first general-purpose computers, the Electronic Numerical Integrator and Computer (ENIAC), for the U.S. Army. Punch cards delivered information to be processed by almost 18,000 vacuum tubes inside the 33-ton machine.

Ⓒ In 1958, developers introduced the integrated circuit, which allowed the development of much smaller computers.

Shrinking **Computer**

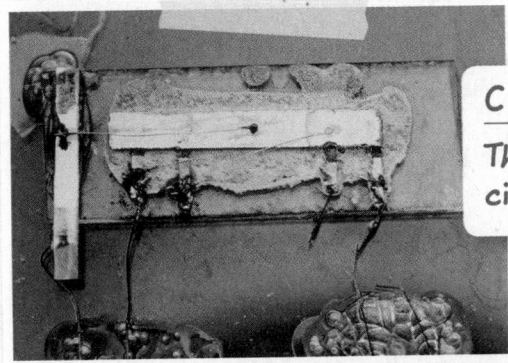

C 1958

The first integrated circuit

_____
_____
_____
_____

_____
_____
_____

Think Outside the Book **Inquiry**

13 Create Design a new electronic device for tomorrow's classrooms. Create a poster describing the advantages of your technology.

1965   **1985**   **2005**

D In 1965, the first commercially successful tabletop computer came on the market. It could sit on a table, but it was too expensive for home computing. It cost what the average person might earn in 15 years!

E In the mid-1970s, personal computers like those used today first appeared. They had monitors, keyboards, and hard drives. These computers could store, process, and output information for people in their homes or businesses.

F In the early 2000s, the first touchscreen smartphones came on the market. Smartphones combined the features of a telephone with a computer. People could make phone calls, send e-mail or messages, and surf the Internet from almost anywhere.

Visual Summary

To complete this summary, fill in each blank with the correct word or phrase. Then, use the key below to check your answers. You can use this page to review the main concepts of the lesson.

Electronic Technology

Electronic devices use integrated circuits to process information.

14 Another word for an integrated circuit is a(n) _____

15 A signal is carried by a(n) _____

A computer is an electronic device that performs tasks by following instructions given to it.

18 A modern computer has devices for handling the input, processing, storage, and _____ of data.

Analog signals change continuously. Digital signals use the binary code, which is a pattern of 1s and 0s.

16 A dimmer switch is a device that sends a(n) _____ signal.

17 A computer is a device that sends a(n) _____ signal.

19 Claims · Evidence · Reasoning Compare the dots and dashes of Morse code with the 1s and 0s of digital binary code. How are they alike and how are they different? Explain your reasoning.

Lesson Review

Vocabulary

Draw a line to connect the following terms to their definitions.

1 electronic device

2 integrated circuit

3 computer

A a tiny circuit with many parts

B device for storing and processing data in binary form

C something that uses electrical energy to process information

Key Concepts

4 Describe Explain the difference between how a lamp and a TV use electrical energy.

_____

_____

_____

_____

5 Identify What device enabled computers to shrink from early models, such as ENIAC, to smartphones that fit in your hand?

_____

_____

6 Compare How do the components that processed information in the ENIAC compare with the components that process information in a modern laptop computer?

_____

_____

_____

7 List What are the four basic functions of a modern computer?

_____

Critical Thinking

8 Relate If water could be used to create digital signals using a drip into a pond as a 1 and no drip as a 0, what would the carrier be?

_____

_____

9 Explain Are digital signals the only signals that use binary code? Explain.

_____

_____

_____

_____

_____

_____

Use this photo to answer the following question.

10 Explain Identify the items shown above and explain the function of each item.

_____

_____

_____

_____

_____

_____

_____

My Notes

Unit 7

Big Idea ▷ An electric current can produce a magnetic field, and a magnetic field can produce an electric current.

Lesson 1
ESSENTIAL QUESTION
What makes something electrically charged?

Describe electric charges in objects and distinguish between electrical conductors and insulators.

Lesson 2
ESSENTIAL QUESTION
What flows through an electric wire?

Describe how electric charges flow as electric current.

Lesson 3
ESSENTIAL QUESTION
How do electric circuits work?

Describe basic electric circuits and how to use electricity safely.

Lesson 4
ESSENTIAL QUESTION
What is magnetism?

Describe magnets and magnetic fields and explain their properties.

Lesson 5
ESSENTIAL QUESTION
What is electromagnetism?

Describe the relationship between electricity and magnetism and how this relationship affects our world.

Lesson 6
ESSENTIAL QUESTION
What are electronics, and how have they changed?

Describe what electronic devices do and how they change as technology changes.

Think Outside the Book

2 Synthesize Choose one of these activities to help synthesize what you have learned in this unit.

☐ Using what you learned in lessons 1 and 4, describe similarities between electricity and magnetism by making a poster presentation. Include captions and labels.

☐ Using what you learned in lessons 2, 3, 5, and 6, explain how electric current, electric circuits, and electromagnetism have affected telecommunication by creating a timeline. Include specific examples from the lessons, your own experience, and history.

Connect ESSENTIAL QUESTIONS
Lessons 4 and 5

1 Synthesize Could a stationary magnet be used to generate an electric current? Explain.

_____

_____

_____

Unit 7 Review

Name _____

Vocabulary

Fill in each blank with the term that best completes the following sentences.

1 A(n) _____ allows electrical charges to move freely.

2 The amount of work required to move a unit electric charge between two points is called _____.

3 A(n) _____ is an electric circuit in which all the parts are connected in a single loop.

4 Magnets exert forces on each other and are surrounded by a(n) _____.

5 A(n) _____ is a signal that is represented as a sequence of separate values made up of zeroes and ones.

Key Concepts

Read each question below, and circle the best answer.

6 Objects can be charged in many ways. In the image below, a student is rubbing a balloon on his head.

What method is he using to charge the balloon?

A friction

B repulsion

C induction

D conduction

7 Which of the following is an electrical insulator?

A copper   **C** aluminum

B rubber   **D** iron

8 Which of the following wires has the lowest resistance?

A a short, thick copper wire at 25 °C

B a long, thick copper wire at 35 °C

C a long, thin copper wire at 35 °C

D a short, thin iron wire at 25 °C

9 There are many devices in the home that use electricity. Below is a diagram of four common electrical devices.

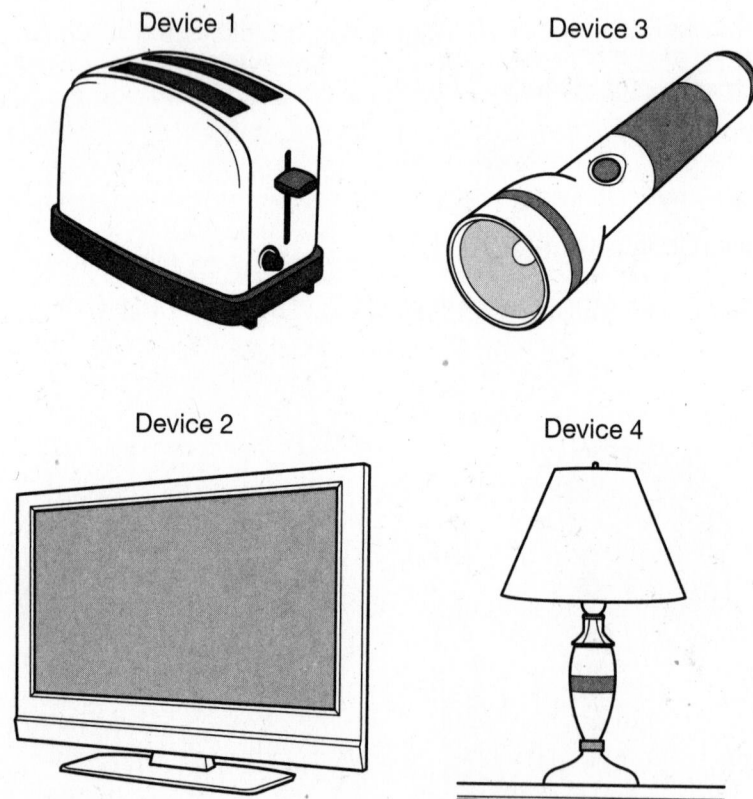

Device 1

Device 3

Device 2

Device 4

Which electrical device runs on direct current?

A Device 1   **C** Device 3

B Device 2   **D** Device 4

10 The diagram below shows two examples of electrical circuits.

Circuit 1

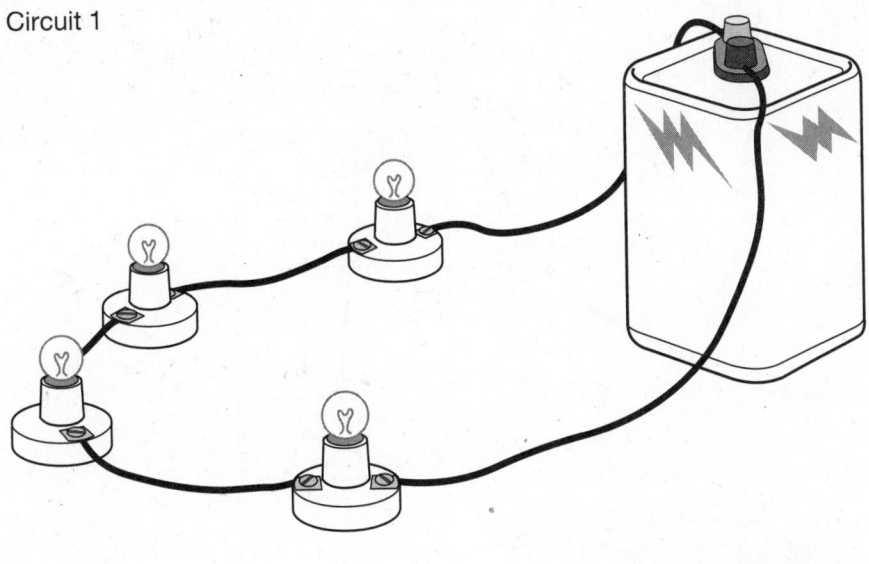

Circuit 2

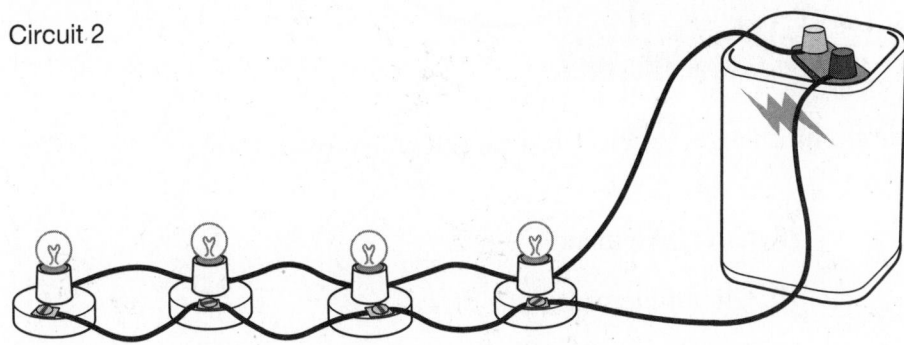

Which of the following statements about the circuits is correct?

A Circuit 1 is a parallel circuit, and Circuit 2 is a parallel circuit.

B Circuit 1 is a series circuit, and Circuit 2 is a parallel circuit.

C Circuit 1 is a parallel circuit, and Circuit 2 is a series circuit.

D Circuit 1 is a series circuit, and Circuit 2 is a series circuit.

11 It is important to practice electrical safety. Which of the following choices is unsafe?

A only using electrical cords that have proper insulation

B seeking shelter on a beach or under a tree during a lightning storm

C keeping electrical appliances away from sinks and bathtubs

D using ground fault circuit interrupters (GFCIs) in the home

12 Here is a diagram of a simple electric circuit. There are four elements to the circuit. They are labeled Circuit Element 1, Circuit Element 2, Circuit Element 3, and Circuit Element 4.

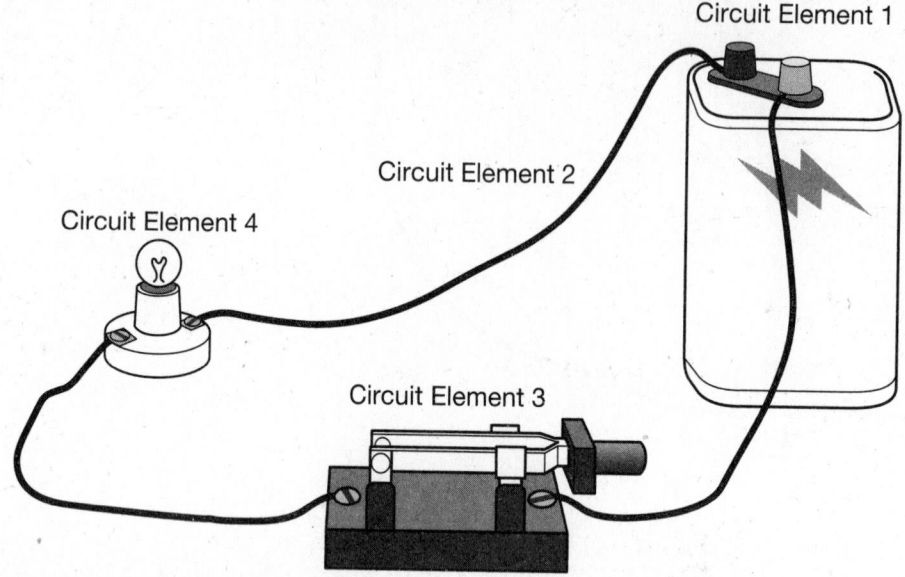

Circuit Element 1

Circuit Element 2

Circuit Element 4

Circuit Element 3

What part of an electric circuit changes the electrical energy into another form of energy?

A Circuit Element 1   **C** Circuit Element 3

B Circuit Element 2   **D** Circuit Element 4

13 Which of the following does not use an electromagnet?

A electric motor   **C** hand-held compass

B galvanometer   **D** doorbell

14 An object can become electrically charged if it gains or loses which particles?

A volts   **C** atoms

B neutrons   **D** electrons

15 Over time, computer size has been greatly reduced because of the introduction of which component?

A memory device   **C** monitor

B microprocessor chip   **D** mouse

16 Binary code is an example of which of the following?

A an analog system   **C** an electronic device

B a digital signal   **D** an integrated circuit

17 Below is an image of a magnet showing the magnetic field.

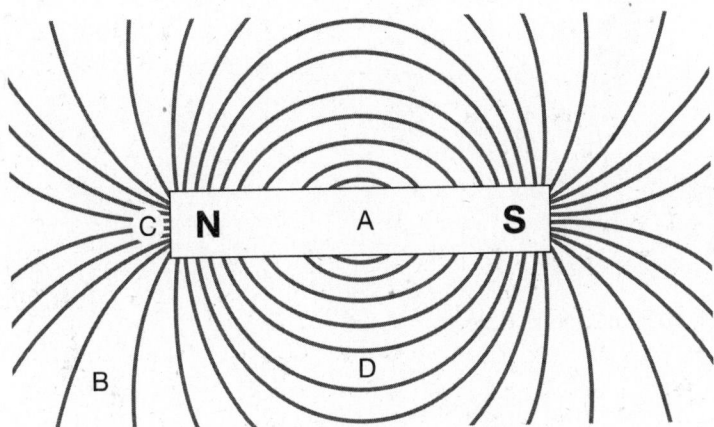

Where is the magnetic force the strongest?

A Position A   **C** Position C

B Position B   **D** Position D

Critical Thinking

Answer the following questions in the space provided.

18 Describe three properties of magnets.

_____

_____

_____

_____

_____

19 List two ways in which the strength of an electromagnet can be increased.

_____

_____

_____

Unit 7 Review continued

20 The image below shows Earth and its magnetic field.

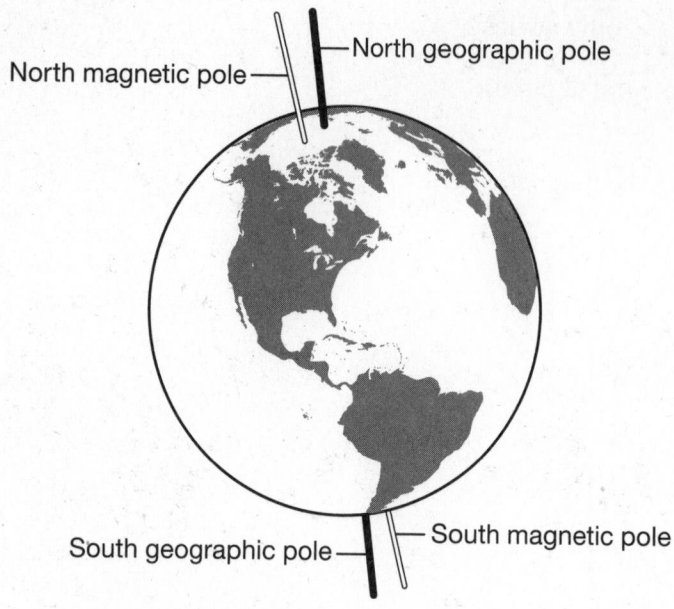

North magnetic pole—

—North geographic pole

South geographic pole—

—South magnetic pole

What is the difference between Earth's magnetic and geographic poles? How do navigators take advantage of this?

_____

_____

_____

_____

_____

_____

Connect ESSENTIAL QUESTIONS
Lessons 4 and 5

Answer the following question in the space provided.

21 There is a close relationship between magnetic forces and the generation of electricity. Explain how magnets can be used to generate electricity and how electric current can be used to create electromagnets. For each process, give an example of a device you would find around the home.

_____

_____

_____

_____

_____

UNIT 8

Introduction to Waves

Big Idea

Waves transfer energy and interact in predictable ways.

S8P4., S8P4.a, S8P4.d, S8P4.e, S8P4.f

The seven undulating waves of the Henderson Waves Bridge, a pedestrian walkway in Singapore, illustrate some of the properties of waves.

The higher the ocean wave, the farther the surfer can travel.

What do you think?

A surfer takes advantage of a wave's energy to catch an exciting ride. What other properties of waves might help a surfer catch a wave? As you explore the unit, gather evidence to help you state and support claims to answer this question.

© Houghton Mifflin Harcourt Publishing Company • Image Credits: (bg) ©Asia File/Alamy Images; (inset) ©Greg Ewing/Getty Images

521

Hit the Airwaves

When you hear the word *waves*, you probably think of waves in an ocean. But you encounter waves every day. For example, radio stations use airwaves to broadcast sounds to an audience.

① Think about It

What do you know about the properties of waves? Sketch and label two full waves in the space below to show your current understanding of waves.

Each number on a radio dial represents a different wave frequency.

② Ask a Question

How does the Federal Communications Commission (FCC) assign the broadcast frequencies for radio and television stations? You might be surprised to discover that the FCC also assigns frequencies for devices that use radio waves. Such devices include garage-door openers and radio-controlled toys. With a partner, research this topic and share your findings with your class.

_____

_____

_____

_____

③ Make a Plan

A Choose a call sign, broadcast frequency (has to be AM), and listening area for a campus radio station based on your research.

_____

_____

B List some other kinds of data you would need to research to start your own campus radio broadcasting station.

_____

_____

_____

_____

C Could you increase the listening area of your radio station?

_____

_____

_____

The airwaves transmit the announcer's voice to listeners far and wide.

Take It Home

Talk with an adult about starting a radio station in your school. What types of programs would students want to hear? Could you actually create a school radio broadcasting station? Write a description of your radio station to turn in to your teacher. See *ScienceSaurus*® for more information about technology design.

Waves

ESSENTIAL QUESTION

What are waves?

By the end of this lesson, you should be able to distinguish between types of waves based on medium and direction of motion.

S8P4.a Electromagnetic and mechanical waves: similarities and differences

Ocean waves can cause great destruction. This woodblock print illustrates a great wave threatening boats off the coast of Japan.

Engage Your Brain

1 Predict Check T or F to show whether you think each statement is true or false.

T	F	
☐	☐	The air around you is full of waves.
☐	☐	Ocean waves carry water from hundreds of miles away.
☐	☐	Sound waves can travel across outer space.
☐	☐	Visible light is a wave.

2 Identify Make a list of items in the classroom that are making waves. Next to each item, write what kind of waves you think it is making. Explain your reasoning.

_____

_____

_____

_____

_____

_____

_____

_____

Active Reading

3 Distinguish Which of the following definitions of *medium* do you think is most likely to be used in the context of studying waves? Circle your answer.

A of intermediate size

B the matter in which a physical phenomenon takes place

C between two extremes

Vocabulary Terms

- **wave**
- **medium**
- **longitudinal wave**
- **transverse wave**
- **mechanical wave**
- **electromagnetic wave**

4 Apply As you learn the definition of each vocabulary term in this lesson, write your own definition or sketch to help you remember the meaning of the term.

Riding the Wave

What are waves?

The world is full of waves. Water waves are just one of many kinds of waves. Sound and light are also waves. A **wave** is a disturbance that transfers energy from one place to another.

Waves Are Disturbances

Many waves travel by disturbing a material. The material then returns to its original place. A **medium** is the material through which a wave travels.

You can make waves on a rope by shaking the end up and down. The rope is the medium, and the wave is the up-and-down disturbance. As the part of the rope nearest your hand moves, it causes the part next to it to move up and down too. The motion of this part of the rope causes the next part to move. In this way, the wave moves as a disturbance down the whole length of the rope.

Each piece of the rope moves up and down as a wave goes by. Then the piece of rope returns to where it was before. A wave transfers energy from one place to another. It does not transfer matter. The points where the wave is highest are called crests. The points where the wave is lowest are called troughs.

Active Reading

5 Identify Underline the names for the highest and lowest points of a wave.

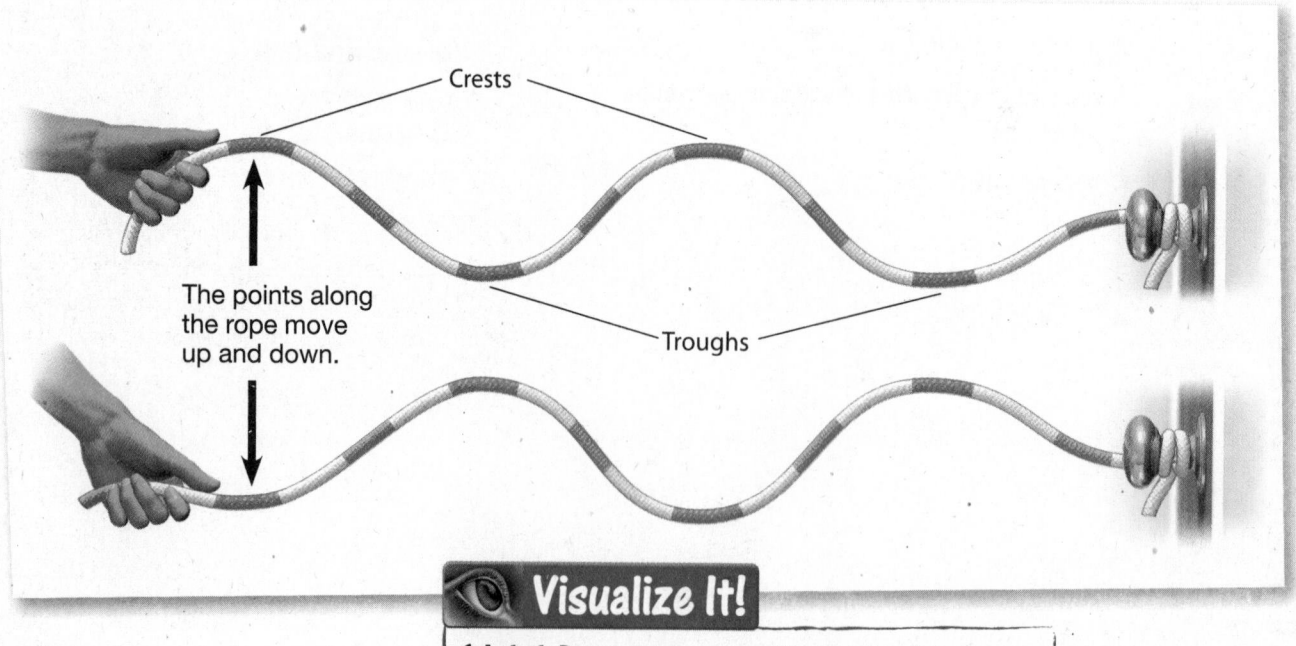

Crests

The points along the rope move up and down.

Troughs

Visualize It!

6 Label Draw an arrow near the rope to show the direction the wave travels.

Waves Are a Transfer of Energy

A wave is a disturbance that transfers energy. Some waves need a medium to transfer energy, such as waves in the ocean that move through water and waves that are carried on guitar or cello strings when they vibrate. Some waves can transfer energy without a medium. One example is visible light. Light waves from the sun transfer energy to Earth across empty space.

Visualize It!

Each snapshot below shows the passage of a wave.
The leaf rises and falls as crests and troughs carry it.

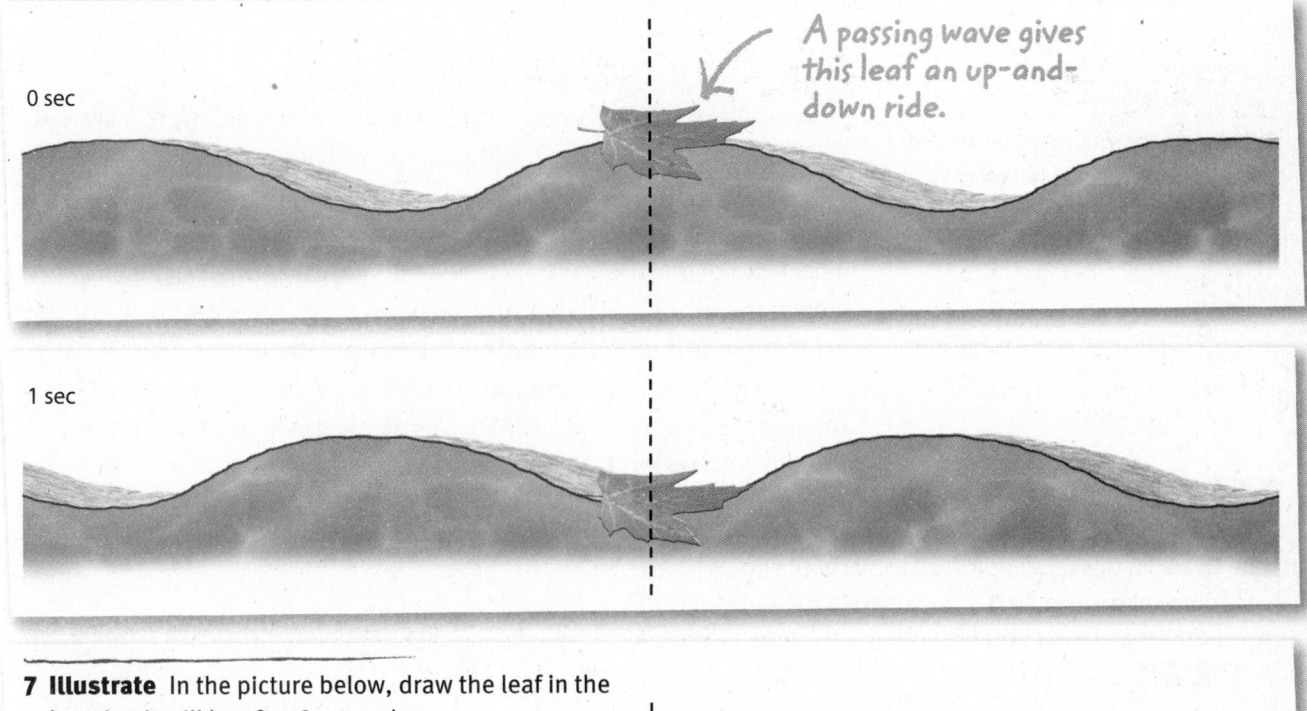

0 sec

A passing wave gives this leaf an up-and-down ride.

1 sec

7 Illustrate In the picture below, draw the leaf in the location it will be after 2 seconds.

2 sec

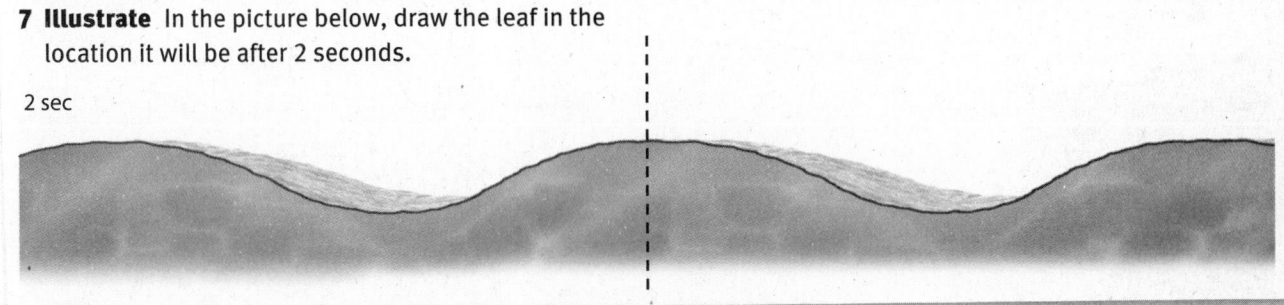

8 Model In the space below, draw the leaf and wave as they will appear after 3 seconds.

3 sec

Different Ways

How does a wave transfer energy?

A wave transfers energy in the direction it travels. However, the disturbance may not be in the same direction as the wave. Each wave can be classified by comparing the direction of the disturbance, such as the motion of the medium, with the direction the wave travels.

As a Longitudinal Wave

When you pull back on a spring toy like the one below, you spread the coils apart and make a *rarefaction*. When you push forward, you squeeze the coils closer together and make a *compression*. The coils move back and forth as the wave passes along the spring toy. This kind of wave is called a longitudinal wave. In a **longitudinal wave** (lahn•jih•TOOD•n•uhl), particles move back and forth in the same direction that the wave travels, or parallel to the wave.

Sound waves are longitudinal waves. When sound waves pass through the air, particles that make up air move back and forth in the same direction that the sound waves travel.

9 Identify As you read, underline the type of wave that sound is.

Visualize It!

10 Label In this longitudinal wave, label the arrow that shows the direction the wave travels with a *T*. Label the arrow that shows how the spring is disturbed with a *D*.

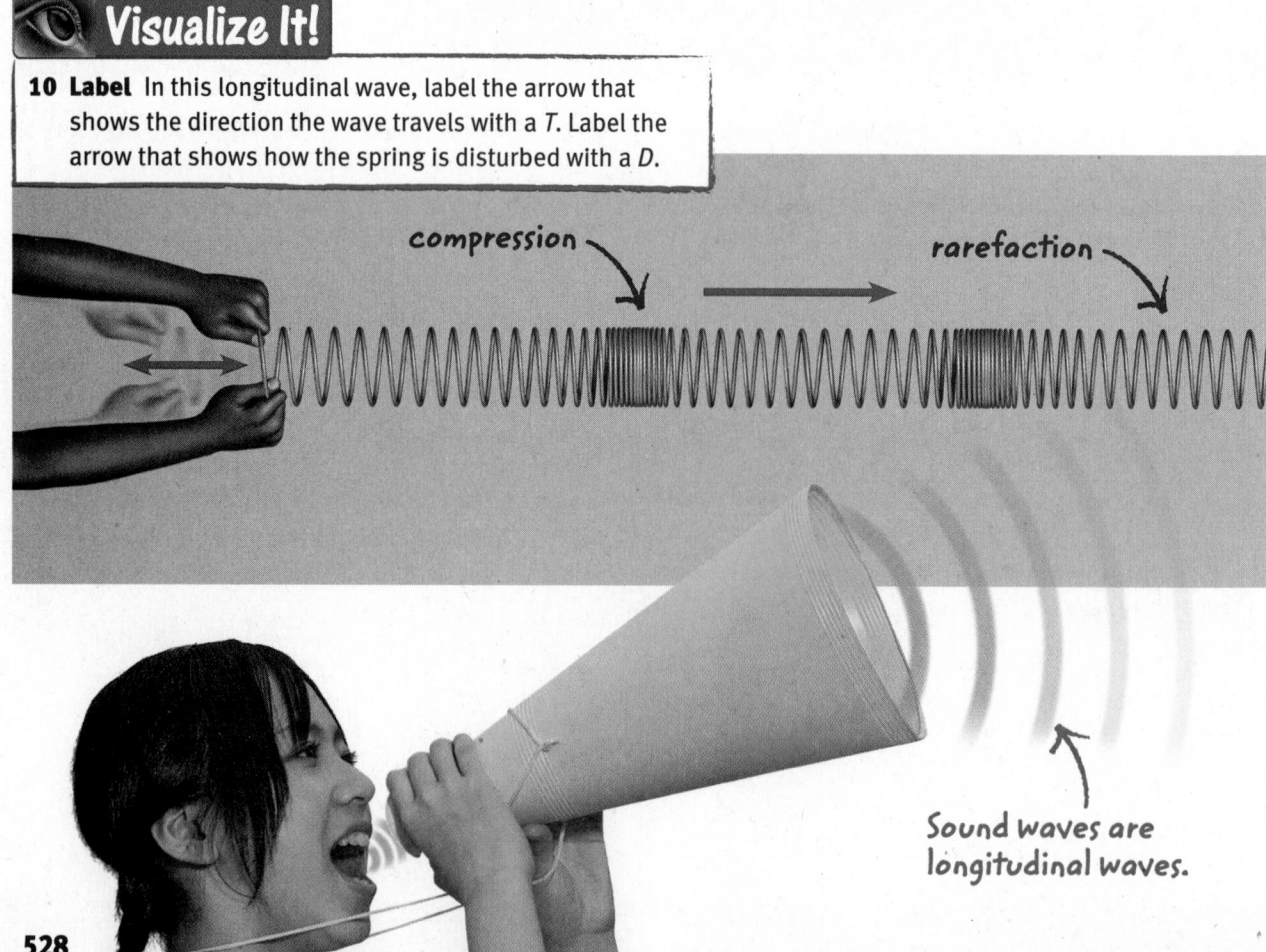

compression

rarefaction

Sound waves are longitudinal waves.

to Transfer Energy

As a Transverse Wave

The same spring toy can be used to make other kinds of waves. If you move the end of the spring toy up and down, a wave also travels along the spring. In this wave, the spring's coils move up and down as the wave passes. This kind of wave is called a **transverse wave**. In a transverse wave, particles move perpendicularly to the direction the wave travels.

Transverse waves and longitudinal waves often travel at different speeds in a medium. In a spring toy, longitudinal waves are usually faster. An earthquake sends both longitudinal waves (called P waves) and transverse waves (called S waves) through Earth's crust. In this case, the longitudinal waves are also faster. During an earthquake, the faster P waves arrive first. A little while later, the S waves arrive. The S waves are slower but usually more destructive.

A transverse wave and a longitudinal wave can combine to form another kind of wave called a surface wave. Ripples on a pond are an example of a surface wave.

When these fans do "The Wave," they are modeling the way a disturbance travels through a medium.

12 Categorize Is the stadium wave shown above a transverse wave or a longitudinal wave? State evidence to support your claim.

Think Outside the Book Inquiry

13 Identify What do the letters *S* in S waves and *P* in P waves stand for? Relate this to earthquakes and discuss it with a classmate.

Visualize It!

11 Label In this transverse wave, label the arrow that shows the direction the wave travels with a *T*. Label the arrow that shows how the spring is disturbed with a *D*.

Water waves are surface waves, a combination of transverse and longitudinal waves.

529

Making Waves

What are some types of waves?

As you have learned, waves are disturbances that transfer energy. Waves can be classified by the direction of disturbance. But they can also be classified by what is disturbed.

Mechanical Waves

Most of the waves we have talked about so far are waves in a medium. For water waves, water is the medium. For earthquake waves, Earth is the medium. A wave that requires a medium through which to travel is called a **mechanical wave**.

Some mechanical waves can travel through more than one medium. For example, sound waves can move through air, through water, or even through a solid wall. The waves travel at different speeds in the different media. Sound waves travel much faster in a liquid or a solid than in air.

Mechanical waves can't travel without a medium. Suppose all the air is removed from beneath a glass dome, or bell jar, as in the photograph below. In a vacuum, there is no air to transmit sound waves. The vibrations made inside the bell jar can't be heard.

Electromagnetic Waves

Are there waves that can travel without a medium? Yes. Sunlight travels from the sun to Earth through empty space. Although light waves can travel through a medium, they can also travel without a medium. Light and similar waves are called electromagnetic (EM) waves. An **electromagnetic wave** is a disturbance in electric and magnetic fields. They are transverse waves. Examples of EM waves include

- visible light
- radio waves
- microwaves
- ultraviolet (UV) light
- x-rays

In empty space, all these waves travel at the same speed. This speed, referred to as the speed of light, is about 300 million meters per second!

The sound from the toy cannot be heard because there is no air to transmit the sound.

Visible light is a type of wave called an electromagnetic wave.

Visualize It!

14 Classify Identify each example of waves in these three photographs as mechanical or electromagnetic.

Sunlight is a(n)
_____

Water waves are
_____

A towel waving displays a(n)
_____

Vocal sounds are
_____

Music is a(n)
_____

Firelight is a(n)
_____

Visual Summary

To complete this summary, fill in the lines below the statement to correct the statement so that it is true. You can use this page to review the main concepts of the lesson.

Waves are disturbances that transfer energy.

15 The water particles in the wave move to the right, along with the wave.

_____

_____

_____

Waves

Waves can be longitudinal or transverse.

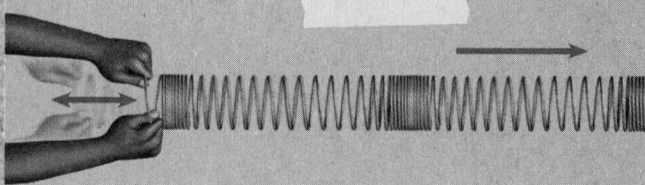

16 The toy above and the toy below both show longitudinal waves.

_____

_____

_____

Waves can be mechanical or electromagnetic.

17 This picture shows only examples of mechanical waves.

_____

_____

_____

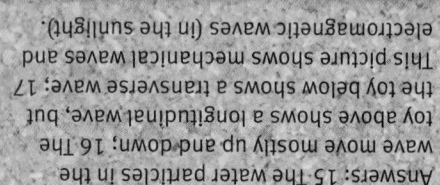

This picture shows mechanical waves and electromagnetic waves (in the sunlight).

Answers: 15 The water particles in the wave move mostly up and down; 16 The toy above shows a longitudinal wave, but the toy below shows a transverse wave; 17

18 **Compare** During a thunderstorm, you experience mechanical waves in the form of sound from thunder. You also experience electromagnetic waves in the form of light from lightning. If you were trying to compare mechanical and electromagnetic waves, what questions could you ask about thunder and lightning to develop explanations about how these two wave types are similar and how they differ?

Lesson Review

Vocabulary

Circle the term that best completes the following sentences.

1 A wave is a disturbance that transfers *matter/energy*.

2 In a *longitudinal/transverse* wave, the disturbance moves parallel to the direction the wave travels.

3 *Mechanical/Electromagnetic* waves require a medium in which to travel.

Key Concepts

4–6 Identify Name the medium for each of the following types of waves.

Type of wave	Medium
ocean waves	**4**
earthquake waves	**5**
sound waves from a speaker	**6**

7 Describe Explain how transverse waves can be produced on a rope. Then describe how pieces of the rope move as waves pass.

_____

_____

_____

_____

_____

8 Analyze Are the sun's rays mechanical waves or electromagnetic waves? How do you know?

_____

_____

Critical Thinking

9 Contrast Mechanical waves travel as disturbances in a physical medium. Make a claim about how electromagnetic waves travel and support your thinking with evidence.

_____

_____

_____

Use this image to answer the following questions.

10 Infer Even though the phone is ringing, no sound comes out of the jar. What does this tell you about the space inside the jar?

_____

_____

_____

11 Claims • Evidence • Reasoning What does this same experiment tell you about light waves? Explain the evidence that supports your claim.

_____

_____

_____

_____

My Notes

Mean, Median, Mode, and Range

You can analyze both the measures of central tendency and the variability of data using mean, median, mode, and range.

Tutorial

Imagine that a group of students records the light levels at various places within a classroom.

Classroom Light Levels	
Area	Illuminance (lux)
1	800
2	300
3	150
4	300
5	200

Mean The mean is the sum of all of the values in a data set divided by the total number of values in the data set. The mean is also called the *average*.	$$\frac{800 + 300 + 150 + 300 + 200}{5}$$ **mean** = 350 lux
Median The median is the value of the middle item when data are arranged in order by size. In a range that has an odd number of values, the median is the middle value. In a range that has an even number of values, the median is the average of the two middle values.	If necessary, reorder the values from least to greatest: 150, 200, **300**, 300, 800 **median** = 300 lux
Mode The mode is the value or values that occur most frequently in a data set. If all values occur with the same frequency, the data set is said to have no mode. Values should be put in order to find the mode.	If necessary, reorder the values from least to greatest: 150, 200, 300, 300, 800 The value 300 occurs most frequently. **mode** = 300 lux
Range The range is the difference between the greatest value and the least value of a data set.	800 − 150 **range** = 650 lux

You Try It!

The data table below shows the data collected for rooms in three halls in the school.

Illuminance (lux)				
	Room 1	Room 2	Room 3	Room 4
Science Hall	150	250	500	400
Art Hall	300	275	550	350
Math Hall	200	225	600	600

①

Using Formulas Find the mean, median, mode, and range of the data for the school.

②

Analyzing Methods The school board is looking into complaints that some areas of the school are too poorly lit. They are considering replacing the lights. If you were in favor of replacing the lights, which representative value for the school's data would you use to support your position? If you were opposed to replacing the lights, which representative value for the school's data would you choose to support your position? Explain your answer.

_____
_____
_____
_____
_____
_____
_____
_____
_____
_____
_____

Language Arts Connection

On flashcards, write sentences that use the keywords *mean*, *median*, *mode*, and *range*. Cover the keywords with small sticky notes. Review each sentence, and determine if it provides enough context clues to determine the covered word. If necessary, work with a partner to improve your sentences.

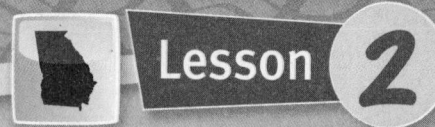

Lesson 2
Properties
of Waves

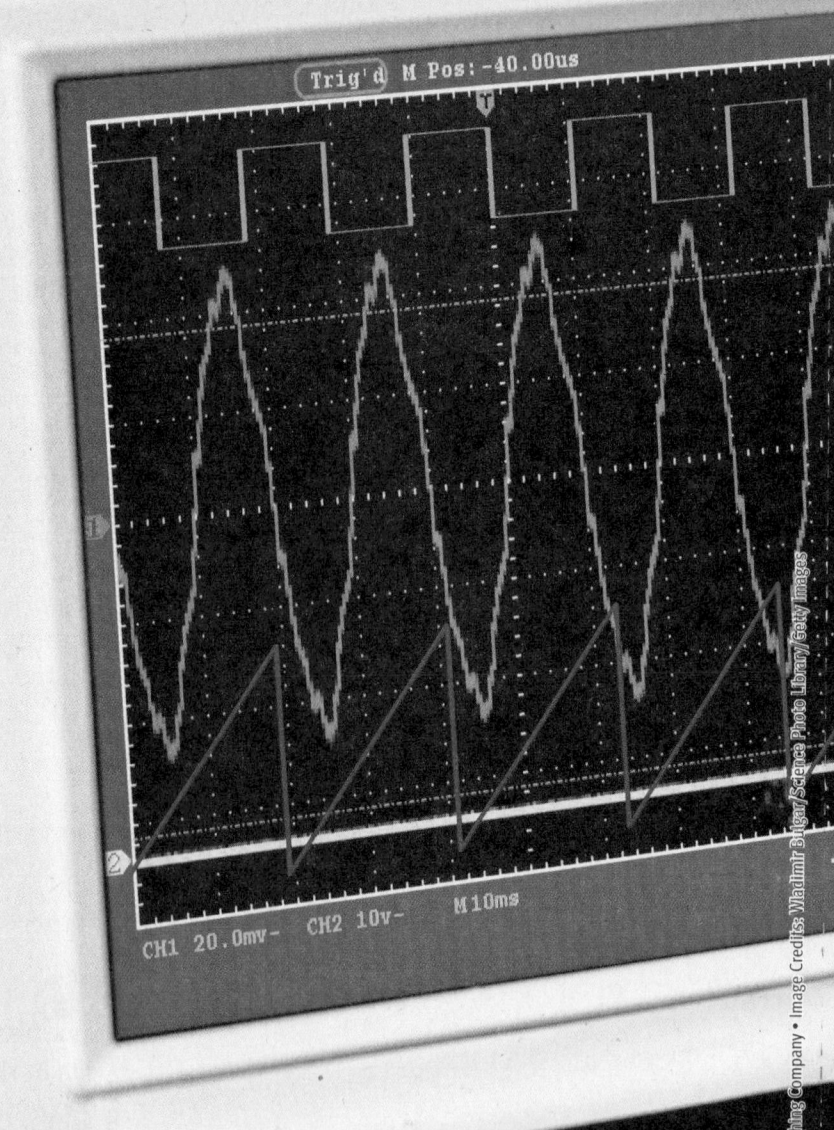

ESSENTIAL QUESTION

How can we describe a wave?

By the end of this lesson, you should be able to identify characteristics of a wave and describe wave behavior.

S8P4.a Electromagnetic and mechanical waves: similarities and differences

S8P4.d Behavior of light and sound waves

S8P4.e Density of media and wave behavior

S8P4.f Properties of waves and energy

A heartbeat monitor displays a wave, the characteristics of which contain information about a patient's heartbeat.

Lesson Labs

Quick Labs
- Investigate Frequency
- Waves on a Spring

Exploration Lab
- Investigate Wavelength

Engage Your Brain

1 Describe Fill in the blank with the word that you think correctly completes the following sentences.

A guitar amplifier makes a guitar sound
_____

FM radio frequencies are measured in
mega- _____

The farther you are from a sound source,
the _____ the sound is.

2 Illustrate Draw a diagram of a wave in the space below. How would you describe your wave so that a friend on the phone could duplicate your drawing?

Active Reading

3 Predict Many scientific words also have everyday meanings. For each of the following terms, write in your own words what it means in common use. Then try writing a definition of what it might mean when applied to waves.

length:
_____
_____
_____
_____

speed:
_____
_____
_____

period (of time):
_____
_____
_____

Vocabulary Terms

- wave
- amplitude
- wavelength
- wave period
- frequency
- hertz
- wave speed

4 Compare This list contains the vocabulary terms you'll learn in this lesson. As you read, circle the definition of each term.

Amp It UP!

How can we describe a wave?

Suppose you are talking to a friend who had been to the beach. You want to know what the waves were like. Were they big or small? How often did they come? How far apart were they? Were they moving fast? Each of these is a basic property that can be used to describe waves.

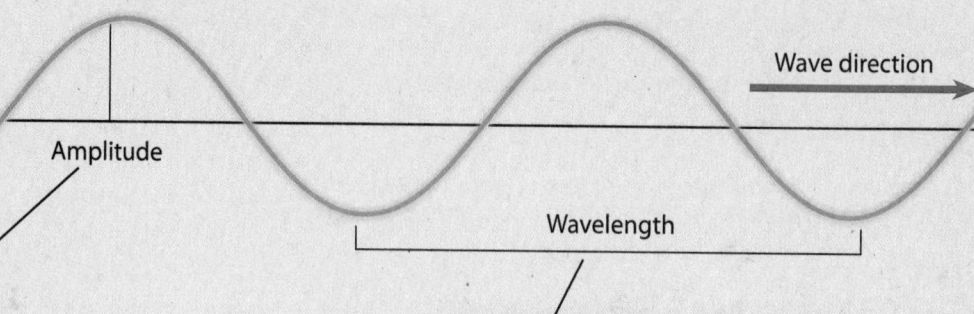

Amplitude

Wave direction

Wavelength

By Its Amplitude

A **wave** is a disturbance that transfers energy from one place to another. As a wave passes, particles in the medium move up and down or back and forth. A wave's **amplitude** is a measure of how far the particles in the medium move away from their normal rest position. The graph above shows a transverse wave. Notice that the amplitude of a wave is also half of the difference between the highest and lowest values.

By Its Wavelength

You can use amplitude to describe the height of an ocean wave, for example. But to describe how long the wave is, you need to know its wavelength. The **wavelength** is the distance from any point on a wave to an identical point on the next wave. For example, wavelength is the distance from one crest to the next, from one trough to the next, or between any other two corresponding points. Wavelength measures the length of one cycle, or repetition.

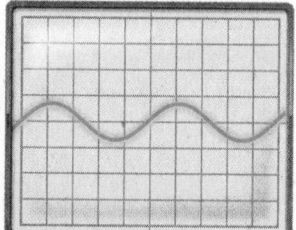 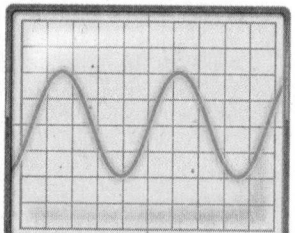

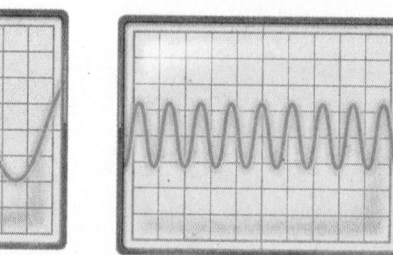 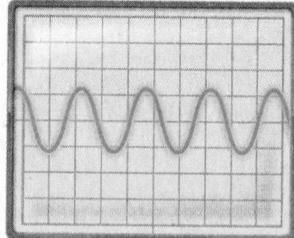

Visualize It!

5 Label Mark the amplitude in the two graphs above. Which wave has the greater amplitude? Explain your reasoning.

_____

_____

_____

6 Label Mark the wavelength in the two graphs above. Which wave has the greater wavelength? Explain your reasoning.

_____

_____

_____

By Its Frequency

Wavelength and amplitude tell you about the size of a wave. Another property tells you how much time a wave takes to repeat. The **wave period** (usually "period") is the time required for one cycle. You can measure the period by finding the time for one full cycle of a wave to pass a given point. For example, you could start timing when one crest passes you and stop when the next crest passes. The time between two crests is the period.

Another way to express the time of a wave's cycle is frequency. The **frequency** of a wave tells how many cycles occur in an amount of time, usually 1 s. Frequency is expressed in **hertz** (Hz). One hertz is equal to one cycle per second. If ten crests pass each second, the frequency is 10 Hz.

> Frequency and period are closely related. Frequency is the inverse of period:
>
> $$\text{frequency} = \frac{1}{\text{period}}$$

Suppose the time from one crest to another—the period—is 5 s. The frequency is then $\frac{1}{5}$ Hz, or 0.2 Hz. In other words, one-fifth (0.2) of a wave passes each second.

The buoy moves down and back up every five seconds as waves pass.

Wave direction

> Frequency is equal to the number of cycles per unit of time:
>
> $$\text{frequency} = \frac{\text{number of cycles}}{\text{time}}$$

Visualize It!

7 Illustrate On the grid below, draw a wave, and then draw another wave with twice the amplitude.

8 Illustrate On the grid below, draw a wave, and then draw another wave with half the wavelength.

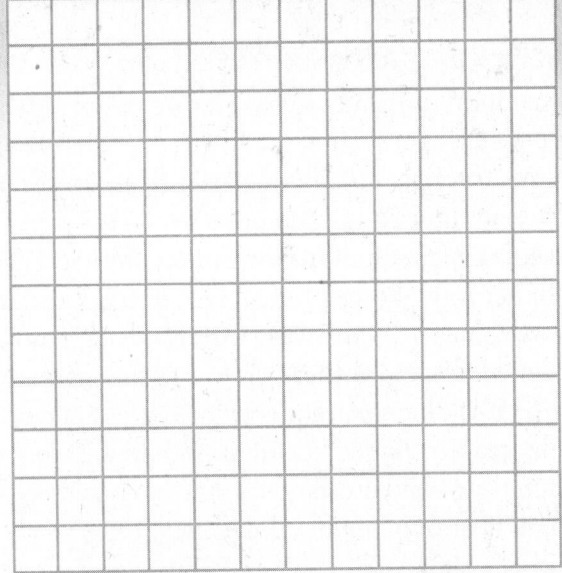

Amp It Down

What affects the energy of a wave?

All waves carry energy from one place to another, but some waves carry more energy than others. A leaf falling on water produces waves so small they are hard to see. An earthquake under the ocean can produce huge waves that cause great destruction.

The Amplitude or The Frequency

For a mechanical wave, amplitude is related to the amount of energy the wave carries. For two similar waves, the wave with greater amplitude carries more energy. For example, sound waves with greater amplitude transfer more energy to your eardrum, so they sound louder.

Greater frequency can also mean greater energy in a given amount of time. If waves hit a barrier three times in a minute, they transfer a certain amount of energy to the barrier. If waves of the same amplitude hit nine times in a minute, they transfer more energy in that minute.

For most electromagnetic (EM) waves, energy is most strongly related to frequency. Very high-frequency EM waves, such as x-rays and gamma rays, carry enough energy to damage human tissue. Lower-frequency EM waves, such as visible light waves, can be absorbed safely by your body.

Active Reading

9 **Identify** As you read, underline the kind of wave whose energy depends mostly on frequency.

Think Outside the Book

10 **Apply** An echo is the reflection of sound waves as they bounce back after hitting a barrier. How can the design of a building, such as a concert hall, reduce unwanted noises and echoes?

Energy Loss to a Medium

A medium transmits a wave. However, a medium may not transmit all of the wave's energy. As a wave moves through a medium, particles may move in different directions or come to rest in different places. The medium may warm up, shift, or change in other ways. Some of the wave's energy produces these changes. As the wave travels through more of the medium, more energy is lost to the medium.

Often, higher-frequency waves lose energy more readily than lower-frequency waves. For example, when you stand far from a concert, you might hear only the low-frequency (bass) sounds.

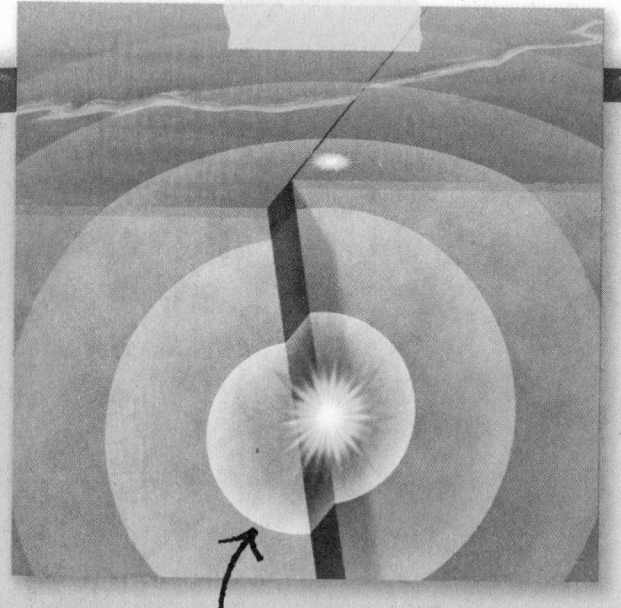

Some of the energy of these earthquake waves is lost to the medium when the ground shifts.

Energy Loss Due to Spreading

So far, we have mostly talked about waves moving in straight lines. But waves usually spread out in more than one dimension. The crests can be drawn as shapes, such as circles or spheres, called *wavefronts*. As each wavefront moves farther from the source, the energy is spread over a greater area. Less energy is available at any one point on the wavefront. If you measure a wave at a point farther from the source, you measure less energy. But the total energy of the wavefront stays the same.

Sound waves expand in three dimensions.

Ripples on a water surface expand in two dimensions.

11 Predict Which type of wave spreading do you think causes faster energy loss—two-dimensional or three-dimensional? Explain.

_____

_____

_____

As the student on the left knocks on the table, the students farther away feel the resulting waves less strongly.

Visualize It! Inquiry

12 Synthesize If these students repeated their experiment using a longer table, what differences would they observe? Explain your answer.

_____

_____

_____

A Happy Medium

What determines the speed of a wave?

Waves travel at different speeds in different media. For example, sound waves travel at about 340 m/s in air at room temperature, but they travel at nearly 1,500 m/s in water. In a solid, sound waves travel even faster.

The Medium in Which It Travels

The speed at which a wave travels—called **wave speed**—depends on the properties of the medium. Specifically, wave speed depends on the interactions of the atomic particles of the medium. In general, waves travel faster in solids than in liquids and faster in liquids than in gases. Interactions, or collisions, between particles happen faster in solids because the medium is more rigid.

How fast the wave travels between particles within the medium depends on many factors. For example, wave speed depends on the density of the medium. Waves usually travel slower in the denser of two solids or the denser of two liquids. The more densely packed the particles are, the more they resist motion, so they transfer waves more slowly.

In a gas, wave speed depends on temperature as well as density. Particles in hot air move faster than particles in cold air, so particles in hot air collide more often. This faster interaction allows waves to pass through hot air more quickly than through the denser cold air. The speed of sound in air at 20 °C is about 340 m/s. The speed of sound in air at 0 °C is slower, about 330 m/s.

Electromagnetic waves don't require a medium, so they can travel in a vacuum. All electromagnetic waves travel at the same speed in empty space. This speed, called the speed of light, is about 300,000,000 m/s. While passing through a medium such as air or glass, EM waves travel more slowly than they do in a vacuum.

Active Reading **13 Identify** Does sound travel faster or slower when the air gets warmer?

Visualize It!

14 Model In each case below, draw a diagram that models the movement of sound. Explain how these models compare to models of light waves through the same boxes.

_____

_____

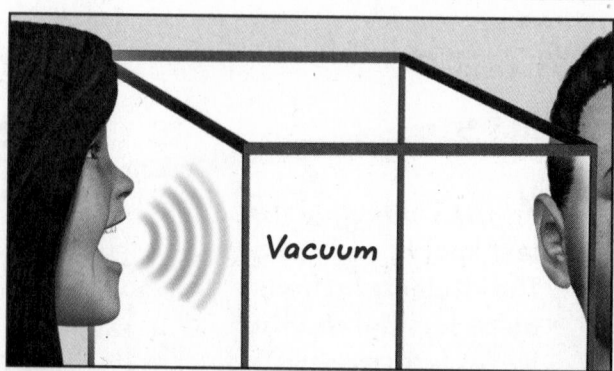

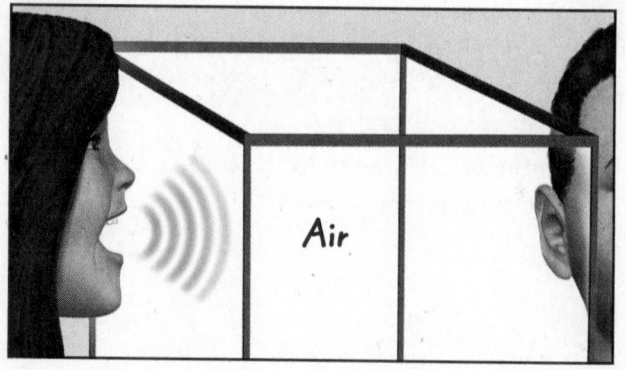

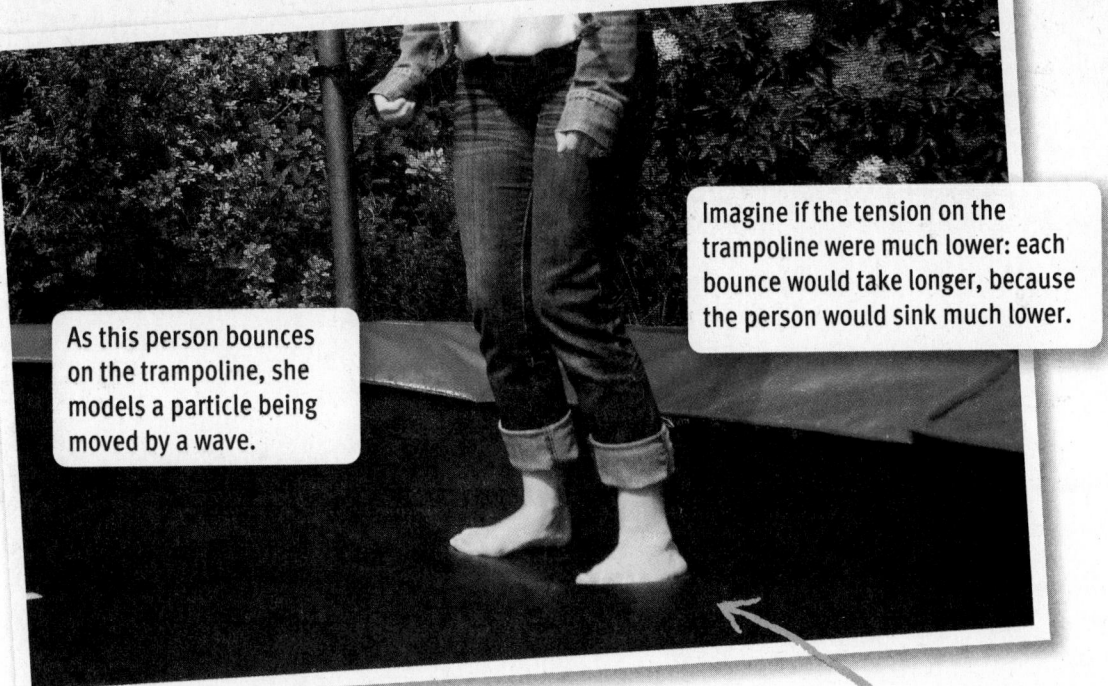

As this person bounces on the trampoline, she models a particle being moved by a wave.

Imagine if the tension on the trampoline were much lower: each bounce would take longer, because the person would sink much lower.

As a medium becomes more flexible, it carries waves more slowly.

Its Frequency and Wavelength

Wave speed can be calculated from frequency and wavelength. To understand how, it helps to remember that speed is defined as distance divided by time:

$$speed = \frac{distance}{time}$$

So if a runner runs 8 m in 2 s, then the runner's speed is 8 m ÷ 2 s = 4 m/s. For a wave, a crest moves a distance of one wavelength in one cycle. The time for the cycle to occur is one period. Using wavelength and period as the distance and time:

$$wave\ speed = \frac{wavelength}{wave\ period}$$

So if a crest moves one wavelength of 8 m in one period of 2 s, the wave speed is calculated just like the runner's speed: 8 m ÷ 2 s = 4 m/s.

Frequency is the inverse of the wave period. So the relationship can be rewritten like this:

$$wave\ speed = frequency \times wavelength$$
or
$$wavelength = \frac{wave\ speed}{frequency}$$

If you already know the wave speed, you can use this equation to solve for frequency or wavelength.

 **Do the Math** You Try It

15 Calculate Complete this table relating wave speed, frequency, and wavelength.

Wave speed (m/s)	Frequency (Hz)	Wavelength (m)
20		5
75	15	
	23	16
625		25
	38	20

© Houghton Mifflin Harcourt Publishing Company • Image Credits: ©Steppenwolf/Alamy Images

Visual Summary

To complete this summary, fill in the blanks with the correct word or phrase. Then use the key below to check your answers. You can use this page to review the main concepts of the lesson.

Amplitude tells the amount of displacement of a wave.

Wavelength tells how long a wave is.

Wave period is the time required for one cycle.

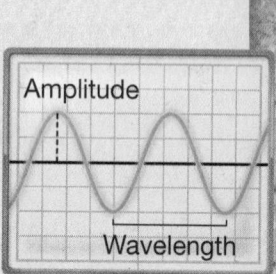

16 _____ = $\dfrac{1}{\text{wave period}}$

17 Hertz is used to express _____

18 One hertz is equal to _____

Wave energy depends on amplitude and frequency.

Most waves lose energy over time as they travel and spread.

20 Some of the wave's energy stays in the _____

Wave Properties

Wave speed depends on the properties of the medium.

In a vacuum, electromagnetic waves all move at the speed of light.

19 wave speed = frequency × _____

Answers: 16 frequency; 17 frequency; 18 one cycle per second; 19 wavelength; 20 medium

21 **Synthesize** Describe how the properties of sound waves change as they spread out in a spherical pattern.

Lesson Review

Lesson 2

Vocabulary

Fill in the blank with the correct letter.

1 frequency

_____

2 wavelength

_____

3 wave speed

_____

4 wave period

_____

5 amplitude

_____

A the distance over which a wave's shape repeats

B the maximum distance that particles in a wave's medium vibrate from their rest position

C the time required for one wavelength to pass a point

D the number of wavelengths that pass a point in a given amount of time

E the speed at which a wave travels through a medium

Key Concepts

6 Describe What measures the amount of displacement in a transverse wave?

_____

7 Relate How are frequency and wave period related?

_____
_____
_____

8 Provide What does the energy of an electromagnetic wave depend on?

_____

9 Claims • Evidence • Reasoning Sound travels slower in colder air than it does in warmer air. Make a claim about the effect of air temperature on the speed of sound. Support your claim with evidence.

_____
_____
_____
_____

Critical Thinking

Use this diagram to answer the following questions. The frequency of the wave is 0.5 Hz.

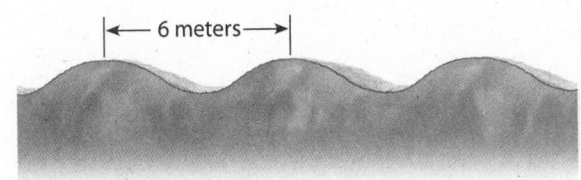

10 Analyze What is the wavelength of these waves?

_____

11 Calculate What is the speed of these waves?

_____

12 Solve If you were sitting in a boat as these waves passed by, how many seconds would pass between wave crests?

_____

13 Infer Why does the energy of a sound wave decrease over time?

_____
_____
_____

14 Infer A wave has a low speed but a high frequency. What can you infer about its wavelength?

_____
_____

15 Predict How do you know the speed of an electromagnetic wave in a vacuum?

_____
_____
_____

© Houghton Mifflin Harcourt Publishing Company

My Notes

Lesson 1

ESSENTIAL QUESTION
What are waves?

Distinguish between types of waves based on medium and direction of motion.

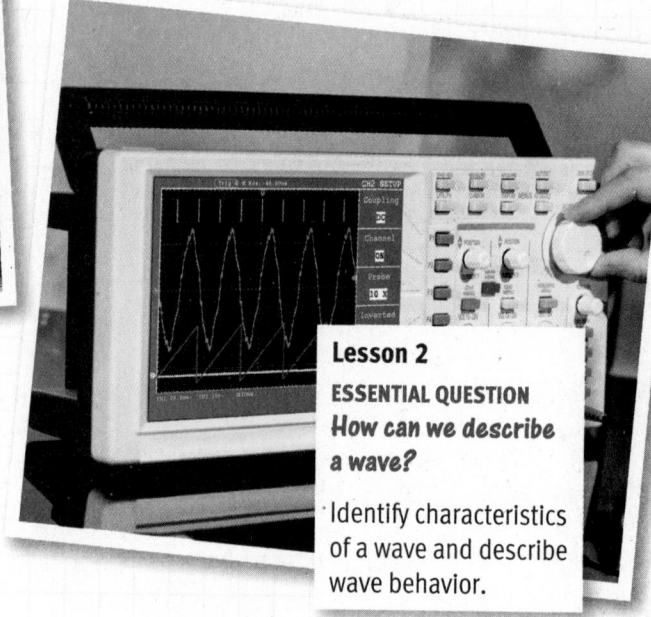

Lesson 2

ESSENTIAL QUESTION
How can we describe a wave?

Identify characteristics of a wave and describe wave behavior.

Connect ESSENTIAL QUESTIONS
Lessons 1 and 2

1 Synthesize What are two properties of waves that affect the energy of waves?

_____

_____

Think Outside the Book

2 Synthesize Choose one of these activities to help synthesize what you have learned in this unit.

☐ Using what you learned in lessons 1 and 2, create a model that compares the parts of a mechanical wave to the parts of an electromagnetic wave.

☐ Using what you learned in lessons 1 and 2, design an experiment to compare mechanical wave speeds through different media. Include all of the steps in your process and provide illustrations where needed.

Vocabulary

Fill in each blank with the term that best completes the following sentences.

1 Light travels as a(n) _____ wave.

2 The distance from the crest of one wave to the crest of the next wave is the _____

3 _____, the number of waves produced in a given amount of time, is expressed in hertz.

4 Sound is a(n) _____ wave because it cannot travel without a medium.

5 The maximum distance that the particles of a medium move away from their rest position is a measure of a wave's _____

Key Concepts

Read each question below, and circle the best answer.

6 Sashita uses the volume control on her TV to make the sound louder or softer. Which property of waves is Sashita's volume control changing?

  A amplitude

  B wave period

  C wavelength

  D wave speed

7 Which statement best explains what waves are?

  A wavy lines on graph paper

  B disturbances that transfer energy

  C light energy that changes into particles of matter

  D circles that move out from a central place

8 The diagram below shows the properties of a transverse wave.

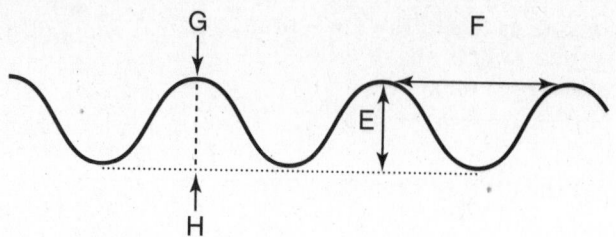

What property of the wave does F measure?

A period

C amplitude

B frequency

D wavelength

9 Which type of electromagnetic waves have the highest frequency?

A radio waves

C light waves

B gamma rays

D microwaves

10 Isabella researched how waves travel through the ground during an earthquake. She drew a diagram of one, called an S wave, moving through Earth's crust.

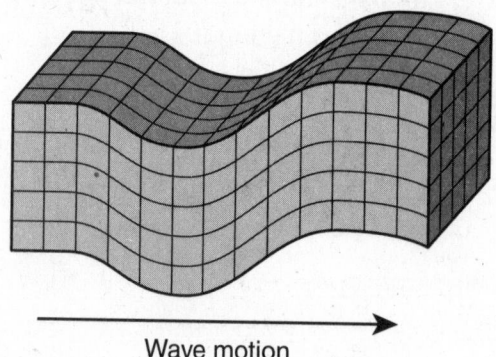

Wave motion

Based on her diagram, what kind of wave is an S wave?

A light

B sound

C longitudinal

D transverse

11 Visible, infrared, and ultraviolet light are electromagnetic waves that travel from the sun to Earth. The diagram below shows some types of electromagnetic waves.

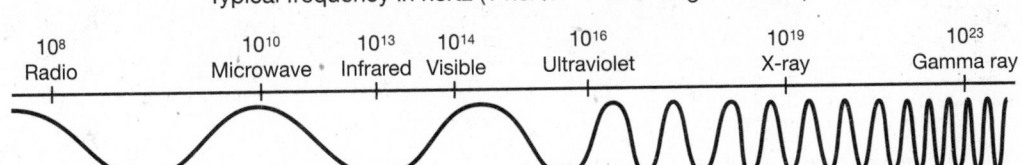

The Electromagnetic Spectrum
Typical frequency in hertz (1 hertz = 1 wavelength/second)

10^8	10^{10}	10^{13}	10^{14}	10^{16}	10^{19}	10^{23}
Radio	Microwave	Infrared	Visible	Ultraviolet	X-ray	Gamma ray

Which statement best explains what electromagnetic waves are?

A waves that vibrate through a medium

B disturbances in the atmosphere of space

C disturbances in electric and magnetic fields

D slow-moving waves

12 Frequency equals the number of wavelengths per unit of time.

$$\text{Frequency} = \frac{\text{Wavelengths}}{\text{Unit of time}}$$

Which unit is used to measure frequency as cycles per second?

A hertz

B period

C crest

D minute

13 Which statement about the effects of medium on the speed of a mechanical wave is true?

A Medium has no effect on the speed of a mechanical wave.

B A mechanical wave generally travels faster in solids than liquids.

C A mechanical wave generally travels faster in gases than liquids.

D A mechanical wave always travels through liquids at the speed of light.

Critical Thinking

Answer the following questions in the space provided.

14 Some waves carry more energy than others. Which wave has more energy, a loud sound or a quiet sound? Why?

_____

_____

15 Tafari worked one summer on a ship that set weather buoys in the ocean. He watched how the buoys moved in the water.

Which wave property describes why the buoys bobbed up and down?

_____

_____

Which wave property determines how fast the buoys bobbed in the water?

_____

_____

He observed that when the wind blew harder, the ocean waves were larger, and the buoys moved away from the ship. What effect, if any, did the waves have on how far the buoys moved? Explain your answer.

_____

_____

_____

_____

Connect ESSENTIAL QUESTIONS
Lessons 1 and 2

Answer the following question in the space provided.

16 Jung arrived at a concert in the park so late that the only seat she could get was almost a block from the stage. The music sounded much fainter to Jung than it did to people near the stage. She could hear the drums and bass guitar fairly well, but she had trouble hearing higher sounds from the singer. Explain the properties and behavior of waves that affected how Jung heard the music.

_____

_____

_____

_____

Sound

Big Idea
Sound waves transfer energy through vibrations.

S8P4., S8P4.d, S8P4.e

The Singing Ringing Tree, located in rural England, enchants visitors with an eerie hum. The sound is created by the wind passing through the galvanized steel pipes.

What do you think?

Music is just one example of sound. What are some sounds you heard today? Are these sounds produced by human activity or by nature? As you explore the unit, gather evidence to help you state and support claims to answer these questions.

The clarinetist uses "wind" to make music.

Unit 9
Sound

Sound It Out!

Have you ever felt a vibrating sensation during a really loud sound? That happens because sound waves transfer energy in the form of vibrations. You can learn how to make sounds louder and quieter by investigating sound sculptures.

(1) Do Additional Research

Investigate the Singing Ringing Tree by finding a book about it in the library or doing an Internet search. How does the sculpture produce sound?

_____

_____

_____

_____

_____

_____

The cheerleader uses a megaphone to make her voice louder.

② Think about It

What would make the sound louder?
What would make the sound quieter?
Write your ideas below.

Louder	Quieter

A mute is used to make
the trumpet quieter.

③ Make A Plan

A You can make your own sound sculpture with
everyday objects. Think about how you would
create sound with some of the following
items: spoons, drinking straws, plastic
bottles, pencils, paper clips, sheets of paper,
cellophane, rubber bands, or plastic cups.
Will wind be the source of your sound? Write a
prediction about how it will sound.

_____

_____

_____

_____

_____

B Sketch your sculpture in the space below.

ear trumpet

Take It Home

With an adult, research devices used by
people who were hard of hearing in 1900, in
1960, and today. Over the years, how have
these devices changed or stayed the same?
See *ScienceSaurus®* for more information
about sound.

Sound Waves
and **Hearing**

ESSENTIAL QUESTION

What is sound?

By the end of this lesson, you should be able to describe what sound is, identify its properties, and explain how humans hear it.

Musical instruments produce sound by making vibrations.

S8P4.e Density of media and wave behavior

© Houghton Mifflin Harcourt Publishing Company • Image Credits: (bg) ©Tim Pannell/Corbis

Engage Your Brain

1 Predict Check T or F to show whether you think each sentence below about sound is correct.

T	F	
☐	☐	Sound reaches our ears as waves.
☐	☐	Loud sounds are not harmful to humans.
☐	☐	All animals hear the same range of frequencies.
☐	☐	Sound can travel in outer space.
☐	☐	Sound can travel in water.

2 Describe Why is this woman wearing ear protection? Write your answer in the form of a caption for this photograph.

_____

_____

_____

Active Reading

3 Apply Use context clues to write your own definition for the term *longitudinal wave*.

Example sentence:
The <u>longitudinal wave</u> traveled back and forth along the length of the coiled spring.

longitudinal wave:

_____

_____

_____

Vocabulary Terms
• sound wave   • loudness
• longitudinal wave   • decibel
• pitch   • Doppler effect

4 Identify As you read, create a reference card for each vocabulary term. On one side of the card, write the term and its meaning. On the other side, draw an image that illustrates or makes a connection to the term. Use your cards as bookmarks in the text so that you can refer to them while studying.

What is sound?

When you beat a drum, the drum skin vibrates and causes the air to vibrate, as shown below. A *vibration* is the complete back-and-forth motion of an object. The vibrations in the air are interpreted as sounds by your brain. No matter how different they are, all sounds are created by vibrations.

What are sound waves?

A **sound wave** is a longitudinal wave that is caused by vibrations and travels through a medium. In a **longitudinal wave** the particles of a medium vibrate in the same direction that the wave travels. Longitudinal waves, also called *compression waves,* are made of compressions and rarefactions (rair•uh•FAK•shuhns). A *compression* is the part of a longitudinal wave where particles are close together. A *rarefaction* is the part where particles are spread apart. As the wave passes through a medium, its particles are compressed together and then spread apart.

Active Reading

5 Identify As you read, underline the properties of longitudinal waves.

Visualize It!

6 Label Write labels for A and B on the sound wave in the diagram.

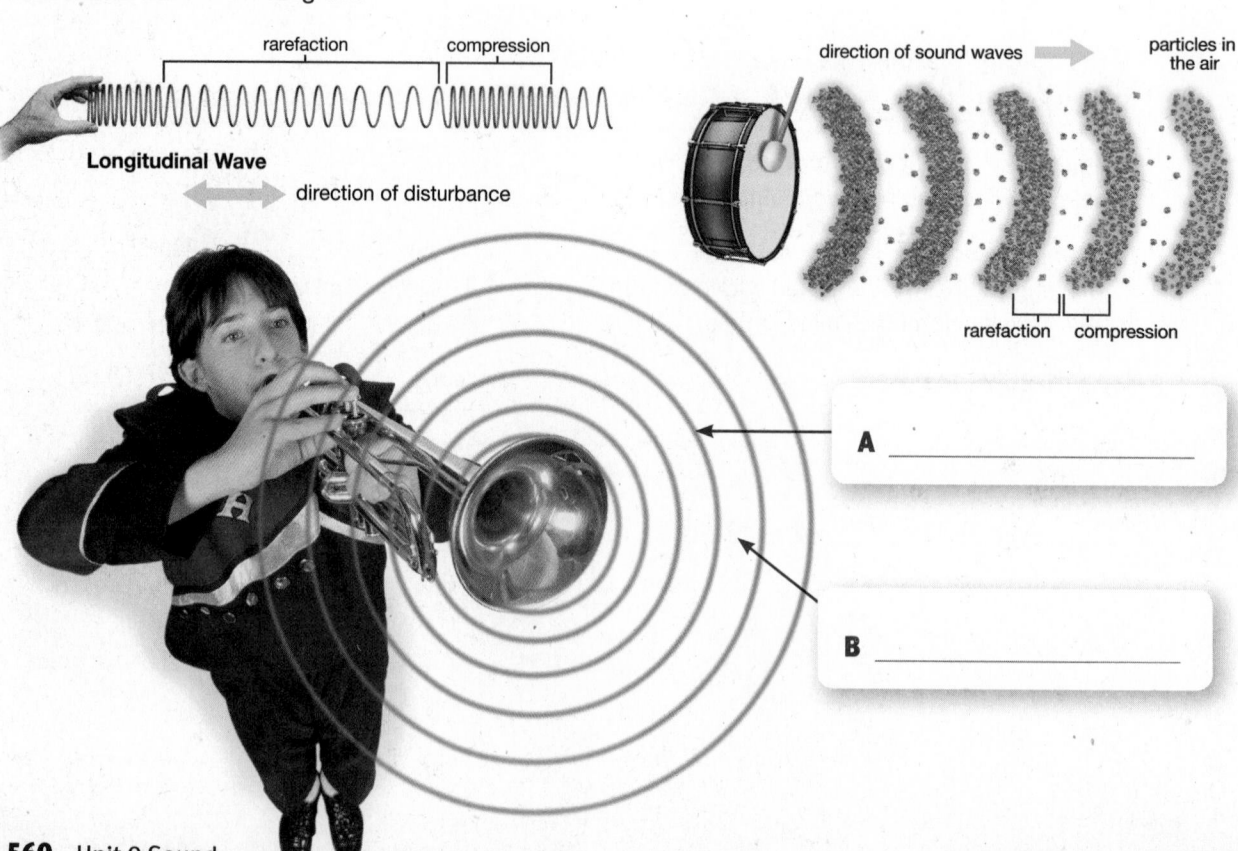

A _____

B _____

How do sound waves travel?

Sound waves travel in all directions away from their source, as shown in the photo of the student playing the trumpet. But this is only possible if there is a medium through which the sound waves can travel.

Through a Medium

All matter—solids, liquids, and gases—is composed of particles. Sound waves travel by disturbing the particles in matter, or a medium. The particles of the medium do not travel with the sound waves themselves. The particles of a medium only vibrate back and forth along the path that the sound wave travels.

Most of the sounds that you hear travel through air at least part of the time. Sound waves can also travel through other materials, such as water, glass, and metal. You have probably heard people talking or dogs barking on the other side of a window or door. When you swim underwater, you may hear the sounds of your swim buddies as they splash and call to each other above the surface.

In a vacuum, there are no particles to vibrate. Therefore, no sound can be made in a vacuum. This fact helps to explain the effect shown in the photograph below. Sound must travel through air or some other medium to reach your ears and be detected.

Active Reading 7 **Explain** Why can't sound travel through a vacuum?

_____

_____

_____

_____

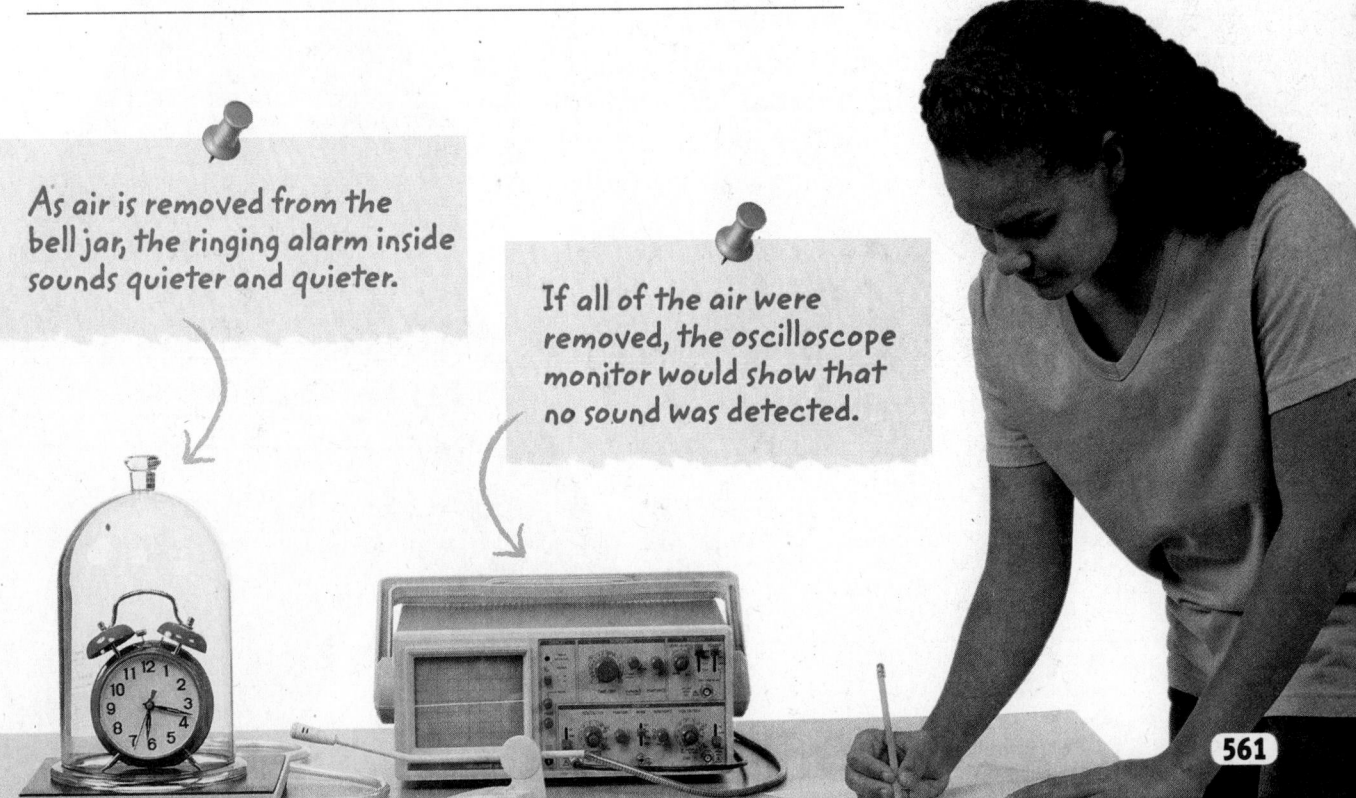

As air is removed from the bell jar, the ringing alarm inside sounds quieter and quieter.

If all of the air were removed, the oscilloscope monitor would show that no sound was detected.

Do You *Hear* That?

How do humans hear sound?

Humans detect sound with their ears. The ear acts like a funnel for sound waves. The ear directs sound vibrations from the environment into the inner ear, where the vibrations are converted to electrical signals. The electrical signals are sent to the brain, which interprets them as sound.

Humans Hear Sound Through Ears

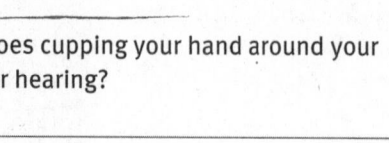 **Active Reading** **8 Match** As you read, match each paragraph to the numbered part of the ear illustration on the facing page.

_____ Sound from the environment enters the outer ear, travels through the ear canal, and reaches the eardrum. The eardrum is a thin membrane that is stretched tightly over the entrance to the middle ear. The compressions and rarefactions in the sound waves make the eardrum vibrate.

_____ The eardrum transfers the vibrations to three tiny, connected bones in the middle ear. These bones are called the hammer, anvil, and stirrup. The bones carry vibrations from the eardrum to the oval window, which is the entrance to the inner ear.

_____ The vibrations pass through the oval window and travel through the fluid in the snail-shaped cochlea (KAHK•lee•uh). The cochlea has thousands of nerve cells, and each nerve cell has thousands of tiny surface hairs. The vibrations of the sound waves cause the cochlea fluid to move. The movement of the fluid bends the tiny hairs. The bending hairs make the nerve cells send electrical signals to the brain through the auditory nerve. The brain receives these electrical signals; then it interprets them as the sound that you hear.

The ear is the organ that detects sound.

9 Analyze Why does cupping your hand around your ear improve your hearing?

_____

_____

_____

_____

The Human Ear

The human ear has many parts that all work together to capture and interpret sound waves.

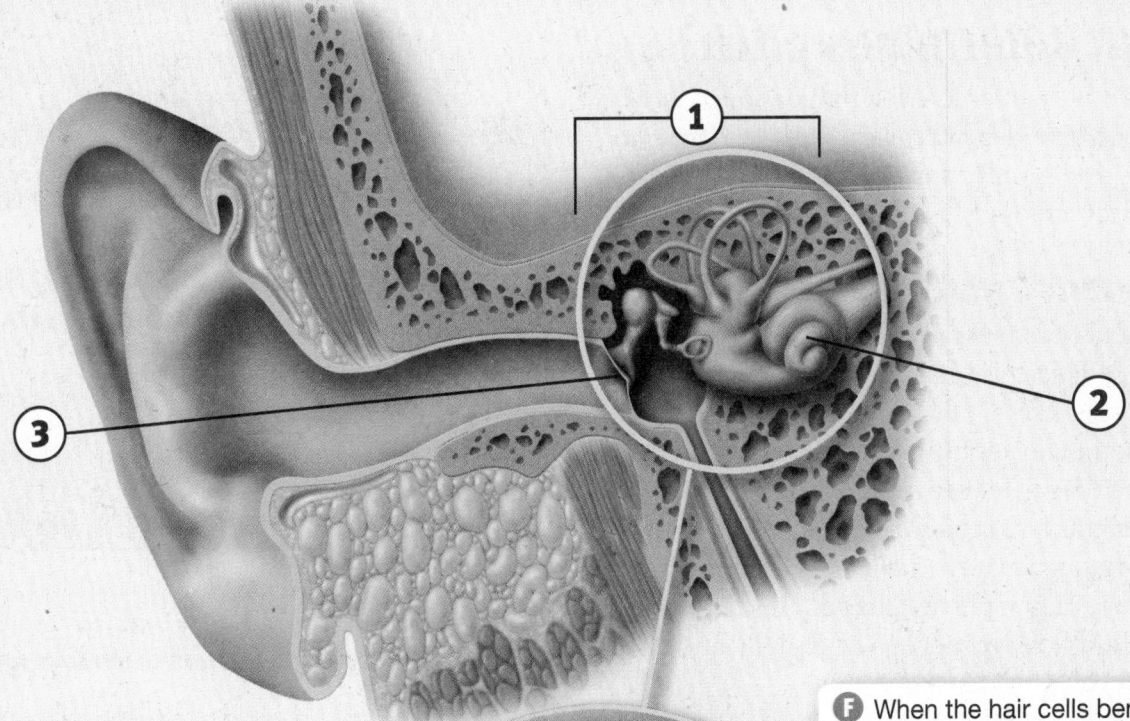

F When the hair cells bend, they stimulate the auditory nerve. The nerve sends electrical signals to the brain, which interprets them as the sounds we hear.

A Sound waves vibrate the eardrum—a tightly stretched membrane that forms the entrance to the middle ear.

E Movement of the liquid causes tiny hair cells inside the cochlea to bend.

B The eardrum vibrates, causing the hammer to vibrate. This in turn makes the anvil and the stirrup vibrate.

D The vibrations of the oval window create waves in the liquid inside the cochlea.

C The stirrup vibrates the oval window—the entrance to the inner ear.

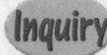 Inquiry

10 Predict If the nerve cells inside the cochlea were damaged, how might hearing be affected?

_____

_____

_____

Can You Hear Me NOW?

What determines pitch?

Pitch is how high or low you think a sound is. The pitch you hear depends on the ear's sensitivity to pitches over a wide range. Pitch depends on the frequency and wavelength of a sound wave.

Frequency and Wavelength

Frequency is expressed in hertz (Hz). One hertz is one complete wavelength, or cycle, per second. In a given medium, the higher the frequency of a wave, the shorter its wavelength and the higher its pitch. High-frequency waves have shorter wavelengths and produce high-pitched sounds. A low-frequency wave has a longer wavelength and makes a low-pitched sound. The diagrams at right show how frequency, wavelength, and pitch are related.

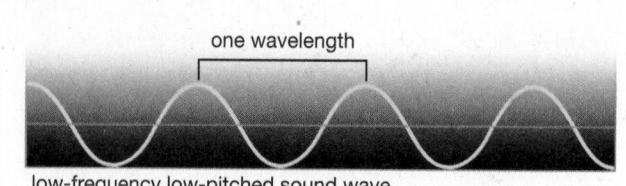

one wavelength

low-frequency low-pitched sound wave

A low-pitched sound has sound waves with a low frequency and a longer wavelength.

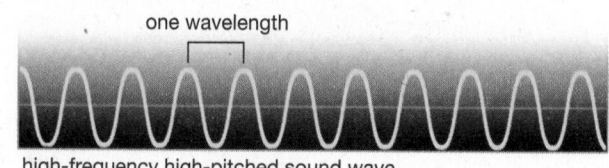

one wavelength

high-frequency high-pitched sound wave

A high-pitched sound has sound waves with a high frequency and a shorter wavelength.

Approximate Sound Frequencies Heard by Animals

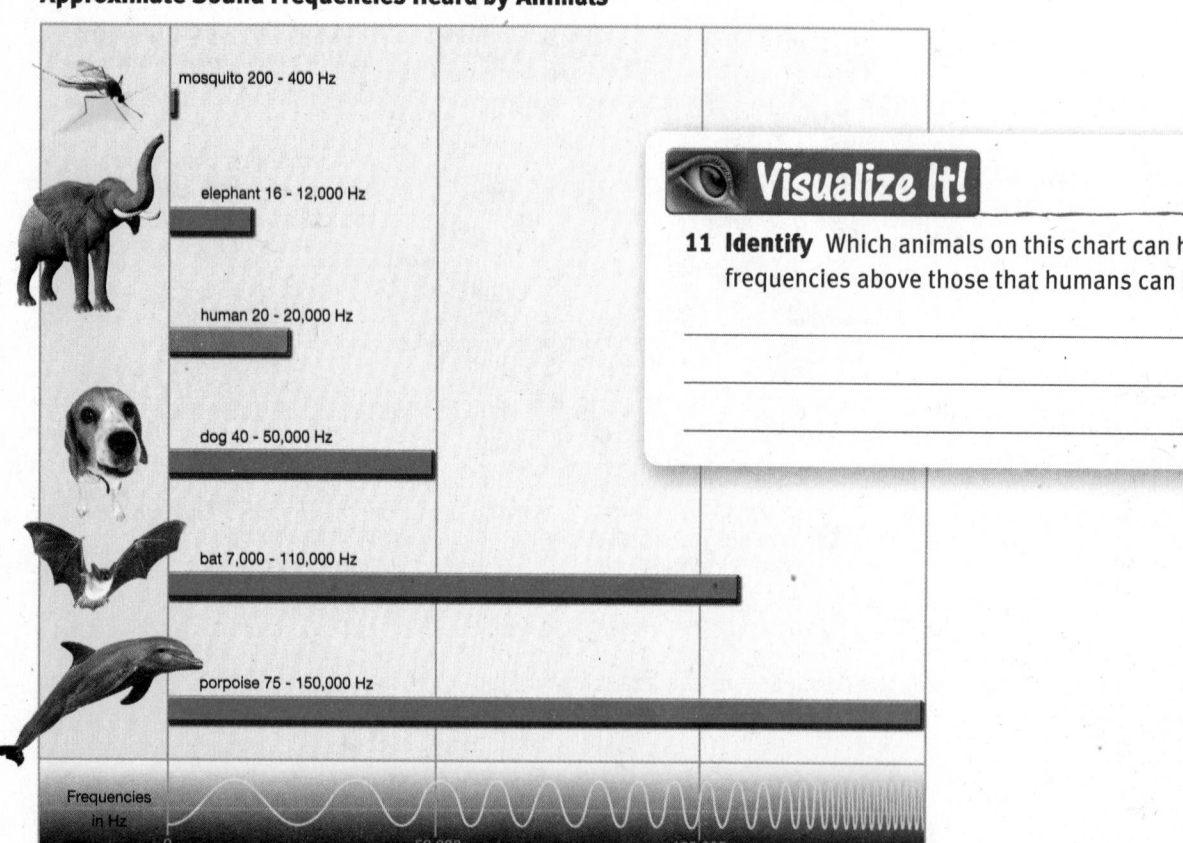

mosquito 200 - 400 Hz

elephant 16 - 12,000 Hz

human 20 - 20,000 Hz

dog 40 - 50,000 Hz

bat 7,000 - 110,000 Hz

porpoise 75 - 150,000 Hz

Frequencies in Hz

0   50,000   100,000

Visualize It!

11 Identify Which animals on this chart can hear frequencies above those that humans can hear?

_____

_____

_____

What makes a sound loud?

If you gently tap a drum, you will hear a soft rumbling. But if you strike the drum much harder, with more force, you will hear a much louder sound. By changing the force you use to strike the drum, you change the loudness of the sound it makes. **Loudness** is a measure of how well a sound can be heard.

Amplitude

The measure of how much energy a sound wave carries is the wave's intensity, or amplitude. The *amplitude* of a sound wave is the maximum distance that the particles of a wave's medium vibrate from their rest position. When you strike a drum harder, you increase the amplitude of the sound waves. The greater the amplitude, the louder the sound; the smaller the amplitude, the softer the sound.

One way to increase loudness is with an amplifier, as shown below. An amplifier receives sound signals in the form of electric current. The amplifier increases the sound wave's energy by increasing the wave's amplitude, which makes the sound louder.

Active Reading

12 Explain What is the relationship between amplitude and the loudness of a sound?

_____

_____

_____

An amplifier increases the amplitude of the sound produced by an electric guitar.

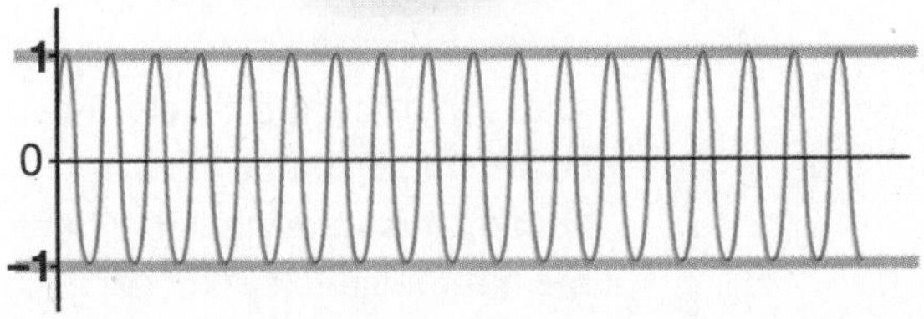

Softer sounds have smaller amplitudes. Observe that the amplitude is 0 to 1, or 0 to −1.

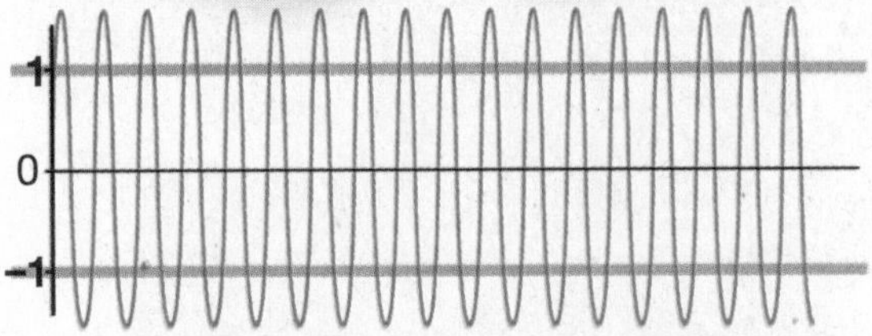

Louder sounds have larger amplitudes. How did the amplitude change? Did the frequency change?

Turn That DOWN!

How is loudness measured?

Loudness is a characteristic of sound that can be calculated from the intensity of a sound wave. The most common unit used to express loudness is the **decibel** (DES•uh•bel). One decibel (dB) is one-tenth of a *bel,* the base unit, although the bel is rarely used. The bel is named after Alexander Graham Bell, who is credited with inventing the telephone.

The softest sounds most humans can hear are at a level of 0 dB. Sounds that are 120 dB or higher can be painful. The table below shows some common sounds and their decibel levels.

How loud is too loud?

Short exposures to sounds that are loud enough to be painful can cause hearing loss. Even loud sounds that are not painful can damage your hearing if you are exposed to them for long periods. Loud sounds can damage the hairs on the nerve cells in the cochlea. Once these hairs are damaged, they do not grow back.

There are simple ways to protect your hearing. Use earplugs to block loud sounds. Lower the volume when using earbuds, and move away from a speaker that is playing loud music. If you double the distance between yourself and a loud sound, you can reduce the sound's intensity by as much as one-fourth of what it was.

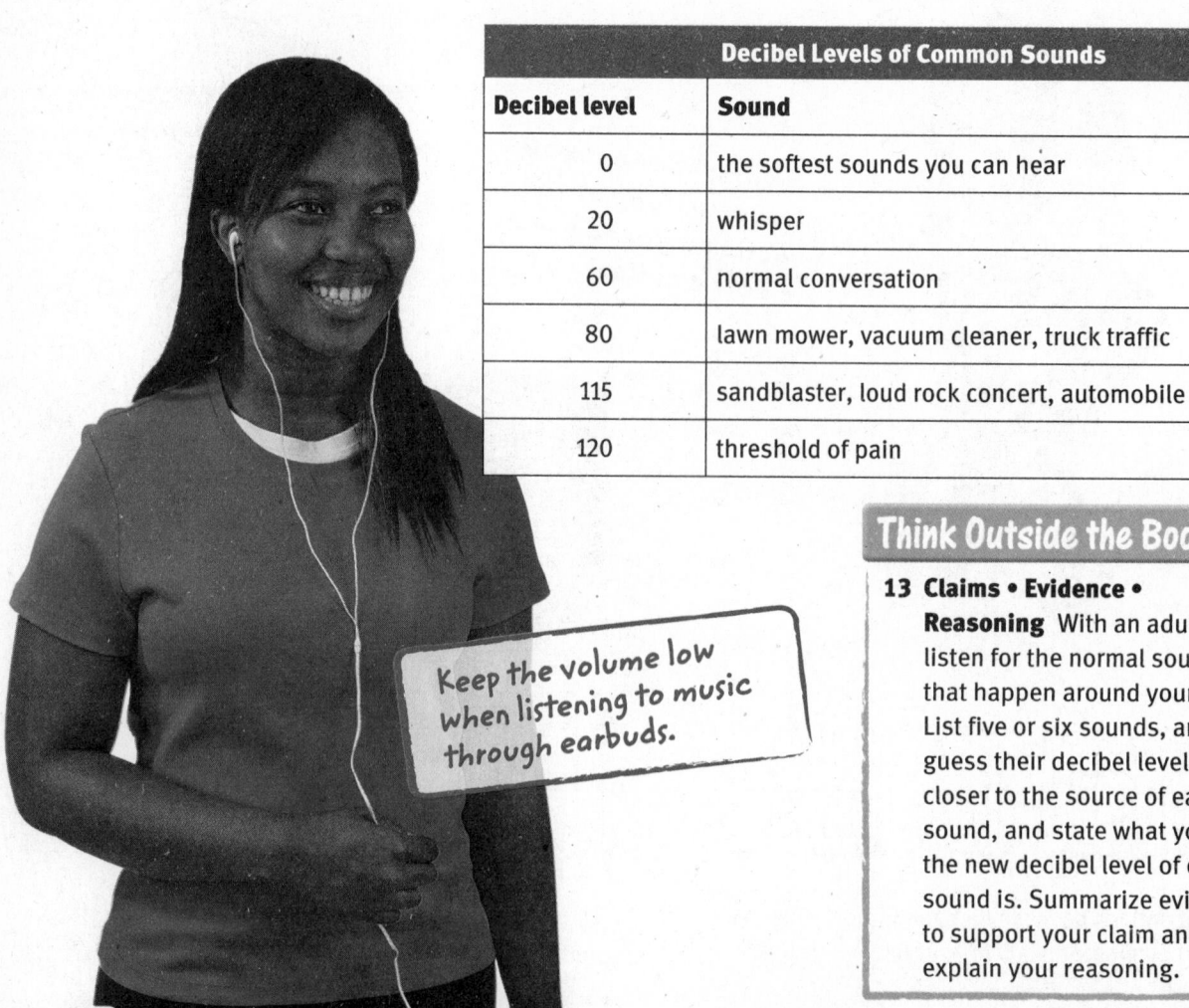

Decibel Levels of Common Sounds	
Decibel level	**Sound**
0	the softest sounds you can hear
20	whisper
60	normal conversation
80	lawn mower, vacuum cleaner, truck traffic
115	sandblaster, loud rock concert, automobile horn
120	threshold of pain

Keep the volume low when listening to music through earbuds.

Think Outside the Book

13 Claims • Evidence • Reasoning With an adult, listen for the normal sounds that happen around your home. List five or six sounds, and guess their decibel levels. Move closer to the source of each sound, and state what you think the new decibel level of each sound is. Summarize evidence to support your claim and explain your reasoning.

What is the Doppler effect?

Have you ever been stopped at a railroad crossing when a train with its whistle blowing went past? You probably noticed the sudden change in the pitch of the whistle as the train passed. This change in pitch is called the Doppler effect (DAHP•ler ih•FEKT). The **Doppler effect** is a change in the observed frequency of a wave when the sound source, the observer, or both are moving.

As shown in the diagram below, when you and the source of the sound are moving closer together, the sound waves are closer together. The sound has a higher frequency and a higher pitch. When you and the source are moving away from each other, the waves are farther apart. The sound has a lower frequency and a lower pitch.

Active Reading

14 Identify As you read, underline the main points that explain the Doppler effect.

Visualize It!

15 Label In the diagram below, consider the sound waves heard by the people as the train passes them. Label the sound wave that has a higher pitch and the sound wave that has a lower pitch.

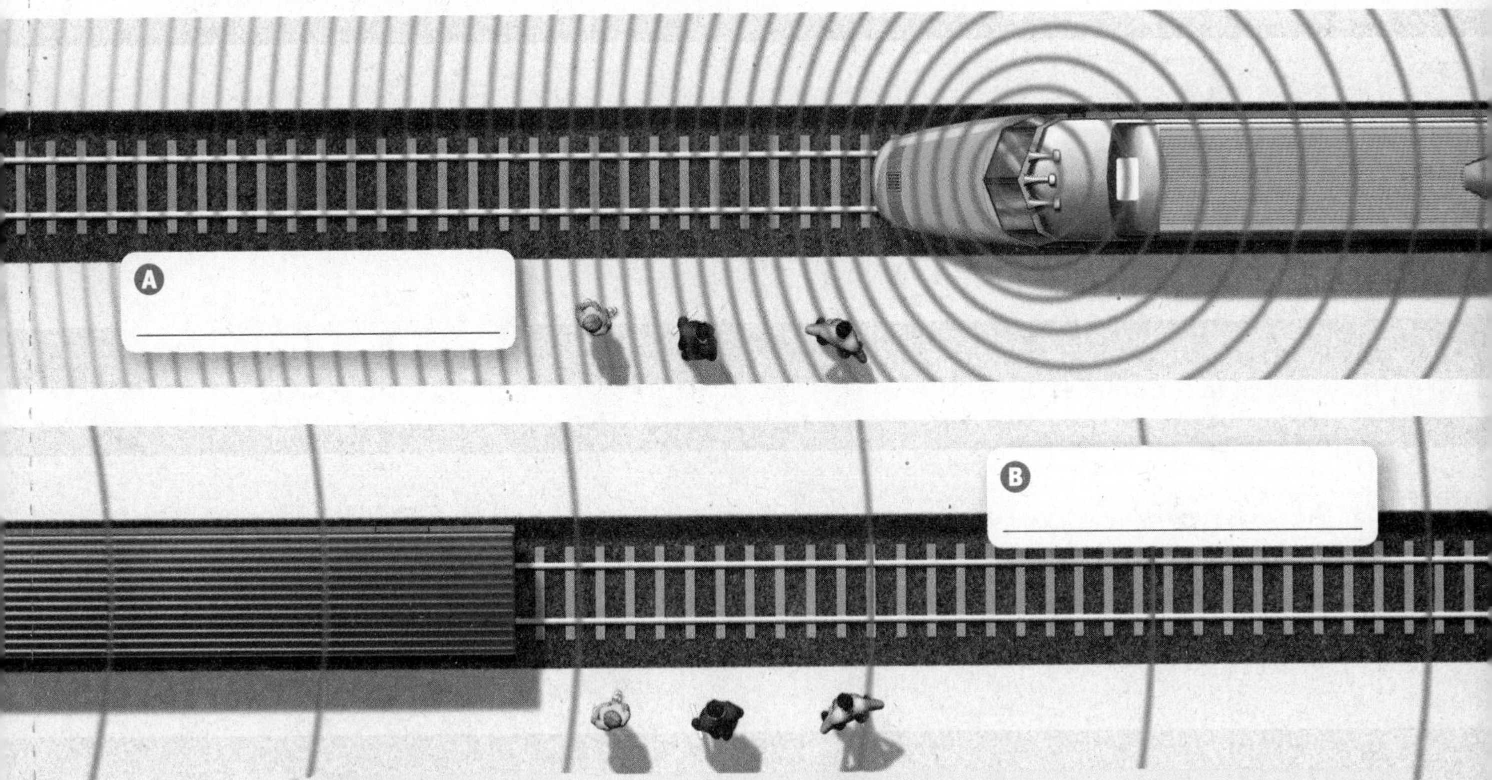

A

B

Inquiry

16 Infer Do you think the Doppler effect occurs only with sound waves? Explain why or why not.

_____

_____

_____

Visual Summary

To complete this summary, fill in the blanks with the correct word or phrase. Then, use the key below to check your answers. You can use this page to review the main concepts of the lesson.

Sound waves are longitudinal waves that cause particles to vibrate.

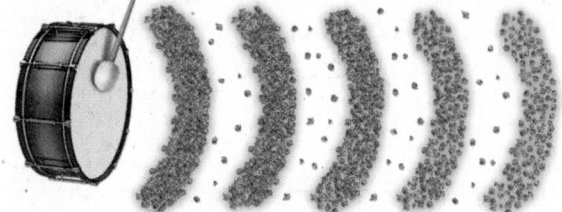

17 Sound waves must travel through a _____

The Doppler effect is the change in pitch you hear when the source of a wave, the observer, or both are moving.

18 As a train approaches, the pitch of its whistle sounds _____

Sound Waves and Hearing

Human ears hear sound when vibrations of sound waves are transmitted to the brain as electrical signals.

19 The surface of the nerve cells in the cochlea contain thousands of _____

Pitch is how high or low a sound is, while amplitude determines loudness.

20 As the amplitude of a sound increases, the sound becomes _____

Answers: 17 medium; 18 higher; 19 tiny hair cells; 20 louder

21 Design Develop a simple demonstration using a coiled spring to model the following wave properties: longitudinal vibration, compression, and rarefaction.

Lesson Review

Vocabulary

Define Fill in the blank with the term that best completes the following sentences.

1 A _____ is an example of a longitudinal wave.

2 _____ is how high or low you think a sound is.

3 Loudness is expressed in _____

Key Concepts

4 Explain Describe the properties of a longitudinal wave.

_____

_____

_____

_____

5 Sequence Describe how the human ear hears sound.

_____

_____

_____

_____

_____

6 Explain How are frequency, wavelength and pitch related? Explain your reasoning.

_____

_____

_____

_____

7 Summarize How does amplitude determine loudness?

_____

_____

_____

_____

Critical Thinking

Use the illustration to answer the following questions.

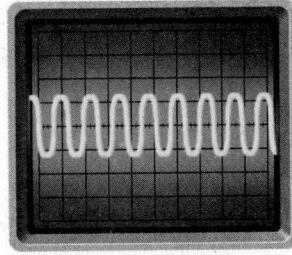 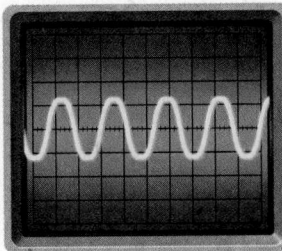

8 Analyze The screens show two sound waves that last the same amount of time. Which wave has a higher frequency? Explain your answer.

_____

_____

_____

_____

9 Analyze Suppose these waves represent the sound of a siren on a passing ambulance. Which wave represents the sound of the siren *after* it has passed you? Explain your answer.

_____

_____

_____

_____

_____

10 Analyze If a meteorite crashed onto the moon, would you be able hear it on Earth? Why or why not? Explain your reasoning.

_____

_____

_____

_____

11 Apply Is it safe to listen to music at a level of 115 decibels? Explain why or why not.

_____

_____

_____

_____

My Notes

Interactions of Sound Waves

ESSENTIAL QUESTION

How do sound waves travel and interact?

By the end of this lesson, you should be able to describe how sound waves interact in many different ways.

S8P4.d Behavior of light and sound waves

S8P4.e Density of media and wave behavior

Bats are one type of animal that uses sound waves to avoid obstacles and to find food.

Lesson Labs

Quick Labs
• Resonance in a Bottle
• The Speed of Sound

S.T.E.M. Lab
• Echoes

Engage Your Brain

1 Predict Check T or F to show whether you think each statement is true or false.

T	F	
☐	☐	Humans can hear sounds at any frequency.
☐	☐	Sound waves can combine to become bigger or smaller.
☐	☐	It is possible to break a crystal glass by singing a certain note.
☐	☐	It is possible to travel faster than the speed of sound.

2 Draw A person standing on the edge of a canyon can make an echo by calling into the canyon. Draw how you think the sound waves travel to make the echo. Use arrows to represent the direction of the sound waves.

Active Reading

3 Synthesize You can often determine the meaning of a term when you have heard some of the words in a different context. Draw a line from the terms on the left to their description on the right.

• constructive interference   • causes sound waves to get smaller

• destructive interference   • causes sound waves to get larger

Vocabulary Terms

• echo   • diffraction
• interference   • resonance

4 Apply As you learn the definition of each vocabulary term in this lesson, create your own definition or sketch to help you remember the meaning of the term.

Some Like It Hot

What affects the speed of sound?

Have you ever seen a flash of lightning, and then heard the sound of thunder a few seconds later? That happens because sound travels more slowly than light. Two main factors affect the speed of sound: the type of medium that the sound travels through, and the temperature of the medium. If we know these factors, we can predict the speed of sound.

Medium

The speed of sound depends on the type of matter, or medium, through which the sound wave travels. When you swim or bathe, you can hear sounds in more than one medium—air and water. The state of matter affects the speed of sound as well. In general, sound travels fastest through solids, slower through liquids, and slowest through gases. Sound travels fastest through solids because solids are denser than liquids or gases. That means that the particles are packed closer together in solids. A sound wave makes the particles of matter move as it travels along, so the wave is fastest when particles are close together.

Active Reading

5 Explain How does the state of matter affect the speed of sound?

_____

_____

_____

Visualize It!

6 Identify Through what medium shown below does sound travel fastest? _____

Slowest? _____

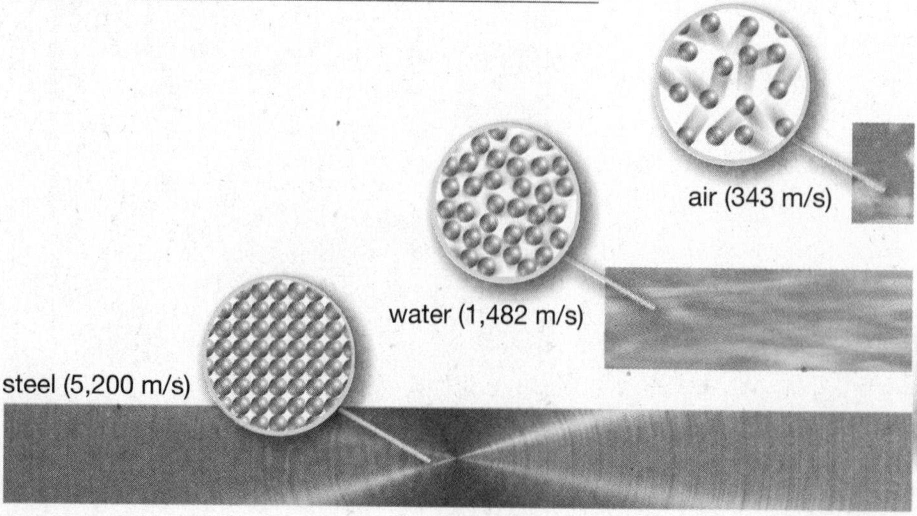

air (343 m/s)

water (1,482 m/s)

steel (5,200 m/s)

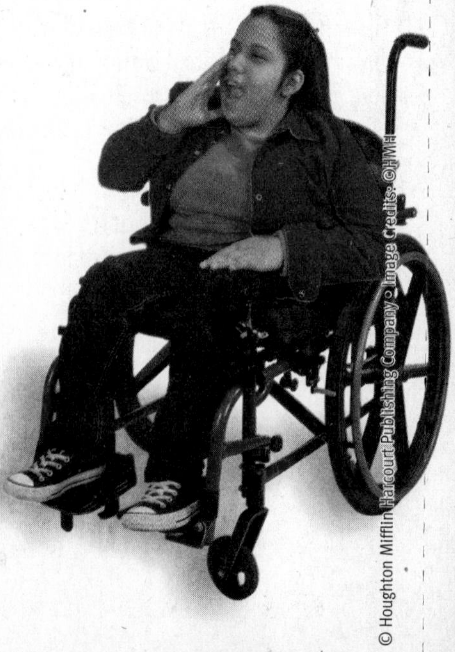

Temperature

The speed of sound also depends on the temperature of a medium. Sound in a medium travels faster at higher temperatures than at lower ones. Consider air, which is a mixture of gases. Particles in a gas are not held together as tightly as particles in a solid are. Instead, the gas particles bounce all around. The higher the temperature, the faster the gas particles move about. Particles of a material move more quickly and transfer energy faster at higher temperatures than at lower temperatures. Therefore, sound travels faster through hot air than through cold air.

Do the Math

Sample Problem

Sound travels at 343 m/s through air at a temperature of 20 °C. How far will sound travel through 20 °C air in 5 s?

$$343 \ m/1 \ s = X \ m/5 \ s$$
$$343 \ m \times 5 = X \ m$$
$$X \ m = 1,715 \ m$$

You Try It

7 Calculate The speed of sound in steel at 20 °C is 5,200 m/s. How far can sound travel in 5 s through steel at 20 °C?

8 Apply Who will hear the sound of an approaching boat first: this diver or his friends above the water? Why?

_____

_____

_____

Speed of Sound in Different Media and Temperatures	
Medium	**Speed (m/s)**
Air (0 °C)	331
Air (20 °C)	343
Air (100 °C)	366
Water (20 °C)	1,482
Steel (20 °C)	5,200

Hello? Hello? Hello?

How do sound and matter interact?

Sound waves do not travel easily through all matter. When a sound wave runs into a barrier, some of the sound waves may bounce away from the front surface of the barrier, and some of the sound waves may be absorbed or transmitted through the barrier.

Matter Can Reflect Sound Waves

Sound waves, like all waves, can reflect off matter. Reflection is the bouncing back of a wave when the wave hits a barrier. The strength of a reflected sound wave depends on the reflecting surface. Sound waves reflect best off smooth, hard surfaces. A sound in a bare room can be loud because the sound waves are reflected off the walls, the floor, and the ceiling. If furniture, drapes, and carpet are added to the room, the same sound is much softer.

Matter Can Absorb Sound Waves

Some types of matter absorb sound waves much better than others. A rough wall will absorb sound better than a smooth wall will. And soft materials absorb sound better than hard materials do. If your school has a music room, it probably has sound-absorbing features, such as carpet and soft, rough acoustic tiles on walls and ceilings. These features help keep the music from being heard throughout the school.

Active Reading

9 Identify As you read, underline features that reflect or absorb sound.

Visualize It!

10 Identify Which features in this room reflect sound waves? Explain your reasoning.

_____

_____

_____

_____

_____

_____

The surfaces in room A interact differently with sound waves than do the surfaces in room B.

Painted ceilings

Hardwood floors

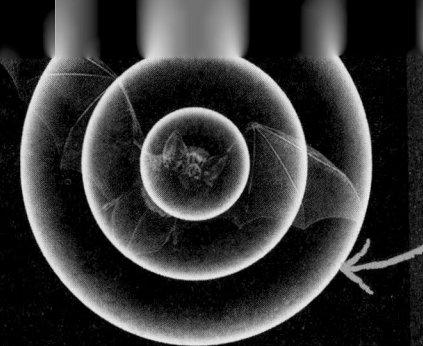

① The sound waves that bats emit while flying are at a higher frequency than humans can hear.

Bats use echoes to navigate.

② The sound waves meet an object and reflect back to the bat. The time it takes these echoes to reach the bat tells it how far the object is.

What is an echo?

Matter that absorbs sound waves will reduce echoes. An **echo** is a reflected sound wave. The strength of a reflecting sound wave depends on the reflecting surface. Echoes can be reduced by the presence of soft materials and rough or irregular surfaces. Rough surfaces reduce echoes by scattering sound waves.

Some animals—such as dolphins, bats, and beluga whales—use echoes to hunt food and to find objects in their paths. The use of reflected sound waves to find objects is called *echolocation*. The illustrations on this page show how echolocation works. Animals that use echolocation can tell how far away something is based on how long it takes sound waves to echo back to the animal.

One example of echolocation technology used by people is sonar (**s**ound **n**avigation **a**nd **r**anging). *Sonar* is a type of electronic echolocation that uses echoes to locate objects underwater.

③ The bat can determine the direction an insect is flying in because the frequency of the echo changes as the insect moves.

Active Reading 11 **Describe** How do some animals use echoes?

_____

_____

Ⓑ

Fabric curtains

Acoustic tiles

12 Describe Explain how the features in this room help reduce echoes.

_____

_____

_____

_____

_____

_____

Interference Patterns

How do sound waves interact with each other?

Sound waves interact through interference. **Interference** happens when two or more waves overlap and combine to form one wave. In music, *beats* happen when two sound waves of nearly equal frequencies interfere. Since the wave frequencies are not quite equal, they form a repeating pattern of constructive and destructive interference that sounds alternately loud and soft.

Active Reading **13 Identify** As you read, underline the main characteristics of constructive interference and destructive interference.

Through Constructive Interference

When *constructive interference* occurs, waves overlap and combine to form a wave with a larger amplitude, or height. The greater amplitude causes the waves to produce a sound that is louder than before. Constructive interference can cause very loud sounds, such as sonic booms.

Through Destructive Interference

In *destructive interference*, waves combine to form a wave with a smaller amplitude. The sound will be softer because the amplitude is decreased. Some noise-canceling headphones use destructive interference. Electronics in the headphones create new sound waves that interfere with outside sounds, so the headphone wearer does not hear them.

When two speakers produce sound at the same frequency, the sound waves combine by both constructive and destructive interference.

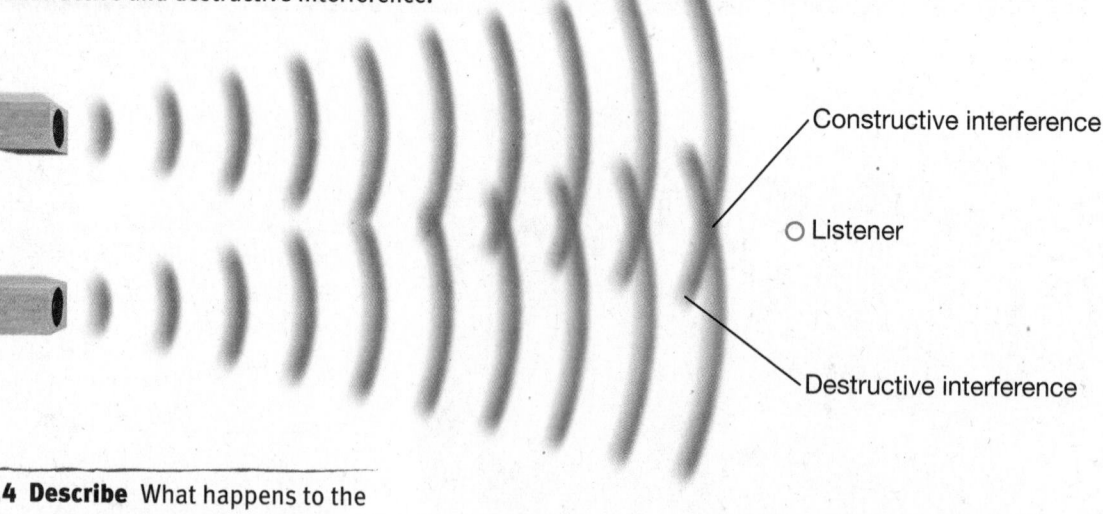

Constructive interference

○ Listener

Destructive interference

14 Describe What happens to the wave amplitude when there is constructive interference? What happens when destructive interference occurs?

_____

_____

_____

_____

© Houghton Mifflin Harcourt Publishing Company • Image Credits: (bg) ©Navy News/PhotoReuters9/Corbis

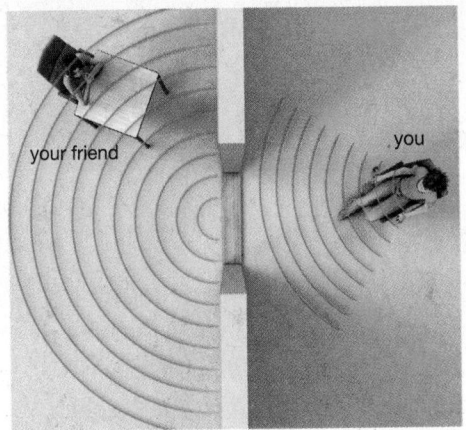

What is diffraction?

Suppose two people are in adjacent rooms. A door between the rooms is open, but neither person is near the door. If one person shouts, will the other hear? The answer has to do with **diffraction**. Diffraction is how a wave changes when it interacts with an obstacle or an opening.

If a wave hits an object it cannot pass through, it bends to move around the object. Similarly, if a wave approaches a small opening, it changes shape to pass through it. When you shout to someone in the next room, the sound wave changes shape as it passes through an opening, such as a door. The person will have a better chance of hearing you if your voice is low in pitch. That's because lower frequency sound waves diffract more efficiently than higher frequency sound waves.

Notice how this wave changes shape as it encounters an obstacle.

Visualize It!

15 Identify Like sound waves, ocean waves can also be diffracted when they encounter an obstacle, such as this seawall. Label the original waves and the object causing the diffraction. Then describe how the obstacle has changed the shape of the waves.

_____

_____

_____

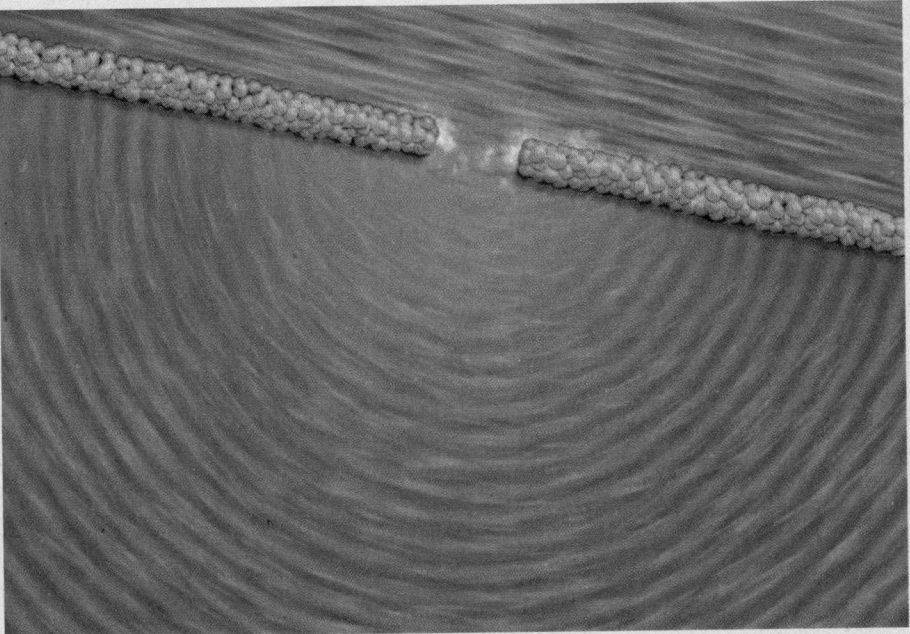

Good Vibrations

![Active Reading]

16 Identify As you read, underline the main characteristics of resonance.

A vibrating tuning fork can cause another object to start vibrating if the fork and the object share the same resonant frequency.

What is resonance?

Have you ever held a seashell to your ear and listened to the "ocean"? What you actually are hearing is resonance. **Resonance** happens when a sound wave matches the natural frequency of an object and causes the object to vibrate. The air in the seashell vibrates at certain frequencies because of the shape of the shell. If a sound wave in the room forces air in the seashell to vibrate at its natural frequency, resonance occurs. This resonance results in a big vibration that sounds like the ocean when you hear it.

Where can resonance occur?

All objects have a frequency, or set of frequencies, at which they vibrate. These are called *natural frequencies,* or *resonant* frequencies. Resonance will happen wherever an object vibrating at or near the natural frequency of a second object causes the second object to vibrate. When an opera singer sings a note that breaks a crystal glass, resonance occurred in the crystal. When you feel the bass of loud music, resonance is happening in your body.

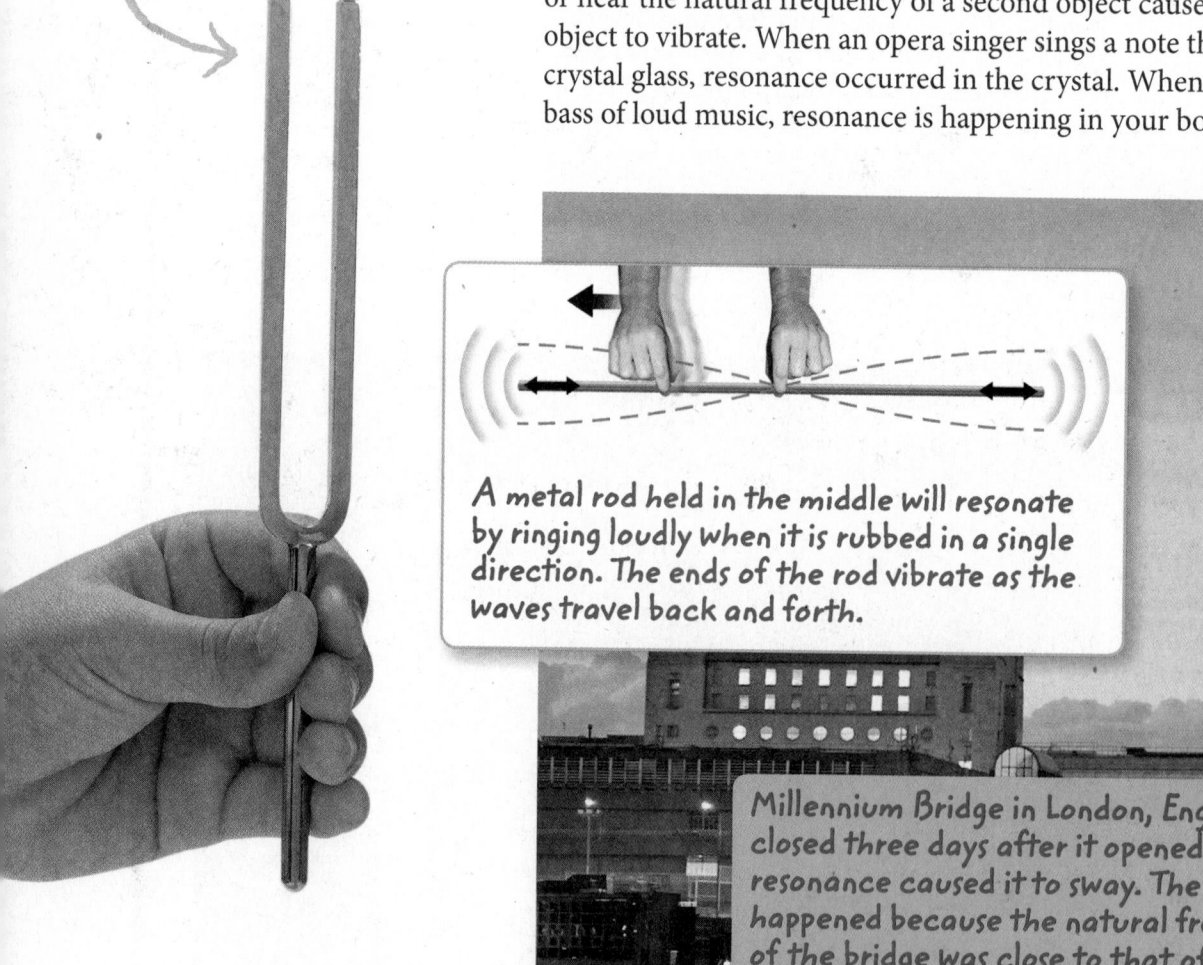

A metal rod held in the middle will resonate by ringing loudly when it is rubbed in a single direction. The ends of the rod vibrate as the waves travel back and forth.

Millennium Bridge in London, England, was closed three days after it opened because resonance caused it to sway. The resonance happened because the natural frequency of the bridge was close to that of human footsteps walking across it.

In Musical Instruments

Active Reading **17 Identify** As you read, underline how resonance occurs in wind instruments.

Resonance is important for making music. In wind instruments, blowing air into the mouthpiece causes vibrations. The vibrations make a sound that gets louder when it forms a standing wave inside the instrument. A *standing wave* is a pattern of vibration that looks like a wave that is standing still. Resonance occurs when standing waves are formed. Waves and reflected waves of the same frequency go back and forth in standing waves inside the instrument.

String instruments also resonate when played. An acoustic guitar has a hollow body. When the strings make a standing wave, the sound waves enter the body of the guitar. Standing waves also form inside the body, and the sound becomes louder.

In Bridges

Resonance can even occur in buildings, towers, and bridges. Because resonance could cause a structure to collapse, engineers plan their designs carefully. For example, some bridges are built in sections with overlapping plates. When the plates move together, they create friction. This friction can change the frequency from one plate to another and keep the resonant wave from becoming destructive. Even simple human activity can create resonance on bridges. For example, rhythmic marching can create resonance and cause a bridge to sway or even collapse. That's why troops always stop marching before crossing a bridge.

This musician creates music by making standing waves on the strings of her cello.

Think Outside the Book Inquiry

18 Apply To better understand how marching can resonate with bridges, form a line with your classmates and march in time around your classroom. As you march, try to be aware of the vibrations and resonance of the classroom floor. Then repeat, but "break step"—march out of time. Do the floor and other objects respond the way they did in the first trial?

Visual Summary

To complete this summary, fill in the word to finish each sentence. Then, use the key below to check your answers. You can use this page to review the main concepts of the lesson.

Interactions of Sound Waves

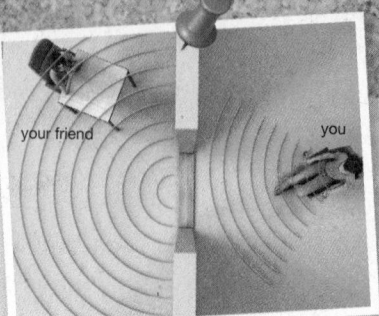
your friend | you

The speed of sound depends on the medium it travels through and on the temperature of the medium.

19 Sound waves travel _____ in solids than in liquids.

Sound waves bend when they encounter an obstacle.

20 _____ occurs when sound waves bend as they pass through an opening in a barrier.

Some surfaces reflect sound waves, while other surfaces absorb sound waves.

21 Sound waves reflect better off _____ surfaces.

Resonance occurs when the frequency of a sound wave matches the natural frequency of an object and makes the object vibrate.

22 Resonance happens when two objects vibrate at _____ frequency.

Answers: 19 faster; 20 Diffraction; 21 hard; 22 the same

23 Summarize What are the results of the two ways that sound waves can interact with each other?

Lesson Review

Vocabulary

Fill in the blank with the term that best completes the following sentence.

1 _____ is the combination of two or more waves, which results in a single wave.

2 _____ happens when a sound wave causes an object to vibrate.

3 A(n) _____ is a reflected sound wave.

Key Concepts

4 Identify How does the state of matter affect the speed of a sound wave traveling through it?

_____

_____

_____

5 Describe How could you reduce the echoes in a music studio? Explain your reasoning.

_____

_____

_____

_____

6 Explain Describe how waves change when they meet an object.

_____

_____

_____

_____

7 Summarize In your own words, explain how resonance occurs when you play a horn.

_____

_____

_____

_____

Critical Thinking

Use this table to answer the following questions.

Speed of Sound in Some Materials	
Material	**Speed of sound (m/s)**
air	330
water	1,480
brain	1,540
blood	1,570

8 Analyze Ultrasound uses high-frequency sound waves to get images of the insides of our bodies. Sound waves would travel the fastest through which of the materials listed in the chart?

_____

9 Infer What two types of matter are closest in density? How do you know?

_____

_____

_____

10 Claims • Evidence • Reasoning Ultrasound waves do not transmit easily through bone. State what you think happens to ultrasound waves when they reach a bone in the body. Give evidence to support your claim and explain your answer.

_____

_____

_____

_____

_____

_____

My Notes

Developing and Using a Model

Scientists often use models to visualize and test different scenarios. In this activity, you will review the basic behaviors of sound waves and then design a model of a room with five speakers in it. You will use your model to predict the behavior of the sound waves coming from the speakers.

Tutorial

The text below describes the basic concepts of the behavior of sound, including reflection, absorption, interference, and diffraction. Consider these concepts as you design your model room.

Reflection Reflection occurs when waves bounce off a barrier, such as a wall. An echo is a reflected sound wave. Smooth, hard surfaces cause the most reflection. Furniture, drapes, and carpet help reduce reflection.

Absorption Absorption occurs when a wave encounters a material that takes the wave in and absorbs the wave's energy. The wave does not reflect off the surface. Soft, rough materials tend to absorb sound.

Interference Interference occurs when waves overlap and combine. Constructive interference forms a larger wave. This produces a louder sound. Destructive interference forms a smaller wave. This produces a quieter sound.

Diffraction Diffraction occurs when a wave encounters an obstacle or an opening. The wave bends or changes to move around the obstacle or through the opening. Low frequency sound waves diffract more efficiently than high frequency waves. As a result, low pitched sounds can be heard better than high pitched sounds.

You Try It!

In the space below, use what you know about sound to design a room with optimal sound quality. In your room, draw five speakers and at least three pieces of furniture. Position the objects strategically. Identify any modifications to surfaces in the room (for example, wall coverings or drapes) to improve sound quality.

1 Making Observations Draw sound waves coming from each speaker to model interactions of sound. Show how the sound waves interact. Label any examples of reflection, absorption, interference, or diffraction.

2 Explain How did the materials you chose affect the behavior of the sounds?

_____

_____

_____

_____

3 Applying Concepts What kinds of interactions reduce sound quality? How did your design limit these kinds of interactions?

_____

_____

_____

4 Assess What were the strengths and weaknesses of your model? What might you change to make this model more useful?

_____

_____

_____

_____

_____

_____

Take It Home

Do you have any kind of sound system in your home? Locate the speakers and analyze the objects in the room. List some ideas for improving the sound quality in the room.

© Houghton Mifflin Harcourt Publishing Company

Lesson 3

Sound Technology

ESSENTIAL QUESTION

How does sound technology work?

By the end of this lesson, you should be able to describe how sound technology is used to extend human senses.

Many radio programs are recorded so that you can listen to them whenever you want.

© Houghton Mifflin Harcourt Publishing Company • Image Credits: ©Zhu Difeng/Shutterstock

Engage Your Brain

1 Predict Check T or F to show whether you think each statement is true or false.

T   F

☐   ☐ Some animals use sound to find food.

☐   ☐ Reflected sound waves can be used to make images.

☐   ☐ Sound waves are sent from one telephone to another telephone.

☐   ☐ Computers can save and store sound waves.

2 Describe List three devices that produce sound waves that you use in your everyday life. Describe how your life would be different without these devices.

_____

_____

_____

_____

_____

_____

_____

Active Reading

3 Synthesize You can often define an unknown word if you know the meaning of its word parts. Use the word part and sentence below to make an educated guess about the meaning of the word *ultrasound*.

Word Part	Meaning
ultra-	beyond

Example sentence
Humans cannot hear <u>ultrasound</u> waves.

ultrasound:

_____

_____

Vocabulary Terms
- echolocation
- sonar
- ultrasound

4 Apply As you learn the definition of each vocabulary term in this lesson, create your own definition or sketch to help you remember the meaning of the term.

Hello Hello Hello

How are echoes used?

You would have difficulty using your sense of hearing to find objects around you. But some animals find food and other objects using *echolocation*. **Echolocation** is the use of echoes, or reflected sound waves to find objects. Animals that use echolocation produce **ultrasound**, which are sound waves that have frequencies greater than 20,000 Hz. The frequencies of these ultrasonic sound waves are too high for humans to hear. But, animals that use echolocation can tell how far away an object is by the time it takes for their ultrasonic waves to bounce off an object and return to them, or *echo*. For example, the dolphin shown below can tell how far away the fish is by sensing the echoes that bounce off of the fish. It takes more time for ultrasonic sound waves to reach and return from objects that are farther away.

Active Reading **5 Explain** What are ultrasonic waves?

_____

_____

 **Visualize It!**

6 Illustrate Draw the sound waves that are reflected from the fish.

7 Analyze Will the echo from the fish or from the boat reach the dolphin first?

_____

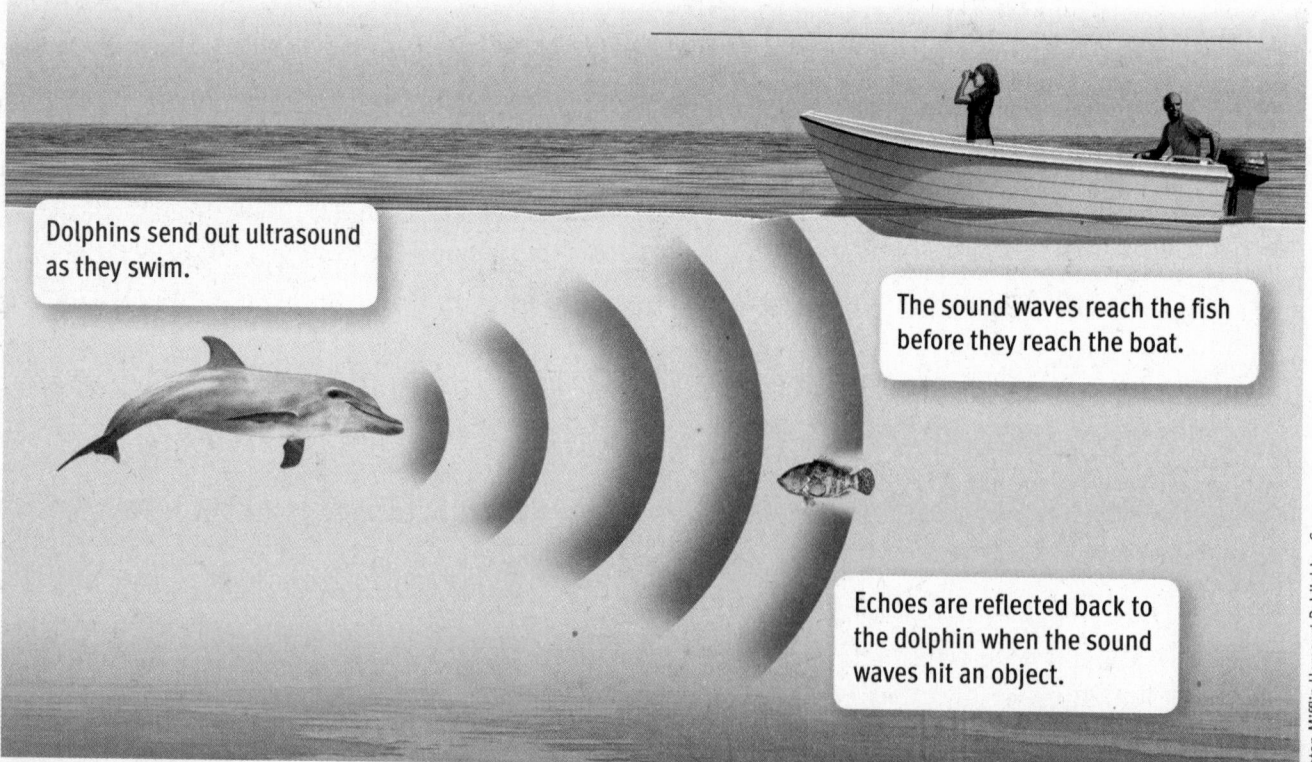

Dolphins send out ultrasound as they swim.

The sound waves reach the fish before they reach the boat.

Echoes are reflected back to the dolphin when the sound waves hit an object.

To Locate Objects

You may not be able to send out or hear ultrasonic waves, but people can use echolocation through various technologies. **Sonar** is a system that uses sound waves to determine the location of objects or to communicate. Visually impaired people can use sonar technology to navigate. Sonar is also used to find shipwrecks, to avoid icebergs, to find fish, and to map the ocean floor as shown in this diagram. An instrument on the boat sends out ultrasonic waves. Then it detects any echoes, or reflected sound waves. The short wavelengths of ultrasonic waves provide more information about objects than the longer wavelengths of sound do.

Emitted Sound Waves

Reflected sound waves are used to map the ocean floor. The red areas are closer to the ship. The blue areas are farther away.

A *more time / less time*

8 Label Circle the correct phrase in each box on the map to show where the reflected sound waves will take more time to return to the ship and where they will take less time to return to the ship.

Reflected Sound Waves

B *more time / less time*

To Make Ultrasound Images

Echoes are used in medicine, too. Ultrasound procedures use ultrasonic sound waves to produce images of the inside of a person's body. Ultrasound that has a frequency of 1 million to 10 million hertz can pass safely into a patient's body. These sound waves reflect when they meet the patient's internal organs. The echoes are detected and used to make images of organs, such as the heart and bladder. Ultrasonic waves do not damage human cells like x-rays can. Ultrasound procedures do not harm fetuses. So ultrasound is often used to check how a fetus is growing inside the mother's body. Health professionals can use ultrasound images to determine the age and sex of a fetus and to diagnose certain disorders.

This ultrasound image shows a 20-week-old fetus.

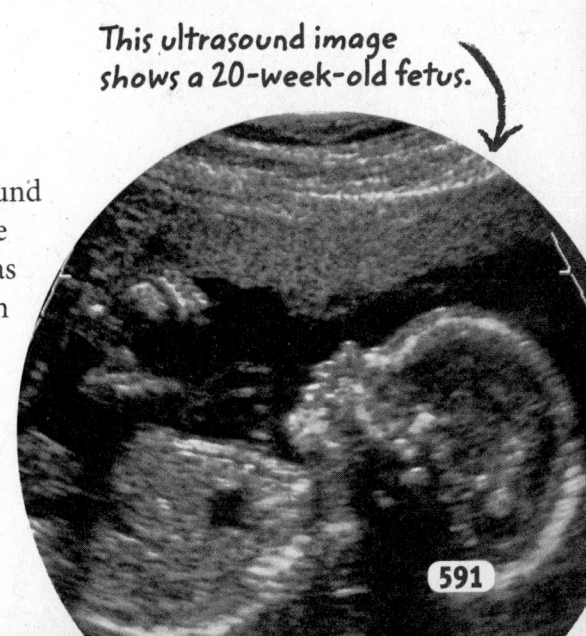

How do telephones transmit sound?

Sound waves lose energy over time. The sound waves of your voice will not reach a friend who is far away. But, you can use a telephone to talk to your friend. Phones change sound waves into other types of signals that can be sent over long distances. Phones also change the signals they receive back into sound waves that you can hear.

All telephones change sound waves into electrical signals. However, electrical signals cannot travel through air. So, in the case of cordless phones, the handset and the base change electrical signals into radio waves that they transmit to each other. These radio waves travel at the speed of light. The base then changes the radio waves back to electrical signals that are sent through wires. A computer sends these signals to the phone of the other caller, where they are changed back into sound waves.

📖 **Active Reading**

9 Identify As you read, underline the types of signals sound waves are changed into by telephones.

The **microphone** in the mouthpiece changes the sound waves from your voice into electrical signals. These electrical signals are then changed into radio waves that are sent to the phone base.

The **earpiece** turns electrical signals into sound waves. The sound you hear is very similar to the sound that was spoken into the phone of the other caller.

The **phone base** receives radio signals from the handset. It changes them into electrical signals. It also receives incoming electrical signals from the wall outlet, which it changes into radio waves that are sent to the handset.

Radio waves

Phone wires send electrical signals outside of the house to a switching station that connects callers. Incoming signals also travel along the wires to the base.

Think Outside the Book Inquiry

10 Apply Create a short cartoon with captions that shows the changes the sound waves go through during a telephone call.

Hello, Operator

For most of human history, people had no way of sending their voices farther than they could shout. The invention of the telephone in 1876 made long-distance communication possible. How has telephone technology changed since then?

Manual Switching
People used to have to call telephone operators whenever they wanted to make a call. The operator plugged wires into a switchboard to connect one phone to another. The switchboard allowed many phone calls to be connected at one time.

Dialing Around
The invention of the rotary dial phone made it possible for people to call a number directly. Human operators were replaced by automated switching centers.

Cell Phones
Modern cell phones use radio waves to send signals. The signals are sent to cell phone towers, which transfer the signals to underground phone cables. Cell phones can also send images and text.

Extend

Inquiry

11 Infer What was a main advantage of a dial phone over an operator-controlled switchboard?

12 Research Make a timeline that shows the following major inventions related to telephones: the telephone, the telephone switching center, the rotary phone, the push-button phone, and the mobile phone. Include pictures and an interesting detail about each invention in your timeline.

13 Compose Write a short paragraph describing how you use telephones in your everyday life. Include one way you would improve your phone.

Groovy

How is sound recorded and played back?

Once sound waves lose their energy, they are gone forever. People make recordings to preserve sound information, such as interviews and music. Thomas Edison invented the phonograph, which could record and play back sound. Later, information in sound was recorded in the grooves of records. Today, most sound recordings are stored on compact discs or in computer files.

On Compact Discs

A compact disc, or CD, is made of hard plastic. The information in sound waves is stored by pressing microscopic pits into the plastic. The pits and lands, which are the spaces between the pits, form a spiral pattern on the CD. This pattern stores digital signals as 1s and 0s that are used to recreate sound waves.

A CD player uses light to read the information stored on the CD. The plastic layer of a CD is coated with a thin layer of shiny aluminum. The light from a laser reflects off the shiny surface as the CD rotates. The pattern on the CD surface produces a pattern of light and dark reflected light. The detector changes this pattern into an electrical signal. The CD player then changes the electrical signal back into sound waves.

Music can be stored in the grooves of records.

Visualize It!

This image shows the pattern on the surface of a CD. Different patterns produce different sounds. CD players use reflected light to read the pattern on CDs.

15 Analyze Suppose the pattern near the arrow represents part of a word of an audio book. How do you think the pattern will appear on the CD the next time that word is repeated? Explain your reasoning.

_____

_____

_____

_____

Compact disc

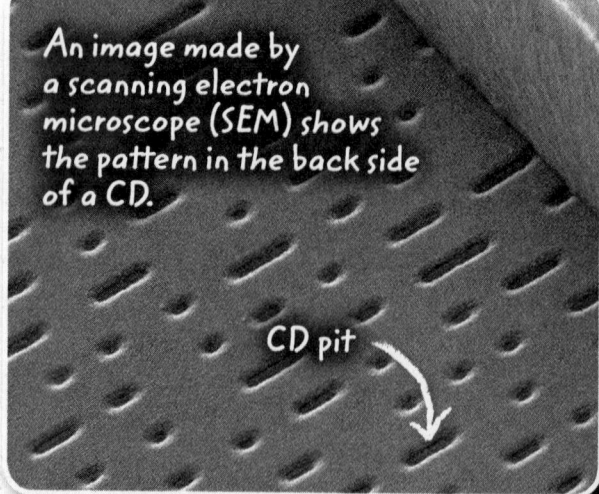

An image made by a scanning electron microscope (SEM) shows the pattern in the back side of a CD.

CD pit

In Computers

Sound can also be stored as digital files in a computer. Digital sound files, such as MP3 files, can store a large amount of sound information. To record sound as a computer file, the original sound is first changed into an electrical signal. Then it is stored as a digital file on the computer hard drive. The digital file is a series of 1s and 0s, similar to the pattern stored on a CD.

Software reads the digital files and produces an electrical signal that is sent to the speakers. The speakers change the signal back into sound waves. Personal MP3 players store and play back sound files in a similar way as larger computers do. But they make it very easy to carry a lot of recordings with you. You would need several CDs to store the hundreds of songs that can be stored in a tiny MP3 player.

Sound is stored in digital files in computers.

16 Summarize Complete the following process chart to show how sound waves can be digitally recorded and played back.

| Original sound waves are played. | → | | → | | → | Sound waves come out of speaker. |

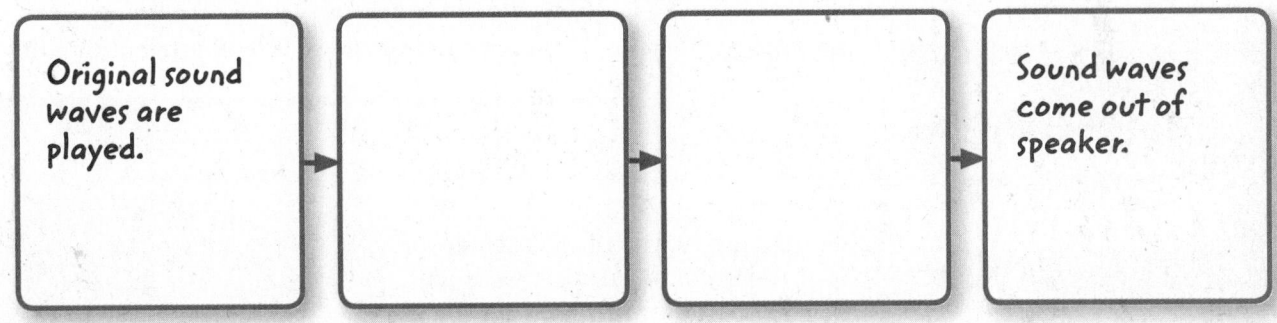

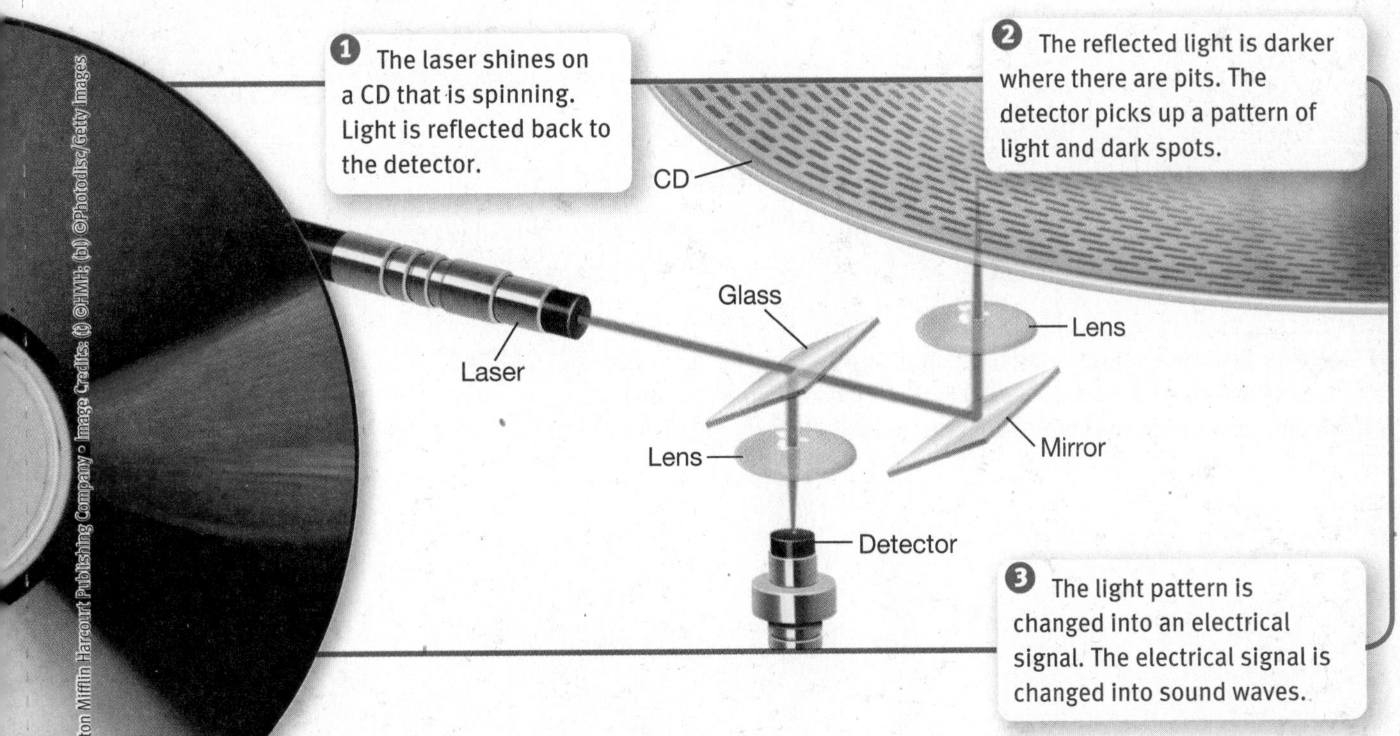

❶ The laser shines on a CD that is spinning. Light is reflected back to the detector.

❷ The reflected light is darker where there are pits. The detector picks up a pattern of light and dark spots.

❸ The light pattern is changed into an electrical signal. The electrical signal is changed into sound waves.

CD

Glass

Lens

Laser

Mirror

Lens

Detector

Visual Summary

To complete this summary, circle the correct word or phrase. Then, use the key below to check your answers. You can use this page to review the main concepts of the lesson.

Echolocation is the use of ultrasound to locate objects.

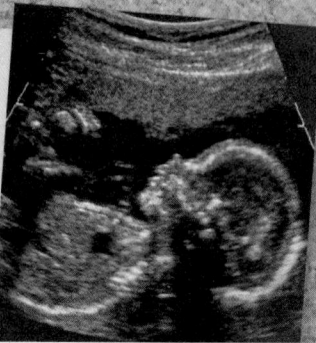

17 A fetus can be viewed using an infrasound / ultrasound procedure.

18 Sonar / Laser light is used to locate objects underwater.

Telephones change sound waves into electrical signals and electrical signals back into sound waves.

19 A cordless phone sends sound / radio waves between the handset and the base.

20 A telephone's earpiece / microphone changes sound waves into electrical signals.

Sound Technology

Sound information is stored digitally on compact discs and in computer files.

21 The information on a CD is stored in a pattern of pits and lands / light waves.

22 Software in a digital music player changes music files into electrical signals / radio waves.

Answers: 17 ultrasound; 18 Sonar; 19 radio; 20 microphone; 21 pits and lands; 22 electrical signals

23 **Claims • Evidence • Reasoning** Explain the way energy in sound waves changes when you and your friend talk on cordless phones. Summarize evidence to support your explanation.

Lesson Review

Vocabulary

In your own words, define the following terms.

1 echolocation

_____

_____

2 ultrasound

_____

_____

3 sonar

_____

_____

Key Concepts

4 Identify Which device can store sound information?

A CD player

B telephone wires

C microphone

D computer

5 Describe How does a telephone handset change the incoming signals from a caller into sound that you can hear?

_____

_____

_____

6 Infer Why do people use echolocation technology to locate objects?

_____

_____

_____

7 Explain Why are sound recordings needed to preserve sound information? Explain your reasoning.

_____

_____

_____

Critical Thinking

8 Explain Describe what happens inside a CD player when you listen to an audio CD.

_____

_____

_____

_____

9 Apply Explain how a doctor can use ultrasound to look at a patient's kidneys.

_____

_____

_____

_____

Use this drawing to answer the following questions.

10 Describe How is sound technology being used by the people in the boat?

_____

_____

11 Analyze Why are the sound waves in the drawing shown to be reflecting from the larger fish but not from the smaller fish under the boat?

_____

_____

_____

My Notes

Unit 9 [Big Idea] Sound waves transfer energy through vibrations.

Lesson 1
ESSENTIAL QUESTION
What is sound?

Describe what sound is, identify its properties, and explain how humans hear it.

Lesson 2
ESSENTIAL QUESTION
How do sound waves travel and interact?

Describe how sound waves interact, and how they can cause echoes and sonic booms.

Lesson 3
ESSENTIAL QUESTION
How does sound technology work?

Describe how sound technology is used to extend human senses.

Connect ESSENTIAL QUESTIONS
Lessons 1 and 2

1 **Synthesize** If you bounce a basketball in an empty gym, you will hear it echo. Describe the path that the sound wave travels from the basketball to your eardrum.

_____

_____

_____

_____

Think Outside the Book

2 **Synthesize** Choose one of these activities to help synthesize what you have learned in this unit.

☐ Using what you learned in lessons 2 and 3, create a brochure to sell a sound absorbing material, explaining why recording studios need this material for the walls and ceiling. Use illustrations with captions and labels.

☐ Using what you learned in lessons 1 and 3, make a poster to explain why communicating in space is a challenge, and show how space scientists have met this challenge.

Name _____

Vocabulary

Check the box to show whether each statement is true or false.

T	F	
☐	☐	**1** A Sound wave is a <u>longitudinal wave</u> that is caused by vibrations in a medium.
☐	☐	**2** <u>Decibels</u> are units that measure the pitch of a sound.
☐	☐	**3** An <u>echo</u> is a sound wave that is absorbed by a soft material.
☐	☐	**4** <u>Interference</u> occurs when two or more waves overlap and combine to form one wave.
☐	☐	**5** <u>Ultrasound</u> technology is used to create medical images and it is based on sound waves with frequencies so high that human ears cannot hear them.

Key Concepts

Read each question below, and circle the best answer.

6 Which statement best describes how humans hear sound?

A Sound waves enter the ear canal and increase in amplitude, which causes you to hear the sound.

B Sound waves cause parts of the ear to vibrate until the waves are converted to electrical signals, which are sent to the brain.

C Sound waves travel into people's ears, and the eardrum sends the sound waves to the brain.

D Sound waves become sounds when they strike the eardrum inside the ear.

7 When Consuelo struck a tuning fork and held it close to a string on a guitar, the string began to vibrate on its own and make a sound. Which statement best explains why the string vibrated without anyone touching it?

A The string vibrated because of destructive inference between its sound waves and those of the tuning fork.

B The tuning fork produced ultrasonic frequencies beyond human hearing.

C The tuning fork and the guitar string both created mechanical waves.

D The string vibrated because of resonance, which happened because the tuning fork and guitar string have the same natural frequency.

8 The diagram below shows a sound wave traveling through a medium.

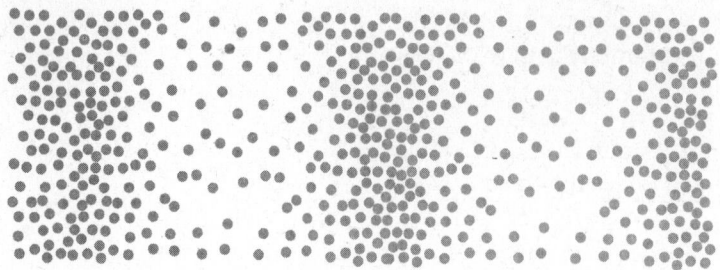

Which statement best describes how the sound wave is moving through a medium?

A The sound wave is creating tensions and accumulations in the medium.

B The sound wave is creating an echo inside the medium.

C The sound wave is creating compressions and rarefactions in the medium.

D The sound wave is creating a mechanical wave in the medium.

9 Which material best absorbs sound waves in a room?

A heavy curtains

B hardwood floors

C brick walls

D cement floors

10 Yorgos drew a diagram of a wave and labeled its parts, as shown below.

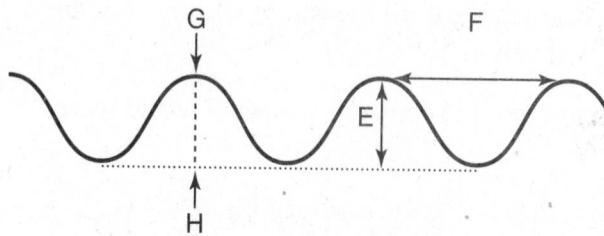

Wavelength is typically measured between the crests to two successive waves. Which labels represent a crest and a wavelength?

A G points to a crest; F is a wavelength

B G points to a crest; E is a wavelength

C H points to a crest; E is a wavelength

D H points to a crest; F is a wavelength

11 Which of the following is not a way in which echolocation is used?

A flying bats avoiding trees and houses at night

B sending messages over telephone lines

C dolphins finding fish in deep water

D mapping the ocean floor

12 Josh observed a bolt of lightning during a thunderstorm. It took more than 15 seconds for Josh to hear the sound of thunder. Why did Josh see the lightning strike before he heard the thunder?

A Thunder always takes 15 seconds to travel through the air after lightning strikes.

B Light waves from the lightning and sound waves from the thunder moved through different media.

C Light waves are electromagnetic waves that travel much faster than mechanical waves, such as the sound waves he heard as thunder.

D The conditions in the air at the time allowed light waves to move faster than the sound waves he heard as thunder.

13 The diagram below shows the distribution of particles in two different kinds of media.

Liquid

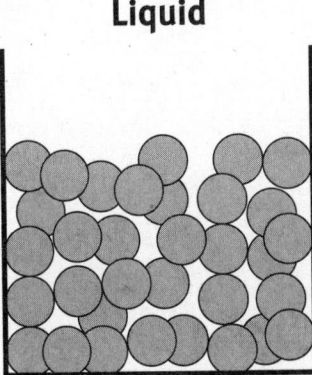

Gas

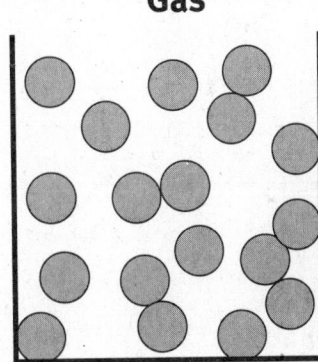

Which statement best compares how sound waves travel through the media shown above?

A Sound waves travel at the same speed through both of the media shown.

B Sound waves move faster through the liquid medium on the left than the gaseous medium on the right.

C Sound waves move faster through the gaseous medium on the right than the liquid medium on the left.

D Sound waves cannot travel through either medium that is shown above.

Critical Thinking

Answer the following questions in the space provided.

14 Describe where the cochlea is located, what parts it contains, and explain the role these parts play in human hearing.

_____

_____

_____

15 Suppose you are at a train station. What changes would you hear in the sound of the whistle as a train comes toward you and then moves away? What causes the changes, and what is this effect called?

_____

_____

_____

_____

Connect ESSENTIAL QUESTIONS

Lesson 2

16 Describe several ways that sound waves interact with each other and with objects. How might you use this information to design a music room in your school? Your goal is to keep the sound within the room so you do not disturb other classrooms.

_____

_____

_____

_____

_____

UNIT 10
Light

What do you think?

We can use large radio telescopes to collect radio waves from space. Other telescopes use mirrors to gather light waves. How can we use different parts of the electromagnetic spectrum to learn about space? As you explore the unit, find evidence to help you state and support your claim.

Unit 10
Light

Looking Into Space

The first telescopes were refracting telescopes, which used a pair of lenses to gather light. Today, astronomers also use reflecting telescopes, which gather light with large mirrors, to observe distant objects.

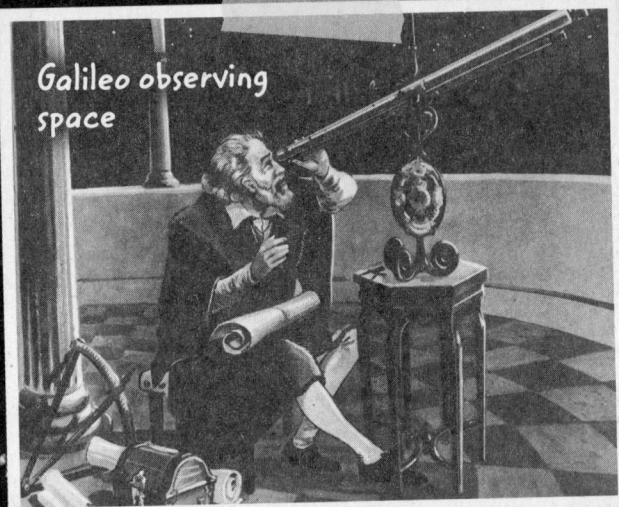

Galileo observing space

1609
Galileo Galilei used a refracting telescope to observe phases of Venus, the moons of Jupiter, the surface of the moon, sunspots, and a supernova.

List other tools that use lenses and think of a use for each one.

_____
_____
_____
_____
_____

Telescope similar to Isaac Newton's

Skylab image of the sun

1973
Telescopes that operate from space, like the sun-observing telescope that was aboard Skylab, can see all kinds of things we can't see from Earth.

1668
Isaac Newton built a reflecting telescope that used a curved mirror to gather light. Newton's mirror did not split light into colors as did the lenses in early refracting telescopes.

Hubble Space Telescope

1990
The orbiting Hubble Space Telescope can capture detailed images of objects very far from Earth. The Hubble Space Telescope has taken images of the most distant galaxies astronomers have ever seen.

Take It Home } Eyes to the Sky

Use a pair of binoculars or a telescope to look at the night sky. Compare what you can see with magnification to what you can see when looking at the same part of the sky without magnification. Draw or write your observations in the chart. See **ScienceSaurus**® for more information about astronomy.

Unmagnified Night Sky	Magnified Night Sky

Lesson 1

The Electromagnetic Spectrum

ESSENTIAL QUESTION

What is the relationship between various EM waves?

By the end of this lesson, you should be able to distinguish between the parts of the electromagnetic spectrum.

S8P4.b The electromagnetic spectrum and energy

S8P4.c Applications of the electromagnetic spectrum

S8P4.d Behavior of light and sound waves

S8P4.f Properties of waves and energy

This iron glows with EM radiation that we normally can't see. The brighter areas represent hotter parts of the iron.

Engage Your Brain

1 Select Circle the word or phrase that best completes each of the following sentences:

Radio stations transmit (*radio waves/gamma rays*).

The dentist uses (*infrared light/x-rays*) to examine your teeth.

Intense (*visible light/ultraviolet light*) from the sun can damage your skin.

2 Predict Imagine that humans had not realized there are other parts of the electromagnetic spectrum besides visible light. How would your day today be different without technology based on other parts of the EM spectrum?

_____

_____

_____

_____

_____

_____

Active Reading

3 Synthesize You can often define an unknown word if you know the meaning of its word parts. Use this table of word parts to make an educated guess about the meanings given.

Word part	Meaning
ultra-	beyond
infra-	below
electro-	related to electricty
-magnetic	related to magnetism

What word means "beyond violet"?

_____

What word means "below red"?

_____

What word means "related to electricity and magnetism"?

_____

Vocabulary Terms

- radiation
- electromagnetic spectrum
- infrared
- ultraviolet

4 Apply As you learn the definition of each vocabulary term in this lesson, think of an example of a real-world use. Practice writing the term and its definition, and then writing or drawing a sketch of the example next to the definition.

Electromagnetic Light Show

What is the nature of light?

Light is a type of energy that travels as waves, but light waves are not disturbances in a medium. Light waves are disturbances in electric and magnetic fields. If you have felt the static cling of fabric and the pull of a magnet, then you have experienced electric and magnetic fields. Because these fields can exist in empty space, light does not need a medium in which to travel.

When an electrically charged particle vibrates, it disturbs the electric and magnetic fields around it. These disturbances, called electromagnetic (EM) waves, carry energy away from the charged particle. The disturbances are perpendicular to each other and to the direction the wave travels. **Radiation** (ray•dee•AY•shuhn) is the transfer of energy as EM waves.

In a vacuum, all EM waves move at the same speed: 300,000,000 m/s, called the speed of light. That's fast enough to circle Earth more than seven times in one second!

Although light and other EM waves do not need a medium, they can travel through many materials. EM waves travel more slowly in a medium such as air or glass than in a vacuum.

Active Reading

5 Identify Underline what produces EM waves.

6 Synthesize Why do we see lightning before we hear the accompanying thunder?

_____

_____

_____

_____

Visualize It!

7 Label Mark and label the wavelength and amplitude of the disturbances in the fields.

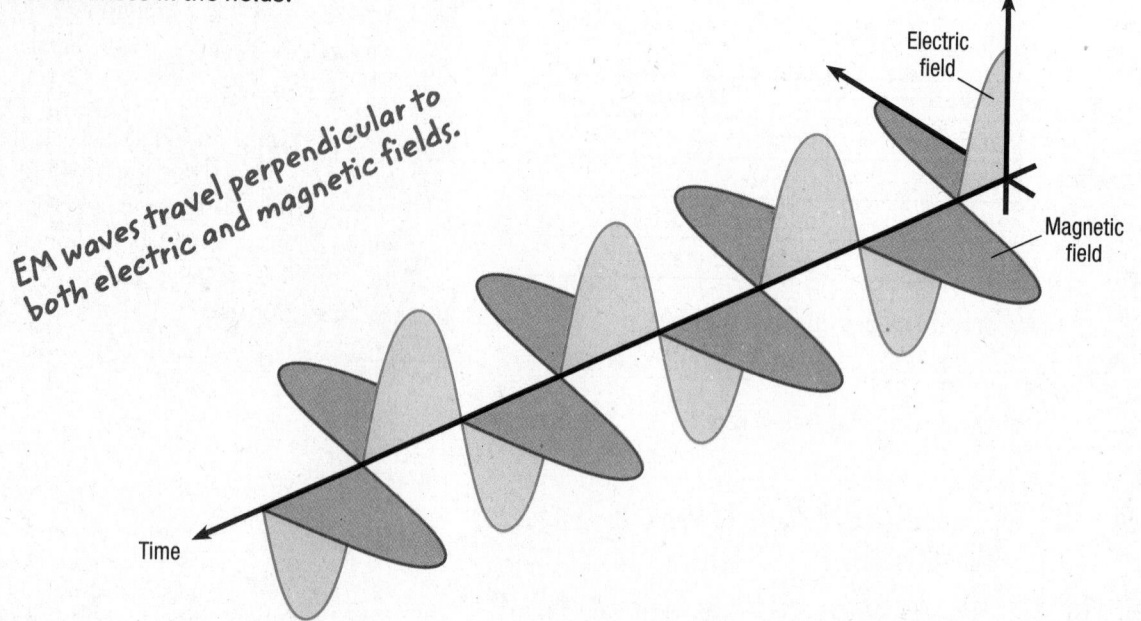

EM waves travel perpendicular to both electric and magnetic fields.

Electric field

Magnetic field

Time

The color with the shortest wavelengths is violet. Violet light has the highest frequencies.

The color with the longest wavelengths is red. Red light has the lowest frequencies.

What determines the color of light?

Light comes in many colors, from red to violet. But what is different about each color of light? Like all waves, light has wavelengths. Different wavelengths of light are interpreted by our eyes as different colors. The shortest wavelengths are seen as violet. The longest wavelengths are seen as red. Even the longest wavelengths we can see are still very small—less than one ten-thousandth of a centimeter.

White light is what we perceive when we see all the wavelengths of light at once, in equal proportions. A prism can split white light into its component colors, separating the colors by wavelength. The various wavelengths of light can also be combined to produce white light.

Our eyes only register three color ranges of light, called the primary colors—red, green, and blue. All other colors we see are a mixture of these three colors. A television or computer screen works by sending signals to make small dots, called pixels, give off red, green, and blue light.

Visualize It!

8 Arrange List the colors of the spectrum in order of increasing wavelength.

_____

_____

_____

_____

_____

_____

Red, green, and blue light combine to appear white.

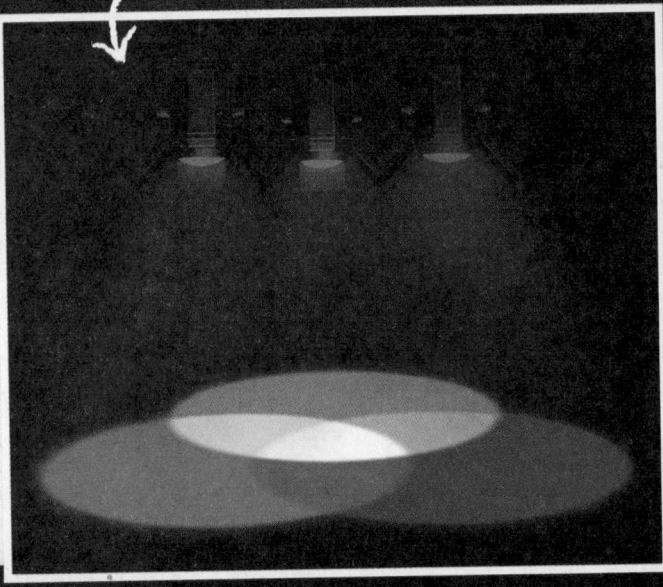

9 Select What combination of primary colors do we perceive as yellow?

_____

_____

Invisible Colors

What are the parts of the EM spectrum?

EM waves are measured by frequency or by wavelength. The light waves we see are EM waves. However, visible light represents only a very small part of the range of frequencies (or wavelengths) that an EM wave can have. This range is called the **electromagnetic (EM) spectrum**. These other EM waves are the same type of wave as the light we're used to. They're just different frequencies.

Two parts of the spectrum are close to visible light. **Infrared**, or IR, light has slightly longer wavelengths than red light. **Ultraviolet**, or UV, light has slightly shorter wavelengths than violet light.

The Electromagnetic Spectrum

Microwaves
Despite their name, microwaves are not the shortest EM waves. Besides heating food, microwaves are used by cellular phones.

Infrared Light
Infrared means "below red." The amount of infrared light an object gives off depends on its temperature. Below, colors indicate different amounts of infrared light.

Radio Waves
Radio waves have the longest wavelengths. They are used to broadcast signals for radios, televisions, alarm systems, and other devices.

Frequency in hertz (1 hertz = 1 cycle/second)

10^2 10^3 10^4 10^5 10^6 10^7 10^8 10^9 10^{10} 10^{11}

Radio Waves

Microwaves

© Houghton Mifflin Harcourt Publishing Company • Image Credits: (t) ©Bjorn Rorslett/Photo Researchers, Inc.; (ml) ©Wiskerke/Alamy; (mc) ©Steve Wisbauer/Photodisc/Getty Images; (mr) ©Nutscode/T Service/Photo Researchers, Inc.

The inner part of these flowers reflects UV light differently than the outer part. A bee's eyes are sensitive to UV light, and the bee can see the difference. However, human eyes cannot detect UV light. Our eyes can detect yellow light, and the center and edges of the flower reflect yellow light equally, so we see an all-yellow flower.

Human eyes see the flowers as entirely yellow.

A bee's eyes see a pattern in UV light.

Think Outside the Book

10 Incorporate The flower shows designs that are visible to bees, which can see light in the ultraviolet range. Research and explain how this adaptation leads to a symbiotic relationship between the flowers and bees.

Visible Light
Visible light is all the colors of the EM spectrum we can see. It is the narrowest part of the EM spectrum.

Ultraviolet Light
Ultraviolet means "beyond violet." Some animals can see ultraviolet light.

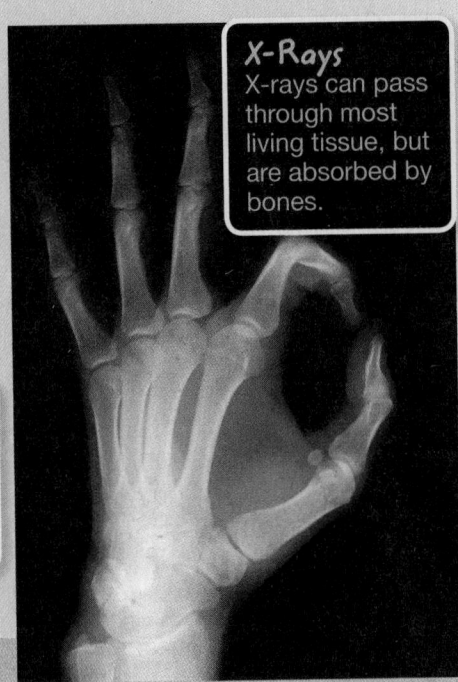

X-Rays
X-rays can pass through most living tissue, but are absorbed by bones.

Gamma Rays
Gamma rays can be used to treat illnesses and in making medical images.

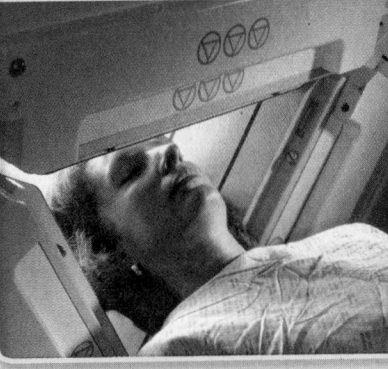

| 10^{12} | 10^{13} | 10^{14} | 10^{15} | 10^{16} | 10^{17} | 10^{18} | 10^{19} | 10^{20} |

| Infrared Light | | Ultraviolet Light | | Gamma Rays |
| | Visible Light | | | X-Rays |

How much of the sun's energy reaches us?

The sun gives off huge amounts of energy in the form of EM radiation. More of this energy is in the narrow visible light range than any other part of the spectrum, but the sun gives off some radiation in every part of the spectrum.

 **Active Reading** **11 Identify** What prevents most of the sun's gamma rays from reaching us?

_____

Visualize It!

The illustration shows how far down each part of the EM spectrum penetrates Earth's atmosphere.

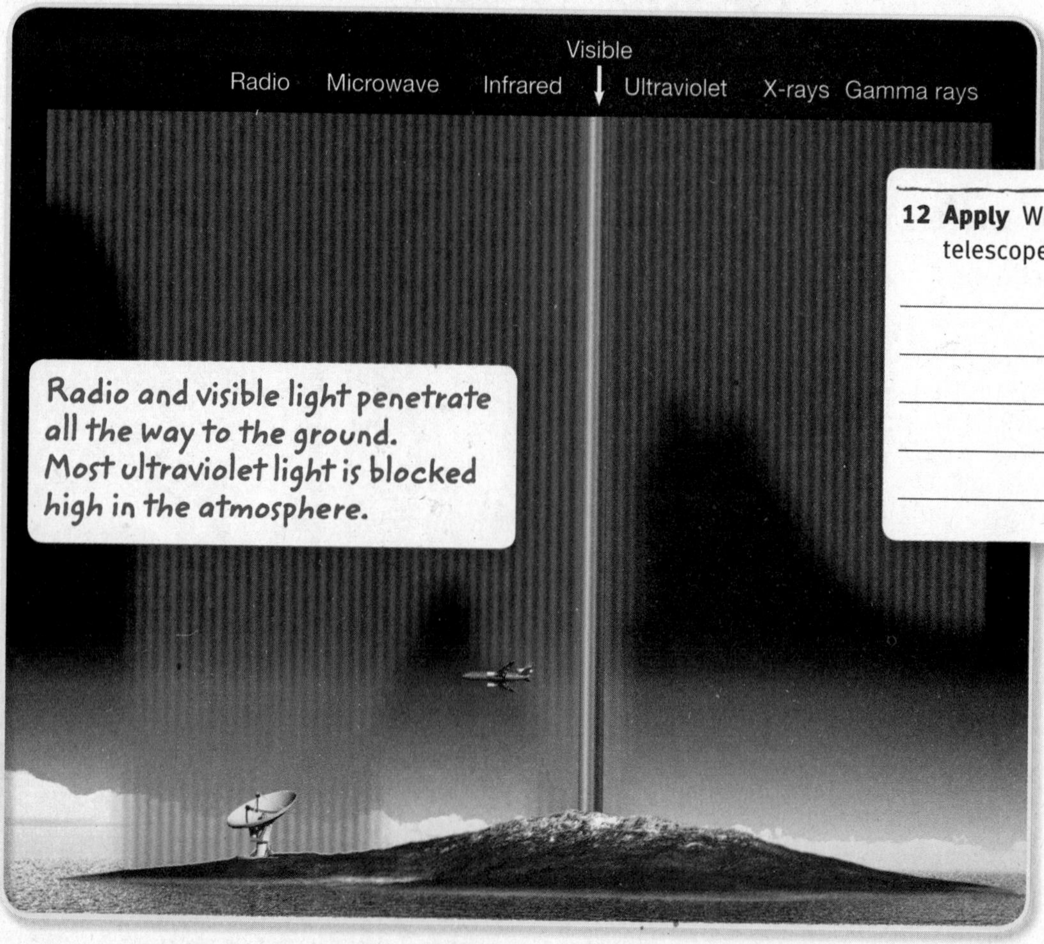

The Earth Shields Us from Some EM Radiation

Between the sun and us lies Earth's atmosphere. In order for us to see anything, some of the sun's light must make it through the atmosphere. However, not all wavelengths of light penetrate the atmosphere equally. The atmosphere blocks most of the higher-frequency radiation like x-rays and gamma rays from reaching us at the ground level, while allowing most of the visible light to reach us. There is a "window" of radio frequencies that are barely blocked at all, and this is why the most powerful ground-based telescopes are radio telescopes.

Radio   Microwave   Infrared   Visible ↓   Ultraviolet   X-rays   Gamma rays

Radio and visible light penetrate all the way to the ground. Most ultraviolet light is blocked high in the atmosphere.

12 Apply Why do we keep some telescopes in space?

_____

_____

_____

_____

Star Bright

13 Hypothesize Why might it be less dangerous to wear no sunglasses than to wear sunglasses that do not block UV light?

_____

_____

_____

_____

Astronauts need extra protection from EM radiation in space.

We Shield Ourselves from Some Radiation

The atmosphere blocks much of the sun's radiation, but not all. Some EM radiation can be dangerous to humans, so we take extra steps to protect ourselves. Receiving too much ultraviolet (UV) radiation can cause sunburn, skin cancer, or damage to the eyes, so we use sunscreen and wear UV-blocking sunglasses to protect ourselves from the UV light that passes through the atmosphere. Hats, long-sleeved shirts, and long pants can protect us, too.

We need this protection even on overcast days because UV light can travel through clouds. Even scientists in Antarctica, one of the coldest places on Earth, need to wear sunglasses, because fresh snow reflects about 80% of UV light back up to where it might strike their eyes.

Outer space is often thought of as being cold, but despite this, one of the biggest dangers to astronauts is from overheating! Outside of Earth's protective atmosphere, the level of dangerous EM radiation is much higher. And, in the vacuum of space, it's much harder to dispose of any energy, because there's no surrounding matter (like air) to absorb the extra energy. This is one reason why astronauts' helmets have a thin layer of pure gold. This highly reflective gold layer reflects unwanted EM radiation away.

Frequency
Asked Questions

How much energy does EM radiation have?

What makes some EM waves safe, and some dangerous? The answer is that different frequencies of EM waves carry different amounts of energy.

Higher Frequency Means More Energy

The energy of an EM wave depends on its frequency. High-frequency, short-wavelength EM waves have more energy than low-frequency, long-wavelength waves.

This chart shows the different amounts of energy that different frequencies of EM waves carry. As the frequency of the wave increases, the amount of energy it carries increases as well.

14 Identify Complete the chart to show which part of the electromagnetic spectrum is described by each frequency and energy. Refer to the illustration of the EM spectrum on the next page for information to help with this task.

Wave Frequency (Hz)	Amount of Energy (eV)	Part of EM Spectrum
10^6	10^{-9}	Radio
10^{12}	10^{-3}	
10^{14}	10^1	
10^{18}	10^3	
10^{24}	10^9	

15 Inquiry Use the data above to construct a graph showing the relationship between the amount of energy and the frequency of the wave. As you graph, concentrate on the exponents of the values to plot your points.

16 Analyze What happens to the amount of energy of a wave as the frequency increases? Use your graph to support your claim.

_____

_____

_____

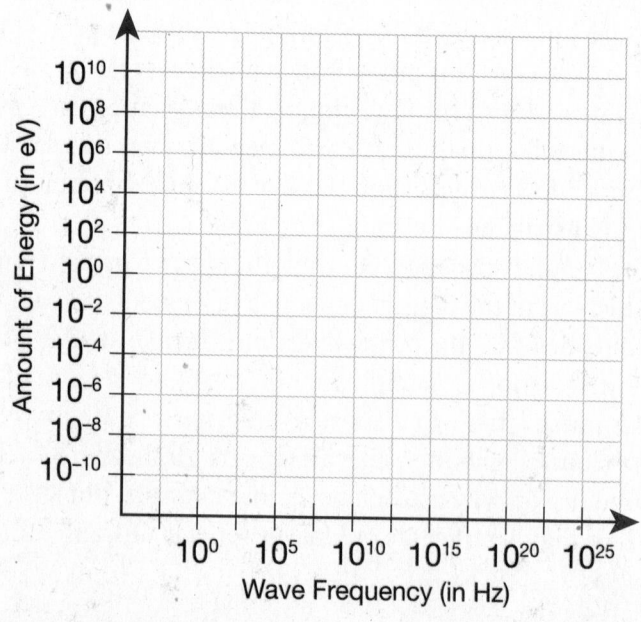

Ionizing Radiation is Dangerous

EM waves with high energy have the ability to ionize. *Ionization* occurs when the atoms making up a material lose one or more electrons. This change can cause the material to lose part or all of its normal function. If the material in question is part of a living thing, such as the cells that make up the human body, ionizing radiation can have damaging effects.

Radiation that is ionizing has higher energy than non-ionizing radiation, and can be more difficult to block. It is also more important to shield living tissue from ionizing radiation, since it can cause more damage than non-ionizing radiation.

17 Apply Use the EM spectrum below to identify the kinds of waves that are ionizing. Shade in that section of your graph. Based on your graph, how much energy is needed for radiation to be ionizing?

_____

_____

_____

_____

_____

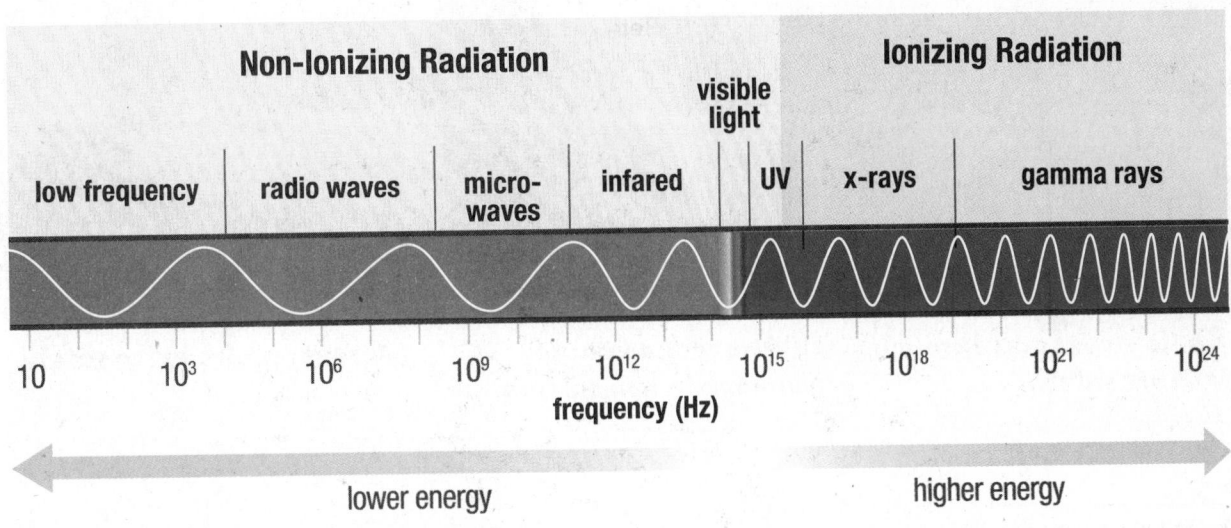

Higher energy waves on the electromagnetic spectrum are ionizing forms of radiation.

More Energy Means More Dangerous

A high-frequency EM wave carries a lot of energy, so it has the possibility of damaging living tissue. But a low-frequency wave carries much less energy, and is safer. This is why radio waves (which have the lowest frequencies) are used so often, such as in walkie-talkies and baby monitors. In contrast, UV light causes sunburn unless you have protection, and when working with even higher-energy waves like x-rays, special precautions must be taken, such as wearing a lead apron to block most of the rays. EM waves that have the ability to ionize have more potential to cause damage to living things. However, when used safely, they can also be very helpful.

Active Reading **18 Conclude** What kind of EM waves are most dangerous to humans?

_____

_____

Think Outside the Book

19 Apply On a separate sheet of paper, write a short story where the main character needs protection from two different kinds of EM radiation.

Radio waves pass through humans safely.

UV waves can cause damage to living tissue.

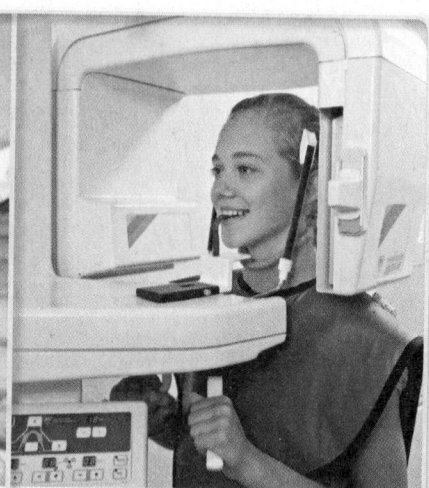
X-rays require extra safety.

20 Claims • Evidence • Reasoning What precautions does a doctor or dentist take to protect themselves and their patients from exposure to x-rays? Make a claim about how those precautions can protect from ionizing radiation. Explain your reasoning.

_____

_____

_____

_____

Fire in the Sky

The sun constantly streams out charged particles. Earth has a strong magnetic field. When particles from the sun strike Earth, the magnetic field funnels them together, accelerating them. When these particles collide with the atmosphere, they give off electromagnetic radiation in the form of light, and near the poles where they usually come together, a beautiful display called an *aurora* (uh•RAWR•uh) sometimes lights up the sky.

Winds of Change
The stream of electrically charged particles from the sun is called the *solar wind*.

What a Gas!
An aurora produced by nitrogen atoms may have a blue or red color, while one produced by oxygen atoms is green or brownish-red.

Pole Position
At the North Pole, this phenomenon is called the *aurora borealis* (uh•RAWR•uh bawr•ee•AL•is), or northern lights. At the south pole, is it called the *aurora australis* (uh•RAWR•uh aw•STRAY•lis), or southern lights.

ughton Mifflin Harcourt Publishing Company • Image Credits: (bg) ©First Light/Alamy; (inset) ©Greg Hense/Alamy

Extend

Inquiry

21 Relate Which color of aurora gives off higher-energy light, green or red?

22 Explain Why don't we see auroras on the moon?

23 Hypothesize Based on what you have learned about auroras, do you think auroras occur on other planets? Why or why not?

Visual Summary

To complete this summary, fill in the blanks with the correct word or phrase. Then use the key below to check your answers. You can use this page to review the main concepts of the lesson.

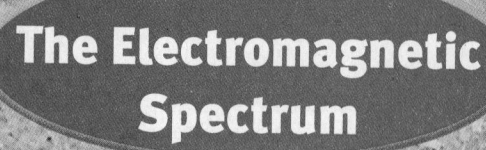

Different wavelengths of light appear as different colors.

24 The color of the longest visible wavelength is _____

25 The color of the shortest visible wavelength is _____

Higher-frequency waves carry more energy. This makes them more dangerous.

26 The energy of an electromagnetic (EM) wave is proportional to its _____

EM waves exist along a spectrum.

27 The waves with the longest wavelengths are _____ waves.

28 The waves with the shortest wavelengths are _____

10^0 10^{19}

Radio Waves

Gamma Rays

Answers: 24 red; 25 violet; 26 frequency; 27 radio; 28 gamma rays

29 Synthesize Suppose you are designing a device to transmit information without wires. What part of the EM spectrum will your device use, and why?

---

620 Unit 10 Light

Lesson Review

Vocabulary

Fill in the blanks with the terms that best complete the following sentences.

1 The transfer of energy as electromagnetic waves is called _____

2 The full range of wavelengths of EM waves is called the _____ _____

3 _____ radiation lies at frequencies just below the frequencies of visible light.

Key Concepts

4 Describe What is an electromagnetic wave?

_____

_____

_____

5 Organize What are the highest-frequency and lowest-frequency parts of the EM spectrum?

_____

_____

_____

6 Compare How fast do different parts of the EM spectrum travel in a vacuum?

_____

_____

Suppose you like to listen to two different radio stations. The opera station broadcasts at 90.5 MHz and the rock and roll station broadcasts at 107.1 MHz.

7 Apply Which station's signal has waves with longer wavelengths?

_____

8 Apply Which station's signal has waves with higher energy?

_____

Use the graph to answer the following questions.

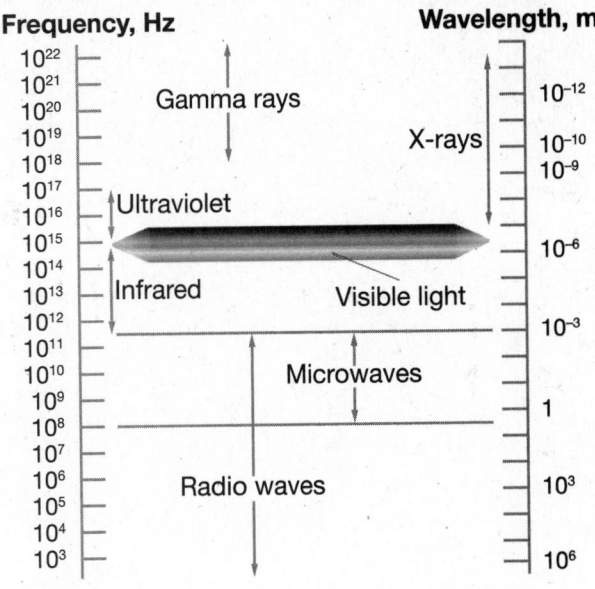

9 Classify How would you classify an EM wave with a frequency of 10^7 Hz?

_____

10 Classify How would you classify an EM wave with a wavelength of 10^{-12} m?

_____

_____

11 Apply What is white light?

_____

_____

Critical Thinking

12 Conclude If you wanted to detect x-rays coming from the sun, where would you place the detector? Explain your reasoning.

_____

_____

_____

_____

_____

My Notes

Engineering Design Process

Skills
Identify a need
Conduct research
✓ Brainstorm solutions
✓ Select a solution
Design a prototype
✓ Build a prototype
✓ Test and evaluate
Redesign to improve
✓ Communicate results

S8P4.d Behavior of light and sound waves

Objectives
• Compare and contrast light and sound waves.
• Demonstrate the effects of different materials on the path of light and sound waves.

Comparing Light and Sound

Light, like sound, is a wave. All waves transfer energy from one place to another, and all have some characteristics in common such as the ability to reflect and diffract. However, waves can differ in other ways. For example, a sound wave is a longitudinal wave, while a light wave is a transverse wave. The way that a specific wave is observed and the way it responds to matter can differ depending on the wave.

1 Predict Look at the photo and identify at least two surfaces or objects. How do you think light waves and sound waves would interact with these surfaces or objects? Would these interactions be the same or different?

_____

_____

_____

_____

Observing Light vs. Sound

Although all waves share certain characteristics and abilities, the way that we observe these characteristics can be very different. A sound wave reflects as it bounces off a smooth surface, and we hear an echo. A light wave reflects as it bounces of a reflective surface, and we see a reflection. How else do we observe these characteristics differently in sound versus light waves?

2 Identify The table below compares different behaviors of sound waves and light waves. Complete the table by filling in the missing descriptions and examples.

	Sound	Light
Reflection	Sound waves bounce off a surface. **Example:** A shout echoes off a canyon wall.	Light waves bounce off a surface. **Example:** We see a reflection in a mirror.
Refraction	_____ **Example:** _____	Light waves bend as they move from one medium to another. **Example:** From above the surface, a fish appears to be in a slightly different location than it actually is.
Absorption	Energy from sound waves is not able to pass through a material. **Example:** Insulation in a recording studio	_____ **Example:** _____
Diffraction	Sound waves bend as they pass by an object **Example:** A police whistle can be heard around the corner of a building.	_____ **Example:** _____
Transmission	_____ **Example:** _____	Light waves pass through a material. **Example:** Objects outside a window appear the same as if the window was not there.

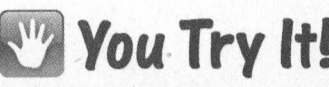 **You Try It!**

Now it's your turn to compare and contrast light and sound waves.

 You Try It!

Design a way to compare and contrast light versus sound for reflection, refraction, absorption, diffraction and transmission. You will brainstorm ways to observe all of these, and then pick one set of designs to complete and evaluate the methods you designed. As you observe these wave behaviors, you will create a model for how the wave is behaving in each scenario.

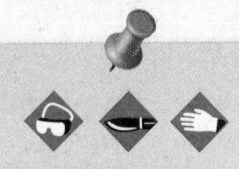

You Will Need

✔ LED flashlight

✔ Pillow

✔ Clear glass with water

✔ Clear tape

✔ Pencils (new, non-mechanical)

✔ Mirror

1 Brainstorm Solutions

Using the materials provided for this activity, brainstorm ways to observe reflection, refraction, absorption, diffraction and transmission of light and sound. Complete the table with a brief explanation of which materials you would use and how you could use them to demonstrate each behavior of light and sound.

	Sound	Light
Reflection		
Refraction		
Absorption		
Diffraction		
Transmission		

2 Select a Solution

Look over your list of ideas, pick one behavior to observe for light and sound. For example, you could compare and contrast reflection of light and sound. Outline the steps of what you will need to do to make your observations.

_____

_____

_____

③ Build a Prototype

Gather your materials and set up your demonstrations! What did you need to adjust as you did so?

_____

_____

_____

_____

④ Test and Evaluate

Complete your demonstration and record your observations.

Sound	Light

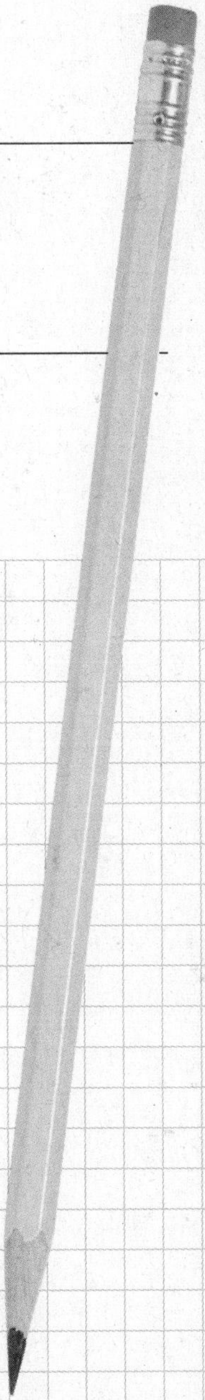

⑤ Communicate Results

Although it is difficult to observe the path of a wave, we can create a model or a sketch to show the path of the wave. Create a sketch showing the set up you designed and showing the path of the wave for both light and sound. Present your findings to your classmates.

Interactions of Light

S8P4.d Behavior of light and sound waves

ESSENTIAL QUESTION

How does light interact with matter?

By the end of this lesson, you should be able to explain how light and matter can interact.

These windows allow different colors of light to pass through. The colorful pattern is then reflected off the floor inside.

 **Lesson Labs**

Quick Labs
• Why is the Sky Blue?
• Refraction with Water

Exploration Lab
• Comparing Colors of Objects in Different Colors of Light

Engage Your Brain

1 Predict Check T or F to show whether you think each statement is true or false.

T   F

☐   ☐   Light cannot pass through solid matter.

☐   ☐   A white surface absorbs every color of light.

☐   ☐   Light always moves at the same speed.

2 Identify Unscramble the letters below to find words about interactions between light and matter. Write your words on the blank lines.

OCRLO _____

RIORMR _____

NABORIW _____

TTRACSE _____

CENFOLRETI _____

 **Active Reading**

3 Synthesize You can often define an unknown word if you know the meaning of its word parts. Use the word parts and sentence below to make an educated guess about the meanings of the words *transmit*, *transparent*, and *translucent*.

Word part	Meaning
trans-	through
-mit	send
-par	show
-luc	light

transmit: _____

_____

transparent: _____

_____

translucent: _____

_____

Vocabulary Terms

• transparent   • reflection
• translucent   • refraction
• opaque   • diffraction
• absorption   • scattering

4 Apply As you learn the definition of each vocabulary term in this lesson, create your own definition or sketch to help you remember the meaning of the term.

Shedding Light

How can matter interact with light?

Interactions between light and matter produce many common but spectacular effects, such as color, reflections, and rainbows. Three forms of interaction play an especially important role in how people see light.

Matter Can Transmit Light

Recall that light and other electromagnetic waves can travel through empty space. When light encounters a material, it can be passed through the material, or transmitted. The medium can transmit all, some, or none of the light.

Matter that transmits light is **transparent** (tranz•PAHR•uhnt). Air, water, and some types of glass are transparent materials. Objects can be seen clearly through transparent materials.

Translucent (tranz•LOO•suhnt) materials transmit light but do not let the light travel straight through. The light is scattered into many different directions. As a result, you can see light through translucent materials, but objects seen through a translucent material look distorted or fuzzy. Frosted glass, some lamp shades, and tissue paper are examples of translucent materials.

Active Reading

5 Identify As you read, underline three words that describe how well matter transmits light.

Objects can be seen clearly through transparent glass.

Objects look distorted when seen through translucent glass.

Think Outside the Book

6 Discuss Write a short story in which it is important that a piece of glass is translucent or transparent.

on the Matter

Matter Can Absorb Light

Opaque (oh•PAYK) materials do not let any light pass through them. Instead, they reflect light, absorb light, or both. Many materials, such as wood, brick, or metal, are opaque. When light enters a material but does not leave it, the light is absorbed. **Absorption** is the transfer of light energy to matter.

The shirt at right absorbs the light that falls on it, and so the shirt is opaque. However, absorption is not the only way an object can be opaque.

The shirt is opaque, because light does not pass through it. We can't see the table underneath.

👁 **Visualize It!**

7 Explain Is the table in the photo at right transparent, translucent, or opaque? Explain your reasoning.

_____

_____

Matter Can Reflect Light

You see an object only when light from the object enters your eye. However, most objects do not give off, or emit, light. Instead, light bounces off the object's surface. The bouncing of light off a surface is called **reflection**.

Most objects have a surface that is at least slightly rough. When light strikes a rough surface, such as wood or cloth, the light reflects in many different directions. Some of the reflected light reaches your eyes, and you see the object.

Light bounces at an angle equal to the angle at which it hit the surface. When light strikes a smooth or shiny surface such as a mirror, it reflects in a uniform way. As a result, a mirror produces an image. Light from a lamp might be reflected by your skin, then be reflected by a mirror, and then enter your eye. You look at the mirror and see yourself.

👁 **Visualize It!**

8 Identify What is the difference between the way light interacts with the shirt above and the way light interacts with the mirror at right?

_____

_____

_____

Light is reflected by the girl's face and by the mirror.

Color Me Impressed!

What determines the color of objects we see?

Visible light includes a range of colors. Light that includes all colors is called white light. When white light strikes an object, the object can transmit some or all of the colors of light, reflect some or all of the colors, and absorb some or all of the colors.

The Light Reflected or Absorbed

The perceived color of an object is determined by the colors of light reflected by the object. For example, a frog's skin absorbs most colors of light, but reflects most of the green light. When you look in the direction of the frog, the green light enters your eyes, so the frog appears green.

An object that reflects every color appears white. An object that absorbs every color appears black.

The frog's body is green because it reflects green light while absorbing other colors of light.

Think Outside the Book

9 **Diagram** Use colored pencils, crayons, or markers to draw light shining on an object. Draw arrows showing the colors of incoming light and arrows showing which colors are reflected.

The Light Transmitted

The color of a transparent or translucent object works differently than it does for opaque objects. Some materials may absorb some colors but let other colors pass through. Green plastic, for example, does not appear green because it reflects green light, but rather, because it transmits green light while absorbing other colors of light. When you look toward a bottle made of green plastic, the transmitted green light reaches your eyes. Therefore, the bottle looks green.

Some matter can absorb visible light but let other kinds of electromagnetic waves pass through. For example, radio waves can easily pass through walls that are opaque to visible light. X-rays pass through skin and muscle, but are stopped by denser bone.

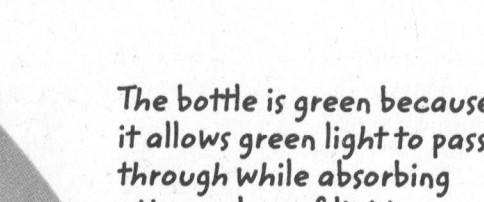

The bottle is green because it allows green light to pass through while absorbing other colors of light.

The Available Light

Sometimes the perceived color of an object depends on the light available in the area. You may have been in a room with a red light bulb. The glass around the bulb filters out all colors except red, plus some orange and yellow. An object that reflects red light would still appear red under such a light bulb. But an object that absorbed all red, orange, and yellow light would appear gray or black. We can't see colors of light that aren't there to be reflected to our eyes!

Filtered Light

Below, the light from the bulb is being filtered before shining on a frog.

The light bulb emits, or gives off, light in all colors.

A filter blocks some colors, transmitting only red light and some orange and yellow light.

The frog absorbs the red, orange, and yellow light, and reflects no light.

 **Visualize It!**

10 Apply Explain why the frog will not look green under the red light.

_____

_____

_____

_____

_____

_____

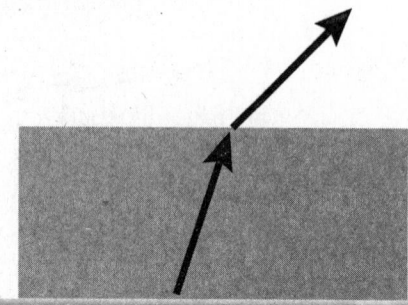

Light changes direction when it leaves the water, making the straw look broken.

Matter Scatter

What happens when light waves interact with matter?

Light waves change when they encounter an object or a new medium.

Light Slows When It Passes Through Matter

Light always travels at the same speed in a vacuum, about 300,000,000 m/s, or the *speed of light*. However, light travels slower in a medium. Light travels only about three-fourths as fast in water as in a vacuum, and only about two-thirds as fast in glass as in a vacuum.

Although light of all wavelengths travels at the same speed in a vacuum, the same is not true in a medium. Shorter wavelengths are slowed more than longer wavelengths. In a medium, the speed of violet light is less than the speed of red light.

Light Changes Direction

A straight object, such as the straw in the picture above, looks bent or broken when part of it is underwater. Light from the straw changes direction when it passes from water to glass and from glass to air. **Refraction** (ri-FRAK-shuhn) is the change in direction of a wave as it passes from one medium into another at an angle. Refraction is due to the change in speed as a wave enters a new medium.

Light Bends Around Objects

Even if the medium doesn't change, waves can change direction if an object is acting as a barrier. **Diffraction** (di-FRAK-shuhn) of waves occurs when a wave bends as it passes through an opening or around an object. The diagram at left shows how a wave diffracts as it passes through a narrow opening. Diffraction depends on a wave's wavelength and the size of the opening. Diffraction of light waves is only noticeable when the opening is very small since the wavelengths of light are so short.

---

12 Compare How are diffraction and refraction different? How are they the same?

_____

_____

Think Outside the Book

11 Apply When a bird tries to catch a fish, it must account for refraction. Draw a picture like the one above to show the path of light from the fish to the bird. Then trace the path backward to show where the fish appears to be to the bird.

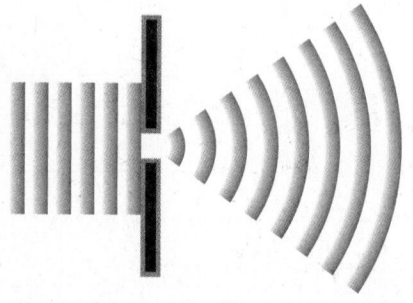

Light bends or diffracts as it passes through an opening in a barrier.

Light Scatters

You don't see a beam of light shining through clear air. But if the beam of light shines through fog, some of the light is sent in many different directions. Some enters your eye, and you see the beam. **Scattering** occurs when light is sent in many directions as it passes through a medium. Dust and other small particles can scatter light.

The color of the sky is due to scattered light. Particles of air scatter short wavelengths—blue and violet light—more than long wavelengths. As sunlight passes through air, blue light is scattered first. The blue light appears to come from all directions, and so the sky appears blue. When the sun is near the horizon in the sky, sunlight passes through more of the atmosphere. As the light passes through more and more air, almost all light of short wavelengths is scattered. Only the longest wavelengths are left. The sun and the sky appear yellow, orange, or red.

 **Active Reading**

13 Identify What color of light is scattered most easily by the atmosphere?

We can see the light beam coming out of the lighthouse because the fog scatters the light.

In the diagram below, the red lines represent paths of light from the sun. The black brackets show the amount of atmosphere the light must pass through to reach our eyes.

In the evening, sunlight travels through a lot of air. The blue light scatters, leaving only redder light.

The daytime sky appears blue because air scatters blue light more than it does other colors.

Not to scale

Visual Summary

To complete this summary, circle the correct word to complete each statement. Then, use the key below to check your answers. You can use this page to review the main concepts of the lesson.

Interactions of Light and Matter

Matter can transmit, reflect, or absorb light.

14 Matter that transmits no light is (transparent/translucent/opaque).

The color of an object depends on what colors of light it reflects or transmits.

15 A frog in white light appears green because it

(reflects/absorbs/transmits)

green light and

(reflects/absorbs/transmits) other colors of light.

A transparent medium can bend, scatter, or change the speed of light.

16 The bending of light as it moves from one medium to another is called (reflection/refraction/diffraction).

Answers: 14 opaque; 15 reflects, absorbs; 16 refraction

17 **Synthesize** Suppose you are looking at a yellow fish in a fish tank. The tank is next to a window. Describe the path that light takes in order for you to see the fish, starting at the sun and ending at your eyes.

Lesson Review

Vocabulary

Fill in the blank with the term that best completes the following sentences.

1 An object appears fuzzy when seen through a(n) _____ material.

2 A(n) _____ material lets light pass through freely.

3 The bouncing of light off a surface is called _____.

4 The bending of light when it changes media is called _____.

5 _____ occurs when light changes direction after colliding with particles of matter.

Key Concepts

6 Identify For each picture below, identify the material enclosing the sandwich as transparent, translucent, or opaque.

a. _____

b. _____

c. _____

d. _____

7 Identify Which material in the pictures above reflects the most light?

_____

8 Identify Which material in the pictures above absorbs the most light?

_____

Critical Thinking

9 Infer Is a mirror's surface transparent, translucent, or opaque? How do you know?

_____

_____

_____

_____

_____

10 Claims • Evidence • Reasoning In the same amount of sunlight, which will become hotter: a black asphalt road, or a white cement sidewalk? Explain your reasoning.

_____

_____

_____

_____

_____

_____

_____

11 Explain Why is the sky blue?

_____

_____

_____

_____

_____

_____

_____

12 Explain Sunlight passing through a window opening creates a distinct window-shaped block of light inside a room. Why does diffraction not cause the window-shaped light to spread out?

_____

_____

_____

_____

_____

_____

_____

My Notes

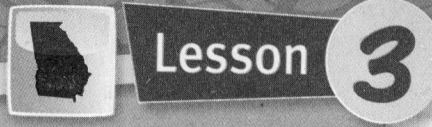
Mirrors and Lenses

ESSENTIAL QUESTION

How do mirrors and lenses work?

By the end of this lesson, you should be able to describe ways that lenses and mirrors form images.

 S8P4.d Behavior of light and sound waves

S8P4.g Lenses and light

The curves on this funhouse mirror produce distorted images of the people and objects nearby.

Lesson Labs

Quick Labs
- Spoon Images
- Mirror Images

S.T.E.M. Lab
- Light Maze

Engage Your Brain

1 Infer Why do you think the word *ambulance* is printed backwards on the front of this emergency vehicle?

_____

_____

_____

2 Predict If your hair is usually parted on the left side, how will it appear in your bathroom mirror?

_____

_____

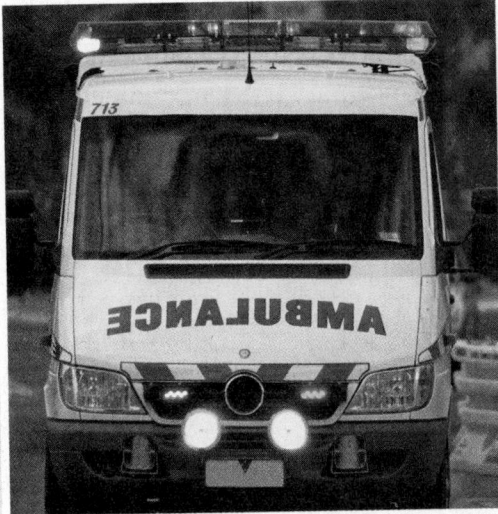

Active Reading

3 Apply Use context clues to write your own definitions for the words *image* and *virtual*.

Example sentence:
When I see myself in a funhouse mirror, my <u>image</u> is distorted and I look weird.

image:

_____

_____

_____

Example sentence:
Some mirrors produce a <u>virtual</u> image; other mirrors produce a real image.

virtual:

_____

_____

Vocabulary Terms

- virtual image
- concave
- converge
- real image
- convex
- diverge
- lens

4 Apply As you learn the definition of each vocabulary term in this lesson, create your own definition or sketch to help you remember the meaning of the term.

Lesson 3 Mirrors and Lenses **641**

Mirror Image

How do mirrors form images?

Light waves travel from their source in all directions. If you could trace the path of one light wave, you would find that it is a straight line. If a light wave hits an object, it may be reflected, or bounce off. Most objects have rough surfaces that reflect light in many different directions. A very smooth surface, such as a mirror, reflects light in a uniform way. Look at the illustrations below. The light from the flashlight hits the mirror at an angle of 40° from an imaginary line perpendicular to the mirror's surface. This imaginary line is called the *normal*. Notice that the angle at which light hits the surface is equal to the angle at which the light is reflected from the surface. This is called the *law of reflection*.

Light reflects off smooth surfaces, such as mirrors, in a uniform way.

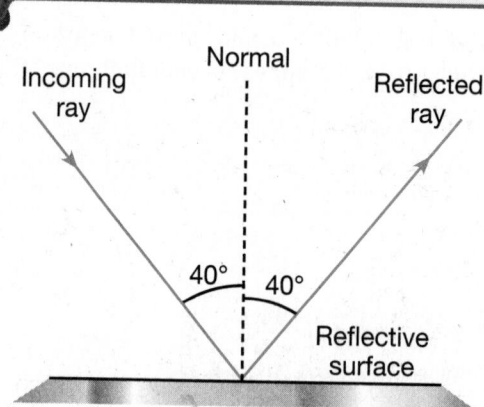

A ray diagram shows a path light can take. The angle at which a light ray hits a mirror is equal to the angle at which the ray reflects.

Do the Math   You Try It

5 Analyze Use a protractor to find the angles at which the light hits the mirror and is reflected from it. Measure from the normal. Write each measurement on the diagram.

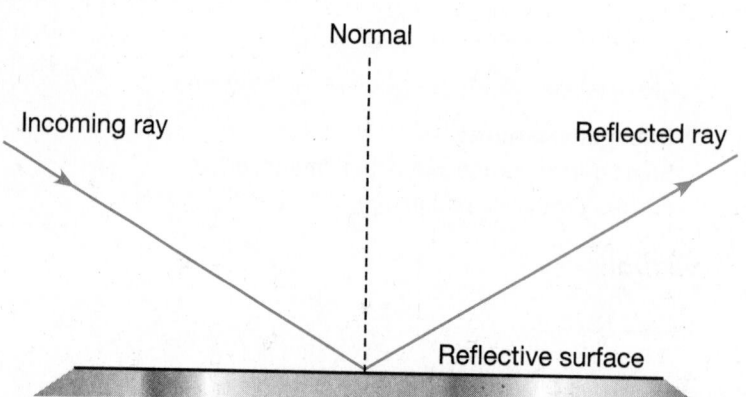

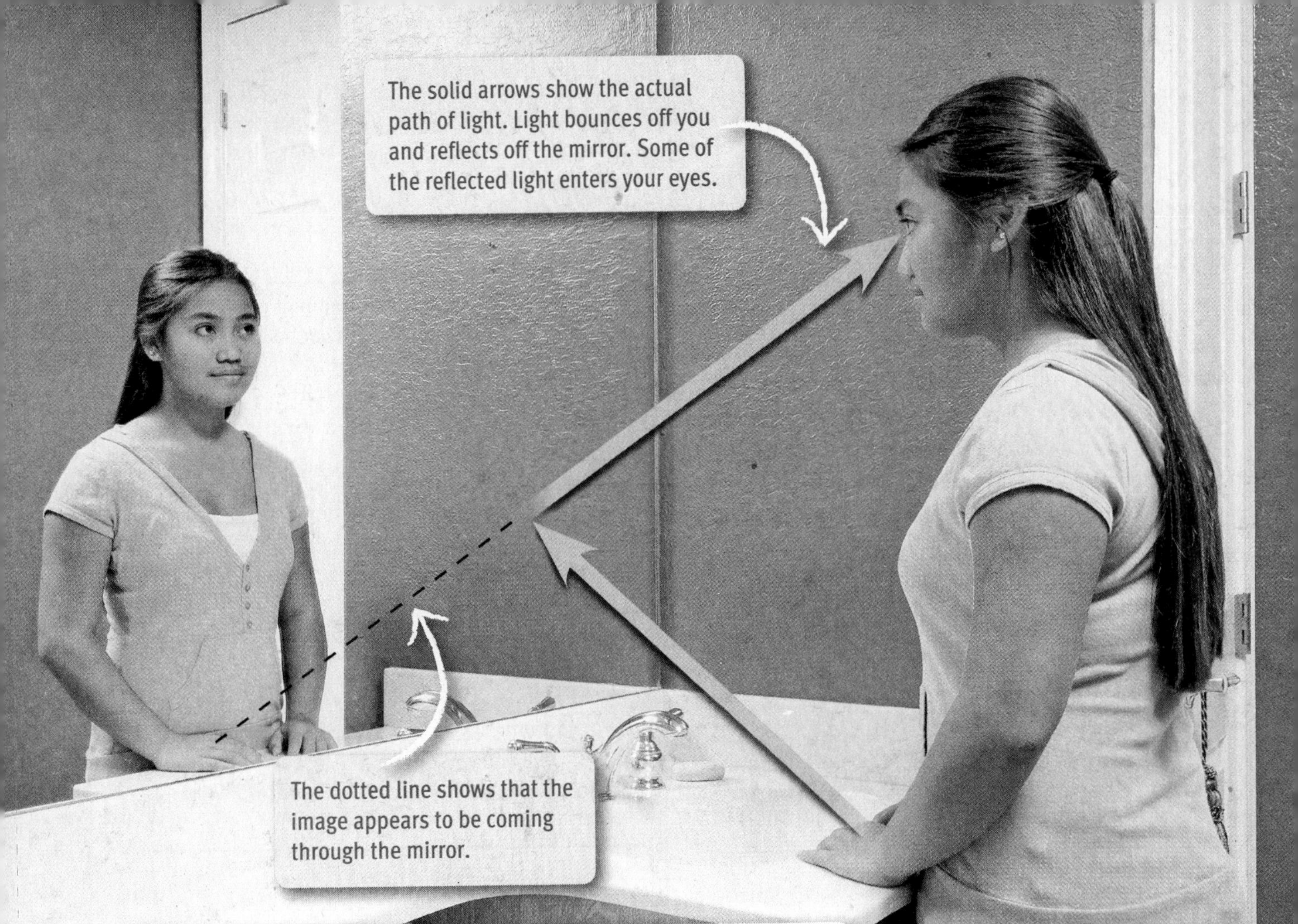

The solid arrows show the actual path of light. Light bounces off you and reflects off the mirror. Some of the reflected light enters your eyes.

The dotted line shows that the image appears to be coming through the mirror.

Plane Mirrors Form Virtual Images

Look in a bathroom mirror and wink with your right eye. Your image will wink with its left eye. Most mirrors are plane mirrors; they have a flat surface. The reflection in a plane mirror is right side up but reversed left to right. Your reflection is the same size as you are. And, it also appears to be the same distance behind the mirror as you are in front of it.

Why does your image seem to be inside the mirror? The picture shows how light is reflected off a plane mirror. When you see reflected light, your brain thinks the light has traveled in a straight line from behind the mirror. In ray diagrams, this type of ray is shown as a dotted line, because it does not represent actual light. Rather, it shows where the light appears to come from. The image formed in a plane mirror is a virtual image. A **virtual image** is an image that appears to come from a place that the light does not actually come from.

Active Reading **6 Analyze** What do all plane mirrors have in common? Explain your reasoning.

_____

_____

_____

© Houghton Mifflin Harcourt Publishing Company • Image Credits: ©HMH

Think Outside the Book

7 Identify Walk through your home and list as many examples of plane mirrors as you can find.

Concave Mirrors Form Real or Virtual Images

Not all mirrors are flat. A **concave** mirror is curved inward like the bowl of a spoon. Concave mirrors cause parallel light waves to **converge**, or come together. If you pointed parallel light rays toward the concave mirror below, they would converge at a point called the *focal point*. Or, if you held a light source at that focal point, the mirror would reflect parallel rays of light. Concave mirrors are useful for producing beams of light and magnifying objects.

All images are formed where two or more rays from the same location on an object converge. Concave mirrors can form either virtual images or real images. But, unlike a virtual image, a **real image** is formed where light from an object converges. A real image can be projected onto a screen; a virtual image cannot.

8 Infer How might concave mirrors be used in car headlights?

_____

_____

_____

_____

_____

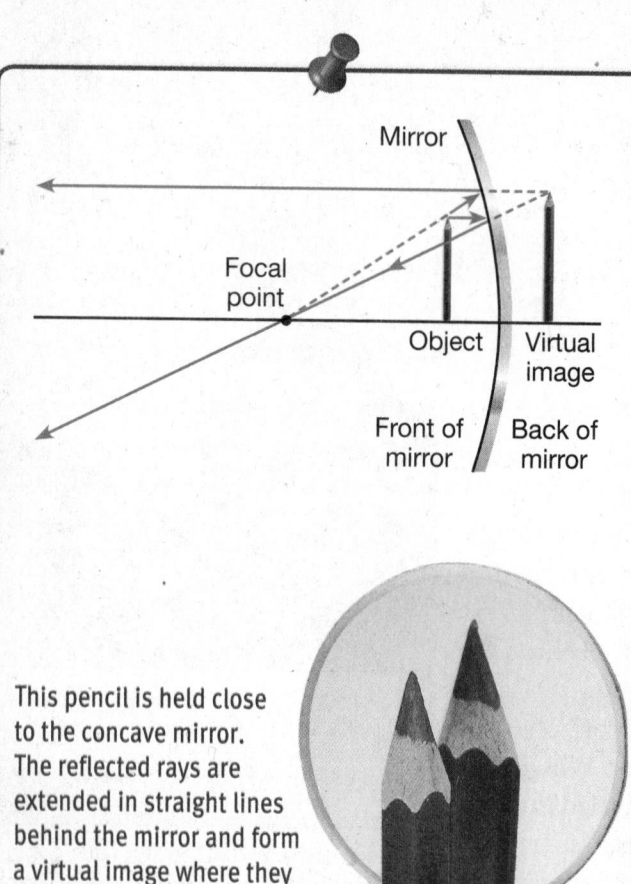

This pencil is held close to the concave mirror. The reflected rays are extended in straight lines behind the mirror and form a virtual image where they cross. The image is right side up and magnified.

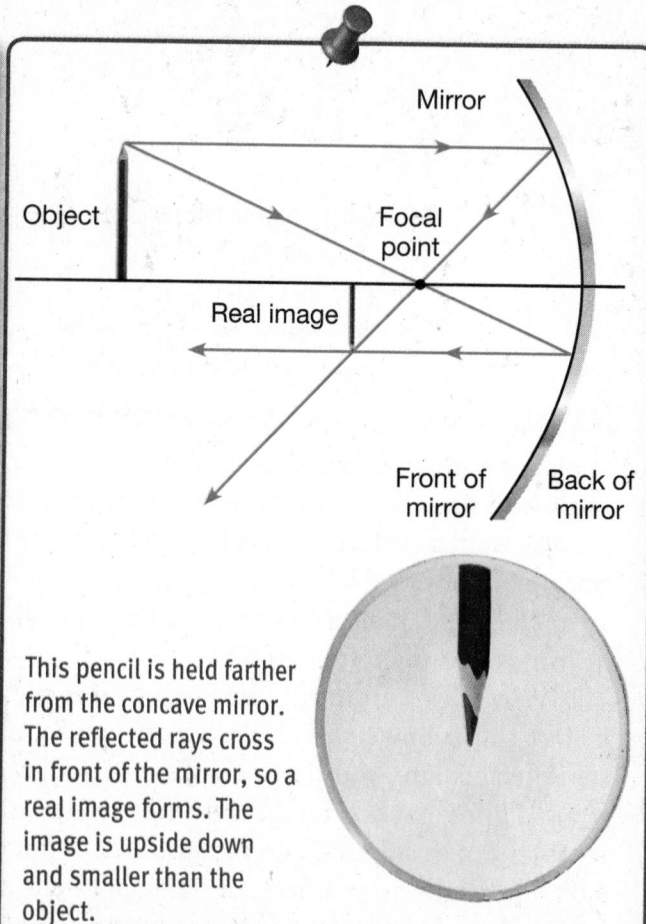

This pencil is held farther from the concave mirror. The reflected rays cross in front of the mirror, so a real image forms. The image is upside down and smaller than the object.

Visualize It! Inquiry

9 Predict What would happen to the size of the image if the green pencil were moved farther away from the mirror? If possible, test your prediction using the inside of a spoon as a mirror.

Convex Mirrors Form Virtual Images

A **convex** mirror curves outward like the back of a spoon. Convex mirrors cause a beam of light to **diverge**, or spread apart, as if it came from a focal point behind the mirror. If you look at your reflection in the back of a spoon, you will notice that your image is right side up and small. You may also be able to see the floor or ceiling around you.

All images formed by convex mirrors are virtual, right side up, and small. Convex mirrors are useful because they make small images of large areas. They are used for security in stores and factories. Many cars, buses, and trucks use convex side mirrors so the driver can see more of the surrounding area.

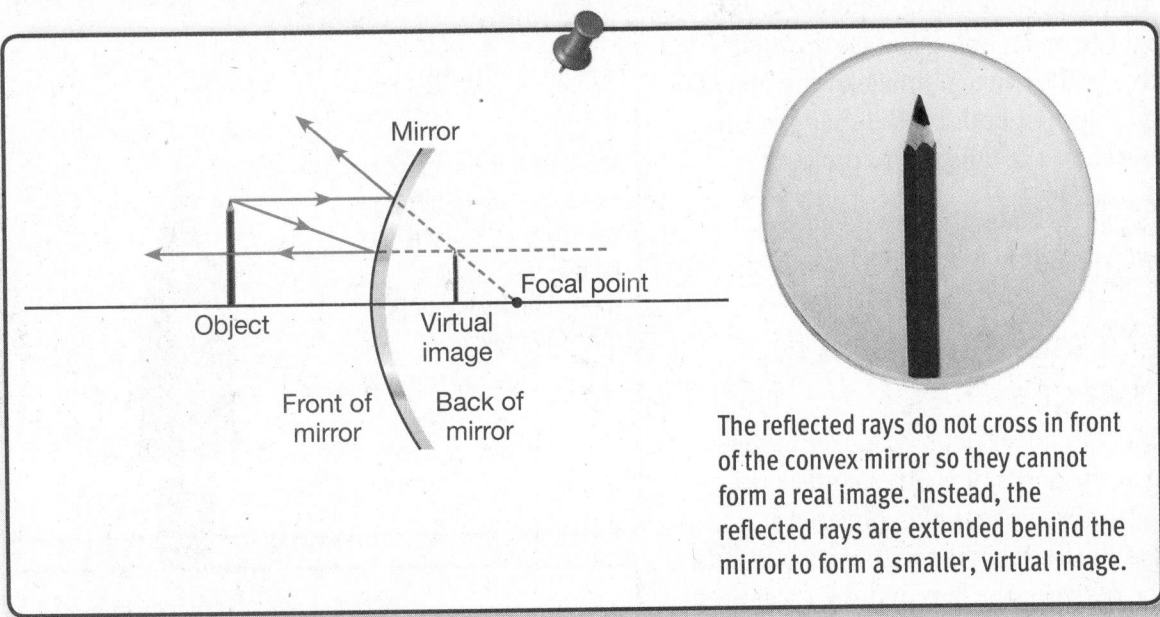

Mirror

Focal point

Object

Virtual image

Front of mirror

Back of mirror

The reflected rays do not cross in front of the convex mirror so they cannot form a real image. Instead, the reflected rays are extended behind the mirror to form a smaller, virtual image.

 **Visualize It!**

10 Diagram In the space below, draw a ray diagram to represent what you might see in the gazing ball on the left.

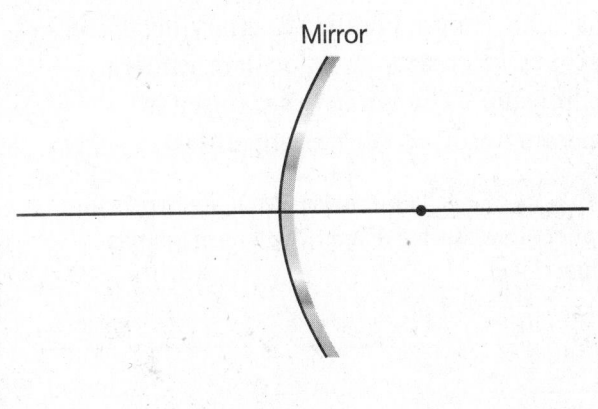

Mirror

Under a Lens

How do lenses form images?

A **lens** is a clear optical tool that refracts light. Refraction occurs when a light wave changes speed as it passes from one medium to another. The change in speed makes the light waves bend and either converge or diverge, depending on the lens. Light from an object passes through a lens to form a real or virtual image of the object. The type of image depends on the shape of the lens and how close the object is to the lens.

Active Reading **11 Identify** As you read, underline seven uses of convex lenses.

Convex Lenses Form Real or Virtual Images

A converging, or convex, lens is thicker at the center than at the edges. It is often convex on both sides. Parallel rays of light converge at a focal point after they pass through a convex lens. The distance between the lens and the focal point is called the focal length. Look at the diagrams on the right. The lens shown in the top diagram is thicker in the center and has a focal length that is longer than the lens shown in the bottom diagram. Also notice that the pencil shown in the top diagram is held closer to the lens than the pencil shown in the bottom diagram.

Convex lenses are used to magnify or to focus light. They are used in magnifying glasses, telescopes, microscopes, binoculars, cameras, and projectors. Convex lenses are used in eyeglasses to correct for farsightedness.

Active Reading **12 Provide** What are two factors that affect how much a magnifying lens magnifies an object?

_____

_____

_____

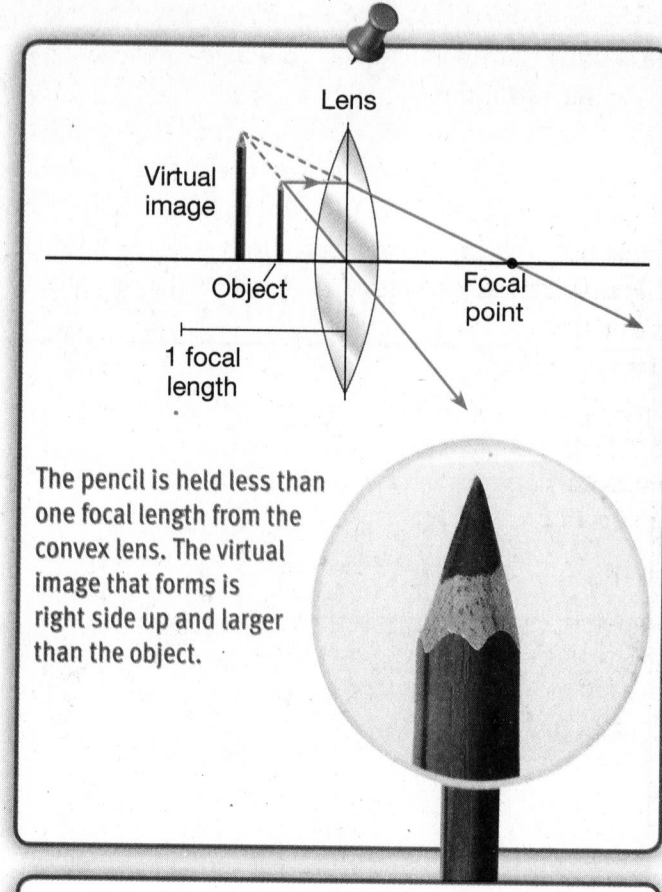

The pencil is held less than one focal length from the convex lens. The virtual image that forms is right side up and larger than the object.

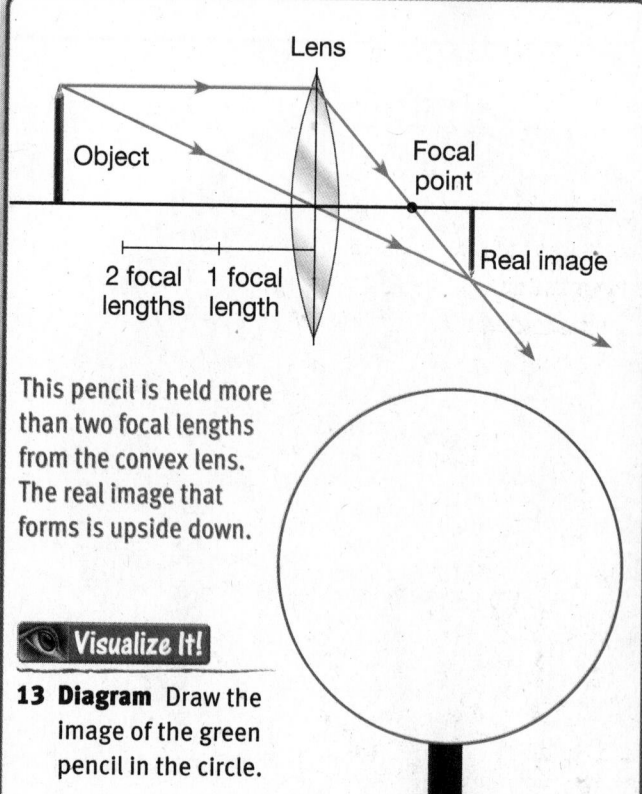

This pencil is held more than two focal lengths from the convex lens. The real image that forms is upside down.

Visualize It!

13 Diagram Draw the image of the green pencil in the circle.

Concave Lenses Form Virtual Images

A diverging, or concave, lens is thinner at the center than at the edges. It is often concave on both sides. Light that passes through a concave lens is refracted outward as if from the focal point.

Because they are refracted away from each other, parallel light waves passing through a concave lens do not meet. The image formed is a virtual image. It is right side up and smaller than the object. In concave lenses, the distance between the object and the lens does not make a difference in the type of image that is formed.

Diverging lenses are used to spread light, often in combination with other lenses in telescopes and binoculars. They are also used in eyeglasses to correct for nearsightedness.

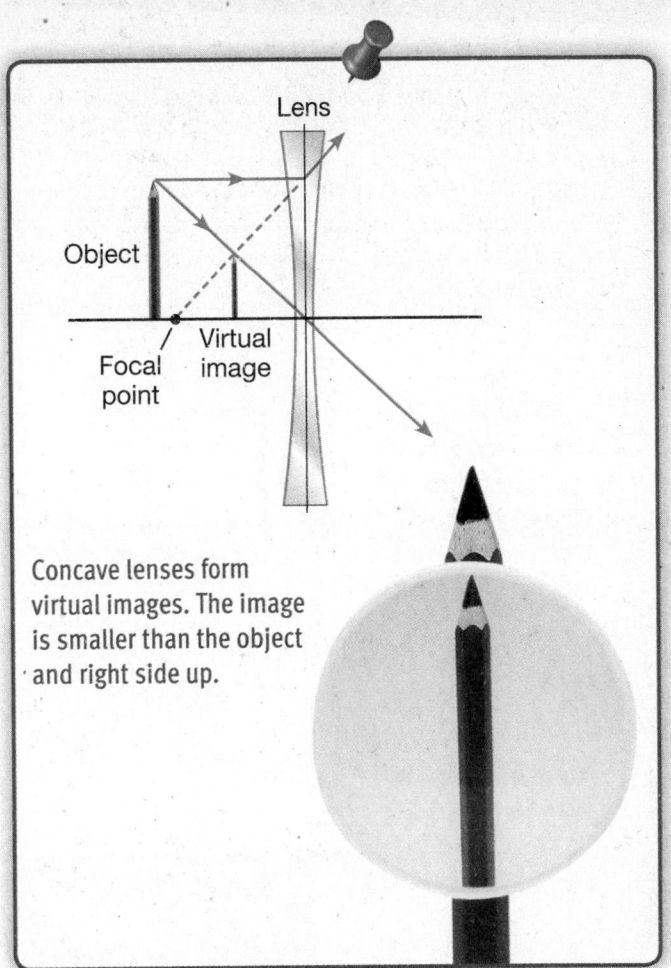

Concave lenses form virtual images. The image is smaller than the object and right side up.

Review: Mirrors and Lenses

14 Summarize Use what you know about mirrors and lenses to write either *concave* or *convex* in the *Optical device* column. Provide a real-world example for each kind of mirror and lens.

Virtual or real?	Orientation of image	Size of image in relation to object	Optical device	Real-world example
virtual	right side up	larger	_____ lens	
real	upside down	smaller	_____ mirror	
virtual	right side up	smaller	_____ lens	
virtual	right side up	larger	_____ mirror	
real	upside down	smaller	_____ lens	
virtual	right side up	smaller	_____ mirror	

Visual Summary

To complete this summary, circle the correct word or phrase. Then, use the key below to check your answers. You can use this page to review the main concepts of the lesson.

Mirrors and Lenses

Concave mirrors form either real or virtual images.

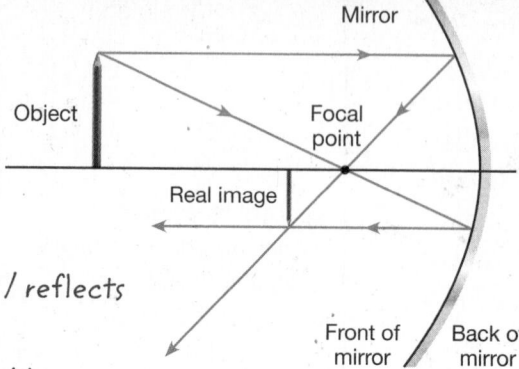

15 A mirror refracts / reflects light.

16 When reflected light converges, a real / virtual image is formed.

Concave lenses produce only virtual images.

19 A concave lens is thinner / thicker in the center than at the edges.

20 A concave lens produces a magnified / smaller image.

Convex mirrors form virtual images.

17 A convex mirror curves inward / outward.

18 Light does / does not pass through a virtual image.

Convex lenses produce real or virtual images.

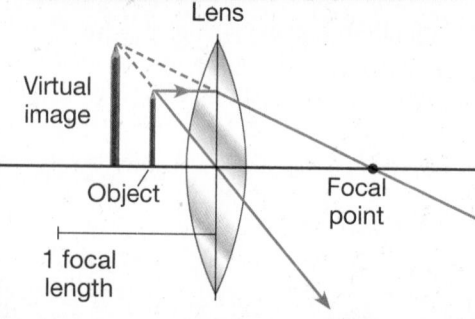

21 A convex lens causes parallel rays of light to spread out / converge.

22 The image produced by a convex lens when the object is close to the lens is real / virtual.

Answers: 15 reflects; 16 real; 17 outward; 18 does not; 19 thinner; 20 smaller; 21 converge; 22 virtual

---

23 Claims • Evidence • Reasoning Using what you know about images and lenses, make a claim about why projectors use convex instead of concave lenses. Use evidence to support your claim.

Lesson Review

Vocabulary

Draw a line to connect the following terms to their definitions.

1 converge   **A** reflected or refracted light converges

2 diverge

3 convex   **B** thick center and thin edges

4 concave   **C** reflected or refracted light does not cross

5 real image   **D** spread apart

6 virtual image   **E** bring together

   F thin center and thick edges

Key Concepts

7 Classify What do you see when you look at yourself in a plane mirror?

   A a real image that appears to be inside the mirror

   B a real image that appears to be in front of the mirror

   C a virtual image that appears to be inside the mirror

   D a virtual image that appears to be in front of the mirror

8 Distinguish What determines whether a real or a virtual image is formed from a concave mirror?

_____

_____

9 Explain How does a concave lens affect rays of light?

_____

_____

10 Apply What can you use a convex lens to do when you hold it close to an object?

_____

_____

Critical Thinking

11 Classify How can you use a screen to determine whether an image is real or virtual?

_____

_____

_____

12 Apply What kind of mirror do you think is used in the side-view mirror of cars? Explain.

_____

_____

_____

_____

13 Justify Why can a ray be used to represent light in a ray diagram?

   A Light waves are electromagnetic waves.

   B Light waves spread out in all directions.

   C Light waves travel in straight lines.

   D Light waves can be reflected or refracted.

Use this drawing to answer the following questions.

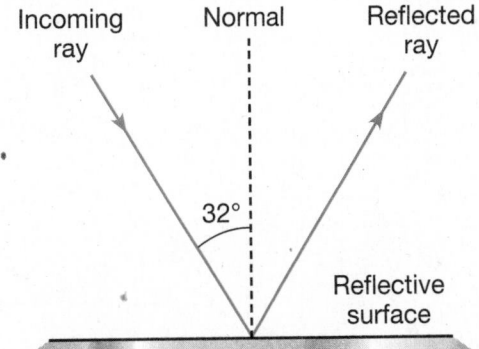

14 Analyze What is the angle of the reflected ray in the diagram above?

_____

15 Diagram On the diagram, draw the incoming and reflected rays for light hitting the mirror at a 50° angle from the normal.

My Notes

S8P4.c Applications of the electromagnetic spectrum

S8P4.g Lenses and light

Engineering Design Process

Skills
Identify a need
Conduct research
✓ Brainstorm solutions
✓ Select a solution
Design a prototype
✓ Build a prototype
✓ Test and evaluate
✓ Redesign to improve
✓ Communicate results

Objectives
• Identify different uses of mirrors and lenses.
• Use mirrors and lenses to design and build a periscope.
• Test and evaluate the periscope you built.

Building a Periscope

A *periscope* is a device that uses mirrors and lenses to help people see around obstacles. You might be surprised to learn how many other important technologies benefit from mirrors and lenses.

Early Uses of Mirrors and Lenses

For many centuries, people have used mirrors and lenses to bend light. In ancient times, people used shiny metal to see their reflections and pieces of curved glass to start fires. In the 17th century, scientists began using lenses and mirrors to make telescopes, microscopes, and other devices that helped them make new discoveries.

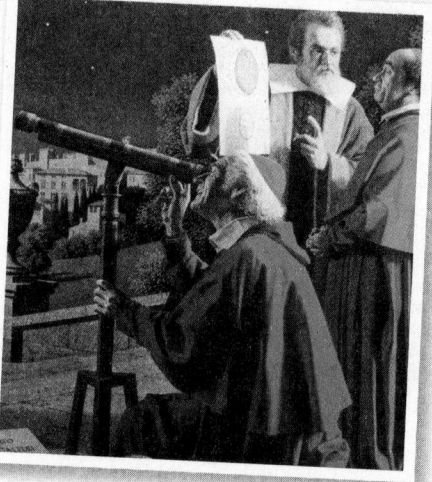

In 1610, Italian astronomer Galileo used a two-lens telescope to discover Jupiter's moons.

1 Identify List devices that use mirrors, lenses, or a combination of both. Then describe the purpose of each device, and identify whether it uses mirrors, lenses, or both.

Device	Purpose	Mirrors, Lenses, or Both
telescope	magnifies far away objects	both

© Houghton Mifflin Harcourt Publishing Company • Image Credits: ©Mehau Kulyk/Photo Researchers, Inc.

Lasers

Mirrors bend light by reflecting it in a different direction. Lenses bend light by slowing it as it passes through the lens material. Many modern technologies also take advantage of mirrors and lenses. Devices such as DVD players and barcode scanners operate by using laser light. A *laser* is a device that produces a coherent beam of light of a specific wavelength, or color. Laser light is created in a chamber that has mirrors on each end. A single color of light is produced by reflecting light back and forth between the two mirrors. The distance between the mirrors determines the wavelength of light that is amplified. When the light is of the proper wavelength, it can exit the transparent center of one of the mirrors. Lenses are often found in devices that use laser light. Lenses can focus the laser light in devices such as DVD players.

2 Identify Conduct research about the uses of laser light. What are some objects that use lasers?

_____

_____

_____

This device uses mirrors and lasers to measure the wind speed during an aircraft test. Wind speed is measured as the laser interacts with dust in the wind.

Periscopes

A periscope is another type of device that uses mirrors and lenses. The mirrors in a periscope bend light in order to allow a person to see around obstacles or above water. Most people think of periscopes in submarines, but periscopes are also used to see over walls or around corners, to see out of parade floats, and to see inside pipes or machinery.

Submarine periscopes use lenses and mirrored prisms to allow people to see above the water without surfacing.

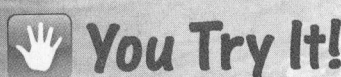 You Try It! ⟶

Now it's your turn to use mirrors and lenses to design and build a periscope.

 You Try It!

Mirrors are used to focus light, and lenses are used to bend light. Now it's your turn to use mirrors and lenses to design and build a periscope that can see at least six inches above eye level.

You Will Need

✔ cardboard boxes or poster board

✔ cardboard or plastic tubes

✔ lenses

✔ mirrors

✔ scissors

✔ tape

① Brainstorm Solutions

A You will build a periscope to see things at least six inches above eye level. Brainstorm some ideas about how your periscope will work. Check a box in each row below to get started.

Length of periscope: ☐ 6 inches ☐ 12 inches ☐ other _____

Shape of periscope: ☐ tube ☐ box ☐ other _____

User will look with: ☐ one eye ☐ both eyes

Your periscope: ☐ will ☐ will not magnify objects

B Once you have decided what your periscope needs to do, look at the materials available to you, and brainstorm how you can build your periscope. Write down the materials you will use and how you will use them.

_____

_____

_____

② Select a Solution

Choose one of the ideas that you brainstormed. In the space below, draw a sketch of how your prototype periscope will be constructed. Include arrows to show the path of light through your periscope.

③ Build a Prototype

Use your materials to assemble the periscope according to your design. Write down the steps you took to assemble the parts.

_____

_____

_____

_____

④ Test, Evaluate, and Redesign to Improve

Test your periscope, and fill in the first row of the table below. Make any improvements, and test your periscope again, filling in an additional row of the table for each revised prototype.

Prototype	What I saw through the periscope	Improvements to be made
1		
2		
3		

⑤ Communicate Results

Write a paragraph summarizing what you wanted the periscope to do, how you designed and built it, whether the finished periscope worked as planned, and how you made improvements.

_____

_____

_____

_____

_____

_____

Light Waves and Sight

ESSENTIAL QUESTION

How do people see?

By the end of this lesson, you should be able to explain how the eye functions and works with the brain to produce vision.

S8P4.g Lenses and light

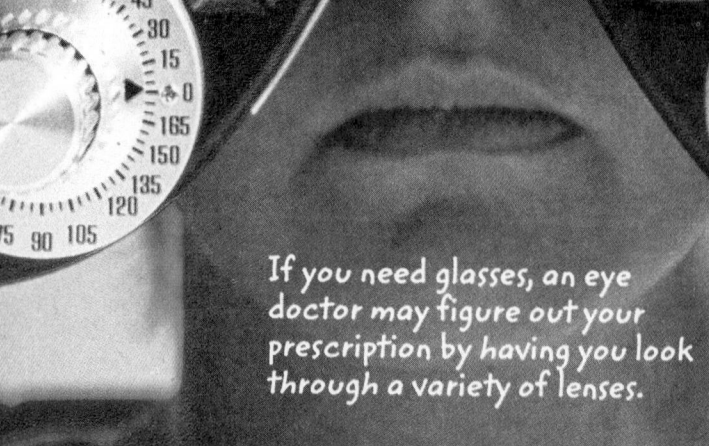

If you need glasses, an eye doctor may figure out your prescription by having you look through a variety of lenses.

Engage Your Brain

1 Predict Check **T** or **F** to show whether you think each statement is true or false.

T   F

☐ ☐ The shape of your eye can make you farsighted or nearsighted.

☐ ☐ One way to correct vision problems is through surgery.

☐ ☐ The cornea of your eye controls the amount of light let in.

☐ ☐ The brain collects signals from the eyes about an image and flips it right side up.

2 Illustrate Draw and label the parts of the eye that you are familiar with.

Active Reading

3 Apply Many scientific words, such as *focus*, also have everyday meanings. Use context clues to write your own definition for each meaning of the word *focus*.

Example sentence
I need to stop listening to music and <u>focus</u> on getting my homework done.

focus:

_____

_____

Example sentence
A convex lens can be used to <u>focus</u> light rays into a point.

focus:

_____

_____

Vocabulary Terms

- cornea
- retina

4 Apply As you learn the definition of each vocabulary term in this lesson, create your own definition or sketch to help you remember the meaning of the term.

Let's Focus

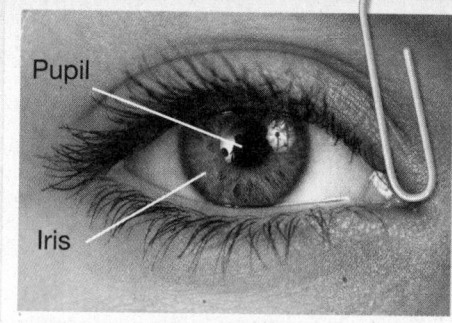

Pupil

Iris

How do people detect and interpret light waves?

How do your eyes and brain work together so that you can see things? You see an object when your eyes detect light and send signals to your brain. Some objects produce their own light, while other objects reflect light. No matter where the light comes from, the light has to enter your eye before you can see anything.

Visualize It!

5 Label After you read, add these labels to the art: cornea, pupil, retina, optic nerve.

Lens

Iris

A

B

Active Reading **6 Identify** As you read, underline two parts of the eye that refract light.

Light Waves Enter the Eye

Light waves enter the eye through the **cornea**, which is the transparent membrane that forms the front part of the eye. The cornea refracts, or bends, the light so that it passes through the pupil at the center of the iris. The iris changes the size of the pupil to control the amount of light let in. The light refracts again as it enters the lens. Muscles around the lens change its thickness so that objects at different distances can be seen in focus.

An Image Is Focused on the Retina

Images are received by the **retina**, the light-sensitive tissue that lines the inside of the eye. The retina is the part of the eye that detects light and sends signals to the brain. The image is actually focused upside down onto the retina. Two types of cells in the retina detect light—rod cells and cone cells. Rods are very sensitive and can detect even dim light. Cones detect brighter light and colors.

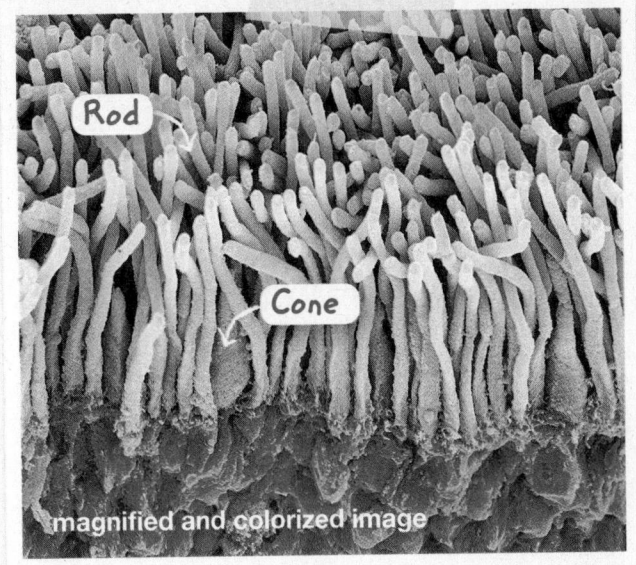

Rod

Cone

magnified and colorized image

C

Image

D

7 Compare Fill in the Venn diagram to compare and contrast rod cells and cone cells.

Rod cells

Cone cells

Both

The Brain Interprets the Signal

The rod and cone cells convert the input they receive into electrical signals. The signals travel to the brain over a bundle of tissue called the *optic nerve*. Different parts of the brain take in these signals and interpret the color, shape, movement, and location of the image. Although the image is sent upside down, the brain understands the image as being right side up. The brain also combines slightly different information from the right and left eyes to produce a sense of distance and depth.

Out of Sight

What are some common vision problems?

Because the eye is complex, there are many things that can affect how well a person's vision works. Common vision problems happen when light is not focused on the retina or when a part of the eye does not work properly.

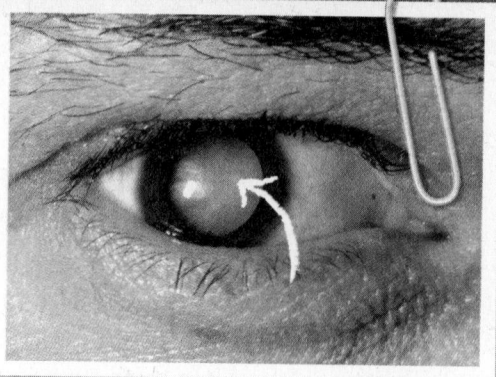

The clouding of an eye lens, called a cataract, interferes with light entering the eye.

Nearsightedness

Nearsightedness happens when a person's eye is too long or their cornea is curved steeply. Nearsighted eyes produce an image in front of the retina rather than on the retina. A nearsighted person can see something clearly only if it is nearby. Faraway objects look blurry.

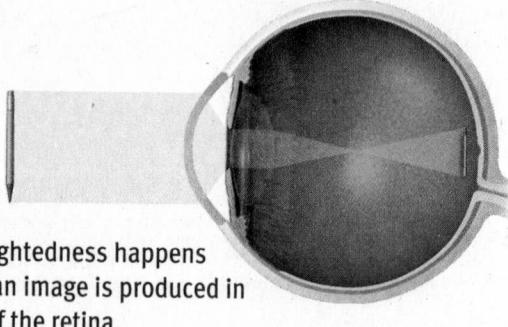

Nearsightedness happens when an image is produced in front of the retina.

Farsightedness

Farsightedness happens when a person's eye is too short or the cornea is not curved enough. Farsighted eyes see distant objects most clearly. Things that are nearby look blurry to a person who is farsighted. People are sometimes born farsighted and grow out of it as they get older.

Farsightedness happens when an image is produced behind the retina.

Color Vision Deficiency

About 5% to 8% of men and 0.5% of women in the world have color vision deficiency. This condition is often called color blindness, but very few people cannot see any color. Color vision deficiency happens when the cones in the retina do not work properly. A person who has normal vision can see all colors of visible light. But in some people, the cones respond to the wrong colors. These people see certain colors, such as red and green, as a different color, such as yellow. Color vision deficiency cannot be corrected.

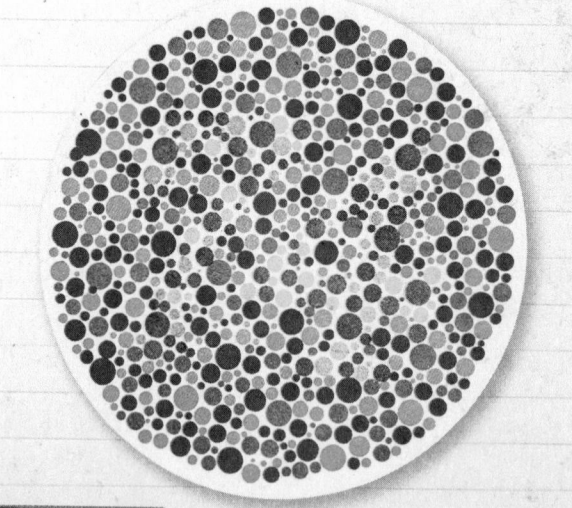

Visualize It!

8 Apply About 8% of males and 0.5% of females have red-green color deficiency. If you can see the number hidden in the test pattern above, write it here.

_____

© Houghton Mifflin Harcourt Publishing Company • Image Credits: (t) ©Sue Ford/Photo Researchers, Inc.; (b) ©Steve Allen/Brand X/Corbis

How can vision problems be corrected?

Nearsightedness and farsightedness are commonly corrected with eyeglasses or contact lenses. But lenses are not the only option. These vision problems can also be corrected with laser surgery.

With Corrective Lenses

Nearsightedness can be corrected with a concave lens. Light bends away from the thin center of a concave lens, and the image moves back to the retina. Farsightedness can be corrected with a convex lens. Light bends toward the wide middle of a convex lens, and the image moves forward to the retina.

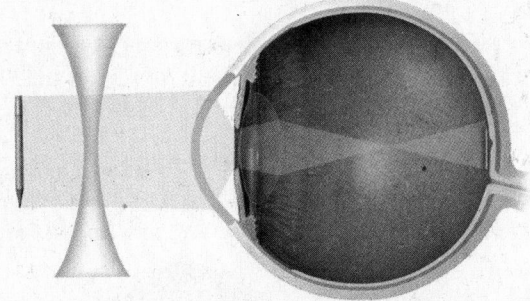

A concave lens placed in front of a nearsighted eye bends the light outward. The lens in the eye can then focus the light on the retina.

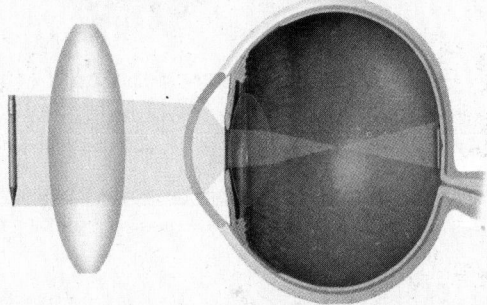

A convex lens placed in front of a farsighted eye focuses the light inward. The lens in the eye can then focus the light on the retina.

Visualize It!

9 Synthesize Why are concave lenses, rather than convex lenses, used to treat nearsightedness? Explain your reasoning.

_____

_____

_____

_____

With Contact Lenses or Surgery

Contact lenses correct vision by bending light in the same way eyeglasses do. Corrective eye surgery also works by reshaping the patient's cornea. Reshaping the cornea changes how light is focused on the retina. During surgery, a thin flap is folded back from the surface of the eye. The cornea is then reshaped with a laser so the patient gains perfect or nearly perfect vision.

Active Reading

10 State What part of the eye is changed by vision correction surgery or contact lenses?

_____

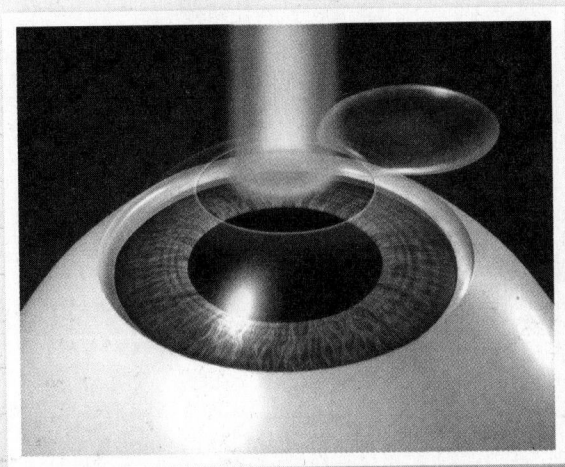

Vision correction surgery works by reshaping the front part of the eye.

Think Outside the Book (Inquiry)

11 Design Build a model that shows how to correct a common vision problem and share the model with your class.

Visual Summary

To complete this summary, choose the word that best completes the sentence. Then use the key below to check your answers. You can use this page to review the main concepts of the lesson.

Light Waves and Sight

Light reflects off objects and enters the eye through the cornea.

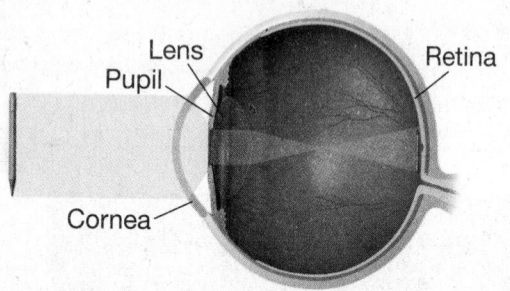

Lens
Pupil
Retina
Cornea

12 The pupil/lens limits how much light enters the eye.

Nearsighted eyes produce an image in front of the retina.

13 Concave lenses spread/focus light so that the image is moved back to the retina.

Farsighted eyes produce an image behind the retina.

14 Convex lenses spread/focus light so that the image is moved up to the retina.

15 Analyze Why is it important for the lens to be attached to muscles in the eye? Use evidence to support your claim.

Lesson Review

Vocabulary

Fill in the blank with the term that best completes the following sentences.

1 The _____ is a clear covering on the surface of an eye that focuses light as it enters the eye.

2 The _____ inside the eye further focuses light.

3 Inside the eye, an image is produced on the _____, and signals are sent to the brain.

Key Concepts

4 Distinguish Compare the function of rod cells and cone cells.

_____

_____

_____

_____

5 Explain How does the brain help with vision?

_____

_____

_____

_____

6 Compare How are nearsighted eyes different from eyes with normal vision?

_____

_____

_____

_____

7 Claims • Evidence • Reasoning Why can even a small injury to the cornea have a major effect on vision? Explain your reasoning.

_____

_____

_____

_____

Critical Thinking

Use these drawings to answer the following questions.

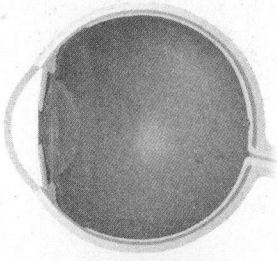

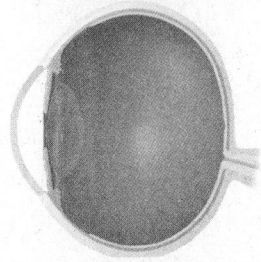

8 Draw Place an X on the top diagram of the eye to show where an image would be in a nearsighted eye.

9 Draw Place an X on the bottom diagram of the eye to show where an image would be in a farsighted eye.

10 Predict Which eye's problem could be corrected with a concave lens?

_____

11 Predict Which eye's problem could be corrected by increasing the curve of the cornea?

_____

12 Infer What might happen to a person's sense of depth or distance if they have only one functioning eye?

_____

_____

_____

_____

_____

My Notes

Light Technology

How can light be used?

By the end of this lesson, you should be able to apply knowledge of light to describe light-related technologies.

The searchlights on these buildings can be seen from miles away.

S8P4.c Applications of the electromagnetic spectrum

Lesson Labs

Quick Labs
• Light Technology in Color Monitors
• Total Internal Reflection

Exploration Lab
• Investigating Artificial Light

Engage Your Brain

1 Predict Check T or F to show whether you think each statement is true or false.

T	F	
☐	☐	Light can be used to perform surgery.
☐	☐	Light cannot be used to transmit sound or data.
☐	☐	Lasers emit light of all frequencies.
☐	☐	Light technology has stayed the same for decades.
☐	☐	Telescopes can use either lenses or mirrors to manipulate light.

2 Describe Do you think this fiber optic lamp is an example of light technology? Explain.

_____
_____
_____
_____

Active Reading

3 Apply Many scientific words, such as *fiber*, also have everyday meanings. Use context clues to write your own definition for each meaning of the word *fiber*.

Example sentence
Clothes can be made of wool fibers.

fiber:
_____
_____

Example sentence
Optical fibers use light to transmit information.

fiber:
_____
_____

Vocabulary Terms
• incandescent light   • laser
• fluorescent light   • optical fiber
• LED

4 Identify As you read, place a question mark next to any words you don't understand. When you finish reading the lesson, go back and review the text that you marked. If the information is still confusing, consult a classmate or a teacher.

I Can See the LIGHT

What are some ways to produce light?

Throughout history, people have developed different ways of producing light to help see things, store and transfer information, and interact with matter. These are considered light technologies. For example, candles were an early invention that helped people see and work even after the sun went down. We now have a wider variety of technologies that produce and use light.

Think Outside the Book **Inquiry**

5 **Research** Investigate light pollution. Write a public service announcement about light pollution, or communicate a new way to produce light while preventing light pollution.

Incandescent Lights

Visible light produced from a very hot material is **incandescent light** (in•kuhn•DES•uhnt LYT). In a typical incandescent bulb, electric current is passed through a thin wire, called a *filament*, inside the bulb. The filament gets hot enough to *emit*, or give off, visible light. Incandescent bulbs are inefficient in producing light compared with other types of bulbs. Only about 8% of the energy given off by an incandescent light bulb is in the form of light. The rest is in the form of heat.

Fluorescent Lights

Electric current can energize some gases and produce ultraviolet light, which is invisible to humans. **Fluorescent light** (flu•RES•uhnt LYT) is produced when a fluorescent coating inside a bulb converts the ultraviolet light into visible light. About 80% of the energy given off by fluorescent bulbs is in the form of visible light. Fluorescent bulbs last about 10 times longer than incandescent bulbs. The screens of many devices produce light using similar technologies.

6 **Compare** Fill in the Venn diagram to compare and contrast incandescent and fluorescent light bulbs.

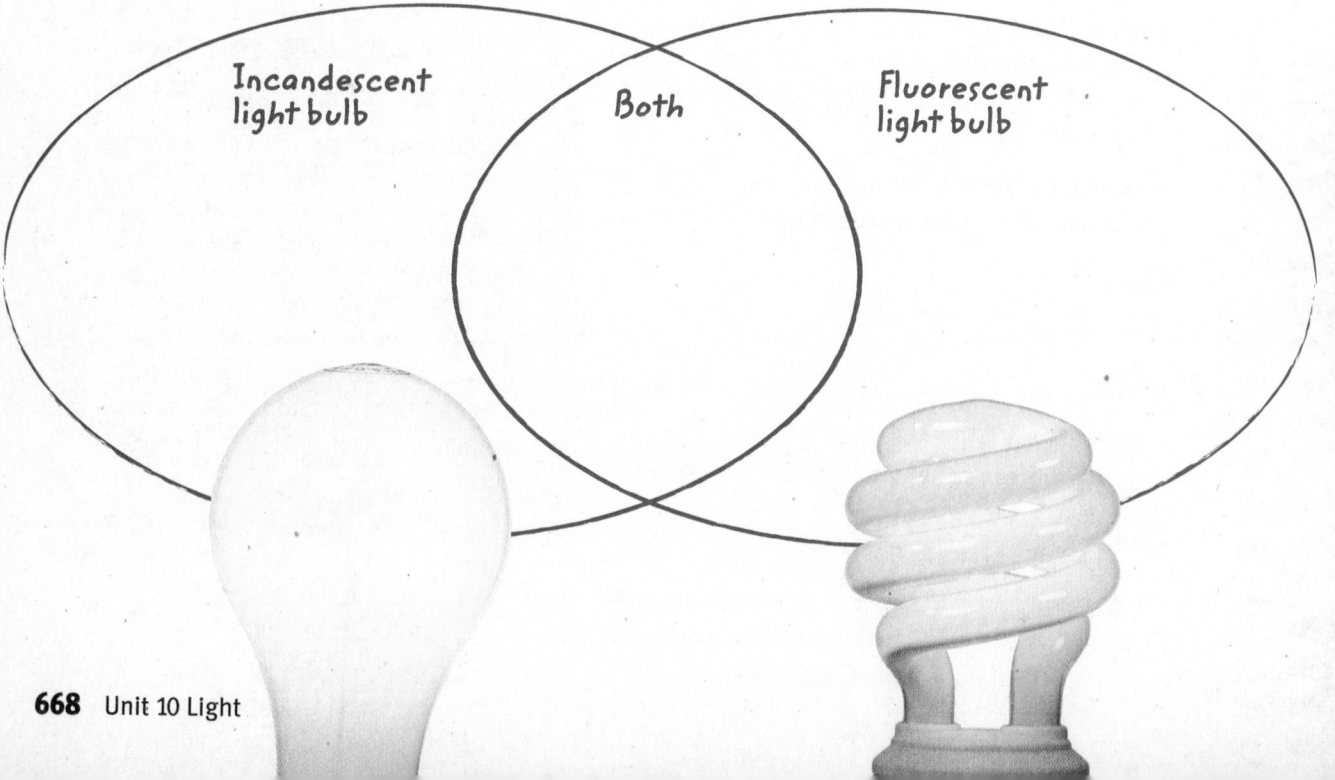

Incandescent light bulb

Both

Fluorescent light bulb

Light-Emitting Diodes

The tiny indicator light on many electronic devices is a *light-emitting diode*, or *LED*. **LEDs** contain solid materials that emit light when energized by an electric current. Unlike other light sources, an LED emits only one color of light. Almost 100% of the energy given off by LEDs is in the form of visible light. This means that LEDs are very efficient and last a long time. Most traffic lights in the United States now use LEDs.

A string of LEDs can provide light for many years.

Lasers

A **laser** is a device that produces intense light of a very small range of wavelengths. Lasers produce light in such a way that causes the light to be more concentrated, or intense, than other types of light. Unlike non-laser light, laser light is *coherent*. When light is coherent, light waves stay together as they travel away from their source. The crests and troughs of coherent light waves are aligned. So the individual waves behave as one wave. The diagram below shows how lasers produce coherent light.

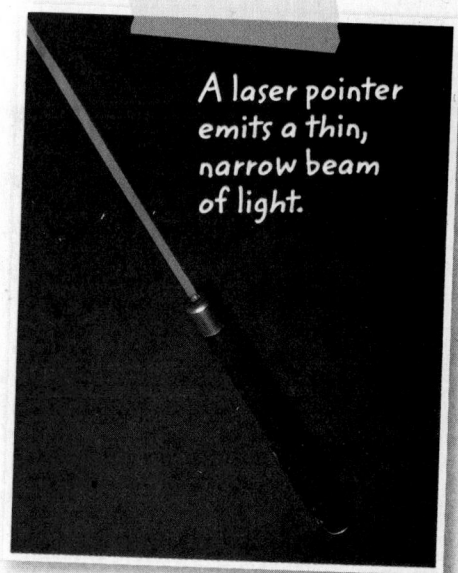

A laser pointer emits a thin, narrow beam of light.

7 Infer What might be an advantage of focusing light into a narrow beam?

_____

_____

_____

How a Helium-Neon Laser Works

A The inside of the laser is filled with helium and neon gases. An electric current in the laser "excites" the atoms of the gases.

B Excited neon atoms release photons of red light. When these photons strike other excited neon atoms, more photons are released that travel together.

C Plane mirrors on both ends of the laser reflect the photons back and forth along the tube.

D Because the photons travel back and forth many times, many more photons are released, and the laser light gets brighter.

E A partial coating on one mirror allows the laser light to escape and form a coherent beam.

Light SPEED

What are some ways light can transfer information?

Some light technologies use light to encode, send, or read signals. For example, a laser inside a CD or DVD player reads the information stored on the disc. Other examples are the bar code scanners in retail stores that record the price of your purchase and TV remote controls that are used to transfer information. Remote controls typically use infrared light.

Infrared Technologies

Infrared radiation is invisible electromagnetic radiation with a wavelength longer than what our eyes can detect. However, several technologies make use of infrared radiation. Some night vision goggles can emit infrared radiation, allowing people to see objects without the help of visible light. Weather satellites can track storms forming at night by taking infrared pictures. Space-based telescopes can determine the temperatures of stars and dust clouds by measuring the infrared radiation coming from them.

Active Reading **8 Identify** As you read, underline three uses of optical fibers.

Fiber Optic Technologies

A thin, transparent glass thread that transmits light over long distances is an **optical fiber**. A bundle of optical fibers is shown on the left. Transmitting information through telephone cables is the most common use of optical fibers. They are also used to network computers and to allow doctors to see inside patients' bodies without performing major surgery.

Optical fibers are like pipes that carry light. Light stays inside an optical fiber because of *total internal reflection*. Total internal reflection is the complete reflection of light back and forth along the inside surface of the material through which it travels. Light is emitted out the end of the fiber.

An optical fiber is flexible and can transmit light with little loss.

Visualize It!

9 Diagram Draw a circle on the fiber optic diagram to show where light is emitted.

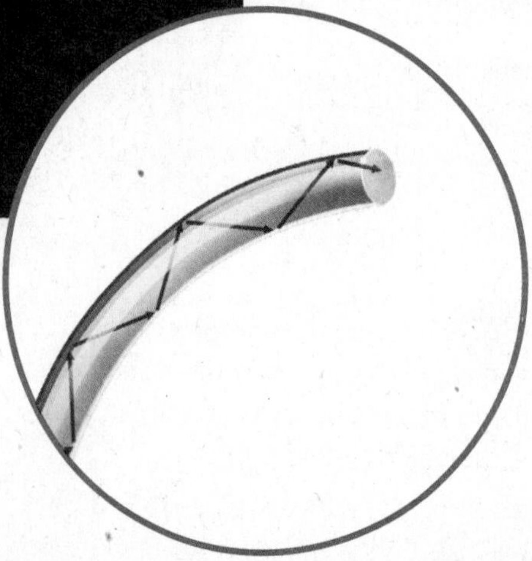

Light traveling through an optical fiber reflects off the sides thousands of times each meter.

© Houghton Mifflin Harcourt Publishing Company • Image Credits: ©Kulka/zefa/Corbis

Satellites in orbit 20,000 km above Earth emit microwaves that are detected by GPS receivers.

Smartphones equipped with GPS receivers can help people navigate a city.

Satellite Technologies

Another technology that uses electromagnetic waves to transmit data is satellite technology. Some satellites are used to send TV, radio, and cell phone data to your home. Weather and government satellites also transmit data using electromagnetic waves.

The Global Positioning System (GPS) is a network of 24 satellites that orbit Earth. These satellites continuously send microwave signals. The signals can be picked up by a GPS receiver on Earth and used to measure positions on Earth's surface. GPS was originally used by the U.S. military. Now, anyone in the world who has a GPS receiver can use the system. Many cars have GPS road maps that help the car's driver navigate to a certain place. Hikers and campers use GPS receivers to find their way in the wilderness.

10 **Compare** What do infrared technologies, fiber optic technologies, and satellite technologies all have in common? Explain your reasoning.

_____

_____

_____

Light
WORK

A truck with a radar dish can follow storm clouds and gather information about them.

What are some ways light can interact with matter?

Light technologies can make use of the ways light interacts with matter to get information about materials. The light emitted, absorbed, or reflected by objects contains an amazing amount of information about the objects' composition, motion, and temperature. Light technologies, such as lasers, can also be used to produce and control energy to actually change matter.

Doppler Radar

Doppler radar uses light in the form of radio waves to measure weather patterns. Radio waves are sent out toward a weather system. They bounce off of the clouds and back to the transmitter, which captures them for analysis. The frequency of the radio waves changes a small amount, depending on how the weather system is moving. The reflected radio waves are received, and the image is used to make a picture of the entire moving weather system. The speed and intensity of the moving system can be determined.

Doppler radar uses light to measure the intensity, location, and movement of a storm system, such as this hurricane. On the radar map, blue is used to show the areas with the lightest rain. Yellow and green represent moderate rain.

 **Active Reading**

11 Identify What form of light does Doppler radar use?

Laser Technologies

The light from lasers can be accurately pointed. The intense energy of the light beam can be used to melt and cut different materials. For example, lasers can be used in manufacturing to cut, weld, and engrave certain metals. Doctors sometimes use lasers for surgery because a laser can be used to make very precise incisions. Lasers are used to shape the cornea of the eye to correct eyesight.

Lasers are found in many everyday devices, too. They are used in the CD drive of computers and in many printers. Laser pointers can be used from a distance, and laser levelers can help you hang pictures in a straight line. Lasers are also used to make holograms, the three-dimensional images seen on credit cards.

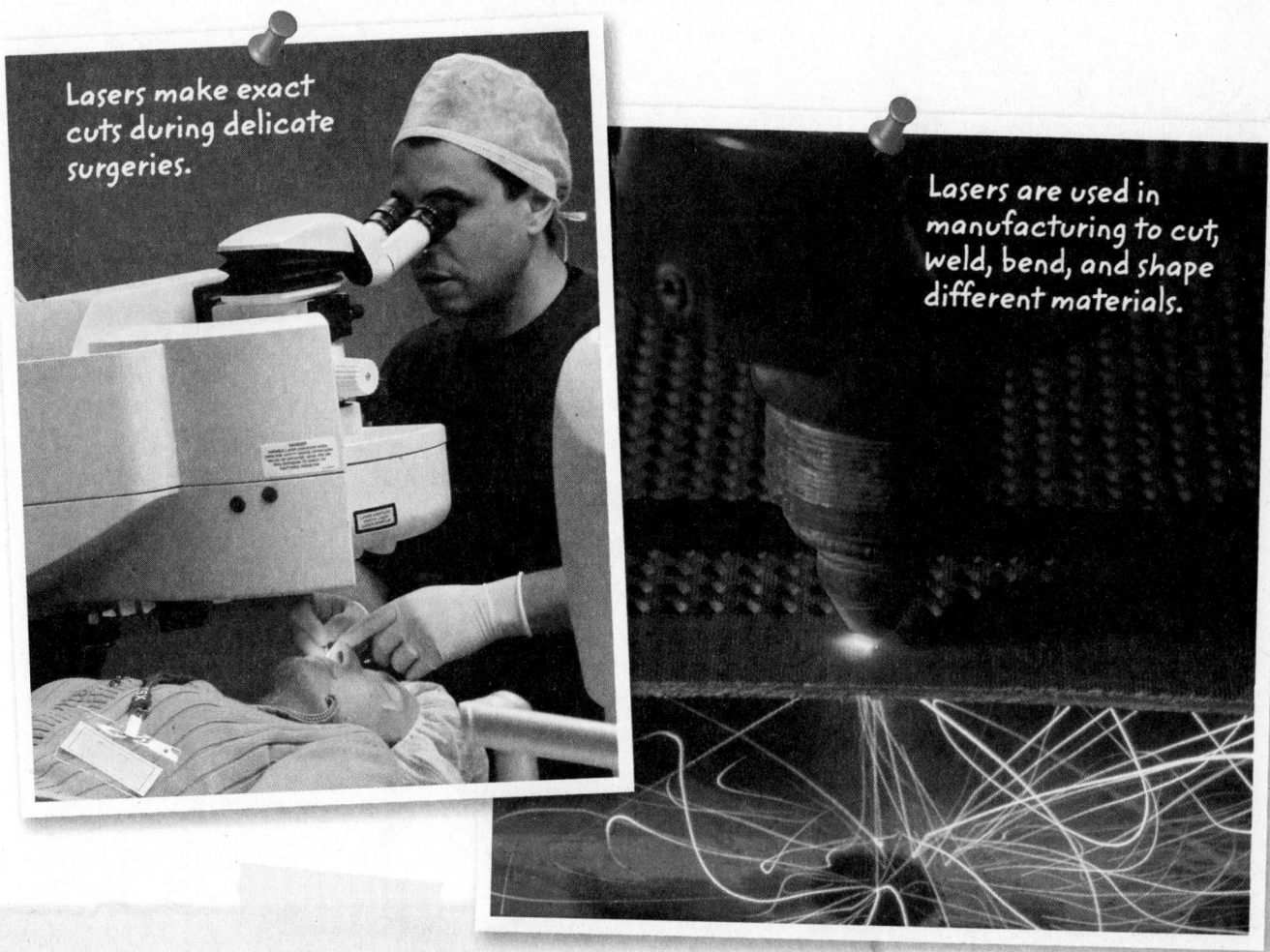

Lasers make exact cuts during delicate surgeries.

Lasers are used in manufacturing to cut, weld, bend, and shape different materials.

© Houghton Mifflin Harcourt Publishing Company • Image Credits: (l) ©Ilene MacDonald/Alamy Images; (r) ©Bruce H. Frisch/Photo Researchers, Inc.

Active Reading

12 Identify As you read, underline five specific uses of laser technology.

13 Infer The photographs on this page show medical and industrial applications of laser technology. Describe a household use of lasers.

_____

_____

_____

_____

Seeing is BELIEVING

What are some ways light can change what people see?

Optical instruments are devices that use mirrors and lenses to control the path of light and change what people can see. These light technologies help people see objects that cannot be observed with the eye alone. Microscopes allow people to see the very small; binoculars and telescopes can allow people to see the very far. Cameras can help people see things that are fast, slow, dangerous, or hard to reach.

Active Reading

14 Identify As you read, underline four examples of light technology that change what people see.

Microscopes

Microscopes are used to see magnified images of tiny, nearby objects. Simple light microscopes have two convex lenses. An objective lens is close to the object being studied. An eyepiece lens is the lens you look through. Light from a lamp or mirror at the bottom shines through the object being studied. The user looks through the eyepiece and focuses on the object.

Visualize It!

15 Identify Label the lenses in the illustration.

A

B

Green chloroplasts inside plant cells.

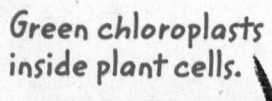

Microscopes allow us to see the very small objects in our world.

Telescopes

Telescopes are used to see images of large, distant objects. Astronomers use telescopes to study known objects, like the moon, and to search for undiscovered objects. Telescopes that use visible light are classified as either refracting or reflecting. Refracting telescopes use lenses to collect light. Reflecting telescopes use mirrors to collect light. Large telescopes are often housed in observatories, high on mountaintops. The less atmosphere the light travels through, the clearer the image appears.

Telescopes allow people to observe objects that are billions of light-years away.

Cameras

Cameras are used to record images. A digital camera controls the light that enters the camera and uses sensors to detect the light. The sensors send an electrical signal to a computer in the camera. This signal contains data about the image that can be stored and transferred. Some cameras also record video using computers. Cameras are useful for scientists who need to see and record things that are fast, slow, dangerous, or hard to reach.

The lens of a digital camera focuses light on the sensors. Moving the lens focuses light from objects at different distances.

Video cameras can record motion data, which can be analyzed later in a laboratory.

The aperture is an opening that lets light into the camera. The larger the aperture is, the more light enters the camera.

Think Outside the Book

16 Summarize Choose one of the technologies on these two pages and research its history. Write a report of your findings.

Visual Summary

To complete this summary, fill in each blank with the correct word or phrase. Then use the key below to check your answers. You can use this page to review the main concepts of the lesson.

Light Technology

Light is produced in many different ways.

17 A(n) _____ bulb produces light more efficiently than a(n) _____ bulb does.

Light can be used to transfer information.

18 _____ can transmit telephone calls, network computers, and allow doctors to see inside the body.

Interactions between light and matter help humans perform tasks.

19 Lasers are useful in manufacturing because the light beam is narrow and carries a great amount of _____

Light can be manipulated to change what people can see.

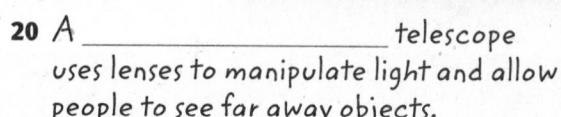

20 A _____ telescope uses lenses to manipulate light and allow people to see far away objects.

21 **Conclude** Describe three areas of human knowledge that would not be as advanced without light technology.

Lesson Review

Vocabulary

Fill in the blank with the term that best completes the following sentences.

1 The coating in a(n) _____ light bulb emits light when it interacts with ultraviolet light.

2 The material inside a(n) _____ light bulb emits light when it is very hot.

3 A(n) _____ contains solid materials that emit light when energized by an electric current.

4 Intense light of a narrow range of wavelengths is called _____ light.

Key Concepts

5 List Give three examples of infrared technologies.

_____

_____

_____

6 Identify What light technology is used by GPS systems?

_____

7 Explain How can a camera help someone see something he or she wouldn't normally be able to see?

_____

_____

_____

_____

_____

8 Distinguish In what way is laser light different from the light produced by other sources?

_____

_____

_____

_____

Critical Thinking

Use this drawing to answer the following questions.

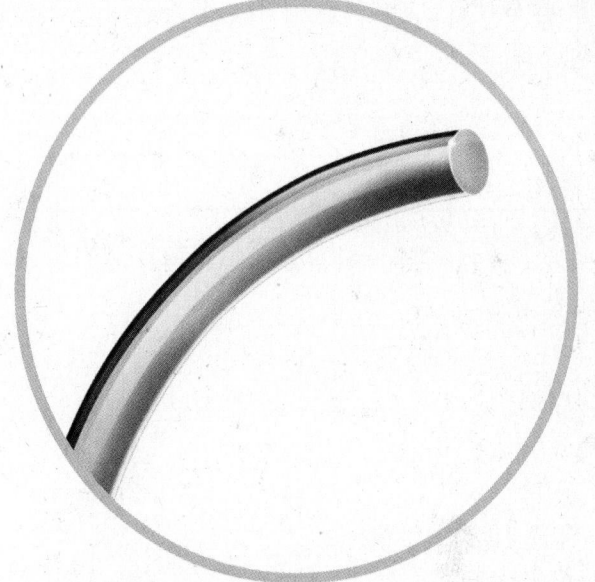

9 Illustrate Draw light rays on the fiber to show how light travels through, and is emitted from, an optical fiber.

10 Evaluate What are some advantages of optical fibers?

_____

_____

_____

_____

_____

11 Claims • Evidence • Reasoning Some streetlights use incandescent bulbs, and others use LEDs. Make a claim about which you would recommend. Use evidence to support your claim and explain your reasoning.

_____

_____

_____

_____

_____

_____

My Notes

Unit 10 | Big Idea

Visible light is the small part of the electromagnetic spectrum that is essential for human vision.

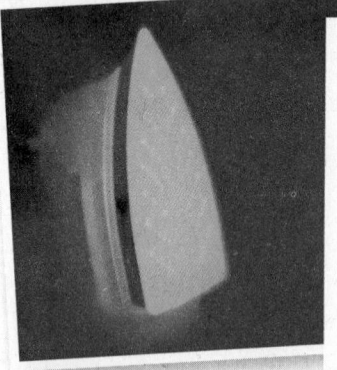

Lesson 1
ESSENTIAL QUESTION
What is the relationship between various EM waves?

Distinguish between the parts of the electromagnetic spectrum.

Lesson 2
ESSENTIAL QUESTION
How does light interact with matter?

Explain how light and matter can interact.

Lesson 3
ESSENTIAL QUESTION
How do mirrors and lenses work?

Describe ways that lenses and mirrors form images.

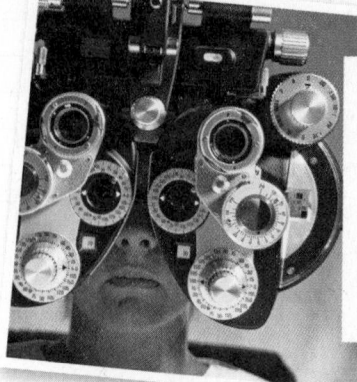

Lesson 4
ESSENTIAL QUESTION
How do people see?

Explain how the eye functions and works with the brain to produce vision.

Lesson 5
ESSENTIAL QUESTION
How can light be used?

Apply knowledge of light to describe light-related technologies.

Connect ESSENTIAL QUESTIONS
Lessons 1, 3, and 4

1 Synthesize What type of light forms a reflected image in a mirror? Would you expect that a mirror would reflect ultraviolet light? Explain.

_____

_____

_____

_____

Think Outside the Book

2 Synthesize Choose one of these activities to help synthesize what you have learned in this unit.

☐ Using what you learned in lessons 3 and 4, make a poster presentation explaining the ways in which lenses help people see better.

☐ Using what you learned in lessons 1, 2, and 5, and research, create a timeline showing how understanding the electromagnetic spectrum and the ways in which to apply it has affected communications technology.

Name _____

Vocabulary

Check the box to show whether each statement is true or false.

T	F	
☐	☐	**1** A <u>convex</u> mirror curves outward like the back of a spoon.
☐	☐	**2** <u>Laser</u> light is more intense than other types of light because it comes from a very small range of wavelengths in the visible spectrum.
☐	☐	**3** Electromagnetic waves travel through a medium by <u>radiation</u>.
☐	☐	**4** <u>Scattering</u> occurs when certain wavelengths of light are reflected by particles, causing the light to spread out in all directions
☐	☐	**5** A material that allows light to pass through it completely is <u>transparent</u>.

Key Concepts

Read each question below, and circle the best answer.

6 Which statement best explains why most people can see colors?

  A The eyes and brain can see all wavelengths in the electromagnetic spectrum.

  B The eyes and brain rely on all of the radiation from the sun to see colors.

  C The eyes and brain interpret different wavelengths of visible light as different colors.

  D The eyes and brain see light waves only when they travel through a medium.

7 What type of cells in the retina are involved in detecting light?

  A the lens and the cornea

  B rod cells and lenses

  C rod cells and cone cells

  D cone cells and corneas

8 The table below lists electromagnetic waves.

Low frequency ↓ High frequency	A	B	C	D
	Radio waves	Gamma rays	Laser light	Visible light
	Microwaves	x-rays	Visible light	x-rays
	Infrared waves	Ultraviolet light	Ultraviolet light	Ultraviolet light
	Visible light	Visible light	x-rays	Radio waves
	Ultraviolet light	Infrared light	Gamma rays	Microwaves

Which column correctly lists waves from lowest to highest frequencies?

A Column A

B Column B

C Column C

D Column D

9 Which statement best tells ways in which light interacts with matter?

A Light can come from the sun, fire, or a light bulb.

B Light waves can be reflected, refracted, or diffracted by matter.

C Laser light goes through matter, and all other light gets stopped by matter.

D Only visible light can interact with matter.

10 Waves of red light and yellow light go through air and strike a piece of glass. The diagram shows how the two kinds of light interact with the glass.

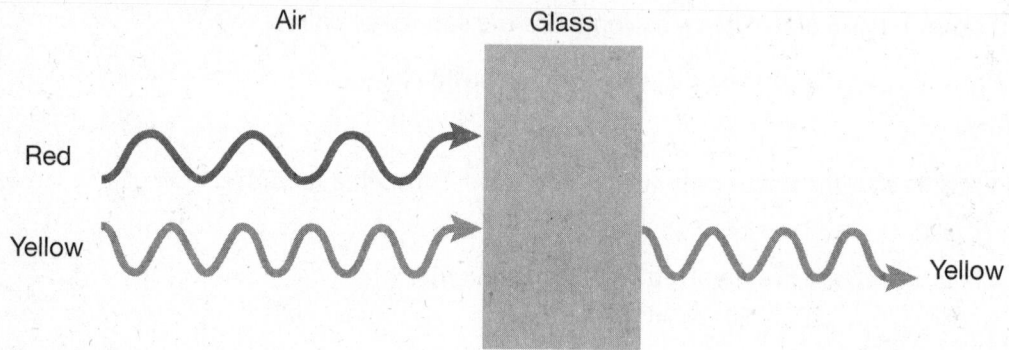

Which statement describes how the glass interacts with red and yellow light?

A The glass absorbs red light and transmits yellow light.

B The glass transmits red light and absorbs yellow light.

C The glass reflects both red and yellow light.

D The glass transmits both red and yellow light.

11 A beam of incoming light strikes a flat mirror. The mirror reflects the light.

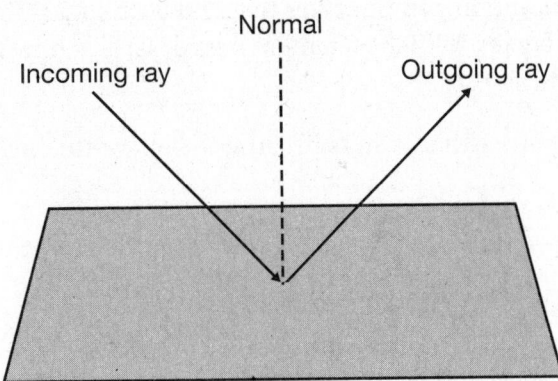

Normal

Incoming ray   Outgoing ray

Which statement best explains what this diagram of a light ray and a mirror is showing?

A A mirror scatters most of the light that strikes its surface.

B The normal absorbs rays of light that strike the surface of a mirror.

C The normal is used to measure the angle of a light ray reflecting off the surface of a flat mirror.

D The angle of an incoming ray is used to predict the angle of the normal when light strikes the surface.

12 When Juan shined a light through the liquid in glass A and then glass B, he saw that the liquids in the two glasses looked different.

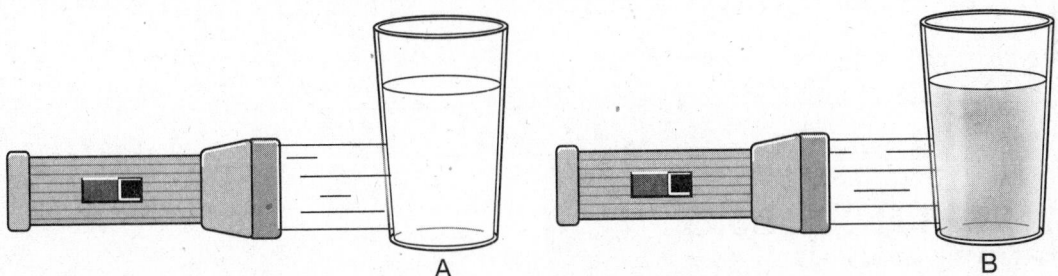

A   B

What did the liquids' appearance tell about how light was interacting with them?

A The liquid in glass A absorbed light; the liquid in glass B reflected light.

B The liquid in glass A was transparent; the liquid in glass B was translucent.

C The liquid in glass A was translucent; the liquid in glass B was transparent.

D The liquids looked different because the liquid in glass A scattered more light than the liquid in glass B.

13 The electromagnetic spectrum includes all electromagnetic waves, from radio waves with long wavelengths and low frequencies to gamma rays with short wavelengths and high frequencies. Which statement best describes how fast these waves travel in a vacuum?

A Gamma rays travel much faster than others because they have the highest frequencies.

B High frequency waves travel somewhat faster than low frequency waves

C Infrared waves travel faster than ultraviolet waves.

D All electromagnetic waves travel at the same speed.

Critical Thinking

Answer the following questions in the space provided.

14 Explain what the cornea is and how it interacts with light. What is the role of the retina in vision?

_____

_____

15 Name three main shapes that mirrors can have. What is the difference between converging and diverging mirrors? Describe real and virtual images.

_____

_____

_____

_____

Connect ESSENTIAL QUESTIONS
Lessons 1, 4, and 5

Answer the following question in the space provided.

16 Give two examples of natural light and two examples of artificial light. How is natural light transmitted? How is artificial light produced?

_____

_____

_____

_____

Resources

Glossary

© Houghton Mifflin Harcourt Publishing Company

Pronunciation Key

Sound	Symbol	Example	Respelling	Sound	Symbol	Example	Respelling
ă	a	pat	PAT	ŏ	ah	bottle	BAHT'l
ā	ay	pay	PAY	ō	oh	toe	TOH
âr	air	care	KAIR	ô	aw	caught	KAWT
ä	ah	father	FAH•ther	ôr	ohr	roar	ROHR
är	ar	argue	AR•gyoo	oi	oy	noisy	NOYZ•ee
ch	ch	chase	CHAYS	o͝o	u	book	BUK
ĕ	e	pet	PET	o͞o	oo	boot	BOOT
ĕ (at end of a syllable)	eh	settee lessee	seh•TEE leh•SEE	ou	ow	pound	POWND
ĕr	ehr	merry	MEHR•ee	s	s	center	SEN•ter
ē	ee	beach	BEECH	sh	sh	cache	CASH
g	g	gas	GAS	ŭ	uh	flood	FLUHD
ĭ	i	pit	PIT	ûr	er	bird	BERD
ĭ (at end of a syllable)	ih	guitar	gih•TAR	z	z	xylophone	ZY•luh•fohn
ī	y eye (only for a complete syllable)	pie island	PY EYE•luhnd	z	z	bags	BAGZ
				zh	zh	decision	dih•SIZH•uhn
îr	ir	hear	HIR	ə	uh	around broken focus	uh•ROWND BROH•kuhn FOH•kuhs
j	j	germ	JERM	ər	er	winner	WIN•er
k	k	kick	KIK	th	th	thin they	THIN THAY
ng	ng	thing	THING	w	w	one	WUHN
ngk	ngk	bank	BANGK	wh	hw	whether	HWETH•er

A

absorption (uhb·SOHRP·shuhn) in optics, the transfer of light energy to particles of matter (631)
absorción en óptica, la transferencia de energía luminosa a las partículas de materia

acceleration (ak·sel·uh·RAY·shuhn) the rate at which velocity changes over time; an object accelerates if its speed, direction, or both change (320)
aceleración tasa a la que la velocidad cambia con el tiempo; un cuerpo acelera si su rapidez cambia, si su dirección cambia, o si tanto su rapidez como su dirección cambian

amplitude (AM·plih·tood) the maximum distance that the particles of a wave's medium vibrate from their rest position (540)
amplitud distancia máxima a la que vibran las partículas del medio de una onda a partir de su posición de reposo

analog signal (AN·uh·lawg SIG·nuhl) a signal whose properties can change continuously in a given range (505)
señal análoga señal cuyas propiedades cambian continuamente en un rango determinado

Archimedes' principle (ar·kuh·MEE·deez PRIN·suh·puhl) the principle that states that the buoyant force on an object in a fluid is an upward force equal to the weight of the volume of fluid that the object displaces (366)
principio de Arquímedes principio que establece que la fuerza flotante de un cuerpo que está en un fluido es una fuerza ascendente cuya magnitud es igual al peso del volumen del fluido que el cuerpo desplaza

atmospheric pressure (at·muh·SFIR·ik PRESH·er) the pressure caused by the weight of the atmosphere (362)
presión atmosférica presión producida por el peso de la atmósfera

atom (AT·uhm) the smallest unit of an element that maintains the properties of that element (60, 181)
átomo unidad más pequeña de un elemento que conserva las propiedades de ese elemento

atomic number (uh·TAHM·ik NUM·ber) the number of protons in the nucleus of an atom; the atomic number is the same for all atoms of an element (186)
número atómico número de protones en el núcleo de un átomo; el número atómico es el mismo para todos los átomos de un elemento

average atomic mass (AV·er·ij uh·TAHM·ik MAS) the weighted average of the masses of all naturally occurring isotopes of an element (198)
masa atómica promedio promedio ponderado de las masas de todos los isótopos de un elemento que se encuentran en la naturaleza

B

boiling (BOYL·ing) the change of state from a liquid to a gas that occurs at a specific temperature (94)
ebullición cambio de estado de líquido a gaseoso que ocurre a una temperatura específica

buoyant force (BOY·uhnt FOHRS) the upward force that keeps an object immersed in or floating on a liquid (366)
fuerza boyante fuerza ascendente por la cual un cuerpo se mantiene sumergido en un líquido o flotando en él

C

calorie (KAL·uh·ree) the amount of energy needed to raise the temperature of 1 g of water 1 °C; the Calorie used to indicate the energy content of food is a kilocalorie (145)
caloría cantidad de energía que se requiere para aumentar la temperatura de 1 g de agua en 1 °C; la Caloría que se usa para indicar el contenido energético de los alimentos es la kilocaloría

carbohydrate (kar·boh·HY·drayt) a class of molecules that includes sugars, starches, and fiber; contains carbon, hydrogen, and oxygen (265)
carbohidrato clase de moléculas entre las que se incluyen azúcares, almidones y fibra; contiene carbono, hidrógeno y oxígeno

centripetal acceleration (sen·TRIP·ih·tl ak·sel·uh·RAY·shuhn) the acceleration directed toward the center of a circular path (323)
aceleración centrípeta aceleración que se dirige hacia el centro de un camino circular

chemical bond (KEM·ih·kuhl BAHND) an interaction that holds atoms or ions together (210)
enlace químico interacción que mantiene unidos los átomos o los iones

chemical change (KEM·ih·kuhl CHAYNJ) a change that occurs when one or more substances change into entirely new substances with different properties (44)
cambio químico cambio que ocurre cuando una o más sustancias se transforman en sustancias totalmente nuevas con propiedades diferentes

chemical equation (KEM·ih·kuhl ih·KWAY·zhuhn) a representation of a chemical reaction that uses symbols to show the relationship between the reactants and the products (245)
ecuación química representación de una reacción química que usa símbolos para mostrar la relación entre los reactivos y los productos

chemical formula (KEM·ih·kuhl FOHR·myuh·luh) a combination of chemical symbols and numbers to represent a substance (245)
fórmula química combinación de símbolos químicos y números que se usan para representar una sustancia

chemical property (KEM·ih·kuhl PRAHP·uhr·tee) a property of matter that describes a substance's ability to participate in chemical reactions (28)
propiedad química propiedad de la materia que describe la capacidad de una sustancia de participar en reacciones químicas

chemical reaction (KEM·ih·kuhl re·AK·shuhn) the process in which atoms are rearranged and chemical bonds are broken and formed to produce a chemical change of a substance (244)

reacción química proceso por el cual los átomos cambian su disposición y se rompen y forman enlaces químicos de manera que se produce un cambio químico en una sustancia

chemical symbol (KEM·ih·kuhl SIM·buhl) a one-, two-, or three-letter abbreviation of the name of an element (198)

símbolo químico abreviatura de una, dos o tres letras del nombre de un elemento

compound (KAHM·pownd) a substance made up of atoms of two or more different elements joined by chemical bonds (61)

compuesto sustancia formada por átomos de dos o más elementos diferentes unidos por enlaces químicos

computer (kuhm·PYOO·ter) an electronic device that can accept data and instructions, follow the instructions, and output the results (508)

computadora aparato electrónico que acepta información e instrucciones, sigue instrucciones, y produce una salida para los resultados

concave (kahn·KAYV) curved or rounded inward like the inside of a spoon (644)

cóncavo curvado o redondeado hacia adentro como la parte interior de una cuchara

condensation (kahn·den·SAY·shuhn) the change of state from a gas to a liquid (95)

condensación cambio de estado de gas a líquido

conduction (kuhn·DUHK·shuhn) the transfer of energy as heat through a material (147)

conducción transferencia de energía en forma de calor a través de un material

conductor (kuhn·DUK·ter) a material that transfers energy easily (147)

conductor material a través del cual se transfiere energía

convection (kuhn·VEK·shuhn) the movement of matter due to differences in density; the transfer of energy due to the movement of matter (148)

convección movimiento de la materia debido a diferencias en densidad; la transferencia de energía debido al movimiento de la materia

converge (kuhn·VERJ) to come together; a converging lens or mirror causes parallel beams of light to come together at a single point (644)

convergir unirse; una lente o espejo convergente hace que los rayos de luz paralelos se unan en un mismo punto

convex (KAHN·veks) curved or rounded outward like the back of a spoon (645)

convexo curvado o redondeado hacia afuera como la parte exterior de una cuchara

cornea (KOHR·nee·uh) a transparent membrane that covers the iris and pupil of the eye; much of the eye's refraction occurs as light passes through the cornea (658)

córnea membrana transparente que cubre el iris y la pupila del ojo; gran parte de la refracción del ojo ocurre cuando la luz pasa a través de la córnea

covalent bond (koh·VAY·luhnt BAHND) a bond formed when atoms share one or more pairs of electrons (226)

enlace covalente enlace formado cuando los átomos comparten uno o más pares de electrones

decibel (DES·uh·bel) the most common unit used to measure loudness (symbol, dB) (566)

decibel unidad más común que se usa para medir el volumen del sonido (símbolo: dB)

degree (dih·GREE) the units of a temperature scale (134)

grado unidad de una escala de temperatura

density (DEN·sih·tee) the ratio of the mass of a substance to the volume of the substance (13)

densidad relación entre la masa de una sustancia y su volumen

deposition (dep·uh·ZISH·uhn) the change of state from a gas directly to a solid (99)

depositación cambio de estado por el cual un gas se convierte directamente en un sólido

diffraction (dih·FRAK·shuhn) the bending of a wave as it passes through an opening or around an object (579, 634)

difracción desviación de una onda cuando pasa por una abertura o alrededor de un cuerpo

digital signal (DIJ·ih·tl SIG·nuhl) a signal that can be represented as a sequence of discrete values (506)

señal digital señal que se puede representar como una secuencia de valores discretos

diverge (dih·VERJ) to move apart; a diverging lens or mirror causes parallel beams of light to spread apart as if they came from a single point (645)

divergir separarse; una lente o espejo divergente hace que los rayos de luz paralelos se separen como si provinieran de un mismo punto

Doppler effect (DAHP·ler ih·FEKT) an observed change in the frequency of a wave when the source or observer is moving (567)

efecto Doppler cambio que se observa en la frecuencia de una onda cuando la fuente o el observador está en movimiento

echo (EK·oh) a reflected sound wave (577)

eco onda de sonido reflejada

echolocation (ek·oh·loh·KAY·shuhn) the process of using reflected sound waves to find objects; used by animals such as bats (590)

ecolocación proceso de usar ondas de sonido reflejadas para buscar objetos; utilizado por animales tales como los murciélagos

electric charge (ee·LEK·trik CHARJ) a fundamental property that leads to the electromagnetic interactions among particles that make up matter (436)

carga eléctrica propiedad fundamental que determina las interacciones electromagnéticas entre las partículas que forman la materia

electric circuit (ee·LEK·trik SER·kit) a set of electrical components connected such that they provide one or more complete paths for the movement of charges (458)
circuito eléctrico conjunto de componentes eléctricos conectados de modo que proporcionen una o más rutas completas para el movimiento de las cargas

electric current (ee·LEK·trik KER·uhnt) the rate at which electric charges pass a given point (448)
corriente eléctrica tasa a la que las cargas eléctricas pasan por un punto dado

electric field (ee·LEK·trik FEELD) the area surrounding a charged particle or object within which electrical force affects other charged particles or objects (437)
campo eléctrico área que rodea a una partícula o un cuerpo cargado en la que se ejerce una fuerza eléctrica sobre otras partículas o cuerpos cargados

electric generator (ee·LEK·trik JEN·uh·ray·ter) a device that converts mechanical energy into electrical energy (496)
generador eléctrico aparato que transforma la energía mecánica en energía eléctrica

electric motor (ee·LEK·trik MO·ter) a device that converts electrical energy into mechanical energy (492)
motor eléctrico aparato que transforma la energía eléctrica en energía mecánica

electrical conductor (ee·LEK·trik·kuhl kuhn·DUHK·ter) a material in which charges can move freely (440)
conductor eléctrico material en el que las cargas se mueven libremente

electrical insulator (ee·LEK·trih·kuhl IN·suh·lay·ter) a material in which charges cannot move freely (440)
aislante eléctrico material en el que las cargas no pueden moverse libremente

electromagnet (ee·lek·troh·MAG·nit) a coil that has a soft iron core and that acts as a magnet when an electric current is in the coil (489)
electroimán bobina que tiene un centro de hierro suave y que funciona como un imán cuando hay una corriente eléctrica en la bobina

electromagnetic induction (ee·lek·troh·mag·NET·ik in·DUHK·shuhn) the process of creating a current in a circuit by changing a magnetic field (494)
inducción electromagnética proceso de crear una corriente en un circuito por medio de un cambio en el campo magnético

electromagnetic spectrum (ee·lek·troh·mag·NET·ik SPEK·truhm) all of the frequencies or wavelengths of electromagnetic radiation (612)
espectro electromagnético todas las frecuencias o longitudes de onda de la radiación electromagnética

electromagnetic wave (ee·lek·troh·mag·NET·ik WAYV) a wave, consisting of changing electric and magnetic fields, that is emitted by vibrating electric charges and can travel through a vacuum (530)
onda electromagnética onda formada por campos eléctricos y magnéticos cambiantes, que es emitida por cargas eléctricas que vibran, y que puede viajar por un vacío

electromagnetism (ee·lek·troh·MAG·nih·tiz·uhm) the interaction between electricity and magnetism (488)
electromagnetismo interacción entre la electricidad y el magnetismo

electron (ee·LEK·trahn) a subatomic particle that has a negative charge (79, 182)
electrón partícula subatómica que tiene carga negativa

electron cloud (ee·LEK·trahn LOWD) a region around the nucleus of an atom where electrons are likely to be found (183)
nube de electrones región que rodea al núcleo de un átomo en la cual es probable encontrar a los electrones

electronic device (ee·lek·TRAHN·ik dih·VYS) a device that produces or is powered by a flow of electrons and contains an integrated circuit (504)
dispositivo electrónico dispositivo que produce o que funciona mediante un flujo de electrones y que contiene un circuito integrado

element (EL·uh·muhnt) a substance that cannot be separated or broken down into simpler substances by chemical means (61)
elemento sustancia que no se puede separar o descomponer en sustancias más simples por medio de métodos químicos

endothermic reaction (en·doh·THER·mik ree·AK·shuhn) a chemical reaction that requires energy input, usually as heat (248)
reacción endotérmica reacción química que requiere la entrada de energía, generalmente en forma de calor

energy (EN·er·jee) the ability to cause change (118, 386)
energía capacidad de producir un cambio

energy transformation (EN·er·jee trans·fohr·MAY·shuhn) the process of energy changing from one form into another (124)
transformación de energía proceso de cambio de un tipo de energía a otro

evaporation (ee·vap·uh·RAY·shuhn) the change of state from a liquid to a gas that usually occurs at the surface of a liquid over a wide range of temperatures (94)
evaporación cambio de estado de líquido a gaseoso que ocurre generalmente en la superficie de un líquido en un amplio rango de temperaturas

exothermic reaction (ek·soh·THER·mik ree·AK·shuhn) a chemical reaction in which energy is released to the surroundings, usually as heat (248)
reacción exotérmica reacción química en la que se libera energía en el ambiente, generalmente en forma de calor

fluid (FLOO·id) a nonsolid state of matter in which the atoms or molecules are free to move past each other, as in a gas or liquid (360)
fluido estado no sólido de la materia en el que los átomos o moléculas tienen libertad de movimiento, como en el caso de un gas o un líquido

fluorescent light (flu·RES·uhnt LYT) visible light emitted by a material when it absorbs energy such as ultraviolet light (668)

luz fluorescente luz visible emitida por un material cuando absorbe energía como la luz ultravioleta

force (FOHRS) a push or a pull exerted on an object in order to change the motion of the object; force has size and direction (330)

fuerza acción de empuje o atracción que se ejerce sobre un cuerpo con el fin de cambiar su movimiento; la fuerza tiene magnitud y dirección

fossil fuel (FAHS·uhl FYOO·uhl) a nonrenewable energy resource formed from the remains of organisms that lived long ago; examples include oil, coal, and natural gas (160)

combustible fósil recurso energético no renovable formado a partir de los restos de organismos que vivieron hace mucho tiempo; algunos ejemplos incluyen el petróleo, el carbón y el gas natural

free fall (FREE FAWL) the motion of a body when only the force of gravity is acting on the body (350)

caída libre movimiento de un cuerpo cuando la única fuerza que actúa sobre él es la fuerza de gravedad

freezing (FREEZ·ing) the change of state from a liquid to a solid (92)

congelación cambio de estado de líquido a sólido

frequency (FREE·kwuhn·see) the number of cycles, such as waves, in a given amount of time (541)

frecuencia número de ciclos, tales como ondas, producidas en una determinada cantidad de tiempo

fulcrum (FUL·kruhm) the point on which a lever pivots (416)

fulcro punto sobre el que pivota una palanca

gas (GAS) a form of matter that does not have a definite volume or shape (79)

gas estado de la materia que no tiene volumen ni forma definidos

gravity (GRAV·ih·tee) a force of attraction between objects that is due to their masses (346)

gravedad fuerza de atracción entre dos cuerpos debido a sus masas

group (GROOP) a vertical column of elements in the periodic table; elements in a group share chemical properties (200)

grupo columna vertical de elementos de la tabla periódica; los elementos de un grupo comparten propiedades químicas

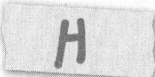

heat (HEET) the energy transferred between objects that are at different temperatures (144)

calor transferencia de energía entre objetos que están a temperaturas diferentes

hertz (HERTS) a unit of frequency equal to one cycle per second (541)

hertz unidad de frecuencia que representa un ciclo por segundo

heterogeneous (het·er·uh·JEE·nee·uhs) describes something that does not have a uniform structure or composition throughout (68)

heterogéneo término que describe algo que no tiene una estructura o composición totalmente uniforme

homogeneous (hoh·muh·JEE·nee·uhs) describes something that has a uniform structure or composition throughout (68)

homogéneo término que describe algo que tiene una estructura o composición global uniforme

hydrocarbon (HY·druh·kar·buhn) an organic compound composed only of carbon and hydrogen (264)

hidrocarburo compuesto orgánico compuesto únicamente por carbono e hidrógeno

incandescent light (in·kuhn·DES·uhnt LYT) the light produced by hot objects (668)

luz incandescente luz producida por objetos calientes

inclined plane (in·KLYND PLAYN) a simple machine that is a straight, slanted surface, which facilitates the raising of loads; a ramp (420)

plano inclinado máquina simple que es una superficie recta e inclinaday que facilita el levantamiento de cargas; una rampa

inertia (ih·NER·shuh) the tendency of an object to resist a change in motion unless an outside force acts on the object (334)

inercia tendencia de un cuerpo a resistir un cambio en el movimiento a menos que actúe una fuerza externa sobre el cuerpo

infrared (in·fruh·RED) electromagnetic wavelengths immediately outside the red end of the visible spectrum (612)

infrarrojo longitudes de onda electromagnéticas inmediatamente adyacentes al color rojo en el espectro visible

insulator (IN·suh·lay·ter) a material that reduces or prevents the transfer of energy (147)

aislante material que reduce o evita la transferencia de energía

integrated circuit (in·tih·GRAY·tid SER·kit) a circuit whose components are formed on a single semiconductor (504)

circuito integrado circuito cuyos componentes están formados en un solo semiconductor

interference (in·ter·FIR·uhns) the combination of two or more waves that results in a single wave (578)

interferencia combinación de dos o más ondas que resulta en una sola onda

ion (EYE·ahn) a charged particle that forms when an atom or group of atoms gains or loses one or more electrons (81, 224)

ion partícula cargada que se forma cuando un átomo o grupo de átomos gana o pierde uno o más electrones

ionic bond (eye·AHN·ik BAHND) the attractive force between oppositely charged ions, which form when electrons are transferred from one atom to another (224)

enlace iónico fuerza de atracción entre iones con cargas opuestas que se forma cuando se transfieren electrones de un átomo a otro

ionization (eye·uh·nih·ZAY·shuhn) a process in which atoms lose or gain electrons to become electrically charged particles called ions (81)

ionización procedimiento a través del cual los átomos pierden o ganan electrones para convertirse en partículas eléctricamente cargadas denominadas iones

isotope (EYE·suh·tohp) one of two or more atoms that have the same number of protons (atomic number) but different numbers of neutrons (atomic mass) (277)

isótopo uno de dos o más átomos que tienen el mismo número de protones (número atómico) pero diferente número de neutrones (masa atómica)

kinetic energy (kih·NET·ik EN·er·jee) the energy of an object that is due to the object's motion (118, 396)

energía cinética energía de un cuerpo debido a su movimiento

kinetic theory of matter (kih·NET·ik THEE·uh·ree UHV MAT·er) a theory that states that all of the particles that make up matter are constantly in motion (132)

teoría cinética de la materia teoría que establece que todas las partículas que forman la materia están en constante movimiento

laser (LAY·zer) a device that produces intense light of a narrow range of wavelength and color; laser is an abbreviation of light amplification by stimulated emission of radiation (669)

láser dispositivo que produce luz intensa de un rango estrecho de longitud de onda y color; "láser" es una abreviatura de las palabras en inglés "amplificación de luz por emisión estimulada de radiación"

law of conservation of energy (LAW UHV kahn·suhr·VAY·shuhn UHV EN·er·jee) the law that states that energy cannot be created or destroyed but can be changed from one form to another (125, 249)

ley de la conservación de la energía ley que establece que la energía ni se crea ni se destruye, sólo se transforma de una forma a otra

law of conservation of mass (LAW UHV kahn·suhr·VAY·shuhn UHV MAS) the law that states that mass cannot be created or destroyed in ordinary chemical and physical changes (48, 246)

ley de la conservación de la masa ley que establece que la masa no se crea ni se destruye por cambios químicos o físicos comunes

LED (el·ee·DEE) an electronic device that converts electrical energy to light; a light-emitting diode (669)

LED dispositivo electrónico que convierte la energía eléctrica en luz; diodo que emite luz

lens (LENZ) a transparent object that refracts light waves such that they converge or diverge to create an image (646)

lente objeto transparente que refracta las ondas de luz de modo que converjan o diverjan para crear una imagen

lever (LEV·er) a simple machine that consists of a bar that pivots at a fixed point called a fulcrum (416)

palanca una máquina simple formada por una barra que gira en un punto fijo llamado fulcro

liquid (LIK·wid) the state of matter that has a definite volume but not a definite shape (79)

líquido estado de la materia que tiene un volumen definido, pero no forma definida

longitudinal wave (lahn·jih·TOOD·n·uhl WAYV) a wave in which the particles of the medium vibrate parallel to the direction of wave motion (528, 560)

onda longitudinal onda en la que las partículas del medio vibran paralelamente a la dirección del movimiento de la onda

loudness (LOWD·nes) the extent to which a sound can be heard (565)

volumen grado al que se escucha un sonido

machine (muh·SHEEN) a device that helps do work by changing the magnitude and/or direction of an applied force (412)

máquina dispositivo que ayuda a realizar trabajos cambiando la magnitud y/o la dirección de una fuerza aplicada

magnet (MAG·nit) any material that attracts iron or materials containing iron (472)

imán cualquier material que atrae hierro o materiales que contienen hierro

magnetic field (MAG·net·ik FEELD) a region where a magnetic force can be detected (473)

campo magnético región donde puede detectarse una fuerza magnética

magnetic force (MAG·net·ik FOHRS) the force of attraction or repulsion generated by moving or spinning electric charges (472)

fuerza magnética fuerza de atracción o repulsión generadas por cargas eléctricas en movimiento o que giran

magnetic pole (MAG·net·ik POHL) one of two points, such as the ends of a magnet, that have opposing magnetic qualities (473)

polo magnético uno de dos puntos, tales como los extremos de un imán, que tienen cualidades magnéticas opuestas

mass (MAS) a measure of the amount of matter in an object (7)

masa medida de la cantidad de materia que tiene un objeto

mass number (MAS NUM·ber) the sum of the numbers of protons and neutrons in the nucleus of an atom (187)

número de masa la suma de los números de protones y neutrones que hay en el núcleo de un átomo

matter (MAT·er) anything that has mass and takes up space (6)

materia cualquier cosa que tiene masa y ocupa un lugar en el espacio

mechanical advantage (mih·KAN·ih·kuhl ad·VAN·tij) a number that tells how many times a machine multiplies input force (414)

ventaja mecánica número que indica cuántas veces una máquina multiplica su fuerza de entrada

mechanical efficiency (mih·KAN·ih·kuhl ih·FISH·uhn·see) a quantity, usually expressed as a percentage, that measures the ratio of work output to work input in a machine (415)

eficiencia mecánica cantidad, generalmente expresada como un porcentaje, que mide la relación entre el trabajo de entrada y el trabajo de salida en una máquina

mechanical energy (mih·KAN·ih·kuhl EN·er·jee) the sum of an object's kinetic energy and potential energy due to gravity or elastic deformation; does not include chemical energy or nuclear energy (120, 400)

energía mecánica suma de las energías cinética y potencial de un cuerpo debido a la gravedad o a la deformación elástica; no incluye la energía química ni nuclear

mechanical wave (mih·KAN·ih·kuhl WAYV) a wave that requires a medium through which to travel (530)

onda mecánica onda que requiere un medio para desplazarse

medium (MEE·dee·uhm) a physical environment in which phenomena occur; for waves, the material through which a wave can travel (526)

medio ambiente físico en el que ocurren fenómenos; para las ondas, el medio a través del cual se desplaza una onda

melting (MELT·ing) the change of state from a solid to a liquid (93)

fusión cambio de estado de sólido a líquido

metal (MET·l) an element that is shiny and that conducts heat and electricity well (199)

metal elemento que es brillante y conduce bien el calor y la electricidad

metallic bond (mih·TAL·ik BAHND) a bond formed by the attraction between positively charged metal ions and the electrons around them (228)

enlace metálico enlace formado por la atracción entre iones metálicos cargados positivamente y los electrones que los rodean

metalloid (MET·l·oyd) an element that has properties of both metals and nonmetals (199)

metaloide elemento que tiene propiedades tanto de metal como de no metal

mixture (MIKS·cher) a combination of two or more substances that are not chemically combined (61)

mezcla combinación de dos o más sustancias que no están combinadas químicamente

molecule (MAHL·ih·kyool) a group of atoms that are held together by chemical forces; a molecule is the smallest unit of a compound that keeps all the properties of that compound (226)

molécula grupo de átomos unidos por fuerzas químicas; una molécula es la unidad más pequeña de un compuesto que conserva todas las propiedades de ese compuesto

motion (MOH·shuhn) an object's change in position relative to a reference point (304)

movimiento cambio en la posición de un cuerpo respecto a un punto de referencia

net force (NET FOHRS) the combination of all of the forces acting on an object (332)

fuerza neta combinación de todas las fuerzas que actúan sobre un cuerpo

neutralization (noo·truh·lih·ZAY·shuhn) a process in which ions lose or gain electrons to become electrically neutral atoms (97)

neutralización procedimiento a través del cual los iones pierden o ganan electrones para convertirse en átomos eléctricamente neutrales

neutron (NOO·trahn) a subatomic particle that has no charge and that is located in the nucleus of an atom (183)

neutrón partícula subatómica que no tiene carga y que está ubicada en el núcleo de un átomo

nonmetal (nahn·MET·l) an element that conducts heat and electricity poorly (199)

no metal elemento que es mal conductor del calor y la electricidad

nonrenewable resource (nahn·rih·NOO·uh·buhl REE·sohrs) a resource that forms at a rate that is much slower than the rate at which the resource is consumed (159)

recurso no renovable recurso que se forma a una tasa que es mucho más lenta que la tasa a la que se consume

nuclear fission (NOO·klee·er FISH·uhn) the process by which the nucleus of a heavy atom splits into two or more fragments; the process releases neutrons and energy (282)

fisión nuclear proceso por medio del cual el núcleo de un átomo pesado se divide en dos o más fragmentos; el proceso libera neutrones y energía

nuclear fusion (NOO·klee·er FYOO·zhuhn) the process by which nuclei of small atoms combine to form a new, more massive nucleus; the process releases energy (286)

fusión nuclear proceso por medio del cual los núcleos de átomos pequeños se combinan y forman un núcleo nuevo con mayor masa; el proceso libera energía

nuclear reaction (NOO·klee·er ree·AK·shuhn) a reaction that affects the nucleus of an atom (276)

reacción nuclear reacción que afecta el núcleo de un átomo

nucleus (NOO·klee·uhs) in physical science, an atom's central region, which is made up of protons and neutrons (183)

núcleo en ciencias físicas, la región central de un átomo, la cual está constituida por protones y neutrones

opaque (oh·PAYK) describes an object that is not transparent or translucent (631)

opaco término que describe un objeto que no es transparente ni translúcido

optical fiber (AHP·tih·kuhl FY·ber) a transparent thread of plastic or glass that transmits light (670)

fibra óptica hilo de plástico o vidrio transparente que transmite luz

orbit (OHR·bit) the path that a body follows as it travels around another body in space (350)

órbita trayectoria que sigue un cuerpo al desplazarse alrededor de otro cuerpo en el espacio

organic acid (ohr·GAN·ik AS·id) an organic chemical compound that contains one or more carboxyl groups; examples are acetic and lactic acid (264)

ácido orgánico compuesto químico orgánico que contiene uno o más grupos carboxílicos; algunos ejemplos son el ácido acético y el ácido láctico

organic compound (ohr·GAN·ik KAHM·pownd) a covalently bonded compound that contains carbon and hydrogen (262)

compuesto orgánico compuesto enlazado de manera covalente que contiene carbono e hidrógeno

parallel circuit (PAIR·uh·lel SER·kit) a circuit in which the parts are joined in branches such that the voltage across each part is the same (463)

circuito paralelo circuito en el que las partes están unidas en ramas de manera tal que el voltaje entre cada parte es la misma

pascal (pa·SKAL) the SI unit of pressure (symbol, Pa) (361)

pascal unidad de presión del sistema internacional de unidades (símbolo: Pa)

period (PIR·ee·uhd) in chemistry, a horizontal row of elements in the periodic table (201)

período química, una hilera horizontal de elementos en la tabla periódica

periodic table (pir·ee·AHD·ik TAY·buhl) an arrangement of the elements in order of their atomic numbers such that elements with similar properties fall in the same column, or group (195)

tabla periódica arreglo de los elementos ordenados en función de su número atómico, de modo que los elementos que tienen propiedades similares se encuentran en la misma columna, o grupo

physical change (FIZ·ih·kuhl CHAYNJ) a change of matter from one form to another without a change in chemical properties (42)

cambio físico cambio de materia de una forma a otra sin que ocurra un cambio en sus propiedades químicas

physical property (FIZ·ih·kuhl PRAHP·er·tee) a characteristic of a substance that does not involve a chemical change, such as density, color, or hardness (24)

propiedad física característica de una sustancia que no implica un cambio químico, tal como la densidad, el color o la dureza

pitch (PICH) a measure of how high or low a sound is perceived to be, depending on the frequency of the sound wave (564)

altura tonal medida de qué tan agudo o grave se percibe un sonido, dependiendo de la frecuencia de la onda sonora

plasma (PLAZ·muh) a state of matter that forms when heat energy is added to a neutral gas, causing its atoms or molecules to lose electrons (79)

plasma estado de la materia que se forma cuando se aplica energía térmica a un gas noble, causando una pérdida de electrones en sus átomos o moléculas

polymer (PAHL·uh·mer) a molecule composed of the same repeating, small groups of atoms joined together in long chains (266)

polímero molécula grande formada a partir de más de cinco monómeros, o unidades pequeñas

position (puh·ZISH·uhn) the location of an object (302)

posición ubicación de un objeto

potential energy (puh·TEN·shuhl EN·er·jee) the energy that an object has because of the position, condition, or chemical composition of the object (119, 398)

energía potencial energía que tiene un cuerpo debido a su posición, condición o composición química

power (POW·er) the rate at which work is done or energy is transformed (388)

potencia tasa a la que se realiza un trabajo o a la que se transforma la energía

pressure (PRESH·er) the amount of force exerted per unit area of a surface (360)

presión cantidad de fuerza ejercida en una superficie por unidad de área

product (PRAHD·uhkt) a substance that forms in a chemical reaction (245)

producto sustancia que se forma en una reacción química

proton (PROH·tahn) a subatomic particle that has a positive charge and that is located in the nucleus of an atom; the number of protons in the nucleus is the atomic number, which determines the identity of an element (183)

protón partícula subatómica que tiene una carga positiva y que está ubicada en el núcleo de un átomo; el número de protones que hay en el núcleo es el número atómico, y éste determina la identidad del elemento

pulley (PUL·ee) a simple machine that consists of a wheel over which a rope, chain, or wire passes (419)

polea máquina simple formada por una rueda sobre la cual pasa una cuerda, cadena, o cable

pure substance (PYOOR SUHB·stuhns) a sample of matter, either a single element or a single compound, that has definite chemical and physical properties (62)
sustancia pura muestra de materia, ya sea un solo elemento o un solo compuesto, que tiene propiedades químicas y físicas definidas

R

radiation (ray·dee·AY·shuhn) the transfer of energy as electromagnetic waves (148, 610)
radiación transferencia de energía en forma de ondas electromagnéticas

radioactive decay (ray·dee·oh·AK·tiv dih·KAY) the process in which a radioactive isotope tends to break down into a stable isotope of the same element or another element (278)
desintegración radiactiva proceso por medio del cual un isótopo radiactivo tiende a desintegrarse y formar un isótopo estable del mismo elemento o de otro elemento

reactant (ree·AK·tuhnt) a substance that participates in a chemical reaction (245)
reactivo sustancia que participa en una reacción química

real image (REE·uhl IM·ij) an image that is formed by the intersection of light rays; a real image can be projected on a screen (644)
imagen real imagen que se forma por la intersección de rayos de luz; una imagen real se puede proyectar en una pantalla

reference point (REF·er·uhns POYNT) a location to which another location is compared (302)
punto de referencia ubicación con la que se compara otra ubicación

reflection (rih·FLEK·shuhn) the bouncing back of a ray of light, sound, or heat when the ray hits a surface that it does not go through (631)
reflexión rebote de un rayo de luz, sonido o calor cuando el rayo golpea una superficie pero no la atraviesa

refraction (rih·FRAK·shuhn) the bending of a wave front as the wave front passes between two substances in which the speed of the wave differs (634)
refracción curvamiento de un frente de ondas a medida que el frente pasa entre dos sustancias en las que difiere la velocidad de las ondas

renewable resource (rih·NOO·uh·buhl REE·sohrs) a natural resource that can be replaced at the same rate at which the resource is consumed (159)
recurso renovable recurso natural que puede reemplazarse a la misma tasa a la que se consume

resistance (rih·ZIS·tuhns) in physical science, the opposition presented to the current by a material or device (450)
resistencia en ciencias físicas, la oposición que un material o aparato presenta a la corriente

resonance (REZ·uh·nuhns) a phenomenon that occurs when two objects naturally vibrate at the same frequency; the sound produced by one object causes the other object to vibrate (580)

resonancia fenómeno que ocurre cuando dos objetos vibran naturalmente a la misma frecuencia; el sonido producido por un objeto hace que el otro objeto vibre

retina (RET·n·uh) the light-sensitive inner layer of the eye, which receives images formed by the lens and transmits them through the optic nerve to the brain (659)
retina capa interna del ojo, sensible a la luz, que recibe imágenes formadas por el lente ocular y las transmite al cerebro por medio del nervio óptico

S

scattering (SKAT·er·ing) an interaction of light with matter that causes light to change direction (635)
dispersión interacción de la luz con la materia que produce un cambio de dirección de la luz

semiconductor (sem·ee·kuhn·DUHK·ter) an element or compound that conducts electric current better than an insulator does but not as well as a conductor does (441)
semiconductor elemento o compuesto que conduce la corriente eléctrica mejor que un aislante, pero no tan bien como un conductor

series circuit (SIR·eez SER·kit) a circuit in which the parts are joined one after another such that the current in each part is the same (462)
circuito en serie circuito en el que las partes están unidas una después de la otra de manera tal que la corriente en cada parte es la misma

solenoid (SOH·luh·noyd) a coil of wire with an electric current in it (489)
solenoide bobina de alambre que tiene una corriente eléctrica

solid (SAHL·id) the state of matter in which the volume and shape of a substance are fixed (78)
sólido estado de la materia en el cual el volumen y la forma de una sustancia están fijos

sonar (SOH·nar) sound navigation and ranging, a system that uses acoustic signals and returned echoes to determine the location of objects or to communicate (591)
sonar navegación y exploración por medio del sonido; un sistema que usa señales acústicas y ondas de eco que regresan para determinar la ubicación de los objetos o para comunicarse

sound wave (SOWND WAYV) a longitudinal wave that is caused by vibrations and that travels through a material medium (560)
onda sonora onda longitudinal que se origina debido a vibraciones y que se desplaza a través de un medio material

speed (SPEED) the distance traveled divided by the time interval during which the motion occurred (305)
rapidez distancia a la cual se desplaza un cuerpo dividida entre el intervalo de tiempo durante el cual ocurrió el movimiento

static electricity (STAT·ik ee·lek·TRIS·ih·tee) electric charge at rest; generally produced by friction or induction (439)
electricidad estática carga eléctrica en reposo; por lo general se produce por fricción o inducción

sublimation (suhb·luh·MAY·shuhn) the change of state from a solid directly to a gas (98)
sublimación cambio de estado por el cual un sólido se convierte directamente en un gas

temperature (TEM·per·uh·chur) a measure of how hot (or cold) something is; specifically, a measure of the average kinetic energy of the particles in an object (134)
temperatura medida del grado de calor (o frío) de un cuerpo; específicamente, una medida de la energía cinética promedio de las partículas de un cuerpo

thermal energy (THER·muhl EN·er·jee) the kinetic energy of a substance's atoms (142)
energía térmica energía cinética de los átomos de una sustancia

thermometer (ther·MAHM·ih·ter) an instrument that measures and indicates temperature (134)
termómetro instrumento que mide e indica la temperatura

transformer (trans·FOHR·mer) a device that increases or decreases the voltage of alternating current (495)
transformador aparato que aumenta o disminuye el voltaje de la corriente alterna

translucent (trans·LOO·suhnt) describes matter that transmits light but that does not transmit an image (630)
traslúcido término que describe la materia que transmite luz, pero que no transmite una imagen

transparent (trans·PAIR·uhnt) describes matter that allows light to pass through with little interference (630)
transparente término que describe materia que permite el paso de la luz con poca interferencia

transverse wave (TRANS·vers WAYV) a wave in which the particles of the medium move perpendicularly to the direction the wave is traveling (529)
onda transversal onda en la que las partículas del medio se mueven perpendicularmente respecto a la dirección en la que se desplaza la onda

ultrasound (UHL·truh·sownd) sound waves with frequencies greater than 20,000 hertz (Hz), the upper limit of typical hearing levels in humans, often used for medical purposes (590)
ultrasonido ondas sonoras con frecuencias mayores de 20,000 hertz (Hz), el límite superior de los niveles de audición típicos en los seres humanos, usadas generalmente con propósitos médicos

ultraviolet (uhl·truh·VY·uh·lit) electromagnetic wave frequencies immediately above the visible range (612)
ultravioleta longitudes de onda electromagnéticas inmediatamente adyacentes al color violeta en el espectro visible

valence electron (VAY·luhns ee·LEK·trahn) an electron that is found in the outermost shell of an atom and that determines the atom's chemical properties (213)
electrón de valencia electrón que se encuentra en la capa más externa de un átomo y que determina las propiedades químicas del átomo

vector (VEK·ter) a quantity that has both size and direction (311)
vector cantidad que tiene tanto magnitud como dirección

velocity (vuh·LAHS·ih·tee) the speed of an object in a particular direction (311)
velocidad rapidez de un cuerpo en una dirección dada

virtual image (VER·choo·uhl IM·ij) an image from which light rays appear to diverge, even though they are not actually focused there; a virtual image cannot be projected on a screen (643)
imagen virtual imagen en la que los rayos de luz parecen divergir, aunque en realidad no se han centrado allí; una imagen virtual no se puede proyectar en una pantalla

voltage (VOHL·tij) the amount of work to move a unit electric charge between two points; expressed in volts (450)
voltaje cantidad de trabajo necesario para transportar una unidad de carga eléctrica entre dos puntos; se expresa en voltios

volume (VAHL·yoom) the amount of space that an object takes up, or occupies (9)
volumen la cantidad de espacio que ocupa un cuerpo

wave (WAYV) a disturbance that transfers energy from one place to another; a wave can be a single cycle, or it can be a repeating pattern (526)
onda alteración que transfiere energía de un lugar a otro; una onda puede ser un ciclo único o un patrón repetido

wave period (WAYV PIR·ee·uhd) the time required for corresponding points on consecutive waves to pass a given point (541)
período de onda tiempo que se requiere para que los puntos correspondientes de ondas consecutivas pasen por un punto dado

wave speed (WAYV SPEED) the speed at which a wave travels; speed depends on the medium (544)
rapidez de onda rapidez a la cual viaja una onda; la rapidez depende del medio

wavelength (WAYV·lengkth) the distance from any point on a wave to the corresponding point on the next wave (540)

longitud de onda la distancia entre cualquier punto de una onda y el punto correspondiente de la siguiente ondaweight

weight (WAYT) a measure of the gravitational force exerted on an object; its value can change with the location of the object in the universe (7)

peso medida de la fuerza gravitacional ejercida sobre un cuerpo; su valor puede cambiar en función de la ubicación del cuerpo en el universo

wheel and axle (WEEL AND AK·suhl) a simple machine consisting of two circular objects of different sizes; the wheel is the larger of the two circular objects, and the axle is attached to the center of the wheel (418)

rueda y eje máquina simple formada por dos objetos circulares de diferentes tamaños; la rueda es el más grande de los dos objetos circulares y el eje está sujeto al centro de la rueda

work (WERK) the transfer of energy to an object by using a force that causes the object to move in the direction of the force (384)

trabajo transferencia de energía a un cuerpo mediante una fuerza que hace que el cuerpo se mueva en la dirección de la fuerza

Index

Italic page numbers represent illustrative material, such as figures, tables, margin elements, photographs, and illustrations. Boldface page numbers represent page numbers for definitions.

absolute zero, 134, **134**
absorption (of light and sound), 576, 582, 586–587, 625, **631,** *632,* 633, 636
acceleration, 320, **320,** *320*
  average, calculating, 321, **321,** *321*
  centripetal, 323, **323,** *323*
  changing direction, 323, **323**
  negative, 322, **322,** *322*
  positive, 322, **322,** *322*
acid, 65
acid rain, 165, **165,** *165*
  aquatic animals, effect on, 165, *165*
  materials, effect on, 165, *165*
  trees, effect on, 165, *165*
Active Reading, lesson opener pages, 23, 41, 59, 77, 89, 117, 131, 141, 157, 179, 193, 209, 223, 243, 257, 275, 301, 319, 329, 345, 359, 383, 395, 411, 435, 447, 457, 471, 487, 503, 525, 539, 559, 573, 589, 609, 629, 641, 657, 667
Afar Depression, 140, *140*
albinism, 251, *251*
alkali metals, 200, *200*
alpha decay, 278, **278,** *278*
alpha particles, 279, **279,** *279*
alternating current (AC), 449, *449,* 453, 492
ampere, 448
amplitude, 540, *540,* 542, 546, 565, 568, 578, 610
analog signal, 505, *505*
Archimedes' principle, 366, **366,** *366*
Aristotle, 180
armature, **493,** *493*
aromatic compounds, 266, **266,** *266*
atmospheric pressure, 362, **362,** *362*
  kilopascal (kPa), 362, **362**

atomic number, 195, 196, **196**
atomic theory, 182–183, **182–183,** *182–183*
  Ernest Rutherford, 183
  J. J. Thomson, 182
  John Dalton, 182
  modern, 183
  Niels Bohr, 183
atoms, 60–61, **60,** *60,* 61, 176, 180–187, 181, **181,** 224
  Aristotle, 180
  bond forming, 215, *215,* 228, *228*
  chemical change and, 211, *211*
  covalent bond, 226, **226,** *226*
  Democritus, 180
  electron cloud, 182, **182,** 184, **184,** *184*
  electrons, 79, **79,** *79,* 182, **182**
  energy level, outermost, 213, **213,** 214, 215
  ions, 184, **184,** 224, **224**
  net charge, 184
  neutrons, 182, **183,** 184, **184,** *184*
  nucleus, 182
  protons, 184, **184,** *184*
atom models,
  Bohr, 212, **212,** *212*
  electron cloud, 212, **212,** *212*
  space-filling, 212, **212,** *212*
auditory nerve, 562–563, *563*
aurora, 123, **477**
  aurora australis, **477, 619**
  aurora borealis, **477,** *477,* **619,** *619*
average atomic mass, 196, **196**
average speed, 305, **305**
  how to calculate, 306, **306,** *306*

balancing chemical equations, 246, **246,** *246*
base, 65, *65*
battery

  as electrical energy source, 458, 461–463, 466
Becquerel, Henri, 276
beta decay, 278, **278,** *278*
beta particles, 279, **279,** *279*
Big Idea, 106, 113, 170, 175, 234, 239, 292, 297, 374, 379, 426, 431, 514, 521, 550, 555, 600, 605, 680
binary code, **506**
biochemicals, 65
  carbohydrates, 65
  lipids, 65
  nucleic acid, 65
  proteins, 65
biomass, 164, **164,** *164*
Bohr model, 212, **212,** *212*
  valence electrons, 213, *213*
boiling, 94, **94,** *94*
boiling point, 27, 94, **94,** *94*
bonds, 215, **215,** *215*
  ionic bond, 224, **224,** 224
  covalent bond, 226, **226,** 226
  metallic, 228, **228,** *228*
bonds, metallic, 228, **228,** *228*
  conductor, electrical, 229, **229,** *229*
  ductile, 229, **229,** *229*
  malleable, 229, **229**
buoyant force, 366, **366,** *366*
  Archimedes' principle, 366, **366,** *366*
  weight, 367

cal (calorie), 145
calorie (cal), **145**
  energy, 145
    heat, 145
    in joules, 145
  temperature, 145
Cal (Calorie), 145, **145**
Calorie (Cal), 145, **145**
  kilocalorie, 145, **145**
cameras, 675, *675*
  aperture, **675,** *675*
carbohydrates, 65, 265, **265,** *265*

N

nuclear chain reaction, 283, **283,** *283*
  Uranium-**235,** 283, **283**
nuclear energy, 122, 162, **162,** *162*
nuclear fission, 282, **282,** *282*
  plutonium isotopes, 282, **282,** *282*
  uranium isotopes, 282, **282,** *282*
nuclear fusion, 286, **286,** *286*
  benefits, potential, 287, **287,** *287*
  challenges, 287, **287,** *287*
nuclear magnetic resonance (NMR), 241
nuclear power,
  advantages, 285
  disadvantages, 285
nuclear power plant, 239, *239,* 284, *284,* 285, *285*
nuclear reaction, 276, **276**
  Becquerel, Henri, 276
  $E = mc^2$, 276
  isotopes, 277, **277,** *277*
  mass changes to energy, 276
  nucleus changes, 277
  polonium, 276
  radioactive decay, 278, **278,** *278*
  uranium, 276, *276*
nucleic acid, 65
nucleus, 182

Oerstad, Hans Christian, 488
Okamoto, Steve, 356
OLED (organic light-emitting diode), 267, **267,** *267*
opaque, 631, *631*
optical fiber, 670, *670,* 676
  total internal reflection, **670**
optic nerve, 659, *659*
orbit, 350, **350,** *350*
organic, 65, *65*
organic compound classification,
  aromatic compounds, 266, **266,** *266*
  carbohydrates, 265, **265,** *265*
  hydrocarbons, 264, **264,** *264*
  monomers, 266, **266,** *266*
  organic acids, 264, **264,** *264*
  plastics, 266, **266**
  polymers, 266, **266**
  rings, 266, **266,** *266*

organic compounds, 65, 262, **262**
  carbon, 262, 263, *263*
  chlorine, 263, *263*
  fluorine, 263, *263*
  hydrogen, 262, 263, *263*
  in living things, 262, **262**
  in nonliving things, 262, **262**
  nitrogen, 263, *263*
  phosphorus, 263, *263*
  sulfur, 263, *263*
organic light-emitting diode (OLED), 267, **267,** *267*
oscilloscope, *561*
output force, 407, **407,** *407,* 412, 414, **414,** *414,* 416, **416,** *416,* 421, *421*
  fulcrum, 416, **416,** *416*
  mechanical advantage, 407, **407,** *407,* 414, **414,** *414*

particles and motion, *132–133,* 133
  in gases, 81, *80–81,* 132–133, **133,** *133*
  in liquids, 81, *80–81,* 132–133, **132,** *132*
  in plasmas, 81, *80–81,* 133, **133,** *133*
  in solids, 80, *80–81,* 132–133, **132,** *132*
parallel circuits, 463, *463,* 466, 482–483
pascal, 361, **361**
periodic table of the elements, 195, **195,** 196–197, **196–197,** *196–197,* 198, **198,** 199, **199**
  atomic number, 196, **196,** 198, **198,** *198,* 201
  average atomic mass, 196, **196,** 198, **198,** *198*
  characteristic prediction, 202, *202*
  chemical symbol, 196, **196,** 198, **198,** *198*
  element name, 196, **196,** 198, **198,** *198*
  family, 196, **196,** 200
  group, 196, **196,** 200, **200**
  isotope, 196, **196**
  Mendeleev, **Dmitri,** 195
  metal, 199, **199,** *199*
  metalloid, 199, **199,** *199*

  Moseley, Henry, 195
  nonmetal, 199, **199,** *199*
  period, 201, **201**
  reactivity, 200, **200,** *200*
  valence electrons, 200, **200,** *200,* 201, 213, **213,** *213,* 214
periscope, 652–655, *653*
permanent magnet, 475, 490, *493*
PET (positron emission tomography), 281, **281,** *281*
petroleum, 160, **160,** *160*
pH, 65
phosphorus, 263, *263*
physical change of matter, 42–43, **42,** *42–43*
  examples of, 43
physical property, 24–27, 32,
  boiling point, 27, 94, **94,** *94*
  characteristic property, 32, **32,** *32*
  density, **26,** *26*
  electrical conductivity, **26,** *26*
  luster, **27,** *27*
  melting point, **27,** *27*
  magnetic attraction, **27,** *27*
  malleability, **27,** *27*
  thermal conductivity, **26,** *26*
pitch, 564, *564,* 567, 568
pixels, 611
planes, inclined, 420, **420,** *420*
  height, 420, *420*
  length, 420, *420*
  mechanical advantage, 420, *420*
  screw, 421, *421*
plasma, 76, 79, **79,** *79,* 81, 133, *133*
  changes shape, 81
  changes volume, 81
  is not electrically neutral, 81
  particles of motion, 81, *80–81,* 133, **133,** *133*
plastics, 266, **266**
plutonium isotopes, 282, **282,** *282*
polymers, 266, **266**
positive charge, *436,* 436–439, *437,* 442
Positron emission tomography (PET), 281, **281,** *281*
potential energy, 119, **119,** *118–119,* 120, 126
  chemical composition, 119, 126
  chemical energy, 122, 126

sound waves, **560,** *560,*
     561–564, *564,* 567, *567,*
     568, 581–582, 586–587,
     590, 592, 594–596, 624–627
southern lights, **619**
south pole
     geographical, 476–478
     magnetic, 473–474
space-filling model, 212, **212,** *212*
space weather, 123, **123**
speed, 305, **305,** 397, *397*
     average speed, 305, **305**
     constant speed, 308, **308,** *308*
speed of light, 530, **544,** 546, 610
speed of sound, 574, *574,*
     575, 582
standard values,
     body temperature, 135, **135**
     boiling point of water, 134 135,
          135
     freezing point of water, 134,
          135, **135**
     room temperature, 135, **135**
standing waves, **581**
states of matter, 78
     change of state, 82, *82,* 90–91
     gas, **76,** 79, **79,** *79*
     liquid, **76,** 79, **79,** *79*
     plasma, **76,** 79, **79,** *79*
     solid, 78, **78,** *78*
static electricity, **439,** *439*
S.T.E.M. Engineering and
     Technology, Engineering
     Design Process
     Building an Electric Circuit,
          482–485
     Building an Insulated Cooler,
          54–57
     Building a Periscope, 652–655
     Comparing Light and Sound,
          624–627
     Testing a Simple Machine,
          406–409
step-down transformer, **495,** *495*
step-up transformer, **495,** *495*
steroids, 241
structural formula, 261, **261,** *261*
     full, 261, **261,** *261*
     simplified, 261, **261,** *261*
sublimation, 98, **98,** *98*
subscript, 245, **245,** *245,* 245,
     260, **260**
sulfur, 263, *263*
sun, 158, 530, 614–615, 619
surface area, 250, **250,** *250*
surface wave, **529,** *529*

suspension, 68, **68,** *68*
S waves, **529,** *529,* 530, 532

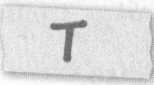

Take It Home, 21, 155, 177, 241,
     299, 317, 381, 433, 523,
     557, 607
technology,
     electronic, 504–509
     space weather and, 123, *123*
telephone, 592–594
     smartphones, **508**–509
telescopes, 652, *652,* **675,** *675*
     Hubble Space Telescope,
          607, *607*
     radio, **605,** *605,* 614
     reflecting, **606, 607,** *607,* 674
     refracting, **606,** 607, 674, 676
     space, 607
temperature, 134–135, **134,** 136,
     136
     heat, 145
     kinetic energy, 134
     reaction rates, 250, **250,** *250*
     thermal energy, 142
temperature scale, 134, **134**
     Celsius, 134, 135, **135**
     Fahrenheit, 134, 135, **135**
     Kelvin, 134, 135, **135**
temporary magnet, 475, 478
thermal conductivity, **26,** *26*
thermal, 122, **122**
thermal energy, 142, **142,**
     150, **150**
     heat, 145
     joules, 142
     kinetic energy, 122, 142, 150
     temperature, 142
thermogram, 113
thermometer, 134, **134,** *135*
     Celsius scale, 135, **135**
     Fahrenheit scale, 135, **135**
     Kelvin scale, 135, **135**
thermostat, programmable,
     114, *114*
Think Science,
     Developing and Using a Model,
          586–587
     Evaluating Scientific Evidence,
          20–21
     Interpreting Graphs,
          316–317
     Mean, Median, Mode, and
          Range, 536–537

Planning an Investigation,
     154–155
transformer, 124, **495,** *495*
translucent, **630,** *630*
transmission
     of light, 625, 630, 636
     of sound, 592, *592*
transparent, **630,** *630*
transverse wave, **529,** *529,* 530,
     532. *See also* **S** waves.
troughs, **526,** *526*
tuning fork, 580, *580*

ultrasound, **590,** *590,* **591,**
     591, 594
Unit Review, 107–112, 171–174,
     235–238, 293–296,
     375–378, 426–430,
     514–520, 550–554,
     600–604, 680–684
Uranium-235, 283, **283**
uranium isotopes, 282, **282,** *282*

vacuum, 530, 544, 546, 561, *561*
valence electrons, 200, **200,** *200,*
     201, 213, **213,** *213,* 214, 226
     Bohr model, 213, *213*
     energy level, outermost, 213,
          213, 214, 215, 224
     in carbon atoms, 258, *258*
Van de Graaff generator,
     438, *438*
vector, 311, **311**
velocity, 311, **311,** *311*
     calculating average acceleration,
          321, **321,** *321*
     final, 321, **321,** *321*
     starting, 321, **321,** *321*
     vector, 311, **311**
velocity, changes in, 320, **320**
     acceleration, 320, **320,** *320*
     calculating average acceleration,
          321, **321,** *321*
vibration, **560,** 580, *580,*
     581–582
virtual image, **643,** 644–648,
     644–648
visible light, 530, 611, 612, 613,
     613, 614, 632
Visual Summary, 16, 36, 50, 72,